Beginning ASP.NET 1.1 E-Commerce: From Novice to Professional

CRISTIAN DARIE AND KARLI WATSON

Apress®

Beginning ASP.NET 1.1 E-Commerce: From Novice to Professional
Copyright ©2004 by Cristian Darie and Karli Watson

ISBN (pbk): 1-59059-254-9

Printed and bound in the United States of America 9 8 7 6 5 4 3

Trademarked names may appear in this book. Rather than use a trademark symbol with every occurrence of a trademarked name, we use the names only in an editorial fashion and to the benefit of the trademark owner, with no intention of infringement of the trademark.

Lead Editor: Ewan Buckingham

Technical Reviewer: Ovidiu Platon

Editorial Board: Steve Anglin, Dan Appleman, Ewan Buckingham, Gary Cornell, Tony Davis, Jason Gilmore, Jonathan Hassell, Chris Mills, Dominic Shakeshaft, Jim Sumser

Project Manager: Tracy Brown Collins

Copy Edit Manager: Nicole LeClerc

Copy Editor: Julie McNamee

Production Manager: Kari Brooks

Production Editor: Janet Vail

Compositor: Kinetic Publishing Services, LLC

Proofreader: Gregory Teague

Indexer: Michael Brinkman

Cover Designer: Kurt Krames

Manufacturing Manager: Tom Debolski

Distributed to the book trade in the United States by Springer-Verlag New York, LLC, 233 Spring Street, Sixth Floor, New York, NY 10013 and outside the United States by Springer-Verlag GmbH & Co. KG, Tiergartenstr. 17, 69112 Heidelberg, Germany.

In the United States: phone 1-800-SPRINGER, email orders@springer-ny.com, or visit http://www.springer-ny.com. Outside the United States: fax +49 6221 345229, email orders@springer.de, or visit http://www.springer.de.

For information on translations, please contact Apress directly at 2560 Ninth Street, Suite 219, Berkeley, CA 94710. Phone 510-549-5930, fax 510-549-5939, email info@apress.com, or visit http://www.apress.com.

The information in this book is distributed on an "as is" basis, without warranty. Although every precaution has been taken in the preparation of this work, neither the author(s) nor Apress shall have any liability to any person or entity with respect to any loss or damage caused or alleged to be caused directly or indirectly by the information contained in this work.

The source code for this book is available to readers at http://www.apress.com in the Downloads section.

Contents at a Glance

Contents

About the Authors

Cristian Darie, currently Technical Lead and Project Manager with the Better Business Bureau Romania, is an experienced programmer specializing in various Microsoft and open source technologies, and relational database management systems. Having worked with computers since he was old enough to press the keyboard, he initially tasted programming success with a first prize in his first programming contest at the age of 12. From there, Cristian moved onto many other similar achievements in the following years. As an eagle-eyed technical reviewer with Wrox Press, Cristian was tempted into writing and has since co-authored several .NET and database books, including *Building Websites with the ASP.NET Community Starter Kit* and *The Programmer's Guide to SQL*. Cristian can be contacted through his personal web site at http://www.CristianDarie.ro.

Karli Watson is the Technical Director of 3form Ltd. (http://www.3form.net) and a freelance writer. He started out with the intention of becoming a world-famous nanotechnologist, so perhaps one day you might recognize his name as he receives a Nobel Prize. For now, though, Karli's computer interests include all things mobile and everything .NET. Karli is also a snowboarding enthusiast and wishes he had a cat.

About the Technical Reviewer

Ovidiu Platon is currently studying computer science and engineering in the Politehnica University of Bucharest, Romania. He is also a Microsoft Student Consultant in his faculty, which has led him to do some cool things the last couple of years, such as organize presentations and trainings within the local Microsoft laboratory that he runs with his team, complete an internship with the CLR team in Redmond, and complete another internship with the Consulting Services Group in Microsoft Romania. Ovidiu is also a Microsoft Certified Professional and will become a computer engineer in about a year.

Whenever he gets more free time, he'd like to spend it hiking (that hasn't happened too much lately) or reading actual books. Ovidiu maintains a weblog on `http://weblogs.studentclub.ro/ovidiupl` (in Romanian) in which he shares his various experiences.

Introduction

WELCOME TO *Beginning ASP.NET 1.1 E-Commerce!* The explosive growth of retail over the Internet is encouraging more small- to medium-sized businesses to consider the benefits of setting up e-commerce web sites. While there are great and obvious advantages to trading online, there are also many hidden pitfalls that may be encountered when developing a retail web site. This book provides the grass-roots reader with a practical, step-by-step guide to setting up an e-commerce site. Guiding you through every step of the design and build process, this book will have you building high quality, extendable e-commerce web sites quickly and easily.

Over the course of the book, you will develop all the skills necessary to get your business up on the web and available to a worldwide audience, without having to use high-end web solutions based on Microsoft Site Server. We present this information in a book-long case study, the complexity of which develops as your knowledge increases through the book.

The case study is presented in three phases. The first phase focuses on getting the site up and running as quickly as possible, and at a low cost. That way, the financial implications if you are not using the site are reduced, and also, should you use the site, you can start to generate revenue quickly. At the end of this phase, you will have a working site that you can play with or go live with if you want to. The revenue generated can be used to pay for further development.

Phase two concentrates on increasing revenue by improving the shopping experience, and actively encouraging customers to buy more by implementing product recommendations. Again at the end of this phase, you'll have a fully working site that you can go live with if you want to.

By the third phase, you'll have a site up and running, and doing very well. During this phase, you'll look at increasing your profit margins by reducing costs through the automating/streamlining of order processing and administration, and by handling credit card transactions yourself.

Who Is This Book For?

Beginning ASP.NET 1.1 E-Commerce is aimed at developers looking for a tutorial approach to building a full e-commerce web site from design to deployment. However, it's assumed that you

- Have some knowledge of using ASP.NET with VB .NET

- Have experience using Visual Basic .NET Standard or Visual Studio .NET Professional or above

- Want to build e-commerce web sites

The book may also prove valuable for ASP3 developers who learn best by example, and want to experience ASP.NET development techniques first hand.

What Does This Book Cover?

In this book you'll learn to

- Build an online product catalog that can be browsed and searched

- Implement the catalog administration pages that allow adding, modifying, and removing products, categories, and departments

- Create your own shopping basket and check out in ASP.NET

- Increase sales by implementing product recommendations

- Handle payments using PayPal, DataCash, and VeriSign Payflow Pro

- Implement a customer accounts system

The Apress forums are a platform for exchanging code and ideas, helping to extend the web site with new modules and modifications.

The following is brief roadmap of where this book is going to take you.

Phase One

Chapter 1: Starting an E-commerce site

In this chapter you'll see some of the principles of e-commerce in the real world. You see the importance of focusing on short-term revenue and keeping risks down. We look at the three basic ways in which an e-commerce site can make money. We then apply those principles to a three-phase plan that provides a deliverable, usable site at each stage and continues to expand throughout the book.

Chapter 2: Laying Out the Foundations

The previous chapter gave an overview of e-commerce in the real world. Now that you've decided to develop a web site, we start to look in more detail at laying down the foundations for its future. We will talk about what technologies and tools you'll use, and even more importantly, how you'll use them.

Chapter 3: Creating the Product Catalog: Part I

After learning about the three-tier architecture and implementing a bit of your web site's main page, it's time to continue your work by starting to create the JokePoint product catalog.

Because the product catalog is composed of many components, you'll create it over two chapters. In this chapter, you'll create the first database table, create a stored procedure, and implement data access methods in the middle tier. By the end of this chapter, you'll have something dynamically generated on your web page.

Chapter 4: Creating the Product Catalog: Part II

The fun isn't over yet! In the previous chapter, you created a selectable list of departments for JokePoint. However, there is much more to a product catalog than a list of departments. In this chapter, you'll add the rest of the product catalog features.

Chapter 5: Searching the Catalog

In the previous chapters, you will have implemented a functional product catalog for JokePoint. However, it lacks the all-important search feature. The goal in this chapter is to allow the visitor to search the site for products by entering one or more keywords. You'll learn how to implement search results ranking, and how to browse through the search results page by page.

You'll see how easy it is to add new functionality to a working site by integrating the new components into the existing architecture.

Chapter 6: Improving Performance

Why walk, when you can run? No, we won't talk about sports cars in this chapter. Instead, we'll analyze a few possibilities to improve the performance of the JokePoint project.

Although having a serious chapter on improving ASP.NET performance is out of the scope of this book, in Chapter 6 you'll learn a few basic principles that you can follow to improve your web site's performance.

Chapter 7: Receiving Payments Using PayPal

Let's collect some money! Your e-commerce web site needs a way of receiving payments from customers. Although the preferred solution for established companies is to open a merchant account, many small businesses choose to start with a solution that's simpler to implement, where they don't have to process card or payment information themselves.

A number of companies and web sites exist to help individuals or small businesses that don't have the resources to process credit card and wire transactions, and can be used to process the payment between companies and their customers. In this chapter, we will demonstrate some of the functionality provided by one such company, PayPal, as we use it on the JokePoint web site in the first two stages of development.

Chapter 8: Catalog Administration

The final detail to take care of before launching a web site is to create its administrative interface. Although this is a part visitors will never see, it's still key to delivering a quality web site to your client.

Phase Two

Chapter 9: The Shopping Basket

Welcome to the second phase of development, where you start improving and adding new features to the already existing, fully functional e-commerce site. In this chapter, you'll implement the custom shopping basket, which will store its data into the local database. This will provide you with more flexibility than the PayPal shopping basket, over which you have no control and which you can't save into your database for further processing and analysis.

Chapter 10: Dealing with Customer Orders

The good news is that the brand new shopping cart implemented in Chapter 9 looks good and is fully functional. The bad news is that it doesn't allow the visitor to actually place an order, making it totally useless in the context of a production system.

As you have probably already guessed, we'll deal with that problem in this chapter, in two separate stages. In the first part of the chapter, you'll implement the client-side part of the order-placing mechanism. In the second part of the chapter, you'll implement a simple orders administration page where the site administrator can view and handle pending orders.

Chapter 11: Making Recommendations

In an e-commerce store, being friendly and helpful equals being efficient. If your web site knows how to suggest more products based on the visitor's preferences, there's a chance the visitor will end up buying more from you than they initially planned. In Chapter 11, you'll learn how to implement a dynamic product recommendation system.

Phase Three

Chapter 12: Customer Details

So far in this book, you've built a basic (but functional) site, and have hooked it into PayPal for taking payments and confirming orders. In this section of the book, you'll take things a little further. By cutting out PayPal from the ordering process, you can gain better control as well as reduce overhead. This isn't as complicated as you might think, but you must be careful to do things right.

This chapter lays the groundwork by implementing a customer account system, as well as looking into the security aspects of exchanging and storing customer and credit card details.

Chapter 13: Order Pipeline

The JokePoint e-commerce application is shaping up nicely. You've added customer account functionality, and you're keeping track of customer addresses and credit card information, which is stored in a secure way. However, you're not currently using this information—you're delegating responsibility for this to PayPal.

In this and the next chapter, you'll build your own order-processing pipeline that deals with credit card authorization, stock checking, shipping, email notification, and so on. We'll leave the credit card processing specifics until Chapter 15, but we'll show you where this process fits in before then.

Chapter 14: Implementing the Pipeline

In this chapter, you implement the class library you built in the last chapter and integrate it into your JokePoint application.

You'll continue building your own order-processing pipeline and learn where the credit card processing fits in. You'll also learn about creating audit trails for orders, and how the administrative side of things works.

Chapter 15: Credit Card Transactions

The last thing you need to do before launching the e-commerce site is enable credit card processing. In this chapter, we will look at how you can build this into the pipeline you created in Chapter 14. You'll see how to use two popular credit card gateways to do this, DataCash and VeriSign Payflow Pro.

By the end of this chapter, JokePoint will be a fully functioning, secure, and usable e-commerce application. All that remains is for you to stock up on stink bombs and wait for the orders to roll in.

What You Need to Use This Book

The examples are designed to be run with Visual Studio .NET Professional and SQL Server 2000 or MSDE, running on Windows 2000 or Windows XP Professional Edition.

The complete source code for all the samples is available in the Downloads section of the Apress web site (http://www.apress.com).

Customer Support and Feedback

We always value hearing from our readers, and we want to know what you think about this book; let us know what you liked, what you didn't like, and what you think we can do better next time.

How to Tell Us Exactly What You Think

You might just want to tell us how much you liked or loathed the book in question. Or you might have ideas about how this whole process could be improved. In either case, you should email support@apress.com. Please be sure to mention the book's ISBN and title in your message. You'll always find a sympathetic ear, no matter what the problem is. Above all, you should remember that we do care about what you have to say, and we'll do our utmost to act upon it.

What We Can't Answer

Obviously with an ever-growing range of books and an ever-changing technology base, there's an increasing volume of data requiring support. Although we endeavor to answer all questions about the book, we can't solve bugs in your own programs that you've adapted from our code. However, do tell us if you're especially pleased with the routine you developed with our help.

Downloading the Source Code for the Book

The source code for this book is available to readers on the Apress web site (http://www.apress.com) in the Downloads section.

Finding Support and Errata on the Apress Web Site

We understand that errors can destroy the enjoyment of a book and can cause many wasted and frustrated hours, so we seek to minimize the distress they can cause. The following sections will explain how to find and post errata on the Apress web site to get book-specific help.

Finding Errata

Before you send in a query, you might be able to save time by finding the answer to your problem on the Apress web site at http://www.apress.com. Locate this book in the online catalog or within the book's category and go to the book's web page. Check to see whether there is a Corrections link. If there is, click the link to see the posted errata.

Adding an Erratum to the Web Site

If you want to point out an erratum or directly query a problem in the book, click the Submit Errata link on the book's web page. Please be sure to include your name and email address, and the chapter number, page number, and a brief description of the problem, as requested.

We won't send you junk mail. We need the details to save your time and ours.

Queries will be forwarded to the book's authors and editor. You may receive a direct email reply, and/or the erratum will be posted to the web site so all readers can benefit. Thank you!

Participating in Peer-to-Peer Forums

For author and peer discussion, join the Apress discussion groups. If you post a query to our forums, you can be confident that many Apress authors, editors, and industry experts are examining it. At forums.apress.com you'll find a number of different lists that will help you, not only while you read this book but also as you develop your own applications. To sign up for the Apress forums, go to forums.apress.com and click the New User link.

CHAPTER 1

Starting an E-Commerce Site

THE WORD "E-COMMERCE" has had a remarkable fall from grace in the past few years. Just the idea of having an e-commerce web site was enough to get many business people salivating with anticipation. Now it's no longer good enough to just say, "E-commerce is the future—get online or get out of business." You now need compelling, realistic, and specific reasons to take your business online.

This book focuses on programming and associated disciplines, such as creating, accessing, and manipulating databases. But before we jump into that, we need to cover the business decisions that lead to the creation of an e-commerce site in the first place.

If you want to build an e-commerce site today, you must answer some tough questions. The good news is these questions do have answers, and we're going to have a go at answering them in this chapter:

- So many big e-commerce sites have failed. What can e-commerce possibly offer me in today's tougher environment?

- Most e-commerce companies seemed to need massive investment. How can I produce a site on my limited budget?

- Even successful e-commerce sites expect to take years before they turn a profit. My business can't wait that long. How can I make money now?

Deciding Whether to Go Online

Although there are hundreds of possible reasons to go online, they tend to fall into the following motivations:

- Getting more customers

- Making customers spend more

- Reducing the costs of fulfilling orders

We'll look at each of these in the following sections.

Getting More Customers

Getting more customers is immediately the most attractive reason. With an e-commerce site, even small businesses can reach customers all over the world. This reason can also be the most dangerous, however, because many people set up e-commerce sites assuming that the site will reach customers immediately. It won't. In the offline world, you need to know a shop exists before you can go into it. This is still true in the world of e-commerce—people must know your site exists before you can hope to get a single order.

Addressing this issue is largely a question of advertising, rather than the site itself. We don't cover this aspect of e-commerce in this book. However, because an e-commerce site is always available, some people may stumble across it. It's certainly easier for customers to tell their friends about a particular web address than to give them a catalog, mailing address, or directions to their favorite offline store.

Making Customers Spend More

Assuming your company already has customers, you probably wish that they bought more. What stops them? If the customers don't want any more of a certain product, there's not a lot that e-commerce can do, but chances are there are other reasons, too:

- Getting to the shop/placing an order by mail is a hassle.

- Some of the things you sell can be bought from more convenient places.

- You're mostly open while your customers are at work.

- Buying some products just doesn't occur to your customers.

An e-commerce site can fix those problems. People with Internet access will find placing an order online far easier than any other method—meaning that when the temptation to buy strikes, it will be much easier for them to give in. Of course, the convenience of being online also means that people are more likely to choose your site over other local suppliers.

Because your site is online 24 hours a day, rather than the usual 9 to 5, your customers can shop with you outside of their working hours. Having an online store brings a double blessing to you if your customers work in offices because they can indulge in retail therapy directly from their desks.

Skillful e-commerce design can encourage your customers to buy things they wouldn't usually think of. You can easily update your site to suggest items of particular seasonal interest or to announce interesting new products.

Many of the large e-commerce sites encourage you to buy useful accessories along with the main product, or to buy a more expensive alternative to the one you're considering. Others give special offers to regular shoppers, or suggest impulse purchases during checkout. You'll learn how to use some of these methods in later chapters, and by the end of the book, you'll have a good idea of how to add more features for yourself.

Finally, it's much easier to learn about your customers via e-commerce than in face-to-face shops, or even through mail order. Even if you just gather e-mail addresses, you can use these to send out updates and news. More sophisticated sites can automatically analyze a customer's buying habits to make suggestions on other products the customer might like to buy.

Another related benefit of e-commerce is that there's no real cost in having people browse without buying. In fact, getting people to visit the site as often as possible can be valuable. You should consider building features into the site that are designed purely to make people visit regularly; for example, you might include community features such as forums, or free content related to the products you're selling. Although we won't be explicitly covering these features, by the end of the book you will have learned enough to easily add them for yourself.

Reducing the Costs of Fulfilling Orders

A well-built e-commerce site will be much cheaper to run than a comparable offline business. Under conventional business models, a staff member must feed an order into the company's order-processing system. With e-commerce, the customer can do this for you—the gateway between the site and the order processing can be seamless.

Of course, after your e-commerce site is up and running, the cost of actually taking orders gets close to zero—you don't need to pay for checkout staff, assistants, security guards, or rent in a busy shopping mall.

If you have a sound business idea, and you execute the site well, you can receive these benefits without a massive investment. What's important is to always focus on the almighty dollar: Will your site, or any particular feature of it, really help you get more customers, get customers to spend more, or reduce the costs and therefore increase your profit margins?

Now it's time to introduce the site we'll be using as the example in this book, and see just how all of these principles relate to our own shop.

Making Money

We're going to build an online joke shop. If you are unfortunate enough to live in a country without joke shops, you should move or read on. They tend to sell fancy dress costumes and accessories, along with equipment for magic tricks and practical jokes. Pepper sweets, soap that makes your face dirty, and weighted dice are freely available.

On all the e-commerce sites we've worked on, there's been a great deal of tension between wanting to produce an amazing site that everybody will love and the need to create a site with a limited budget that will make money. Usually, we're on the trigger-happy, really amazing site side, but we're always grateful that our ambitions are reined in by the actual business demands. If you're designing and building the site for yourself, and you are the client, then you have a challenge: keeping your view realistic while maintaining your enthusiasm for the project.

This book shows you a logical way to build an e-commerce site that will deliver what it needs to be profitable. However, when designing your own site, you need to think carefully about exactly who your customers are, what they need, how they want to place orders, and what they are most likely to buy. Most important of all, you need to think about how they will come to your site in the first place. You should consider the following points before you start to visualize or design the site, and certainly before you start programming:

- *Getting customers*: How will you get visitors to the site in the first place?

- *Offering products*: What you will offer, and how will you expect customers to buy? Will they buy in bulk? Will they make a lot of repeat orders? Will they know what they want before they visit, or will they want to be inspired? These factors will influence how you arrange your catalog and searching, as well as what order process you use. A shopping basket is great if people want to browse. If people know exactly what they want, then they may prefer something more like an order form.

- *Processing orders*: How will you turn a customer order into a parcel ready for mailing? Your main consideration here is finding an efficient way to process payments and deliver orders to whoever manages your stocks or warehouse. How will you give your customers confidence in your ability to protect their data and deliver their purchases on time?

- *Servicing customers*: Will customers require additional help with products that they buy from you? Do you need to offer warranties, service contracts, or other support services?

- *Bringing customers back*: How will you entice customers back to the site? Are they likely to only visit the site to make a purchase, or will there be e-window shoppers? Are your products consumables and can you predict when your customers will need something new?

After you've answered these questions, you can start to design your site, knowing that you're designing for your customers—not just doing what seems like a good idea at the time. Determining the answers to these questions will also help ensure that your design covers all the important areas, without massive omissions that will be a nightmare to fix.

The example presented in this book has deliberately kept a generic approach to show you the most common e-commerce techniques. But to really lift yourself above the competition, you don't need fancy features or Flash movies—you just need to understand, attract, and serve your customer better than anybody else. Think about this before you launch into designing and building the site itself.

Considering the Risks and Threats

All this might make it sound as if your e-commerce business can't possibly fail. Well, it's time to take a cold shower and realize that even the best-laid plans often go wrong. Some risks are particularly relevant to e-commerce companies, such as

- Hacking

- Credit-card scams

- Hardware failure

- Unreliable shipping services

- Software errors

- Changing laws

You can't get rid of these risks, but you can try to understand them and defend yourself from them. The software developed in this book goes some way to meeting these issues, but many of the risks have little to do with the site itself.

An important way to defend your site from many risks is to keep backups. You already know backups are important. But if you're anything like us, when it gets to the end of the day, saving five minutes and going home earlier seems even more important. When you have a live web site, this simply isn't an option.

We haven't talked much about the legal side of e-commerce in this book because we're programmers, not lawyers. However, if you're setting up an e-commerce site that goes much beyond an online garage sale, you'll need to look into these issues before putting your business online.

While we're on the subject of risks and threats, one issue that can really damage your e-commerce site is unreliable order fulfillment. This is a programming book, and it focuses on offering products to customers and communicating their orders to the site's owner. An essential part of the processes is getting the products delivered, and to do this you need a good logistics network set up before launching your shop. If your store doesn't deliver the goods, customers won't come back or refer their friends.

 TIP *Webmonkey provides an excellent general e-commerce tutorial, which covers taxation, shipping, and many of the issues you'll face when designing your site, at* `http://hotwired.lycos.com/webmonkey/e-business/building/tutorials/tutorial3.html`. *Check this out before you start designing your own site.*

Designing for Business

Building an e-commerce site requires a significant investment. If you design the site in phases, you can reduce the initial investment, and therefore cut your losses if the idea proves unsuccessful. You can use the results from an early phase to assess whether it's worthwhile to add extra features, and even use revenue from the site to fund future development. If nothing else, planning to build the site in phases means that you can get your site online and receiving orders much earlier than if you build every possible feature into the first release.

Even after you've completed your initial planned phases, things may not end there. Whenever you plan a large software project, it's important to design in a way that makes unplanned future growth easy. In Chapter 2, where we'll start dealing with the technical details of building e-commerce sites, you'll learn how to design the web site architecture to allow for long-term development flexibility.

If you're building sites for clients, they will like to think their options are open. Planning the site, or any other software, in phases will help your clients feel comfortable doing business with you. They will be able to see that you are getting the job done, and they can decide to end the project at the end of any phase if they feel—for whatever reason—that they don't want to continue to invest in development.

Phase I: Getting a Site Up

Chapters 2 through 8 concentrate on establishing the basic framework for a site and putting a product catalog online. We'll start by putting together the basic site architecture, deciding how the different parts of our application will work together. We'll then build the product catalog into this architecture. You'll learn how to

- Design a database for storing a product catalog, containing categories, subcategories, and products.

- Write the SQL (Structured Query Language) and VB.NET (Visual Basic .NET) code for accessing that data.

- Provide a free-text search engine for that database.

- Give the site's administrators a private section of the site where they can modify the catalog online.

After you've built this catalog, you'll see how to offer the products for sale by integrating it with PayPalPayPal's shopping cart and order-processing system, which will handle credit card transactions for you and e-mail you with details of orders. These orders will be processed manually, but in the early stages of an e-commerce site, the time you lose processing orders will be less than the time it would have taken to develop an automated system.

Phase II: Creating Your Own Shopping Cart

Using PayPal's shopping cart is okay, and really easy, but it does mean we lose a lot of advantages. For example, we can't control the look and feel of PayPal's shopping cart, but if we use our own, we can make it an integral part of the site.

This is a significant advantage, but it's superficial compared to some of the others. For example, with our own shopping cart, we can store complete orders in our database as part of the order process, and use that data to learn about our customers. With additional work, we also can use the shopping basket and checkout as a platform for selling more products. How often have you been tempted by impulse purchases near the checkout of your local store? Well, this also works with e-commerce. Having our own shopping cart and checkout gives us the option of later offering low-cost special offers from there. We can even analyze the contents of the cart, and make suggestions based on this. These optional features are outside the scope of this book, but will be easy to plug into the infrastructure you develop here—remember, your site is designed for growth!

Chapters 9 through 11 show you how to

- Build your own ASP.NET (Active Server Pages .NET) shopping cart.

- Pass a complete order through to PayPal for credit card processing.

- Create an orders administration page.

- Implement a product recommendations system in the form of a "customers who bought these products also bought:" list, in the visitor's shopping cart.

Once again, at the end of Phase II, your site will be fully operational. If you want, you can leave it as it is or add features within the existing PayPal-based payment system. But when the site gets serious, you'll want to start processing orders and credit cards yourself. This is the part where things get complicated, and you need to be serious and careful about your site's security.

Phase III: Processing Orders

The core of e-commerce, and the bit that really separates it from other web-development projects, is handling orders and credit cards. PayPal is your friend because it's helped you put this off, but there are many good reasons why—eventually—you'll want to part company with PayPal:

- *Cost*: PayPal is not expensive, but the extra services it offers must be paid for somehow. Moving to a simpler credit-card processing service will mean lower transaction costs, although developing your own system will obviously incur upfront costs.

- *Freedom*: PayPal has a fairly strict set of terms and conditions and is designed for residents of a limited number of countries. By taking on more of the credit-card processing responsibility yourself, you can better control the way your site works. As an obvious example, you can accept payment using regional methods such as the Switch debit cards common in the United Kingdom.

- *Integration*: If you deal with transactions and orders using your own system, you can integrate your store and your warehouse to whatever extent you require. You could even automatically contact a third-party supplier and have them ship the goods straight to the customer.

- *Information*: When you handle the whole order yourself, you can record and collate all the information involved in the transaction—and then use it for marketing and research purposes.

By integrating the order processing with the warehouse, fulfillment center, or suppliers, you can reduce costs significantly. This might mean that it reduces the need for staff in the fulfillment center, or at least mean that business can grow without requiring additional staff.

Acquiring information about customers can feed back into the whole process, giving you valuable information about how to sell more. At its simplest, you could e-mail customers with special offers, or just keep in touch with a newsletter. You also could analyze buying patterns and use that data to formulate targeted marketing campaigns.

During Phase III (in Chapters 12 through 15), you will learn how to

- Build a customer accounts module, so that customers can log in and retrieve their details every time they make an order.

- Establish secure connections using SSL (Secure Socket Layer), so that data sent by users is encrypted on its travels across the Internet.

- Authenticate and charge credit cards using third-party companies such as DataCash and VeriSign, and their XML (Extensible Markup Language) web services.

- Store credit card numbers securely in a database.

This third phase will be the most involved of all of them, and will require some hard and careful work. By the end of Phase III, however, you will have an e-commerce site with a searchable product catalog, shopping cart, secure checkout, and complete order-processing system.

The Joke Shop

As we said earlier, we're going to build an online joke shop called JokePoint. Figure 1-1 shows the way JokePoint will look like at some point during the first stage of development.

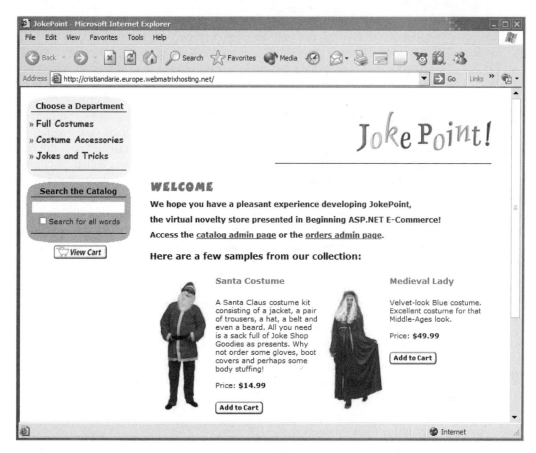

Figure 1-1. JokePoint during Phase I of development

TIP   *You can preview the online version of JokePoint at* http://cristiandarie.europe.webmatrixhosting.net/. *Many thanks go to* http://www.the-joke-shop.com, *who allowed us to use some of their products to populate our virtual JokePoint store.*

For the purposes of this book, we'll assume that the client already exists as a mail-order company, and has a good network of customers. The company is not completely new to the business, and wants the site to make it easier and more enjoyable for its existing customers to buy—with the goal that they'll end up buying more.

Knowing this, we suggest the phased development because

- The company is unlikely to get massive orders initially, so you should keep the initial cost of building the web site down as much as possible.

- The company is accustomed to manually processing mail orders, so manually processing orders e-mailed by PayPal will not introduce many new problems.

- The company doesn't want to invest all of its money in a massive e-commerce site, only to find that people actually prefer mail order after all! Or it might find that, after Phase I, the site does exactly what it wants and there's no point in expanding it further. Either way, you hope that offering a lower initial cost gives your bid the edge. (It might also mean you can get away with a higher total price.)

Because this company is already a mail-order business, it probably already has a merchant account, and can therefore process credit cards. Thus, moving on to Phase III as soon as possible would be best for this company so it can benefit from the preferential card-processing rates.

Summary

In this chapter, we've covered some of the principles of e-commerce in the real, hostile world. We've shown the importance of focusing on short-term revenue and keeping risks down. We've discussed the three basic motivations for taking your business online:

- Acquiring more customers

- Making customers spend more

- Reducing the costs of fulfilling orders

We've shown you how to apply those principles to a three-phase plan that provides a deliverable, usable site at each stage. We'll continue to expand on this plan throughout the book.

You've presented your plan to the owners of the joke shop. In the next chapter, you'll put on your programming hat, and start to design and build your web site (assuming you get the contract, of course).

CHAPTER 2

Laying Out
the Foundations

NOW THAT YOU HAVE convinced the client that you can create a cool web site to complement the client's store activity, it's time to stop celebrating and start thinking about how to put into practice all the promises made to the client. As usual, when we lay down on paper the technical requirements we must meet, everything starts to seem a bit more complicated than initially anticipated.

In order to ensure this project's success, you need to come up with a smart way to implement what you've signed the contract for. You want to make your life easy and develop the project smoothly and quickly, but the ultimate goal is to make sure the client is satisfied with your work. Consequently, you should aim to provide your site's increasing number of visitors with a pleasant web experience by creating a nice, functional, and responsive web site, by implementing each one of the three development phases described in the first chapter.

The requirements are pretty high, but this is normal for an e-commerce site nowadays. To maximize the chances of success, we'll try to analyze and anticipate as many of the technical requirements as possible, and implement the solution in such a way as to support changes and additions with minimal effort.

In this chapter we'll lay down the foundations for the future JokePoint web site. We'll talk about what technologies and tools you'll use, and even more important, how you'll use them. Let's consider a quick summary of the goals for this chapter before moving on:

- Analyze the project from a technical point of view.

- Analyze and choose an architecture for your application.

- Decide which technologies, programming languages, and tools to use.

- Discuss naming and coding conventions.

- Create the basic structure of the web site and set up the database.

Designing for Growth

The word *design* in the context of a Web Application can mean many things. Its most popular usage probably refers to the visual and user interface design of a web site.

This aspect is crucial because, let's face it, the visitor is often more impressed with how a site looks and how easy it is to use than about which technologies and techniques are used behind the scenes, or what operating system the web server is running. If the site is slow, hard to use, or easy to forget, it just doesn't matter what rocket science was used to create it.

Unfortunately, this truth makes many inexperienced programmers underestimate the importance of the way the invisible part of the site is implemented—the code, the database, and so on. The visual part of a site gets the visitor interested to begin with, but its functionality makes them come back. A web site can sometimes be implemented very quickly based on certain initial requirements, but if not properly architected, it can become difficult, if not impossible, to change.

For any project of any size, some preparation must be done before starting to code. Still, no matter how much preparation and design work is done, the unexpected does happen and hidden catches, new requirements, and changing rules always seem to work against deadlines. Even without these unexpected factors, site designers are often asked to change or add new functionality many times after the project is finished and deployed. This will also be the case for JokePoint, which will be implemented in three separate stages, as discussed in Chapter 1.

You'll learn how to create the web site so that the site (or you) will not fall apart when functionality is extended or updates are made. Because this is a programming book, instead of focusing on how to design the user interface or on marketing techniques, we'll pay close attention to designing the code that makes them work.

The phrase "designing the code" can have different meanings; for example, we'll need to have a short talk about naming conventions. Still, the most important aspect that we need to take a look at is the **architecture** to use when writing the code. The architecture refers to the way you split the code for a simple piece of functionality (for example, the product search) into smaller components. Although it might be easier to implement that functionality as quickly and as simply as possible, in a single component, you gain great long-term advantages by creating more components that work together to achieve the desired result.

Before considering the architecture itself, you must determine what you want from this architecture.

Meeting Long-Term Requirements with Minimal Effort

Apart from the fact that you want a fast web site, each of the phases of development we talked about in Chapter 1 brings new requirements that must be met.

Every time you proceed to a new stage, you want to be able to **reuse** most of the already existing solution. It would be very inefficient to redesign the whole site (not just the visual part, but the code as well!) just because you need to add a new feature. You can make it easier to reuse the solution by planning ahead, so any new functionality that needs to be added can slot in with ease, rather than each change causing a new headache.

When building the web site, implementing a **flexible architecture** composed of pluggable components allows you to add new features—such as the shopping cart, the departments list, or the products search feature—by coding them as separate components and plugging them into the existing application. Achieving a good level of flexibility is one of the goals regarding the application's architecture, and this chapter shows how you can put this into practice. You'll see that the flexibility level is proportional to the amount of time required to design and implement it, so we'll try to find a compromise that will provide the best gains without complicating the code too much.

The last major requirement that is common to all online applications is a **scalable architecture**. Scalability is defined as the capability to increase resources to yield a linear (ideally) increase in service capacity. In other words, scalability refers to the way the application reacts when the number of clients increases. You might expect that at first, your small web store won't have much traffic, and in these conditions any web site would handle the small number of requests. But because we're optimistic about the number of customers, we must be sure that the site will be able to deliver its functionality to a large number of clients without throwing out errors or performing sluggishly.

Revealing the Magic of Three-Layered Architecture

Generally, the architecture refers to splitting each piece of the application's functionality into separate components based on what they do, and grouping each kind of component into a single logical tier.

The three-tier architecture has become popular today because it answers most of the problems discussed so far by splitting an application's functionality into three logical tiers:

- The presentation tier

- The business tier

- The data tier

Almost every module that you'll create for the site will have components in all these three tiers.

The **presentation tier** contains the user interface elements of the site, and includes all the logic that manages the interaction between the visitor and the client's business. This tier makes the whole site feel alive, and the way you design it has a crucial importance for the site's success. Because your application is a web site, its presentation tier is composed of dynamic web pages.

The **business tier** (also called the *middle tier*) receives requests from the presentation tier and returns a result to the presentation tier depending on the business logic it contains. All events that happen in the presentation tier usually result in the business tier being called. For example, if the visitor is doing a product search, the presentation tier calls the business tier and says, "Please send me back the products that match this search criterion." Almost always, the business tier needs to call the data tier for information to be able to respond to the presentation tier's request.

The **data tier** (sometimes referred to as the *database tier*) is responsible for storing the application's data, and sending it to the business tier when requested. For the

JokePoint e-commerce site, you'll need to store data about products—their categories and their departments—users, shopping carts, and so on. Almost every client request finally results in the data tier being interrogated for information (excepting when previously retrieved data has been cached at business tier or presentation tier levels), so it is important to have a fast database system. In this chapter and Chapter 4, you'll learn how to design the database for optimum performance.

Note that these tiers are purely logical—there is no constraint on the physical location of each tier. You're free to place all of the application, and implicitly all of its tiers, on a single server machine; place each tier on a separate machine; or even split the components of a single tier over multiple machines. Your choice depends on the particular performance requirements of the application. This kind of flexibility allows you to achieve many benefits, as you'll soon see.

An important constraint in the three-layered architecture model is that information must flow in sequential order between tiers. The presentation tier is only allowed to access the business tier, and never directly the data tier. The business tier is the "brain" in the middle that communicates with the other tiers and processes and coordinates all the information flow. If the presentation tier directly accessed the data tier, the rules of three-tier architecture programming would be broken. When you implement a three-tier architecture, you must be consistent and obey its rules to reap the benefits.

Figure 2-1 is a simple representation of the way data is passed in an application that implements the three-tier architecture.

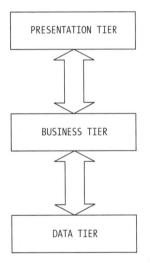

Figure 2-1. The three-tier architecture

A Simple Scenario

It is easier to understand how data is passed and transformed between tiers if you take a closer look at a simple example. To make the example even more relevant to the project, let's analyze a situation that will actually happen in JokePoint. This scenario is typical for three-tier applications.

Like most e-commerce sites, JokePoint will have a shopping cart, which we'll discuss later in the book. For now, it's enough to know that the visitor will add products to the shopping cart by clicking an "Add to Cart" button. Figure 2-2 shows how the information flows through the application when that button is clicked.

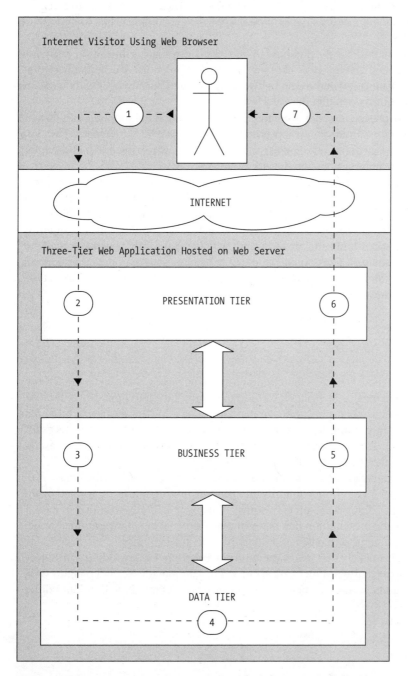

Figure 2-2. Internet visitor interacting with a three-tier application

When the user clicks the "Add to Cart" button for a specific product (Step 1), the presentation tier (which contains the button) forwards the request to the business tier—"Hey, I want this product added to my shopping cart!" (Step 2). The business tier receives the request, understands that the user wants a specific product added to the shopping cart, and handles the request by telling the data tier to update the visitor's shopping cart by adding the selected product (Step 3). The data tier needs to be called because it stores and manages the entire web site's data, including users' shopping cart information.

The data tier updates the database (Step 4) and eventually returns a success code to the business tier. The business tier (Step 5) handles the return code and any errors that might have occurred in the data tier while updating the database, and then returns the output to the presentation tier.

Finally, the presentation tier generates an updated view of the shopping cart (Step 6). The results of the execution are wrapped up by generating an HTML (Hypertext Markup Language) web page that is returned to the visitor (Step 7), where the updated shopping cart can be seen in the visitor's favorite web browser.

Note that in this simple example, the business tier doesn't do a lot of processing and its business logic isn't very complex. However, if new business rules appear for your application, you would change the business tier. If, for example, the business logic specified that a product could only be added to the shopping cart if its quantity in stock was greater than zero, an additional data tier call would have been made to determine the quantity. The data tier would only be requested to update the shopping cart if products are in stock. In any case, the presentation tier is informed about the status and provides human-readable feedback to the visitor.

What's in a Number?

It's interesting to note how each tier interprets the same piece of information differently. For the data tier, the numbers and information it stores have no significance because this tier is an engine that saves, manages, and retrieves numbers, strings, or other data types—not product quantities or product names. In the context of the previous example, a product quantity of 0 represents a simple, plain number without any meaning to the data tier (it is simply 0, a 32-bit integer).

The data gains significance when the business tier reads it. When the business tier asks the data tier for a product quantity and gets a "0" result, this is interpreted by the business tier as "Hey, no products in stock!" This data is finally wrapped in a nice, visual form by the presentation tier, for example, a label saying, "Sorry, at the moment the product cannot be ordered."

Even if it is unlikely that you want to forbid a customer from adding a product to the shopping cart if the product isn't in stock, the example (described in Figure 2-3) is good enough to present in yet another way how each of the three tiers has a different purpose.

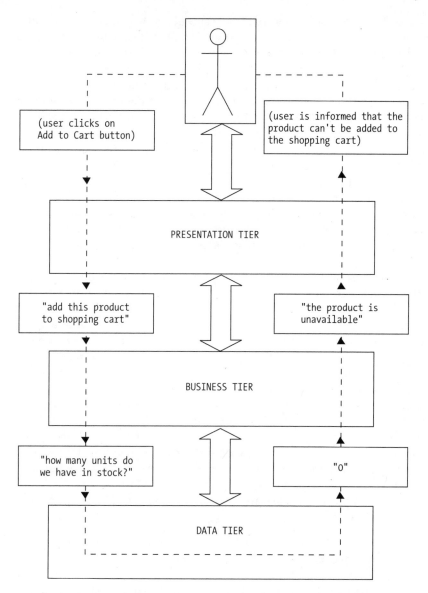

Figure 2-3. Internet visitor interacting with a three-tier application

The Right Logic for the Right Tier

Because each layer can contain its own logic, sometimes it can be tricky to decide where exactly to draw the line between the tiers. In the previous scenario, instead of reading the product's quantity in the business tier and deciding whether the product is available based on that number, you could have a stored procedure in the database named `IsProductAvailable` that simply returns a value of `True` or `False` depending on the availability of the product. This way, the simple logic (an `if` statement) of deciding whether a product is available would be transferred from the business tier to the data tier.

As an alternative, instead of first checking whether the product is available and then adding it to the shopping cart, you could directly call a database stored procedure named `AddProductToCart`, which first tests whether the product is available before adding it or returning an error code if the product isn't available. This way the whole operation is made with a single call to the data tier, which can result in better performance.

Note that in both of the hypothetical changes presented previously, some logic is transferred from the business tier to the data tier. Many other scenarios exist in which the same logic can be placed in one tier or another, or maybe in both. In most cases, there is no single best way to implement the three-tier architecture, and many times you'll need to make a compromise or a choice based on personal preference or external constraints.

Furthermore, there are occasions in which even though you know the *right* way (in respect to the architecture) to implement something, you might choose to break the rules to get a performance gain. As a general rule, if performance can be improved this way, it is okay to break the strict limits between tiers *just a little bit* (for example, add some of the business rules to the data tier or vice versa), *if* these rules aren't likely to change in time. Otherwise, keeping all the business rules in the middle tier is preferable because it generates a "cleaner" application that is easier to maintain.

Finally, don't be tempted to access the data tier directly from the presentation tier. This is a common mistake that is the shortest path to a complicated, hard-to-maintain, and inflexible system. In many data access tutorials or introductory materials, you'll be shown how to perform simple database operations using a simple user interface application. In these kinds of programs, all the logic is probably written in a short, single file, instead of separate tiers. Although the materials might be very good, keep in mind that most of these texts are meant to teach you how to do different individual tasks (for example, access a database), and not how to correctly create a flexible and scalable application.

A *Three-Tier Architecture for JokePoint*

Implementing a three-tiered architecture for the JokePoint web site will help achieve the goals listed at the beginning of the chapter. The coding discipline imposed by a system that might seem rigid at first sight allows for excellent levels of flexibility and extensibility in the long run.

Splitting major parts of the application into separate, smaller components also encourages reusability. More than once when you add new features to the site you'll see that you can reuse some of the already existing bits. Adding a new feature without needing to change much of what already exists is, in itself, a good example of reusability. Also, smaller pieces of code placed in their correct places are easier to document and analyze later.

Another advantage of the three-tiered architecture is that, if properly implemented, the overall system is resistant to changes. When bits in one of the tiers change, the other tiers usually remain unaffected, sometimes even in extreme cases. For example, if for some reason the backend database system is changed (say, the manager decides to use Oracle instead of SQL Server), you only need to update the data tier. The existing business tier should work the same with the new database.

Why Not Use More Tiers?

The three-tier architecture we've been talking about so far is a particular (and the most popular) version of the *n*-Tier Architecture, which is a commonly used buzzword these days. **n-Tier architecture** refers to splitting the solution into a number (*n*) of logical tiers. In complex projects, sometimes it makes sense to split the business layer into more than one layer, thus resulting in an architecture with more than three layers. However, for this web site, it makes most sense to stick with the three-layered design, which offers most of the benefits while not requiring too many hours of design or a complex hierarchy of framework code to support the architecture.

Maybe with a more involved and complex architecture, you would achieve even higher levels of flexibility and scalability for the application, but you would need much more time for design before starting to implement anything. As with any programming project, you must find a fair balance between the time required to design the architecture and the time spent to implement it. The three-tier architecture is best suited to projects with average complexity, like the JokePoint web site.

You also might be asking the opposite question, "Why not use fewer tiers?" A two-tier architecture, also called *client-server* architecture, can be appropriate for less complex projects. In short, a two-tier architecture requires less time for planning and allows quicker development in the beginning, although it generates an application that's harder to maintain and extend in the long run. Because we're expecting to have to extend the application in the future, the client-server architecture isn't appropriate for this application, so it won't be discussed further in this book.

Now that the general architecture is known, let's see what technologies and tools you'll use to implement it. After a brief discussion of the technologies, you'll create the foundation of the presentation and data tiers by creating the first page of the site and the backend database. You'll start implementing some real functionality in each of the three tiers in Chapter 3 when you start creating the web site's product catalog.

Choosing Technologies and Tools

No matter which architecture is chosen, a major question that arises in every development project is which technologies, programming languages, and tools are going to be used, bearing in mind that external requirements can seriously limit your options.

NOTE   *In this book we're creating a web site using Microsoft technologies. We really like these technologies, but it doesn't necessarily mean they're the best choice for any kind of project, in any circumstances. Additionally, there are many situations when you must use specific technologies because of client requirements. The System Requirements and Software Requirements stages in the software development process will determine which technologies you must use for creating the application. Please see Appendix B for more details.*

This book is about programming e-commerce web sites with ASP.NET (Active Server Pages .NET) and VB .NET (Visual Basic .NET). We'll also talk about Visual Studio .NET and SQL Server 2000. Although the book assumes a little previous experience with each of these, we'll take a quick look at them and see how they fit into the project and into the three-tier architecture.

Using ASP.NET

ASP.NET is Microsoft's newest technology for building dynamic, interactive web content. Perhaps the simplest example of dynamic web content is the search results page of a search engine. If you go to http://www.google.com and search for "Beginning E-Commerce," the response you get is a web page that obviously doesn't exist on the web server as a static HTML document. It would be impossible to store a separate web document for each possible search string, not to mention updating this tremendous number of result pages. ASP.NET pages contain a template that applies to all response pages, but their content is dynamically generated by the underlying code.

ASP.NET is not the only server-side technology around for creating dynamic web pages. Among its most popular competitors are JSP (JavaServer Pages), PHP (Hypertext Preprocessor), ColdFusion, and even the outdated ASP (Active Server Pages) and CGI (Common Gateway Interface). Between these technologies are many differences, but also some fundamental similarities. For example, pages written with any of these technologies are composed of basic HTML, which draws the static part of the page (the template), and code that generates the dynamic part. Even Google's dynamically generated search pages have a static structure that applies to all of them.

NOTE   *You might want to check out* Beginning PHP 5 E-Commerce *(ISBN: 1-59059-392-8), also published by Apress, which explains how to build e-commerce web sites with PHP 5 and MySQL.*

The Code Behind the Page

Figure 2-4 shows what happens to an ASP.NET web page from the moment the client browser requests it to the moment the browser actually receives it.

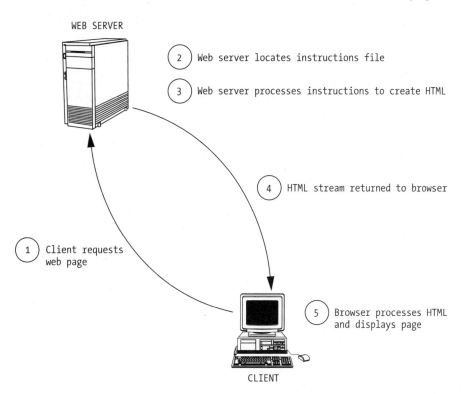

WEB SERVER

2　Web server locates instructions file

3　Web server processes instructions to create HTML

4　HTML stream returned to browser

1　Client requests web page

5　Browser processes HTML and displays page

CLIENT

Figure 2-4. Web server processing client requests

The page is first processed at the server before being returned to the client, this being the reason ASP.NET and the other mentioned technologies are called **server-side technologies**. When an ASP.NET page is requested, its underlying code is first executed on the server. This code can be written in a number of .NET-compatible languages, and it is used to populate or generate the dynamic part of the page. After the final page is composed, the resulting HTML is returned to the visitor's browser.

The returned HTML can optionally contain client-side script code, which can be part of the page template or can be dynamically generated. The client-side script code is named as such because the client's browser always directly interprets it. The most popular client-side scripting technologies are JavaScript and VBScript. JavaScript is usually the better choice because it has wider acceptance, whereas only Internet Explorer recognizes VBScript. Other important client-side technologies are Macromedia Flash and Java applets, but these are somewhat different because the web browser does not directly parse them—Flash requires a specialized plug-in and Java applets require a JVM (Java Virtual Machine). Internet Explorer also supports ActiveX controls and .NET assemblies.

Regarding the server-side code, ASP.NET has the advantage of allowing this code to be written separately from the static part of the file. All the code that belongs to a certain page can be saved as a **code-behind file**, which is an advance over regular ASP in which the HTML layout and the server-side code were mixed in a single file. These mixed files are the subject of both designers' and programmers' work, and are hard to document, change, and maintain.

Before moving on, let's summarize the most important general features of ASP.NET:

- The server-side code can be written in the .NET language of your choice. The .NET Framework is supplied with three languages (C#, VB .NET, and JScript .NET), but the whole infrastructure is designed to support additional languages. These languages are powerful and fully object oriented.

- The server-side code of ASP.NET pages is fully compiled and executed—as opposed to being interpreted line by line—which results in optimal performance, and offers the possibility to detect a number of errors at compile-time instead of runtime.

- The concept of code-behind files helps separate the visual part of the page from the (server-side) logic behind it. This is an advantage over ASP, in which both the HTML and the server-side code resided in the same file (often resulting in the popular "spaghetti code").

- Visual Studio .NET, an excellent and complete visual editor, represents a good weapon in the ASP.NET programmer's arsenal even though you don't have to have it to create ASP.NET Web Applications.

ASP.NET Web Forms and Web User Controls

An ASP.NET web page along with its code-behind file is called an **ASP.NET Web Form**. The Web Form is composed of server-side code and HTML (which can contain client-side script).

Web Forms are files with the .aspx extension. Their code-behind files don't have to follow any particular naming convention except for the final extension specific to the language they are programmed in. The recommended naming system is the one implicitly used by Visual Studio, which automatically creates .aspx.vb code-behind files for VB .NET projects, .aspx.cs if working with C#, and .aspx.js for JScript .NET. So, in your project, the default Web Form will be created in a file named default.aspx, and its code-behind file will be default.aspx.vb.

A Web Form can include server-side controls. Server-side controls generically refers to three kinds of controls: **Web User Controls**, **Web Server Controls**, and **HTML Server Controls**.

Web User Controls are files with the .ascx extension that have a structure similar to the structure of Web Forms (they can have code-behind files and so on), but they can't be requested directly by a client web browser. Instead, they are included in Web Forms, the parent Web Form being the container of the control.

Web Server Controls are compiled .NET classes that, when executed, generate HTML output (eventually including client-side script). You can use them in Web Forms or in Web User Controls. A number of Web Server Controls are provided by the .NET Framework, including simpler controls such as Label, TextBox, or Button, and more complex controls such as DataGrid or Calendar. The main advantage of

Web Server Controls is the ability to programmatically access them and set their properties, just as in Windows Forms applications or old VB6 programs. With ASP.NET it's not unusual to set a label's property like this, in the code-behind file:

```
descriptionLabel.Text = "This is an interesting description"
```

HTML Server Controls allow you to programmatically access HTML elements from the page that would normally be programmatically inaccessible. Most HTML Server Controls are doubled by Web Server Controls (such as labels, buttons, and so on). For consistency, we'll stick with Web Server Controls most of the time, but in some cases you'll need to use HTML Server Controls. For example, as you'll see later in this chapter, you'll need to use an HTML Server Control to programmatically access an HTML table cell (which isn't available as a Web Server Control).

For the JokePoint project, you'll use some of the existing .NET Web Server Controls (although in more advanced ASP.NET books you can learn how to create your own), and you'll create a number of Web User Controls.

Because you can develop Web User Controls independently of the main web site, and then just plug them in when they're ready, having a site structure based on Web User Controls provides an excellent level of flexibility and reusability.

ASP.NET and the Three-Tier Architecture

The collection of Web Forms and Web User Controls form the presentation tier of the application. They are the part that creates the HTML code loaded by the visitor's browser.

The logic of the user interface is stored in code-behind files for both Web Forms and Web User Controls. Note that although with ASP.NET you don't need to use code-behind files (you're free to mix code and HTML just as you did with ASP), we'll exclusively use code-behind files for the presentation-tier logic.

In the context of a three-tier application, the logic in the presentation tier usually refers to the various event handlers, such as `Page_Load` and `someButton_Click`. As you learned earlier, these event handlers should call business-tier methods to get their jobs done (and never call the data tier directly).

Using VB .NET

VB .NET is one of the languages that can be used to code the Web Forms' logic. Unlike its previous version (VB6), VB .NET is a fully object-oriented language and takes advantage of all the features provided by the .NET Framework.

Because of its similarity to VBScript, which was the server-side language for ASP files, VB .NET is currently the most popular programming language for developing presentation-tier logic for projects developed with the .NET Framework.

This doesn't mean that using VB .NET is an absolute requirement. On the contrary, Visual Studio .NET 2003 (and .NET 1.1) ships with three languages that you can use for ASP.NET development: VB .NET, C#, and JScript .NET.

Moreover, you can use different .NET languages for different modules of the project, because they will be perfectly interoperable. For more information about how the .NET Framework works, you should read a general-purpose .NET book.

Apart from using VB .NET for the code-behind files, you'll use the same language to code the middle tier classes. You'll create the first classes in Chapter 3 when building the product catalog, and you'll learn more details there.

Using Visual Studio .NET

Visual Studio is by far the most powerful tool you can find to develop .NET applications. Visual Studio is a complete programming environment capable of working with many types of projects and files, including Windows and Web Forms projects, setup and deployment projects, and many others. Visual Studio also can be used as an interface to the database to create tables and stored procedures, implement table relationships, and so on.

Although we'll exclusively use Visual Studio for writing this project, it is important to know that you don't have to. ASP.NET and the C#, VB .NET, and JScript .NET compilers are available as free downloads at http://www.microsoft.com as part of the .NET Framework SDK (Software Developers Kit), and a simple editor like Notepad is enough to create any kind of web page.

TIP *An alternative to Visual Studio .NET is Web Matrix, which is a free ASP.NET development tool that you can download at* http://www.asp.net/webmatrix *(its installer kit is only 1.3MB). Web Matrix doesn't support all the features you can find in Visual Studio .NET, such as support for code-behind files, IntelliSense, or debugging, but it can be useful for developing small ASP.NET applications. Web Matrix isn't used in this book, but if you're interested in more details, read the articles at* http://aspnet.4guysfromrolla.com/articles/061803-1.aspx *or* http://www.aspnetpro.com/productreviews/2003/06/asp200306KM_p/asp200306KM_p.asp.

You'll explore the various features of Visual Studio as you create JokePoint.

Using SQL Server

SQL Server is Microsoft's player in the relational database management systems (RDBMS) field. This complex software program's purpose is to store, manage, and retrieve data as quickly and reliably as possible. You'll use SQL Server to store all the information regarding your web site, which will be dynamically placed on the web page by the application logic. Simply said, all data regarding the products, departments, users, shopping carts, and so on will be stored and managed by SQL Server.

SQL Server in its commercial versions ships with various management utilities. Perhaps the most popular is the Enterprise Manager, a program that allows you to perform almost any operation on a database, including set-up security and backup strategies. The other utility much loved by programmers is the Query Analyzer, a simple yet powerful application that allows you to execute and analyze SQL statements. If you aren't familiar with SQL, you'll learn more about it in the next chapter.

Microsoft Database Engine (MSDE)

Visual Studio .NET ships with a lightweight, free version of SQL Server named MSDE (Microsoft Database Engine), which you'll use as the database backend system. If you have SQL Server Standard or Enterprise edition, you can use that instead.

MSDE has some performance limitations, but it is free and totally compatible with the commercial and expensive version of SQL Server. This means that you can use MSDE on your development machines and then simply transfer the database to the full SQL Server versions at the client site. This is an important advantage over the old technique of using Access on development machines and then upsizing to SQL Server when moving the application to the client site.

MSDE doesn't ship with the management programs mentioned earlier, so you'll use Visual Studio to interact with the database engine. The first steps in interacting with SQL Server come a bit later in this chapter when you create the JokePoint database.

SQL Server and the Three-Tier Architecture

It should be clear by now that SQL Server is somehow related to the data tier. However, if you haven't worked with databases until now, it might be less than obvious that SQL Server is more than a simple store of data. Apart from the actual data stored inside, SQL Server is also capable of storing logic in the form of **stored procedures**. The stored procedures are stored internally in the database, and can be called from external programs. In your architecture, the stored procedures will be called from the business tier. The stored procedures in turn access the data store, get the results, and return them to the business tier (or perform the necessary operations).

Figure 2-5 shows the technologies associated with every tier in the three-tier architecture. SQL Server contains the data tier of the application (stored procedures that contain the logic to access and manipulate data), and also the actual data store.

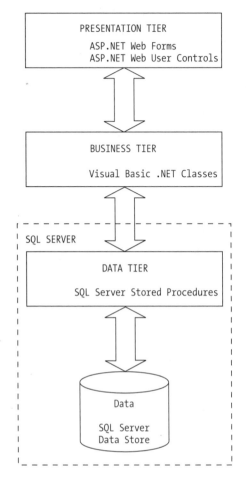

Figure 2-5. Microsoft technologies and the three-tier architecture

The stored procedures in the database are written in a language called T-SQL (Transact-SQL), which is the SQL dialect recognized by SQL Server. SQL, or Structured Query Language, is the language used to interact with the database. SQL is used to transmit to the database instructions such as "Send me the last 10 orders" or "Delete product #123."

Following Coding Standards

Although coding and naming standards might not seem that important at first, they definitely shouldn't be overlooked. Not following a set of rules for your code will almost always result in code that's hard to read, understand, and maintain. On the other hand, when you follow a consistent way of coding, you can say your code is already half documented, which is an important contribution toward the project's maintainability, especially when many people are working at the same project at the same time.

> **TIP** *Some companies have their own policies regarding coding and naming standards, while in other cases you'll have the flexibility to use your own preferences. In either case, the golden rule to follow is* be consistent *in the way you code.*

Naming conventions refer to many elements within a project, simply because almost all of a project's elements have names: the project itself, Web Forms, Web User Controls, instances of Web User Controls, and other interface elements, classes, variables, methods, method parameters, database tables, database columns, stored procedures, and so on. Without some discipline when naming all those elements, after a week of coding, you won't understand a line of what you've written.

This book tries to stick to Microsoft's recommendations regarding naming conventions. Now the philosophy is that a variable name should express what the object does, and not its data type. We'll talk more about naming conventions while building the site. Right now, it's time to play.

Creating the Visual Studio .NET Project

So far we have dealt with theory regarding the application you're going to create. Now it's time to start implementing it.

> **NOTE** *Before reading on, note that we assume you have Visual Studio .NET, ASP.NET, IIS (Internet Information Services) 5.0, and MSDE or SQL Server installed on your computer. If you're not sure, please consult Appendix A, which explains how to do all the installation work.*

The first step toward building the successful JokePoint site is to open Visual Studio .NET and create an ASP.NET Web Application. You'll do this step-by-step in the exercises that follow. From Visual Studio, you'll be able to manage all of the application's code for all three tiers.

Visual Studio .NET does a great job of automating many tasks. For example, when creating a new ASP.NET Web Application, you just need to specify the web location where you want it to be created, for example `http://localhost/JokePoint`. If you do this, Visual Studio will create the project files in a new folder named `JokePoint` in the `web root` folder (by default located at `\Inetpub\wwwroot`), and also a `JokePoint` virtual directory that points to that folder. This way, when loading `http://localhost/JokePoint` using a web browser, the new Web Application will be executed.

For our purposes, we prefer to have the project physically located in a different folder on the disk than \Inetpub\wwwroot\JokePoint, which is the default path used by Visual Studio. To achieve this, you must manually create the virtual directory http://localhost/JokePoint.

Exercise: Creating the JokePoint Project in a Custom Location

Follow the steps in this exercise to create the virtual directory for the Visual Studio project, and the project itself:

1. Create a new folder named MyCommerceSite, which will be used for all the work you'll do in this book. We are creating it in the root folder of C:\ so it will be easier to work with it, but we'll use relative paths in the code so you may choose another location or drive if you prefer.

2. In the MyCommerceSite folder, create another folder named JokePoint. This folder will contain the JokePoint project. If you created MyCommerceSite in C:\, right now the complete path to JokePoint should be C:\MyCommerceSite\ JokePoint.

3. In Windows, open Control Panel, go to Administrative Tools, and double-click the Internet Information Services tool. Here make sure the Default Web Site located in *local computername*\Web Sites is visible. If you're using Windows XP, your IIS tool should look like Figure 2-6.

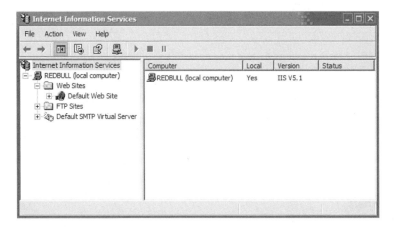

Figure 2-6. The IIS Administration tool

4. Right-click Default Web Site, and select New ➤ Virtual Directory. Click Next, and in the Wizard that pops up, type **JokePoint** for Alias as shown in Figure 2-7.

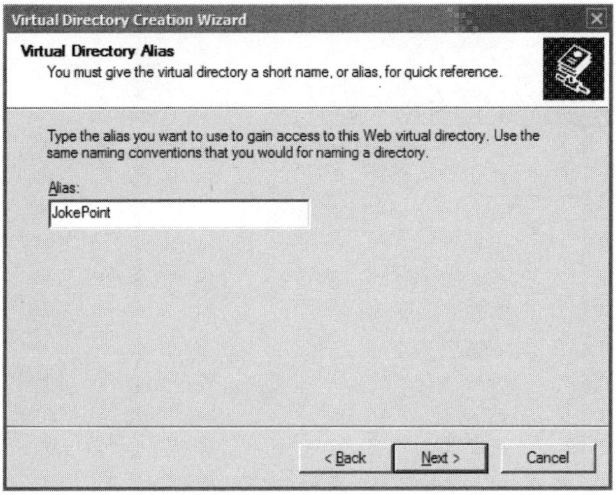

Figure 2-7. Choosing a name for the virtual folder

5. Click Next. In the window that appears, type or browse to the JokePoint folder that you just created (see Figure 2-8).

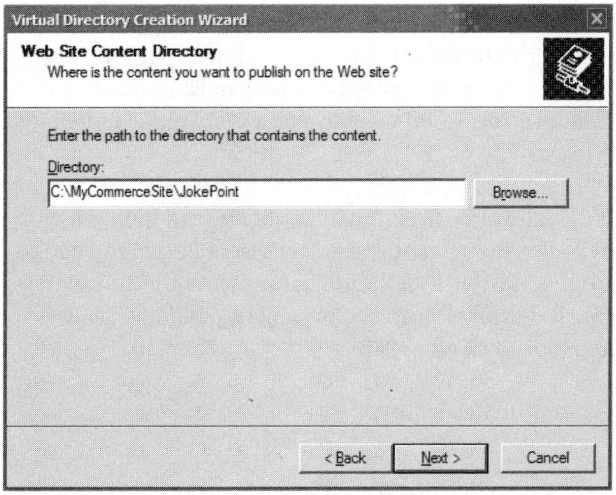

Figure 2-8. Choosing a physical folder to associate with the virtual folder

6. Click Next. In the next window, leave the default options of Read and Run scripts checked. Click Next again, and then Finish to close the wizard. At this point, the JokePoint virtual directory should be selected in the IIS management console (see Figure 2-9).

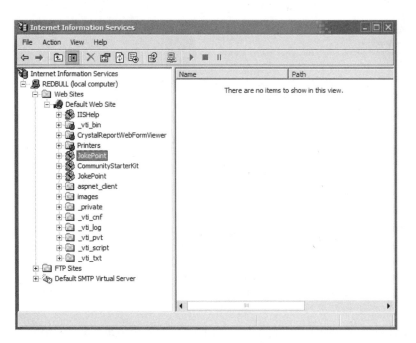

Figure 2-9. JokePoint virtual folder in the IIS Administration tool

After creating this virtual directory, if you try to load the address
http://localhost/JokePoint in Internet Explorer, it would attempt to load
the site located in the MyCommerceSite\JokePoint folder. Because the location
is empty, you would get an error. So, let's create a new Web Application in the
mentioned folder.

7. Start Visual Studio .NET, select File from the main menu, and then select
    New ➤ Project. In the dialog box that opens, select Visual Basic Projects as
    the project type, and then ASP.NET Web Application from the Templates
    panel. Enter **http://localhost/JokePoint** for the project location. The New
    Project window should look like Figure 2-10.

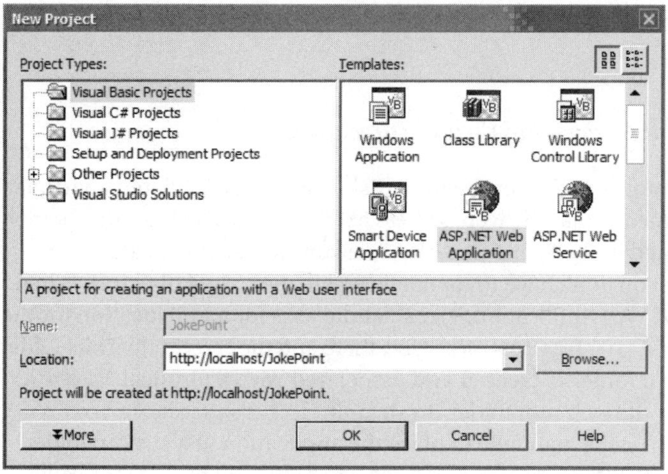

Figure 2-10. Choosing the web location for the new Web Application

8. Click OK. Visual Studio now creates the new project in the JokePoint folder that you created at the beginning of this exercise.

9. In the new project, a new Web Form called WebForm1.aspx is created by default as shown in Figure 2-11.

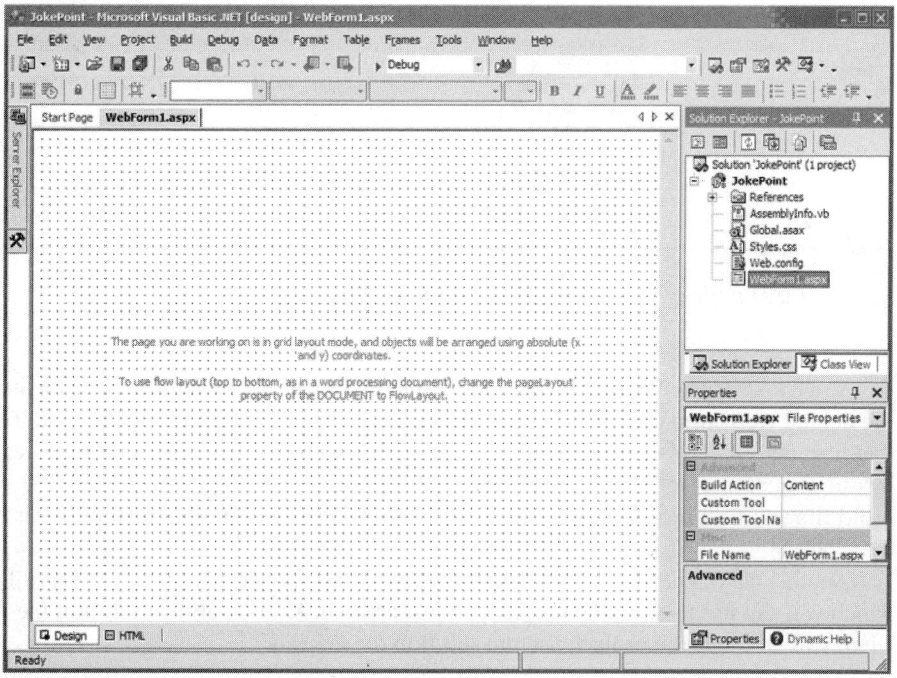

Figure 2-11. Visual Studio .NET

Congratulations! You have just completed the first step in creating your e-commerce store!

How It Works: Physical Folders and Virtual Directories

You have created a physical folder on the hard disk, and then associated a virtual directory with it. This means that the web address `http://localhost/JokePoint` points to the application located in the `MyCommerceSite\JokePoint` folder you created.

Keep in mind that you don't have to manually create the virtual directory. When creating a new ASP.NET Web Application, Visual Studio asks for a web location for the application. If you type `http://localhost/JokePoint` there and the `JokePoint` virtual folder doesn't exist, the virtual folder is created and associated with a physical `JokePoint` folder that is created in the web root folder (by default `InetPub\wwwroot`).

We have done these steps manually to place the application in a custom folder instead of the default one. If you're curious to see which files were automatically created by Visual Studio, open the `MyCommerceSite\JokePoint` folder in Explorer (see Figure 2-12).

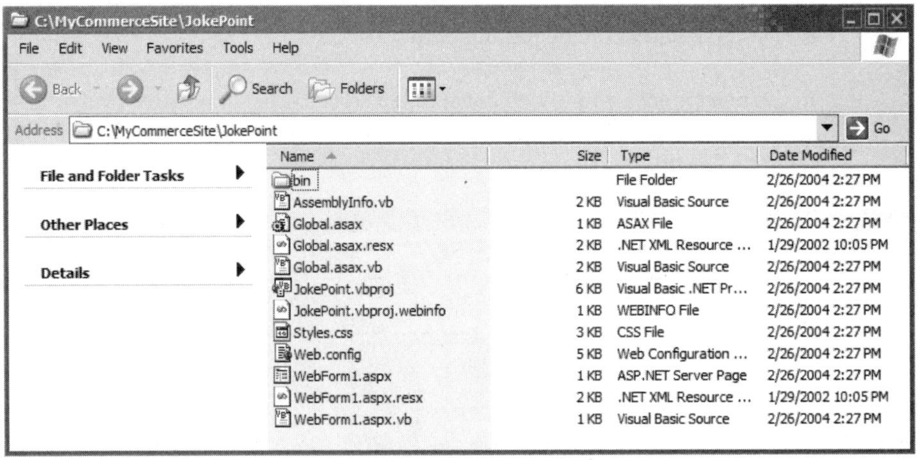

Figure 2-12. The files generated by Visual Studio .NET

You'll take a look at some of these files later. Probably the most interesting file is the default Web Form created by Visual Studio, `WebForm1.aspx` and the code behind it, `WebForm1.aspx.vb`. This Web Form (empty by default) can be loaded in Internet Explorer by opening `http://localhost/JokePoint/WebForm1.aspx`, although you should first build the solution by going to Build ➤ Build Solution (the default shortcut key is **Ctrl+Shift+B**).

Another file you need to know about is the Visual Basic project file (`jokepoint.vbproj`), which you can use to open the project you just created. After creating a solution file when you first save the project, use the solution file instead.

Implementing the Site Skeleton

The visual and functional design of the site is usually agreed upon after a discussion with the client, and in collaboration with a professional web designer. As noted earlier, because this is a programming book, we won't focus too much on visual design issues. Furthermore, we want to have a fairly simple design that will allow you to learn how to create an e-commerce site quickly, without spending time with unnecessary details.

All pages in JokePoint, including the first page, will have the structure shown in Figure 2-13.

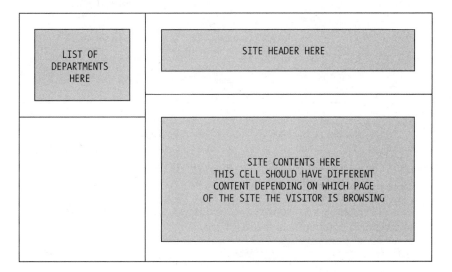

Figure 2-13. Web page structure in JokePoint

Although we'll discuss the detailed structure of the product catalog in the next chapter, right now you know that you'll have a main list of departments that needs to be displayed on every page of the site. You also want the site header to be visible in any page the visitor browses.

To implement this structure as simply as possible, you'll use user controls to create the separate parts of the page as shown in Figure 2-14.

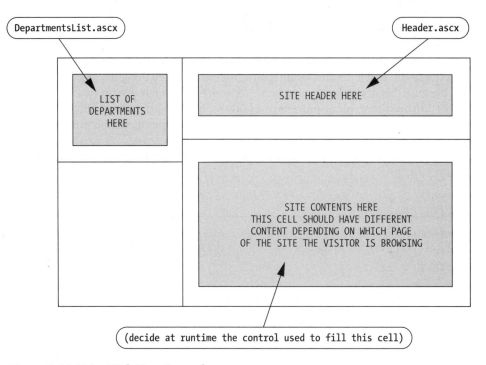

Figure 2-14. Using Web User Controls to generate content

As Figure 2.14 suggests, you'll create two Web User Controls, DepartmentsList and Header, which will help you populate the first page.

> **TIP** *You have a number of options for filling the lower-left part of the page, which we'll leave empty in JokePoint. For example, you can fill that table cell with an AdRotator control, to display ads on your web site. Please see the .NET Framework documentation for more information on the AdRotator Web Server Control.*

As we talked about earlier in the chapter, having user controls to implement different pieces of functionality is beneficial. Having different, unrelated pieces of functionality logically separated from one another gives you the flexibility to modify them independently, and even reuse them in other pages without having to write HTML code and the supporting code-behind file again. It's also extremely easy to extend the functionality, or change the place of a feature implemented as a user control in the parent web page; changing the location of a Web User Control is anything but a complicated and lengthy process.

The list of departments and the site header will be present in every page of the site. The only part that changes while browsing through the site will be the contents cell, which will update itself depending on the site location requested by the visitor. For implementing that cell, you have two main options. You can either add a user control that changes itself depending on the location or use different user controls to populate that cell depending on the location being browsed. There is no rule about which method to use, because it mainly depends on the specifics of the project. For JokePoint, you'll create a number of user controls that will fill that location.

The remainder of this chapter will show you how to create the main web page and the header Web User Control. We'll deal with the other user controls in the following chapters. Finally, at the end of the chapter, you'll create the JokePoint database, which will be the last step in laying the foundations of the project.

Building the First Page

At the moment, you have a single Web Form in the site, WebForm1.aspx, which was automatically added by Visual Studio when you created the project. To work with more familiar names, in the next exercise you'll delete this form from the project and add a new form called default.aspx. You also can rename WebForm1.aspx to default.aspx, but this wouldn't change the contents of the code-behind file, so it's preferable to start with a new, clean form.

You now will learn how to write default.aspx with placeholders for the three major parts of the site: the header, the table of departments, and the page contents cell.

Exercise: Creating the Main Web Page

Follow these steps to write default.aspx for the three major parts of the site:

1. Download the files for this chapter from the Downloads section of the Apress web site at http://www.apress.com or from http://www.CristianDarie.ro. You'll need to use the Images folder, which contains background pictures for the main web page. Copy the Images folder from the downloaded files to the JokePoint folder that you created in the previous section.

2. Open the JokePoint project in Visual Studio, if it isn't already open. Let's first delete the automatically generated Web Form file, WebForm1.aspx. To do this, make sure Solution Explorer is visible by selecting View ➤ Solution Explorer (the default shortcut is **Ctrl+Alt+L**). Right-click WebForm1.aspx in Solution Explorer and select Delete. Click OK when asked for confirmation.

3. To add a new Web Form, right-click the project's name, JokePoint, in Solution Explorer, and then choose Add ➤ Add Web Form. Enter **default.aspx** for the name of the new Web Form. If you type **default**, Visual Studio will add the .aspx extension for you. Click Open.

4.   Right-click default.aspx, and click the Set As Start Page option (see Figure 2-15). This marks default.aspx as the default Web Form that is loaded when browsing to http://localhost/JokePoint in a web browser. Also, now when you start your Web Application in debug mode (**F5** is the default key), default.aspx will be loaded by default in Internet Explorer. If you test this, make sure you stop the project from execution (you can do this by simply closing the Internet Explorer instance opened by Visual Studio) before proceeding to the next step.

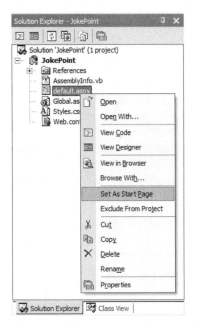

Figure 2-15. Setting default.aspx *as the start page*

5.   Now open the default.aspx Web Form by double-clicking it in Solution Explorer. You should be presented with a form like the one shown in Figure 2-16.

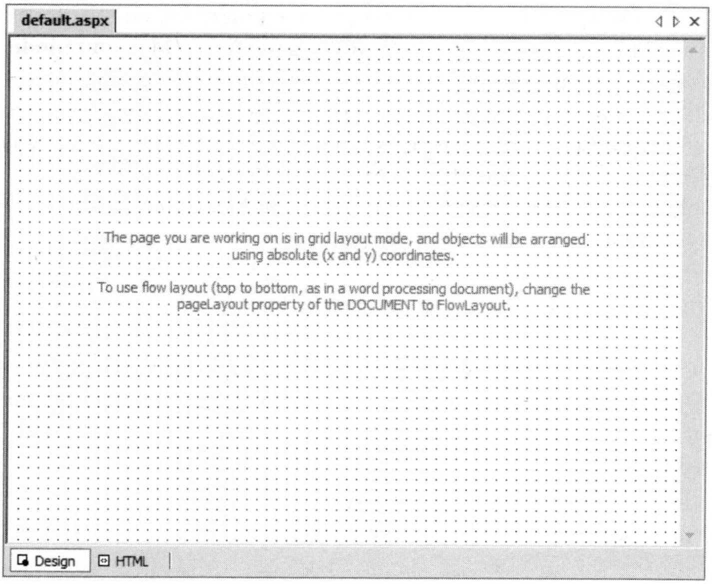

Figure 2-16. `default.aspx` *in Design View*

Figure 2-16 shows the **design window** of Visual Studio .NET. This window allows you to edit a Web Form using either the **Design View** or the **HTML View** modes. You can see the Web Form in Design View mode in Figure 2-16, indicated by the highlighted Design button at the bottom of the window.

When using Design View, you can visually edit the form in a WYSIWYG (What You See Is What You Get) editor by dragging and dropping components from the toolbox into the form or by directly writing text on the form. The other way of editing a Web Form is using HTML View mode, where you can directly edit the HTML of the Web Form.

No matter which edit mode you use, Visual Studio always keeps both views synchronized. If you edit the form in Design View and then switch to HTML View, you'll see the changes there; when directly changing the HTML, you'll see the results when switching back to Design View.

While creating JokePoint, you'll use both Design View and HTML View, depending on which one takes less time for the task at hand. Also, sometimes HTML View will be used to gain better control of the code.

When using the Design View, you can use two layout modes to edit the form. As you can see in Figure 2-16, the default working mode is **grid layout mode**. This means when you drag and drop components from the toolbox, they are placed at the exact position where you dropped them because their location is stored using absolute coordinates. This mode is similar to the way controls are placed in VB6, or in Windows Forms projects in Visual Studio .NET. However, many developers prefer to work in the **flow layout mode**, where the HTML generated is similar to that which of "regular" web pages.

You'll use the flow layout mode while developing JokePoint.

6. If the Properties window isn't visible, select View ➤ Properties to see it (the default shortcut key is **F4**). Make sure the design window is selected by clicking it, and then modify its pageLayout property to FlowLayout in the Properties window (see Figure 2-17).

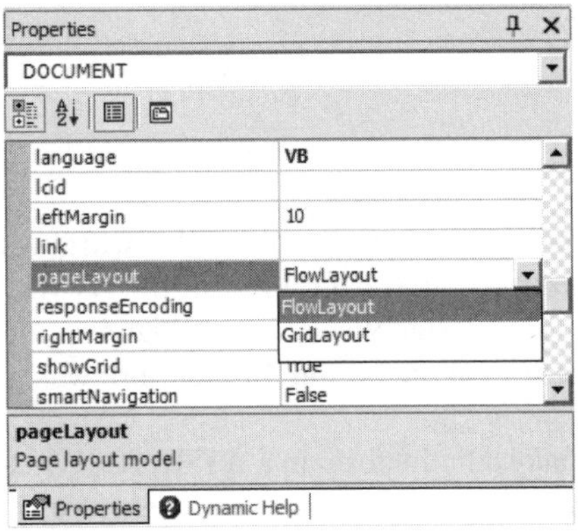

Figure 2-17. Setting default.aspx *to use flow layout*

7. Enter HTML View by selecting the HTML button at the bottom of the designer window as shown in Figure 2-18.

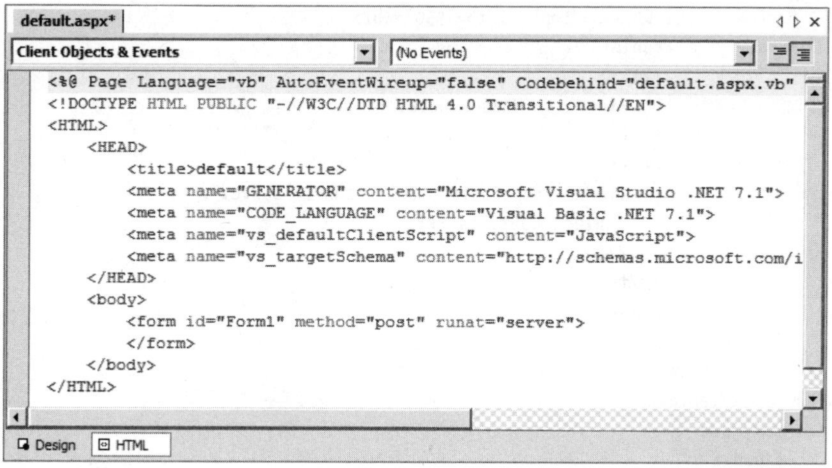

Figure 2-18. default.aspx *in HTML View*

8. Here you can see the code Visual Studio generated. While in HTML View update the Web Form like this:

```
<%@ Page Language="vb" AutoEventWireup="false" Codebehind="default.aspx.vb"
Inherits="JokePoint._default"%>
<!DOCTYPE HTML PUBLIC "-//W3C//DTD HTML 4.0 Transitional//EN">
<html>
  <head>
    <title>JokePoint</title>
      <meta name="GENERATOR" content="Microsoft Visual Studio .NET 7.1">
      <meta name="CODE_LANGUAGE" content="Visual Basic .NET 7.1">
      <meta name="vs_defaultClientScript" content="JavaScript">
      <meta name="vs_targetSchema"
                    content="http://schemas.microsoft.com/intellisense/ie5">
  </HEAD>
  <body>
    <form id="Form1" runat="server">
      <table height="100%" cellSpacing="0" cellPadding="0" width="770" border="0">
        <tr>
          <td width="190" height="100%">
            <table height="100%" width="190" cellspacing="0" cellpadding="0">
              <tr>
                <td vAlign="top" height="100%">Place List of Departments Here
                </td>
              </tr>
            </table>
          </td>
```

```
        <td vAlign="top" width="550"><br>
          <table>
            <tr>
              <td>Place Header Here</td>
            </tr>
            <tr>
              <td id="pageContentsCell" runat="server">
                Place Contents Here
              </td>
            </tr>
          </table>
        </td>
      </tr>
    </table>
  </form>
</body>
</html>
```

9. After making these changes, switch back to Design View mode. If no errors were made, the page you see should resemble Figure 2-19.

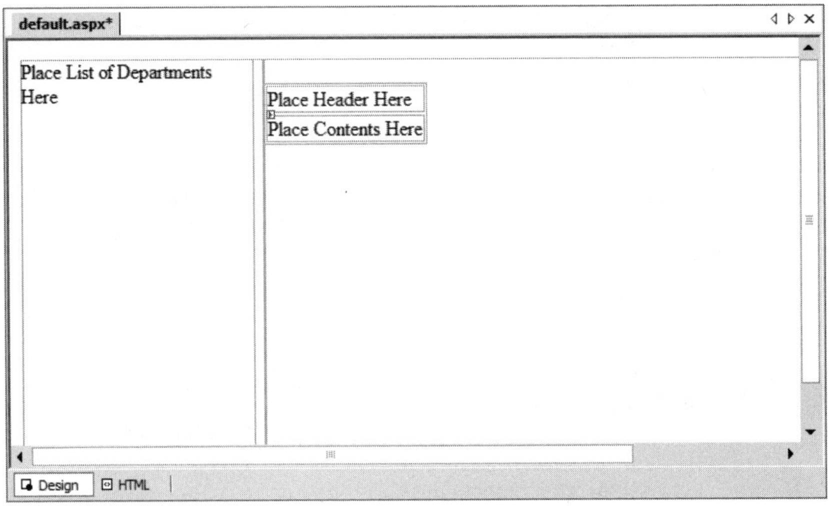

Figure 2-19. `default.aspx` *in Design View*

10. If you haven't changed the default behavior of Visual Studio .NET, you'll see that the Place Contents Here table cell is marked with a little green arrow sign (which is probably hardly visible in the printed screenshot). This indicates that the control is marked to be executed at server-side (on the server). If you look at the HTML, you'll see the `runat="server"` clause:

```
<td id="pageContentsCell" runat="server">
  Place Contents Here
</td>
```

pageContentsCell is an HTML Server Control that allows you to programmatically access the page contents table cell. You need the page contents cell to be executed server-side because you'll need to programmatically fill it with contents when the page is loaded. For the other cells, you know for sure which user controls will be used, and you'll populate them at design time, but the page contents cell must be populated from code.

All server-side controls (including Labels, TextBoxes, and so on) on the page will be marked with the same green symbol.

When adding an HTML Server Control to the form (by adding the runat="server" clause to a simple HTML element), Visual Studio automatically adds an object declaration in the code-behind file, which will allow you to access the control programmatically. To access the code-behind file default.aspx.vb, right-click default.aspx in Solution Explorer and select View Code. Alternatively, you can click the View Code icon at the top of the Solution Explorer window when default.aspx is selected.

Figure 2-20 shows the declaration of the pageContentsCell object, at the beginning of the file.

```
default.aspx*   default.aspx.vb*

_default                                         (Declarations)

Public Class _default
    Inherits System.Web.UI.Page

#Region " Web Form Designer Generated Code "

    'This call is required by the Web Form Designer.
    <System.Diagnostics.DebuggerStepThrough()> Private Sub InitializeComponent()

    End Sub
    Protected WithEvents pageContentsCell As System.Web.UI.HtmlControls.HtmlTableCell

    'NOTE: The following placeholder declaration is required by the Web Form Designer.
    'Do not delete or move it.
    Private designerPlaceholderDeclaration As System.Object
```

Figure 2-20. The code-behind file of default.aspx *(default.aspx.vb)*

In certain situations when adding the control while in HTML mode, Visual Studio forgets to generate that line automatically for you. If this is the case, make sure that line is there by manually adding it as a protected member of the _default class:

```
Protected WithEvents pageContentsCell As _
                System.Web.UI.HtmlControls.HtmlTableCell
```

How It Works: The Main Web Page

You've done a lot in this exercise and learned about some of the features Visual Studio .NET provides.

The main web page contains three major sections. There are three table cells that you'll fill with user controls. The contents cell is the only one that changes while browsing the site—the other two cells will be filled with the same controls no matter what page is visited. This explains why the contents cell is the only one marked to run at the server.

Now you'll see how to create a Web User Control by implementing Header.ascx.

Adding the Header to the Main Page

Finally, after learning so much about how useful user controls are, you get to create one. The Header control will populate the upper-right part of the main page and will look like Figure 2-21.

JokePoint!

Figure 2-21. The JokePoint logo

To keep your site's folder organized, you'll create a separate folder for all the user controls. Having them in a centralized location is helpful, especially when the project grows and contains lots of files.

Exercise: Creating the Header User Control

Follow these steps to create a folder to hold your user controls:

1. Make sure Solution Explorer is visible in Visual Studio. If it isn't, click View ➤ Solution Explorer (**Ctrl+Alt+L** by default). Right-click JokePoint and select Add ➤ New Folder (see Figure 2-22).

Figure 2-22. Adding a new folder to the JokePoint project

2. Enter **UserControls** as the name of the new folder.

3. Now create the Header user control in the UserControls folder. Right-click
    UserControls in Solution Explorer, and then choose Add ➤ Add Web User
    Control.

4. You'll be asked for the name of the new user control. Type **Header.ascx** and
    press **Enter** (see Figure 2-23).

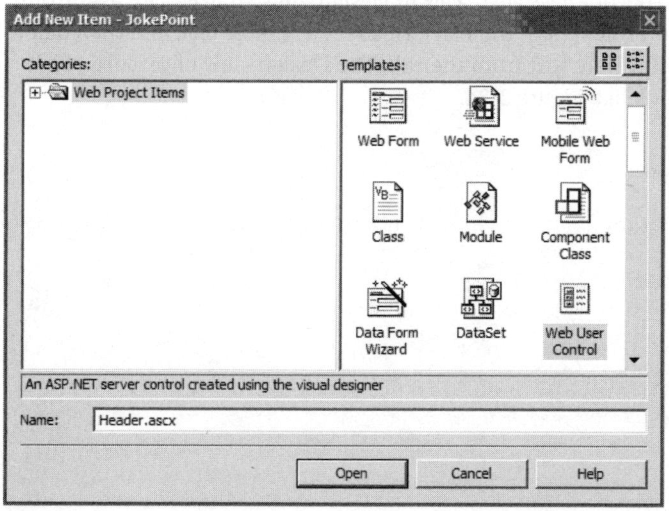

Figure 2-23. Adding a new Web User Control to the project

5. Now open the `Header` Web User Control by double-clicking it in Solution Explorer. Enter the HTML View mode by clicking the HTML button at the bottom of the design window. Modify the HTML code like this:

```
<%@ Control Language="vb" AutoEventWireup="false"
Codebehind="Header.ascx.vb" Inherits="JokePoint.Header"
TargetSchema="http://schemas.microsoft.com/intellisense/ie5" %>

<table border="0" width="550" cellspacing="0" cellpadding="0">
  <TR align="right">
    <td>
      <a href="default.aspx">
        <img src="Images/JokePointLogo.gif" border="0">
      </a>
    </td>
  </TR>
</table>
```

NOTE *If you switch the control to Design View right now, you won't see the image. This happens because the relative path to the* Images *folder points to a different absolute path at design time than at runtime. At runtime, the control will be included and run from within* default.aspx, *not from its current location (the* UserControls *folder).*

6. Select Build ➤ Build Solution (the default shortcut is **Ctrl+Shift+B**) to build the solution. Now open default.aspx in Design View, drag Header.ascx from Solution Explorer, drop it in the Place Header Here table cell, and then delete the Place Header Here text from the cell. The Design view of default.aspx should now look like Figure 2-24.

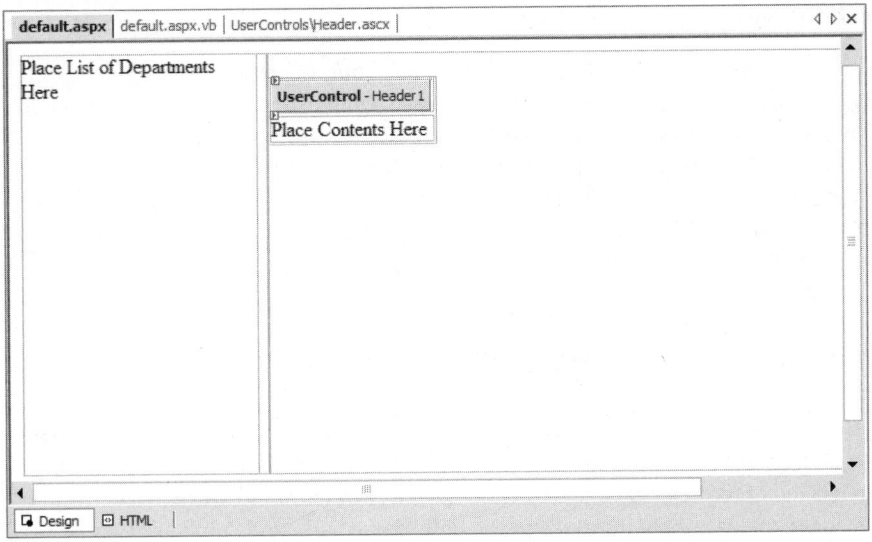

Figure 2-24. Using the Header.ascx *control in* default.aspx

7. Click Debug ➤ Start (**F5** by default) to execute the project. The web page will
    look like Figure 2-25.

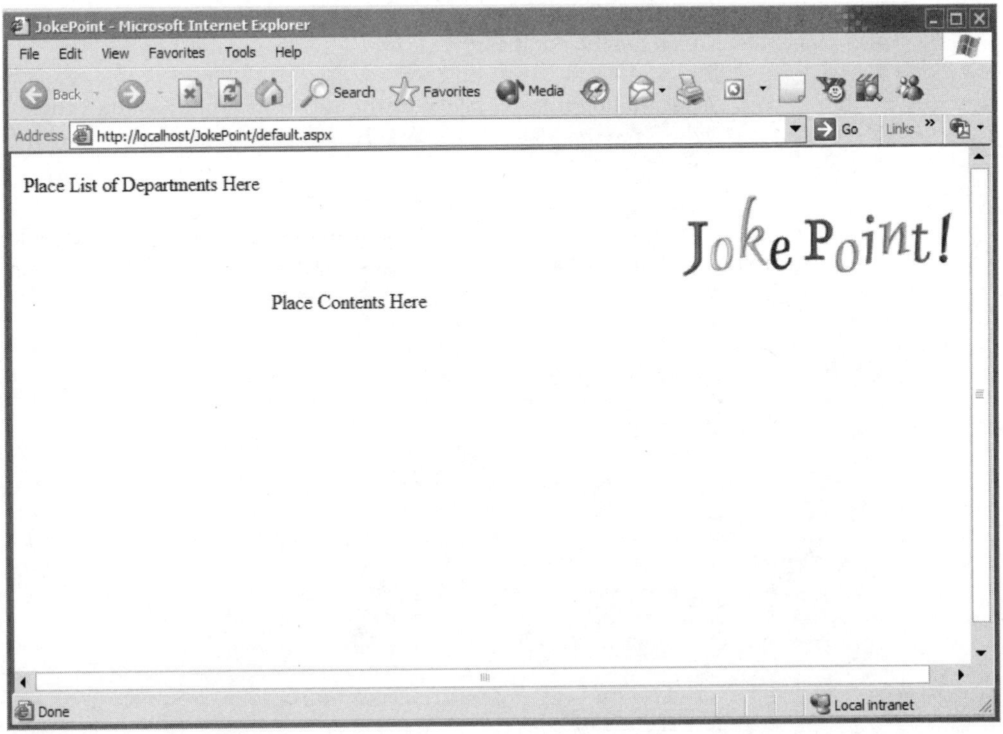

Figure 2-25. JokePoint in action

How It Works: The Header User Control

You created this control by editing its HTML source, but it's possible to use the Design View to drag and drop items to the form as well. When executed alone, this piece of HTML generates the JokePoint logo.

The Header control isn't particularly exciting, but you saw how to create a user control and then add it to a Web Form. This user control can now be reused on other Web Forms, or even on other Web User Controls; hence, it is an easy way to create toolbars, menus, headers (obviously), and other reusable elements.

Creating the SQL Server Database

The final step in this chapter is to create the SQL Server database, although you won't get to effectively use it until the next chapter. If you have SQL Server, you might prefer to use the Enterprise Manager to create the data structures. However, Visual Studio .NET does provide a great interface to the database engine and you'll use that to work with the database.

All the information that needs to be stored for your site, such as data about products, customers, and so on, will be stored in a database named, unsurprisingly, JokePoint.

Exercise: Creating a New Database Using Visual Studio .NET

Follow these steps to create the database:

1. In your Visual Studio project, make sure the Server Explorer window is open. If it isn't, you can either select View ➤ Server Explorer or press the default shortcut keys **Ctrl+Alt+S**.

2. In Server Explorer, open Servers/*localservername*/SQL Servers. Right-click the name of your SQL Server instance, and select New Database as shown in Figure 2-26.

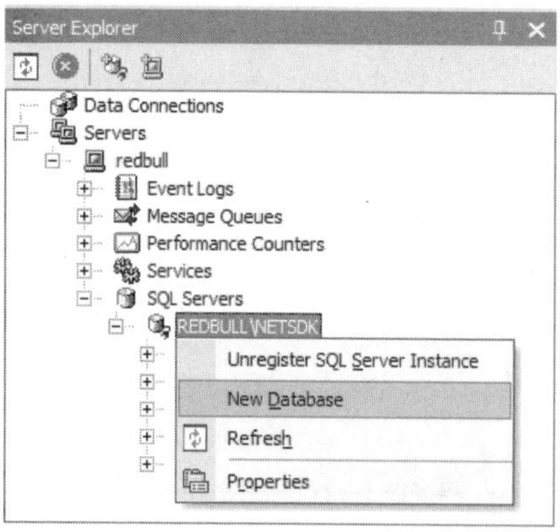

Figure 2-26. Creating a new SQL Server database

3. In the dialog box that appears, you need to choose a name for the new database and the way to log in to SQL Server (see Figure 2-27). The database name will be JokePoint, and for authentication, you can select either Use Windows NT Integrated Security or SQL Server Authentication.

NOTE *With Windows NT Integrated Security, your local Windows account will be used to log in to SQL Server. If you installed MSDE or SQL Server yourself, everything will run smoothly, otherwise you'll need to make sure you're provided with administrative privileges on the SQL Server instance. With SQL Server Authentication, you need to provide a username and password, but note that this authentication mode can be disabled from SQL Server.*

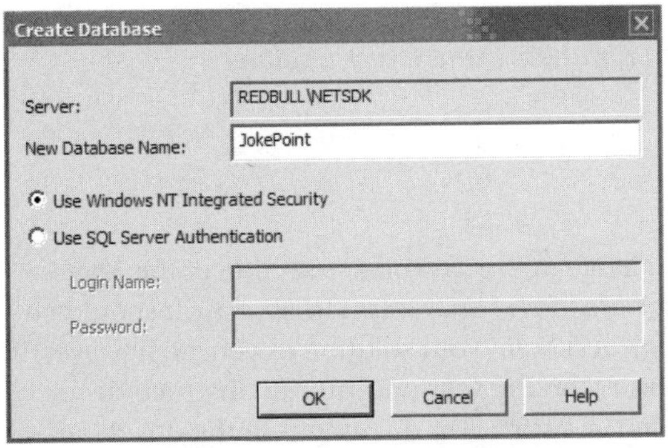

Figure 2-27. Choosing a name from the new database

How It Works: The SQL Server Database

That's it! You have just created a new SQL Server database. The Server Explorer window in Visual Studio is powerful and allows you to control many details of the SQL Server instance. After creating the JokePoint database, you can expand its nodes and see what it contains as shown in Figure 2-28. Because you just created an empty database, its nodes are also empty, but you'll take care of this detail in the following chapters.

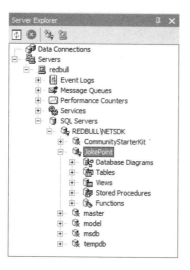

Figure 2-28. Accessing the JokePoint database from Server Explorer

Downloading the Code

The code you have just written is available in the Downloads section of the Apress web site at `http://www.apress.com` or from `http://www.CristianDarie.ro`. It should be easy for you to read through this book and build your solution as you go; however, if you want to check something from our working version, you can. Instructions on loading the chapters are available in the `README.TXT` document in the download. On `http://www.CristianDarie.ro`, you can also find a link to an online version of JokePoint.

Summary

We covered a lot of ground in this chapter, didn't we? We talked about the three-tier architecture and how it helps you create great flexible and scalable applications. You also saw how each of the technologies used in this book fits into the three-tier architecture.

So far you have a very flexible and scalable application because it only has a main web page and a `Header` user control, but you'll feel the real advantages of using a disciplined way of coding in the next chapters. In this chapter, you have only coded the basic, static part of the presentation tier and created the JokePoint database, which is the support for the data tier. In the next chapter, you'll start implementing the product catalog and learn a lot about how to dynamically generate visual content using data stored in the database with the help of the middle tier and with smart and fast controls and omponents in the presentation tier.

CHAPTER 3

Creating the Product Catalog: Part I

AFTER LEARNING ABOUT the three-tier architecture and implementing a bit of your web site's main page, it's time to continue your work by starting to create the JokePoint product catalog.

Because the product catalog is composed of many components, you'll create it over two chapters. In this chapter, you'll create the first database table, create a stored procedure, and implement data access methods in the middle tier. By the end of this chapter, you'll finally have something dynamically generated on your web page.

The main topics we'll touch on in this chapter are

- Thinking about what you want the catalog to look like and what functionality it should support

- Creating the database structures for the catalog and the data tier of the catalog

- Implementing the business tier objects required to make the catalog run

- Implementing a functional user interface for the product catalog

Showing the Visitor Your Products

One of the essential features required in any e-store is to allow the visitor to easily browse through the products. Just imagine what Amazon.com would be like without its excellent product catalog!

Whether your visitors are looking for something specific or just browsing, it is important to make sure their experience with your site is a pleasant one. When looking for a specific product or product type, you want the visitor to find it as easily as possible. This is why you'll want to add search functionality to the site, and also find a clever way of structuring products into categories so they can be quickly and intuitively accessed.

Depending on the size of the store, it might be enough to group products under a number of categories, but if there are a lot of products, you need to find even more ways to categorize and structure the product catalog.

Determining the structure of the catalog is one of the first tasks to accomplish in this chapter. Once this is done, we'll move to the technical details that will make the catalog work.

What Does a Product Catalog Look Like?

Today's web surfers are more demanding than they used to be. They expect to find information quickly on whatever product or service they have in mind, and if they don't find it, they are likely to go to the competition before giving the site a second chance. Of course, you don't want this to happen to *your* visitors, so you need to structure the catalog to make it as intuitive and helpful as possible.

Besides, if you *do* have the product in your catalog, wouldn't it be a shame if your visitor didn't buy it because they couldn't find it? You need to place the products exactly where the visitor expects them to be and make them easily accessible with an easy-to-use interface.

Because the e-store will start with around 100 products and will probably have many more in the future, it's not enough to just group them in categories. The store also has a number of departments and each department will contain a number of categories. Each category can then have any number of products attached to it.

 NOTE *Even if you have a pretty clear idea of the categories and departments, the client wants these to be configurable from the administrative part of the web site. This requirement is not unusual, because it is likely that categories and even departments will change in time. Of course, one solution would be for you to manually change these whenever needed, but this solution would be highly unprofessional. You'll create the administrative part of the product catalog, which will allow the client to manage the departments, categories, and products, in Chapter 7.*

Another particularly important detail that you need to think about is whether a category can exist in more than one department, and whether a product can exist in more than one category. As you might suspect, this is the kind of decision that can have implications on the way you code the product catalog, so you need to consult your client on this matter.

For the JokePoint product catalog, each category can exist in only one department, but a product can exist in more than one category. For example, the product "Deadly Phantom Costume" will appear in both "Costumes for Men" and "Costumes for Women" categories. This decision will have some implications in the way we design the database, and we'll highlight them when we get there.

Finally, apart from having the products grouped in categories, we also want to have featured products. For this web site, a product can be featured either on the front page or in the department pages. Let's look at a few screenshots that will explain this by themselves.

Previewing the Product Catalog

Although we'll have the fully functional product catalog finished by the end of the next chapter, taking a look at it right now will help us have a better idea about we're heading. In Figure 3-1, you can see the JokePoint front page and two of its featured products.

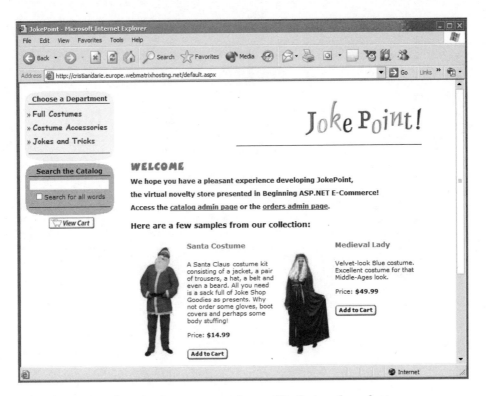

Figure 3-1. The JokePoint front page and two of its featured products

Note the departments list in the upper-left corner of the page. The list of departments is dynamically generated with data gathered from the database; we'll implement the list of departments in this chapter.

When site visitors click a department in the departments list, they go to the main page of the specified department. This will replace the store's list of catalog-featured products with a page containing information specific to the selected department—including the list of featured products for that department. In Figure 3-2, you see the page that will appear when the Full Costumes department is clicked.

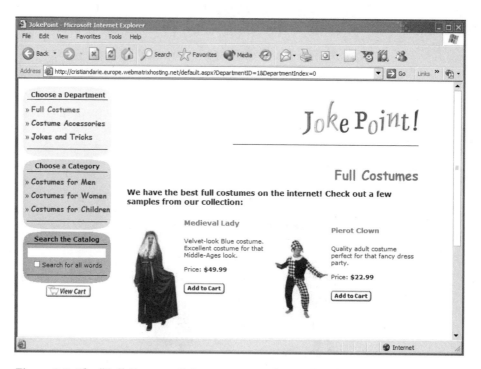

Figure 3-2. The "Full Costumes" department and two of its featured products

Under the list of departments, you can now see the list of categories that belong to the selected department. In the right side of the screen you can see the name, description, and featured products of the selected department. We decided to list only the featured products in the department page, in part because the complete list would be too long. The text above the list of featured products is the description for the selected department, which means you'll need to store in the database both a name and a description for each department.

In this page, when a particular category from the categories list is selected, all of its products are listed, along with updated title and description text. In Figure 3-3 you can see how that page appears when selecting the "Costumes for Children" category.

Figure 3-3. The "Costumes for Children" category

Planning the Departments List of Your Catalog

As you can see, the product catalog, although not very complicated, has more parts that need to be covered. In this chapter, you'll only create the departments list (see Figure 3-4), located in the upper left of the page.

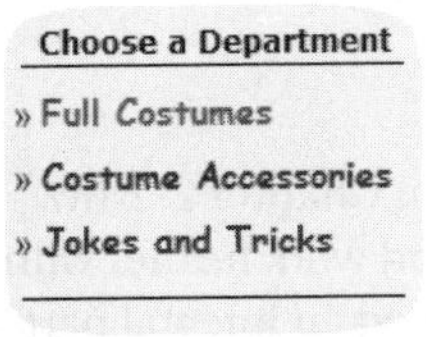

Choose a Department
» Full Costumes
» Costume Accessories
» Jokes and Tricks

Figure 3-4. The departments list

This departments list will be the first dynamically generated data in your site because the names of the departments will be extracted from the database.

We cover just the creation of the department list in this chapter, which is actually a user control, because we'll also take a closer look at the mechanism that makes the control work. After you understand what happens behind the list of departments, you'll quickly implement the other components in Chapter 4.

In Chapter 2, we discussed the three-tiered architecture that you'll use to implement the Web Application. The product catalog part of the site makes no exception to the rule, and its components (including the departments list) will be spread over the three logical layers. Figure 3-5 previews what you'll create at each tier in this chapter to achieve a functional departments list.

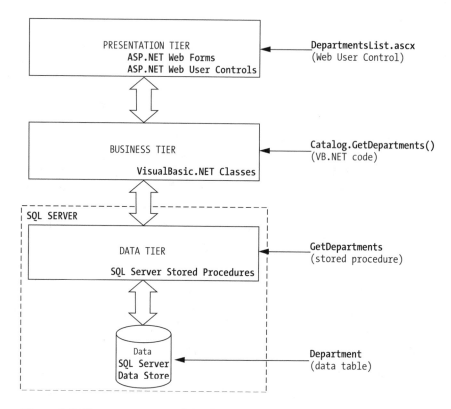

Figure 3-5. The components of the departments list

So far you have only played a bit with the presentation tier in Chapter 2. Now, when building the catalog, you'll finally meet the other two tiers and work further with the JokePoint database. The database backend itself is not considered an integral part of the three-tiered architecture.

These are the main steps you will take toward having your own dynamically generated department list. Note that you'll start with the database, and make your way to the presentation tier:

1. You'll create the Department table in the database. This table will store data regarding the store's departments. Before adding this table, you'll learn the basic concepts of working with relational databases.

2. You'll add the GetDepartments stored procedure to the database, which (like all the other stored procedures you'll write) is logically located in the data tier part of the application. At this step, you'll learn how to speak with the database using SQL.

3. You'll create the business tier components of the departments list. You'll learn how to communicate with the database by calling the stored procedure and sending the results to the presentation tier.

4. Finally you'll implement the `DepartmentsList.ascx` control, which represents the goal of this chapter.

So, let's start with the database.

Storing Catalog Information

Although this is not a book about databases or relational database design, you'll learn all you need to know to understand the product catalog and make it work. For more information about database programming using SQL Server, read *Professional SQL Server 2000 Programming* (ISBN: 1-86100-448-6), published by Wrox Press, or Robin Dewson's *Beginning SQL Server 2000 Programming* (ISBN: 1-59059-252-2), published by Apress.

Essentially, a relational database is made up of **data tables** and the **relationships** that exist between them. Because in this chapter you'll work with a single data table, we'll cover only the database theory that applies to the table as a separate, individual database item. In the next chapter, when you'll add the other tables to the picture, we'll take a closer look at the theory behind relational databases by analyzing how the tables relate to each other.

 NOTE *In a real world situation, you would probably design the whole database (or at least all the tables relevant to the feature you build) from the start. However, we chose to split the development over two chapters to maintain a better balance of theory and practice.*

So, let's start with a little bit of theory, after which we'll create the Department data table and the rest of the required components:

Understanding Data Tables

This section is a quick database lesson that covers the essential information you need to know to design simple data tables. We'll briefly discuss the main parts that make up a database table:

- Primary Keys

- SQL Server data types

- Unique columns

- Nullable columns and default values

- Identity columns

- Indexes

NOTE *If you have enough experience with SQL Server, you might want to skip this section and go directly to the "Creating the Table" section.*

This book assumes you know the basic database concepts. Still, let's make sure we use the same terms. The data in Figure 3-6 is extracted from the pubs database that comes with SQL Server.

```
                        Authors Table

                        data column
                        (data field)


                Author              Phone          Address
                ---------------     ----------     ----------------
                White, Johnson      408 496-7223   10932 Bigge Rd.
                Green, Marjorie     415 986-7020   309 63rd St. #411
data row        Carson, Cheryl      415 548-7723   589 Darwin Ln.
(data record)   O'Leary, Micheal    408 286-2428   22 Cleveland Av. #14
                Straight, Dean      415 834-2919   5420 College Av.
                Smith, Meander      913 843-0462   10 Mississippi Dr.
                Bennet, Abraham     415 658-9932   6223 Bateman St.
                Dull, Ann           415 836-7128   3410 Blonde St.
                Gringlesby, Burt    707 938-6445   PO Box 792
                Locksley, Charlene  415 585-4620   18 Broadway Av.
                Green, Morningstar  615 297-2723   22 Graybar House Rd.
```

Figure 3-6. Sample data from the pubs database

A data table is made up of columns and rows. Columns are also referred to as **fields**, and rows are sometimes also called **records**.

Still, in a relational database, a good deal of hidden logic exists behind a simple list of data rows.

The Department Table

The database element of the product catalog is composed of tables, table relationships, and stored procedures. Because this chapter only covers the departments list, you'll only need to create one data table: the Department table. This table will store your departments' data, and is one of the simplest tables you'll work with.

With the help of tools such as the SQL Server Enterprise Manager or Visual Studio .NET, it's easy to create a data table in the database *if* you know for sure what kind of data it will store. When designing a table, you must consider which fields it should contain and which data types should be used for those fields. Besides a field's data type, there are a few more properties to consider; we'll learn about them in the following pages.

To determine which fields you need for the Department table, write down a few examples of records that would be stored in that table. Remember from the previous figures that there isn't much information to store about a department—just the name and description for each department. The table containing the departments' data might look like Figure 3-7.

Name	Description
Full Costumes	We have the greatest costumes on the internet! Here are a few samples from our collection:
Costume Accessories	Improve your costumes with these cool accessories. These products are on promotion:
Jokes and Tricks	Funny or scary, but all interesting and harmless! Take a look at these featured products befc

Figure 3-7. Data from the Department *table*

From a table like this, the names would be extracted to populate the list in the upper-left part of the web page, and the descriptions would be used as headers for the featured products list.

Primary Keys

The way you work with data tables in a relational database is a bit different from the way you usually work on paper. A fundamental requirement in relational databases is that each data row in a table must be *uniquely identifiable*. This makes sense because you usually save records into a database so that you can retrieve them later. But you can't do that if each row isn't uniquely identifiable. For example, suppose you add another record to the departments table shown previously in Figure 3-7, making it look like the table shown in Figure 3-8.

Name	Description
Full Costumes	We have the greatest costumes on the internet! Here are a few samples from our collection:
Costume Accessories	Improve your costumes with these cool accessories. These products are on promotion:
Jokes and Tricks	Funny or scary, but all interesting and harmless! Take a look at these featured products befc
Jokes and Tricks	This is the Jokes and Tricks department in JokeShop. Here are its products:

Figure 3-8. Having two departments with the same name

Look at this table, and then describe the "Jokes and Tricks" department. Yep, we have a problem! The problem arises because there are two departments with the name

"Jokes and Tricks". If you queried the table using the Name column, you would get two results.

The solution to the problem consists in using a **primary key**, which allows you to uniquely identify a specific row out of many rows. Technically, a PRIMARY KEY is a *constraint* applied on a table column that guarantees that the column will have unique values across the table.

A table can have a single PRIMARY KEY constraint, which can be composed of one or more columns. Note that the primary key is not a column itself; it is a **constraint** that applies to one or more of the existing columns. Constraints are rules that apply to data tables and make up part of the **data integrity** rules of the database. The database takes care of its own integrity and makes sure these rules aren't broken. If, for example, you try to add two identical values for a column that has a PRIMARY KEY constraint, the database will refuse the operation and generate an error. We'll do some experiments later in this chapter to show this.

NOTE   *Although a* PRIMARY KEY *is not a column, but a constraint that applies to that column, from now on when we refer to primary key, we'll be talking about the column that has the* PRIMARY KEY *constraint applied to it.*

Back to the example, setting the Name column as the primary key of the Department table would solve the problem because two departments would not be allowed to have the same name. If Name is the primary key of the Department table, searching for a row with a specific Name will always produce exactly one result if the name exists, or no results if no records have the specified name.

An alternative solution, and usually the preferred one, is to have an additional column in the table, called an ID column, to act as its primary key. With an ID column, the Department table would look like Figure 3-9.

DepartmentID	Name	Description
1	Full Costumes	We have the greatest costumes on the internet! Here are a few sa
2	Costume Accessories	Improve your costumes with these cool accessories. These product
3	Jokes and Tricks	Funny or scary, but all interesting and harmless! Take a look at the

Figure 3-9. Adding an ID *column as the primary key of* Department

The primary key column is named DepartmentID. We'll use the same naming convention for primary key columns in the other data tables we'll create.

There are two main reasons it's better to create a separate numerical primary key column than to use the Name (or another existing column) as the primary key:

- *Performance*: The database engine handles sorting and searching operations much faster with numerical values than with strings. This becomes even more relevant in the context of working with multiple related tables that need to be frequently joined (you'll learn more about this in Chapter 4).

- *Department name changes*: If you need to rely on the ID value being stable in time, creating an artificial key solves the problem, because it's unlikely you'll ever want to change the ID.

In Figure 3-9, the primary key is composed of a single column, but this is not a requirement. If the primary key is composed of more than one column, the group of primary key columns (taken as a unit) is guaranteed to be unique (but the individual columns that form the primary key can have repeating values in the table). In Chapter 4, you'll see an example of a multi-valued primary key. For now, it's enough to know that they exist.

Unique Columns

UNIQUE is yet another kind of constraint that can be applied to table columns. This constraint is similar to the PRIMARY KEY constraint because it doesn't allow duplicate data in a column. Still, there are differences. Although there is only one PRIMARY KEY constraint per table, you are allowed to have as many UNIQUE constraints as you like.

Columns having the UNIQUE constraint are useful when you already have a primary key, but still have columns for which you want to have unique values. You can set Name to be unique in the Department table if you want to forbid repeating values, in the situation where the DepartmentID column is the primary key. (We won't use the UNIQUE constraint in this book, but we mention them here for completeness.) We decided to allow identical department names because only site administrators will have the privilege to modify or change department data.

Another difference between primary keys and columns with the UNIQUE constraint is that columns with the UNIQUE constraint can be set to accept NULL values (in which case, it can only accept *one* NULL value).

TIP *Indexes are automatically created on columns with the* PRI-MARY KEY *and* UNIQUE *constraints.* **Indexes** *are database objects meant to improve data access performance, and we'll cover them a bit later in this chapter.*

Columns and Data Types

Each column in a table has a particular data type. By looking at the previously shown Figure 3-9 with the Department table, DepartmentID has a numeric data type, while Name and Description contain text.

It's important to consider the many data types that SQL Server supports so that you'll be able to make correct decisions about how to create your tables. Table 3-1 isn't an exhaustive list of SQL Server data types, but it focuses on the main types you might come across in your project. Please refer to SQL Server 2000 Books Online (http://www.microsoft.com/sql/techinfo/productdoc/2000/books.asp) for a more detailed list.

To keep the table short, under the *Data Type* heading we have listed only the most frequently used types, while similar data types are explained under the *Description and Notes* heading. You don't need to memorize the list, but you should get an idea of which data types are available.

Table 3-1. SQL Server 2000 Data Types

Data Type	Size in Bytes	Description and Notes
Int	4	Stores whole numbers from -2,147,483,648 to 2,147,483,647. Related types are SmallInt and TinyInt. A Bit data type is able to store values of 0 and 1.
Money	8	Stores monetary data with values from -2^{63} to 2^{63} -1 with a precision of four decimal places. SQL Server supports the Float data type, which holds floating-point data, but it is not recommended to store monetary information because of its lack of precision. A variation of Money is SmallMoney that has a smaller range, but the same precision.
DateTime	8	Supports date and time data from January 1, 1753, through December 31, 9999, with an accuracy of three hundredths of a second. A SmallDateTime type has a range from January 1, 1900 to June 6, 2079, with an accuracy of one minute.
UniqueIdentifier	16	Stores a numerical Globally Unique Identifier (GUID). A GUID is guaranteed to be unique; this property makes it very useful in certain situations.
VarChar, NVarChar	Variable	Stores variable-length character data. NVarChar stores Unicode data with a maximum length of 4,000 characters, and VarChar non-Unicode data with a maximum length of 8,000 characters.
Char, NChar	Fixed	Stores fixed-length character data. Values shorter than the declared size are padded with spaces. NChar is the Unicode version and goes to a maximum 4,000 characters, while Char can store 8,000 characters.
Text, NText	Fixed	Stores large fixed-length character data. NText is the Unicode version and has a maximum size of 1,073,741,823 characters. Text has double this maximum size. Using these data types can slow down the database, and it's highly recommended to use Char, VarChar, NChar, or NVarChar instead. When adding Text or NText fields, their length is fixed to 16. This is the length of the pointer that points to the place where the actual text is stored.
Binary, VarBinary	Fixed/Variable	Store binary data with a maximum length of 8,000 bytes.

Table 3-1. SQL Server 2000 Data Types (continued)

Data Type	Size in Bytes	Description and Notes
Image	Variable	Stores binary data of maximum 231 - 1 bytes. Despite its name, this field can store any kind of binary data, not just pictures. For performance reasons, if there are alternatives, it is not recommended to store binary data directly in the database. For your products' pictures, for example, you'll store just a path in the Product table that points to an image file on the hard disk.

Note that the table was written with SQL Server 2000 in mind. SQL Server 7 comes close, but there are a few different details, such as the maximum size for character data. Also, keep in mind that data type names are case insensitive; in most database interface programs, data type names aren't capitalized.

Now let's get back to the Department table and determine which data types to use. Don't worry that you don't have the table yet in your database; you'll create it a bit later. For now, you just need to understand how data types work with SQL Server.

If you know what these data types mean, Figure 3-10 is self-explanatory. DepartmentID is an int, and Name and Description are varchar data types. The little golden key at the left of DepartmentID specifies that the column is the primary key of the Department table.

Department				
Column Name	Data Type	Length	Allow Nulls	▲
🔑 DepartmentID	int	4		
Name	varchar	50		
Description	varchar	200	✓	▼

Figure 3-10. Designing the Department *table*

You can also see the length of each field. Note that Length means different things for different data types. For numerical data types, Length specifies the number of bytes, while for text data, Length specifies the number of characters. This is a subtle but important difference, because for Unicode text data (nchar, nvarchar, ntext), the actual space needed is 2 bytes per character.

For the int data type, this value is not configurable, but for varchar, you can set different values depending on your requirements. We choose to have 50 characters available for the department's name and 200 for the description.

Some prefer to use nvarchar instead of varchar—this is actually a requirement when you need to store Unicode characters (such as Chinese text). Otherwise, the non-Unicode versions are usually preferred because they occupy half of the size their Unicode pairs need. With large databases, the difference becomes noticeable.

Nullable Columns and Default Values

Observe the Allow Nulls option in the design window of the Department table—some fields have this option checked, while others don't. If the option is checked, the column will be allowed to store the NULL value.

The best and shortest definition for NULL is "undefined." In your Department table, only DepartmentID and Name are really required, while Description is optional—meaning that you are allowed to add a new department without supplying a description for it. If you add a new row of data without supplying a value for columns that allow nulls, NULL is automatically supplied for them.

Especially for character data, there is a subtle difference between the NULL value and an "empty" value. If you add a product with an empty string for its description, this means that you actually set a value for its description; it's an empty string, not an undefined (NULL) value.

The primary key field never allows NULL values. For the other columns, it's up to you (and your client) as to which fields are required and which are not.

In some cases, instead of allowing NULLs, you'll prefer to specify default values. This way, if the value is unspecified when creating a new row, it will be supplied with the default value. The default value can be a literal value (such as 0 for a Salary column or "Unknown" for a Description column), or it can be a system value (such as the GETDATE function, which returns the current date). In Chapter 10, you'll have a DateCreated column, which can be set to have the default value supplied by the GETDATE function. You'll learn how to set default column values later in this chapter.

Identity Columns

Identity columns are "auto-numbered" columns. This behavior is similar to AutoNumber columns in Microsoft Access. When a column is set as an identity column, SQL Server automatically provides values for it when inserting new records into the table; by default, the database doesn't permit manually specifying values for identity columns.

SQL Server guarantees that the generated values are always unique, which makes them especially useful when used in conjunction with the primary key constraint. You already know that primary keys are used on columns that uniquely identify each row of a table. If you set a primary key column to also be an identity column, SQL Server automatically fills that column with values when adding new rows (in other words, it generates new IDs), ensuring that the values are unique.

When setting an identity column, you must specify an **identity seed**, which is the first value that SQL Server will provide for that column, and an **identity increment value**, which specifies the number of units to increase between two consecutive records.

By default, identity seed and identity increment values are both set to 1, meaning that the first value will be 1 and the following ones will be generated by adding 1 to the last created value. You don't need to specify other values because you don't care what values are generated anyway. A value that was generated once will never be generated again, even if you delete rows from the table.

Although it wasn't shown in the earlier Figure 3-10, DepartmentID in your Department table is an identity column. You'll learn how to set identity columns a bit later, when creating the Department table.

Indexes

Indexes are related to SQL Server performance tuning, so we'll mention them only briefly. For more in-depth information about SQL Server indexes, read Robin Dewson's *Beginning SQL Server 2000 Programming* (ISBN: 1-59059-252-2).

Indexes are database objects meant to increase the overall speed of database operations. Indexes work on the presumption that the vast majority of database operations are read operations. Indexes increase the speed of search operations, but slow down insert, delete and update operations. Usually, the gains of using indexes considerably outweigh the drawbacks.

On a table, you can create one or more indexes, with each index working on one column or on a set of columns. When a table is indexed on a specific column, its rows are either indexed or physically arranged based on the values of that column and of the type of index. This makes search operations on that column very fast. If, for example, an index exists on DepartmentID and then you do a search for department 934, the search would be performed very quickly.

The drawback of indexes is that they can slow down database operations that add new rows or update existing ones because the index must be actualized (or the table rows rearranged) each time these operations occur.

You should keep the following in mind about indexes:

- Indexes greatly increase search operations on the database, but they slow down operations that change the database (delete, update, and insert operations).

- Having too many indexes can slow down the general performance of the database. The general rule is to set indexes on columns frequently used in WHERE or ORDER BY clauses, used in table joins, or having foreign key relationships with other tables.

- By default, indexes are automatically created on primary key and unique table columns.

You can use dedicated tools to test the performance of a database under stress conditions with and without particular indexes; in fact, a serious database administrator will want to make some of these tests before deciding on a wining combination for indexes. Two popular tools are the Index Tuning Wizard that can be accessed through SQL Server's Enterprise Manager, and the Query Analyzer, which has the capability to show the execution plan of a particular SQL command. Please consult a specialized SQL Server book for more details on these subjects.

In your application, you'll rely on the indexes that are automatically created on the primary key columns.

Creating the Table

You created the JokePoint database in Chapter 2. In the following exercise, you'll add the Department table to it. Alternatively, you can use the SQL scripts from the Downloads section of the Apress web site to create and populate the Department table.

 NOTE *You can find the database creation scripts for this book in the Downloads section of the Apress web site* (http://www.apress.com) *or at* http://www.CristianDarie.ro. *The script file that creates the* Department *table is named* CreateDepartment.sql. *Read Appendix A to learn how to execute SQL script files using the* osql *command-line utility that ships with MSDE.*

Exercise: Creating the Department Table

1. Using the Server Explorer in Visual Studio .NET, navigate to your SQL Server instance, and then to the JokePoint database that you created in Chapter 2. Remember, if Server Explorer is not visible, activate it using View ➤ Server Explorer (or use the default shortcut **Ctrl+Alt+S**).

2. Expand the JokePoint database node—this makes sure Visual Studio .NET connects to the database. Go to the Database menu (which appears when JokePoint or any of its nodes is selected in the tree) and select the New Table item. Alternatively, you can right-click Tables and select New Table (see Figure 3-11).

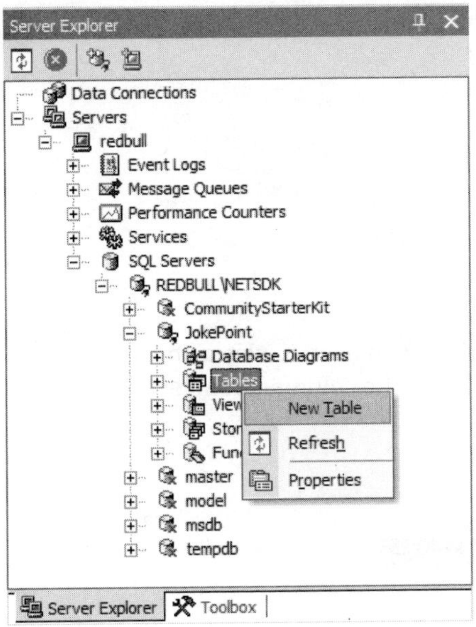

Figure 3-11. Creating a new table

3. After clicking New Table, you'll see a form where you can add columns to the new table (see Figure 3-12).

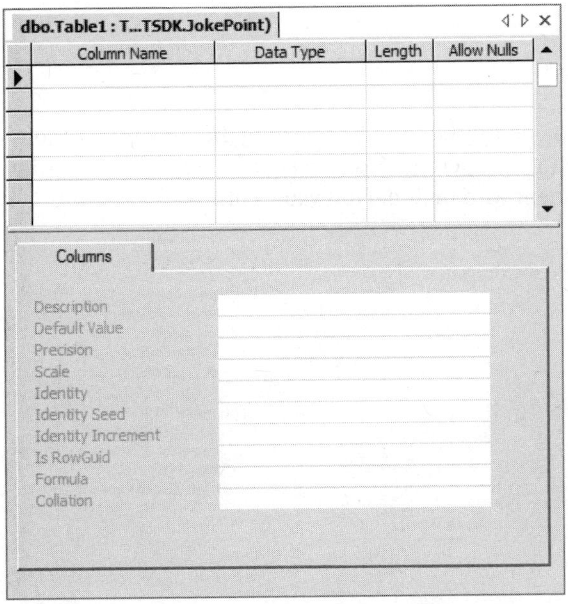

Figure 3-12. Adding the fields for the new table

4. Using this form, add three columns, as shown in Figure 3-13.

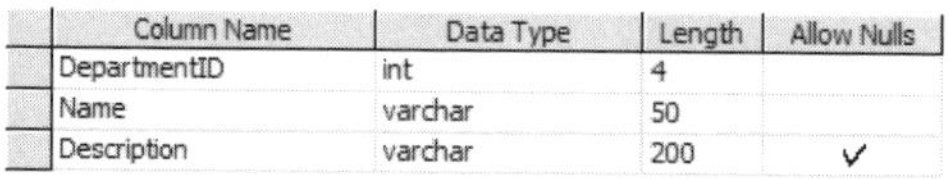

Column Name	Data Type	Length	Allow Nulls
DepartmentID	int	4	
Name	varchar	50	
Description	varchar	200	✓

Figure 3-13. The three fields of the Department table

5. Now that you have the columns in place, you need to play a little bit with the DepartmentID column. First, right-click the column and select Set Primary Key, as shown in Figure 3-14.

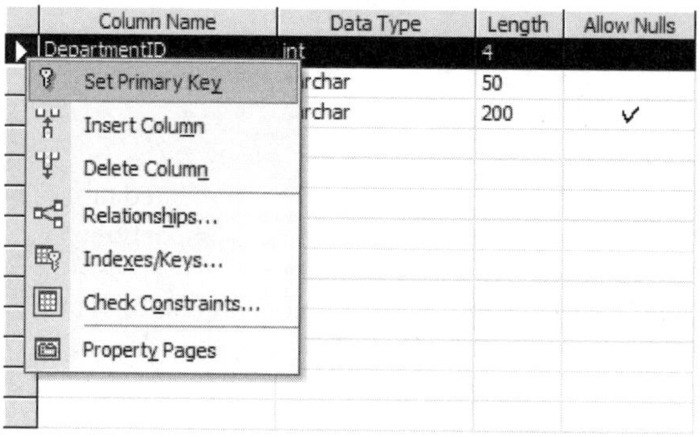

Column Name		Data Type	Length	Allow Nulls
DepartmentID		int	4	
♀ Set Primary Key		rchar	50	
ꝥ Insert Column		rchar	200	✓
ꝝ Delete Column				
⚬⚬ Relationships...				
⌨ Indexes/Keys...				
▦ Check Constraints...				
▣ Property Pages				

Figure 3-14. Setting a primary key

6. Make the DepartmentID an identity column by selecting the DepartmentID column, and setting its Identity property to Yes (see Figure 3-15). Leave Identity Seed and Identity Increment with their default values of 1.

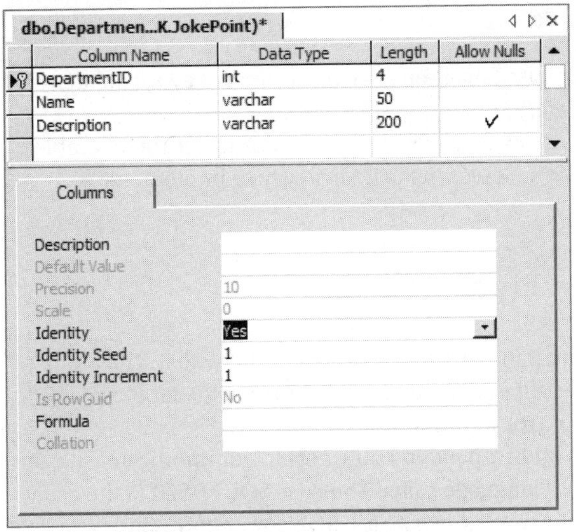

Figure 3-15. Setting an identity column

7. Now that everything is in place, you need to save the newly created table. Press **Ctrl+S** or select File ➤ Save Table 1. When asked, type **Department** for the table name.

8. Having the table structure saved in the database, you can open it to add some data. To open the Department table for editing, just double-click its name in the Server Explorer. Using the editor integrated with Visual Studio, you can start adding rows. Because DepartmentID is an Identity column, you cannot manually edit its data—SQL Server automatically fills this field, depending on the Identity Seed and Identity Increment values that you specified when creating the table.

9. Add three departments, as shown in Table 3-2.

Table 3-2. Three Sample Rows for the Department Table

DepartmentID	Name	Description
1 (autonumbered)	Full Costumes	We have the best costumes on the Internet! Check out a few samples from our collection:
2 (autonumbered)	Costume Accessories	Accessories and fun items to jazz up that special costume. These products are on promotion:
3 (autonumbered)	Jokes and Tricks	Funny or frightening, but all harmless! Take a look at these featured products before browsing the categories:

How It Works: The Database Table

You have just created your first database table! You also set a primary key, set an identity column, and filled it with some data.

As you can see, as soon as you have a clear idea about the structure of a table, Visual Studio .NET and MSDE or SQL Server make it very easy to implement.

Implementing the Data Tier

Now that you have a table filled with data, let's do something useful with it. The ultimate goal with this table is to get the list of department names from a Visual Basic .NET program and populate the user control with that list.

To get data from a database, you first need to know how to communicate with the database. SQL Server understands a language called Transact-SQL (T-SQL). The usual way of communicating with SQL Server is to write a T-SQL command, send it to SQL Server, and get the results back. However, these commands can be sent either directly from the business tier to SQL Server (without having an intermediary data tier), or can be centralized and saved as stored procedures. In a three-tier application, the logic that interacts with the database is always saved in stored procedures.

Stored procedures are database objects that store programs written in T-SQL. Much like normal functions, stored procedures accept input and output parameters and have return values.

You don't need to use stored procedures if you want to perform database operations. You can directly send the SQL commands from an external application to SQL Server. When using stored procedures, instead of passing the SQL code you want executed to the database, you just pass the name of the stored procedure, and the values for any parameters it might have. Using stored procedures for data operations has the following advantages:

- Storing SQL code as a stored procedure usually results in better performance because SQL Server generates and caches the stored procedure execution plan when it is first executed.

- Using stored procedures allows for better maintainability of the data access code, which can be stored in a central place, and permits easier implementation of the three-tier architecture (the stored procedures forming the data tier).

- Security can be better controlled because SQL Server permits setting different security permissions for each individual stored procedure.

- This might be a matter of taste, but the data access code in the business tier looks much better and cleaner when you call the name of a stored procedure, than when you join strings to create an SQL query that you finally pass to the database

Your goal for this section is to write the `GetDepartments` stored procedure, but first, let's take a quick look at SQL.

Speaking with the Database

SQL (Structured Query Language) is the language used to communicate with modern relational database management systems (RDBMS). Most database systems support a particular dialect of SQL, such as T-SQL (Transact-SQL) for SQL Server and PL/SQL (Procedural Language extensions to SQL) for Oracle. Because T-SQL can be a pretty big subject when analyzed in detail, we'll give only a brief introduction and cover just enough so you'll understand the code in your stored procedures.

 TIP *If you are interested in entering the world of SQL, we recommend another book we've authored called The Programmer's Guide to SQL, published by Apress. It covers the SQL standard and its dialects implemented in SQL Server, Oracle, DB2, MySQL, and Access. To get more information about this book, visit* `http://www.CristianDarie.ro`*.*

The basic and most important SQL commands are `SELECT`, `INSERT`, `UPDATE`, and `DELETE`. Their names are self-explanatory, and they allow you to perform basic operations on the database.

If you have SQL Server, you can use Query Analyzer to play with these SQL statements. Unfortunately, Query Analyzer is not included with MSDE or with Visual Studio .NET, so you might not be able to test your T-SQL skills right now. If this is the case, don't worry, because you'll be able to do a lot of testing later, when you create the stored procedure.

Be aware that each of these commands has more optional arguments and they can become more complex than those presented here. Still, to keep the presentation short and simple, you'll learn the most important and frequently used parameters.

SELECT

The `SELECT` statement is used to query the database and retrieve selected data that match the criteria you specify. Its basic structure is

```
SELECT <column list>
FROM <table name(s)>
[WHERE <restrictive condition>]
```

 NOTE *In this book, the SQL commands and queries appear in uppercase for consistency and clarity although SQL is not case sensitive. The* `WHERE` *clause appears in brackets because it's optional.*

The following command returns the name of the department that has the DepartmentID of 1. In your case, the returned value is "Full Costumes", but you would receive no results if there were no departments with an ID of 1.

```
SELECT Name FROM Department WHERE DepartmentID = 1
```

If you want more columns to be returned, you simply list them, separated by commas. Alternatively, you can use *, which means "all columns." However, for performance reasons, if you need only certain specific columns, you should list them separately instead of asking for them all. With your current Department table, the following two statements return the same results:

```
SELECT DepartmentID, Name, Description FROM Department
WHERE DepartmentID = 1

SELECT * FROM Department WHERE DepartmentID = 1
```

If you don't want to place any condition on the query, simply remove the WHERE clause. The following SELECT statement returns all rows and all columns from the Product table:

```
SELECT * FROM Product
```

INSERT

The INSERT statement is used to insert or add a row of data into the table. Its syntax is as follows:

```
INSERT [INTO] <table name> (column list) VALUES (column values)
```

The following INSERT statement adds a department named "Mysterious Department" to the Department table:

```
INSERT INTO Department (Name) VALUES ('Mysterious Department')
```

We didn't specify any value for the Description field because it was marked to allow NULLs in the Department table. This is why you can omit specifying a value, if you want to. However, the Name field is required, so if you tried, for example, to specify a description without specifying a name, you would have got an error:

```
INSERT INTO Department (Description) VALUES ('Some Description Here')
```

The error message specifies

```
Cannot insert the value NULL into column ' Name ',
table 'JokePoint.dbo.Department'; column does not allow NULLs. INSERT fails.
```

Also please note that we didn't specify a `DepartmentID`. Because `DepartmentID` was set as an identity column, you're not allowed to manually specify values for this column. SQL Server can guarantee this has unique values, but only if you don't interfere with it.

So, if you can't specify a value for `DepartmentID`, how can you determine which value was automatically supplied by SQL Server? For this, you have a special variable named `@@IDENTITY`. You can type its value by using the `SELECT` statement. The following two SQL commands add a new record to `Department`, and return the `DepartmentID` of the row just added:

```
INSERT INTO Department (Name) Values ('Some New Department')
SELECT @@IDENTITY
```

 TIP *The* `INTO` *keyword is optional, but including it makes the statement more readable.*

UPDATE

The `UPDATE` statement is used to modify existing data, and has the following syntax:

```
UPDATE <table name>
SET <column name> = <new value> [, <column name> = <new value> ...]
[WHERE <restrictive condition>]
```

The following query changes the name of the department with the ID of 43 to `Cool Department`. If there were more departments with that ID, all of them would have been modified, but because `DepartmentID` is the primary key, you can't have more departments with the same ID.

```
UPDATE Department SET Name='Cool Department' WHERE DepartmentID = 43
```

Be careful with the `UPDATE` statement, because it makes it easy to mess up an entire table. If the `WHERE` clause is omitted, the change is applied to every record of the table, which you usually don't want to happen. SQL Server will be happy to change all of your records; even if all departments in the table would have the same name and description, they would still be perceived as different entities because they have `DepartmentID`s.

DELETE

The syntax of the `DELETE` command is actually very simple:

```
DELETE [FROM] <table name>
[WHERE <restrictive condition>]
```

The FROM keyword is optional and can be omitted. We generally use it because it makes the query sound more like normal English.

Most times, you'll want to use the WHERE clause to delete a single row:

```
DELETE FROM Department
WHERE DepartmentID = 43
```

As with UPDATE, be careful with this command, because if you forget to specify a WHERE clause, you'll end up deleting all of the rows in the specified table. The following query deletes all the records in Department. The table itself isn't deleted by the DELETE command.

```
DELETE FROM Department
```

TIP *As with* INSERT [INTO], *the* FROM *keyword is optional. Add it if you feel it makes the statement easier to understand.*

Creating the Stored Procedure

In this section, you'll create the GetDepartments stored procedure, which will return the department information from the Department table. This stored procedure is part of the data tier and will be accessed from the business tier. The final goal is to have this data displayed in the user control. Before writing the stored procedure, you first need to know the SQL code that does the necessary action.

Asking for a List of Department Names

To ask for a list of department names, you need to query the database using a SELECT statement. The command could look like this:

```
SELECT * FROM Department
```

This command would return all of the department information. Asking for *all* of the columns is useful when the columns might change in time and you want to be sure you get all of them. But when you know exactly what info you want from a table, it's always better to be specific. Asking for more data than necessary will not make the program stop working, but it can slow down its performance.

To display the department list, you need to know the name and ID for each department. You need to know the ID because it's the ID, and not the name, that makes a department unique. When the visitor wants more information about a specific department, you'll search for that information based on its ID, not on its name.

The SELECT statement that works best for your situation is

```
SELECT DepartmentID, Name
FROM Department
```

Saving the Query as a Stored Procedure

As with data tables, once you know the structure, implementing the stored procedure is a piece of cake. Now that you know the SQL code, the tools will help you save the query as a stored procedure very easily.

The syntax for creating a stored procedure that has no input or output parameters is as follows:

```
CREATE PROCEDURE <procedure name>
AS
  <stored procedure body>
```

If the procedure already exists and you just want to update its code, use ALTER PROCEDURE instead of CREATE PROCEDURE.

Stored procedures can have input or output parameters. Because GetDepartments doesn't have any parameters, you don't have to bother with them right now. You'll learn how to use input and output parameters in Chapter 4.

In the following exercise, you'll add the GetDepartments stored procedure to your database.

NOTE *Alternatively, you can execute the* GetDepartments.sql *script file, which creates the* GetDepartments *stored procedure. Read Appendix A to learn how to execute SQL script files using the* osql *command-line utility that ships with MSDE.*

Exercise: Writing the GetDepartments *Stored Procedure*

1. Make sure the JokePoint database is selected in Server Explorer. Choose Database ➤ New Stored Procedure. Alternately, you can use the context menu by right-clicking the Stored Procedures node and selecting New Stored Procedure.

2. Replace the default text with your GetDepartments stored procedure:

    ```
    CREATE PROCEDURE GetDepartments AS

    SELECT DepartmentID, Name
    FROM Department

    RETURN
    ```

3. Press **Ctrl+S** to save the stored procedure. Unlike with the tables, you won't be asked for a name because the database already knows that you're talking about the GetDepartments stored procedure.

NOTE *After saving the procedure, the* CREATE *keyword becomes* ALTER. *This happens because* ALTER *is used to change the code of an existing procedure.*

4. Now test your first stored procedure to see that it is actually working. In Server Explorer, under your JokePoint database, open the Stored Procedures node.

5. Right-click GetDepartments and select Run Stored Procedure as shown in Figure 3-16.

🗗	<u>E</u>dit Stored Procedure
	R<u>u</u>n Stored Procedure
	Step <u>I</u>nto Stored Procedure
	New Stored <u>P</u>rocedure
🔁	Re<u>f</u>resh
📑	Cop<u>y</u>
✕	<u>D</u>elete
📑	Pr<u>o</u>perties

Figure 3-16. Executing a stored procedure from Visual Studio .NET

After running the stored procedure, you can see the results in the Output window (see Figure 3-17).

```
Output                                              ⚐  ✕
Database Output                                        ▾
  Running dbo."GetDepartments".

  DepartmentID Name
  ------------ --------------------------------------------------
  1            Full Costumes
  2            Costume Accessories
  3            Jokes and Tricks
  No more results.
  (3 row(s) returned)
  @RETURN_VALUE = 0
  Finished running dbo."GetDepartments".

◀         ⫼⫼                                        ▶
```

Figure 3-17. The Output window shows the results.

How it Works: the GetDepartments *Stored Procedure*

You've just finished coding the data tier part that reads the departments list!

The results in the Output window confirm your stored procedure works as expected. If you have the full version of SQL Server, you can use the Query Analyzer utility to connect to the JokePoint database, and execute and test SQL code or stored procedures. In Query Analyzer, you can connect to the JokePoint database and execute the GetDepartments stored procedure with the following commands:

```
USE JokePoint
EXEC GetDepartments
```

Now it's time to learn how to execute the stored procedure from the business tier, using Visual Basic .NET code.

Implementing the Business Tier

In this section, you'll learn how to access the database and call a stored procedure from Visual Basic .NET code. We'll create the middle-tier code that gets department data by calling the GetDepartments stored procedure.

The middle tier (business tier) part of the product catalog will consist of a Catalog class written in Visual Basic .NET, which will contain the necessary logic to get the catalog's data from the database and send it to the user interface layer. For the departments list, you'll only need to add a single method—GetDepartments—to the Catalog class.

Accessing SQL Server from VB.NET

The .NET technology that permits accessing a database from Visual Basic .NET code is called **ADO.NET**. All .NET classes that are related to database access are collectively known as ADO.NET. This is the most modern Microsoft data-access technology, and it can be used from any .NET language, not only with Visual Basic .NET.

ADO.NET is a complex subject that requires a separate book by itself, so we will cover just enough to help you understand how your business tier works. For more information about ADO.NET, please refer to *Beginning ASP.NET Databases in VB .NET: From Novice to Professional* forthcoming from Apress.

You will notice that we use classes like SqlConnection, SqlCommand, and SqlDataReader. These objects and all the others whose names start with Sql are specifically created for SQL Server, and are part of the SQL Server Managed Data Provider. The SQL Server Managed Data Provider is the low-level interface between the database itself and your program. The ADO.NET objects that use this provider are grouped in the System.Data.SqlClient namespace, so you'll need to import this namespace when you want to access SQL Server.

Because we use SQL Server in this book, you will only work with the objects that are part of the SQL Server provider; however, keep in mind that if you need to, you can easily update the program to use other database systems.

Each *database operation* always consists of three steps:

1. *Open* a connection to the database.

2. *Perform* the needed operations with the database and get back the results.

3. *Close* the connection to the database.

You should always try to make the second step (executing the commands) as fast as possible. As you'll learn, keeping a data connection open for too long or having too many database connections open at the same time is expensive for your application's performance. The golden rule is to open the connection as late as possible, perform the necessary operations, and then close it immediately. You'll learn how to do each of these steps in the following sections.

Connecting to SQL Server

The class used to connect to SQL Server is SqlConnection. When creating a new database connection, you always need to specify at least three important pieces of data: the name of the SQL Server instance you're connecting to, the authentication information that will permit you to access the server, and the database you want to work with.

This connection data is grouped in a **connection string**, which needs to be passed to the SqlConnection object. The following code snippet demonstrates how to create and open a database connection:

```
' Create the connection object
Dim connection As New SqlConnection()

' Set the connection string
connection.ConnectionString = _
   "Server=(local);" _
   & "User ID=johnny; Password=qwerty;" _
   & "Initial Catalog=JokePoint"

' Open the connection
connection.Open()
```

The code is fairly straightforward: you first create a SqlConnection object, then set its ConnectionString property, and finally open the connection. A connection needs to be opened before using it for any operations.

Understanding the connection string is important—if your program has problems connecting to the database, it's likely that these problems can be solved by "fixing" the connection string (assuming that SQL Server is properly configured and that you actually have access to it).

The connection string contains the three important elements. The first is the name of the SQL Server instance you're connecting to. For the MSDE version that comes with Visual Studio .NET, the instance name is (local)\VSdotNET or (local)\NetSDK. You will want to change this if your SQL Server instance has another name. You can use your computer name instead of (local). Of course, if you connect to a remote SQL Server instance, you'll need to specify the complete path instead of (local).

After specifying the server, you need to supply security information needed to log in to the server. You can log in to SQL Server by either using SQL Server Authentication (in which case you need to supply a SQL Server username and password, as shown in the code snippet), or by using Windows Authentication (also named Windows Integrated Security). With Windows Integrated Security, you don't have to supply a username and password because SQL Server uses the Windows login information of the currently logged in user.

To log in using Windows Authentication, you'll need to supply `Integrated Security=True` (or `Integrated Security=SSPI`) instead of `User ID=username; Password= password`.

By default when installing SQL Server or MSDE, there is a System Administrator (sa) account with a blank password. Be very careful with this account, and never use it in a production system because it has full access to all database resources. On a production system, the sa account should be renamed, and shouldn't have a blank password. If you want to use SQL Server authentication and you don't have access to the sa account, you'll need to ask for permission from the database administrator for an account that has access to the JokePoint database.

The final part of the connection string specifies the database you will be working with.

You can provide the connection string right when creating the `SqlConnection` object, instead of setting the `ConnectionString` separately:

```
' Create the connection object
Dim connection As New SqlConnection(" ... connection string here ... ")
' Open the connection
connection.Open()
```

A final note about the connection string is that several synonyms can be used inside it; for example, instead of `Server`, you can use `Data Source`, or `Data Server`, and instead of `Initial Catalog`, you can use `Database`. The list is much longer, and the complete version can be found in MSDN or SQL Server 2000 Books Online (`http://www.microsoft.com/sql/techinfo/productdoc/2000/books.asp`).

Configuring SQL Server Security

Because SQL Server connection problems are common, let's talk about configuring SQL Server or MSDE to accept connections from within your web site.

SQL Server can work with either Windows Authentication or in Mixed Mode. In Mixed Mode, SQL Server accepts connections through both Windows Authentication and SQL Server Authentication. You can't set SQL Server to accept connection only through SQL Server Authentication.

 NOTE *You can find more details about the SQL Server Authentication modes at* `http://msdn.microsoft.com/library/default.asp?url=/ library/en-us/adminsql/ad_security_47u6.asp`.

If you don't specify otherwise at installation, by default SQL Server works in Windows Authentication mode. There are two problems with this scenario:

- With the default security settings, you can't use SQL Server Authentication.

- When using Windows Authentication, ASP.NET applications connect to SQL Server under the credentials of a special account named ASPNET (Windows 2003 Server uses the "Network Service" account). So even if you installed SQL Server yourself and have full privileges to it, the Web Application will use the credentials of a username that doesn't have any privileges to SQL Server.

There are three ways to connect to SQL Server from within ASP.NET applications. You'll only need to apply one of them.

TIP *The configuration details can be boring, so you can skip these sections for now, if you want. If the JokePoint project throws a connectivity exception when executed, you can come back and see what's wrong.*

Method 1: Using SQL Server Authentication

The first solution is to enable SQL Server security by switching SQL Server to use Mixed Mode authentication. If you have SQL Server, you can start Enterprise Manager and use its visual interface to change the server's security options.

MSDE doesn't have visual management utilities, and the easiest way to enable SQL Server Authentication is by using a special parameter at installation (see more details in Appendix A). If you already installed MSDE, you need to manually edit the Windows Registry to enable Mixed Mode.

NOTE *For more details, please see the "Enable Mixed Mode Authentication During Installation" and "Enable Mixed Mode After Installation" sections in the article at* http://support.microsoft.com/default.aspx?scid=kb;EN-US;319930. *Another useful article about connecting with SQL Server Authentication is found at* http://support.microsoft.com/default.aspx?scid=kb;EN-US;321698.

Method 2: Adding the ASPNET Account to SQL Server

If you want to use Windows Authentication, the first alternative is to grant the *MachineName/ASPNET* account access to the SQL Server database (where *MachineName* is the name of your machine). If you have SQL Server, you can start Enterprise Manager and use its visual interface to add the *MachineName/ASPNET* user account and grant it access to the JokePoint database.

If you have MSDE, meaning that you don't have access to the visual client, you'll need to connect using the `osql` utility and perform the necessary actions. The typical sequence is to do something like this:

1. In command-prompt mode, connect to your SQL Server instance using `osql`. If your instance name is *MachineName*\NetSDK and you installed MSDE (so you can connect to it using Windows Authentication), type this `osql` command:

   ```
   osql -E -S MachineName\NetSDK
   ```

    NOTE *Learn more about* `osql` *and connecting to SQL Server in interactive mode using* `osql` *at*
   http://msdn.microsoft.com/library/default.asp?url=/library/
   en-us/coprompt/cp_osql_1wxl.asp *and*
   http://msdn.microsoft.com/library/default.asp?url=/library/
   en-us/acdata/ac_8_mta_01_5zxi.asp.

2. In `osql`, call the `sp_grantlogin` stored procedure, which adds a Windows user account to the SQL Server database:

   ```
   exec sp_grantlogin 'MachineName\ASPNET'
   go
   ```

    NOTE *Learn more about the* `sp_grantlogin` *stored procedure at*
   http://msdn.microsoft.com/library/default.asp?url=/library/
   en-us/tsqlref/ts_sp_ga-gz_8dri.asp.

3. After giving the ASPNET account the privilege to connect to SQL Server, you need to give it access to the JokePoint database:

   ```
   use JokePoint
   go
   exec sp_grantdbaccess 'MachineName\ASPNET'
   go
   ```

    NOTE *Learn more about* `sp_grantdbaccess` *at*
   http://msdn.microsoft.com/library/default.asp?url=/library/
   en-us/tsqlref/ts_sp_ga-gz_290z.asp.

4. Finally, you need to give the ASPNET account privileges to the objects inside the JokePoint database, such as the privilege to execute stored procedures, read and modify tables, and so on. The simplest way is to assign the ASPNET account with the db_owner role in the JokePoint database. Assuming that you already connected to the JokePoint database at the previous step (with use JokePoint), type the following:

```
exec sp_addrolemember 'db_owner', 'MachineName\ASPNET'
go
```

That's it, now you can connect to SQL Server from your Web Application using Windows Authentication.

> **NOTE** *Learn more about* sp_addrolemember *at* http://msdn.microsoft.com/library/default.asp?url=/library/ en-us/tsqlref/ts_sp_addp_4boy.asp.

Method 3: Using ASP.NET Impersonation

The second alternative that allows you to use Windows Authentication is to use ASP.NET impersonation. When using impersonation, the ASP.NET application is executed under the credentials of the logged in user (who is supposed to have access to SQL Server), instead of the ASP.NET account. There are a number of articles about ASP.NET impersonation on MSDN, such as the one at http://msdn.microsoft.com/library/default.asp?url=/ library/en-us/cpguide/html/cpconaspnetimpersonation.asp.

Issuing Commands

After you have an open connection, you usually need to create an SqlCommand object to perform operations. Because there are more tricks you can do with the SqlCommand object, we'll take them one at a time.

Creating an SqlCommand Object

SqlCommand will be your best friend when implementing the business tier. It is capable of storing information about what you want to do with the database—it can store a SQL query or the name of a stored procedure that needs to be executed. The SqlCommand is also aware of stored procedure parameters—you'll learn more about these in Chapter 4, since GetDepartments doesn't have any parameters.

Following is the standard way of creating and initializing an SqlCommand object

```
' Create the command object
Dim command As SqlCommand = New SqlCommand()
command.Connection = connection
command.CommandText = "GetDepartments"
command.CommandType = CommandType.StoredProcedure
```

Once again, there's no mystery about the code. You first create an `SqlCommand` object, and then set some of its properties. The most important property that needs to be set is `Connection`, because each command needs to be executed on a specific connection. The other important property is `CommandText`, which specifies the command that needs to be executed. This can be a SQL query such as `SELECT * FROM Departments`, but in your application this will always be the name of a stored procedure.

By default, the `CommandText` property receives SQL queries. Because you are supplying the name of a stored procedure (instead of an SQL query), you need to inform the `SqlCommand` object about this by setting its `CommandType` property to `CommandType.StoredProcedure`.

The previous code snippet shows a simple and structured way to create and configure the `SqlCommand` object. However, it's possible to achieve the same result using less code by passing some of the information when creating the `Command` object:

```
' Create the command object
Dim command As New SqlCommand("GetDepartments", connection)
command.CommandType = CommandType.StoredProcedure
```

Executing the Command

This is the moment of glory—finally, after creating a connection, creating a `SqlCommand` object, and setting various parameters, you are ready to execute the command.

You can execute the command in many ways, depending on the specifics. Does it return any information? If so, what kind of information, and in which format? You'll analyze the various scenarios later, when you actually put the theory into practice, but for now let's take a look at the three `Execute` methods of the `SqlCommand` class: `ExecuteNonQuery`, `ExecuteScalar`, and `ExecuteReader`.

`ExecuteNonQuery` is used to execute an SQL statement or stored procedure that doesn't return any records. You'll use this method when executing operations that update, insert, or delete information in the database. `ExecuteNonQuery` has an integer return value that specifies the number of rows affected by the query—this proves useful if you want to know, for example, how many rows were deleted by the last delete operation.

`ExecuteScalar` is like `ExecuteNonQuery` in that it returns a single value, although it returns a value that has been read from the database instead of the number of affected rows. It is used in conjunction with `SELECT` statements that select a single value. If `SELECT` returns more rows and/or more columns, only the first column in the first row is returned.

`ExecuteReader` is used with `SELECT` statements that return multiple records (with any number of fields). `ExecuteReader` returns an `SqlDataReader` object, which contains the results of the query. An `SqlDataReader` object reads and returns the results one by one, in a forward-only and read-only manner. This object is particularly useful because it's quick, and many objects work with it. For example, for displaying the departments in the Web User Control, you'll use a `DataList` control that will take an `SqlDataReader` object as a parameter.

NOTE *The* SqlDataReader *object requires an open connection when it reads values from the data source. In other words, it doesn't store any information locally: it reads records from the database one by one, and only when finished can you close the connection. You also need to close the* SqlDataReader *after you finish using it. No other operations can be performed via the same connection until the* SqlDataReader *is closed.*

Because the user control in the presentation tier reads all the rows from the SqlDataReader without any additional processing, the operation is performed very quickly and the database connection stays open for only a short period of time. The SqlDataReader is the fastest choice for this kind of operation.

In other circumstances, the SqlDataReader might not be a good choice because it is read only and is only aware of the current row read from the database; it doesn't store any other rows in memory.

 NOTE *ADO.NET contains a number of other important and powerful objects, such as* SqlDataAdapter *and* DataSet, *but they aren't used in this book. Instead we'll use* SqlDataReader, *which is powerful enough for our purposes and the fastest means to retrieve data from the SQL Server database. Please consult MSDN or a specialized ADO.NET book for advanced details on .NET and SQL Server data access.*

You'll take a closer look at SqlDataReader when you build the middle tier a bit later in this chapter.

Closing the Connection

It is important always to close the connection because open connections consume server resources, finally resulting in poor performance if not managed carefully.

For this reason, it is recommended to open the connection as late as possible, just before executing the command. After the command is executed, close it immediately. Here's an example from one of the methods you'll implement in Chapter 4:

```
connection.Open()
command.ExecuteNonQuery()
command.Close ()
```

When you execute the command with ExecuteReader, you pass the returned SqlDataReader to the calling method of the presentation tier, which needs an open connection to operate. In this situation, the connection can't be closed in the business tier. Instead, you rely on the SqlDataReader to close the connection itself after all its records have been read:

```
connection.Open()
Return command.ExecuteReader(CommandBehavior.CloseConnection)
```

Implementing the Business-Tier Functionality

The business layer part of the product catalog will consist of a file named Catalog.vb, which holds the Catalog class.

In this section, after creating the Catalog class, you implement the GetDepartments method, which will be called to populate the user control. In Chapter 4, you'll keep adding methods to this class to support the new pieces of functionality.

Adding the Catalog Class to the Solution

Let's start building the business layer by creating the Catalog.vb file, which will hold the Catalog class. For now, you can close the Server Explorer window, if it is still present on your development environment.

Exercise: Creating the Catalog Class

1. Make sure the Solution Explorer is visible in Visual Studio .NET. If it isn't, go to View ➤ Solution Explorer, or press **Ctrl+Alt+L**. Right-click JokePoint and select Add ➤ New Folder (see Figure 3-18).

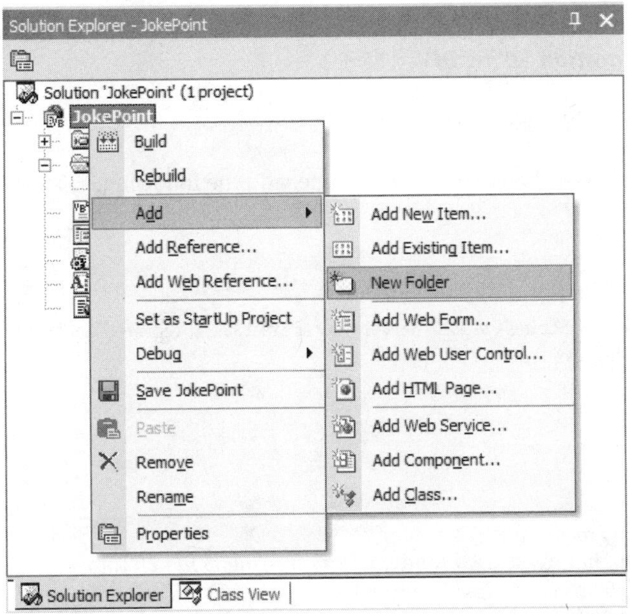

Figure 3-18. Creating a new folder

2. Choose BusinessObjects as the name of your new folder.

3. Right-click the BusinessObjects folder, and select Add ➤ Add New Item.

4. In the dialog box that appears, select Class from the Templates window, and call it Catalog.vb in the Name text box. Click Open.

You created a new folder named BusinessObjects, which will hold the classes of your business tier. There's yet one more step you need to make before writing the code.

Storing the Connection String in a Central Location

You learned that in every database operation, three steps always happen: opening the connection, issuing commands on it, and then closing it. Because you will create a new connection for every method of the business tier that performs database operations, it is a good programming practice to have the connection string saved in a central location. That way, if, for example, the password or the server name changes, you only need to change the connection string in one place rather than modifying many methods.

A common place to store configuration settings in ASP.NET Web Applications is their Web.config file. This is an external configuration file managed by ASP.NET, written in the XML format. Web.config is a complex and powerful file and it can include many options regarding the application's security, performance, behavior, and so on. Studying this file is beyond the scope of this book, but we'll take a look at its features that are directly related to our tasks. Right now you'll see how to save your own configuration settings to Web.config and retrieve them from Visual Basic .NET code.

Exercise: Storing the Connection String in Web.config

1. In Solution Explorer, double-click the Web.config file.

2. In Web.config, just below the <configuration> line, add the following:

```
<configuration>

  <appSettings>
    <add key="ConnectionString" value="Server=(local)\NetSDK;Integrated Security=
True;Initial Catalog=JokePoint" />
  </appSettings>

  <system.web>
```

 NOTE *You might need to adapt the connection string to match your particular SQL Server configuration.*

CAUTION *Make sure you type the* <add> *element on a single line, not split in two lines as shown in the previous code snippet, otherwise you'll receive a runtime error.*

3. Now that you have just saved the connection string to the application's configuration file, open the `Catalog.vb` file by double-clicking it in Solution Explorer. Add the `connectionString` property to the `Catalog` class:

```
Public Class Catalog
   Private Shared ReadOnly Property connectionString() as String
      Get
         Return ConfigurationSettings.AppSettings("ConnectionString")
      End Get
   End Property
End Class
```

How It Works: `Web.config` *and the Connection String*

`Web.config` is an XML file that stores configuration data that applies to the whole application; the data saved in `Web.config` can be easily accessed from anywhere within your application, and consists of *(key, value)* pairs. We chose to save the database connection string to a key named `ConnectionString`, allowing you to access it by calling `ConfigurationSettings.AppSettings("ConnectionString")`. You can create a new connection object like this:

```
Dim connectionString as String
connectionString = ConfigurationSettings.AppSettings("ConnectionString")
Dim connection As New SqlConnection(connectionString)
```

Because you'll need to read the connection string in more places, we created the `connectionString` property in the `Catalog` class. This property returns the value of the connection string, and comes in handy when creating new connections:

```
Dim connection As New SqlConnection(connectionString)
```

Looking at the definition of `connectionString`, you can see it is `Private`, `ReadOnly`, and `Shared`.

`connectionString` is `Private` because it is an internal property of the `Catalog` class. No client of the `Catalog` class needs to access it directly. Unlike public methods and properties, private class members can only be accessed from within the class.

`connectionString` is `ReadOnly` because you only implemented its `Get` accessor; you don't need to write the connection string in code.

`connectionString` needs to be `Shared` because you want to access it from other methods of the `Catalog` class (such as `GetDepartments`) without creating instances of the class. A shared method is called directly on its class, like in Catalog.GetDepartments, and not on an instance of the class. This is the way you'll access GetDepartments from the presentation tier.

Adding the GetDepartments Method to the Catalog Class

The Catalog class stores all the methods that carry out database operations regarding the product catalog. Almost all methods of the Catalog class have a one-to-one relationship with the stored procedures that reside in SQL Server, and their names are self-explanatory.

In the following exercise, you'll implement the GetDepartments method to get the list of departments from the database. It calls the GetDepartments stored procedure, and returns the results as a SqlDataReader.

Exercise: Implementing GetDepartments

1. Add the following line at the beginning of Catalog.vb:

   ```
   Imports System.Data.SqlClient
   ```

2. Add the GetDepartments function to the Catalog class:

   ```
   Imports System.Data.SqlClient

   Public Class Catalog
     Public Shared Function GetDepartments() As SqlDataReader
       ' Create the connection object
       Dim connection As New SqlConnection(connectionString)
       ' Create and initialize the command object
       Dim command As New SqlCommand("GetDepartments", connection)
       command.CommandType = CommandType.StoredProcedure
       ' Open the connection
       connection.Open()
       ' Return a SqlDataReader to the calling function
       Return command.ExecuteReader(CommandBehavior.CloseConnection)
     End Function

     Private Shared ReadOnly Property connectionString() As String
       Get
         Return ConfigurationSettings.AppSettings("ConnectionString")
       End Get
     End Property
   End Class
   ```

3. Go to Build ➤ Build Solution (or press **Ctrl+Shift+B**) to make sure the project compiles correctly.

How It Works: The GetDepartments *Method*

In this exercise, we first imported the System.Data.SqlClient namespace:

```
Imports System.Data.SqlClient
```

This line specifies that you're going to use objects from the System.Data.SqlClient namespace. This namespace groups the objects that belong to the SQL Server managed data provider (the classes whose names start with Sql). When you import a namespace using Imports, you no longer have to type the fully qualified name for classes in that namespace (such as System.Data.SqlClient.SqlConnection).

The GetDepartments method employs the main steps of working with a database that you studied earlier. First, it creates a database connection and passes the connection string using the connectionString property you wrote earlier:

```
' Create the connection object
Dim connection As New SqlConnection(connectionString)
```

Next, you create an SqlCommand object and set its CommandText, Connection, and CommandType properties. You supply the values for the first two of these when creating the object:

```
' Create and initialize the command object
Dim command As New SqlCommand("GetDepartments", connection)
command.CommandType = CommandType.StoredProcedure
```

Just before executing the command, you open the connection:

```
' Open the connection
connection.Open()
```

Finally, you execute the command using the ExecuteReader method. The return type of ExecuteReader is an SqlDataReader object, which is returned to the calling function:

```
' Return a SqlDataReader to the calling function
Return command.ExecuteReader(CommandBehavior.CloseConnection)
```

NOTE *Remember, when passing back* SqlDataReader *objects, you don't manually close the connection after executing the command. This would be pointless, because the code after* Return *doesn't get to execute anyway, and the* SqlDataReader *needs an open connection when it is read at presentation tier level. Still, because you pass the* CommandBehavior.CloseConnection *parameter to the* ExecuteReader *method, the connection will be automatically closed after retrieving all the records.*

Implementing the Presentation Tier

Now that everything is in place in the other tiers, all you have to do is create the presentation tier part—the final goal you've been working toward from the beginning. As you saw in the figures at the beginning of this chapter, the departments list needs to look something like Figure 3-19, when the site is loaded in the web browser.

Choose a Department

» Full Costumes

» Costume Accessories

» Jokes and Tricks

Figure 3-19. The departments list when loaded in the web browser

You'll implement this as a separate Web User Control named DepartmentsList, just as you did with the Header control in Chapter 2, and then you'll add the user control to default.aspx.

The header and footer of the user control are simple images from the Images folder, the same folder that contains the JokePoint logo used in Chapter 2. However, the list of departments needs to be dynamically generated based on what you have in the database. Fortunately, the .NET Framework provides a few very useful web controls that can help you solve this problem without writing too much code. For example, the DataList control can be set to simply take a SqlDataReader object as input and generate a list based on its data.

Before actually writing the user control, however, you need to set up a CSS file for your web site.

Preparing the Field: Setting the Styles

Cascading Style Sheets (CSS) files are used to store centralized font and formatting information that can be easily applied to various parts of the site. Instead of setting fonts, colors, and dimensions for a Label control, you can set its CssClass to one of the existing styles.

In the following exercise, you set up a new CSS file for your site, and then add three styles that will be used in DepartmentsList for the fonts and colors of the listed departments.

Exercise: Preparing the Styles

1. Delete the Styles.css file from the project. In Solution Explorer, right-click the Styles.css file and click Delete on the menu that appears. Click OK when asked for confirmation.

2. Right-click JokePoint in Solution Explorer, and then choose Add ➤ Add New Item. From the Templates window, choose Style Sheet and call it JokePoint.css (see Figure 3-20).

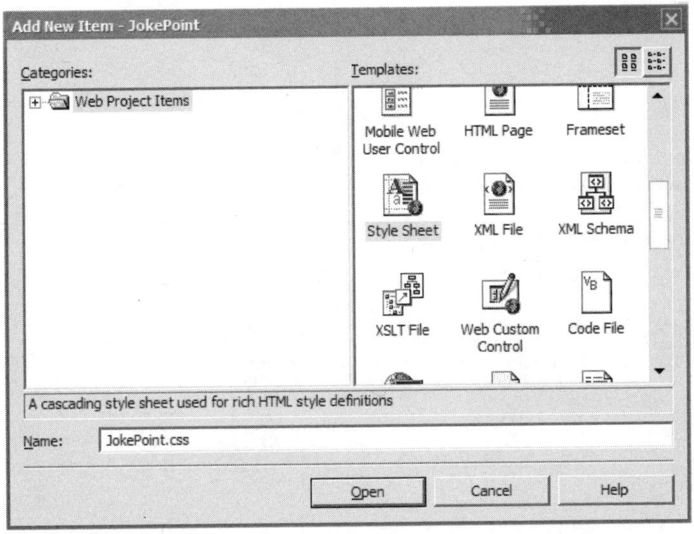

Figure 3-20. Adding a CSS file to the project

3. Open JokePoint.css by double-clicking it in Solution Explorer. Delete its contents and add these three styles to it:

```
A.DepartmentUnselected
{
    color: Blue;
    font-family: Comic Sans MS;
    text-decoration: none;
    font-size:   14px;
    font-weight: bold;
    line-height: 25px;
    padding-left: 0px
}
```

```
A.DepartmentUnselected:hover
{
  color: red;
  padding-left: 0px
}

A.DepartmentSelected
{
  color: green;
  font-family: Comic Sans MS;
  text-decoration: none;
  font-size:  14px;
  font-weight: bold;
  line-height: 25px;
  padding-left: 0px
}
```

4. Finally, open `default.aspx` in HTML View and modify it as shown here:

```
<HTML>
  <HEAD>
    <title>JokePoint</title>
    <meta name="GENERATOR" content="Microsoft Visual Studio .NET 7.1">
    <meta name="CODE_LANGUAGE" content="Visual Basic .NET 7.1">
    <meta name="vs_defaultClientScript" content="JavaScript">
    <meta name="vs_targetSchema"

content="http://schemas.microsoft.com/intellisense/ie5">
    <link href="JokePoint.css" type="text/css" rel="stylesheet">
  </HEAD>
```

How It Works: `JokePoint.css`

Having a central place to store style information helps you to easily change the look of the site without changing a line of code.

You deleted `Styles.css`, which was created by default by Visual Studio .NET, and created a new CSS file named `JokePoint.css`. Another method, perhaps a simpler one, would have been to simply rename the existing `Styles.css` file and then delete its contents (its default contents are not appropriate for JokePoint).

You then added to `JokePoint.css` the three styles you'll use in `DepartmentsList`. These styles refer to the way department names should look when they are unselected, unselected but with the mouse hovering over them, or selected.

You finally modified the `default.aspx` file to be aware of the newly created CSS file. This enables you to apply the styles that exist in `JokePoint.css` to any component that exists in `default.aspx`, or in the Web User Controls it includes.

Before moving on, let's highlight the built-in features Visual Studio .NET has for editing CSS files. While `JokePoint.css` is open in edit mode, right-click one of its styles and look at the menu that appears (see Figure 3-21).

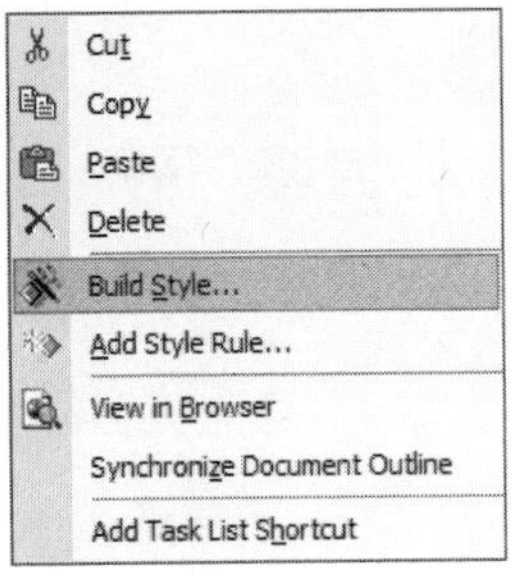

Figure 3-21. Editing a style in the CSS file

Clicking the Build Style option opens a window where the selected style can be edited visually.

Creating the `DepartmentsList` Web User Control

Now everything is in place, the only missing part being the user control itself. Your user control will contain a DataList control that will generate the list of departments.

The DataList control will have a header (consisting of the "Choose a Department" image), a footer, and the template that will generate the list of departments.

Optionally, instead of using the header and footer of the DataList, you could have implemented this using an HTML table with three cells; however, allowing DataList to handle these details is simpler.

In this exercise, you'll implement most functionality by using the Design View of Visual Studio .NET, and you'll see the HTML code that it generates. In other exercises, you'll work directly in HTML View mode.

Exercise: Creating DepartmentsList.ascx

1. First create a new Web User Control in the UserControls folder. Right-click the UserControls folder, and then choose Add ➤ Add Web User Control.

2. You'll be asked for the name of the new user control. Type **DepartmentsList.ascx**. (You also can type only **DepartmentsList**, and Visual Studio .NET will add the extension for you.)

3. You are presented with the design window of your new DepartmentsList control. Make sure the toolbox is visible (**Ctrl+Alt+X**), and double-click the DataList entry. This will add a DataList to the user control.

4. Change the name of the DataList from DataList1 to list by clicking the DataList control to select it, and changing the (ID) to list in the Properties window (see Figure 3-22).

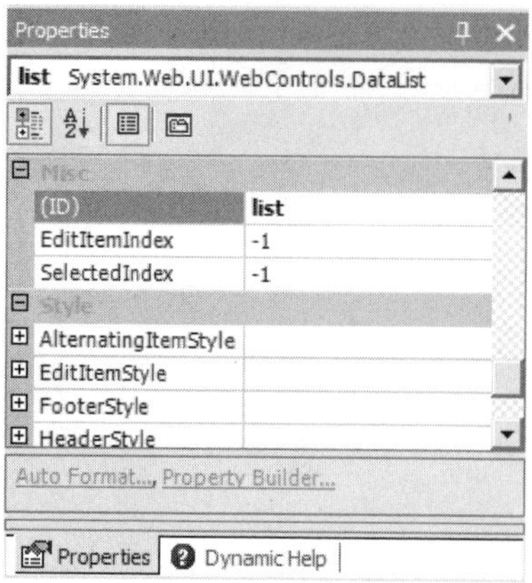

Figure 3-22. Editing the DataList *properties*

5. Now, it's time to deal with the header and footer images. You can add the images by either using the Image ASP.NET web control (available under the Web Forms tab in the toolbox), or the <IMG> HTML tag (available under the HTML tab in the toolbox), but you should use the latter variant because it requires less processing at the server side.

   Right-click the DataList, go to Edit Template, and select Header and Footer Templates. The DataList will look like Figure 3-23.

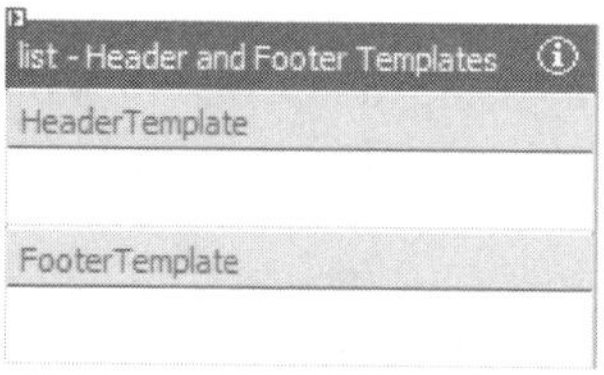

Figure 3-23. Editing the Header and Footer templates of the DataList

6. Click the white cell below HeaderTemplate to ensure it has the focus. Click the HTML tab in the toolbox, and double-click Image. A new empty image will be added as shown in Figure 3-24.

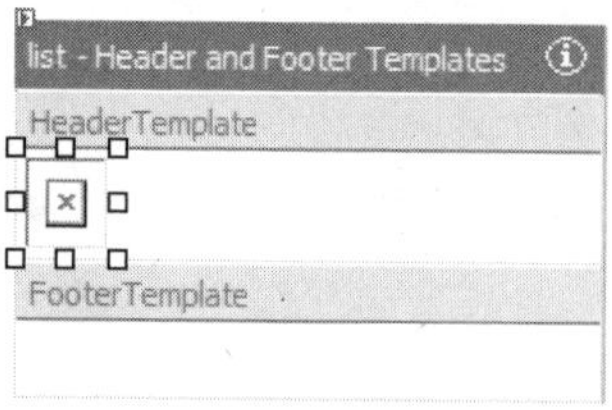

Figure 3-24. Adding an image to the Header template

7. While the Image is selected, press F4 to highlight its Properties window. Set border to 0 and src to Images/DeptHeader.gif.

> **TIP** *Usually, it is good practice to also specify the width and height of the image at design time. This makes rendering easier for browsers and browsing easier for users (because the page layout doesn't change after the page is loaded).*

8. Using the same technique, add an image to the FooterTemplate cell. Set its border property to 0 and src to Images/DeptFooter.gif.

> **NOTE** *Because the image paths are relative to the place where* default.aspx *resides (because your user control will be included in* default.aspx*), at this moment the images don't appear in Design View, but they will show up when running the page.*

9. Now close the edit mode by right-clicking the DataList and selecting End Template Editing. Before moving on to editing the item templates (which will generate the list of departments), select the DataList, and set the following properties:

    - Expand the ItemStyle node, and set BackColor to "Yellow".

    - Expand the HeaderStyle node, and set BackColor to "Yellow".

    - Set the CellPadding property to 0.

    These changes set the yellow background used in the list of departments, and ensure you'll have no white spaces between the header, templates, and footer in the DataList.

10. Right-click the DataList control, go to Edit Template, and then select the Item Templates option. You should be presented with a form as shown in Figure 3-25.

Figure 3-25. Editing the Item templates of the DataList

11. You need to add two HyperLink controls, one to the Item template and the other one to the SelectedItem template. First click the Web Forms tab in the toolbox, and then drag and drop two HyperLink controls to the mentioned template locations.

12. For the first hyperlink, set the CssClass property to DepartmentUnselected. For the second, set the CssClass property to DepartmentSelected. Set the Text property of both controls to an empty string (in other words, clear the Text property). The list control should then look like Figure 3-26.

Figure 3-26. Using HyperLink controls in the Item templates.

13. Enter the HTML View by clicking the HTML tab at the bottom of the designer window. You need to make a few changes to the HyperLink controls here. This is the full code, with the changes highlighted; take particular care about the NavigateUrl and Text fields of the HyperLink objects.

 CAUTION *Ensure that the code in each* asp:Hyperlink *section is on a single line rather than split over multiple lines as shown here.*

```
<%@ Control Language="vb" AutoEventWireup="false"

Codebehind="DepartmentsList.ascx.vb" Inherits="JokePoint.DepartmentsList"

TargetSchema="http://schemas.microsoft.com/intellisense/ie5" %>

<asp:datalist id="list" runat="server" CellPadding="0">
  <HeaderTemplate>
    <IMG alt="" src="Images/DeptHeader.gif" border="0">
  </HeaderTemplate>
  <SelectedItemTemplate>
     &raquo;
    <asp:HyperLink id=HyperLink2 runat="server"
        NavigateUrl='<%# "../default.aspx?DepartmentID=" &amp;
                      DataBinder.Eval(Container.DataItem, "departmentID") &amp;
                      "&amp;DepartmentIndex=" &amp; Container.ItemIndex %>'
        Text='<%# DataBinder.Eval(Container.DataItem, "Name") %>'
        CssClass="DepartmentSelected">
    </asp:HyperLink>
  </SelectedItemTemplate>
  <FooterTemplate>
    <IMG alt="" src="Images/DeptFooter.gif" border="0">
  </FooterTemplate>
  <ItemStyle BackColor="Yellow"></ItemStyle>
  <ItemTemplate>
     &raquo;
    <asp:HyperLink id=HyperLink1 runat="server"
        NavigateUrl='<%# "../default.aspx?DepartmentID=" &amp;
                      DataBinder.Eval(Container.DataItem, "departmentID") &amp;
                      "&amp;DepartmentIndex=" &amp; Container.ItemIndex  %>'
        Text='<%# DataBinder.Eval(Container.DataItem, "Name") %>'
        CssClass="DepartmentUnselected">
    </asp:HyperLink>
  </ItemTemplate>
  <HeaderStyle BackColor="Yellow"></HeaderStyle>
</asp:datalist>
```

14. Now open the code-behind file for the user control. Select it in Solution Explorer and then either click the View Code button or right-click the DepartmentList.ascx file and select View Code.

15. After you click the View Code button, Visual Studio .NET opens the code-behind file named DepartmentsList.ascx.vb. Within the automatically generated code, you can see a blank Page_Load method. Modify this method like this:

```
Private Sub Page_Load(ByVal sender As System.Object, _
                      ByVal e As System.EventArgs) Handles MyBase.Load
    ' The departmentIndex parameter is added to the query string when
    ' a department link is clicked. You need this because when the
    ' page is reloaded, the DataList forgets which link was clicked.
    Dim listIndex As String = Request.QueryString("departmentIndex")
```

```
' If listIndex has a value, this tells you that the visitor
' has clicked a department, and you inform the DataList about that
' (so it can apply the correct template for the selected item)
If Not listIndex Is Nothing Then
  list.SelectedIndex = CInt(listIndex)
End If

' GetDepartments returns a SqlDataReader object that has
' two fields: DepartmentID and Name. These fields are read in
' the SelectedItemTemplate and ItemTemplate of the DataList
list.DataSource = Catalog.GetDepartments()

' Needed to bind the child controls (the HyperLink controls)
' to the data source
list.DataBind()
End Sub
```

16. Press **Ctrl+Shift+B** to compile the project.

17. Open default.aspx in Design View. Drag DepartmentsList.ascx from the Solution Explorer and drop it over the cell that reads "Place List of Departments Here". Delete the text from the cell, so that only the user control should be there, as shown in Figure 3-27.

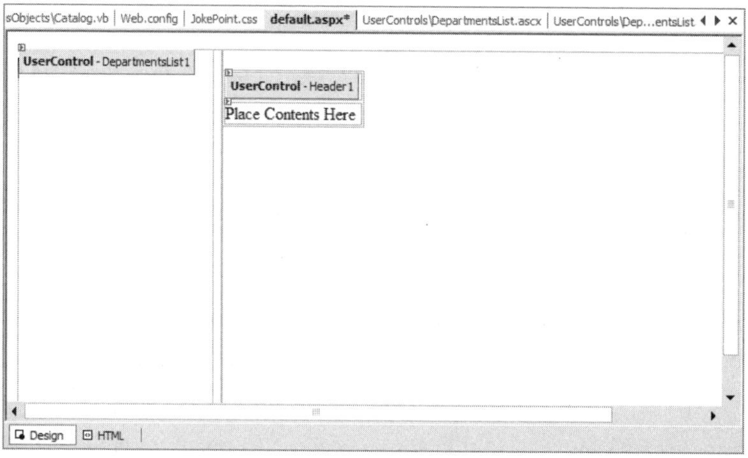

Figure 3-27. Using the DepartmentsList *control in* default.aspx

18. Make sure default.aspx is set as the start page for the project. If it isn't, right-click default.aspx and select Set As Start Page.

19. Press **F5** to execute the project (see Figure 3-28).

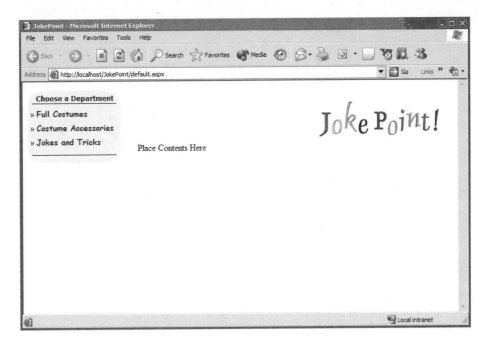

Figure 3-28. DepartmentsList *in action*

 CAUTION *If you get an error at this point, you either didn't enter the code correctly, or there is a problem connecting to SQL Server. Review the "Configuring SQL Server Security" section earlier in this chapter.*

20. Now you can see what happens when you click a department. Figure 3-29 shows the web page after a user clicked the Costume Accessories link. Note that default.aspx was reloaded, but with a different query string, and the Costume Accessories link is now listed using the DepartmentSelected style.

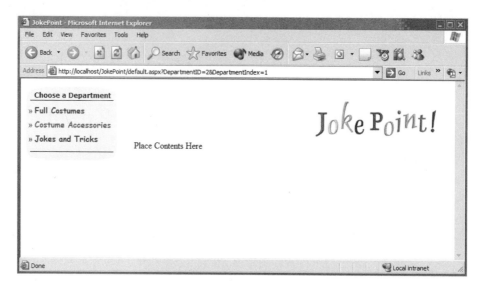

Figure 3-29. Selecting a department

You can always click the JokePoint header image to return to the main page.

How It Works: The DepartmentsList *User Control*

The heart of the DepartmentsList user control is its DataList control, which generates the list of departments. To make a DataList work, you need to edit its ItemTemplate property at the least. You also edited its SelectedItemTemplate, HeaderTemplate, and FooterTemplate. Editing the SelectedItemTemplate allows you to display a different look for a selected item.

The templates can be edited either in Design View mode or in HTML View mode. It is easier to work with the designer, but editing the HTML directly is more powerful and allows some tweaks that aren't possible with the designer. For the DataList, you wanted to have links so the reader could click a department. For this reason, you added HyperLink controls to ItemTemplate and SelectedItemTemplate boxes in the designer. This created a part of the HTML code for you, which you built upon later.

The DataList control is flexible and configurable. The first steps for configuring are to set its Item and SelectedItem templates. The ItemTemplate applies to "normal" list items, while the SelectedItemTemplate applies to the currently selected item. It is easy to create a DataList and its templates directly in HTML—you just need to implement the templates in a schema like the following:

```
<asp:DataList id="list" runat="server">
  <HeaderTemplate>
    <!- contents -->
  </HeaderTemplate>
  <SelectedItemTemplate>
    <!- contents -->
  </SelectedItemTemplate>
  <ItemTemplate>
```

```
    <!- contents -->
  </ItemTemplate>
  <AlternatingItemTemplate>
    <!- contents -->
  </AlternatingItemTemplate>
  <FooterTemplate>
    <!- contents -->
  </FooterTemplate>
</asp:DataList>
```

The templates that require closer attention are `ItemTemplate` and `SelectedItemTemplate`. These contain `HyperLink` controls that contain links to the respective departments.

Because of the way you implement the presentation layer, `default.aspx` is the only page that gets called, but you specify the department that was clicked by adding parameters to the query string. When a department is clicked in the department list, `default.aspx` is loaded with a query string like the following:

```
http://localhost/JokePoint/default.aspx?DepartmentID=2&DepartmentIndex=1
```

In the next chapter, you'll learn how `default.aspx` can update its contents depending on the supplied parameters. Right now, apart from having a different style for the selected item, the page doesn't change much when changing the department.

Apart from the different `CssClass` property, the links in `ItemTemplate` and `SelectedItemTemplate` have much the same definition. Here's the definition for the hyperlink in ItemTemplate:

```
<asp:HyperLink id=HyperLink1 runat="server"
    NavigateUrl='<%# "../default.aspx?DepartmentID=" &amp;
                DataBinder.Eval(Container.DataItem, "departmentID") &amp;
                "&amp;DepartmentIndex=" &amp; Container.ItemIndex  %>'
    Text='<%# DataBinder.Eval(Container.DataItem, "Name") %>'
    CssClass="DepartmentUnselected">
</asp:HyperLink>
```

The `DataBinder.Eval` function is used to extract data from the data source—in this case, the `SqlDataReader` object that you get from the business tier. Basically, the previous HTML code specifies that each department link should link to a page with the following form:

```
http://webservername/default.aspx?DepartmentID=XXX&DepartmentIndex=YYY
```

When a department is clicked, `default.aspx` and its controls are reloaded, and the `DataList` control doesn't know which link was clicked. For this reason, you pass the `DepartmentID` and `DepartmentIndex` in the query string.

DepartmentIndex is used to tell the DataList which item was clicked, so it will apply the correct style to it (DepartmentSelected). This will give the visitor a visual confirmation about the department currently selected.

DepartmentID will be read by other user controls that need more information about the selected department (such as needing to extract its description, or its list of categories). When working with the database, you identify a department by its ID, not by its placement in the departments list, so you can't use DepartmentsIndex instead.

DepartmentID and DepartmentIndex are not related in any way. A department can have the DepartmentID of 123 in the database, but if it's the first department displayed in the list, the DepartmentIndex will be 0 (it is a zero-based list).

Page_Load is the method that gets called every time the page is loaded, including after the visitor clicks any of the links on the page. In the Page_Load method of DepartmentsList, you first search for the DepartmentIndex parameter in the query string—if it has been passed, that means one of the departments was selected, and you tell the list which one is the selected item:

```
' The departmentIndex parameter is added to the query string when
' a department link is clicked. You need this because when the
' page is reloaded, the DataList forgets which link was clicked.
Dim listIndex As String = Request.QueryString("departmentIndex")

' If listIndex has a value, this tells you that the visitor
' has clicked a department, and you inform the DataList about that
' (so it can apply the correct template for the selected item)
If Not listIndex Is Nothing Then
  list.SelectedIndex = CInt(listIndex)
End If
```

Also in Page_Load, the DataList is loaded with data. This means that every time the reader clicks one of the departments (or when default.aspx gets reloaded for whatever reason), Page_Load is called again and the DataList is filled again with data. In Page_Load, you call the GetDepartments methods of the Catalog class (which is part of the business layer), and ask for the list of departments:

```
' GetDepartments returns a SqlDataReader object that has
' two fields: DepartmentID and Name. These fields are read in
' the SelectedItemTemplate and ItemTemplate of the DataList
list.DataSource = Catalog.GetDepartments()

' Needed to bind the child controls (the HyperLink controls)
' to the data source
list.DataBind()
```

Keep in mind that you're working on the presentation tier right now. It doesn't matter how the Catalog class or the GetDepartments method are implemented. You just need to know that GetDepartments returns a list of (DepartmentID, Name) pairs. While you are on the presentation tier, you don't really care how Catalog.GetDepartments does what it's supposed to do.

Downloading the Code

The code you have just written is available in the Downloads section of the Apress web site at http://www.apress.com or at http://www.CristianDarie.ro. You should be able to read through this book and build your solution as you go; however, if you want to check something from our working version, you can. Instructions on loading the chapters are available in the README.TXT document in the download.

Summary

This long chapter was well worth the effort, when you consider how much theory you've learned, and applied to the JokePoint project! In this chapter, you accomplished the following:

- Created the Department table and populated it with data

- Added a stored procedure to the database and added code to access this stored procedure from the middle tier

- Added the database connection string to the project to allow simple access to the database

- Added the DepartmentList Web User Control to the site

In the next chapter, you will continue building the site to include further exciting functionality.

CHAPTER 4

Creating the Product Catalog: Part II

THE FUN ISN'T OVER YET! In the previous chapter, you created a selectable list of departments for JokePoint. However, there's much more to a product catalog than a list of departments. In this chapter, you'll add the rest of the product catalog features.

In this chapter, you will

- Learn about relational data and the types of relationships that occur between data tables, and then implement the necessary relationships between the tables in your database.

- Learn about database diagrams, and create one for your database.

- Learn how to use the SQL WHERE and JOIN clauses, and how to use input and output parameters while writing the stored procedures in the data tier.

- Implement error handling in the business tier methods.

- Create the presentation tier Web User Controls to support the new catalog functionality.

- Learn how to load web controls dynamically at runtime.

- Create a custom error page and email the site administrator in case an error happens.

That's a lot of material to get through, so let's get started!

Determining the New Functionality

In Chapter 2, you established the general structure of your future web site. You decided that each page would have the header in the upper-right side and the list of departments in the upper-left side of the page. You achieved this part in Chapters 2 and 3, and right now JokePoint looks like Figure 4-1.

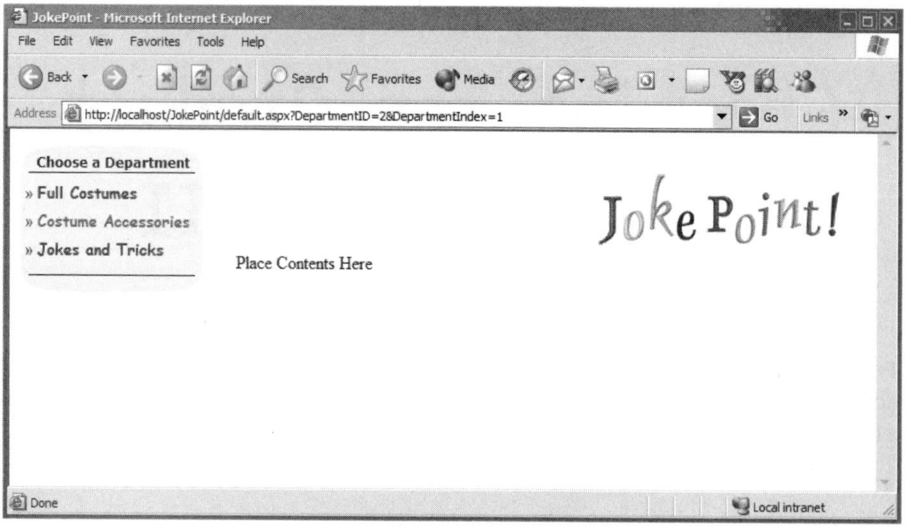

Figure 4-1. JokePoint

Unlike the departments list or the header, the part of the site that provides the actual content has a different structure depending on the page being visited. To better understand how to implement the contents area of the web site, let's look once again at what you want to achieve. At the beginning of Chapter 3, you saw how the full product catalog will look; let's take another look at how the dynamically generated part of the page looks for the parts of the site that you can browse.

For the main web page, the dynamically generated part should look like Figure 4-2.

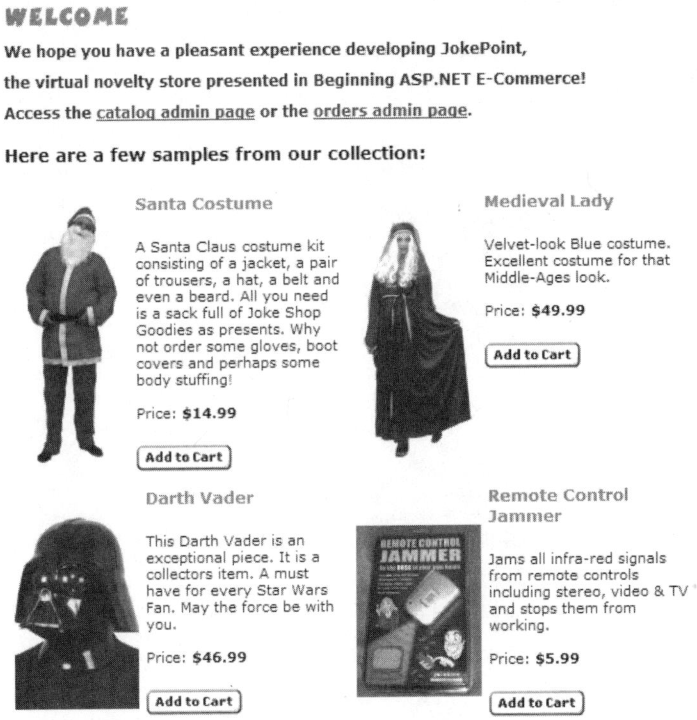

WELCOME

We hope you have a pleasant experience developing JokePoint,
the virtual novelty store presented in Beginning ASP.NET E-Commerce!
Access the catalog admin page or the orders admin page.

Here are a few samples from our collection:

Santa Costume

A Santa Claus costume kit consisting of a jacket, a pair of trousers, a hat, a belt and even a beard. All you need is a sack full of Joke Shop Goodies as presents. Why not order some gloves, boot covers and perhaps some body stuffing!

Price: **$14.99**

[Add to Cart]

Medieval Lady

Velvet-look Blue costume. Excellent costume for that Middle-Ages look.

Price: **$49.99**

[Add to Cart]

Darth Vader

This Darth Vader is an exceptional piece. It is a collectors item. A must have for every Star Wars Fan. May the force be with you.

Price: **$46.99**

[Add to Cart]

Remote Control Jammer

Jams all infra-red signals from remote controls including stereo, video & TV and stops them from working.

Price: **$5.99**

[Add to Cart]

Figure 4-2. The contents area of the JokePoint main page

When you visit a department, apart from it being highlighted in the list of departments, you are presented with a page like that shown in Figure 4-3.

Figure 4-3. Visiting the Full Costumes department

Finally, when you select a category, the page will look like Figure 4-4.

Figure 4-4. Visiting the Costumes for Women category

These are the three main parts that you need to implement. First we'll create the data structures to hold the necessary data. As you can see from the figures, now there's more information to store than just the list of departments, and you'll learn about some interesting new theory issues. The business tier comes with some new tricks of its own. Finally, you'll implement the presentation tier, which has some new surprises as well.

Okay, enough talking. Here we go ...

Storing the New Data

Given the new functionality needed for this chapter, it's not surprising that you need to add more data tables to the database. However, this isn't just about adding new data tables. You also need to learn about relational data and the relationships that can be implemented between the data tables, so that you can obtain more significant information from your database.

What Makes a Relational Database

It's no mystery that a database is something that stores data; however, today's modern relational database management systems (RDBMS) such as SQL Server, Oracle, DB2, and others, have extended this basic role by adding the capability to store and manage relational data.

So what does relational data mean? It's easy to see that every piece of data ever written in a real-world database is somehow related to some already existing information. Products are related to categories and departments, orders are related to products and customers, and so on. A relational database keeps this information stored in data tables, but is also aware of the relations between those tables.

These related tables form the relational database, which becomes an object with a significance of its own, rather than simply being a group of unrelated data tables. It is said that data becomes information only when you give significance to it, and establishing relations with other pieces of data is a good means of doing that.

Let's look at the product catalog and see what pieces of data it needs, and how you can transform this data into information.

For the product catalog, you'll need at least three data tables: one for departments, one for categories, and one for products. It is important to note that physically each data table is an independent database object, even if logically it is part of a larger entity; in other words, even though we say, "a category contains products," the table that contains the products is not inside the table that contains categories. This is not in contradiction with the relational character of the database. Figure 4-5 shows a simple representation of three data tables, including some selected sample data.

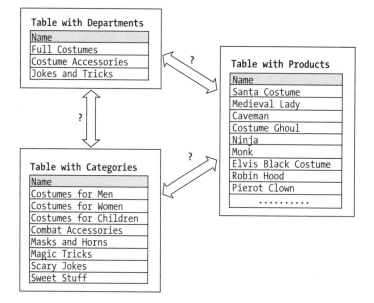

Figure 4-5. Unrelated departments, categories, and products

Note that when two tables are related, that means the records of those tables are related. So, if the products table is related to the categories table, this translates into each product record being somehow related to one of the records in the categories table.

Figure 4-5 doesn't show the physical representation of the database. For that reason, the table names aren't listed there. Diagrams like this are used to decide what needs to be stored in the database. After you know what to store, the next step is to decide how the listed data is related, which will lead you to the physical structure for the database. In Figure 4-5, you can see three kinds of data to store, but as you'll see later, to implement this structure in the database you'll use four tables, not three.

So, now that you know what data to store, let's think about how the three parts relate to each other. Apart from knowing that the records are related somehow, you also need to know the kind of relationship between them. Let's take a closer look at the different ways in which two tables can be related.

Relational Data and Table Relationships

To continue your discovery of the world of relational databases, let's further analyze the three logical tables we've been looking at so far. To make life easier, let's give them names now: the table containing products is Product, the table containing categories is Category, and the last one is our old friend, Department. No surprises here! Luckily, these tables implement the most common kinds of relationships that exist between tables, the **One-to-Many** and **Many-to-Many** relationships, so you have the chance to learn about them.

NOTE *Some variations of these two relationship types exist, as well as the less popular* One-to-One *relationship. In the One-to-One relationship, each row in one table matches exactly one row in the other. For example, in a database that allowed patients to be assigned to beds, you would hope that there would be a one-to-one relationship between patients and beds! The database doesn't support enforcing this kind of relationship, because you would have to add matching records in both tables at the same time. Moreover, two tables with a One-to-One relationship can be joined to form a single table. No One-to-One relationships are used in this book.*

One-to-Many Relationships

The One-to-Many relationship happens when one record in a table can be associated with multiple records in the related table, but not vice versa. In the sample table, this happens for the Department – Category relation. A specific department can contain any number of categories, but each category belongs to exactly one department. Figure 4-6 better represents the One-to-Many relationship between departments and categories.

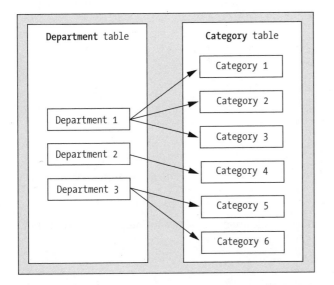

Figure 4-6. A One-to-Many relationship between departments and categories

Another common scenario in which you see the One-to-Many relationship is with the Order – Order Details tables, where Order contains general details about the order (such as date, total amount, and so on) and Order Details contains the products related to the order.

Many-to-Many Relationships

The other common type of relationship is the Many-to-Many relationship. This kind of relationship is implemented when records in both tables of the relationship can have multiple matching records in the other.

This kind of relationship happens between the Product and Category tables, because a product can exist in more than one category (one product—many categories), and also a category can have more than one product (one category—many products).

If a product belonged to a single category, you would have another One-to-Many relationship, just like that between departments and categories (where a category can't belong to more than one department).

If a diagram represented this relationship like that shown in Figure 4-6, you get something Figure 4-7.

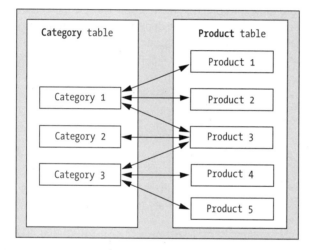

Figure 4-7. The Many-to-Many relationship between categories and products

You need to know a few more details about the Many-to-Many relationship, and we'll discuss them later when you implement it in the JokePoint database.

The FOREIGN KEY *Constraint*

Relationships between tables are physically implemented in the database using FOREIGN KEY constraints, or simply foreign keys.

You learned in the previous chapter about the PRIMARY KEY and UNIQUE constraints. They were covered there because they apply to the table as an individual entity. Foreign keys, on the other hand, always occur between two tables: the table in which the foreign key is defined (the referencing table) and the table the foreign key references (the referenced table).

SQL Server Books Online defines a foreign key as being a column or combination of columns used to establish or enforce a link between data in two tables. Foreign keys are used both as a method of ensuring data integrity and to establish a relationship between tables.

FOREIGN KEY constraints, like the other types of constraints, apply certain restrictions to enforce data integrity. Unlike PRIMARY KEY and UNIQUE constraints that apply to a single table, the FOREIGN KEY constraint applies restrictions on both the referencing and referenced tables. When establishing a One-to-Many relationship between the Department table and the Category table by using a FOREIGN KEY constraint, the database will include this relationship as part of its integrity. The foreign key will not allow you to add a category to a nonexistent department, and it will not allow deleting a department if categories belong to it.

You learned the general theory of foreign keys here. You'll implement them in the following exercise, where you'll have the chance to learn more about how foreign keys work. A bit later, in the "Creating a Database Diagram" exercise, you'll learn how to visualize and implement foreign keys using the integrated diagramming feature in Visual Studio .NET.

Implementing Table Relationships

So you have an idea about the two main kinds of table relationships. You also know that these relationships are implemented in the database using a special kind of constraint: FOREIGN KEYS. In the following exercises, you'll add all the tables and table relationships required for the product catalog to the JokePoint database.

Departments, Categories, and the One-to-Many Relationship

Essentially, creating the Category table is pretty much the same as the Department table you've already created, so we'll move pretty quickly. Still, you'll have fun in this exercise as well, because this is where you implement the One-to-Many relationship between the Category and Department tables.

Let's first create the new table and implement the relationship, and then you'll get the details in the "How It Works" section afterwards.

Exercise: Creating the Category **Table and Relating It to** Department

1. Using the Server Explorer (**Ctrl+Alt+S**), navigate to your SQL Server instance, and then to the JokePoint database. Also, expand the JokePoint node to make sure Visual Studio establishes a connection with it. When the database is selected, choose Database ➤ New Table. Alternatively, you can right-click the Tables node under JokePoint and select New Table.

2. Add the following columns using the form that appears (see Figure 4-8).

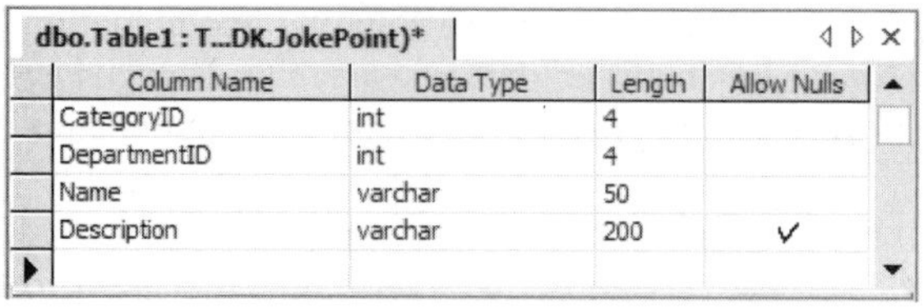

dbo.Table1 : T...DK.JokePoint)*			◁ ▷ ×
Column Name	Data Type	Length	Allow Nulls ▲
CategoryID	int	4	
DepartmentID	int	4	
Name	varchar	50	
Description	varchar	200	✓
▶			▼

Figure 4-8. Designing the `Category` *table*

3. Right-click the `CategoryID` field and select Set Primary Key. You also want `CategoryID` to be an identity column, so set it as shown in Figure 4-9.

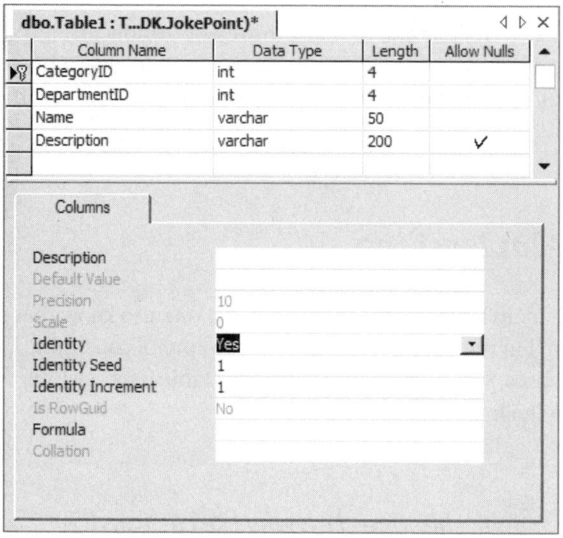

dbo.Table1 : T...DK.JokePoint)*			◁ ▷ ×
Column Name	Data Type	Length	Allow Nulls ▲
▶🗝 CategoryID	int	4	
DepartmentID	int	4	
Name	varchar	50	
Description	varchar	200	✓
			▼

Columns

Description	
Default Value	
Precision	10
Scale	0
Identity	Yes ▾
Identity Seed	1
Identity Increment	1
Is RowGuid	No
Formula	
Collation	

Figure 4-9. Setting a primary key and an identity column

4. Press **Ctrl+S** to save the table. When asked, type Category for the table's name.

5. While the `Category` table is still selected, choose View ➤ Relationships. Here is where you specify the details for the foreign-key relationship. This works by relating a column of the referencing table (`Category`) to a column of the referenced table (`Department`). You need to relate the `DepartmentID` column in `Category` with the `DepartmentID` column of the `Department` table.

6. In the dialog box that appears, click New.

7. In the Primary key table combo box, select `Department`. Make sure that `Category` is selected for the Foreign key table.

8. Under `Department`, select `DepartmentID` as the primary key column. Do the same for `Category`—choose `DepartmentID` (not `CategoryID`!). Right now, the Property Pages dialog box should look like Figure 4-10.

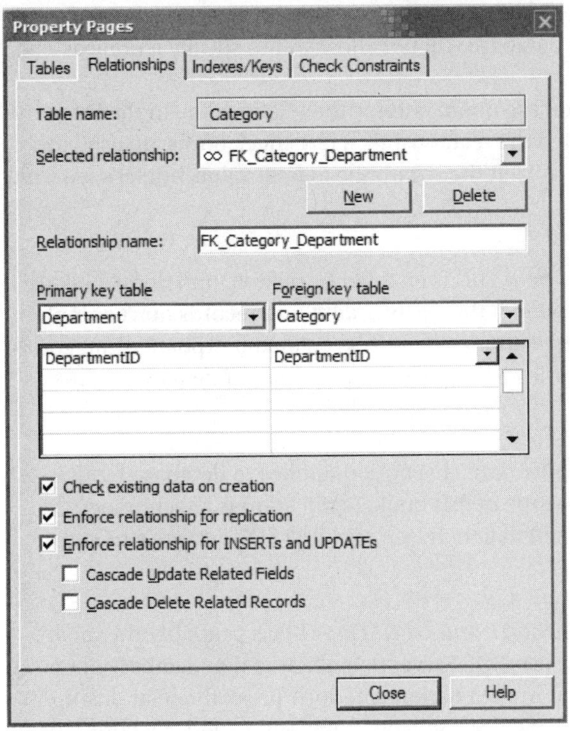

Property Pages

Tables | Relationships | Indexes/Keys | Check Constraints

Table name: Category

Selected relationship: ∞ FK_Category_Department

New   Delete

Relationship name: FK_Category_Department

Primary key table   Foreign key table
Department   Category

DepartmentID	DepartmentID

☑ Check existing data on creation
☑ Enforce relationship for replication
☑ Enforce relationship for INSERTs and UPDATEs
☐ Cascade Update Related Fields
☐ Cascade Delete Related Records

Close   Help

Figure 4-10. Adding a table relationship

TIP   *If anything goes wrong, click Delete to delete the relationship, and then create it again.*

9. Click Close to save the relationship.

10. Press **Ctrl+S** to save the table again. You will be warned about the Category and Department tables being updated and asked for confirmation. This confirms once again that a foreign-key relationship affects both tables that take part in the relationship. Click Yes.

How It Works: The One-to-Many Relationship

Okay, so you created a relationship between the Category and Department tables. But how does it work, and how does it affect your work and life? Let's study how you implemented this relationship.

In the Category table, apart from the primary key and the usual Name and Description columns, you added a DepartmentID column. This column stores the department each category belongs to. Because the DepartmentID field in Category doesn't allow NULLs, you will be required to supply a department for each category. Furthermore, because of the foreign-key relationship, the database will not allow you to specify a nonexistent department.

Actually, you can ask the database not to enforce the relationship. In the Property Pages dialog box where you created the relationship, a few check boxes are used to set some options for the foreign key. We left them with the default value, but let's see what they do:

- *Check existing data on creation*: This is enabled by default, and doesn't allow the creation of the relationship if the existing database records don't comply with it. In other words, the relationship can't be created if orphaned categories are in the database (categories with a DepartmentID that references an nonexistent department).

- *Enforce relationship for replication*: This option applies to database replication, which is beyond the scope of this book. Replication is a technology that allows the synchronization of data between multiple SQL Servers situated at different locations.

- *Enforce relationship for INSERTs and UPDATEs*: This is probably the most important of the options. It tells SQL Server to make sure that database operations on the tables involved in the relationship don't break the relationship. When this option is selected, SQL Server won't allow you to add categories to nonexistent departments or delete departments that have related categories.

- *Cascade Update Related Fields*: This option allows SQL Server to update existing data if this is required for keeping data integrity. If the DepartmentID field of an existing department is changed, SQL Server also changes the DepartmentID fields of the categories that belong to that department—this way, even after you change the ID of the department, its categories will still belong to it. You can leave this option unchecked because you won't need to change departments IDs.

- *Cascade Delete Related Records*: This is a radical solution for keeping data integrity. If this is selected and you delete a department from the database, all its related categories would be automatically deleted by SQL Server. This is a sensitive option and you should be very careful with it. You won't use it in the JokePoint project.

In the One-to-Many relationship (and implicitly the FOREIGN KEY constraint), you link two columns from two different tables. One of these columns is a primary key, and it defines the One part of the relationship. In the sample case, DepartmentID is the primary key of Department, so Department is the one that connects to many categories. A primary key must be on the One part to ensure it is unique—a category can't be linked to a department if you can't be sure that the department ID is unique; you must ensure that no two departments have the same ID, otherwise, the relationship wouldn't make much sense.

Categories Linked to Existing Departments

Now that you've created the Categories table, you can populate it with some data. We'll also try to add data that would break the relationship that you established between the Department and Category tables.

 TIP *Remember that you can use the code in the Downloads section of the Apress web site (http://www.apress.com) to create and populate the data tables.*

Exercise: Adding Categories

1. Open the Category table for editing by double-clicking the table in Server Explorer.

2. Using the editor integrated with Visual Studio, you can start adding rows. Because CategoryID has been set as an identity column, you cannot manually edit its data—SQL Server automatically fills this field for you. However, you'll need to manually fill the DepartmentID field with ID values of existing departments. Add categories as shown in Figure 4-11.

CategoryID	DepartmentID	Name	Description
1	1	Costumes for Men	Childish costumes for adult gangsters:
2	1	Costumes for Women	Here is our complete list of costumes for women:
3	1	Costumes for Children	Sweet costumes for your kid:
4	2	Combat Accessories	Choose one of these lethal weapons:
5	2	Masks and Horns	This is our complete list of masks and horns:
6	3	Magic Tricks	Impress your friends with these unique magic items:
7	3	Scary Jokes	This is our complete list of scary jokes:
8	3	Sweet Stuff	Can they get any sweeter than that?

Figure 4-11. Populating the Category *table*

 TIP *Please keep the* CategoryID *numbers in sequential order. This will make your life easier when associating them with product IDs, later in this chapter.*

---

3. Now, try to break the database integrity by adding a category to a nonexistent department (for example, set the DepartmentID to 500). After filling the new category data, press Tab or click the next row. At this point, Visual Studio will submit the newly written data to SQL Server. If you have created the relationship properly, an error should occur (see Figure 4-12). For more detailed information about the error, click the Help button.

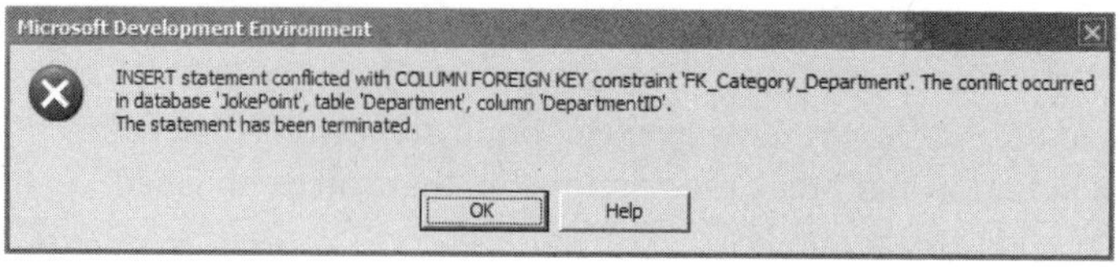

Figure 4-12. You can't break the FOREIGN KEY *constraint.*

How It Works: Populating the Categories Table

Visual Studio .NET makes it very easy to add new records to a data table. The only trick it to keep the generated CategoryID numbers in sequential order, as shown in Figure 4-11. Otherwise, you won't be able to use the SQL scripts from the code download to populate the tables that relate to Category.

This can be tricky if you delete and add records in the table, because the autogenerated number keeps increasing, and you can't specify the ID manually.

Categories, Products, and the Many-to-Many Relationship

Now that you've added categories and departments to the database, the next logical step is to add products. This is a bit more complicated than just creating a Product table and adding data to it, as you did for Category. This is because Product and Category have a different kind of relationship from the one between categories and departments.

You'll implement a Many-to-Many relationship between Product and Category. Although logically the Many-to-Many relationship happens between two tables, SQL Server doesn't have the means to physically enforce this kind of relationship, so we cheat by adding a third table to the mix. This third table, called a junction table (also known as a linking table or associate table) and two One-to-Many relationships (two FOREIGN KEY constraints) will help you achieve the Many-to-Many relationship.

The junction table is used to associate products and categories, with no restriction on how many products can exist for a category, or how many categories a product can be added to. Figure 4-13 explains the role of the junction table:

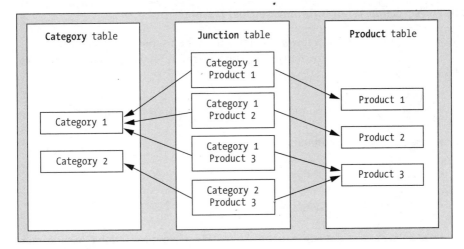

Figure 4-13. Implementing the Many-to-Many relationship with a junction table

Note that each record in the junction table links one category with one product. You can have many records in the junction table, linking any category to any product. The linking table contains two fields, each one being a foreign key to the primary key of one of the two linked tables. In our case, the junction table will contain two fields: CategoryID and ProductID.

Each record in the junction table will consist of a (ProductID, CategoryID) pair, which will be used to associate a particular product with a particular category. By adding more records to the ProductCategory table, you can associate a product with more categories or a category with more products, effectively implementing the Many-to-Many relationship.

We can't give a definitive recommendation for a naming convention to use for the junction table. Most of the time, it will be okay to just join the names of the two linked tables—in our case, the junction table will be named ProductCategory. However, there are times when the junction table has a "meaning" of its own and can be named otherwise. For example, in the Northwind database that is supplied with Access and SQL Server, you see the [Order Details] junction table, which links orders with products.

NOTE   *Because the Many-to-Many relationship is implemented using a third table that makes the connection between the linked tables, there is no need to add additional fields to the related tables in the way that you added the* DepartmentID *field to the* Category *table.*

The Product *Table: What Information Does It Store?*

The Product table contains a few more fields than the usual ProductID, Name, and Description. Most of them are pretty self-explanatory but for completeness, let's have a look at each of them:

- ProductID stores the unique ID of each product. This is the primary key.

- Name contains the product's name.

- Description contains the product's description.

- Price contains the product price.

- ImagePath stores the name (or could be a more complex relative path) of the file that contains the product's picture. SQL Server is able to store binary data, including pictures, directly in the database, but this usually results in poor database performance. It is wiser to store only the picture location and file name in the database, and store the actual picture files in the Windows file system. This method also allows you to have the images saved in a separate physical location (for example, another hard disk), further improving performance for high-traffic web sites.

- OnCatalogPromotion is a bit field (can be set to either 0 or 1) that specifies whether the product is featured on the front page of the web site. The main page of the site will list the products that have this bit set to 1. This field doesn't accept NULLs and has a default value of 0.

- OnDepartmentPromotion is a bit field that specifies whether the product is featured on the department pages. Remember that when visiting a department, the visitor is shown only the featured products of that department. If a product belongs to more than one department (remember, it can belong to more than one category), it will be listed as featured on all those departments. This field doesn't accept NULLs and has a default value of 0.

Using those bit fields allows you to let the site administrators highlight a set of products that are of particular importance for a department at a specific time (for example, before Christmas they will add Santa costumes and accessories, and so on). Okay, enough talk; let's add the Product table to the database.

Exercise: Creating the Product *Table and Relating It to* Category

1. Using the steps that you already know, create a new Product table that looks like Figure 4-14.

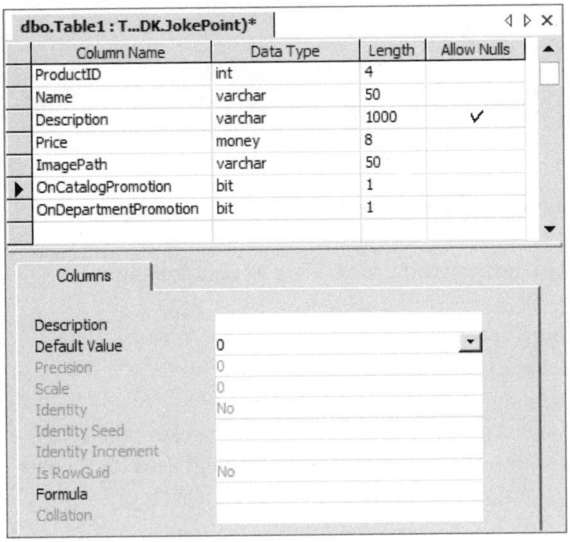

Figure 4-14. Designing the Product *table*

2. Set ProductID as the primary key, and also make it an identity column with the default values for Identity Seed and Identity Increment. Also, set OnCatalogPromotion and OnDepartmentPromotion to a default value of 0.

3. Press **Ctrl+S** to save the table, and type Product for its name. Now you have a brand new Product table!

4. Because there are many products, please populate this table with the script provided in the Downloads section of the Apress web site (http://www.apress.com).

    Now, implement the Many-to-Many relationship between Product and Category by creating the junction table.

5. Create a new table with two fields, as shown in Figure 4-15.

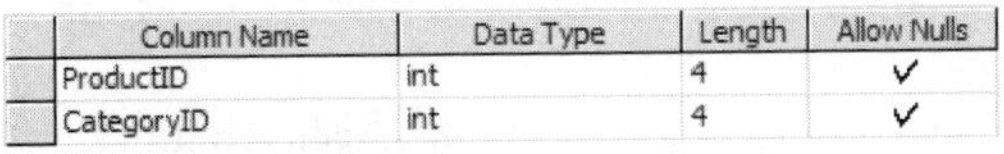

Figure 4-15. Designing the ProductCategory *table*

6. Now select both fields, ProductID and CategoryID, and choose Diagram ➤ Set Primary Key. Two golden keys appear on the left side, and the Allow Nulls check boxes are automatically unchecked (see Figure 4-16).

Column Name	Data Type	Length	Allow Nulls
ProductID	int	4	
CategoryID	int	4	

Figure 4-16. Setting the composite primary key on ProductCategory

7. Press Ctrl+S to save the newly created table. Its name is ProductCategory.

8. While ProductCategory is in design mode, click View ➤ Relationships.

9. In the Property Pages dialog box that appears, click New to create a new relationship.

10. For the Primary key table, choose Category, and for the Foreign key table, choose ProductCategory. For both tables, choose CategoryID as the field used for the relationship. The relationship is automatically named FK_ProductCategory_Category.

11. Click the New button again, because you now want to create the relationship between Product and ProductCategory.

12. Select Product for the Primary key table, select ProductCategory for the Foreign key table, and then select ProductID as the field to implement the relationship for both of them. This relationship is automatically named FK_ProductCategory_Product.

13. Click Close to close the Property Pages dialog box.

14. Press Ctrl+S to save the changes you made by adding the relationships. You will be warned that Product, Category, and ProductCategory will be saved to the database. Click Yes to confirm.

15. You can now populate this new table by running the script from the Downloads section of the Apress web site (http://www.apress.com).

How It Works: The Many-to-Many Relationship

In this exercise, you created the Product table, and implemented a Many-to-Many relationship with Category.

Many-to-Many relationships are created by adding a third table, called a junction table, which, in this case, is named ProductCategory. This table contains (ProductID, CategoryID) pairs, and each record in the table associates a particular product with a particular category. So, if you see a record such as (1,4) in ProductCategory, you know that the product with ProductID 1 belongs to the category with CategoryID 4.

The Many-to-Many relationship is physically enforced through two One-to-Many relationships—one between Product and ProductCategory, the other between ProductCategory and Category. In English, this means, "one product can be associated with many product-category entries, each of those being associated with one category." The relationship ensures that the products and categories that appear in the

ProductCategory table actually exist in the database, and won't allow you to delete a product if you have a category associated with it and vice versa.

This is also the first time that you set a primary key consisting of more than one column. The primary key of ProductCategory is formed by both its fields: ProductID and CategoryID. This means that you won't be allowed to have two identical (ProductID, CategoryID) pairs in the table. However, it is perfectly legal to have a ProductID or CategoryID more than once, as long as it is part of a unique (ProductID, CategoryID) pair.

This makes sense, because you don't want to have two identical records in this table. A product can be associated with a particular category, or not; it cannot be associated with a particular category multiple times.

At first all the theory about table relationships can be a bit confusing, until you get used to them. To understand the relationship more clearly, you can get a picture by using database diagrams.

Database Diagrams

Database diagrams are very useful because they provide a way to visualize not only the data tables, but also the relationships between them. Diagrams can also be used to create tables, and they allow you to create table relationships using drag and drop.

Let's create a diagram containing the tables you've created so far.

Exercise: Creating a Database Diagram

1. Make sure the JokePoint database is selected in Server Explorer. Choose Database ➤ New Diagram. Alternatively, you can right-click the Database Diagrams node under JokePoint and select New Diagram.

2. In the dialog box that appears, you are invited to select which tables to add to the diagram. Because you want all of them, click Add four times. Click Close.

3. After closing the dialog box, you can see the tables and their relationships in the newly created diagram. You should see something like Figure 4-17.

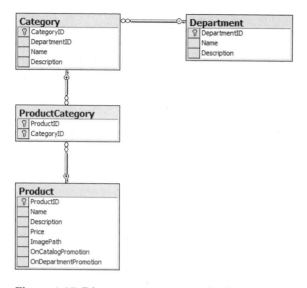

Figure 4-17. Diagram representing the four tables of the JokePoint database

4.   Press Ctrl+S to save the diagram. Select JokePoint for the name.

How It Works: Database Diagrams

Database diagrams are useful things. If, until now, you could only imagine the relationships between the different tables, the diagram allows you to see what actually happens. The diagram shows the three One-to-Many relationships you created earlier.

The diagram also shows the type and direction of the relationships. Note that a key symbol appears at the one part of each relationship, and an infinity symbol at the many side of the relationship. The table whose primary key is involved in the relationship is at the one side of the relationship and is marked with the little golden key.

One of the most useful things about diagrams is that you can edit database objects directly from the diagram. If you right-click a table or a relationship, you'll see a lot of features there. Feel free to experiment a bit to get a feeling of the features available. Although you won't use this feature here, keep in mind that it's possible to create foreign-key relationships by simply dragging one column from one table to a different column of another (or even the same) table. This automatically opens the Create Relationship dialog box.

You can also create new tables, or design existing ones, directly within the diagram. To design one of the existing tables, you must switch the table to normal mode by right-clicking a table, and then choosing Table View ➤ Standard, as shown in Figure 4-18.

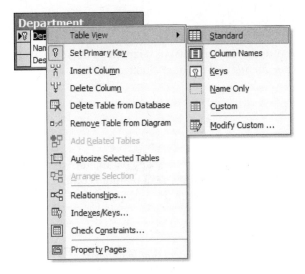

Figure 4-18. Setting Standard Table View

After the table is in normal mode, you can edit it directly in the diagram, as shown in Figure 4-19.

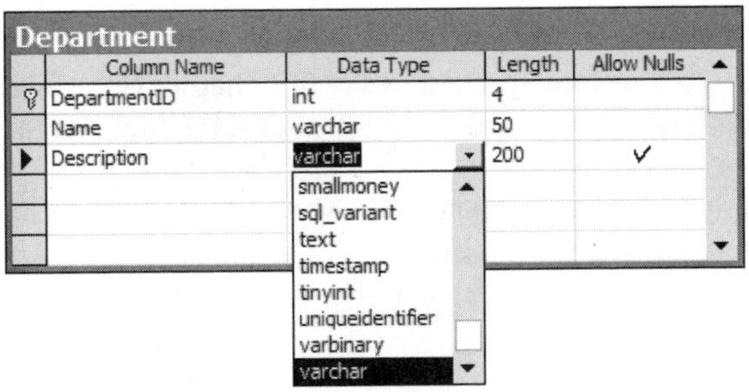

Figure 4-19. Editing a table directly in the diagram

Implementing the Data Tier

Now you have a database with a wealth of information just waiting to be read by somebody. As usual, you'll implement the data-access logic in stored procedures.

For this chapter, the data-tier logic is a bit more complicated than in the previous chapter. It will need to answer to queries like "give me the list of categories for a specific department" or "give me the details for this specific department or category." To accomplish the new requirements, you must get data from multiple data tables and/or use input (and output) parameters.

Filtering SQL Query Results

Remember the simple SQL Query you used in the previous chapter? In that case, you wanted to get the whole list of departments and the query looked like this:

```
SELECT DepartmentID, Name FROM Department
```

There is a single table involved, the query doesn't have any parameters, and the records aren't even filtered with the WHERE clause. Things get a bit more complicated in this chapter, but don't worry; we still don't talk about rocket science!

NOTE   *Before continuing, there is a detail you should be aware of. Almost every SQL query, except maybe for the simplest ones, can be written in a number of alternative ways. Advanced database programming books have entire chapters explaining how to get the same result using different interrogation techniques, the performance implications of each of them, and so on. In this book, we employ techniques that are generally recommended as good programming practices, and which work best for the joke shop.*

The first new element to introduce to the stored procedures in this chapter is the SQL WHERE clause, which is used to filter the records acted on by SELECT, UPDATE, and DELETE SQL statements.

Say you wanted to retrieve the Name and Description of a particular department. You'll need this query when the visitor clicks a department to get more data about it. The SQL query that returns the Name and Description of the department with an ID of 3 is

```
SELECT Name, Description FROM Department
WHERE DepartmentID = 3
```

A similar query can be used to retrieve the list of categories that belong to a particular department:

```
SELECT Name, Description FROM Category
WHERE DepartmentID = 3
```

These two queries were simple enough, because they queried data from a single table. Things get a bit more complicated when you need to gather data from more tables.

Joining Data Tables

Because the data is stored in several tables, you'll frequently run into situations in which not all of the information you want is in one table. Take a look at the list shown in Figure 4-20, which contains data from both the Department and Category tables.

	Department Name	Category Name	Category Description
1	Full Costumes	Costumes for Men	Childish costumes for adult gangsters:
2	Full Costumes	Costumes for Women	Here is our complete list of costumes for women:
3	Full Costumes	Costumes for Children	Sweet costumes for your kid:
4	Costume Accessories	Combat Accessories	Choose one of these lethal weapons:
5	Costume Accessories	Masks and Horns	This is our complete list of masks and horns:
6	Jokes and Tricks	Magic Tricks	Impress your friends with these unique magic items:
7	Jokes and Tricks	Scary Jokes	This is our complete list of scary jokes:
8	Jokes and Tricks	Sweet Stuff	Can they get any sweeter than that?

Figure 4-20. Fictive table containing data gathered from two tables

In other cases, all the information you need is in just one table, but you need to place conditions on it, based on the information in another table. The list shown in Figure 4-21 contains data extracted from the Product table, but only the products that belong to the Costumes for Children category:

	ProductID	Name	Description	Price
1	2	Medieval Lady	Velvet-look Blue costume. Excellent costume for t...	49.9900
2	21	Mystic Witch	An adorable mystic witch costume for kids. Broom...	25.0000
3	23	Space Warrior	A space warrior costume by Star Orangutan. Idea...	10.9900
4	24	Hippie	A cool seventies hippie costume for kids. Don't fo...	9.9900
5	25	Sheriff hat	A children's sheriff hat in black felt with a silver b...	6.5000

Figure 4-21. Sample data from the Product table

When extracting the products that belong to a category, the SQL query isn't the same as when extracting the categories that belong to a department. This is because products and categories are linked through the ProductCategory associate table.

To get the list of products in a category, first look in the ProductCategory table and get all the (ProductID, CategoryID) pairs where CategoryID is the ID of the category you're looking for. That list contains the IDs of the products in that category. Using these IDs, you can generate the required product list.

Although this sounds pretty complicated, it can be done using a single SQL query. The real power of SQL lies in its capability to perform complex operations on large amounts of data using simple queries.

How to Use JOIN

The results shown in the previous figures are the result of table joins. When you need to get a result set based on data from multiple tables, you probably need to use JOIN.

You'll learn how to use JOIN by analyzing the Product and ProductCategory tables, and analyzing how to get a list of products that belong to a certain category. Suppose you want to get all the products in the category where CategoryID = 3. Figure 4-22 shows the records that you want returned.

(selection from **ProductCategory** table)

CategoryID	ProductID
2	18
2	19
2	20
3	2
3	21
3	23
3	24
3	25
4	26
4	28
4	32

(selection from **Product** table)

ProductID	Name	Description
2	Medieval Lady	Velvet-look Blue costume. E...
21	Mystic Witch	An adorable mystic witch c...
23	Space Warrior	A space warrior costume by...
24	Hippie	A cool seventies hippie cost...
25	Sheriff hat	A children's sheriff hat in blu...

Figure 4-22. Joining the ProductCategory *and* Product *tables on the* ProductID *field*

Tables are joined in SQL using the JOIN clause. Joining one table with another table results in the columns (not the rows) of those tables being joined. When joining two tables, there always needs to be a common column on which the join will be made. The query that joins the Product and ProductCategory tables is as follows:

```
SELECT *
FROM ProductCategory INNER JOIN Product
ON Product.ProductID = ProductCategory.ProductID
```

The result will look something like Figure 4-23 (to save space, the picture doesn't include the full results).

	ProductID	CategoryID	ProductID	Name	Description	Price
1	1	1	1	Santa Costume	A Santa Claus costume kit consis...	14.9900
2	2	2	2	Medieval Lady	Velvet-look Blue costume. Excellen...	49.9900
3	2	3	2	Medieval Lady	Velvet-look Blue costume. Excellen...	49.9900
4	3	1	3	Caveman	Go back in time and dress up as a ...	12.9900
5	4	1	4	Costume Ghoul	A Ghoul costume in Black. Simplisti...	18.9900
6	5	1	5	Ninja	A Ninja costume in Black. Check o...	15.9900
7	6	1	6	Monk	Adult Fancy Dress costume of one...	13.9900
8	7	1	7	Elvis Black Costume	The king would be proud to wear t...	35.9900
9	8	1	8	Robin Hood	Robin Hood - He steals from the ri...	18.9900
10	9	1	9	Pierot Clown	Quality adult costume perfect for t...	22.9900

Figure 4-23. Results of the table join between Product *and* ProductCategory

The resultant table is composed of the fields from the joined tables synchronized on the ProductID column, which was specified as the column to make the join on.

Looking at the resultant table, it's easy to see that a `WHERE` clause is needed to provide just the records that have a `CategoryID` of 3. The new query would look like this:

```
SELECT *
FROM ProductCategory INNER JOIN Product
ON Product.ProductID = ProductCategory.ProductID
WHERE ProductCategory.CategoryID = 3
```

When you work with multiple tables in the same query, you sometimes need to prefix the column names with the table name so that SQL Server will know for sure which column you are talking about. This is a requirement in the case of columns that exist in both tables (such as `ProductID`); for the other columns, SQL Server doesn't require us to specify the table, but this is considered good practice anyway. The previous query can also be written as

```
SELECT *
FROM ProductCategory INNER JOIN Product
ON Product.ProductID = ProductCategory.ProductID
WHERE CategoryID = 3
```

The results are shown in Figure 4-24.

	ProductID	CategoryID	ProductID	Name	Description
1	2	3	2	Medieval Lady	Velvet-look Blue costume. Excellen...
2	21	3	21	Mystic Witch	An adorable mystic witch costume...
3	23	3	23	Space Warrior	A space warrior costume by Star ...
4	24	3	24	Hippie	A cool seventies hippie costume fo...
5	25	3	25	Sheriff hat	A children's sheriff hat in black felt...

Figure 4-24. Results of the table join between Product *and* ProductCategory

Except that the list of columns is too long (they didn't all fit in the figure), this table has all that you need. The last step is to specify the columns you're interested in:

```
SELECT Product.Name, Product.Description
FROM ProductCategory INNER JOIN Product
ON Product.ProductID = ProductCategory.ProductID
WHERE ProductCategory.CategoryID = 3
```

This finally provides the results we were looking for, as shown in Figure 4-25.

	Name	Description
1	Medieval Lady	Velvet-look Blue costume. Excellent costume for that Middle-Ages look.
2	Mystic Witch	An adorable mystic witch costume for kids. Broomstick not included but avail...
3	Space Warrior	A space warrior costume by Star Orangutan. Ideal Halloween Costume. Come...
4	Hippie	A cool seventies hippie costume for kids. Don't forget to check out the adult ...
5	Sheriff hat	A children's sheriff hat in black felt with a silver badge.

Figure 4-25. Results of the table join between Product *and* ProductCategory

The Stored Procedures

You're pretty close now to start writing the stored procedures required for the new features of JokePoint. Before doing that, there's still another little thing (this time, it is really is little, honest!) you need to learn about: stored procedure parameters.

In the previous example with table joins, you used a hard-coded `CategoryID`. In the stored procedures, you'll need to receive various data as input parameters, and sometimes return values as output parameters. Let's look at these in more detail.

Input and Output Stored Procedure Parameters

The syntax used to create a stored procedure with parameters is

```
CREATE PROCEDURE <procedure name>
[(
    <parameter name> <parameter type> [=<default value>] [INPUT|OUTPUT],
    <parameter name> <parameter type> [=<default value>] [INPUT|OUTPUT],
    ...
    ...
)]
AS
    <stored procedure body>
```

Remember that the portions between the square brackets are optional. Specifying parameters is optional, but if you specify them, they must be within parentheses. For each parameter, you must supply at least its name and data type.

You can optionally supply a default value for the parameter. In this case, if the calling function doesn't supply a value for this parameter, the default value will be used instead. Also you can specify whether the parameter is an input parameter or output parameter. By default, all parameters are input parameters. The value of output parameters can be set in the stored procedure and read by the calling function.

Stored procedure parameters are treated just like any other SQL variables, and their names start with @, as in `@DepartmentID`, `@CategoryID`, `@ProductName`, and so on. The simplest syntax for setting the value of an output parameter, inside the stored procedure, is as follows:

```
SELECT @DepartmentID = 5
```

Implementing the Stored Procedures

Now let's add the stored procedures to the JokePoint database, and then you'll have the chance to see them in action. For each stored procedure, you'll need its functionality somewhere in the presentation tier. To understand the purpose of the stored procedures even better, refer to the beginning of the chapter to review figures of the product catalog in action.

Add the stored procedures discussed in the following sections to the database.

GetDepartmentDetails

The GetDepartmentDetails stored procedure is needed when the user selects a particular department in the product catalog. When this happens, the database must be queried again to find out the name and the description of the particular department.

The stored procedure receives the ID of the selected department as a parameter and returns its name and description in the form of output parameters. A bit later, when you create the business tier, you'll learn how to extract the values of these parameters after executing the stored procedure.

The code for GetDepartmentDetails is as follows:

```
CREATE PROCEDURE GetDepartmentDetails
     (@DepartmentID int,
      @DepartmentName varchar(50) OUTPUT,
      @DepartmentDescription varchar(200) OUTPUT)
AS
SELECT @DepartmentName=[Name], @DepartmentDescription=[Description]
FROM Department
WHERE DepartmentID = @DepartmentID
RETURN
```

The SELECT statement is used to store the Name and Description of the specified DepartmentID (which is an input parameter here) to the @DepartmentName and @DepartmentDescription output parameters. These are the output parameters that will be read by the business tier when calling the GetDepartmentDetails stored procedure.

GetCategoriesInDepartment

When the visitor selects a particular department, apart from showing the department's details, you also want to display the categories that belong to that department. This will be done using the GetCategoriesInDepartment procedure, which returns the list of categories in a specific department.

GetCategoriesInDepartment returns the IDs and names for the categories that belong to the department mentioned by the @DepartmentID input parameter:

```
CREATE PROCEDURE GetCategoriesInDepartment
     (@DepartmentID int)
AS
SELECT CategoryID, [Name]
FROM Category
WHERE DepartmentID = @DepartmentID
RETURN
```

Because you can't know ahead of time how many categories will be returned, using output parameters to send back the data is not an option. You simply SELECT the needed categories, just like you did in the previous chapter with the list of departments; the list gets to the presentation tier in the form of an SqlDataReader, which will be used to populate a DataList control.

GetCategoryDetails

The GetCategoryDetails stored procedure is called when the visitor clicks a particular category, and wants to find out more information about it, namely its name and description. Here's the code:

```
CREATE PROCEDURE GetCategoryDetails
      (@CategoryID int,
        @CategoryName varchar(50) OUTPUT,
        @CategoryDescription varchar(200) OUTPUT)
AS
SELECT
        @CategoryName = [Name],
        @CategoryDescription = [Description]
FROM Category
WHERE CategoryID = @CategoryID
RETURN
```

GetProductsInCategory

When a visitor selects a particular category from a department, you'll want to list all the products that belong to that category. For this, you'll use the GetProductsInCategory stored procedure. You saw how this procedure works earlier when you learned about table joins. The single difference is that here you return more data about each product to the calling function than just its name and description. Later in this chapter, you'll learn how to use the returned information to create a nice looking list of products.

```
CREATE PROCEDURE GetProductsInCategory
      (@CategoryID int)
AS
SELECT Product.ProductID,Product.[Name], Product.[Description],
        Product.Price, Product.ImagePath, Product.OnDepartmentPromotion,
        Product.OnCatalogPromotion
FROM Product INNER JOIN ProductCategory
ON Product.ProductID = ProductCategory.ProductID
WHERE ProductCategory.CategoryID = @CategoryID
RETURN
```

GetProductsOnDepartmentPromotion

When the visitor selects a particular department, apart from needing to list its name, description, and list of categories (you wrote the necessary stored procedures for these tasks earlier), you also want to display the list of featured products for that department.

GetProductsOnDepartmentPromotion needs to return all the products that belong to a specific department with the OnDepartmentPromotion bit set to 1. In GetProductsInCategory, you needed to make a table join to find out the products that belong to a specific category. Now that you need to do this for departments, the task is a bit more complicated because you can't directly know which products belong to which departments.

You know how to find categories that belong to a specific department (you did this in GetCategoriesInDepartment), and you know how to get the products that belong to a specific category (you did that in GetProductsInCategory). By combining this information, you can determine the list of products in a department. For this, you need two table joins. You'll also filter the final result to get only the products that have the OnDepartmentPromotion bit set to 1.

You'll also use the DISTINCT clause to filter the results to make sure you don't get the same record multiple times. This can happen when a product belongs to more than one category, and these categories are in the same department. In this situation, you would get the same product returned for each of the matching categories, unless you filter the results using DISTINCT.

```
CREATE PROCEDURE GetProductsOnDepartmentPromotion
  (@DepartmentID int)
AS
SELECT DISTINCT Product.ProductID,Product.[Name], Product.[Description],
                Product.Price, Product.ImagePath
FROM Product
INNER JOIN ProductCategory
ON Product.ProductID = ProductCategory.ProductID
INNER JOIN Category
ON ProductCategory.CategoryID = Category.CategoryID
WHERE Product.OnDepartmentPromotion = 1
      AND Category.DepartmentID=@DepartmentID
RETURN
```

GetProductsOnCatalogPromotion

GetProductsOnCatalogPromotion returns all the products that have the OnCatalogPromotion bit field set to 1.

```
CREATE PROCEDURE GetProductsOnCatalogPromotion
AS
SELECT Product.ProductID,Product.[Name], Product.[Description],
       Product.Price, Product.ImagePath
FROM Product
WHERE Product.OnCatalogPromotion = 1
RETURN
```

Well, that's about it. Right now the data store is ready to hold and process the product catalog information, so it's time to move to the next step: implementing the business tier of the product catalog.

Implementing the Business Tier

In this section, you'll learn a few more tricks for ADO.NET, mainly regarding dealing with stored procedure parameters. Let's start with the usual theory part, after which you'll write the code.

Working with Stored Procedure Parameters

The ADO.NET class that deals with input and output stored procedure parameters is SqlCommand. This shouldn't come as a big surprise—SqlCommand is responsible for executing commands on the database, so it makes sense that it should also deal with their parameters.

Using Input Parameters

The following code snippet demonstrates how you can add an input parameter to an SqlCommand object named command:

```
' Add an input parameter and supply a value for it
command.Parameters.Add("@DepartmentID", SqlDbType.Int, 4)
command.Parameters("@DepartmentID").Value = value
```

The first line adds a new stored procedure parameter named @DepartmentID, of type SqlDbType.Int and size 4 (in bytes) to the Parameters collection of the SqlCommand object. When adding a new parameter to the SqlCommand object, a new SqlParameter object is created. The Parameters collection of SqlCommand contains objects of type SqlParameter, which represent stored procedure parameters.

To specify the data type of a stored procedure parameter, you use the SqlDbType class, which knows SQL Server's data types. However, specifying a size is optional. For most numerical types, the size is fixed by SQL Server.

NOTE *For numerical columns, specify the parameter size in bytes. For columns that store strings (such as* char, varchar, *or even* text), *specify the size in number of characters. Longer strings will be automatically truncated to the size specified for the parameter.*

The second line assigns a value to the parameter. Because @DepartmentID is a required input parameter (it doesn't have a default value defined in the stored procedure), you need to specify a value for it.

If the stored procedure has more than one parameter, the order you define them in here has no importance.

TIP *The previous two lines of code that add a stored procedure parameter and set its value can be written as a single line:*

```
' Add an input parameter and supply a value for it
command.Parameters.Add("@DepartmentID", SqlDbType.Int, ➥
4).Value = value
```

This works because the Add *method returns the* SqlParameter *object that was just added, which is then assigned a value.*

Stored Procedure Parameters Are Not Strongly Typed

When adding stored procedure parameters, you should use exactly the same name, type, and size as in the stored procedure. Actually, you can break this rule, although it isn't recommended. For example, you could add @DepartmentID as a varchar or even nvarchar; as long as the value you set it to is a string containing a number; the database doesn't complain, and automatically makes the conversion. If you don't want to supply the data type when creating a new parameter, you can use the shortened version that adds a parameter and sets its value at the same time:

```
command.Parameters.Add("@DepartmentID", value)
```

However, we recommend always specifying the correct data type for a parameter. There are two main reasons it's good to handle the data type in the business tier. First, this allows the business tier to have control over the validity of the data types that pass through it. Second, sending bogus information to a stored procedure can corrupt your data.

The VB .NET methods in the business tier always take their parameters as strings. We chose this approach for the architecture because we don't want the presentation tier to be bothered with the data types. The presentation tier, as you'll see, gets and receives the parameters as strings; for this reason, it doesn't care what kind of product IDs we have (the ID of 123 is just as welcome as KSJ222). It's the role of the business tier to interpret the data and test for its correctness. Moreover, if at some time, a change occurs in the database and suddenly you have character-based product IDs, you would only need to make the change in the data tier and the business tier, leaving the presentation tier untouched.

Using Output Parameters

The code that creates an output parameter is as follows:

```
' Add an output parameter
command.Parameters.Add("@DepartmentDescription", SqlDbType.VarChar, 200)
command.Parameters("@DepartmentDescription").Direction = _
                                        ParameterDirection.Output
```

This is almost the same as the code for the input parameter, except instead of supplying a value for the parameter, you set its Direction property to ParameterDirection.Output. This tells the command that @DepartmentDescription is an output parameter.

Parameters Are Independent Objects

As mentioned earlier, stored procedure parameters are represented in VB .NET code by a specialized class called SqlParameter. To keep the code compact, you don't create SqlParameter objects by hand, but you could if you wanted to. The following code

snippet demonstrates how you can create an `SqlParameter` object and add it to the
`Parameters` collection of the command object:

```
Dim param As New SqlParameter("@MyBit", SqlDbType.Bit, 1)
param.Direction = ParameterDirection.Output
' or:
' param.Value = 5
command.Parameters.Add(param)
```

Getting the Results Back from Output Parameters

After executing a command that has output parameters, you'll probably want to read
the values returned in those parameters. You can do this by reading the parameters'
values from the `SqlCommand` object after executing it and closing the connection.

Here's an example that demonstrates getting the value back from a `VarChar` output
parameter to a `String` variable:

```
' Open the connection, execute the command, and close the connection
connection.Open()
command.ExecuteNonQuery()
connection.Close()
' Get the results back
Dim name As String
name = command.Parameters("@DepartmentName").Value.ToString()
```

In this example, `ToString` is called to convert the returned value to a string. This
is a recommended practice, even if the type of the output parameter is `VarChar` or
another string character type (which wouldn't normally require a conversion). The
reason for this has to do with the `NULL` SQL value.

If the output parameter comes back with a `NULL`, it translates to `Nothing` in Visual
Basic, and trying to store it in a `String` object (like `name` in the example) would generate a runtime exception. Calling `ToString` on the return value makes sure you always
get a string—`NULL` values returned from the database are converted to empty strings
instead of breaking your code.

When dealing with numerical values instead of strings, the challenge involves
not only checking for the returned value not being `NULL`, but also actually making sure
that you received an actual number. Visual Basic .NET provides the `IsNumeric` function,
which is handy in this situation. Take a look at an example:

```
' Get the results back
Dim iValue As Integer
Dim oValue As Object
oValue = command.Parameters("@DepartmentId").Value
If IsNumeric(oValue) Then
    iValue = CType(oValue, Integer)
Else
    iValue = 0
End If
```

In this example, you store the returned value in an `Object` variable named `oValue`. This variable is capable of storing any kind of value, including `NULL`s, and no exception will be generated no matter what you receive from the database. You then use `IsNumeric` to determine whether this variable contains a number. If it does, cast it to `Integer` and store it in an `Integer` variable named `iValue`.

A Little Bit of Theory About Exception Handling

Now you'll learn how to deal with the unexpected errors that might occur while processing the client requests. After practicing in this chapter, you'll be able to apply the techniques to the code you wrote in Chapter 3.

Although the code is designed to work without any unpleasant surprises, there's always a possibility that something might go wrong. For example, an error might be generated when you're trying to execute a database stored procedure, for reasons that you didn't anticipate, or for reasons that are out of your control (say, a database failure). The error also could have originated at the business-tier class, for example, because of bad user input data.

When such an error happens, a runtime exception is raised. If you don't handle the error in code, the execution of your program terminates immediately, which usually results in an ugly error page shown to the visitor. The general strategy to deal with runtime exceptions is as follows:

- If the error is not critical, deal with it in code, allowing the code to continue executing normally, and the visitor will never know an error happened

- If the error is critical, handle it partially with code to reduce the possible negative effects as much as possible, and then let the error propagate to the presentation tier that will show the visitor a nice looking "Houston, there's a problem" page.

- For the errors that you can't anticipate, the last line of defense is still the presentation tier, which politely asks the visitor to come back later.

For the latter two cases, it's good to let the site administrator (or the technical staff) know about the problem. Possible options include sending details about the error to a custom database table, to the Windows event log, or by email. At the end of this chapter we'll learn how to email the site administrator with detailed information when an error happens.

As for dealing with the exception in code, you can do this at the business-tier or presentation-tier levels, or even both. As you're programming VB .NET, your best friend is the `Try-Catch-Finally` construct:

```
Try
    ' code that might generate an exception
Catch
    ' code that executed only in case of an exception
Finally
```

```
' code that executes at the end, no matter if
' an exception was generated or not
End Try
```

You place inside the Try block any code that you suspect might possibly generate errors. In case an exception is generated, the execution is passed to the Catch block. If no errors are generated, the Catch block is bypassed completely. In the end, no matter whether an exception occurred or not, the Finally block is executed (in case it exists).

The Finally block is important because it is guaranteed to execute no matter what happens. If any database operations happen in the Try block, it's a standard practice to close the database connection in the Finally block, to ensure no open connections will remain active on the database server. This is useful because open connections consume resources on the database server, and can even keep database resource locked, creating problems for other connections that have database activities at the same time or after the error has occurred.

Runtime exceptions propagate from the point they were raised through the call stack of your program. So if an exception is generated in the database stored procedure, it will be immediately passed to the business tier. If the business tier handles the error using a Try-Catch construct, then everything's fine and the presentation tier will never know that an error occurred. If the business tier doesn't handle the exception, the exception is then propagated to the presentation tier. If the error isn't handled in the presentation tier, the exception is finally propagated to the ASP.NET runtime that will deal with it by presenting an error page to the visitor.

If no Catch block exists (and you have only Try and Finally), the exception is not handled; the code stops executing and the exception propagates to the higher levels in the class hierarchy, but not before executing the Finally block (which, as stated previously, is guaranteed to execute no matter what happens).

TIP   *Learn more about the* Try-Catch-Finally *construct from the Visual Basic .NET language reference in MSDN (http:// msdn.microsoft.com/library/default.asp?url=/library/en-us/vblr7/ html/vastmTryCatchFinally.asp).*

Let's start writing some code, and see the theory in action.

Completing the Catalog Class

Let's now implement the business-tier methods. Each method calls exactly one stored procedure, and they are named exactly like the stored procedures they are calling. In Visual Studio, open the Catalog.vb file you created in the previous chapter, and prepare to fill it with business logic.

GetDepartmentDetails

GetDepartmentDetails will be called from the presentation tier when a department is clicked to display its name and description. The presentation tier will pass the ID of the selected department, and you need to send back the name and the description of the selected department. Remember that the GetDepartmentDetails stored procedure has exactly two output parameters: Name and Description. You extract them here and wrap them into a separate object.

What object, you say? The technique is to create a separate class for the particular purpose of storing data that you want to pass around. This class is named DepartmentDetails and looks like this:

```
Public Class DepartmentDetails
    Public Name As String
    Public Description As String
End Class
```

You wrap the department's name and description into one DepartmentDetails object and send it back to the presentation tier. The DepartmentDetails class can be either added in a separate file in the BusinessObjects folder, or added to one of the existing files. Most of the time, you'll want to create a separate file for each class, but because in this case DepartmentDetails is more like a tool for the Catalog class, we chose to add it to Catalog.vb.

Add the DepartmentDetails class at the beginning of Catalog.vb (but not inside the Catalog class) like this:

```
Imports System.Data.SqlClient
Public Class DepartmentDetails
    Public Name As String
    Public Description As String
End Class
Public Class Catalog
    ' ... code here
```

Next, add the GetDepartmentDetails function to the Catalog class. It doesn't matter where you place this function; for example, it doesn't need to be placed after the connectionString property, even if it uses that property.

```
Public Shared Function _
GetDepartmentDetails(ByVal departmentId As String) As DepartmentDetails
    ' Create the connection object
    Dim connection As New SqlConnection(connectionString)
    ' Create and initialize the command object
    Dim command As New SqlCommand("GetDepartmentDetails", connection)
    command.CommandType = CommandType.StoredProcedure
    ' Add an input parameter and supply a value for it
    command.Parameters.Add("@DepartmentID", SqlDbType.Int, 4)
    command.Parameters("@DepartmentID").Value = departmentId
```

```
' Add an output parameter
command.Parameters.Add("@DepartmentName", SqlDbType.VarChar, 50)
command.Parameters("@DepartmentName").Direction = _
                                    ParameterDirection.Output
' Add an output parameter
command.Parameters.Add("@DepartmentDescription", _
                                    SqlDbType.VarChar, 200)
command.Parameters("@DepartmentDescription").Direction = _
                                    ParameterDirection.Output
' Open the connection, execute the command, and close the connection
Try
     connection.Open()
     command.ExecuteNonQuery()
Finally
     connection.Close()
End Try
' Populate a DepartmentDetails object with data from output parameters
Dim details As New DepartmentDetails()
details.Name = command.Parameters("@DepartmentName").Value.ToString()
details.Description = _
        command.Parameters("@DepartmentDescription").Value.ToString()
' Return the DepartmentDetails object to the calling function
Return details
End Function
```

You know what happens in this function fairly well because we analyzed portions of it while learning about stored procedure parameters. Its main purpose in life is to send back the name and description of the relevant department. To do this, it calls the GetDepartmentDetails stored procedure, supplying it with a department ID. After execution, the function reads the @DepartmentName and @DepartmentDescription output parameters, saves them into a DepartmentDetails object, and sends this object back to the calling function.

The error-handling part in this method ensures that the database connection is closed in case something bad happens when opening the database connection or executing the stored procedure:

```
' Open the connection, execute the command, and close the connection
Try
     connection.Open()
     command.ExecuteNonQuery()
Finally
     connection.Close()
End Try
```

There is no Catch block; for this reason, if an exception is raised, it still propagates to the presentation tier. The execution of the GetDepartmentDetails function will be terminated, but not before closing the database connection in the Finally block (which was the point of introducing the error-handling mechanism).

GetCategoriesInDepartment

The GetCategoriesInDepartment function is called when you need to display the details of a department in the product catalog. Apart from the department name and description (returned by the previous function), you also need the list of categories that belong to that department. Add this function to the Catalog class:

```
Public Shared Function _
GetCategoriesInDepartment(ByVal departmentId As String) As SqlDataReader
    ' Create the connection object
    Dim connection As New SqlConnection(connectionString)
    ' Create and initialize the command object
    Dim command As New SqlCommand("GetCategoriesInDepartment", connection)
    command.CommandType = CommandType.StoredProcedure
    ' Add an input parameter and supply a value for it
    command.Parameters.Add("@DepartmentID", SqlDbType.Int, 4)
    command.Parameters("@DepartmentID").Value = departmentId
    Try
        ' Open the connection
        connection.Open()
        ' Return an SqlDataReader to the calling function
        Return command.ExecuteReader(CommandBehavior.CloseConnection)
    Catch e As Exception
        ' Close the connection and throw the exception
        connection.Close()
        Throw e
    End Try
End Function
```

In this method, regarding the exception-handling code, things are a bit different than with the previous method because now you return an SqlDataReader to the calling function (which is a presentation-tier method).

The problem with SqlDataReader is that it needs an open connection to operate. For this reason, never close the SqlConnection object in the business tier when sending back SqlDataReader objects—instead, execute them passing CommandBehavior.CloseConnection as parameter, and they'll close the connection themselves when they finish processing:

```
Return command.ExecuteReader(CommandBehavior.CloseConnection)
```

So, when passing back SqlDataReader objects, you can't close the connection in the Finally block, like you did in GetDepartmentDetails. The following code wouldn't work, because the Finally block executes, closes the connection, and then passes back to the presentation tier a connectionless SqlDataReader object.

```
' bad code - don't try this at home!
Try
```

```
    ' Open the connection
    connection.Open()
    ' Return an SqlDataReader to the calling function
    Return command.ExecuteReader(CommandBehavior.CloseConnection)
Finally
    connection.Close()
End Try
```

TIP *When I said the* Finally *block is guaranteed to execute no matter what happens, I really meant that. When executing the previous code, the* Finally *block is always executed before the method finishes executing, even if the* Try *block contains a* Return *command (in other conditions,* Return *causes the method to exit immediately).*

In methods that return SqlDataReaders, close the connection manually only if an error occurs when executing the command (in which case the SqlDataReader object, which was supposed to close the connection, never gets created and sent to the presentation tier):

```
Try
    ' Open the connection
    connection.Open()
    ' Return an SqlDataReader to the calling function
    Return command.ExecuteReader(CommandBehavior.CloseConnection)
Catch e As Exception
    ' Close the connection and throw the exception
    connection.Close()
    Throw e
End Try
```

If an exception occurs, close the connection and then re-throw the exception. The purpose of the error-handling mechanism at this level is to make sure the connection is closed, not stop the error from propagating. You still want the presentation tier to intercept the error, display an error page to the visitor, and mail the site administrator about the problem.

GetCategoryDetails

History repeats itself in this section. Just as you needed to return a name and description for the selected department, now you need to do the same thing for the categories. You'll use the same technique here, and wrap the data into a separate class.

Add the CategoryDetails class at the beginning of Catalog.vb. Don't place it inside the Catalog class!

```
Imports System.Data.SqlClient
Public Class DepartmentDetails
    Public Name As String
    Public Description As String
End Class
Public Class CategoryDetails
    Public Name As String
    Public Description As String
End Class
Public Class Catalog
    // ... class code here ...
```

Next, add the GetCategoryDetails method to the Catalog class. Except for the fact that it calls another stored procedure and uses another class to wrap the return information, it is identical to GetDepartmentDetails:

```
Public Shared Function _
GetCategoryDetails(ByVal categoryId As String) As CategoryDetails
    ' Create the connection object
    Dim connection As New SqlConnection(connectionString)
    ' Create and initialize the command object
    Dim command As New SqlCommand("GetCategoryDetails", connection)
    command.CommandType = CommandType.StoredProcedure
    ' Add an input parameter and supply a value for it
    command.Parameters.Add("@CategoryID", SqlDbType.Int, 4)
    command.Parameters("@CategoryID").Value = categoryId
    ' Add an output parameter
    command.Parameters.Add("@CategoryName", SqlDbType.VarChar, 50)
    command.Parameters("@CategoryName").Direction = _
                                        ParameterDirection.Output
    ' Add an output parameter
    command.Parameters.Add("@CategoryDescription", SqlDbType.VarChar, 200)
    command.Parameters("@CategoryDescription").Direction = _
                                        ParameterDirection.Output
    ' Open the connection, execute the command, and close the connection
    Try
        connection.Open()
        command.ExecuteNonQuery()
    Finally
        connection.Close()
    End Try
    ' Populate a CategoryDetails object with data from output parameters
    Dim details As New CategoryDetails()
    details.Name = _
            command.Parameters("@CategoryName").Value.ToString()
    details.Description = _
            command.Parameters("@CategoryDescription").Value.ToString()
    ' Return the CategoryDetails object to the calling function
    Return details
End Function
```

GetProductsInCategory

GetProductsInCategory returns the list of products that belong to a particular category.
You return the list using an SqlDataReader, which feeds a DataList object that displays
the list of products:

```
Public Shared Function _
GetProductsInCategory(ByVal categoryId As String) As SqlDataReader
    ' Create the connection object
    Dim connection As New SqlConnection(connectionString)
    ' Create and initialize the command object
    Dim command As New SqlCommand("GetProductsInCategory", connection)
    command.CommandType = CommandType.StoredProcedure
    ' Add an input parameter and supply a value for it
    command.Parameters.Add("@CategoryID", SqlDbType.Int, 4)
    command.Parameters("@CategoryID").Value = categoryId
    Try
        ' Open the connection
        connection.Open()
        ' Return an SqlDataReader to the calling function
        Return command.ExecuteReader(CommandBehavior.CloseConnection)
    Catch e As Exception
        ' Close the connection and throw the exception
        connection.Close()
        Throw e
    End Try
End Function
```

GetProductsOnDepartmentPromotion

The GetProductsOnDepartmentPromotion function returns the list of products featured
for a particular department. The department's featured products must be displayed
when the customer visits the home page of a department.

```
Public Shared Function _
GetProductsOnDepartmentPromotion(ByVal departmentId As String) _
As SqlDataReader
    ' Create the connection object
    Dim connection As New SqlConnection(connectionString)
    ' Create and initialize the command object
    Dim command As New SqlCommand("GetProductsOnDepartmentPromotion", _
                                                        connection)
    command.CommandType = CommandType.StoredProcedure
    ' Add an input parameter and supply a value for it
    command.Parameters.Add("@DepartmentID", SqlDbType.Int, 4)
    command.Parameters("@DepartmentID").Value = departmentId
    Try
        ' Open the connection
        connection.Open()
        ' Return an SqlDataReader to the calling function
        Return command.ExecuteReader(CommandBehavior.CloseConnection)
    Catch e As Exception
```

```
            ' Close the connection and throw the exception
            connection.Close()
            Throw e
        End Try
    End Function
```

GetProductsOnCatalogPromotion

The GetProductsOnCatalogPromotion method is needed to get the list of products featured on the main page of the site.

```
    Public Shared Function GetProductsOnCatalogPromotion() As SqlDataReader
        ' Create the connection object
        Dim connection As New SqlConnection(connectionString)
        ' Create and initialize the command object
        Dim command As New SqlCommand("GetProductsOnCatalogPromotion", _
                                                        connection)
        command.CommandType = CommandType.StoredProcedure

        Try
            ' Open the connection
            connection.Open()
            ' Return an SqlDataReader to the calling function
            Return command.ExecuteReader(CommandBehavior.CloseConnection)
        Catch e As Exception
            ' Close the connection and throw the exception
            connection.Close()
            Throw e
        End Try
    End Function
```

Implementing the Presentation Tier

Believe it or not, right now the data and business tiers of the product catalog are complete for this chapter. All you have to do is use their functionality in the presentation tier. In this final section, you'll create a few Web User Controls and integrate them into the existing project.

Execute the JokePoint project (or load http://localhost/JokePoint in your favorite web browser) to see once again what happens when the visitor clicks a department. After the page loads, click one of the departments. The main page, default.aspx, is reloaded, but this time with a query string at the end:

http://localhost/JokePoint/default.aspx?DepartmentID=2&DepartmentIndex=1

This happens because of the way you designed the departments' links in Chapter 3. You learned then that DepartmentIndex is used to select the department that was clicked so that it would be displayed using a different style.

Now you'll use the other parameter that appears when someone clicks a department: if you know the DepartmentID, you can obtain any information about the selected department. The value of DepartmentID must be read each time default.aspx is reloaded to get its description, its list of categories, and the list of featured products in that department (this happens every time the visitor clicks another department).

In the following sections, you'll create the controls that display the list of categories associated with the selected department, and the products for the selected department, category, or main web page.

Displaying the List of Categories

You start completing the presentation tier by implementing the list of categories that appears when a department is selected. This consists of a new Web User Control named CategoriesList.ascx.

CategoriesList is similar to the DepartmentsList web control. It consists of a DataList control that is populated with data from the Catalog class. The DataList control will contain links to default.aspx, but this time the query string will also contain a CategoryID, showing that a category has been clicked, like this:

```
default.aspx?DepartmentID=1&DepartmentIndex=0&CategoryID=1&CategoryIndex=0
```

The steps in the following exercise are like the steps for the DepartmentsList user control, so we'll move a bit more quickly this time.

Exercise: Creating the CategoriesList *Web User Control*

1. Add a new Web User Control named CategoriesList.ascx to the UserControls folder by right-clicking the UserControls folder, and then choosing Add ➤ Add Web User Control.

2. Add a DataList object to the user control, and change its name to list.

3. Right-click DataList, go to Edit Template, and select Header and Footer Templates.

4. Click the HTML tab in Toolbox, and add an Image to HeaderTemplate and to FooterTemplate.

5. Set the border property of both images to 0. For the first image, set src to Images/CategHeader.gif, and for the second image to Images/CategFooter.gif.

6. Now close the edit mode by right-clicking DataList and selecting End Template Editing. Before moving on to editing the item templates (which will generate the list of categories), select DataList, and set the following properties to it:

- Expand the ItemStyle node, and set BackColor to PaleGoldenrod.

- Expand the HeaderStyle node, and set BackColor to PaleGoldenrod.

- Set the CellPadding property to 0.

These changes set the PaleGoldenrod background used in the list of categories, and ensure that no white spaces appear between the header, templates, and footer in DataList.

7. Now, edit the item templates. Right-click DataList, go to Edit Template, and select the Item Templates option.

8. Go back to the Web Forms tab in Toolbox, and add a HyperLink control to the ItemTemplate, and a Label control to the SelectedItemTemplate.

9. For the HyperLink control, set the CssClass property to CategoryUnselected. For the Label control, set the CssClass property to CategorySelected.

10. Add the following styles to JokePoint.css:

```
A.CategoryUnselected
{
  color:Blue;
  font-family: Comic Sans MS;
  text-decoration: none;
  font-size:  14px;
  font-weight: bold;
  line-height: 25px;
  padding-left: 0px
}
A.CategoryUnselected:hover
{
  color: red;
}
.CategorySelected
{
  color: green;
  font-family: Comic Sans MS;
  text-decoration: none;
  font-size:  14px;
  font-weight: bold;
  line-height: 25px;
  padding-left: 0px
}
```

11. Go back to `CategoriesList.ascx`. Enter the HTML View mode by clicking the HTML tab at the bottom of the design window. You need to make a few changes to the `HyperLink` controls. This is the full code, with the changes highlighted:

 CAUTION *Ensure that the code in the* `<asp:Hyperlink>` *and* `<asp:Label>` *sections is on a single line rather than split over multiple lines as shown here.*

```
<%@ Control Language="vb" AutoEventWireup="false"

Codebehind="CategoriesList.ascx.vb" Inherits="JokePoint.CategoriesList"

TargetSchema="http://schemas.microsoft.com/intellisense/ie5" %>
<asp:DataList id="list" runat="server" CellPadding="0">
  <HeaderTemplate>
    <IMG alt="" src="Images/CategHeader.gif" border="0">
  </HeaderTemplate>
  <SelectedItemTemplate>
     &raquo;
    <asp:Label id="Label1" runat="server"
               Text='<%# DataBinder.Eval(Container.DataItem, "Name") %>'
               CssClass="CategorySelected">Label
               </asp:Label>
  </SelectedItemTemplate>
  <FooterTemplate>
    <IMG alt="" src="Images/CategFooter.gif" border="0">
  </FooterTemplate>
  <ItemStyle BackColor="PaleGoldenrod"></ItemStyle>
  <ItemTemplate>
         &raquo;
      <asp:HyperLink id="HyperLink1" runat="server"
                   NavigateUrl='<%# "../default.aspx?DepartmentID=" &amp;
                   Request.QueryString("DepartmentID") &amp;
                   "&amp;DepartmentIndex=" &amp;
                   Request.QueryString("DepartmentIndex") &amp;
                   "&amp;CategoryID=" &amp;
                   DataBinder.Eval(Container.DataItem, "categoryID") &amp;
                   "&amp;CategoryIndex=" &amp; Container.ItemIndex  %>'
                   Text='<%# DataBinder.Eval(Container.DataItem, "Name") %>'
            CssClass="CategoryUnselected">HyperLink
          </asp:HyperLink>
  </ItemTemplate>
  <HeaderStyle BackColor="PaleGoldenrod"></HeaderStyle>
</asp:DataList>
```

12. Now, open the code-behind file of the CategoriesList user control. You need to populate DataList and mark the selected item when the user control loads. Modify Page_Load like this:

```
Private Sub Page_Load(ByVal sender As System.Object, _
              ByVal e As System.EventArgs) Handles MyBase.Load
  ' The department for which we are loading the categories
  Dim departmentId As String = Request.QueryString("DepartmentID")
  ' Don't load categories if no department was selected
  If Not departmentId Is Nothing Then
    ' The index of the selected DataList item.
    Dim listIndex As String = Request.QueryString("CategoryIndex")
    ' The DataList item that was clicked is set as the selected item
    If Not listIndex Is Nothing Then
      list.SelectedIndex = CInt(listIndex)
    End If
    ' GetCategoriesInDepartment returns an SqlDataReader object that has
    ' two fields: CategoryID and Name. These fields are read in
    ' the SelectedItemTemplate and ItemTemplate of the DataList
    list.DataSource = Catalog.GetCategoriesInDepartment(departmentId)
    ' Needed to bind the child controls(the HyperLink and Label controls)
    ' to the data source
    list.DataBind()
  End If
End Sub
```

13. Press **Ctrl+Shift+B** to compile the project.

14. Add the CategoriesList control default.aspx. Open default.aspx in Design View. Drag the CategoriesList user control from Solution Explorer and drop it below Departments.ascx (see Figure 4-26).

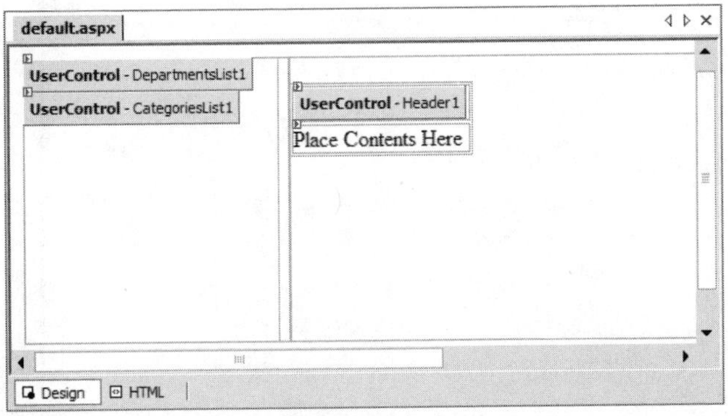

Figure 4-26. default.aspx *in Design View*

15. Press **F5** to execute the project, or save the file and load `http://localhost/JokePoint` in your favorite web browser. When the page loads, click one of the departments. You'll see the categories list appear in the chosen place, as shown in Figure 4-27.

Figure 4-27. JokePoint in action

16. When you click a category, the query string updates accordingly (see Figure 4-28).

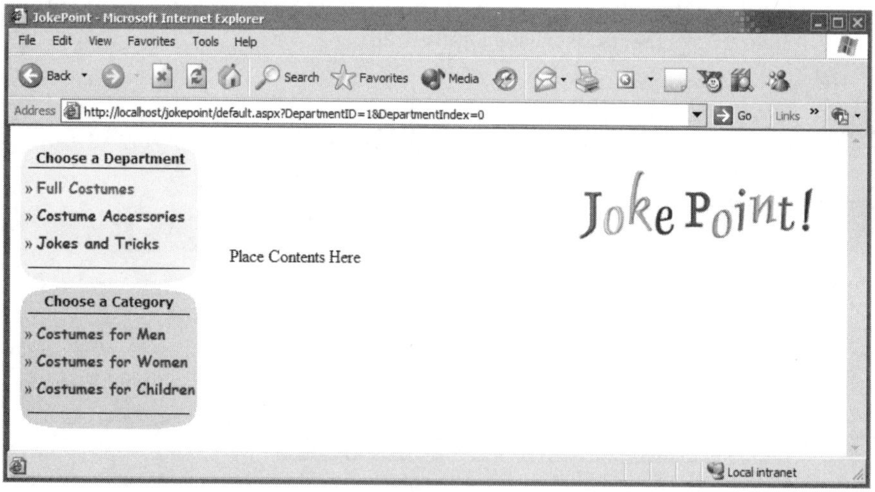

Figure 4-28. Visiting a JokePoint department

How It Works: The CategoriesList *User Control*

The important detail to know about CategoriesList is what happens when you click a category link: default.aspx is reloaded, but this time, CategoryID and CategoryIndex are also in the query string. In some of the other controls you'll create, we check for CategoryID—when it is present, this is an indication that the visitor is browsing a category.

CategoriesList works like DepartmentsList and they are both placed in default.aspx, and both get loaded at the same time. However, when CategoriesList gets loaded and its Page_Load function executes, the code checks to determine whether a department was selected:

```
Private Sub Page_Load(ByVal sender As System.Object, _
            ByVal e As System.EventArgs) Handles MyBase.Load
  ' The department for which we are loading the categories
  Dim departmentId As String = Request.QueryString("DepartmentID")
  ' Don't load categories if no department was selected
  If Not departmentId Is Nothing Then
    ...
    ...
    ...
```

If the DataList isn't populated with data, it doesn't show at all (not even its header or footer are displayed). This is important, because if the visitor is on the main page and a department was not selected, no categories should show up.

On the other hand, if a department was selected, the code first determines whether a category was also clicked, in which case, it informs DataList about this, so the selected category will be drawn with the appropriate style:

```
' The index of the selected DataList item.
Dim listIndex As String = Request.QueryString("CategoryIndex")
' The DataList item that was clicked is set as the selected item
If Not listIndex Is Nothing Then
  list.SelectedIndex = CInt(listIndex)
End If
```

Finally, you populate the DataList object with category names by calling the business-tier method Catalog.GetCategoriesInDepartment:

```
' GetCategoriesInDepartment returns an SqlDataReader object that has
' two fields: CategoryID and Name. These fields are read in
' the SelectedItemTemplate and ItemTemplate of the DataList
list.DataSource = Catalog.GetCategoriesInDepartment(departmentId)
' Needed to bind the child controls(the HyperLink and Label controls)
' to the data source
list.DataBind()
```

> **NOTE** *A final note about* CategoriesList *is that you're free to use it in other pages or even for other user controls. For example, you might want to add* CategoriesList *to the* SelectedItemTemplate *of* DepartmentsList *instead of placing it in* default.aspx. *This way, the list of categories would be displayed inside the list of departments, just below the currently selected department. Feel free to do this experiment and see how easy it is to change the look of the web site with just a few clicks!*

Displaying Department and Category Information

Now the visitor can visit the main web page, and select a department or a category. In each of these cases, you must fill the pageContentsCell in default.aspx with information regarding the page being visited.

Remember that when you created default.aspx in Chapter 2, you marked pageContentsCell to run at server side. That means you can fill that table cell at runtime with different user controls, depending on the page being visited. This is opposed to placing the web controls at design time, like you did with CategoriesList and DepartmentsList.

If the visitor is on the main page of the site, populate pageContentsCell with a custom web control named FirstPage.ascx. The first page will look like Figure 4-29.

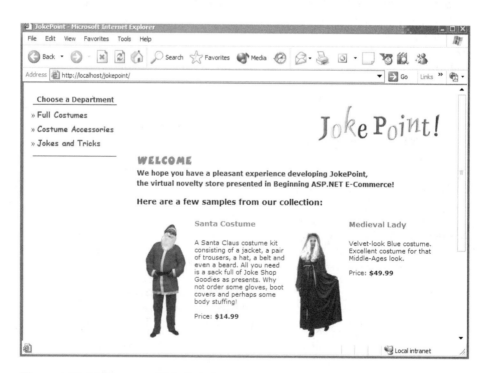

Figure 4-29. Main page of JokePoint

If the visitor is browsing a department or category, you fill `pageContentsCell` with a web control named `Catalog.ascx`. You use the same control for displaying departments and categories data because their pages have similar structures. On the top, place the name of the department or category, then its description, and finally the list of products. Figure 4-30 shows the page of one of the categories:

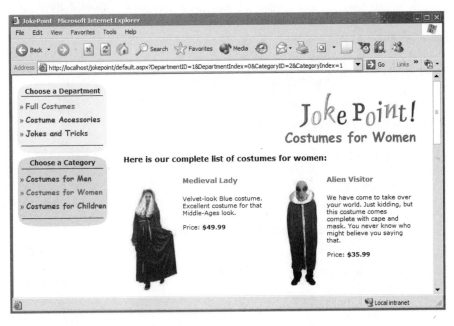

Figure 4-30. The Costumes for Women department

Note that both `Catalog.ascx` and `FirstPage.ascx` contain only the pages' header; you'll implement the actual list of products using yet another Web User Control—`ProductsList.ascx`—a bit later. You'll then use `ProductsList.ascx` in `Catalog.ascx` and `FirstPage.ascx` to add the list products to these pages.

In the following exercise, you implement `FirstPage.ascx` and `Catalog.ascx` Web User Controls, and teach `default.aspx` to load them at runtime depending on the page being visited.

Exercise: Creating the `FirstPage` *and* `Catalog` *Web User Controls*

1. Start by creating `FirstPage.ascx`. Right-click the `UserControls` folder, and then choose Add ➤ Add Web User Control, and choose `FirstPage` or `FirstPage.ascx` for the name.

2. Edit its HTML code as shown here:

```
<%@ Control Language="vb" AutoEventWireup="false" Codebehind="FirstPage.ascx.vb"

Inherits="JokePoint.FirstPage"

TargetSchema="http://schemas.microsoft.com/intellisense/ie5" %>
<br><img src="Images/welcome.gif" border="0" width="102" height="18"><br>
<font class="FirstPageText">
   <br>We hope you have a pleasant experience developing JokePoint,<br><br>
   the virtual novelty store presented in Beginning ASP.NET E-Commerce!
</font>
<br><br>
<font class="ListDescription">
   Here are a few samples from our collection:
</font>
<br><br>
<EM>[Place List of Products Here]</EM>
```

3.   Enter the following styles in JokePoint.css:

```
.FirstPageText
{
   color: Navy;
   font-family: Verdana, Helvetica, sans-serif;
   text-decoration: none;
   font-size:  12px;
   font-weight: bold;
   line-height: 9px;
   padding-left: 10px
}
.ListDescription
{
   color: Black;
   font-family: Verdana, Helvetica, sans-serif;
   font-weight: bold;
   font-size: 14px;
}
```

4.   Right now, FirstPage should look like Figure 4-31 in Design View.

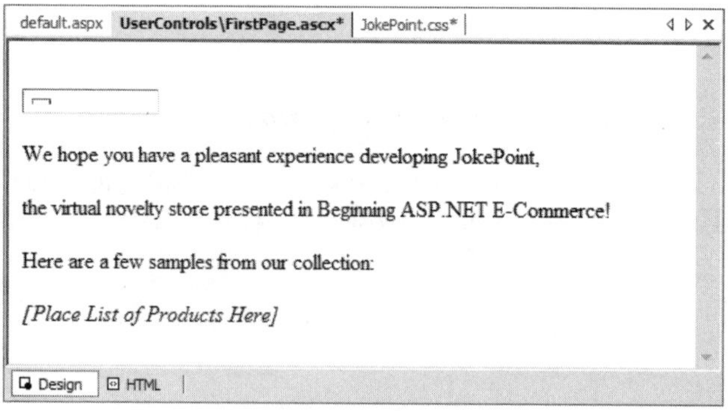

Figure 4-31. FirstPage.ascx *in Design View*

5. Now create another control in the `UserControls` folder, named `Catalog.ascx`.

6. Switch to HTML View and modify it like this:

```
<%@ Control Language="vb" AutoEventWireup="false" Codebehind="Catalog.ascx.vb"

Inherits="JokePoint.Catalog1"

TargetSchema="http://schemas.microsoft.com/intellisense/ie5" %>
<P align="right">
  <asp:label id="sectionTitleLabel" CssClass="SectionTitle" runat="server">
  </asp:label>
</P>
<asp:label id="descriptionLabel" CssClass="ListDescription" runat="server">
</asp:label>
<br><br>
<EM>[Place List of Products Here]</EM>
```

7. Enter the following style to `JokePoint.css`:

```
.SectionTitle
{
  color: red;
  font-family: Comic Sans MS;
  text-decoration: none;
  font-size:  24px;
  font-weight: bold;
  line-height: 15px;
  padding-left: 10px
}
```

8. Change `Catalog.ascx` to Design View. The page should look like Figure 4-32.

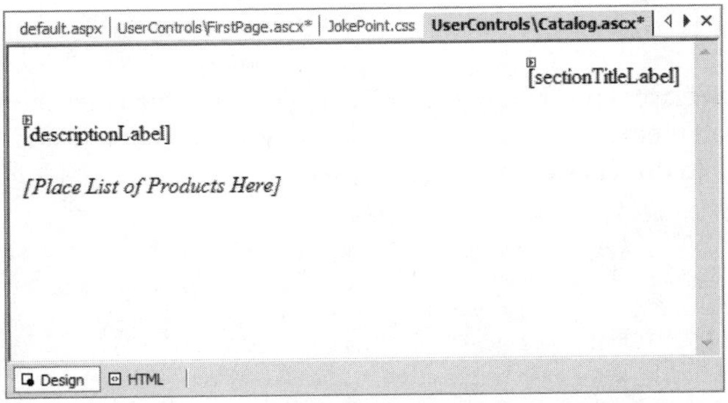

Figure 4-32. `Catalog.ascx` *in Design View*

9. Open the code-behind file of the user control. First make sure the objects corresponding to the server-side components were added by Visual Studio inside the " Web Form Designer Generated Code " region:

```
Protected WithEvents sectionTitleLabel As System.Web.UI.WebControls.Label
Protected WithEvents descriptionLabel As System.Web.UI.WebControls.Label
```

10. Catalog.ascx is loaded only if the visitor is browsing a category or a department. Its Page_Load function gathers category or department data from the business tier and shows it in the Label controls:

```
Private Sub Page_Load(ByVal sender As System.Object, ByVal e As
System.EventArgs) Handles MyBase.Load
    ' Retrieve DepartmentID from the query string
    Dim departmentId As String = Request.QueryString("DepartmentID")
    ' Retrieve CategoryID from the query string
    Dim categoryId As String = Request.QueryString("CategoryID")
    ' If the visitor is browsing a category ...
    If Not categoryId Is Nothing Then
        ' Obtain category data in a CategoryDetails object
        Dim categoryDetails As New CategoryDetails()
        categoryDetails = Catalog.GetCategoryDetails(categoryId)
        ' Display category info in the label controls
        sectionTitleLabel.Text = categoryDetails.Name
        descriptionLabel.Text = categoryDetails.Description
    ' If the visitor is browsing a department ...
    ElseIf Not departmentId Is Nothing Then
        ' Obtain department data in a DepartmentDetails object
        Dim departmentDetails As New DepartmentDetails()
        departmentDetails = Catalog.GetDepartmentDetails(departmentId)
        ' Display department info in the label controls
        sectionTitleLabel.Text = departmentDetails.Name
        descriptionLabel.Text = departmentDetails.Description
    End If
End Sub
```

11. Right now, FirstPage.ascx and Catalog.ascx are complete. It's time to teach default.aspx to load them in pageContentsCell. Open the code-behind file of default.aspx and add this code to Page_Load:

```
Private Sub Page_Load(ByVal sender As System.Object, ByVal e As
System.EventArgs) Handles MyBase.Load
    ' Save DepartmentID from the query string to a variable
    Dim departmentId As String = Request.QueryString("departmentID")
    ' Are we on the main web page or browsing the catalog?
    If Not departmentId Is Nothing Then
        Dim control As Control
        control = Page.LoadControl("UserControls/Catalog.ascx")
        pageContentsCell.Controls.Add(control)
    Else
        Dim control As Control
```

```
        control = Page.LoadControl("UserControls/FirstPage.ascx")
        pageContentsCell.Controls.Add(control)
    End If
End Sub
```

12. Remove "`Place Contents Here`" from the `pageContentsCell` in `default.aspx`, and then execute the project. The first page should look Figure 4-33.

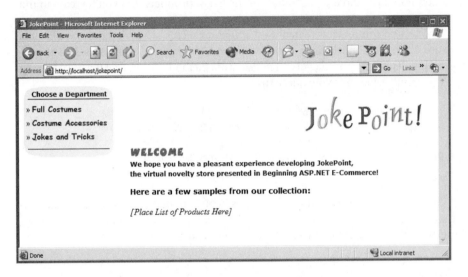

Figure 4-33. JokePoint in action

13. Now click one of the departments, as shown in Figure 4-34.

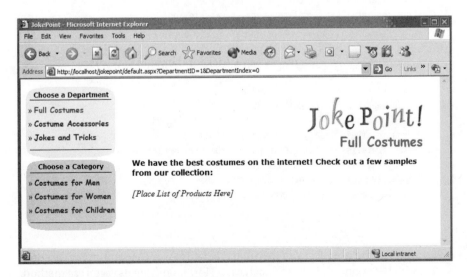

Figure 4-34. The Full Costumes department

14. Now if you click a category, its name and description will replace the department's name and description.

How It Works: `FirstPage.ascx` *and* `Catalog.ascx`

You started this exercise by implementing `FirstPage.ascx`. This is a simple web control that displays information for the main page of your site. At this moment, you only have a "hello!" message, and a placeholder for the list of products that you'll create in the next exercise.

The second control you created was `Catalog.ascx`. This was a bit more complicated, because it also had some logic in its code-behind file. `Catalog.ascx` displays data about the current department or category. In its `Page_Load` method, you first get the `DepartmentID` and `CategoryID` values from the query string:

```
' Retrieve DepartmentID from the query string
Dim departmentId As String = Request.QueryString("DepartmentID")
' Retrieve CategoryID from the query string
Dim categoryId As String = Request.QueryString("CategoryID")
```

Next you determine whether a value has been supplied for `CategoryID`; if the visitor is browsing a department and didn't click a category, `CategoryID` will be `Nothing`. Otherwise, the two `Label` controls are populated with the category data:

```
' If the visitor is browsing a category ...
If Not categoryId Is Nothing Then
  ' Obtain category data in a CategoryDetails object
  Dim categoryDetails As New CategoryDetails()
  categoryDetails = Catalog.GetCategoryDetails(categoryId)
  ' Display category info in the label controls
  sectionTitleLabel.Text = categoryDetails.Name
  descriptionLabel.Text = categoryDetails.Description
```

If `CategoryID` is `Nothing`, you do the same trick for the value of `DepartmentID`:

```
' If the visitor is browsing a department ...
ElseIf Not departmentId Is Nothing Then
  ' Obtain department data in a DepartmentDetails object
  Dim departmentDetails As New DepartmentDetails()
  departmentDetails = Catalog.GetDepartmentDetails(departmentId)
  ' Display department info in the Label controls
  sectionTitleLabel.Text = departmentDetails.Name
  descriptionLabel.Text = departmentDetails.Description
End If
```

At the end of the exercise, you instructed `default.aspx` to load the `Catalog` or `FirstPage` Web User Controls in its `pageContentsCell` by modifying its `Page_Load` method. In this method, you determine whether a `DepartmentID` was supplied in the query string.

If it was, the visitor is either browsing a department or a category, and Catalog.ascx is loaded dynamically. Otherwise, FirstPage.ascx is loaded:

```
' Save DepartmentID from the query string to a variable
Dim departmentId As String = Request.QueryString("departmentID")
' Are we on the main web page or browsing the catalog?
If Not departmentId Is Nothing Then
  Dim control As Control
  control = Page.LoadControl("UserControls/Catalog.ascx")
  pageContentsCell.Controls.Add(control)
Else
  Dim control As Control
  control = Page.LoadControl("UserControls/FirstPage.ascx")
  pageContentsCell.Controls.Add(control)
End If
```

Displaying the Products

Finally, you're at the last Web User Control for this chapter. In this section, you'll create the ProductsList control, which will be integrated in FirstPage.ascx and Catalog.ascx and display their products.

ProductsList will generate a list of products that looks like Figure 4-35.

Figure 4-35. Sample output from the ProductsList *control*

When loaded in the main page (through FirstPage.ascx), ProductsList displays the products on catalog promotion (remember, the ones that have the OnCatalogPromotion bit set to 1 in the database). When the visitor selects a department, the ProductsList control displays the products featured for that department. Finally, when the visitor clicks a category, the control displays all the products that belong to that category.

When loaded in any of those pages, `ProductsList` decides which products to display based on the information it gets from the query string. If both `DepartmentID` and `CategoryID` are present, this means the products of that category should be listed. If only `DepartmentID` is present, this means the visitor is visiting a department, so it should display its featured products. If `DepartmentID` is not present, this means the visitor is on the main page, so the catalog's featured products should appear.

Exercise: Creating the `ProductsList` *Web User Control*

1. Add a new Web User Control named `ProductsList` to the `UserControls` folder.

2. Open the control in Design View, and drag a `DataList` control from the toolbox on to the control.

3. Rename the ID of `DataList` to list, and set its `RepeatColumns` property to 2, and `RepeatDirection` to `Horizontal`.

   Setting `RepeatColumns` to 2 specifies two products listed per row.

4. Edit the `DataList`'s `ItemTemplate` directly it HTML View:

```
<%@ Control Language="vb" AutoEventWireup="false"
Codebehind="ProductsList.ascx.vb" Inherits="JokePoint.ProductsList"
TargetSchema="http://schemas.microsoft.com/intellisense/ie5" %>
<asp:datalist id="list" RepeatColumns="2" runat="server"
RepeatDirection="Horizontal">
  <ItemTemplate>
    <table cellPadding="0" align="left">
      <tr>
        <td align="center" width="110">
          <img src='ProductImages/<%# DataBinder.Eval(Container.DataItem,
"ImagePath") %>' border="0" vspace="10"></a>
        </td>
        <td vAlign="top" width="200" height="200">
          <font class="ProductName">
            <%# DataBinder.Eval(Container.DataItem, "Name") %>
          </font>
          <br>
          <br>
          <font class="ProductDescription">
            <%# DataBinder.Eval(Container.DataItem, "Description") %>
            <br>
            <br>
            Price: </font><font class="ProductPrice">
            <%# DataBinder.Eval(Container.DataItem, "Price", "{0:c}") %>
          </font>
      </tr>
    </table>
  </ItemTemplate>
</asp:datalist>
```

5.   The way ASP.NET outputs product prices to the visitor depends on the culture of the computer running the site. You told ASP.NET which numbers represent prices by specifying the {0:C} formatting parameter to DataBinder.Eval. For example, if the default culture is set to fr-FR, instead of $1.23 you would see 1,23€. (For more information on internationalization issues, consult an advanced ASP.NET book). For now, to make sure the prices are expressed in the same currency (US dollars for this example), double-click Web.config in Solution Explorer and find the following line:

```
<globalization requestEncoding="utf-8" responseEncoding="utf-8" />
```

Modify the line like this:

```
<globalization requestEncoding="utf-8" responseEncoding="utf-8" culture="en-US"/>
```

This ensures that no matter how the development (or production) machine is set up, your prices will always be expressed in the same currency.

6.   Modify the Page_Load event handler of ProductsList like this:

```
Private Sub Page_Load(ByVal sender As System.Object, _
        ByVal e As System.EventArgs) Handles MyBase.Load
  ' Retrieve DepartmentID from the query string
  Dim departmentId As String = Request.QueryString("DepartmentID")
  ' Retrieve CategoryID from the query string
  Dim categoryId As String = Request.QueryString("CategoryID")
  ' Are we retrieving products for a Category, for a Department
  ' or for the main page?
  If Not categoryId Is Nothing Then
    ' category
    list.DataSource = Catalog.GetProductsInCategory(categoryId)
    list.DataBind()
  ElseIf Not departmentId Is Nothing Then
    ' department
    list.DataSource=Catalog.GetProductsOnDepartmentPromotion(departmentId)
    list.DataBind()
  Else
    ' main page
    list.DataSource = Catalog.GetProductsOnCatalogPromotion()
    list.DataBind()
  End If
End Sub
```

7. Add these styles to the `JokePoint.css` file:

```css
.ProductName
{
  color: Red;
  font-family: Verdana, Helvetica, sans-serif;
  font-weight: bold;
  font-size: 13px;
}
.ProductDescription
{
  color: Black;
  font-family: Verdana, Helvetica, sans-serif;
  font-size: 11px;
}
.ProductPrice
{
  color: Black;
  font-family: Verdana, Helvetica, sans-serif;
  font-weight: bold;
  font-size: 11px;
}
```

8. Build the solution by pressing Ctrl+Shift+B.

9. Open `FirstPage.ascx` in Design View. Drag the `ProductsList.ascx` user control from Solution Explorer, drop it near the [Place List of Products Here] text, and then delete the text, as shown in Figure 4-36.

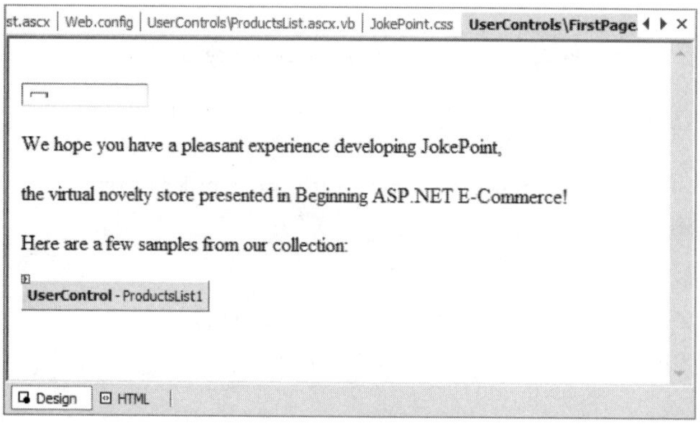

Figure 4-36. `FirstPage.ascx` *in Design View*

10. Now do the same in `Catalog.ascx` (see Figure 4-37).

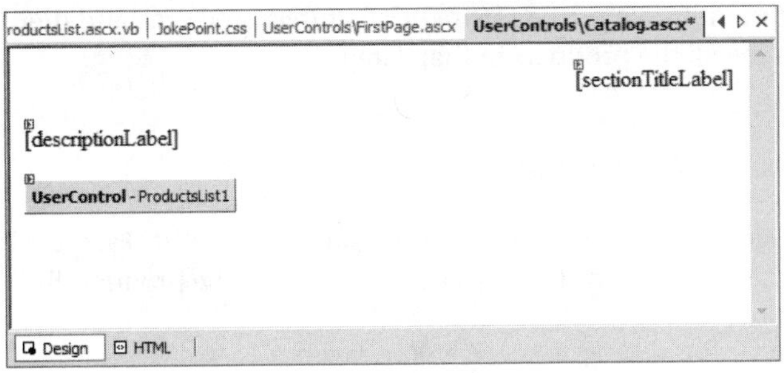

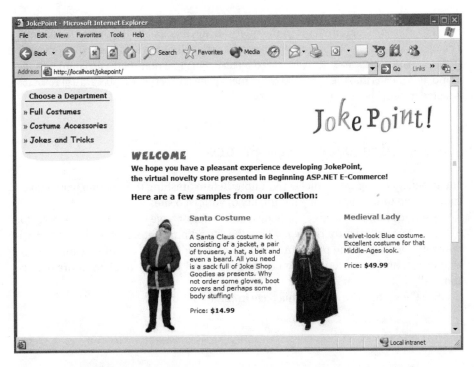

Figure 4-37. `Catalog.ascx` *in Design View*

11. Press F5 to execute the project. The main page should now be populated with its featured products (see Figure 4-38).

NOTE *To see the product images, make sure you have the* `ProductImages` *folder from the code download located in your project's folder.*

Figure 4-38. JokePoint in action

12. Now click a department to see the department's featured products, and then click a category to see all the products in that category.

How It Works: The ProductsList *User Control*

The ProductsList control is similar to CategoriesList and DepartmentsList. Its Page_Load event handler decides which method of the Catalog class to use to get the products list:

```
' Are we retrieving products for a Category, for a Department
' or for the main page?
If Not categoryId Is Nothing Then
   ' category
   list.DataSource = Catalog.GetProductsInCategory(categoryId)
   list.DataBind()
ElseIf Not departmentId Is Nothing Then
   ' department
   list.DataSource = Catalog.GetProductsOnDepartmentPromotion(departmentId)
   list.DataBind()
Else
   ' main page
   list.DataSource = Catalog.GetProductsOnCatalogPromotion()
   list.DataBind()
End If
```

If a CategoryID parameter is in the query string, this means the visitor is visiting a category, so Catalog.GetProductsInCategory is called. If only a DepartmentID is present, GetProductsOnDepartmentPromotion is called instead. Finally, if none of these parameters are found, this means that the visitor is on the main page and GetProductsOnCatalogPromotion is called to provide the list.

Dealing with Unexpected Errors

The product catalog works nicely right now. Before finishing this chapter, you'll take another step toward improving the quality of your web site.

A serious web site needs to provide a custom error page to be shown to the visitor when an unexpected error happens. Also, the site administrator needs to be automatically informed about the problem. ASP.NET provides several techniques for dealing with errors, and we encourage you to read a general ASP.NET book for more details about all of them.

Say the visitor tries to load this page in the web browser:

http://*JokePoint*/default.aspx?DepartmentID=999999999999&DepartmentIndex=0

If the visitor tries to load this page, the DepartmentID is interpreted as a string by the presentation tier. Because the data type isn't checked within the presentation tier, the value 999999999999 is sent directly as a string to the business tier.

The fact that there is no department with an ID of 999999999999 wouldn't be a big deal—you would simply get a void list of categories, an empty name, and an empty department description—except for the fact that 999999999999 is not a valid Int32 value. When the business tier tries to convert this to an integer to send it to the database, an error is generated and an error page appears like the one in Figure 4-39.

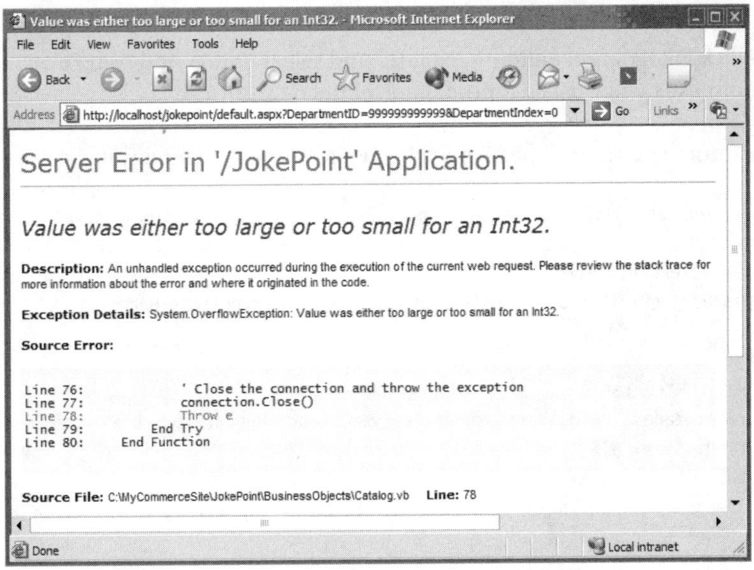

Figure 4-39. JokePoint shows debugging information on errors

Changing the Default Error Page

You don't want the visitor to see those kind of errors. Apart from the fact that it looks ugly, you certainly don't want the visitor to see the debugging info. Luckily, by default, the debugging information is only available to requests on the local machine (http://localhost/JokePoint/...). Requests from other domains will display an error page without the debugging details.

For JokePoint, you'll implement a custom error page in the following exercise.

Exercise: Adding a Custom Error Page to JokePoint

1. In Solution Explorer, double-click Web.config.

2. In Web.config file, find this line:

   ```
   <customErrors mode="RemoteOnly" />
   ```

   Modify the line like this:

   ```
   <customErrors defaultRedirect="/JokePoint/error.aspx" />
   ```

> **NOTE** *After this change, remote clients will be forwarded to* error.aspx *in case of any errors, but on the local machine, you'll still receive detailed error information. If you want to see* error.aspx *as well, add* mode="On" *to the* <customErrors> *element.*

3. Right-click JokePoint in Solution Explorer and select Add ➤ Add Web Form. Type error.aspx when asked for the name of the new form.

4. Set the form to FlowLayout mode, open it in HTML View, and modify it like this:

```
<%@ Page Language="vb" AutoEventWireup="false" Codebehind="error.aspx.vb"

Inherits="JokePoint._error"%>
<%@ Register TagPrefix="uc1" TagName="Header" Src="UserControls/Header.ascx" %>
<HTML>
  <body>
    <P align="center">
      <uc1:Header id="Header1" runat="server"></uc1:Header><br><br>
      <font size="5">
      Our website is experiencing temporary problems.<br><br>
      Thanks for visiting us - we hope we'll be seeing you again<br><br>
      in better circumstances. :)
      </font>
    </P>
  </body>
</HTML>
```

5. Press **Ctrl+Shift+B** to build the solution. Right now, remote clients trying to load http://JokePoint/default.aspx?DepartmentID=999999999999&DepartmentIndex=0 would get the page shown in Figure 4-40.

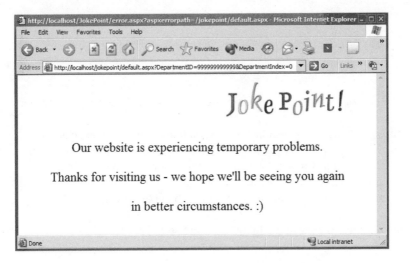

Figure 4-40. A custom error page for JokePoint

How It Works: The Custom Error Page

The custom error page was enabled by modifying the Web.config configuration file. You'll meet this file again in the following chapters and will learn a few more tricks. Web.config is a powerful file—you can find out much more information about it in MSDN or an advanced ASP.NET book.

Notifying the Site Administrator About the Problem

Common ways to inform the site administrator when an error occurs include

- Writing error information to the Event Log

- Saving error information to the base

- Mailing the administrator

You can take these actions in the Page_Error event of a web form, which gets called when an error occurs in that page, or in the Application_Error method, which resides in the Global.asax.vb code-behind file, and gets called when an unhandled error occurs in any place of an application.

For the example site, an email will be sent to the administrator containing error information in the Application_Error method.

The .NET Framework provides the System.Web.Mail namespace, which contains three classes that can be used to create and send mail messages:

- MailMessage

- MailAttachment

- SmtpMail

MailMessage has four important properties that you set when sending a message: From, To, Subject, and Body.

After setting up the MailMessage object, you send it using the SmtpMail class. You can set the SmtpServer property of the SmtpMail class if you want to send using an external SMTP (Simple Mail Transfer Protocol) server; otherwise, the mail is sent by default through the SMTP service in Windows.

To send a message, you just pass a MailMessage object as a parameter to SmtpMail.Send.

Let's implement this theory in the following exercise.

Exercise: Emailing the Site Administrator

1. Double-click Global.asax in Solution Explorer, and switch to Code View.

2. Import System.Web.Mail at the beginning of the file:

    ```
    Imports System.Web
    Imports System.Web.SessionState
    Imports System.Web.Mail
    ```

3. Find the Application_Error method and modify it like this:

    ```
    Sub Application_Error(ByVal sender As Object, ByVal e As EventArgs)
      ' Create an email message
      Dim email As New MailMessage()
      email.From = "server@jokepoint.com"
      email.To = "jokepoint@CristianDarie.ro"
      email.Subject = "JokePoint error"
      email.Body = Server.GetLastError().ToString()
      ' Send the email message
      SmtpMail.SmtpServer = "SMTP Server Address"
      SmtpMail.Send(email)
    End Sub
    ```

How It Works: Emailing the Site Administrator

The code is pretty straightforward. You create a MailMessage object, and send it using SmtpMail.Send. Note that if you don't specify an SMTP server, the mail will be sent through the SMTP service on the local machine.

The body of the email you send contains detailed error information, extracted using Server.GetLastError. After this method finishes executing, the visitor is forwarded to the error.aspx page you wrote earlier.

Optionally, after sending the email, you can call `Server.ClearError`, and the visitor will not be redirected to `error.aspx`. In this case, you would need to manually redirect the visitor to another page in the site using `Response.Redirect` or `Server.Transfer`. You'll learn more about these in the following chapters.

Summary

You've done a lot of work in this chapter. You finished building the product catalog by implementing the necessary logic in the data, business, and presentation tiers. On the way, you learned about many new theory issues, including

- Relational data and the types of relationships that can occur between tables

- Database diagrams, and why they can be useful

- How to obtain data from multiple tables in a single result set using `JOIN`, and how to filter the results using `WHERE`

- How to work with stored procedure input and output parameters in stored procedures and in Visual Basic .NET code

- How to handle errors in the business tier, and how to catch them in the presentation tier

- How to email the administrator in case something bad happens

Chapter 5 will be at least as exciting as this one: you'll learn how to add search functionality to your web site!

CHAPTER 5

Searching the Catalog

IN THE PREVIOUS CHAPTERS, you implemented a functional product catalog for JokePoint. However, it lacks the all-important search feature. Our goal in this chapter is to allow the visitor to search the site for products by entering one or more keywords.

You'll see how easy it is to add new functionality to a working site by integrating the new components into the existing architecture.

Determining the Kind of Search You Want

As always, there are a few things you need to think about before starting to code. When analyzing the technical requirements of a new feature you want to add, it's good to look at that feature from the visitor's perspective.

So what kind of search would be most useful for the visitor? Most of the time, the answer to this comes from the customer for whom you are building the site. For the visual part, the answer is fairly simple—all types of searches require a text box where the visitor can enter one or more words to search for.

In our site, the words entered by the visitor will be searched for in the products' names and descriptions. There are a few ways you can treat the text entered by the visitor:

- *Exact-match search*: If the visitor enters an entire phrase, this would be searched in the database as it is, without splitting the words and searching for them separately.

- *All-words search*: The phrase entered by the visitor is split into words, causing a search for products that contain every word entered by the visitor. This is like the exact-match search in that it still searches for all the entered words, but this time the order of the words is no longer important.

- *Any-words search*: Products must contain at least one of the entered words.

This simple classification isn't by any means complete. The search engine can be as complex as the one offered by Google (http://www.google.com), which provides many options and features and shows a ranked list of results, or as simple as searching the database for the exact string provided by the visitor.

JokePoint will support the any-words and all-words search modes. This decision leads to the visual design of the search feature (see Figure 5-1).

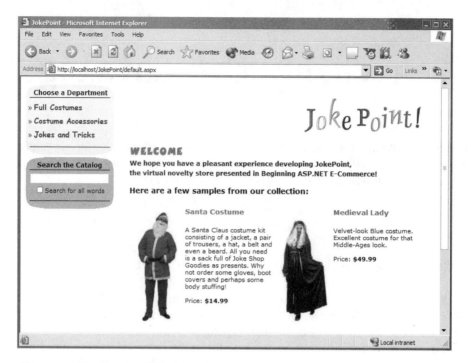

Figure 5-1 The design of the search feature

The text box is there, as expected, along with a check box that allows the visitor to choose between an all-words search and an any-words search.

Another decision you need to make here is the way in which the search results are displayed. How should the search results page look? You want to display, after all, a list of products that match the search criteria.

The simplest solution to display the search results would be to reuse the ProductsList.ascx web control you built in the previous chapter. A sample search page will look like Figure 5-2.

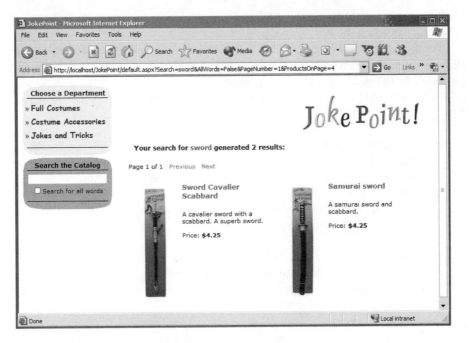

Figure 5-2. A sample search page

You can also see in the figure that the site employs paging. If there are a lot of search results, you'll only present a fixed (but configurable) number of products per page, and allow the visitor to browse through the pages using Previous and Next links.

Let's begin implementing the functionality, by starting, as usual, with the data tier.

Implementing the Data Tier

As usual, we'll start with a little bit of theory (you'll love it, I promise!), and then you'll practice by implementing the data tier functionality for JokePoint.

Teaching the Database to Search Itself

Within the database, there are two main ways to implement searching. One way is to use SQL Server's Full-Text Search feature. This advanced feature—available with SQL Server Developer, Standard, and Enterprise editions—allows for advanced keyword searches. These include searching using the Boolean operators (AND, AND NOT, OR), and searching for inflected forms of words, such as plurals and various verb tenses, or words located in close proximity. Additionally, the Full-Text Search feature can also sort the results based on rank, placing the most likely matches at the top.

The problem with the Full-Text Search feature is that it's not available with MSDE (the free version of SQL Server that is used for this book), and most likely your client won't want to invest the money for a Standard or Enterprise version of SQL Server at this stage of building the site.

For these reasons, we won't use the Full-Text Search feature for JokePoint. If the client decides to make a software upgrade, all you would need to change in the data tier would be the SearchCatalog stored procedure.

Before starting to implement the search functionality, it's good to know the disadvantages of the custom search method from the start:

- Manual searches of the catalog are slower than SQL Server's Full-Text Search feature. SQL Server's Full-Text Search creates internal search indexes and features advanced search algorithms. An internal SQL Server function always performs faster than having the same functionality coded within a stored procedure. However, this will not be a problem for your site until the site has a very high number of visitors.

- You can't implement all the features that you could use with SQL Server's Full-Text Search, such as searching using Boolean operators (AND, OR). Also, manually implementing advanced features such as searching for similar words adds even more performance penalties.

When it comes to manually searching the catalog, you have some options to choose from, as detailed in the following sections.

Searching Using WHERE *and* LIKE

The straightforward solution, most widely used in such situations, consists of using LIKE in the WHERE clause of the SELECT statement. The following query returns all the products that have the word "mask" somewhere in their Description:

```
SELECT Name FROM Product WHERE Description LIKE '%mask%'
```

The percent (%) wildcard is used to specify any string of zero or more characters. Placing it before and after the word to be searched for guarantees that you'll get all the products whose description contains the word "mask".

This technique—using WHERE and LIKE—was used when building the SearchCatalog stored procedure for the first edition of this book, and is also presented in the Product Catalog case study in *The Programmer's Guide to SQL* (Apress, 2003). This is the fastest method for manually searching the catalog. In this edition of the book, we chose to present two other methods, which are not as fast as this one, but provide better search results.

Searching for Product Data in the Search String

This is yet another search strategy that doesn't provide the best search results, but it's worth taking a look at. This is the search method used in the Community Starter Kit (CSK).

NOTE *The CSK is a complex, free, and customizable application (provided with full source code) from Microsoft that allows you to build powerful community web sites quickly and easily. By default, the CSK comes with out-of-the box functionality with support for nine types of content including articles, books, events, photo galleries, downloads, user polls, and more. It also supports features such as moderation, upload quotas, comments, ratings, newsletters, advertisements, web services, and security. You can download the CSK at* `http://www.asp.net`.

Like with JokeShop, the CSK also implements a custom search feature instead of relying on SQL Server's Full-Text Search, making it possible to use MSDE as the database server.

The typical search method when Full-Text Search is not available is to split the search string into words, and then look into the database for these words. However, the search algorithm in the CSK goes the other way round: it takes every word from the searchable database content and verifies whether it exists in the search string. The method doesn't offer much search flexibility, but it works.

In JokeShop, the searchable content would be the product's name and description. These are split in separate words called **search keys**. The search keys are saved into a special data table in the database whenever new content is added or updated in the database.

TIP *To learn more about the CSK, check out another book I co-authored, named "Building Websites with the ASP.NET Community Starter Kit" (Packt Publishing, 2004). Find more details about it at* `http://www.CristianDarie.ro/books.html`.

These two methods are okay, but in JokeShop, you'll implement something even better.

Searching by Counting the Number of Appearances

The disadvantage when searching with `LIKE` is that the search results are returned in random order. Today's smart search engines provide a ranking system that places the results with higher rankings at the top of the search results page.

An intuitive solution for implementing a simple ranking system is to count how many times the words you're searching for appear in the product's name or description. Moreover, you can give higher ranking to products that have matching words in their names, rather than in their descriptions.

This solution can't be implemented with `LIKE` and `WHERE`. `LIKE` returns `True` or `False`, specifying whether you have a match or not, but can't tell you how many times a word appears in a phrase.

Because SQL Server doesn't provide an easy way to count how many times a substring appears in a string, you'll manually implement this functionality as an SQL Server User-Defined Function.

SQL Server User-Defined Functions (better knows as UDFs) implement common logic that can be called from stored procedures. Unlike stored procedures, which can be accessed from client applications, UDFs are created for database internal usage, and can be called from stored procedures or from other UDFs. UDFs must return data to the caller function or stored procedure before exiting (their last command must be RETURN), and are not allowed to modify data—their role is to return information.

For the catalog, you'll create a UDF named WordCount. It will take as parameters two strings, and will return a SMALLINT value specifying how many times the first string appears in the second.

TIP *Don't implement anything just yet—right now you're only studying the theory. You'll add the WordCount function and SearchCatalog stored procedure to the JokePoint database a bit later.*

The definition of WordCount is

```
CREATE FUNCTION dbo.WordCountt
(@Word VARCHAR(20),
@Phrase VARCHAR(1000))
RETURNS SMALLINT
```

It looks a lot like the way you create stored procedures, except that you use FUNCTION instead of PROCEDURE, and you need to explicitly specify the user who owns the function (which, in the example, is dbo).

NOTE *dbo is a special database user that has full privileges on the database. If you're not permitted to use dbo, use the username under which you have privileges on the database.*

Inside WordCount, the challenge is to find an effective way to count how many times @Word appears in @Phrase, because SQL Server doesn't provide a function for this (otherwise, you would have used that function instead of creating your own, right?).

The straightforward solution, which implies splitting the phrase where it has spaces (or other delimiter characters), and comparing word by word, is very slow. We've found a trick that performs the same functionality about five times faster.

SQL Server provides the REPLACE function, which replaces all occurrences of a substring in a string with another substring. REPLACE doesn't tell you how many replacements it did, but it returns the modified initial string. REPLACE works much faster than a custom created UDF or stored procedure, because its code is compiled and optimized by SQL Server.

We'll use REPLACE to replace the word to search for with a word that is one character longer. Say you want to count how many times the word "red" appears in "This is a red, red mask". Replacing "red" with "redx" generates "This is a redx, redx mask". The length difference between the initial phrase and the modified phrase tells you how many times the word "red" appears in the initial phrase.

The code that does this appears as follows:

```
/* @BiggerWord is a string one character longer than @Word */
DECLARE @BiggerWord VARCHAR(21)
SELECT @BiggerWord = @Word + 'x'

/* Replace @Word with @BiggerWord in @Phrase */
DECLARE @BiggerPhrase VARCHAR(2000)
SELECT @BiggerPhrase = REPLACE (@Phrase, @Word, @BiggerWord)

/* The length difference between @BiggerPhrase and @phrase
   is the number we're looking for */
RETURN LEN(@BiggerPhrase) - LEN(@Phrase)
```

Searching for Similar Words

The implementation shown earlier is fast, but has one drawback: it can't be used to search for words that are similar to (sound alike) the words entered by the visitor. For example, in the current database, searching for "costume" generates many results, while searching for "costumes" doesn't generate any results.

This problem can be fixed by changing the WordCount function. However, the version that looks for similar versions of each word is very slow because you can't use the REPLACE function anymore—you need to manually split the phrase word by word in SQL code, which is a time-consuming process.

We'll present the modified version of WordCount at the end of the chapter for your reference.

Introducing the SearchCatalog Stored Procedure

SearchCatalog is the stored procedure that will perform the actual database search. When building it, you need to address three main issues:

- The form in which you will pass the search string to the stored procedure

- The way to use the WordCount UDF to calculate ranking within search results

- The need to support the paging functionality for the presentation tier. If the search generated ten results and the visitor is seeing only four products per page, you'll return only the first four products. When the visitor clicks Next, you'll return the next four products.

Let's analyze these requirements one at a time.

Passing the Search String to the Stored Procedure

The SearchCatalog stored procedure will receive the words to search for as separate INPUT parameters. But wait, how do you know how many keywords the search string will contain? Well, you don't, and the workaround is to assume a maximum number of keywords.

In this case, you'll have five input parameters named @Word1 through @Word5. These parameters will have a default value of NULL, so the business tier won't have to supply values for all of them, if the visitor is searching for less than five words.

The obvious disadvantage is that you'll always have a maximum number of keywords that can be accepted (five words, in this example). If a visitor ever introduces more than the maximum number of words, the additional words are simply ignored—the business tier doesn't send them to the stored procedure at all. This suggests the second drawback: the business tier needs to know about the data-tier logic (regarding the maximum number of allowed words); this is a data-tier limitation that has to be handled by the business tier.

 NOTE *You might not like the limitation about the number of words you can search for in the database. However, if you set the limit high enough, the visitors are not likely to feel this limitation. Even Google has a maximum number of allowed search words (ten), and we haven't heard anyone complaining about this, so far.*

The alternative to sending separate words to SearchCatalog is to send the entire search string from the business tier, and then split it into separate words in the stored procedure. Then, after extracting the words, you have to build the SQL query that does the search by joining strings, and save it in a varchar variable. When you have a query saved in a varchar variable, named say @SearchQuery, you can execute it using sp_executesql as follows:

```
/* Execute the query using the SQL Server's sp_executesql stored procedure*/
EXEC sp_executesql @SearchQuery
```

This solution isn't preferred because it results in messy SQL code (don't we all like simple and clear solutions?), and dynamically creating SQL queries isn't an elegant solution (it's almost like building the query in the business tier by joining strings). Also, the query will probably perform slower because SQL Server can't precompile and save the execution plan of a dynamically created query, as it does with stored procedures.

Calculating Product Ranking Using WordCount

You've decided SearchCatalog will receive the search string as separate words, named @Word1 to @Word5. The second challenge with this stored procedure is how to calculate a ranking for each matching product, so you can place the higher-ranking records first.

To assign a rank to each product in the database when doing an any-words search, you need a query like this one:

```
SELECT Product.Name,
         3*dbo.WordCount(@Word1, Name)+dbo.WordCount(@Word1, Description)+
         3*dbo.WordCount(@Word2, Name)+dbo.WordCount(@Word2, Description)+
         ...
         AS TotalRank
FROM Product
```

TIP TotalRank, *in this example, is a calculated column. It doesn't exist in the database, but it is generated using a formula you define.*

This query gives three ranking points for each time one of the search string words are found in the product's name, and one ranking point for each time the words are found in the description. The query uses the WordCount function, which returns how many times a word appears in a phrase.

If none of the search words are found in a product's name or description, its ranking will be 0. If any of the words are found, the ranking will be a positive number. The search results will consist of the products that have a positive ranking number.

In case the business tier sends less than five words to the procedure, the remaining @Word parameters are NULL, in which case WordCount returns 0. This is okay for any-words searches, because you don't want any ranking points added for nonmatching words, and you also don't want a product eliminated because of a nonmatching word.

Things are a bit more complicated for all-words searches. With all-words searches, when a single word isn't found in the product's name or description, the product must not be included in the search results.

One solution to implement the all-words search is to multiply the individual rankings of each word (using 1 for NULL @Word parameters), instead of adding them; this way, if a word has a ranking of 0, the total rank will be 0, and the product is excluded from the list.

The query that returns the names and rankings for each product in the Product table for an all-words search looks like the following:

```
SELECT Product.Name,
         (3*dbo.WordCount(@Word1, Name)+dbo.WordCount(@Word1, Description)) *
         CASE
             WHEN @Word2 IS NULL THEN 1
             ELSE 3*dbo.WordCount(@Word2, Name)+dbo.WordCount(@Word2, Description)
         END *
         ...
         AS TotalRank
FROM Product
```

TIP   *Unlike with the any-words search, the all-words search must have at least one matching word. For this reason, there isn't a* CASE *block for the first word here.*

If for any reason you want to avoid multiplying the partial rank numbers, the workaround is to continue adding the partial ranks, while granting negative ranks for the words that don't match. So, if the WordCount function returns a positive number, that number is used as the word's partial rank; if WordCount returns 0, that number is substituted with a negative number (-1000 in the following code) that ensures the total sum is negative. Here's how to do that:

```
SELECT Product.Name,
       CASE
         WHEN @Word1 IS NULL THEN 0
         ELSE ISNULL(NULLIF(dbo.WordCount(@Word1, Name+' '+Description),0),-1000)
       END +
       CASE
         WHEN @Word2 IS NULL THEN 0
         ELSE ISNULL(NULLIF(dbo.WordCount(@Word2, Name+' '+Description),0),-1000)
       END +
       ...
       AS TotalRank
FROM Product
```

NOTE   *We used* ISNULL *and* NULLIF *functions to avoid calling* WordCount *twice for each word (this trick significantly improves performance). Visit SQL Server 2000 Books Online (*http://www.microsoft.com/sql/techinfo/productdoc/2000/books.asp*) for more information about how these functions work.*

Implementing Paging

Here comes the last bit of theory for the data tier. After learning how to calculate search rankings, the final challenge for the SearchCatalog stored procedure is to send back only the page of results the visitor is currently visiting.

Remember that when searching the catalog, you count for the possibility that the search might return a large number of products. In this case, it's better to let the visitor browse through the results, page by page, with a fixed number of products per page.

Of course, you might even want to implement paging for the rest of the catalog, when displaying categories or departments. In this client's site, you'll implement paging only for the search results, but it would be easy for you to extend this functionality for the rest of site, if necessary.

Paging functionality can be implemented either at the presentation/business tier levels, or at data tier level.

In the first case, you always send back all the search results from the database to the business tier (not just for the page the visitor is currently visiting). There, you store all the search results in memory, using an object named DataSet. DataSet is a very smart object that represents something like an "in-memory" database. DataSet is capable of storing data tables, their data types, relationships between tables, and so on. When storing all the data in a DataSet, you can use an object named DataGrid at the presentation tier. Based on the data received from the DataSet, DataGrid can automatically implement a working paging system.

The other solution, and the one you'll implement in this chapter, is to retrieve from the database only the range of products you're interested in. Say, the first time the visitor searches for something, only the first *n* matching products are retrieved from the database. Then, when the visitor clicks Next page, the next *n* rows are retrieved from the database, and so on.

Each of these two methods has its advantages and disadvantages. The advantage of using DataSets is that a single query is performed on the database, requesting all the search results. When the visitor browses through the resulting pages, no additional database calls are made. However, the drawback is that the whole table of search results needs to be stored in memory on the web server. Retrieving a long list of products from the server can hurt performance at the server side.

Using SqlDataReader objects, like you've done so far, doesn't consume much memory on the server—the results are gathered from the database and sent directly to the presentation tier, which displays them for the visitor. Apart from consuming less memory, SqlDataReader objects perform faster than DataSets. The drawback is that every time the visitor wants to see another page of products when browsing through multiple result pages, another database call is made.

NOTE *Implementing output page caching can improve the performance in some cases (we'll discuss this in the next chapter).*

For the purposes of the sample commerce site, we chose the latter variant, for two main reasons:

- Retrieving data using SqlDataReader objects is faster than using DataSets.

- This solution also allows you to learn some interesting programming techniques, including how to ask the database for a range of results from a query (say, products from 6 to 10). The solution isn't well known and not straightforward (as SQL Server doesn't have an explicit mechanism for this), and knowing how to do this will come in handy when you develop your own web sites. On the other hand, a simple search on Google for DataGrid and DataSet paging will provide many resources that will show you how to implement paging using DataSets and the DataGrid control.

This being said, let's see how to tell SQL Server that you don't want to get back all the list of searched products, but only a portion of it.

Requesting a Range of Records

When the visitor searches the catalog, a set of records is calculated using queries like the ones shown earlier in this chapter. You need a way to retrieve a range of records from that data set, knowing the row number of the first record to be returned (say, the sixth record), and the number of records to be returned (say, five records). How do you do that?

The solution we're implementing for JokePoint consists of using a temporary table. When the visitor makes a product search, that table is populated with all the matching products, sorted in descending order by their search ranking. The temporary table has an Identity column, which generates sequential numbers, starting with 1, for each record.

Having created this table, you simply need to read the records where the Identity column has a value between 6 and 10.

NOTE   *You might be aware that SQL Server provides the* TOP *keyword, which allows you to get the first* N *records from a data set. Unfortunately,* TOP *cannot be used to get then the following ten products from the same list. Using a temporary table as shown in this chapter is one of the workarounds to this problem (and the one we like best). The* Product Catalog *case study in* The Programmer's Guide to SQL *(Apress, 2003) shows a few additional methods that serve the same purpose.*

This is the first (and last) time you'll work with temporary tables in this book. **Temporary tables** are special SQL Server tables that exist in the database only for a limited period of time. A temporary table created in a stored procedure will automatically be deleted by the database when the stored procedure finishes execution.

Temporary tables can be created just like normal data tables, except their names begin with # or ##. Using # specifies a *local temporary table* and ## marks a *global temporary table*. Local temporary tables are unique to the connection that created them, whereas global temporary tables are visible to all connections.

In the SearchCatalog stored procedure, you'll create a local temporary table named #SearchedProducts. Because it is a local temporary table, if multiple users are performing searches at the same time, each user will create a separate version of the #SearchedProducts table, because different users will access the database on different database connections. This is important, because it would be awkward if the search results from multiple visitors were messed in on a single table (not to mention potential errors and erroneous results).

You'll learn more about using the temporary table to get a range of products, after you implement the code in the next sections.

Writing the Code

You're probably eager to write some code! Let's implement the WordCount function and the SearchCatalog stored procedure in the following exercises.

Exercise: Implementing the WordCount *Function*

Navigate to the JokePoint database in Server Explorer, right-click Functions and choose New Scalar-valued Function. Change the function skeleton Visual Studio created for you with the following code:

```
CREATE FUNCTION dbo.WordCount
(@Word VARCHAR(20),
@Phrase VARCHAR(1000))
RETURNS SMALLINT
AS
BEGIN

/* If @Word or @Phrase is NULL the function returns 0 */
IF @Word IS NULL OR @Phrase IS NULL RETURN 0

/* @BiggerWord is a string one character longer than @Word */
DECLARE @BiggerWord VARCHAR(21)
SELECT @BiggerWord = @Word + 'x'

/* Replace @Word with @BiggerWord in @Phrase */
DECLARE @BiggerPhrase VARCHAR(2000)
SELECT @BiggerPhrase = REPLACE (@Phrase, @Word, @BiggerWord)

/* The length difference between @BiggerPhrase and @phrase
   is the number we're looking for */
RETURN LEN(@BiggerPhrase) - LEN(@Phrase)
END
```

How It Works: The WordCount *Function*

WordCount returns the number of times the @Word string appears in @Phrase (@Word and @Phrase are its input parameters).

We discussed how this function works earlier in this chapter. Let's continue by implementing the SearchCatalog stored procedures, which makes use of WordCount to calculate the search results.

Exercise: Implementing the SearchCatalog *Stored Procedure*

Using the well-known steps, add this stored procedure to your JokePoint database:

```
CREATE PROCEDURE SearchCatalog
(
@PageNumber tinyint,
@ProductsOnPage tinyint,
@HowManyResults smallint OUTPUT,
@AllWords bit,
@Word1 varchar(15) = NULL,
@Word2 varchar(15) = NULL,
```

```
@Word3 varchar(15) = NULL,
@Word4 varchar(15) = NULL,
@Word5 varchar(15) = NULL)
AS


/* Create the temporary table that will contain the search results */
CREATE TABLE #SearchedProducts
(RowNumber SMALLINT NOT NULL IDENTITY(1,1),
 ProductID INT,
 Name VARCHAR(50),
 Description VARCHAR(1000),
 Price MONEY,
 ImagePath VARCHAR(50),
 Rank INT)


/* Populate #SearchedProducts for an any-words search */
IF @AllWords = 0
    INSERT INTO #SearchedProducts
            (ProductID, Name, Description, Price, ImagePath, Rank)
    SELECT Product.ProductID, Product.Name, Product.Description,
            Product.Price, Product.ImagePath,
            3*dbo.WordCount(@Word1, Name)+dbo.WordCount(@Word1, Description)+
            3*dbo.WordCount(@Word2, Name)+dbo.WordCount(@Word2, Description)+
            3*dbo.WordCount(@Word3, Name)+dbo.WordCount(@Word3, Description)+
            3*dbo.WordCount(@Word4, Name)+dbo.WordCount(@Word4, Description)+
            3*dbo.WordCount(@Word5, Name)+dbo.WordCount(@Word5, Description)
            AS TotalRank
    FROM Product
    ORDER BY TotalRank DESC


/* Populate #SearchedProducts for an all-words search */
IF @AllWords = 1
    INSERT INTO #SearchedProducts
            (ProductID, Name, Description, Price, ImagePath, Rank)
    SELECT Product.ProductID, Product.Name, Product.Description,
            Product.Price, Product.ImagePath,
            (3*dbo.WordCount(@Word1, Name)+dbo.WordCount(@Word1, Description)) *
            CASE
              WHEN @Word2 IS NULL THEN 1
              ELSE 3*dbo.WordCount(@Word2, Name)+dbo.WordCount(@Word2, Description)
            END *
            CASE
              WHEN @Word3 IS NULL THEN 1
              ELSE 3*dbo.WordCount(@Word3, Name)+dbo.WordCount(@Word3, Description)
            END *
            CASE
              WHEN @Word4 IS NULL THEN 1
              ELSE 3*dbo.WordCount(@Word4, Name)+dbo.WordCount(@Word4, Description)
            END *
```

```
            CASE
                WHEN @Word5 IS NULL THEN 1
                ELSE 3*dbo.WordCount(@Word5, Name)+dbo.WordCount(@Word5, Description)
            END
            AS TotalRank
    FROM Product
    ORDER BY TotalRank DESC

/* Save the number of searched products in an output variable */
SELECT @HowManyResults=COUNT(*) FROM #SearchedProducts WHERE Rank>0

/* Send back the requested products */
SELECT ProductID, Name, Description, Price, ImagePath, Rank
FROM #SearchedProducts
WHERE Rank > 0
    AND RowNumber BETWEEN (@PageNumber-1) * @ProductsOnPage + 1
                     AND @PageNumber * @ProductsOnPage
ORDER BY Rank DESC
```

How it Works: The SearchCatalog *Stored Procedure*

First of all, let's analyze the stored procedure's parameters:

- @PageNumber specifies the page of results the visitor has requested.

- @ProductsOnPage specifies how many records to return. If @PageNumber is 3 and @ProductOnPage is 5, you'll need the 11th to 15th records from the search results.

- @HowManyResults is an output parameter, which you'll set to the total number of search results. This will be read from the VB. NET code to calculate the number of search results pages.

- @AllWords is a bit input parameter that specifies whether you should do an all-words or any-words search.

- @Word1 to @Word5 are the words to be searched for. They all have a default value of NULL.

The stored procedure starts by creating the #SearchedProducts temporary table. Here is the first time you see a table created in SQL code. You can see that the SQL syntax to create a table is pretty self-explanatory:

```
/* Create the temporary table that will contain the search results */
CREATE TABLE #SearchedProducts
(RowNumber SMALLINT NOT NULL IDENTITY(1,1),
 ProductID INT,
 Name VARCHAR(50),
 Description VARCHAR(1000),
 Price MONEY,
 ImagePath VARCHAR(50))
```

The key field in #SearchedProducts is RowNumber. This is an Identity column with a seed value of 1 and an increment value of 1. This column could have been the primary key of the table. However, in this case it's better, for performance reasons, not to have a primary key. Remember that indexes are automatically created for primary keys. Because most operations with this table are insert operations, having an index on it would hurt its performance a little bit.

After creating the temporary table, you populate it by searching the product catalog. For this, the stored procedure reads the @AllWords bit parameter and decides what kind of search to do depending on its value. The logic of searching the catalog was explained earlier in this chapter.

After searching the catalog and populating #SearchedProducts, you set the value of the @HowManyResults output parameter (which will be read from the business tier), by counting the number of rows in #SearchedProducts:

```
/* Save the number of searched products in an output variable */
SELECT @HowManyResults=COUNT(*) FROM #SearchedProducts WHERE Rank>0
```

Finally, you get back the portion of records from #SearchedProducts based on the @PageNumber and @ProductsOnPage input parameters:

```
/* Send back the requested products */
SELECT ProductID, Name, Description, Price, ImagePath, Rank
FROM #SearchedProducts
WHERE Rank > 0
  AND RowNumber BETWEEN (@PageNumber-1) * @ProductsOnPage + 1
                    AND @PageNumber * @ProductsOnPage
ORDER BY Rank DESC
```

Implementing the Business Tier

The business tier consists of the SearchCatalog method, which calls the SearchCatalog stored procedure.

You'll learn two new theory issues when implementing SearchCatalog:

- *The* Session *object*: Through this object you can store data on the server, associated to the current visitor session. The visitor's session data is preserved between client requests (while the visitor is browsing the site), and is accessible from any Web Form or user control. The session data is stored and handled at the server side, and is not passed to the client and back during requests. This means that storing large quantities of data in the visitor's session occupies the server's memory, but doesn't increase network traffic.

- *The* DataTable *object*: So far, you've been passing data from the business tier to the presentation tier through SqlDataReader objects. As mentioned, SqlDataReaders read records one by one from the database and pass them directly to whoever reads them. SqlDataReader objects need an open connection to operate. The DataTable object is capable of storing any number of records without needing an open database connection (it stores them in memory).

TIP *Earlier in this chapter, we mentioned* DataSet *objects, which are also capable of storing information without needing an open database connection. In fact, the* DataSet *is capable of storing information from more data tables through an internal structure composed of* DataTable *objects.*

So why do you need to know about the DataTable and Session objects? The data SearchCatalog extracts from the database will be needed in two different controls: SearchResults.ascx (which you'll build later) will need to know the total number of search results, and ProductsList.ascx will need the list of products for the current page.

In Figure 5-3, you can see SearchResults.ascx in action. SearchResults informs the visitor about the total number of matching products, and implements the search results paging system. It contains some header text, the Previous and Next links, and then the actual list of products, generated using ProductsList.ascx:

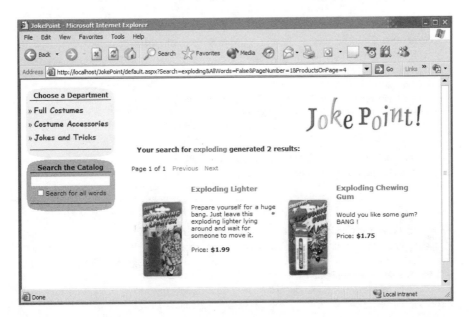

Figure 5-3. SearchResults.ascx *in action*

When executing the web page at server side, SearchResults.ascx and its code-behind file execute before ProductsList.ascx. For this reason, you'll call the SearchCatalog method from SearchResults.ascx, and you'll need a way to save the retrieved list of products (corresponding to the current search page) to be retrieved later from ProductsList.ascx (so ProductsList.ascx won't have to call SearchCatalog and query the database again). You'll do this by storing the list of products in a DataTable object, and saving it to the user's session through the Session object.

We'll talk more about these objects after implementing the `SearchCatalog` method in the next exercise.

Exercise: Implementing the `SearchCatalog` Method

Add the following method to the `Catalog` class in the business tier, and then we'll comment on it:

```
Public Shared Function SearchCatalog(ByVal searchString As String, _
                    ByVal pageNumber As String, _
                    ByVal productsOnPage As String, _
                    ByVal allWords As String) _
                    As Integer
  ' Create the connection object
  Dim connection As New SqlConnection(connectionString)

  ' Create and initialize the command object
  Dim command As New SqlCommand("SearchCatalog", connection)
  command.CommandType = CommandType.StoredProcedure

  ' Add the @AllWords parameter
  ' Guard against bogus values here - if you receive anything
  ' different than "TRUE" assume it's "FALSE"
  If allWords.ToUpper = "TRUE" Then
    ' only do an "all words" search
    command.Parameters.Add("@AllWords", SqlDbType.Bit)
    command.Parameters("@AllWords").Value = 1
  Else
    ' only do an "any words" search
    command.Parameters.Add("@AllWords", SqlDbType.Bit)
    command.Parameters("@AllWords").Value = 0
  End If

  ' Add the @PageNumber parameter
  command.Parameters.Add("@PageNumber", SqlDbType.TinyInt)
  command.Parameters("@PageNumber").Value = pageNumber

  ' Add the @ProductsOnPage parameter
  command.Parameters.Add("@ProductsOnPage", SqlDbType.TinyInt)
  command.Parameters("@ProductsOnPage").Value = productsOnPage

  ' Add the @HowManyResults output parameter
  command.Parameters.Add("@HowManyResults", SqlDbType.SmallInt)
  command.Parameters("@HowManyResults").Direction = ParameterDirection.Output

  ' Eliminate separation characters
  searchString = searchString.Replace(",", " ")
  searchString = searchString.Replace(";", " ")
  searchString = searchString.Replace(".", " ")
  searchString = searchString.Replace("!", " ")
  searchString = searchString.Replace("?", " ")
  searchString = searchString.Replace("-", " ")
```

```vbnet
' Create an array that contains the words
Dim words() As String = Split(searchString, " ")
' wordsCount contains the total number of words in the array
Dim wordsCount As Integer = words.Length
' index is used to parse the list of words
Dim index As Integer = 0
' this will store the total number of added words
Dim addedWords As Integer = 0

' Allow a maximum of five words
While addedWords < 5 And index < wordsCount
   ' Add the @WordN parameters here
   ' Only add words having more than two letters
   If Len(words(index)) > 2 Then
     addedWords += 1
     ' Add an input parameter and supply a value for it
     command.Parameters.Add("@Word" + addedWords.ToString, words(index))
   End If
   index += 1
End While

' Time to execute the command
Try
   ' Open the connection
   connection.Open()
   ' Create and initialize an SqlDataReader object
   Dim reader As SqlDataReader
   reader = command.ExecuteReader(CommandBehavior.CloseConnection)
   ' Store the search results to a DataTable
   Dim table As New DataTable()
   ' Copy column information from the SqlDataReader to the DataTable
   Dim fieldCount As Integer = reader.FieldCount
   Dim fieldIndex As Integer
   For fieldIndex = 0 To fieldCount - 1
     table.Columns.Add(reader.GetName(fieldIndex), _
               reader.GetFieldType(fieldIndex))
   Next
   ' Copy data from the SqlDataReader to the DataTable
   Dim row As DataRow
   While reader.Read()
     row = table.NewRow()
     For fieldIndex = 0 To fieldCount - 1
       row(fieldIndex) = reader(fieldIndex)
     Next
     table.Rows.Add(row)
   End While
   ' Close the reader and return the number of results
   reader.Close()

   ' Save the search results to the current session
   HttpContext.Current.Session("SearchTable") = table
```

```
    ' return the total number of matching products
    Return command.Parameters("@HowManyResults").Value
  Catch e As Exception
    ' Close the connection and throw the exception
    connection.Close()
    Throw e
  End Try
End Function
```

How it Works: The `SearchCatalog` Method

Although this method isn't complicated, there are a few new tricks. We'll be brief and take a closer look only at the new elements.

This method's purpose is to search the database using the `SearchCatalog` stored procedure. It returns the total number of matching products, and stores the search results in a `DataTable`, in the `Session` object. Later, the `ProductsList.ascx` user control reads the `DataTable` object from the session to display the current page of products to the visitor. Again, `SearchCatalog` is defined like this:

```
Public Shared Function SearchCatalog(ByVal searchString As String, _
                    ByVal pageNumber As String, _
                    ByVal productsOnPage As String, _
                    ByVal allWords As String) _
                    As Integer
```

The first detail in `SearchCatalog` worth noticing is it handles the `allWords` parameter:

```
' Add the @AllWords parameter
' Guard agains bogus values here - if you receive anything
' different than "TRUE" assume it's "FALSE"
If allWords.ToUpper = "TRUE" Then
  ' only do an "all words" search
  command.Parameters.Add("@AllWords", SqlDbType.Bit)
  command.Parameters("@AllWords").Value = 1
Else
  ' only do an "any words" search
  command.Parameters.Add("@AllWords", SqlDbType.Bit)
  command.Parameters("@AllWords").Value = 0
End If
```

We expect `allWords` to contain "TRUE" or "FALSE" because this will be the value of the check box that sets the kind of search to be performed. However, guarding against receiving other values is a good thing—if you send this value directly to the data tier, and expect it to do the conversion, it would generate an error if the value was not `True` or `False`.

This verification makes the business tier better protected. At some point in the presentation tier, the value of `allWords` is read from the query string; the visitor could change it to any value—without proper handling, this has the potential to generate an application exception, which you want to avoid.

After adding the other stored procedure parameters, you have a code block that eliminates unnecessary elements from the search string, such as punctuation elements:

```
' Eliminate separation characters
searchString = searchString.Replace(",", " ")
searchString = searchString.Replace(";", " ")
searchString = searchString.Replace(".", " ")
searchString = searchString.Replace("!", " ")
searchString = searchString.Replace("?", " ")
searchString = searchString.Replace("-", " ")
```

This is necessary because later you'll split the search string where it has spaces to get the individual words. If you didn't replace the punctuation marks with spaces, a search for "red,mask" wouldn't generate any results. Although not present here, a common practice is also to separately eliminate the so-called "noise" words that are not relevant to a search, such as "a", "or", "and", "on", and so on. You might want to add these too.

However, to automatically remove most noise words, we filter all words that are one or two characters long. Otherwise, simply typing a vowel into the search string would return the entire product catalog, and you certainly don't want that!

To split the search string into individual words, you use the Split Visual Basic function. This function returns an array of words. In the sample, the string is split on the space character:

```
' Create an array which contains the words
Dim words() As String = Split(searchString, " ")
```

Finally, with the individual words in the array, you add them as parameters for the stored procedure. You send a maximum of five words, while filtering out the words of one or two characters:

```
' wordsCount contains the total number of words in the array
Dim wordsCount As Integer = words.Length
' index is used to parse the list of words
Dim index As Integer = 0
' this will store the total number of added words
Dim addedWords As Integer = 0

' You allow a maximum of five words
While addedWords < 5 And index < wordsCount
  ' Add the @WordN parameters here
  ' Only add words having more than two letters
  If Len(words(index)) > 2 Then
    addedWords += 1
    ' Add an input parameter and supply a value for it
    command.Parameters.Add("@Word" + addedWords.ToString, words(index))
  End If
  index += 1
End While
```

At the end of the procedure, you execute the command, return the total number of matching products, and store the search results in a DataTable object in the current session.

 NOTE *You could have used other methods to share data between user controls and Web Forms. Alternatives to using* Session *include using the application state (via the* Application *object), or using a shared public property in the* Catalog *class. However, these solutions share data between all the visitors, which is not what we want.*

Let's see how all this happens, step by step. You first open the connection, execute the stored procedure, and retrieve the SqlDataReader object in the usual way:

```
' Time to execute the command
Try
    ' Open the connection
    connection.Open()
    ' Create and initialize an SqlDataReader object
    Dim reader As SqlDataReader
    reader = command.ExecuteReader(CommandBehavior.CloseConnection)
```

Next, create the DataTable object:

```
' Store the search results to a DataTable
Dim table As New DataTable()
```

Before copying the actual data from SqlDataReader to DataTable, you must initialize the fields of the DataTable. The following code block creates the DataTable columns using column names and data types extracted from the SqlDataReader:

```
' Copy column information from the SqlDataReader to the DataTable
Dim fieldCount As Integer = reader.FieldCount
Dim fieldIndex As Integer
For fieldIndex = 0 To fieldCount - 1
    table.Columns.Add(reader.GetName(fieldIndex), _
                      reader.GetFieldType(fieldIndex))
Next
```

Once the column definitions are in place, we start copying information from the SqlDataReader, row by row. Here note the Read() method of SqlDataReader. This moves the cursor to the next row from the search results; if there are no more records, the method returns False, causing the While loop to end:

```
' Copy data from the SqlDataReader to the DataTable
Dim row As DataRow
While reader.Read()
    row = table.NewRow()
    For fieldIndex = 0 To fieldCount - 1
```

```
    row(fieldIndex) = reader(fieldIndex)
  Next
  table.Rows.Add(row)
End While
```

Inside the `While` loop for each record in the `SqlDataReader`, a new `DataRow` object is created using the `NewRow` function of the `DataTable`. Most of the internal data of a `DataTable` is stored as a collection of `DataRow` objects.

`NewRow` creates a `DataRow` object with the same structure as the `DataTable`. You fill that row with information from the `SqlDataReader` using the `For` loop. Finally, the `DataRow` is added to the `DataTable` through its `Rows` collection.

NOTE   *The way information is read from the* `SqlDataReader` *is similar to the way* `DataList` *objects in the presentation tier operate when being populated using* `SqlDataReader` *objects.* `SqlDataReaders` *are very fast, but are limited to moving forward through the results using the* `Read` *method, and cannot be used to perform updates on the data source.*

When the reader gets at the end of the result set, `reader.Read` returns `False`, and the `While` loop exits. At that moment, you close the `SqlDataReader`, and its connection is also closed because you created the `SqlDataReader` by passing `CommandBehavior.CloseConnection` to the `ExecuteReader` method of `SqlCommand`.

NOTE   *Even if you didn't have to store the query results in the* `Session` *object, you would still have to use an intermediary* `DataTable` *object. This happens because you can't read the value of* `OUTPUT` *parameters from the* `SqlCommand` *object while the* `SqlDataReader` *is open. The* `SqlDataReader` *needs to be closed first, but not before saving the retrieved data to the* `DataTable` *object.*

After the data is stored in the `DataTable` and the `SqlDataReader` and its connection are closed, you can finally read the `@HowManyResults` output parameter from the `SqlCommand` object. Before returning the value, you save the results table to the `Session` object.

```
' Close the reader and return the number of results
reader.Close()

' Save the search results to the current session
HttpContext.Current.Session("SearchTable") = table

' return the total number of matching products
Return command.Parameters("@HowManyResults").Value
```

We wrote more code than usually for retrieving data from the database because we wanted to retrieve the total number of matching products without performing an additional database call.

Let's now create the presentation tier, where you'll use all the logic implemented so far.

Implementing the Presentation Tier

Yep, it's time to see some colors in front of your eyes! The Search Catalog feature has two separate interface elements that you need to implement. The first one is the place where the visitor enters the search string, shown in Figure 5-4. You have seen it already in the previous screenshots.

Search the Catalog
Search for all words

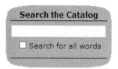

Figure 5-4. The `SearchBox` *control in action*

This part of the user interface will be implemented as a separate user control named `SearchBox.ascx`, which provides a text box and a check box for the visitor. The other part of the user interface consists of the search results control (`SearchResults.ascx`), which displays the products matching the search criteria. Figure 5-5 shows an example.

Your search for mask generated 5 results:
Page 1 of 2 Previous Next
Black Screamer Cape & Mask
Want to scare all your friends senseless. This costume will do the job. Just organize the party and put on a cd of horror sounds. And wear this Cape and Mask.
Price: $30.99
Beast Mask
Scary mask with red eyes and open mouth
Price: $5.99

Figure 5-5. The `SearchResults` *control in action*

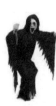

Implementing the `SearchBox` Web User Control

In the next exercise, you'll create the first user control, `SearchBox.ascx`.

Exercise: Creating the SearchBox *Web User Control*

1. First, create a Web User Control named `SearchBox.ascx` in the `UserControls` folder.

2. You can create the control either by using the Design View window, or by directly modifying the HTML. In this case, let's simply write the HTML for this file using HTML View:

```
<%@ Control Language="vb" AutoEventWireup="false"
Codebehind="SearchBox.ascx.vb" Inherits="JokePoint.SearchBox"
TargetSchema="http://schemas.microsoft.com/intellisense/ie5" %>
<table border="0" width="168" cellspacing="0" cellpadding="0"
bgcolor="LightSteelBlue">
  <tr>
    <td>
      <img src="Images/SearchBoxHeader.gif" border="0">
    </td>
  </tr>
  <tr bgcolor="LightSteelBlue">
    <td align="middle">
      <asp:TextBox id="searchTextBox" runat="server" Width="90%"
                   CssClass="SearchBox" BorderStyle="Dotted" MaxLength="100">
      </asp:TextBox>
    </td>
  </tr>
  <tr>
    <td align="middle">
      <asp:CheckBox id="allWordsCheckBox" CssClass="SearchBox" runat="server"
                   Text="Search for all words">
      </asp:CheckBox>
    </td>
  </tr>
</table>
<img  src="Images/SearchBoxFooter.gif" border="0">
```

3. Switch to Design View. The control should look like Figure 5-6.

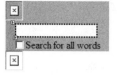

Figure 5-6. The Switch to Design View control

Remember that the header and footer pictures aren't visible right now because their paths are relative to the location of default.aspx, not the UserControls folder. For this reason, the pictures' image paths do not point to the correct location when designing the control, but they will when the page is executed.

Note the CssClass used for both controls, and the fact that a maximum size of 100 characters was set for the text box.

4. Add the following style to JokePoint.css. This style is used for the text in the searchTextBox and allWordsCheckBox controls:

```
.SearchBox
{
  font-family: Verdana, Helvetica, sans-serif;
  font-size: 11px;
  color: Black;
}
```

5. Open SearchBox.ascx in Design View, double-click the text box control (named searchTextBox). A searchTextBox_TextChanged method is automatically generated. This method executes when the visitor types something in the text box and presses the **Enter** key. Modify the TextChanged event handler method like this:

```
Private Sub searchTextBox_TextChanged(ByVal sender As System.Object, _
                                ByVal e As System.EventArgs) _
                                Handles searchTextBox.TextChanged
    ExecuteSearch()
End Sub

Private Sub ExecuteSearch()
    If Trim(searchTextBox.Text) <> "" Then
        Response.Redirect(Request.Url.AbsolutePath + _
                "?Search=" + searchTextBox.Text + _
                "&AllWords=" + allWordsCheckBox.Checked.ToString() + _
                "&PageNumber=1&ProductsOnPage=4")
    End If
End Sub
```

6. Press Ctrl+Shift+B to build the solution.

7. Add the newly created user control to `default.aspx` by dragging it from the Solution Explorer and dropping it just below the `CategoriesList` user control (see Figure 5-7).

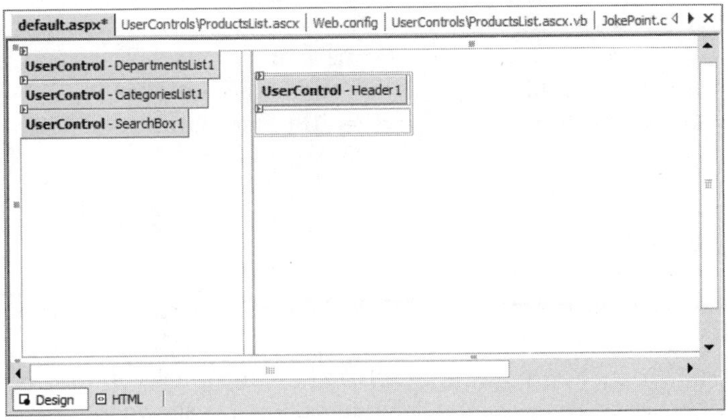

Figure 5-7. Adding a new user control to `default.aspx`

8. Press **F5** to execute the project. The search box should rest nicely in its place. Enter the words **red mask** and press **Enter**. You'll notice the page doesn't change a bit, except for the query string that appears:

```
default.aspx?Search=red%20mask&AllWords=False&PageNumber=1&ProductsOnPage=4
```

How It Works: The `SearchBox` Web User Control

The `SearchBox` user control isn't very complicated. When the visitor enters a new search string and presses **Enter**, `default.aspx` is reloaded with a few new parameters in the query string:

- `Search` specifies the search string

- `AllWords` specifies whether to do an all-words or an any-words search. You find its value by checking `allWordsCheckBox.Checked`, which returns `True` or `False`.

- `PageNumber` is the page requested by the visitor. On the first search, this is 1.

- `ProductsOnPage` specifies the number of products per page. You hard-coded its value at 4, but it will be easy to let the visitor choose a different value.

We use `Request.Url.AbsolutePath` to obtain the address of `default.aspx` when building the redirect path.

In `default.aspx`, we'll check for the `Search` parameter in the query string. If it appears, we'll load the `SearchResults` user control (which you'll build next) in `pageContentsCell` using the same technique we applied for browsing departments, categories, and the main web page.

Displaying the Search Results

You will now create the control that displays the search results. To simplify the work, you'll reuse the ProductsList user control to display the actual list of products. This is the control that you have used so far to list products for the main page, for departments, and for categories. Of course, if you wanted to have the searched products displayed in another format, you would need to create another user control.

In the following exercise, you'll create the SearchResults user control and update ProductsList.

Exercise: Displaying Search Results

1.   Create a new user control in the UserControls folder named SearchResults.ascx.

2.   While in Design View, add two Label controls and two HyperLink controls, and then drag ProductsList.ascx from Solution Explorer, as shown in Figure 5-8.

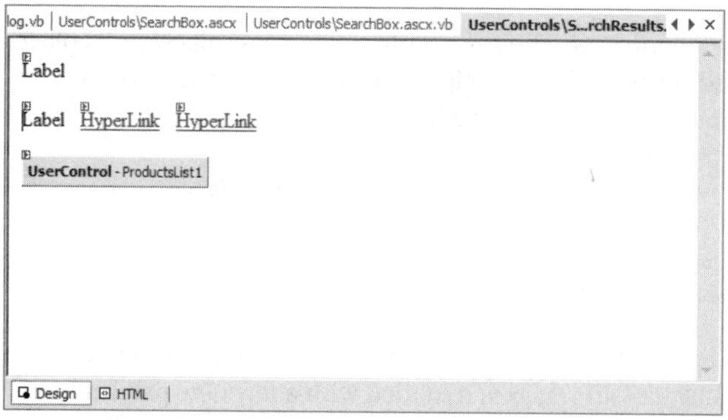

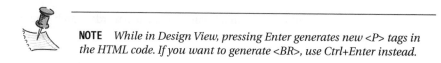

Figure 5-8. Creating SearchResults.ascx *in Design View*

> **NOTE**   *While in Design View, pressing Enter generates new <P> tags in the HTML code. If you want to generate <BR>, use Ctrl+Enter instead.*

3.   Clear the Text property of the Label controls. Set the text of the first HyperLink to "Previous", and the text of the second HyperLink to "Next".

4.   Set the name of the first label to titleLabel. The second label should be named pageNumberLabel. The HyperLink controls are previousLink and nextLink.

5.   Set the CssClass property of the first Label control to FirstPageText. Set the CssClass property of the other controls to SearchResults.

The HTML code of the control should be like this, at this moment:

```
<%@ Control Language="vb" AutoEventWireup="false"
Codebehind="SearchResults.ascx.vb" Inherits="JokePoint.SearchResults"
TargetSchema="http://schemas.microsoft.com/intellisense/ie5" %>
<%@ Register TagPrefix="uc1" TagName="ProductsList" Src="ProductsList.ascx" %>
<P>
  <asp:Label id="titleLabel" runat="server" CssClass="FirstPageText">
  </asp:Label>
</P>
<P>
  <asp:Label id="pageNumberLabel" runat="server" CssClass="SearchResults">
  </asp:Label>  
  <asp:HyperLink id="previousLink" runat="server" CssClass="SearchResults">
  Previous</asp:HyperLink>  
  <asp:HyperLink id="nextLink" runat="server" CssClass="SearchResults">
  Next</asp:HyperLink></P>
<P>
  <uc1:ProductsList id="ProductsList1" runat="server"></uc1:ProductsList>
</P>
```

Figure 5-9 shows how the control looks in Design View:

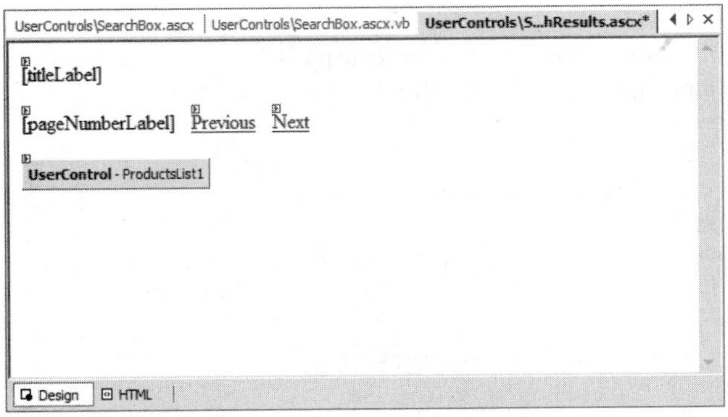

Figure 5-9. SearchResults.ascx *in Design View*

6. Add the following style to JokePoint.css:

```
.SearchResults
{
  font-family: Verdana, Helvetica, sans-serif;
  font-size: 11px;
  color: Black;
}
```

7. Open the code-behind file SearchResults.ascx.vb, and modify Page_Load like this:

```
Private Sub Page_Load(ByVal sender As System.Object, _
ByVal e As System.EventArgs) Handles MyBase.Load

  ' Save the search string parameters to String variables
  Dim searchString As String = Request.QueryString("Search")
  Dim allWords As String = Request.QueryString("AllWords")
  Dim pageNumber As String = Request.QueryString("PageNumber")
  Dim productsOnPage As String = Request.QueryString("ProductsOnPage")

  ' Perform the search and get back the number of results
  ' The search results will be read from ProductsList.ascx
  Dim howManyResults As Integer
  howManyResults = Catalog.SearchCatalog(searchString, pageNumber, _
                     productsOnPage, allWords)

  ' Do you have any results?
  If howManyResults = 0 Then
    titleLabel.Text = "Your search for <font color=red>" + searchString + _
            "</font> generated no results."
    previousLink.Visible = False
    nextLink.Visible = False
    pageNumberLabel.Visible = False
  Else
    titleLabel.Text = "Your search for <font color=red>" + searchString + _
            "</font> generated " + howManyResults.ToString + _
            " results:"

    ' Calculate how many pages of results
    Dim howManyPages As Integer = _
      Math.Ceiling(howManyResults / (CType(productsOnPage, Integer)))

    ' Show "Page x of y" text
    pageNumberLabel.Text = "Page " + pageNumber + _
                " of " + howManyPages.ToString

    ' Initialize the "Previous" link
    If pageNumber = "1" Then
      previousLink.Enabled = False
    Else
      previousLink.NavigateUrl = _
          Request.Url.AbsolutePath + _
          "?Search=" + searchString + _
          "&AllWords=" + allWords + _
          "&PageNumber=" + (CType(pageNumber, Integer) - 1).ToString + _
          "&ProductsOnPage=" + productsOnPage
    End If

    ' Initialize the "Next" link
    If pageNumber = howManyPages.ToString() Then
      nextLink.Enabled = False
```

```
        Else
          nextLink.NavigateUrl = _
              Request.Url.AbsolutePath + _
              "?Search=" + searchString + _
              "&AllWords=" + allWords + _
              "&PageNumber=" + (CType(pageNumber, Integer) + 1).ToString + _
              "&ProductsOnPage=" + productsOnPage
        End If
      End If
    End Sub
```

8. Now modify the code-behind file of `default.aspx` to load `SearchResults.ascx` in case the `Search` parameter is found in the query string:

```
    Private Sub Page_Load(ByVal sender As System.Object, _
                  ByVal e As System.EventArgs) Handles MyBase.Load
      ' Save DepartmentID from the query string to a variable
      Dim departmentId As String = Request.QueryString("departmentID")

      ' Save the search string from the query string to a variable
      Dim searchString As String = Request.QueryString("Search")

      ' Are you on the main web page or browsing the catalog?
      If Not searchString Is Nothing Then
        ' you're searching the catalog
        Dim control As Control
        control = Page.LoadControl("UserControls/SearchResults.ascx")
        pageContentsCell.Controls.Add(control)
      ElseIf Not departmentId Is Nothing Then
        ' you're visiting a department or category
        Dim control As Control
        control = Page.LoadControl("UserControls/Catalog.ascx")
        pageContentsCell.Controls.Add(control)
      Else
        ' you're on the main page
        Dim control As Control
        control = Page.LoadControl("UserControls/FirstPage.ascx")
        pageContentsCell.Controls.Add(control)
      End If
    End Sub
```

9. Finally, modify the code-behind file of `ProductsList.ascx` like this:

```
    Private Sub Page_Load(ByVal sender As System.Object, _
                  ByVal e As System.EventArgs) Handles MyBase.Load
      ' Retrieve DepartmentID from the query string
      Dim departmentId As String = Request.QueryString("DepartmentID")

      ' Retrieve CategoryID from the query string
      Dim categoryId As String = Request.QueryString("CategoryID")

      ' Retrieve the SearchString from the query string
      Dim searchString As String = Request.QueryString("Search")
```

```
If Not searchString Is Nothing Then
  ' search results
  list.DataSource = Session("SearchTable")
  list.DataBind()
  Session.Remove("SearchTable")
ElseIf Not categoryId Is Nothing Then
  ' category
  list.DataSource = Catalog.GetProductsInCategory(categoryId)
  list.DataBind()
ElseIf Not departmentId Is Nothing Then
  ' department
  list.DataSource = Catalog.GetProductsOnDepartmentPromotion(departmentId)
  list.DataBind()
Else
  ' main page
  list.DataSource = Catalog.GetProductsOnCatalogPromotion()
  list.DataBind()
End If
End Sub
```

10. Press **F5** to execute the project. Type **"black costume"** in the search text box to get an output similar to Figure 5-10.

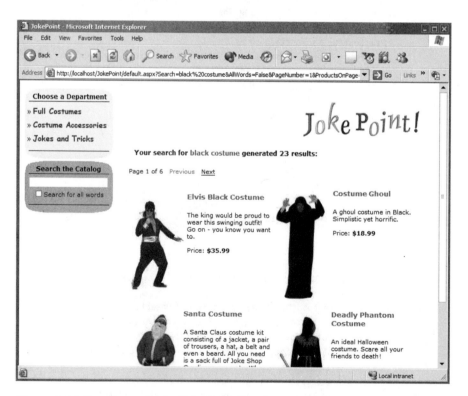

Figure 5-10. Search results for "black costume"

How It Works: Displaying Search Results

You've now finished implementing the search functionality of the catalog. Although you had quite a bit to write, the code wasn't that complicated, was it?

There were three main steps you needed to do:

- Implement the SearchResults.ascx Web User Control. This reads the query string, and calls the business tier SearchCatalog method to perform the search. SearchCatalog returns the number of matching products (five, in this example, when searching for "mask"), and saves the products in the current page (four products, in this example) in the visitor's session.

- Update default.aspx to load SearchResults when Search appears in the query string.

- Update ProductsList.ascx to display the products saved in the visitor's session if a Search appears in the query string. Right after displaying the products, the table is removed from the session. Otherwise, it would be kept for the entire visitor's session, occupying the server's memory.

Review these steps by taking a closer look at the code. Because there aren't any new challenging new issues with the code, we won't analyze it step by step here.

A Final Trick: Searching for Similar Words

Okay, the search feature is working fine. Do some tests with both all-words and any-words modes to ensure that the search feature really does work. You'll notice that it's fast, too.

The major problem with the search feature is that it doesn't recognize similar word forms. If you search for "costume" you'll be shown 19 results, but if you search for "costumes" no results will be retrieved.

Depending on your client's requests, this might not be acceptable. Let's analyze another search algorithm that deals this problem.

Searching Smarter but Slower

Searching smarter equals searching slower. To improve the search functionality to recognize different word forms, you'll need to change the WordCount function. The SearchCatalog stored procedure doesn't need to change! (nice one, right?)

The key SQL Server feature that allows you to implement this functionality is the SOUNDEX function. If the return value of SOUNDEX is the same for two different words, this means they sound very similar. SOUNDEX was initially created to find similar person names—SOUNDEX will return the same value for, say, Charlie and Charly. However, the function is useful in our scenario as well (although still not as accurate as SQL Server's full-text feature).

TIP   *Please read more about* SOUNDEX *in SQL Server 2000 Books Online* (http://www.microsoft.com/sql/techinfo/productdoc/2000/ books.asp). *You might also want to take a look at* DIFFERENCE, *which returns the degree of similarity between two words based on their* SOUNDEX *value.*

Unfortunately, in WordCount, when using SOUNDEX you must manually split the phrase into separate words and compare their SOUNDEX value to the SOUNDEX value of the word you're searching for. This isn't very fast.

In tests, we discovered that the new version of WordCount is about five times slower than the previously presented one. In the next chapter, you'll learn some techniques to further improve the web site's performance. However, if the business has grown large enough and the SQL Server can't successfully deal any more with client requests, this is an indication that a commercial version of SQL Server should probably be purchased (which also come with the advanced Full-Text Search functionality).

NOTE   *The main performance penalty in this version of* WordCount *isn't because of the* SOUNDEX *calls, as you might think. Manually splitting the phrase into separate words is what takes a lot of time. The* WordCount *algorithm solution you applied earlier using the* REPLACE *function, was cool because it allowed you to "trick" SQL Server and void to manually split the phrase.*

After all that, here's the code for the "smarter" version of WordCount:

```
CREATE FUNCTION dbo.WordCount
(@Word VARCHAR(20),
@Phrase VARCHAR(1000))
RETURNS SMALLINT
AS
BEGIN

/* If @Word or @Phrase is NULL the function returns 0 */
IF @Word IS NULL OR @Phrase IS NULL RETURN 0

/* Calculate and store the SOUNDEX value of the word */
DECLARE @SoundexWord CHAR(4)
SELECT @SoundexWord = SOUNDEX(@Word)

/* Eliminate bogus characters from phrase */
SELECT @Phrase = REPLACE(@Phrase, ',', ' ')
SELECT @Phrase = REPLACE(@Phrase, '.', ' ')
SELECT @Phrase = REPLACE(@Phrase, '!', ' ')
SELECT @Phrase = REPLACE(@Phrase, '?', ' ')
SELECT @Phrase = REPLACE(@Phrase, ';', ' ')
SELECT @Phrase = REPLACE(@Phrase, '-', ' ')
```

```
/* Necessary because LEN doesn't calculate trailing spaces */
SELECT @Phrase = RTRIM(@Phrase)

/* Check every word in the phrase */
DECLARE @NextSpacePos SMALLINT
DECLARE @ExtractedWord VARCHAR(20)
DECLARE @Matches SMALLINT

SELECT @Matches = 0

WHILE LEN(@Phrase)>0
  BEGIN
      SELECT @NextSpacePos = CHARINDEX(' ', @Phrase)
      IF @NextSpacePos = 0
        BEGIN
          SELECT @ExtractedWord = @Phrase
          SELECT @Phrase=''
        END
      ELSE
        BEGIN
          SELECT @ExtractedWord = LEFT(@Phrase, @NextSpacePos-1)
          SELECT @Phrase = RIGHT(@Phrase, LEN(@Phrase)-@NextSpacePos)
        END

      IF @SoundexWord = SOUNDEX(@ExtractedWord)
        SELECT @Matches = @Matches + 1
  END

/* Return the number of occurences of @Word in @Phrase */
RETURN @Matches
END
```

Summary

In this chapter, you implemented the search functionality of JokePoint. You learned many useful tricks about SQL Server and Visual Basic programming.

While implementing the data tier, you learned two ways of counting how many times a substring appears in a longer string while building the WordCount function. You learned how to use that function to implement search results ranking in the SearchCatalog procedure. You also learned how to select only a portion of the entire search results by using a temporary table.

When building the business tier, you learned how to read information from an SqlDataReader object, store it in a DataTable, and save the DataTable in the visitor's session.

Finally, in the presentation tier, you used the DataTable from the Session object to populate the list of products.

In Chapter 6, you'll learn a few methods to improve the web site's performance.

CHAPTER 6

Improving Performance

WHY WALK, when you can run? No, we won't talk about sports cars in this chapter. Instead, we'll analyze a few possibilities to improve the performance of the JokePoint project.

For now, rest assured that you've already implemented good programming practices when building JokePoint, such as:

- Carefully designing the database; for example, having indexes on the columns used in table joins significantly improves query performance (remember that indexes are automatically created on primary key columns!).

- Storing data logic in stored procedures (which, because they are stored in a compiled state by SQL Server, run faster than ad-hoc queries).

- Writing efficient SQL code and storing it within stored procedures for maximum performance.

- Using smart data access techniques in the business tier: making use of fast SqlDataReader objects, opening the database connections as late as possible, and closing the connections as soon as possible.

However, you can gain even more performance by using a few more tricks. In this chapter, you'll briefly learn about some of the most important performance tricks.

In this chapter, you'll learn how to

- Avoid populating controls with data during postback events

- Disable ViewState to pass less data in client-server roundtrips

- Enable output page caching

 NOTE *This chapter is meant as an introduction to a few topics regarding ASP.NET performance. For more serious coverage of these subjects, you should read an advanced ASP.NET book, such as* Performance Tuning and Optimizing ASP.NET Applications *(Apress, 2003).*

Handling Postback

Postback is the mechanism by which the client (the web browser) informs the server about the events that happen to its server-side controls. When an event happens at the client side (say, a button is clicked), the data about this event is posted back to the server, where it is handled using server-side code (the VB .NET code from the code-behind files).

For example, if you have a Button control and the visitor clicks it, the data about this event is posted back on the server. At the server side, the button's Click event method executes, and the results are sent back to the client as HTML code.

The problem is, every time such an event happens, the ASP.NET page and all its controls (including user controls) get reloaded. This incurs a performance penalty, because every time a user control such as DepartmentsList.ascx gets reloaded, it performs an additional database query to update itself with information in its Page_Load method.

In the JokePoint site, there's an example of event handling in the SearchBox control. In SearchBox.ascx, you have a TextBox control. After the visitor writes the search string and presses Enter, its TextChanged event-handling method is executed at the server side:

```
Private Sub searchTextBox_TextChanged(ByVal sender As System.Object, _
                      ByVal e As System.EventArgs) _
                      Handles searchTextBox.TextChanged
    ExecuteSearch()
End Sub

Private Sub ExecuteSearch()
  If Trim(searchTextBox.Text) <> "" Then
    Response.Redirect(Request.Url.AbsolutePath + _
            "?Search=" + searchTextBox.Text + _
            "&AllWords=" + allWordsCheckBox.Checked.ToString() + _
            "&PageNumber=1&ProductsOnPage=4")
  End If
End Sub
```

The code in this method redirects the visitor to the search results page. However, in the postback process, the original default.aspx page is reloaded once before being redirected.

That means that all the composing controls, including DepartmentsList.ascx, CategoriesList.ascx, and any other controls on the page are loaded twice: once for the original page, and then after the page is reloaded with the new query string parameters.

You can significantly improve performance by preventing Web User Controls or Web Forms from performing certain tasks (such as refreshing the DataList controls with information from the database), in case they are being reloaded as a result of a postback event.

NOTE *During postback events, the state of server-side controls (includ-ing user controls) is maintained by an internal ASP.NET mechanism called* ViewState—*we'll talk about it a bit later.*

The IsPostBack function helps with this problem. Let's see how it works by updating DepartmentsList and CategoriesList in the following exercise.

Exercise: Updating DepartmentsList ***and*** CategoriesList

Open the code-behind file of DepartmentsList, and update it by adding two lines of code, as shown here:

```
Private Sub Page_Load(ByVal sender As System.Object, _
           ByVal e As System.EventArgs) Handles MyBase.Load
  If Not IsPostBack Then
    ' The departmentIndex parameter is added to the query string when
    ' a department link is clicked. We need this because when the
    ' page is reloaded the DataList forgets which link was clicked.
    Dim listIndex As String = Request.QueryString("DepartmentIndex")

    ' If listIndex has a value, this tells us that the visitor
    ' has clicked on a department, and we inform the DataList about that
    ' (so it can apply the correct template for the selected item)
    If Not listIndex Is Nothing Then
      list.SelectedIndex = CInt(listIndex)
    End If

    ' GetDepartments returns an SqlDataReader object that has
    ' two fields: DepartmentID and Name. These fields are read in
    ' the SelectedItemTemplate and ItemTemplate of the DataList
    list.DataSource = Catalog.GetDepartments()

    ' Needed to bind the child controls (the HyperLink controls)
    ' to the data source
    list.DataBind()
  End If
End Sub
```

Now, do the same to CategoriesList.ascx.vb:

```
Private Sub Page_Load(ByVal sender As System.Object, _
                  ByVal e As System.EventArgs) Handles MyBase.Load
  If Not IsPostBack Then
    ' The department for which we are loading the categories
    Dim departmentId As String = Request.QueryString("DepartmentID")
    ' Don't load categories if no department was selected
    If Not departmentId Is Nothing Then
      ' The index of the selected DataList item.
      Dim listIndex As String = Request.QueryString("CategoryIndex")
```

```
' The DataList item that was clicked is set as the selected item
If Not listIndex Is Nothing Then
    list.SelectedIndex = CInt(listIndex)
End If
' GetCategoriesInDepartment returns an SqlDataReader object that has
' two fields: CategoryID and Name. These fields are read in
' the SelectedItemTemplate and ItemTemplate of the DataList
list.DataSource = Catalog.GetCategoriesInDepartment(departmentId)
' Needed to bind the child controls(the HyperLink and Label controls)
' to the data source
list.DataBind()
      End If
    End If
End Sub
```

How It Works: The IsPostBack *Function*

In Departments.ascx.vb, the list of departments is populated in Page_Load. However, during postback events, its state is maintained anyway by ASP.NET using the ViewState mechanism (which we'll discuss next). Also, there are no postback events that should affect the way the departments list looks. For this reason, it's more efficient to query the database for the list of departments only the first time the page is loaded, and never reload the list of departments during postback events.

Here, the IsPostBack function is your best friend. IsPostBack indicates whether the page is being loaded in response to a client postback, or whether it's being loaded and accessed for the first time.

NOTE   IsPostBack *is, in fact, a property of the* Page *class. You can use* Me.IsPostBack *instead of* IsPostBack *to achieve the same results.*

You can apply the same technique for other controls that work with the database or perform additional processing that is not related to the events happening in the page.

NOTE   *Performance tuning can be fun to play with, but never do experiments on a production system, because you can get strange results.*

Managing ViewState

HTTP (Hypertext Transfer Protocol) is a stateless protocol—the server doesn't retain any information about the previous client request. Without an additional mechanism over this protocol, the server can't retain the state of a simple HTML page between client requests (say, which check boxes or radio buttons are selected, and so on).

ASP.NET has a built-in technique for dealing with this problem. When sending the HTML response to the client, by default ASP.NET encodes the current state of every control in a string called ViewState, in the form of a hidden form field called __VEWSTATE.

ViewState is used to maintain the state of the web page during client postbacks. In other words, when the visitor performs any action that triggers a postback event, the page maintains its state after the event handler method executes at the server.

For this reason, in the previous exercise, you modified DepartmentsList.ascx to first verify whether the control is being loaded as a result of a client postback. If it is, you don't need to query the database again, because you know it was already loaded once, and ASP.NET already contains the control's state in the ViewState string.

The problem with ViewState is that it's transferred between the client and the server on every request. With pages that contain a large number of controls, the ViewState information can grow significantly, causing a lot of network traffic.

To see the encoded ViewState information for a page, you can do a simple test. Load JokePoint in your web browser, right-click the page and select View Source. Inside the page HTML code, you can see the ViewState information encoded as a hidden form element named __VIEWSTATE:

```
<input type="hidden" name="__VIEWSTATE"
value="dDwyMTAxNDE4MzM303Q802w8aTwxPjs+02w8dDw7bDxpPDE+02k8Mz47aTwxMT47PjtsPHQ802
w8aTwwPjs+02w8dDxAMDxwPHA8bDxTZWxlY3R1ZEluZGV4400RhdGFLZX1z0 ............" />
```

NOTE *The value of the* ViewState *is not in human-readable form, but it isn't encrypted either. The information is stored as name-value pairs using the* System.Web.UI.StateBag *object. The simplest way to decipher the value stored in your* ViewState *is by going to a web site such as* http://www.wilsondotnet.com/Demos/ViewState.aspx, *which reveals what the* ViewState *string actually contains.*

In the JokePoint web site, you're mainly concerned about the ViewState for ProductsList.ascx, which can get quite large for a lot of products. The total page ViewState has about 4KB if the page has 12 products, and only 1KB if no products are displayed on the page.

The professional way to view how much space the ViewState occupies for every element on the page is to enable **page tracing** by opening default.aspx and modifying its Page directive like this:

```
<%@ Page Trace="true" Language="vb" AutoEventWireup="false"
Codebehind="default.aspx.vb" Inherits="JokePoint._default"%>
```

After making this change when loading default.aspx, tracing information will be appended at the bottom of the page (see Figure 6-1). You can see a lot of info about your page, including the ViewState size for every control.

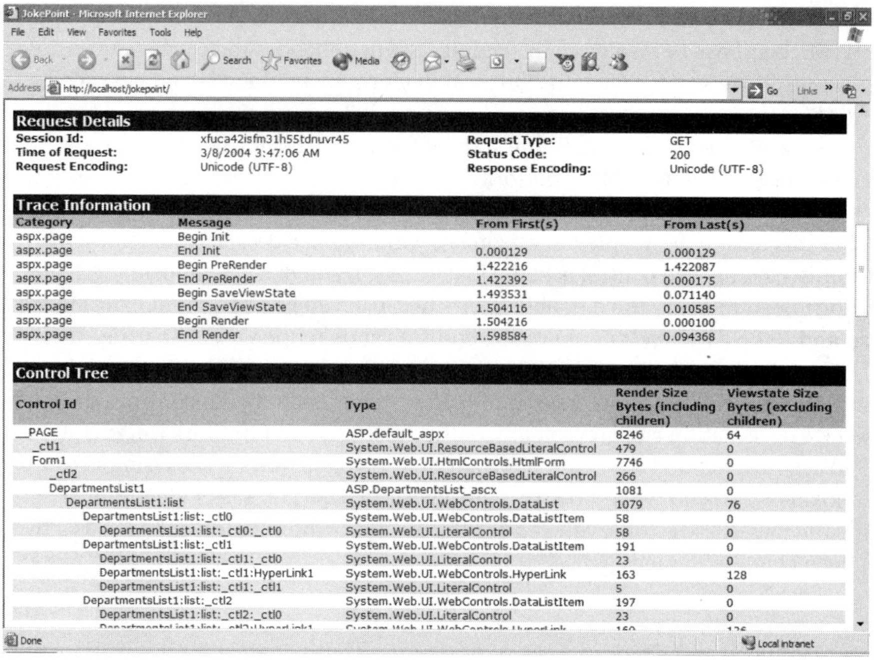

Figure 6-1. Viewing tracing information

NOTE   *This is obvious, but it has to be said: Always remember to turn off tracing and debug mode before releasing your pages to the web.*

By default, ViewState is enabled for all server controls. However, it can be disabled for a specific control, or even for an entire page. Because ProductsList.ascx is populated from the database in every occasion, ASP.NET doesn't need to hold its state, so it makes sense to disable ViewState for this control, or for the DataList it contains.

To disable ViewState for a control, change its EnableViewState property to False (by default it's True). Let's disable ViewState for the DataList control in ProductsList.ascx, and for all the controls in SearchBox.ascx, in the following exercise.

Exercise: Disabling ViewState for Server-Side Controls

1. Open ProductsList.ascx in Design View, select the DataList, and open its Properties window by pressing F4.

2. Set the EnableViewState property to False, as shown in Figure 6-2.

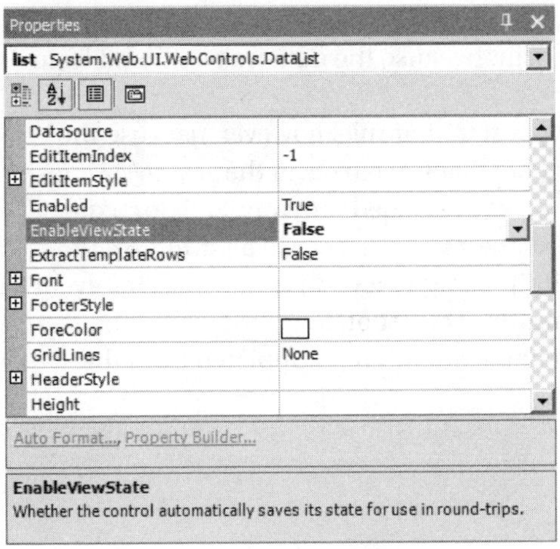

Figure 6-2. Disabling ViewState *for the* DataList *control*

3. Now disable the ViewState for all the controls in SearchBox.ascx. Instead of disabling the ViewState for every control it contains, you can disable it for the whole user control. Open SearchBox.ascx in Design View and set enableViewState to False in its Properties window, as shown in Figure 6-3.

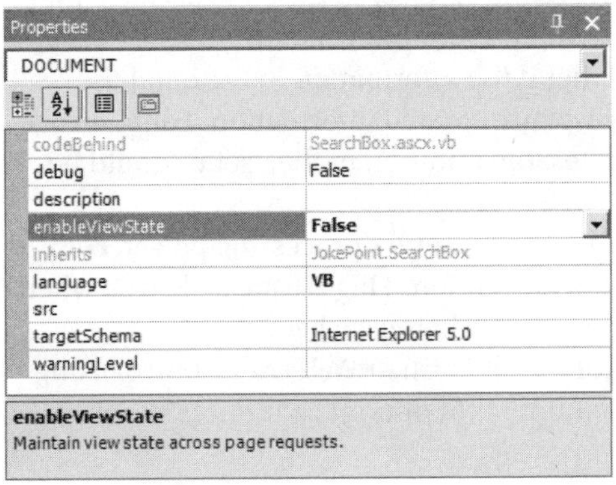

Figure 6-3. Setting SearchBox.ascx's enableViewState *to* False

How It Works: Disabling ViewState to Improve Performance

Now you have disabled ViewState for some of your controls. For your particular solutions, you'll decide for which controls it's best to disable ViewState.

So far, you've learned about letting ASP.NET manage the state of your controls, in which case you don't reload the controls with data from the database (by verifying the IsPostBack value), like you did with DepartmentsList.ascx. You also learned how to disable the ViewState information, in which case you rely on the control reading the database on every request.

Most of the time, you must not apply both techniques—you risk ending up with "empty" controls when client postbacks occur, because the data isn't gathered from the database or from the ViewState.

So far your client's web site is an exception to that rule, however, because the only occasion (until now) in which a client postback occurs is in the SearchBox control, at which time the page is redirected (and so reloaded) anyway. Still, for a quick test, you can now disable ViewState for DepartmentsList.ascx, add a button somewhere on default.aspx, and double-click it (in Design View) to create its Click event handler. Execute the page, and click the button. The list of departments should disappear, because its ViewState is not maintained, and it's not populated from the database either.

Using Output Cache

Output page caching is an ASP.NET feature that increases the performance of your Web Application by caching the HTML content generated from dynamic pages.

In other words, a page or user control that has output caching enabled will only be executed the first time it is requested. On subsequent requests, the page or control is served directly from the cache, instead of being executed again.

This can have an important effect on performance for JokePoint, because most controls access the database to populate themselves with information. With output caching enabled, the controls only read the database the first time they are accessed. You can set the interval of time at which the cache expires, so the controls have the chance to execute again, and refresh them with current information.

The drawback with output caching is that if the information in the database changes in the meantime, your page will display outdated information. For controls whose data is susceptible to frequent updates, the duration of the cache should be shorter.

Also, enabling output caching, although it saves server processing power, consumes server memory, and should be used with caution. This is especially true when storing multiple versions of the page or user control being cached.

You can enable output page caching for a Web Form or Web User Control using the OutputCache page directive, which has a number of optional parameters:

```
<%@ OutputCache
    Duration="#ofseconds"
    Location="Any | Client | Downstream | Server | None"
    Shared="True | False"
    VaryByControl="controlname"
    VaryByCustom="browser | customstring"
    VaryByHeader="headers"
    VaryByParam="parametername" %>
```

- *Duration*: Specifies the number of seconds the page will be stored in cache. A page is stored in cache the first time it is generated, which happens the first time a visitor asks for it. All the subsequent requests for that page, during the period mentioned by Duration, will be served directly from cache instead of being processed again. After the cache duration expires, it is removed from the cache.

- *Location*: Specifies the place the actual data for the cache is stored. The default value (Any) caches the page on the client browser, on the web server, or on any proxy servers supporting HTTP 1.1 caching located between the client and the server.

- *Shared*: Applies only to user controls, and specifies whether the output of the user control should be cached once for all the pages that include the control, or if multiple versions of the control should be cached for each page that contains it.

- *VaryByControl*: Used to vary the output cache depending on the values of server-side controls contained in the control or page being cached.

- *VaryByCustom*: Used to identity custom caching requirements. Its most popular value is "browser", which results in having different versions of the page cached at the server for each type of client-side browser. This feature is very useful if your dynamic web pages generate different HTML outputs depending on the client browser (this isn't the case for JokePoint, though). If varying the output by browser type, the server will retain different versions of the page that were generated for each kind and version of client browser.

- *VaryByHeader*: Used to vary the output cache by the value of different HTTP headers. When you set the value of VaryByHeader to a list of HTTP headers (separated by semicolons), multiple versions of the page will be cached depending on the values of the mentioned headers. A typical value for VaryByHeader is "Accept-Language", which instructs ASP.NET to cache multiple versions of the page for different languages.

- *VaryByParam*: Varies the output cache based on the values of the parameters passed to the server, which include the query string parameters. You'll see in the exercise how to vary the output page cache based on the query string parameters.

 NOTE *In this chapter, you learn how to enable page caching declaratively, but it's also possible to control page caching programmatically. Please check an advanced ASP.NET book for more details.*

You can enable output caching for DepartmentsList.ascx by editing the file in HTML View, and adding the following line at the beginning of the file:

```
<%@ OutputCache Duration="1000" VaryByParam="DepartmentIndex" %>
```

After adding this directive, ASP.NET will retain the different output versions of DepartmentsList.ascx, depending on the value of the DepartmentIndex query string parameter.

 CAUTION *Implementing output caching can easily affect the behavior of your web site in unexpected ways. Also, the way output caching should be implemented depends on the exact stage of your web site. For now, you shouldn't use output caching, but only keep its possibilities in mind. You can start improving performance and tweaking your Web Forms or Web User Controls after you have a working and viable Web Application.*

For controls whose output also depends on the CategoryIndex, such as CategoriesList.ascx and Catalog.ascx, you can implement caching like this:

```
<%@ OutputCache Duration="1000" VaryByParam="DepartmentIndex;CategoryIndex" %>
```

Because ProductsList.ascx has many output versions (especially if you take searching into account), it's not recommended to implement caching for it. However, if you still want to do this, you need to make it vary on every possible query string parameter that could influence its output, with an OutputCache directive like this:

```
<%@ OutputCache Duration="1000"

VaryByParam="DepartmentIndex;CategoryIndex;Search;AllWords;PageNumber;ProductsOnP
age" %>
```

Alternatively, the "*" wildcard can be used, to vary the output cache on any possible query string parameter:

```
<%@ OutputCache Duration="1000" VaryByParam="*" %>
```

NOTE *You can test caching to make sure it actually works by either placing breakpoints in code (the code shouldn't execute at all when caching is enabled), or even by temporarily stopping SQL Server and then browsing through pages that were stored in cache (although for this to work, you'll need to implement caching on all the controls that perform data access).*

Although implementing output page caching saves the database, it occupies web server memory. For this reason, it isn't feasible to implement output caching for controls such as ProductsList, which have a very large number of display possibilities. ProductsList has a different output for every department and category, not to mention the endless search possibilities.

NOTE *For your own solutions, you'll need to carefully decide on which user controls to implement output page caching. You can start experimenting by playing with the different controls that you implemented for JokePoint so far. One thing you should be aware of is that output page caching doesn't always behave as expected during client postbacks generated by other user controls in the page. For this reason, it's advisable to test your solution seriously every time you change output cache options.*

Summary

This was a very short, but interesting chapter! Although ASP.NET performance tuning is out of the scope of this book, you took a quick look at the most useful features that allow you to improve a web site's performance.

In the next chapter, you'll learn how to accept payments for JokePoint using PayPal.

CHAPTER 7

Receiving Payments Using PayPal

LET'S COLLECT SOME MONEY! Your e-commerce web site needs a way of receiving payments from customers. While the preferred solution for established companies is to open a merchant account, many small businesses choose to start with a solution that's simpler to implement, where they don't have to process credit card or payment information themselves.

A number of companies and web sites can help individuals or small businesses that don't have the resources to process credit card and wire transactions. These companies can be used to intermediate the payment between online businesses and their customers. Many of these payment-processing companies are relatively new and the handling of any individual's financial details is very sensitive. Additionally, a quick search on the Internet will produce reports from both satisfied and unsatisfied customers for almost all of these companies. For these reasons, we are not recommending any third-party company.

Instead, this chapter lists some of the companies currently providing these services, and then demonstrates some of the functionality they provide with PayPal. You'll learn how to integrate PayPal with JokePoint in the first two stages of development. In this chapter, you will

- Learn how to create a new PayPal account

- Learn how to integrate PayPal in stage 1 of development, where you'll need a shopping cart and custom checkout mechanism

- Learn how to integrate PayPal in stage 2 of development, where you'll have your own shopping cart, so you'll need to guide the visitor directly to a payment page

- Learn how to configure PayPal to automatically calculate shipping costs

 NOTE *This chapter is not a PayPal manual, but a quick guide to using PayPal. For any complex queries about the services provided, please contact PayPal, or the Internet Payment Service Provider you decide to use.*

Considering Internet Payment Service Providers

Take a look at this list of Internet Payment Service Provider web sites. This is a diverse group, each having its advantages. Some of the providers transfer money person to person and payments need to be verified manually; others have sophisticated integration with your web site. Some work anywhere on the globe, while others work only for a single country.

The following list is not complete—you can find more detailed lists of payment systems on a number of web sites, such as http://www.online-payment-processing.com, or http://www.computerbits.com/archive/2003/0800/credicards.html.

- *2Checkout*: http://www.2checkout.com

- *AnyPay*: http://www.anypay.com

- *CCNow*: http://www.ccnow.com

- *Electronic Transfer*: http://www.electronictransfer.com

- *Moneybookers*: http://www.moneybookers.com

- *MultiCards*: http://www.multicards.com

- *Pay By Web*: http://www.paybyweb.com

- *Paymate*: http://www.paymate.com.au

- *PayPal*: http://www.paypal.com

- *PaySystems:* http://www.paysystems.com

- *ProPay*: http://www.propay.com

- *QuickPayPro*: http://www.quickpaypro.com

- *WorldPay*: http://worldpay.com

For the demonstration in this chapter we chose to use PayPal. Apart from being quite popular, PayPal offers the services that fit very well into our web site for the first two stages of development. PayPal is available in a number of countries—the most up-to-date list can be found at http://www.paypal.com.

For the first stage of development—where you only have a searchable product catalog—and with only a few lines of HTML code, PayPal enables you to add a shopping cart with checkout functionality. For the second stage of development, in which you need to manually record orders in the database, PayPal has a feature called Single Item Purchases that can be used to send the visitor directly to a payment page without the intermediate shopping cart. You'll use this feature of PayPal in Chapter 10.

For a summary of the features provided by PayPal, point your browser to http://www.paypal.com and click the Merchant Tools link. That page contains a few other useful links that will show you the main features available.

Getting Started with PayPal

Probably the best description of this service is the one found on its web site: "PayPal is an account-based system that lets anyone with an email address securely send and receive online payments using their credit card or bank account."

PayPal is one of the companies that allow a small business like our electronic novelty store to receive payments from its customers. The visitor, instead of paying the client directly, pays PayPal using a credit card or bank account. The client then uses its PayPal account to get the money received from the customers. At the time of writing, there is no cost involved in creating a new PayPal account and the service is free for the buyer. The fees involved when receiving money are shown at http://www.paypal.com/cgi-bin/webscr?cmd=_display-fees-outside.

Please visit the PayPal web site to get updated and complete information, and, of course, visit its competitors before making a decision for your own e-commerce site. You will also want to check which of the services are available in your country, and what kind of credit cards and payment methods each company accepts.

If you want to use PayPal beyond the exercises with JokePoint, you'll want to learn more about its service. On the main PayPal web page, click the Help link, which opens up the Help pages. These pages are well structured and provide a search feature. You might also want to check the PayPal Developer Network site at https://www.paypal.com/pdn. Another useful web site for PayPal developers is http://www.paypaldev.org, which according to the site is an "independent forum for PayPal developers." This web site provides a number of useful links, including links to the five PayPal manuals in PDF format (Single Item Purchases, Shopping Cart, Instant Payment Notification, Donations, Subscriptions).

In the following exercise, you'll create a new PayPal account, and then integrate it with JokePoint.

 TIP *These steps are also described in more detail in the PayPal manuals mentioned earlier.*

Exercise: Creating the PayPal Account

1. Browse to http://www.paypal.com using your favorite web browser.

2. Click the Sign Up link.

3. PayPal supports two account types: Personal account and Business accounts. To receive credit card payments, you need to open a Business account. Choose your country from the combo box, and click Continue.

4. Complete all of the requested information and you will receive an email asking you to revisit the PayPal site to confirm the details you have entered.

How It Works: The PayPal Account

After the PayPal account is set up, the email address you provided will be your PayPal ID.

A lot of functionality is available within the PayPal service—because the site is easy to use and many of the functions are self-explanatory, we won't describe everything here. Remember that these sites are there for your business, so they're more than happy to assist with any of your queries.

Now let's see now how you can actually use the new account for the web site.

Integrating the PayPal Shopping Cart and Checkout

In the first stage of development (the current stage), you need to integrate the shopping cart and checkout functionality from PayPal. In the second stage of development, after you create your own shopping cart, you'll only need to rely on PayPal's checkout mechanism.

To accept payments, you need to add two important elements to the user interface part of the site: Add to Cart buttons for each product and a View Cart button somewhere on the page. PayPal makes adding these buttons a piece of cake.

The functionality of those buttons is performed by secure links to the PayPal web site. For example, the following form represents the Add to Cart button for a product named Beast Mask that costs $5.99:

```
<form target="paypal" action="https://www.paypal.com/cgi-bin/webscr"
      method="post">
  <input type="hidden" name="cmd" value="_cart">
  <input type="hidden" name="business" value="your_email_address">
  <input type="hidden" name="item_name" value="Beast Mask">
  <input type="hidden" name="amount" value="$5.99">
  <input type="image" src="Images/AddToCart.gif" name="submit">
  <input type="hidden" name="add" value="1">
</form>
```

The View Cart button can be generated using a similar structure. In your web site, because ASP.NET works by default using a main form (and forms cannot be nested), we choose to generate the buttons using links such as

```
https://www.paypal.com/cgi-bin/webscr?
cmd=_cart&business=your_email_address&item_name=Beast Mask&amount=$5.99&add=1
```

NOTE *The fields are predefined and their names are self-explanatory. The most important is* business, *which must be the email address you used when you registered the PayPal account (the email address that will receive the money). Please consult PayPal's Shopping Cart Manual for more details. You can download it at* https://www.paypal.com/en_US/pdf/shopping_cart.pdf.

You need to make sure this HTML code gets added to each product, so you'll have Add to Cart buttons for each product. To do this, you must modify the ItemTemplate of the DataList control in the ProductsList user control. Then, you'll add the View Cart button somewhere on default.aspx, so it will be accessible at any time for the visitor.

TIP *Although we won't use them for our site, it's good to know that PayPal provides button generators that based on certain data you provide (product name, product price), give you an HTML block similar to the one shown previously. These button generators are found by clicking the* Developers *link at the bottom of the first page, and then clicking* PayPal Solutions *in the menu on the left.*

In JokePoint, you'll need to add links such as the one shown previously (Add to Cart links) for each displayed product (so you'll need to update ProductsList.acx), and you'll need to add a View Cart link on the main web page (so you'll update default.aspx as well).

After adding the Add to Cart and View Cart buttons, the web site will look like Figure 7-1.

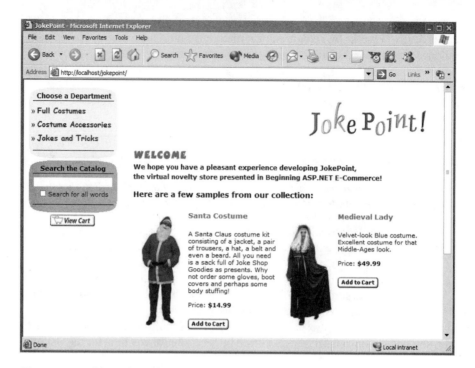

Figure 7-1. Adding the Add to Cart buttons

You'll implement the PayPal integration in the next exercise.

Exercise: Integrating with the PayPal Shopping Cart and Custom Checkout

1. Open default.aspx in HTML View, and add the following JavaScript function inside the <HEAD> element:

```
<HEAD>
  <title>JokePoint</title>
  <meta content="Microsoft Visual Studio .NET 7.1" name="GENERATOR">
  <meta content="Visual Basic .NET 7.1" name="CODE_LANGUAGE">
  <meta content="JavaScript" name="vs_defaultClientScript">
  <meta content="http://schemas.microsoft.com/intellisense/ie5"
name="vs_targetSchema">
  <LINK href="JokePoint.css" type="text/css" rel="stylesheet">

  <script language="JavaScript">
  <!--
  var PayPalWindow = null;

  function OpenPayPalWindow(url)
  {
    if ((!PayPalWindow) || PayPalWindow.closed)
```

```
        // If the PayPal window doesn't exist, we open it
        PayPalWindow = window.open(url,"cart","height=300, width=500");
      else
      {
        // If the PayPal window exists, we make it show
        PayPalWindow.location.href=url;
        PayPalWindow.focus();
      }
    }


    // -->
    </script>
  </HEAD>
```

NOTE *JavaScript is case sensitive, so you need to be very careful to reproduce the code exactly, otherwise it won't work as expected.*

2. Now, add the View Cart button on the main page, just below the SearchBox control. Open default.aspx in HTML View and modify it like this:

```
<td vAlign="top" height="100%">
  <uc1:DepartmentsList id="DepartmentsList1" runat="server">
  </uc1:DepartmentsList>
  <uc1:CategoriesList id="CategoriesList1" runat="server">
  </uc1:CategoriesList>
  <uc1:SearchBox id="SearchBox1" runat="server">
  </uc1:SearchBox>
  <br>         
  <a href=
  "JavaScript: OpenPayPalWindow('https://www.paypal.com/cgi-bin/webscr?
        cmd=_cart
        &business=youremail@yourserver.com
        &display=1
        &return=www.yourwebsite.com
        &cancel_return=www.yourwebsite.com')">
    <IMG src="Images/ViewCart.gif" border="0">
  </a>
</td>
```

NOTE *You must write the OpenPayPalWindow call on a single line in the HTML source. We split it on multiple lines in the code snippet to make it easier to read.*

3. Add the PayPal Add to Cart button in ProductsList.ascx, just below the product price:

```
<br><br>
<a href=
  'JavaScript: OpenPayPalWindow("https://www.paypal.com/cgi-bin/webscr?
    cmd=_cart
    &business=youremail@yourserver.com
    &item_name=<%# DataBinder.Eval(Container.DataItem, "Name")%>
    &amount=<%# DataBinder.Eval(Container.DataItem, "Price", "{0:c}")%>
    &add=1
    &return=www.yourwebsite.com
    &cancel_return=www.yourwebsite.com")'>
  <IMG src="Images/AddToCart.gif" border="0">
</a>
```

NOTE *You must write the* OpenPayPalWindow *call on a single line in the HTML source. We split it on multiple lines in the code snippet to make it easier to read.*

4. Please make sure you replace youremail@yourserver.com with the email address you submitted when you created your PayPal account for both Add to Cart and View Cart buttons! Also, replace www.yourwebsite.com with the address of your e-commerce store. Alternatively, you can remove the return and cancel_return variables if you don't want PayPal to redirect to your web site after the customer completes or cancels a payment.

CAUTION *You need to use the correct email address if you want the money to get into your account!*

5. Press **F5** to execute the project. Your first page should look like Figure 7-2 now.

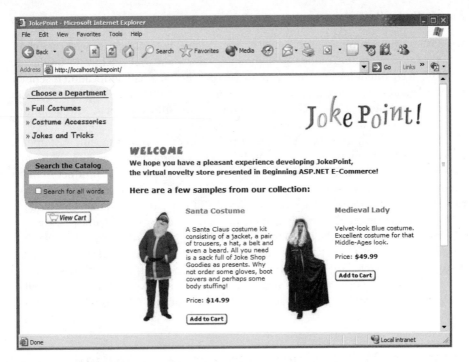

Figure 7-2. Integrating the PayPal shopping cart

Experiment with the PayPal shopping cart to see that it works as advertised. Figure 7-3 shows the PayPal shopping cart in action.

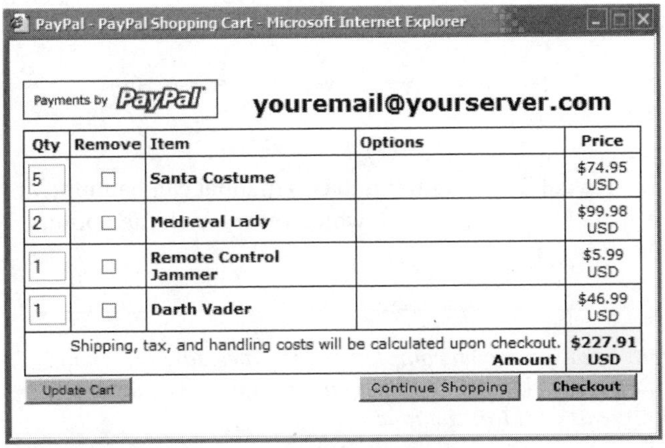

Qty	Remove	Item	Options	Price
5	☐	Santa Costume		$74.95 USD
2	☐	Medieval Lady		$99.98 USD
1	☐	Remote Control Jammer		$5.99 USD
1	☐	Darth Vader		$46.99 USD

Payments by **PayPal** — **youremail@yourserver.com**

Shipping, tax, and handling costs will be calculated upon checkout. **Amount** — **$227.91 USD**

Update Cart   Continue Shopping   Checkout

Figure 7-3. The PayPal shopping cart

How It Works: PayPal Integration

Yes, it was just that simple. Right now, all visitors became potential customers! They can click the Checkout button of the PayPal shopping cart, where they can buy the products!

After a customer makes a payment on the web site, an email notification is sent to the email address registered on PayPal, and also to the customer. Your PayPal account will reflect the payment, and you can view the transaction information in your account history or as a part of the history transaction log.

After PayPal confirms the payment, you can ship the products to your customer. On each payment, you need to carefully check that the product prices correspond to the correct amounts, because it's very easy for anyone to add a fake product to the shopping cart, or an existing product with a modified price. This can be done by fabricating one of those PayPal `Add to Cart` links and navigating to it. You can read a detailed article about this problem at `http://www.alphabetware.com/pptamper.asp`.

We touched a few of the details of the PayPal shopping cart, but for a complete description of its functionality, you should read the PayPal Shopping Cart manual, which is available for download at `https://www.paypal.com/en_US/pdf/shopping_cart.pdf`.

If you decide to use PayPal for your own web site, make sure you learn about all its features. For example, you can teach PayPal to automatically calculate shipping costs and tax for each order.

Using the PayPal Single Item Purchases Feature

Single Item Purchases is a PayPal feature that allows you to send the visitor directly to a payment page instead of the PayPal shopping cart. The PayPal shopping cart will become useless in Chapter 9, where you'll create your own shopping cart.

In Chapter 10, Dealing with Customer Orders, you'll implement the "Place Order" button in the shopping cart, which saves the order into the database and forwards to a PayPal payment page. To call the PayPal payment page (bypassing the PayPal shopping cart), we redirect to a link like the following:

```
https://www.paypal.com/xclick/business=youremail@yourserver.com&item_name=Order#1
23&item_number=123&amount=$123
```

The latest version of the PayPal Single Item Purchases manual can be found at `https://www.paypal.com/en_US/pdf/single_item.pdf`, which includes all the options available for this feature.

 TIP *You will create your own complete order-processing system in the third phase of development (starting with Chapter 12), where you'll process credit card transactions.*

When you implement the PayPal Single Item Purchases in Chapter 10 (just after creating the Place Order button), you'll need to add the following code to `placeOrderButton_Click` in the code-behind file of `ShoppingCart.ascx`:

```vb
Private Sub placeOrderButton_Click(ByVal sender As System.Object, ByVal e As
System.EventArgs) Handles placeOrderButton.Click
        ' We need to store the total amount because the shopping cart
        ' is emptied when creating the order
        Dim amount As Decimal = ShoppingCart.GetTotalAmount()
        ' Create the order and store the order ID
        Dim orderId As String = ShoppingCart.CreateOrder()
        ' This will contain the PayPal request string
        Dim redirect As String
        ' Create the redirect string
        redirect += "https://www.paypal.com/xclick/business=youremail@server.com"
        redirect += "&item_name=JokePoint Order " & orderId
        redirect += "&item_number=" & orderId
        redirect += "&amount=" & String.Format("{0:c}", amount)
        redirect += "&return=http://www.YourWebSite.com"
        redirect += "&cancel_return=http://www.YourWebSite.com"
        ' Load the PayPal payment page
        Response.Redirect(redirect)
    End Sub
```

Of course, don't forget to replace youremail@server.com with your registered PayPal email address, and http://www.YourWebSite.com with the address of your e-commerce store. The return and cancel_return parameters specify the web pages to return to after the payment is made, or canceled. Figure 7.4 shows the PayPal Single Item Purchase screen.

Figure 7-4. The PayPal Single Item Purchase screen

Summary

In this chapter, you saw how to integrate PayPal into an e-commerce site—a simple payment solution that many small businesses choose so they don't have to process credit card or payment information themselves.

First we listed some of the alternatives to PayPal, before we guided you through the creation of a new PayPal account. We then covered how to integrate PayPal in stages 1 and 2 of development, first discussing a shopping cart, a custom checkout mechanism, and then how to direct the visitor directly to the payment page.

In the next chapter, we will move on to look at a catalog administration page for JokePoint.

CHAPTER 8

Catalog Administration

THE FINAL DETAIL TO take care of before launching a web site is to create its administrative interface. Although this is a part visitors will never see, it's still key to delivering a quality web site to your client.

In the previous chapters, you worked with catalog information that already existed in the database. You have probably inserted some records yourself, or maybe you downloaded the department, category, and product information from the Downloads section of the Apress web site. Obviously, for a real web site both ways are unacceptable, so you need to write some code to allow easy management of the web store data.

In this chapter, you'll implement a catalog administration page. With this feature, you complete the first stage of your web site's development!

Because this page can be done in many ways, a serious discussion with the client is required to get the specific list of required features. In our case, the catalog administration page should allow the client to

- Add or remove departments

- Modify existing departments' information (name, description)

- View the list of categories that belong to a department

- Add/remove new categories to/from a department

- Edit existing categories' information (name, description)

- View the list of products in a specific category

- Edit product details

- Assign an existing product to an additional category (a product can belong to multiple categories), or move it to another category

- Remove a product from a category

- Delete a product from the catalog

The administration page also needs to ask for a username and password, so only the site administrators will be allowed to perform administrative tasks.

Preparing to Create the Catalog Administration Page

Although the long list of objectives might look intimidating at first, it will be easy to implement. We have already covered most of the theory in the previous chapters, but you'll still learn a few new bits of information in this chapter.

The first step toward creating the catalog administration page is to create a simple login mechanism.

Next, you build the site administration part of the site by creating its main page and the constituent user controls. There is a single Web Form named admin.aspx that has the structure shown in Figure 8-1.

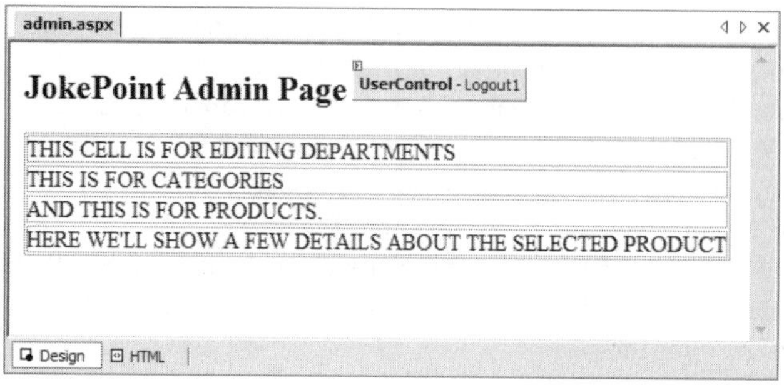

Figure 8-1. Structure of the catalog administration page

The Logout user control near the title displays the logout text. When first loading the administration page, the user is presented with the list of departments, as shown in Figure 8-2.

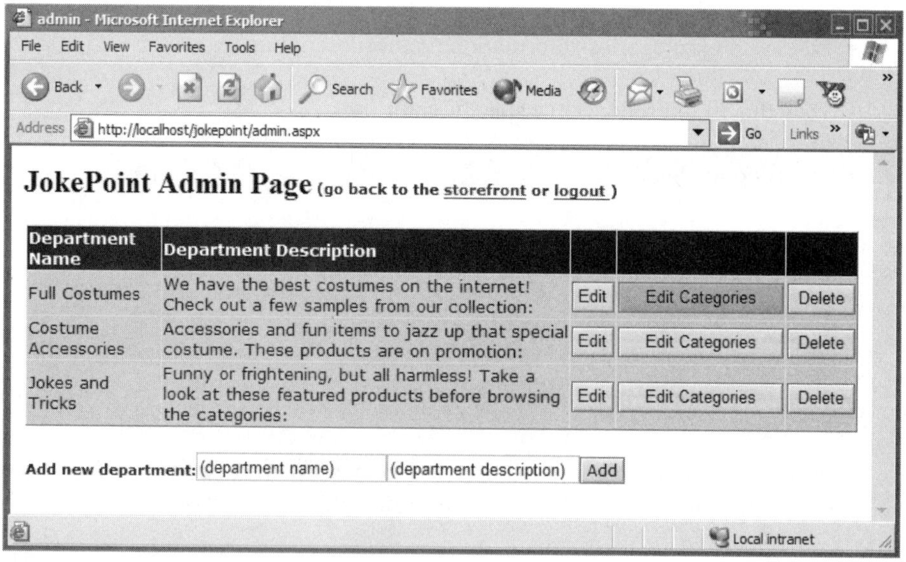

Figure 8-2. Administering departments

TIP *Although this looks like a* DataList *control, it is a* DataGrid. *You'll learn more about this control later, when you create the* DepartmentsAdmin *Web User Control. For now, it's important to know that it allows for easy integration of edit, select, and delete functionality. When the Edit, Edit Categories (Select), or Delete buttons are clicked, events are generated that can be handled in code.*

The functionality you'll implement for departments is much the same you'll see for categories and products. More specifically, the administrator can

- Edit the department's name or description when the user clicks the Edit button.

- Edit the categories for a specific department by clicking the Edit Categories button.

- Completely remove a department from the database by clicking the Delete button (this will work only if the department has no related categories).

When clicking the Edit button, the grid enters edit mode and its fields become editable TextBox controls, as shown in Figure 8-3. Also, as you can see, instead of the Edit button, you get Update and Cancel buttons. Clicking Update results in having the database updated with the changes, while clicking Cancel simply quits edit mode.

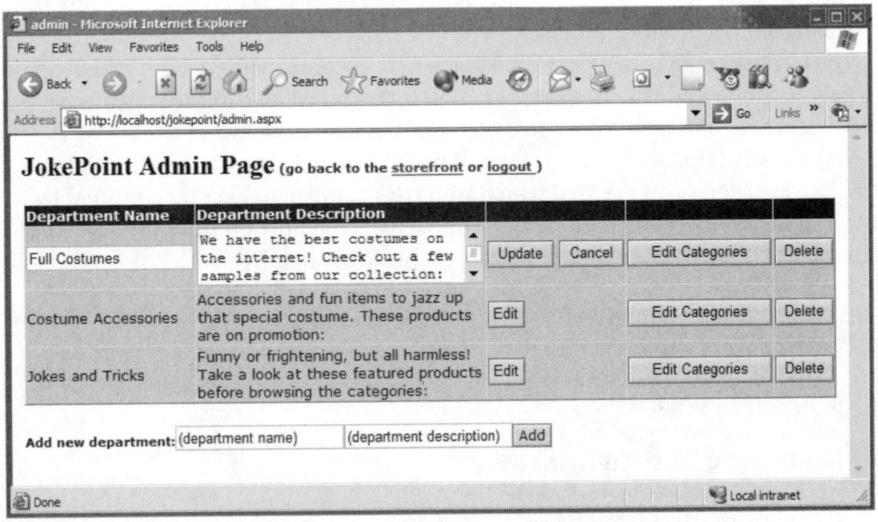

Figure 8-3. Editing department information

The administrator can add new departments by writing the new department's name and description in the TextBox controls below the grid, and clicking the Add button.

When clicking the Edit Categories button, the page is reloaded, but with an additional parameter in the query string: `DepartmentID`. The user is presented with a similar page where he or she can edit the categories that belong to the selected department (see Figure 8-4).

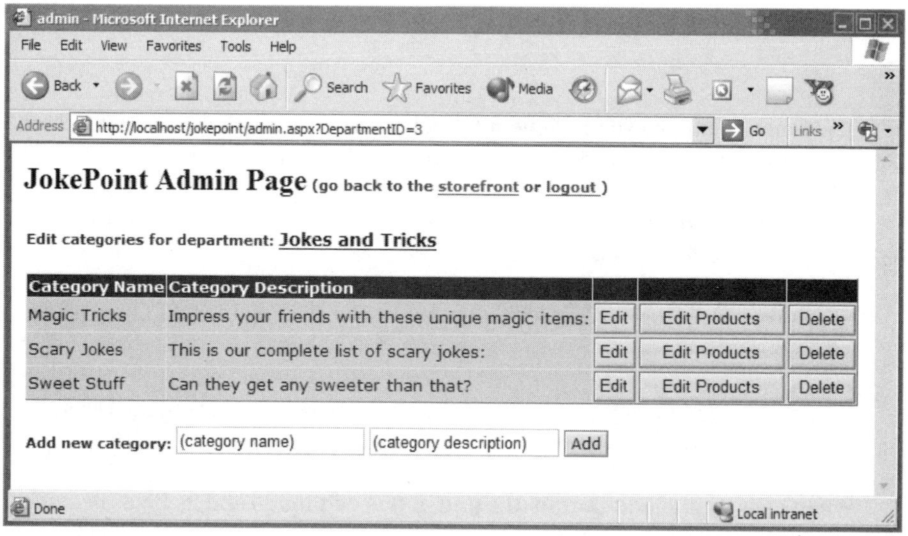

Figure 8-4. Administering categories

This page works similar to the one for editing departments. Here, the name of the currently selected department ("Jokes and Tricks" in this case) becomes a link to the department's administration page.

The navigation logic between the department, category, and product administration pages is done using query string parameters. As you can see in the previous figure, when a department is selected, its `ID` is appended to the query string.

You already implemented this kind of functionality in the code-behind file for `default.aspx`. There, you decided which Web User Control to load (at runtime) by analyzing the query string parameters. Following is the portion from the `Page_Load` method in `default.aspx.vb` that implements this functionality:

```
' Are you on the main web page or browsing the catalog?
If Not searchString Is Nothing Then
  ' you're searching the catalog
  Dim control As Control
  control = Page.LoadControl("UserControls/SearchResults.ascx")
  pageContentsCell.Controls.Add(control)
ElseIf Not departmentId Is Nothing Then
  ' you're visiting a department or category
  Dim control As Control
  control = Page.LoadControl("UserControls/Catalog.ascx")
  pageContentsCell.Controls.Add(control)
Else
  ' you're on the main page
```

```
    Dim control As Control
    control = Page.LoadControl("UserControls/FirstPage.ascx")
    pageContentsCell.Controls.Add(control)
End If
```

For the catalog administration page, you'll implement a different technique: you'll add all the controls at design time (not at runtime), but you'll make the unnecessary ones invisible.

We'll discuss more about admin.aspx and its four user controls later, while you're building them. For now, let's deal with the security measures.

Authenticating Administrators

Because you want only certain persons to access the catalog administration page, you need to implement some sort of security mechanism that controls access to the sensitive pages in the site.

Implementing security implies dealing with two important concepts: **authentication** and **authorization**. Authentication is the process in which users are uniquely identified (most often by supplying a username and password); authorization refers to which resources the authenticated user can access.

Users who want to access the catalog administration page should first *authenticate* themselves. Once you know who they are, you decide whether they are authorized to access the administration page.

In JokePoint, you'll use an authentication method called **Forms authentication**, which allows you to control the login process through a Web Form. After the client is authenticated, ASP.NET automatically generates a cookie on the client, which is used to authenticate all subsequent requests. If the cookie is not found, the client is redirected to the login Web Form.

 TIP *You should know that ASP.NET supports more authentication methods, which are presented in the MSDN article on ASP.NET authentication at* http://msdn.microsoft.com/library/default.asp?url=/ library/en-us/vsent7/html/vxconASPNETAuthentication.asp. *Two other interesting and detailed articles on ASP.NET security are "Building Secure ASP.NET Applications: Authentication, Authorization, and Secure Communication"* (http://msdn.microsoft.com/library/ default.asp?url=/library/en-us/dnnetsec/html/secnetlpMSDN.asp), *and "Improving Web Application Security: Threats and Countermeasures"* (http://msdn.microsoft.com/library/default.asp?url=/library/enus/ dnnetsec/html/ThreatCounter.asp).

The username and password combinations can be physically stored in various ways. For example, in Chapter 12, you'll see how to store hashed (encrypted) customer passwords in the database.

A simpler method is to store the username and password combinations allowed to access various resources directly in the Web.config file. This method isn't as flexible as using the database, but it's fast and easy to implement.

> **TIP** *Hashing is a common method for storing passwords. The hash value of a password is calculated by applying a mathematical function (hash algorithm) to it. When the user tries to authenticate, the password is hashed, and the resulted hash value is compared to the hash value of the original (correct) password. If the two values are identical, then the entered password is the correct one. The essential property about the hash algorithm is that you cannot obtain the original password from its hash value (the algorithm is one-way).*

When storing the username/password combination in Web.config, you can choose to store the password either in clear text, or hashed with one of the two hashing algorithms known by ASP.NET (MD5 or SHA1). To calculate the hash value of a password for storing in web.config, you can use the very intuitively named function FormsAuthentication.HashPasswordForStoringInConfigFile. You can find examples about how to use this function in MSDN and in a number of other articles, such as the ones at http://www.stardeveloper.com/articles/display.html?article=2003062001&page=1 or http://www.c-sharpcorner.com/Code/2003/Feb/HashPassword.asp.

In the following example, you'll simply store the password in clear text, but it's good to know you have other options as well.

Exercise: Implementing a Simple Security Check

1. Double-click Web.config in Solution Explorer, and add the following sections to it. Be aware that the default authentication mode is Windows, and you'll need to change it to Forms:

```
<?xml version="1.0" encoding="utf-8" ?>
<configuration>
  <appSettings>
    <add key="ConnectionString" value="your_connection_string" />
  </appSettings>

  <location path="admin.aspx">
    <system.web>
      <authorization>
        <allow users="admin" />
        <deny users="*" />
      </authorization>
    </system.web>
  </location>
```

```
<system.web>

    <!-- ... various settings here ... -->

    <authentication mode="Forms">
      <forms name="JokePoint"
          loginUrl="login.aspx" path="/" protection="All" timeout="60">
        <credentials passwordFormat="Clear">
          <user name="user" password="user"/>
          <user name="admin" password="admin"/>
        </credentials>
      </forms>
    </authentication>
```

 NOTE *Make sure you have the* <forms> *element on a single line, not split in two lines as shown in the code listing.*

We'll explain these additions in the "How It Works" section. For now, it's enough to know that all users except admin will be denied access to admin.aspx—the administration page you'll write a bit later. Right now, two users are registered: admin (password: admin) and user (password: user).

2. Add the login.aspx form now. Right-click the JokePoint project in Solution Explorer and select Add ➤ Add Web Form. When asked for the form name, type **login** or **login.aspx**.

3. Change the pageLayout property of login.aspx to FlowLayout. Then, add controls to the form, as shown in Figure 8-5.

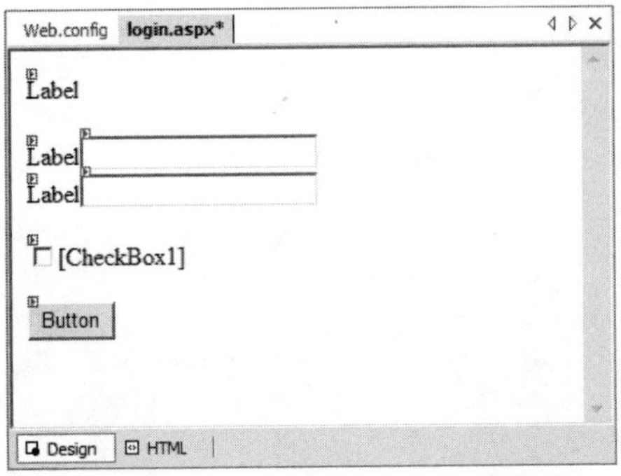

```
Web.config   login.aspx*                          ◁ ▷ ✕
Label

Label
Label

  □ [CheckBox1]

  Button

 ▭ Design   ▣ HTML
```

Figure 8-5. login.aspx *in Design View*

Note that after the Label control you should press Enter, and after the text boxes you should press Shift+Enter.

TIP   *While editing an HTML file in Design View, pressing Shift+Enter generates <BR> tags, and pressing Enter generates <P> paragraph tags.*

4.   Set the properties of each control to the values shown in Table 8-1.

Table 8-1. Setting Controls' Properties in login.aspx

Control Type	ID	Text
Label	loginMessageLabel	(Clear this property)
Label	userNameLabel	User Name:
TextBox	userNameTextBox	
Label	passwordLabel	Password:
TextBox	passwordTextBox	
CheckBox	persistCheckBoxu	Persist Security Info
Button	loginButton	Login

Also, set the TextMode property of passwordTextBox to Password.

After setting these properties, the form will look like Figure 8-6.

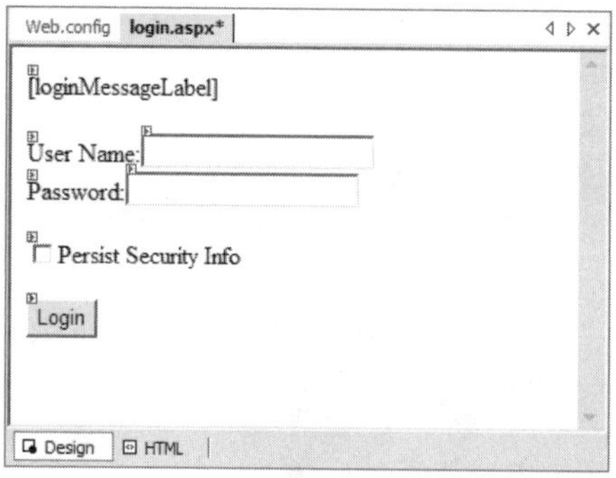

```
Web.config   login.aspx*                           ◁ ▷ ✕
[loginMessageLabel]

User Name:[                    ]
Password:[                    ]

☐ Persist Security Info

[Login]


  🔲 Design   ⊟ HTML
```

Figure 8-6. The form with the control properties set

5.   Now it's time to deal with the code. Switch to the code-behind file, login.aspx.vb, and add this as the first line:

```
Imports System.Web.Security
```

You'll use some classes from this namespace in the login mechanism.

6. Now modify Page_Load to set the welcome text in the first label:

```
Private Sub Page_Load(ByVal sender As System.Object, _
    ByVal e As System.EventArgs) Handles MyBase.Load
  loginMessageLabel.Text = "Hello! Please enter the magic formula:"
End Sub
```

7. Add the code for the button's Click event handler. To have Visual Studio .NET write the signature for you, switch back to Design View and double-click the Button control. Modify the event handler by adding this code:

```
Private Sub loginButton_Click(ByVal sender As System.Object, _
    ByVal e As System.EventArgs) Handles loginButton.Click
  ' Store the entered user name in a variable
  Dim user As String = userNameTextBox.Text
  ' Store the entered password in a variable
  Dim pass As String = passwordTextBox.Text
  ' This variable is True when persistCheckBox is checked
  Dim persist As Boolean = persistCheckBox.Checked
  ' Check if the (user, pass) combination exists
  If FormsAuthentication.Authenticate(user, pass) Then
    ' Attempt to load the originally solicited page using
    ' the supplied credentials
    FormsAuthentication.RedirectFromLoginPage(user, persist)
  End If
End Sub
```

8. Now create the admin.aspx Web Form in the existing solution by right-clicking the project name in Solution Explorer and selecting Add ➤ Add Web Form. Enter **admin.aspx** for the name.

9. Compile the project by pressing Ctrl+Shift+B, and then try to load the admin page by browsing to http://localhost/JokePoint/admin.aspx. Because you aren't authenticated yet, you'll be redirected to the login.aspx page that you created earlier. After entering the correct username-password combination (admin/admin), you'll be forwarded to admin.aspx, the page you initially requested.

How It Works: The Security Mechanism

The mechanism is fairly simple, and uses the Web.config configuration file. As pointed out in previous chapters, a lot of power is hidden behind this file, and you need to read an advanced ASP.NET book to learn about its subtleties.

First, you modified Web.config by adding these lines to it:

```
<location path="admin.aspx">
  <system.web>
    <authorization>
      <allow users="admin" />
```

```
        <deny users="*" />
      </authorization>
    </system.web>
  </location>
```

This sets the authorization options for the admin.aspx file. The user admin is granted access, while all other users are denied:

```
<allow users="admin" />
<deny users="*" />
```

Note that the authorization list is interpreted in sequential order. The following combination would reject all login attempts:

```
<deny users="*" />
<allow users="admin" />
```

The * wildcard is used for "all identities." The other wildcard character, ?, means "anonymous users." If you wanted all anonymous users to be denied, you could have used:

```
<location path="admin.aspx">
  <system.web>
    <authorization>
      <deny users="?" />
    </authorization>
  </system.web>
</location>
```

With this setting, both user and admin identities would be allowed access to the admin page.

TIP   *By default, all visitors are allowed access to all pages, so you need to explicitly deny access to the sensitive pages.*

The other addition to Web.config specifies how to authenticate visitors that try to visit admin.aspx. You specified the Forms authentication mode through the login.aspx login page. You also added the username/password combinations for two users:

```
<authentication mode="Forms">
  <forms name="JokePoint"
    loginUrl="login.aspx" path="/" protection="All" timeout="60">
    <credentials passwordFormat="Clear">
      <user name="user" password="user"/>
      <user name="admin" password="admin"/>
    </credentials>
  </forms>
</authentication>
```

The `passwordFormat` attribute of the `credentials` element specifies the format in which the passwords are stored in the `Web.config` file. In this example, they are stored as clear text, which is a potential security risk (even if `Web.config` is not accessible to visitors).

After adding the security bits to `Web.config`, unauthenticated visitors that try to access `admin.aspx` will be automatically redirected to `login.aspx`. The login form doesn't look extraordinary, but it is functional (see Figure 8-7).

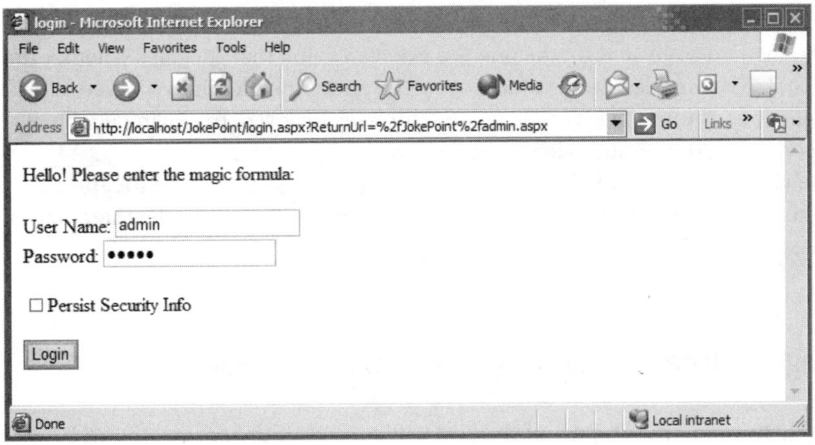

Figure 8-7. The login form

Notice the query string, which looks interesting although we didn't do anything about it. This is part of ASP.NET's security mechanism, and it's designed to make your life easy. If there are more pages that require authentication, the login form doesn't need to change—after the login is successful, you will be redirected to the correct page, the one you tried to access in the first place.

In `login.aspx`, the information supplied by the visitor is verified in the `loginButton_Click` event handler. You used the `FormsAuthentication` class from the `System.Web.Security` namespace to verify whether the username and password combination was valid. As you can see, there are only two lines of code to do the trick:

```
' Store the entered user name in a variable
Dim user As String = userNameTextBox.Text
' Store the entered password in a variable
Dim pass As String = passwordTextBox.Text
' This variable is True when persist CheckBox is checked
Dim persist As Boolean = persistCheckBox.Checked
' Check if the (user, pass) combination exists
If FormsAuthentication.Authenticate(user, pass) Then
    ' Attempt to load the originally solicited page using
    ' the supplied credentials
    FormsAuthentication.RedirectFromLoginPage(user, persist)
End If
```

The FormsAuthentication.Authenticate method simply returns True if the user is authenticated (the user exists and the password is correct), but it doesn't necessarily mean they are authorized to access the solicited page. Remember that with the supplied Web.config data, user is not allowed to access the admin page.

Anyway, if the user is authenticated, you try to redirect them to the solicited page using the FormsAuthentication.RedirectFromLoginPage method. At this stage, the *authorization* check is made—if the user isn't allowed to access the page, the login page gets loaded again. Otherwise, the user is redirected to the originally solicited page.

RedirectFromLoginPage has two parameters: the first represents the user trying to access the secured page, and the second is a Boolean value that specifies whether the security cookie is durable. If that value is True, the authentication info is saved across browser sessions. If the value is False, and the browser is closed, the login page shows up again on the next attempt to load a secured page.

If the visitor accesses the login.aspx page directly, and the authentication is successful, the visitor is then automatically redirected by default to the main page, default.aspx.

Setting Up the Catalog Administration Page

The catalog administration part of the site will consist of the admin.aspx Web Form, and four user controls: DepartmentsAdmin, CategoriesAdmin, ProductsAdmin, and ProductDetailsAdmin. You will build each of these components one at a time. For each one, you'll first implement the presentation layer, then write the business-tier sections, and finally write the stored procedures in the database.

You'll also create an additional user control named Logout.ascx, which contains the logout and go back to the storefront links. You'll reuse this control in other administration pages you'll build in the following chapters.

Exercise: Creating the Logout *Control*

1.   Right-click JokePoint in Solution Explorer, and choose Add ➤ New Folder. Type **AdminUserControls** for the name of the new folder.

> **NOTE**   *The* AdminUserControls *folder will contain all the Web User Controls you create for the administrative pages in JokePoint.*

2.   In Solution Explorer, right-click the AdminUserControls folder and select Add ➤ Add Web User Control. Type **Logout.ascx** for the name and click Open.

3.   In HTML View, add the following code:

```
<font class="AdminPageText">
  (go back to the
  <a href="default.aspx">storefront</a> or
  <asp:LinkButton id="logoutButton" runat="server">logout
  </asp:LinkButton>)
</font>
```

4. While in Design View, double-click the logout LinkButton (which appears as a hyperlink), and modify its Click event handler like this:

```
Private Sub logoutButton_Click(ByVal sender As System.Object, _
               ByVal e As System.EventArgs) Handles logoutButton.Click
  System.Web.Security.FormsAuthentication.SignOut()
  Response.Redirect("default.aspx")
End Sub
```

How It Works: The logout *Control*

That's it! Using a logout control will make your life easier when implementing the same functionality in other administrative pages of the site. The logout button signs out the currently logged in user, forcing the user to log in again when trying to access a secure part of the site (even if on the previous login, he or she checked the Persist Security Info check box).

Let's continue with the serious stuff now.

Exercise: Creating the Skeleton of the Catalog Administration Page

1. You created admin.aspx in the previous exercise, when you implemented the security mechanism. Now add a link to this page in the main web site—this will come in handy in the development stage. Open the FirstPage.ascx Web User Control in HTML View and add this link to it:

```
<font class="FirstPageText">
  <br>
  We hope you have a pleasant experience developing JokePoint,<br>
  <br>
  the virtual novelty store presented in Beginning ASP.NET E-Commerce!
  <br><br>
  Press here for the <a href="admin.aspx">catalog admin page</a>.
</font>
<br><br>
```

2. Open admin.aspx, and change the pageLayout property to FlowLayout.

3. Now open the file in HTML View, and add the following table to the automatically created code:

```
<body>
  <form id="Form1" method="post" runat="server">
    <strong><font size="5">JokePoint Admin Page</font></strong>
    <br><br>
      <table border="0" cellpadding="0">
        <tr>
          <td>
            THIS CELL IS FOR EDITING DEPARTMENTS
          </td>
        </tr>
        <tr>
          <td>
            THIS IS FOR CATEGORIES
          </td>
        <tr>
          <td>
            AND THIS IS FOR PRODUCTS.
          </td>
        </tr>
        <tr>
          <td>
            HERE WE'LL SHOW A FEW DETAILS ABOUT THE SELECTED PRODUCT
          </td>
        </tr>
      </table>
  </form>
</body>
```

4. Switch to Design View. The Form should look like Figure 8-8.

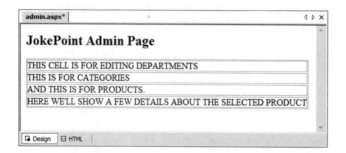

Figure 8-8. admin.aspx *in Design View*

NOTE   *The text in each table cell is just an indication about what will be placed in that cell. You can keep the text for now, but remember to remove it after implementing the user controls that will fill the table cells.*

5.   From Solution Explorer, drag the Logout.ascx control and drop it next to "JokePoint Admin Page," as shown in Figure 8-9.

```
admin.aspx                                              ◁ ▷ ×

JokePoint Admin Page  UserControl - Logout1

THIS CELL IS FOR EDITING DEPARTMENTS
THIS IS FOR CATEGORIES
AND THIS IS FOR PRODUCTS.
HERE WE'LL SHOW A FEW DETAILS ABOUT THE SELECTED PRODUCT


 ⊡ Design   ⊞ HTML
```

Figure 8-9. Adding the Logout.ascx *control*

6.   Now insert a reference to JokePoint.css, and add a few styles to this file to be used in the administration page. Add this line in the <HEAD> section of admin.aspx:

```
<link href="JokePoint.css" type="text/css" rel="stylesheet">
```

7.   Add a new file and a new class to the BusinessObjects folder. You could have used Catalog.vb and the Catalog class, but that one was created specifically for the client functionality. For administering the catalog, apart from it being cleaner to have a separate class, you also get better flexibility (for example, it's easier to place it on a separate machine this way, if you want to) and better performance (because the catalog administration code is loaded just when needed in admin.aspx).

In Solution Explorer, right-click BusinessObjects, and then select Add ➤ Add New Item. In the Templates window, select Class and write CatalogAdmin or CatalogAdmin.vb for the Name.

8.   Modify CatalogAdmin.vb with the following code:

```
Imports System.Data.SqlClient

Public Class CatalogAdmin

    ' Add methods here
```

```
Private Shared ReadOnly Property connectionString() As String
   Get
      Return ConfigurationSettings.AppSettings("ConnectionString")
   End Get
End Property
End Class
```

How It Works: The Catalog Administration Page

You still don't have anything that you can actually test, except for the `logout` link on the main page and the security mechanism that you built at the beginning of the chapter.

Still, you've put down the basic structure that you'll start filling throughout the rest of the chapter. You need to create the four user controls that populate the table in `admin.aspx`.

You've also created the `CatalogAdmin.vb` file, which will be your business object responsible for the catalog administration part of the site. For now, you have only added the `connectionString` property that returns the connection string stored in the `Web.config` file. You've used the same property in `Catalog.vb` in Chapter 3, so you should already know where and how to use it.

Administering Departments

The department administration section will allow our customer to add, remove, or change department information. To implement this functionality, you'll need to write the code for the presentation, business, and data layers. Although so far you've always started with the data tier, in this chapter, the order is reversed.

One fundamental truth regarding *n*-Tiered applications (which also applies to our particular case) is that the business and database tiers are ultimately created to support the presentation tier. Drawing on paper and establishing exactly how you want the site to look (in other words, what functionality needs to be supported by the UI [User Interface]) is a good indication of what the database and business tier will contain.

With the proper design work, you would know exactly what to place in each tier, so the order of writing the code wouldn't matter. When the design is clearly established, a team of programmers can work at the same time and implement the three tiers concurrently, which is one of the benefits of having a tiered architecture.

However, this rarely happens in practice, except for the largest projects that really need very careful design and planning. In our case, usually the best way is to start with the lower levels (the database), to have the basics established before creating the UI. For this to happen, you need to analyze first what functionality is required for the UI, otherwise you won't know what to write in the data and business tiers.

As stated before, in this chapter, we always start with the presentation tier. You can do this because now you have a good overview of the architecture, and know beforehand how you'll implement the other two tiers. This knowledge is necessary because in the presentation tier, you call methods from the business tier (which you haven't created yet), and in the business tier, you call stored procedures from the data tier (which, again, you haven't yet created). If you don't have a clear idea of how to implement the other tiers, starting with the presentation tier can be trickier in the long run.

Because you already have a working architecture, it will be simple to write components as needed for each tier. Of course, if you had to implement something new or more complicated, we would have spent some time analyzing the full implications, but here you won't do anything more complicated than the code in the previous chapters.

You'll apply the same technique for all Web User Controls you'll build in this chapter.

The DepartmentsAdmin *User Control*

Let's take another look at what the DepartmentsAdmin Web User Control looks like in action (see Figure 8-10).

Department Name	Department Description			
Full Costumes	We have the best costumes on the internet! Check out a few samples from our collection:	Edit	Edit Categories	Delete
Costume Accessories	Accessories and fun items to jazz up that special costume. These products are on promotion:	Edit	Edit Categories	Delete
Jokes and Tricks	Funny or frightening, but all harmless! Take a look at these featured products before browsing the categories:	Edit	Edit Categories	Delete

Add new department: (department name)   (department description)   Add

Figure 8-10. The DepartmentsAdmin *Web User Control*

The control is formed from a list populated with the departments' information, and it also has four additional controls (a label, two text boxes and a button) used to add new departments to the list.

The list control you see in Figure 8-10 is not a DataList, but a DataGrid control.

TIP *The* DataGrid *object is more powerful than the* DataList, *but its power comes at the expense of speed. For this reason, when the* DataGrid's *extra features are not used, it's good to stick with the* DataList. *ASP.NET also provides an even simpler and faster object, named* Repeater. *We don't use the* Repeater *object in this book, but you should take a look at its documentation for more information.*

The DataGrid is more powerful than a DataList, and has many more features; in this chapter, we will only use a few of DataGrid's possibilities, particularly the ones that allow for easy integration of Edit, Select, and Delete buttons, and database-bound column editing in Design View. You can see the mentioned controls in Figure 8-10, where the Select button is called Edit Categories.

All that you do here with the DataGrid is also possible to do with a DataList, but using the DataGrid eases your work considerably because of its rich set of built-in features.

You don't have to worry about the performance penalty for using a more complex control, because the administration page will not be frequently accessed, compared to the main web site.

NOTE *If you're worried about the performance, one way to improve things is to move the administration parts of the site to another server. You would need to create another project on the other server to contain the* `admin.aspx` *page, its related user controls, and its supporting business-tier class,* `CatalogAdmin`*. The data tier wouldn't need to change because it's located in the database, which is the same for both visitors and administrators. Alternatively, for improving performance, you can move the whole business tier to another server, by including it in a separate Class Library project. You'll learn in Chapter 12 how to create independent class libraries.*

You'll implement `DepartmentsAdmin.ascx` in the following exercise, and then we'll discuss the details in the "How it Works" section.

Exercise: Implementing `DepartmentsAdmin.ascx`

1. Create a new Web User Control named `DepartmentsAdmin` in the `AdminUserControls` folder.

2. From the toolbox, add a new `DataGrid` control, a `Label` control, two `TextBox` controls, and a `Button` control to the form, as shown in Figure 8-11.

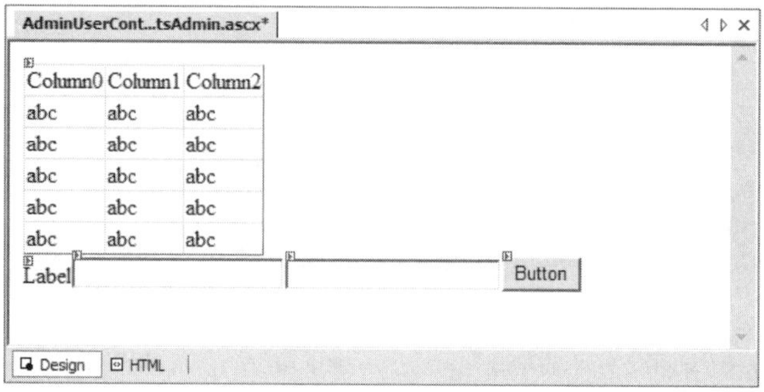

AdminUserCont...tsAdmin.ascx*
Column0 Column1 Column2
abc abc abc
abc abc abc
abc abc abc
abc abc abc
abc abc abc
Label
Button
Design
HTML

Figure 8-11. Adding controls to the form

3. Now, start editing the controls' properties, starting with the `DataGrid`. Set the `ID` of the grid to `departmentsGrid`, and the `Width` property to `100%`.

4. Open the Property Builder of `departmentsGrid`. Right-click the `DataGrid` and select the Property Builder item from the menu shown in Figure 8-12.

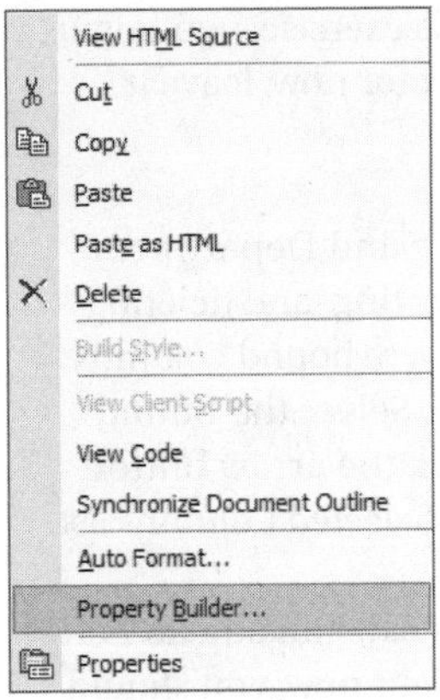

Figure 8-12. Selecting Property Builder from the DataGrid *menu*

Alternatively, when the DataGrid is selected, you can click the Property Builder link at the bottom of the Properties window, as shown in Figure 8-13.

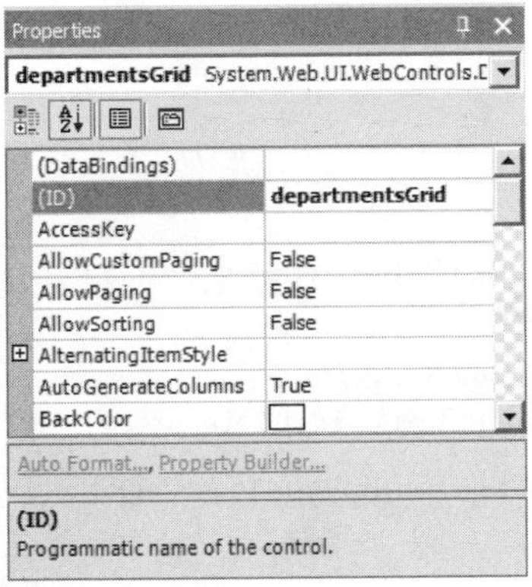

Figure 8-13. The Properties window with the Property Builder *link*

5. The Property Builder window has several tabs that allow you to customize almost anything about the data grid regarding both its functionality and appearance. Right now, you need to specify which columns the data grid will display after being connected to the data source. By default the DataGrid displays all the columns received from the data source, but you need to customize the information presented. In the Property Builder, click the Columns tab in the left side of the window.

6. Deselect the Create Columns Automatically at Runtime check box. This tells the DataGrid that you want to manually specify which columns to display. If you leave this check box checked, when you set a data source for the DataGrid (for example using an SqlDataReader object), it gets all its columns, and then

appends the manually created ones. At the end of this exercise, you might want to experiment with checking this check box, but for now, leave it unchecked.

7. You need to add two columns for Department Name and Department Description, and then three columns for editing, selecting, and deleting rows. Department Name and Department Description are bound columns (they get their values directly from the data source). Select the Bound Column in the Available Columns list, and then click the arrow button twice. This will add two Bound Column records to the Selected Columns list.

8. Expand the Button Column in the Available Columns list, and add an Edit, Update, Cancel field, Select field, and Delete field. Right now, you should have five columns in the Selected Columns list.

9. Set the properties for the five columns as shown in Table 8-2.

Table 8-2. Setting DataGrid's *Field Properties*

Column Type	Header Text	Data Field	Other Properties
Bound Column	Department Name	Name	
Bound Column	Department Description	Description	
Edit, Update, Cancel			Change Button type to PushButton
Select			Change Button type to PushButton; change Text to Edit Categories
Delete			Change Button type to PushButton

The most important field is Data Field, which refers to the database field that will be used to populate this column.

10. To improve the look of the DataGrid a little bit, you can play with the colors. In the left tab of the window, click Format. From the Objects list, select Header, and set the values as shown in Figure 8-14.

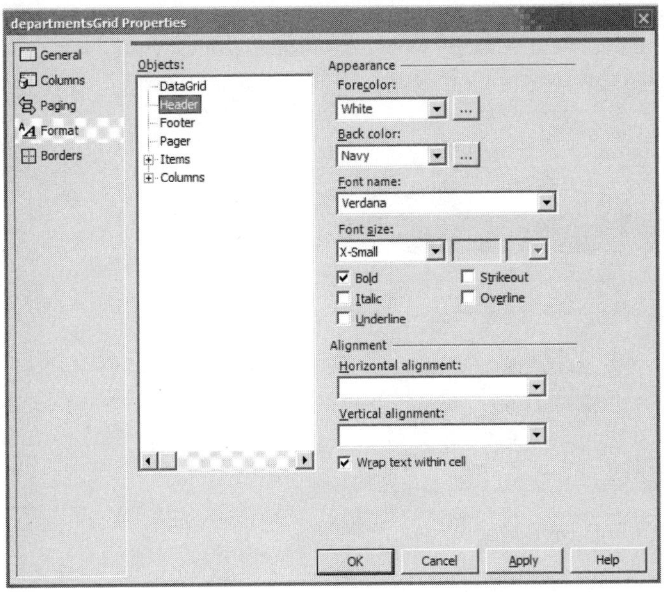

Figure 8-14. Setting DataGrid *properties*

11. Expand the Items category, select Normal Items, and set their properties as shown in Figure 8-15.

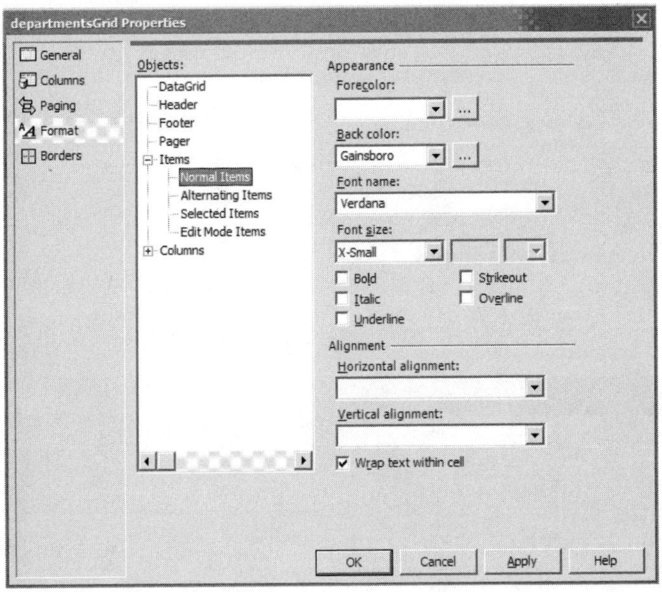

Figure 8-15. Setting DataGrid *properties*

As you can see, you can also change fonts, colors, styles, and alignments, and customize the look of the data grid in many ways. After the changes, your DataGrid should look like Figure 8-16 in Design View.

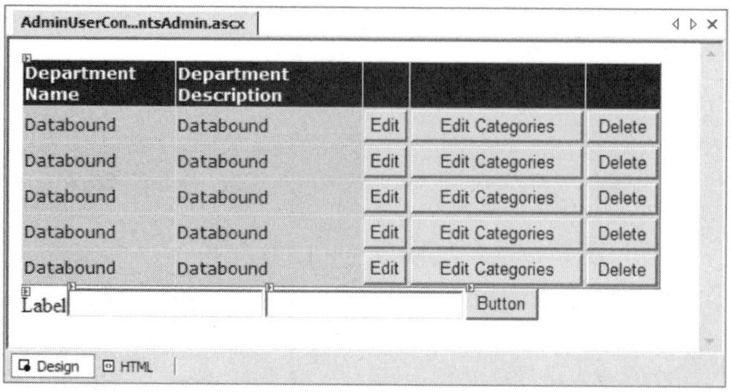

Figure 8-16. The DataGrid *in Design View*

12. Now, change the other controls' properties as described in Table 8-3.

Table 8-3. Setting Controls' Properties in DepartmentsAdmin.ascx

Control Type	ID Property	Text Property	CssClass Property
Label		Add new department:	AdminPageText
TextBox	nameTextBox	(department name)	
TextBox	descriptionTextBox	(department description)	
Button	addDepartmentButton	Add	AdminButtonText

Figure 8-17 shows the new design window.

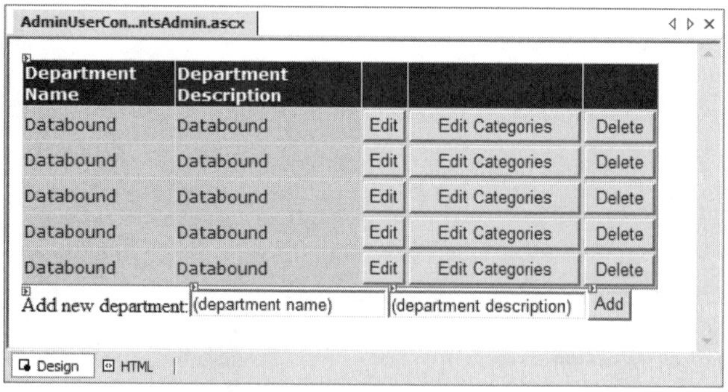

Figure 8-17. The DataGrid *in Design View*

13. Open the `JokePoint.css` file and add these two styles to the file:

```css
.AdminPageText
{
  color: Navy;
  font-family: Verdana, Helvetica, sans-serif;
  text-decoration: none;
  font-size:  11px;
  font-weight: bold;
  line-height: 12px;
}

.AdminButtonText
{
  color: Black;
  font-family: Verdana, Helvetica, sans-serif;
  font-size: 12px;
}
```

You'll see these styles applied when executing the page; right now they don't have any effect because the `JokePoint.css` file is referenced from `default.aspx`, not from the user control.

14. The first step to make the data grid functional is to populate it with data in the `Page_Load` method:

```vb
Private Sub Page_Load(ByVal sender As System.Object, ByVal e As
System.EventArgs) Handles MyBase.Load
    ' Save DepartmentID from the query string to a variable
    Dim departmentId As String = Request.QueryString("DepartmentID")
    ' If no department is selected, this control should be invisible
    If IsNumeric(departmentId) Then
      Me.Visible = False
    ElseIf Not Page.IsPostBack Then
      ' Update the data grid
      BindDepartments()
    End If
End Sub

Private Sub BindDepartments()
    ' Supply the data grid with the list of departments
    departmentsGrid.DataSource = _
                        CatalogAdmin.GetDepartmentsWithDescriptions
    ' The DataKey of each row is the department's ID. We will use this
    ' when we need to get the department ID of a selected data row
    departmentsGrid.DataKeyField = "DepartmentID"
    ' Bind the data grid to the data source
    departmentsGrid.DataBind()
End Sub
```

In BindDepartments, you call a method from CatalogAdmin, named GetDepartmentsWithDescriptions, which hasn't been written yet. Until you implement this method, the line that calls it will be underlined by Visual Studio to mark the problem.

BindDepartments is the method that will be called by all the methods that make changes to the database—it updates the information in the DataGrid control.

15. Next, you need to write the event handlers for the Edit, Edit Categories (Select), and Delete buttons. Visual Studio .NET helps generate the method signatures for these event handlers. First, while editing the code-behind file of DepartmentsAdmin, select the departmentsGrid from the first combo box as shown in Figure 8-18.

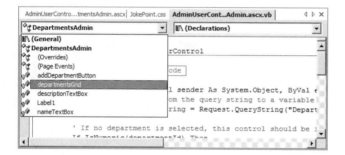

Figure 8-18. Selecting departmentsGrid *from the first combo box*

16. Select the event you want to handle in the second combo box, as shown in Figure 8-19.

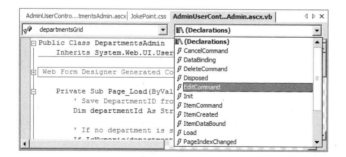

Figure 8-19. Selecting an event to handle in the second combo box

17. After clicking the `EditCommand` event, the method prototype is automatically added to the code. Now modify it like this:

```
Private Sub departmentsGrid_EditCommand(ByVal source As Object, _
ByVal e As System.Web.UI.WebControls.DataGridCommandEventArgs) _
Handles departmentsGrid.EditComman78d
    ' We enter edit mode
    departmentsGrid.EditItemIndex = e.Item.ItemIndex
    ' Update the data grid
    BindDepartments()
End Sub
```

18. When the Edit button is clicked, the grid enters into edit mode, as shown in Figure 8-20 (note that you can't test this yet, because the business and data tiers are not there yet).

Department Name	Department Description				
Full Costumes	We have the best costum	Update	Cancel	Edit Categories	Delete
Costume Accessories	Accessories and fun items to jazz up that special costume. These products are on promotion:	Edit		Edit Categories	Delete
Jokes and Tricks	Funny or frightening, but all harmless! Take a look at these featured products before browsing the categories:	Edit		Edit Categories	Delete

Add new department: (department name) (department description) Add

Figure 8-20. Editing department information

NOTE *The problem with automatically generated editing controls is that they aren't configurable. You'll learn later how to transform the Department Description column into a* **template column**, *which will allow you to customize its look (for example, use a multiline* TextBox *for easier editing).*

19. While in edit mode, instead of the Edit button, the `DataGrid` places two buttons: Update and Cancel. To make editing functional, you need to supply code that reacts when these buttons are clicked. When the Update button is clicked, an `UpdateCommand` event is raised, and when Cancel is clicked, a `CancelCommand` data grid event is generated. Visual Studio .NET can help you generate the method signatures for these events in the same fashion as with the `EditCommand` event, in the previous step. Now add the following code for these two events:

```
Private Sub _
departmentsGrid_UpdateCommand(ByVal source As System.Object, _
ByVal e As System.Web.UI.WebControls.DataGridCommandEventArgs) _
Handles departmentsGrid.UpdateCommand
  Dim departmentId As String
  Dim departmentName As String
  Dim departmentDescription As String
  ' DepartmentID is the DataKey field (set in BindDepartments)
  departmentId = departmentsGrid.DataKeys(e.Item.ItemIndex)
  ' We get the department name from the data grid
  departmentName = CType(e.Item.Cells(0).Controls(0), TextBox).Text
  ' We get the department description from the data grid
  departmentDescription = _
                    CType(e.Item.Cells(1).Controls(0), TextBox).Text
  ' Pass the values to the business tier to update department info
  CatalogAdmin.UpdateDepartment( _
        departmentId, departmentName, departmentDescription)
  ' Cancel edit mode
  departmentsGrid.EditItemIndex = -1
  ' Update the data grid
  BindDepartments()
End Sub

Private Sub departmentsGrid_CancelCommand(ByVal source As Object, _
ByVal e As System.Web.UI.WebControls.DataGridCommandEventArgs) _
Handles departmentsGrid.CancelCommand
  ' Cancel edit mode
  departmentsGrid.EditItemIndex = -1
  ' Update the data grid
  BindDepartments()
End Sub
```

20. Now, add the code that reacts to the Edit Categories button. In fact, this is a Select button that, when clicked, triggers the SelectedIndexChanged event. Use Visual Studio .NET to add the signature for this event handler, and then add the highlighted code.

 TIP SelectedIndexChanged *is the default event for* DataGrid; *its signature can be generated by double clicking* DataGrid *in the Design View window.*

```
Private Sub departmentsGrid_SelectedIndexChanged(ByVal sender As _
Object, ByVal e As System.EventArgs) _
Handles departmentsGrid.SelectedIndexChanged
  Dim departmentId As String
  ' DepartmentID is the DataKey field (set in BindDepartments)
  departmentId = _
            departmentsGrid.DataKeys(departmentsGrid.SelectedIndex)
  ' We reload the page with a DepartmentID parameter in the query string
  Response.Redirect("admin.aspx?DepartmentID=" & departmentId)
End Sub
```

21. Finally, here's the code for the DeleteCommand event handler. Let Visual Studio generate its signature for you, and then add the following code:

```
Private Sub departmentsGrid_DeleteCommand(ByVal source As Object, _
ByVal e As System.Web.UI.WebControls.DataGridCommandEventArgs) _
Handles departmentsGrid.DeleteCommand
  Dim departmentId As String
  ' DepartmentId is the DataKey field (set in BindDepartments)
  departmentId = departmentsGrid.DataKeys(e.Item.ItemIndex)
  ' We try to delete the department, but if it has related categories the
  ' database will generate an exception because this would violate its
  ' integrity
  Try
    CatalogAdmin.DeleteDepartment(departmentId)
    ' Update the data grid
    BindDepartments()
  Catch ex As Exception
    ' Here you can show an error message specifying the department
    ' can't be deleted. At the moment we simply redisplay the grid
    ' Update the data grid
    BindDepartments()
  End Try
End Sub
```

22. The last bit of code to write in this exercise consists of adding the addDepartmentButton_Click event handler method. Generate its signature by double-clicking the Add button in the Design View window.

```
Private Sub addDepartmentButton_Click(ByVal sender As System.Object, _
ByVal e As System.EventArgs) Handles addDepartmentButton.Click
  ' Add the new department to the database
  CatalogAdmin.AddDepartment(nameTextBox.Text,descriptionTextBox.Text)
  ' Update the data grid
  BindDepartments()
End Sub
```

TIP   *The presentation tier should do input validation when possible—for example, you can check whether the department name and description are valid before trying to add them to the database. Later in this chapter, you'll learn how to implement validation using the .NET validator controls.*

23. Finally, open `admin.aspx` in Design View, and drag and drop `DepartmentsAdmin.ascx` from Solution Explorer to the first cell in the table, as shown in Figure 8-21.

```
admin.aspx*                                                    ◁ ▷ ×

JokePoint Admin Page  UserControl - Logout1

  UserControl - DepartmentsAdmin1
  THIS IS FOR CATEGORIES
  AND THIS IS FOR PRODUCTS.
  HERE WE'LL SHOW A FEW DETAILS ABOUT THE SELECTED PRODUCT


  ⬚ Design   ⊞ HTML
```

Figure 8-21. Dragging `DepartmentsAdmin.ascx` *to the first cell in the table*

How It Works: `DepartmentsAdmin.ascx`

You wrote a lot of code in this exercise, and you still can't test anything. This is the tough part when creating the UI first.

Still, the code is not that complicated if you look at it. It's mostly about working with the `DataGrid` control. For example, to enter a row into edit mode, you just need to set the `DataGrid`'s `EditItemIndex` property to the index of the column you want to change in the `EditCommand` event handler method:

```
Private Sub departmentsGrid_EditCommand(ByVal source As Object, _
    ByVal e As System.Web.UI.WebControls.DataGridCommandEventArgs) _
    Handles departmentsGrid.EditCommand
  ' We enter edit mode
  departmentsGrid.EditItemIndex = e.Item.ItemIndex
  ' Update the data grid
  BindDepartments()
End Sub
```

The `EditCommand` event handler receives a `DataGridCommandEventArgs` object named e, which contains, among other details, the index of the row on which the Edit button was clicked (`e.Item.ItemIndex`). You use this value to inform the DataGrid to enter in edit mode for that row.

You take similar action in the `CancelCommand` event handler, where you cancel edit mode by setting `EditItemIndex` to `-1`:

```
Private Sub departmentsGrid_CancelCommand(ByVal source As Object, _
    ByVal e As System.Web.UI.WebControls.DataGridCommandEventArgs) _
    Handles departmentsGrid.CancelCommand
  ' Cancel edit mode
  departmentsGrid.EditItemIndex = -1
  ' Update the data grid
  BindDepartments()
End Sub
```

The way these two event handlers work is fairly standard.

The methods that modify data (the event handlers for the Update and Delete buttons) need to read information from the data grid, and more. Let me explain.

The "and more" bit refers to the ID of the item on which the action happens. For example, when the user wants to delete or update a department, you need to obtain somehow the ID of the department. This is necessary because all database operations are based on IDs. The problem is that you can't extract DepartmentID from the DataGrid, because it wasn't included in the data grid (it is a low-level detail, useless for the user). So, how do you know the ID associated with a DataGrid row? Fortunately, the designers of the DataGrid control anticipated this problem and added a DataKeys property to the DataGrid, which holds a key for each row in the grid.

The mechanism works like this: when binding the DataGrid to the data source, you specify a DataKeyField in BindDepartments:

```
Private Sub BindDepartments()
  ' Supply the data grid with the list of departments
  departmentsGrid.DataSource = _
                        CatalogAdmin.GetDepartmentsWithDescriptions
  ' The DataKey of each row is the department's ID. We will use this
  ' when we need to get the department ID of a selected data row
  departmentsGrid.DataKeyField = "DepartmentID"
  ' Bind the data grid to the data source
  departmentsGrid.DataBind()
End Sub
```

The highlighted line tells the DataGrid that it should read the DepartmentID for each row and save it as the DataKey for the specified row. This make it very easy to obtain the ID associated with a particular row:

```
' DepartmentID is the DataKey field (set in BindDepartments)
departmentId = departmentsGrid.DataKeys(e.Item.ItemIndex)
```

When updating a department, you also need to read the updated values from the data grid. The code that reads the Department Name and Department Description text boxes into two String variables is shown here:

```
' We get the department name from the data grid
departmentName = CType(e.Item.Cells(0).Controls(0), TextBox).Text
' We get the department description from the data grid
departmentDescription = CType(e.Item.Cells(1).Controls(0), TextBox).Text
```

The DataGrid is very powerful, and has the capability to hold any kind of data in each of its cells. If you want, you can make a column being edited contain more controls, not just a TextBox.

Because a DataGrid cell can contain multiple objects, you must be specific about which object you're interested in. For example, to get the name of the department, you read the first cell of the row, e.Item.Cells(0), and get the first control from the cell, e.Item.Cells(0).Controls(0). You know for sure that the text box is the first control, because it's the only control.

Note that the first control of that cell could be any kind of control, so before reading its Text property, you need to manually convert it to a TextBox. This can be done using the CType method, which takes two parameters: the object to be converted and the destination type, and returns the object converted to the desired type. After getting a reference to the TextBox object, you read its Text property.

Let's review again the line that reads the department name:

```
departmentName = CType(e.Item.Cells(0).Controls(0), TextBox).Text
```

To make the functionality even clearer, take a look at the following code block, which performs exactly the same functionality:

```
' Get an entire row from the grid
Dim dataGridItem As DataGridItem
dataGridItem = e.Item
' Get the first cell (one which contains the name)
Dim tableCell As TableCell
tableCell = dataGridItem.Cells(0)
' Get the first control in the cell
Dim control As Control
control = tableCell.Controls(0)
' Access the control through a TextBox reference
Dim textBox As TextBox
textBox = CType(control, TextBox)
' Get the text from the TextBox
Dim departmentName As String
departmentName = textBox.Text
```

After finding the department ID, name, and description, you call CatalogAdmin.UpdateDepartment, which takes care of updating catalog information:

```
' Pass the values to the business tier to update department info
CatalogAdmin.UpdateDepartment( _
        departmentId, departmentName, departmentDescription)
' Cancel edit mode
departmentsGrid.EditItemIndex = -1
' Update the data grid
BindDepartments()
```

Of course, right now CatalogAdmin is empty and there is no UpdateDepartment class, but you'll to write it in the next exercise. We knew how to call the method even though it hasn't been written yet because we anticipate that it will have the three mentioned parameters.

The final piece of code to consider here is the SelectedIndexChanged event handler, which happens when the Edit Categories button is clicked in the data grid. You redirect to admin.aspx, adding the selected department's ID to the query string. With the new element in the query string, the admin page will know to display the list of categories in the selected department, instead of the list of departments.

```
Dim departmentId As String
' DepartmentID is the DataKey field (set in BindDepartments)
departmentId = _
            departmentsGrid.DataKeys(departmentsGrid.SelectedIndex)
' We reload the page with a DepartmentID parameter in the query string
Response.Redirect("admin.aspx?DepartmentID=" & departmentId)
```

Middle-Tier Methods for Departments Administration

You called four middle-tier methods from DepartmentsAdmin:

- GetDepartmentsWithDescriptions

- UpdateDepartment

- DeleteDepartments

- AddDepartment

GetDepartmentsWithDescriptions is called from BindDepartments to populate the data grid with a list of departments:

```
' Sub: BindDepartments
' Supply the data grid with the list of departments
departmentsGrid.DataSource = CatalogAdmin.GetDepartmentsWithDescriptions
```

UpdateDepartment changes a department's data. Its parameters are the department ID, its new name, and its new description.

```
' Sub: departmentsGrid_UpdateCommand
' Pass the values to the business tier to update department info
CatalogAdmin.UpdateDepartment( _
   departmentId, departmentName, departmentDescription)
```

When deleting a department, you simply need to supply a department ID to DeleteDepartment:

```
' Sub: departmentsGrid_DeleteCommand
CatalogAdmin.DeleteDepartment(departmentId)
```

Finally, when adding a new department, you call AddDepartment. This needs the name and description for the new department, because the ID will be automatically generated by the database (the DepartmentID column in the Department table is an IDENTITY column). You might want to take another look at the section about identity columns in Chapter 3.

```
' Sub: addDepartmentButton_Click
' Add the new department to the database
CatalogAdmin.AddDepartment(nameTextBox.Text, descriptionTextBox.Text)
```

You'll include these methods in a #Region section (which ends with #End Region) named Departments. #Region isn't part of the Visual Basic language, but a feature of Visual Studio .NET that lets you group a number of methods. These methods can be shrunk or expanded like any other method in Visual Studio .NET (see Figure 8-22).

```
BusinessObjec...atalogAdmin.vb                                    ◁ ▷ ×
Ⅱ\ (General)                        ▼  Ⅱ\ (Declarations)           ▼
    Imports System.Data.SqlClient                                    ▲
⊟ Public Class CatalogAdmin

⊞    Departments

⊟       Private Shared ReadOnly Property connectionString() As String
⊟          Get
                Return ConfigurationSettings.AppSettings("ConnectionString")
            End Get
        End Property
└ End Class
```

Figure 8-22. Using code regions in Visual Studio .NET

Exercise: Adding the Methods

Now it's time to implement each one of the methods. Add this code to the CatalogAdmin class in CatalogAdmin.vb:

```
Imports System.Data.SqlClient

Public Class CatalogAdmin

#Region " Departments "
  Public Shared Function GetDepartmentsWithDescriptions() As SqlDataReader
    ' Create the connection object
    Dim connection As New SqlConnection(connectionString)
    ' Create and initialize the command object
    Dim command As New SqlCommand("GetDepartmentsWithDescriptions", connection)
    command.CommandType = CommandType.StoredProcedure
    Try
      ' Open the connection
      connection.Open()
```

```
      ' Return an SqlDataReader to the calling function
      Return command.ExecuteReader(CommandBehavior.CloseConnection)
    Catch e As Exception
      ' Close the connection and throw the exception
      connection.Close()
      Throw e
    End Try
End Function

Public Shared Function UpdateDepartment(ByVal departmentId As String, _
    ByVal departmentName As String, ByVal departmentDescription As String)
    ' Create the connection object
    Dim connection As New SqlConnection(connectionString)
    ' Create and initialize the command object
    Dim command As New SqlCommand("UpdateDepartment", connection)
    command.CommandType = CommandType.StoredProcedure
    ' Add an input parameter and supply a value for it
    command.Parameters.Add("@DepartmentID", SqlDbType.Int)
    command.Parameters("@DepartmentID").Value = departmentId
    ' Add an input parameter and supply a value for it
    command.Parameters.Add("@DepartmentName", SqlDbType.VarChar, 50)
    command.Parameters("@DepartmentName").Value = departmentName
    ' Add an input parameter and supply a value for it
    command.Parameters.Add("@DepartmentDescription", SqlDbType.VarChar, 200)
    command.Parameters("@DepartmentDescription").Value = departmentDescription
    ' Open the connection, execute the command, and close the connection
    Try
      connection.Open()
      command.ExecuteNonQuery()
    Finally
      connection.Close()
    End Try
End Function

Public Shared Function DeleteDepartment(ByVal departmentId As String)
    ' Create the connection object
    Dim connection As New SqlConnection(connectionString)
    ' Create and initialize the command object
    Dim command As New SqlCommand("DeleteDepartment", connection)
    command.CommandType = CommandType.StoredProcedure
    ' Add an input parameter and supply a value for it
    command.Parameters.Add("@DepartmentID", SqlDbType.Int)
    command.Parameters("@DepartmentID").Value = departmentId
    ' Open the connection, execute the command, and close the connection
    Try
      connection.Open()
      command.ExecuteNonQuery()
    Finally
      connection.Close()
    End Try
End Function
```

```
  Public Shared Function AddDepartment(ByVal departmentName As String, _
                                  ByVal departmentDescription As String)
    ' Create the connection object
    Dim connection As New SqlConnection(connectionString)
    ' Create and initialize the command object
    Dim command As New SqlCommand("AddDepartment", connection)
    command.CommandType = CommandType.StoredProcedure
    ' Add an input parameter and supply a value for it
    command.Parameters.Add("@DepartmentName", SqlDbType.VarChar, 50)
    command.Parameters("@DepartmentName").Value = departmentName
    ' Add an input parameter and supply a value for it
    command.Parameters.Add("@DepartmentDescription", SqlDbType.VarChar, 200)
    command.Parameters("@DepartmentDescription").Value = departmentDescription
    ' Open the connection, execute the command, and close the connection
    Try
      connection.Open()
      command.ExecuteNonQuery()
    Finally
      connection.Close()
    End Try
  End Function
#End Region

  Private Shared ReadOnly Property connectionString() As String
    Get
      Return ConfigurationSettings.AppSettings("ConnectionString")
    End Get
  End Property
End Class
```

How It Works: The Middle-Tier Methods

From other chapters, you already know what these methods do; the interesting part is to see how the data-tier logic is implemented in the stored procedures.

Stored Procedures for Departments Administration

Four stored procedures perform the four basic tasks for departments: retrieve departments, update departments, delete departments, and insert departments. These stored procedures are called from the business-tier methods you just added.

GetDepartmentsWithDescriptions

GetDepartmentsWithDescriptions is the simplest stored procedure you'll implement here. It returns the complete list of departments with their identities, names, and descriptions. This is similar to the GetDepartments stored procedure called to fill the departments list from the storefront, but this one also returns the descriptions.

```
CREATE PROCEDURE GetDepartmentsWithDescriptions AS

SELECT DepartmentID, Name, Description FROM Department

RETURN
```

UpdateDepartment

The UpdateDepartment stored procedure updates the name and description of an existing department using the UPDATE SQL statement:

```
CREATE PROCEDURE UpdateDepartment
(@DepartmentID int,
@DepartmentName varchar(50),
@DepartmentDescription varchar(1000))
AS

UPDATE Department
SET Name = @DepartmentName, Description = @DepartmentDescription
WHERE DepartmentID = @DepartmentID

RETURN
```

DeleteDepartment

DeleteDepartment deletes an existing department from the database:

```
CREATE PROCEDURE DeleteDepartment
(@DepartmentID int)
AS

DELETE FROM Department
WHERE DepartmentID = @DepartmentID

RETURN
```

AddDepartment

AddDepartment inserts a new department into the database:

```
CREATE PROCEDURE AddDepartment
(@DepartmentName varchar(50),
@DepartmentDescription varchar(1000))
AS

INSERT INTO Department ([Name], [Description])
VALUES (@DepartmentName, @DepartmentDescription)

RETURN
```

Testing the DepartmentsAdmin Web User Control

You've added a lot of code, and now finally everything is put together and ready to execute. Run the solution using either the Start button or F5. If you prefer to load the project directly in a web browser, be sure to compile the project first (Ctrl+Shift+B).

After supplying the admin credentials (admin as both username and password in this case), you are allowed to see the catalog administration page, shown in Figure 8-23.

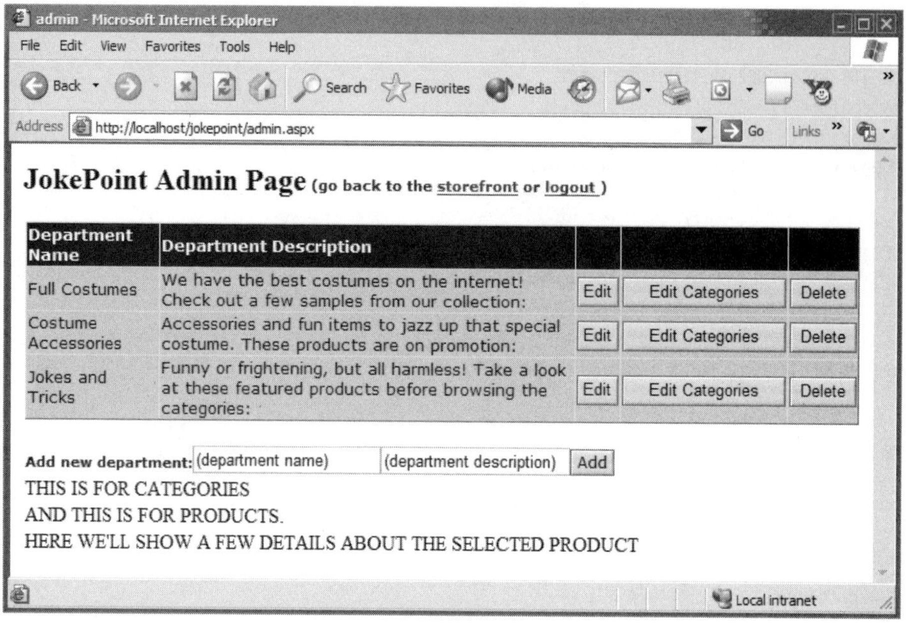

Figure 8-23. The catalog administration page

All the functionality regarding department administration works fine, except the Edit Categories link. When this link is clicked, the page is reloaded with a DepartmentID parameter in the query string; you'll deal with this parameter in the next section. For now, test adding, editing, and deleting departments to see the buttons work as advertised.

Customizing the DataGrid *with* Template *Columns*

It was so easy to implement the editable DataGrid! You configured the DataGrid in the Design View window, and Visual Studio generated the following five DataGrid columns in DepartmentsAdmin.ascx:

```
<Columns>
  <asp:BoundColumn DataField="Name" HeaderText="Department Name">
  </asp:BoundColumn>
  <asp:BoundColumn DataField="Description" HeaderText="Department Description">
  </asp:BoundColumn>
  <asp:EditCommandColumn ButtonType="PushButton" UpdateText="Update"
                 CancelText="Cancel" EditText="Edit"></asp:EditCommandColumn>
  <asp:ButtonColumn Text="Edit Categories" ButtonType="PushButton"
                 CommandName="Select"></asp:ButtonColumn>
  <asp:ButtonColumn Text="Delete" ButtonType="PushButton"
                 CommandName="Delete"></asp:ButtonColumn>
</Columns>
```

The interesting aspect is that you can't see any Label or TextBox controls, even though DataGrid generates them when showing its data, or when entering edit mode. The BoundColumn, EditCommandColumn, and ButtonColumn fields take care of rendering themselves without your intervention. Take a close look at the HTML code in DepartmentsAdmin.ascx, and observe the data you entered in the Property Builder window.

The problem with these automated controls is that you don't have much flexibility with how they show their data. Although you can use the Format tab in DataGrid's Property Builder to set styles, fonts, and colors for various elements of the DataGrid, it's still impossible to customize the controls generated for displaying data, or to use other controls (for example, a CheckBox for True/False columns).

The way to fully customize any column of the DataGrid is to transform it into a **template column**. When using template columns, you need to manually supply the HTML code for its various display templates. You'll do that in the following exercise, where you'll implement a MultiLine TextBox for editing the department description.

Exercise: Implementing a Template Column

1. Edit the DataGrid's properties once again using Property Builder. Select the Department Description field, shown in Figure 8-24.

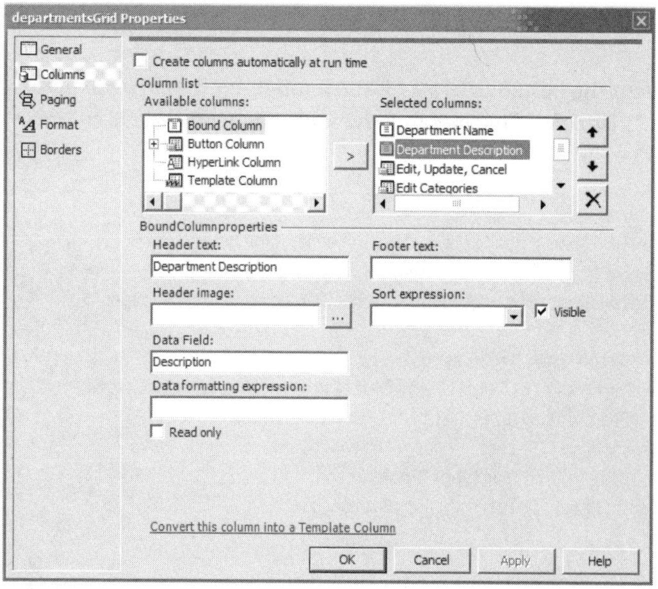

Figure 8-24. Selecting the Department Description field

2. Click the `Convert this column into a Template Column` link. Because the `DataGrid` no longer takes care of these details (you're supposed to manually supply them in the templates), the Data Field, Data Formatting Expression, and Read Only options disappear, as shown in Figure 8-25.

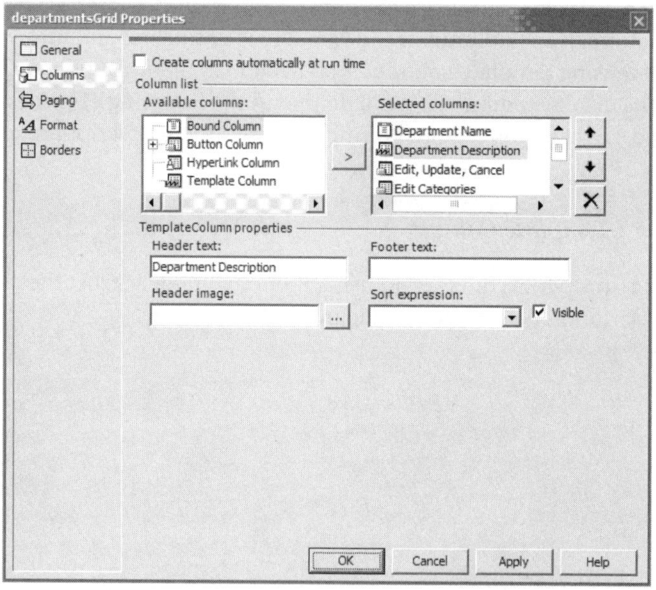

Figure 8-25. Working with template columns in Property Builder

3. Visual Studio was smart enough to generate the `ItemTemplate` and `EditItem-Template` for the Department Description column to preserve the existing functionality. However, now you have access to the `Label` that displays text in view mode, and to the `TextBox` used to edit the column in edit mode:

```
<asp:TemplateColumn HeaderText="Department Description">
  <ItemTemplate>
    <asp:Label id=Label2 runat="server"
      Text='<%# DataBinder.Eval(Container, "DataItem.Description") %>'>
    </asp:Label>
  </ItemTemplate>
  <EditItemTemplate>
    <asp:TextBox id=TextBox1 runat="server"
      Text='<%# DataBinder.Eval(Container, "DataItem.Description") %>'>
    </asp:TextBox>
  </EditItemTemplate>
</asp:TemplateColumn>
```

4. The goal is to enlarge the `TextBox` used for editing, and make it `MultiLine`. Visual Studio even allows you to perform these changes in Design View: right-click the `DataGrid`, and select Edit Template ➤ Columns[1] - Department Description (see Figure 8-26).

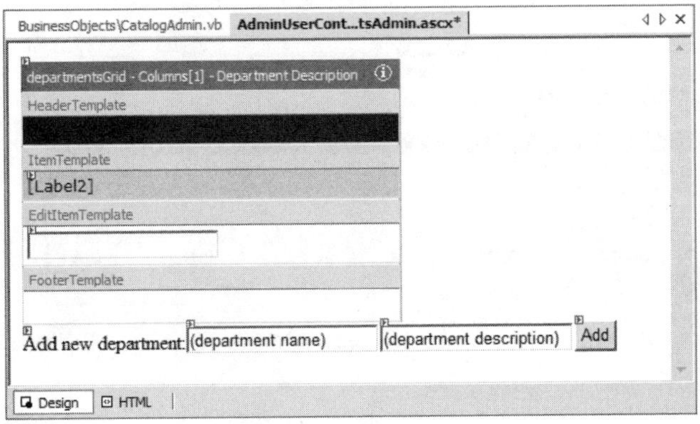

Figure 8-26. Using Design View to modify the Edit Template

5. Select the `TextBox` of the `EditItemTemplate`, set its `ID` to `editDescriptionTextBox`, `TextMode` to `MultiLine`, `Rows` to 3, and `Width` to 100% (see Figure 8-27).

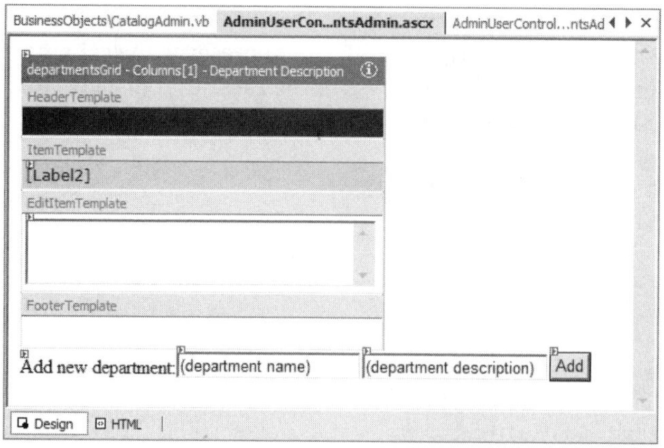

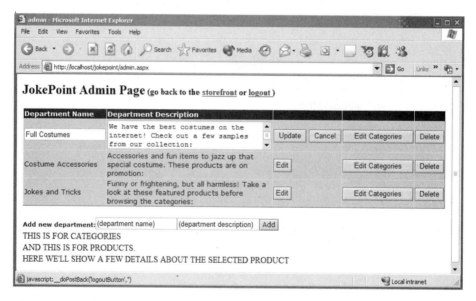

Figure 8-27. Using Design View to modify the Edit Template

6. You can end editing by right-clicking the grid and selecting End Template Editing. After you save the file and reload the project, you should have a nice surprise when editing a department (see Figure 8-28).

Figure 8-28. Editing a department

7. In the code-behind file, you need to modify the way the new TextBox is located in the DataGrid (this is something that happens only when updating a department). Locate this line in departmentsGrid_UpdateCommand:

```
departmentDescription= CType(e.Item.Cells(1).Controls(0), TextBox).Text
```

Change it to

```
departmentDescription = _
        CType(e.Item.FindControl("editDescriptionTextBox"), TextBox).Text
```

How It Works: Using Template Columns with the DataGrid Control

Execute the project and test the updated functionality to ensure it works as explained. Template columns are useful because they allow you to control how each DataGrid column looks. In this exercise, you modified the TextBox used for editing the department description, but now you can use the same technique to change any field in the table.

You'll see some other examples of template columns later in this chapter, when we'll use CheckBox controls instead of Labels and TextBoxes for displaying the value of True/False fields.

Administering Categories

The category administration bits are quite similar compared to what you did for departments, so we won't have too much explanation this time.

The main player in the whole categories administration part is the CategoriesAdmin user control. When you click Edit Categories in the Jokes and Tricks department, CategoriesAdmin will look like Figure 8-29.

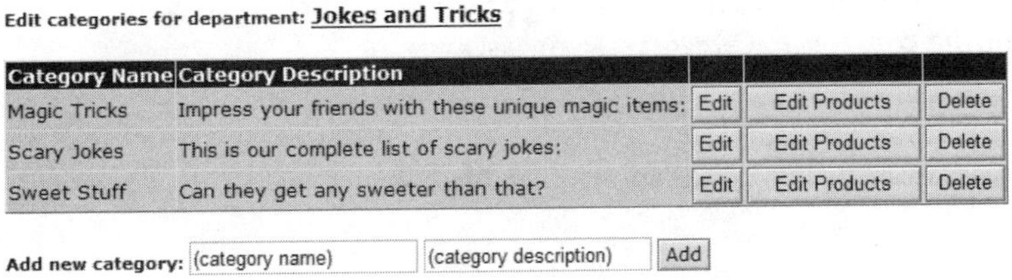

Edit categories for department: Jokes and Tricks

Category Name	Category Description			
Magic Tricks	Impress your friends with these unique magic items:	Edit	Edit Products	Delete
Scary Jokes	This is our complete list of scary jokes:	Edit	Edit Products	Delete
Sweet Stuff	Can they get any sweeter than that?	Edit	Edit Products	Delete

Add new category: (category name) (category description) Add

Figure 8-29. Editing categories

You'll add the CategoriesAdmin user control to admin.aspx at design time, so it will always get loaded, not only when the DepartmentID parameter is present in the query string. However, you'll make it invisible if DepartmentID is not present, or if it has an invalid value.

DepartmentID is added to the query string in the SelectedIndexChanged event of the departmentsGrid (which is triggered when an Edit Categories button is clicked), in DepartmentsAdmin.ascx.vb:

```
Response.Redirect("admin.aspx?DepartmentID=" & departmentId)
```

The CategoriesAdmin Web User Control

The steps here are similar to what you know from the DepartmentsAdmin control.

Exercise: Implementing CategoriesAdmin.ascx

1. Create a new Web User Control named CategoriesAdmin.ascx in the AdminUserControls folder.

2. From the toolbox, add a new Label control, LinkButton, DataGrid control, another Label control, two TextBox controls, and a Button control to the form, as shown in Figure 8-30.

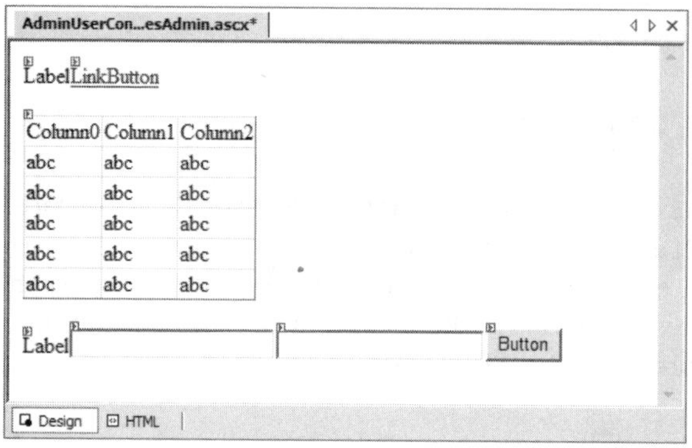

Figure 8-30. Adding controls to CategoriesAdmin.ascx

3. Set the controls' properties as shown in Table 8-4.

Table 8-4. Setting Controls' Properties in CategoriesAdmin.ascx

Control Type	ID **Property**	Text **Property**	CssClass **Property**
Label		Edit categories for department:	AdminPageText
LinkButton	departmentNameLink	*(should be empty)*	ListDescription
DataGrid	categoriesGrid		
Label		Add new category:	AdminPageText
TextBox	nameTextBox	(category name)	
TextBox	descriptionTextBox	(category description)	
Button	addCategoryButton	Add	AdminButtonText

4. Now, set up the properties for the data grid. First, set its Width property to 100%.

5. Open the Property Builder form of the data grid and select the Columns tab. Uncheck the Create Columns Automatically at Runtime check box. Add two Bound Column fields, and then add Edit, Update, Cancel, Select, and Delete fields to the Selected Columns list. Set their properties as shown in Table 8.5.

Table 8-5. Setting DataGrid's *Column Properties*

Column Type	Header Text	Data Field	Other Properties
Bound Column	Category Name	Name	
Bound Column	Category Description	Description	
Edit, Update, Cancel			Change Button type to PushButton
Select			Change Button type to PushButton; change Text to Edit Products
Delete			Change Button type to PushButton

6. Transform the Category Description field into a Template column. Select it in the Selected Columns list, and click the Convert this column into a Template Column link.

7. Modify the colors for the data grid just as you did for the grid in the DepartmentsAdmin user control. In the left tab of the window, click Format. From the Objects list, select Header, and set the values as shown in Figure 8-31.

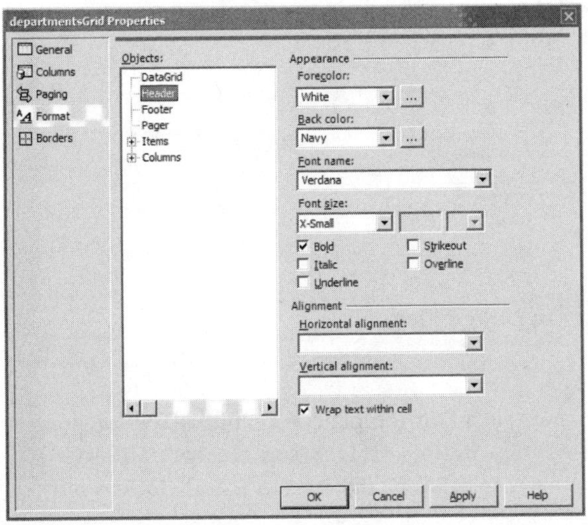

Figure 8-31. Setting DataGrid *properties*

8. Then expand the Items category, select Normal Items, and set their properties as shown in Figure 8-32.

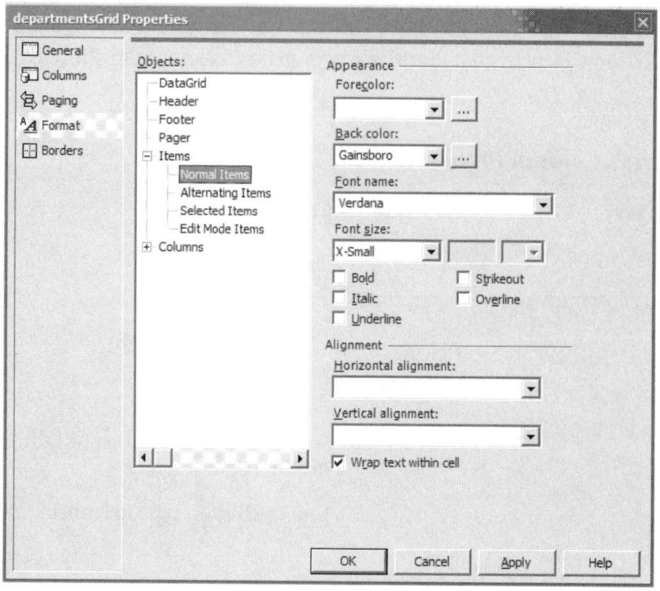

Figure 8-32. Setting DataGrid *properties*

9. Click OK. Your control should now look like Figure 8-33.

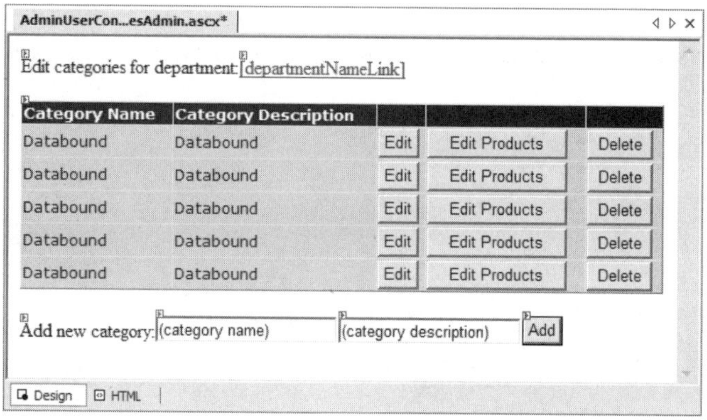

Figure 8-33. CategoriesAdmin.ascx *in Design View*

10. Right-click the DataGrid, and select Edit Template ➤ Columns[1] - Category Description. Select the TextBox in the EditItemTemplate, set its ID to editDescriptionTextBox, TextMode to MultiLine, Rows to 3, and Width to 100% (see Figure 8-34).

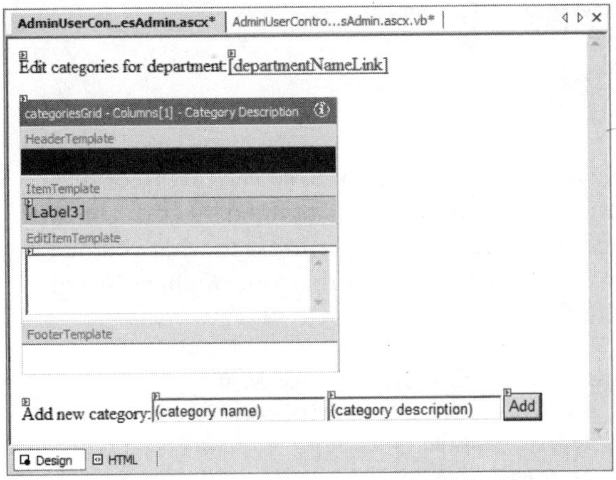

Figure 8-34. Editing a template column

11. Let's now deal with the code-behind file. Double-click somewhere on the CategoriesAdmin control, but not on one of its constituent controls. This should open the Page_Load method. Add the following code to it:

```
Private Sub Page_Load(ByVal sender As System.Object, ByVal e As
System.EventArgs) Handles MyBase.Load
    ' Save DepartmentID from the query string to a variable
    Dim departmentId As String = Request.QueryString("DepartmentID")
    ' Save CategoryID from the query string to a variable
    Dim categoryId As String = Request.QueryString("CategoryID")
    ' If no department is selected, or if a category is selected
    ' this control should be invisible
    If Not IsNumeric(departmentId) Or IsNumeric(categoryId) Then
      Me.Visible = False
    ElseIf Not Page.IsPostBack Then
      ' Update the data grid
      BindCategories()
      ' Retrieve the name of the department
      Dim departmentDetails As DepartmentDetails
      departmentDetails = Catalog.GetDepartmentDetails(departmentId)
      ' Set the text of departmentNameLabel
      departmentNameLink.Text = departmentDetails.Name
    End If
End Sub

Private Sub BindCategories()
    ' Save DepartmentID from the query string to a variable
    Dim departmentId As String = Request.QueryString("DepartmentID")
    ' Supply the data grid with the list of categories
    categoriesGrid.DataSource = _
      CatalogAdmin.GetCategoriesWithDescriptions(departmentId)
    ' The DataKey of each row is the category ID.
```

```
                    categoriesGrid.DataKeyField = "CategoryID"
                     ' Bind the data grid to the data source
                    categoriesGrid.DataBind()
                End Sub
```

12. Now you need to handle the EditCommand, UpdateCommand, CancelCommand, SelectedIndexChanged, and DeleteCommand events of the data grid. This will make the grid fully functional, and the code is similar to what you had in the DepartmentsAdmin user control. Remember that you can have Visual Studio .NET generate their signatures:

```
Private Sub categoriesGrid_EditCommand(ByVal source As Object, _
    ByVal e As System.Web.UI.WebControls.DataGridCommandEventArgs) _
    Handles categoriesGrid.EditCommand
   ' Enter the category into edit mode
   categoriesGrid.EditItemIndex = e.Item.ItemIndex
   ' Update the data grid
   BindCategories()
End Sub

Private Sub categoriesGrid_UpdateCommand(ByVal source As Object, _
    ByVal e As System.Web.UI.WebControls.DataGridCommandEventArgs) _
    Handles categoriesGrid.UpdateCommand
  Dim categoryId As String
  Dim categoryName As String
  Dim categoryDescription As String
   ' CategoryID is the DataKey field (set in BindDepartments)
  categoryId = categoriesGrid.DataKeys(e.Item.ItemIndex)
   ' We get the category name from the data grid
  categoryName = CType(e.Item.Cells(0).Controls(0), TextBox).Text
   ' We get the category description from the data grid
  categoryDescription = _
    CType(e.Item.FindControl("editDescriptionTextBox"), TextBox).Text
   ' Pass the values to the business tier to update department info
  CatalogAdmin.UpdateCategory(categoryId, categoryName, _
                                              categoryDescription)
   ' Cancel edit mode
  categoriesGrid.EditItemIndex = -1
   ' Update the data grid
  BindCategories()
End Sub

Private Sub categoriesGrid_CancelCommand(ByVal source As Object, _
    ByVal e As System.Web.UI.WebControls.DataGridCommandEventArgs) _
    Handles categoriesGrid.CancelCommand
   ' Cancel edit mode
  categoriesGrid.EditItemIndex = -1
   ' Update the data grid
  BindCategories()
End Sub
```

```
      Private Sub categoriesGrid_SelectedIndexChanged(ByVal sender As
    Object, ByVal e As System.EventArgs) _
    Handles categoriesGrid.SelectedIndexChanged
          ' Get the department ID from the query string
          Dim departmentId As String= Request.QueryString("DepartmentID")
          ' CategoryID is the DataKey field for categoriesGrid
          Dim categoryId As String
          categoryId = categoriesGrid.DataKeys(categoriesGrid.SelectedIndex)
          ' Reload admin.aspx by specifying a DepartmentID and CategoryID
          Response.Redirect("admin.aspx?DepartmentID=" & departmentId & _
                    "&CategoryID=" & categoryId)
      End Sub

      Private Sub categoriesGrid_DeleteCommand(ByVal source As Object, _
    ByVal e As System.Web.UI.WebControls.DataGridCommandEventArgs) _
    Handles categoriesGrid.DeleteCommand
        Dim categoryId As String
        ' CategoryID is the DataKey field for categoriesGrid
        categoryId = categoriesGrid.DataKeys(e.Item.ItemIndex)
        ' We try to delete the category, but this will generate an
        ' exception if the category has related products in the database
        Try
          CatalogAdmin.DeleteCategory(categoryId)
          BindCategories()
        Catch ex as Exception
          ' Here we can show an error message specifying that the category
          ' can't be deleted. At the moment we simply redisplay the grid
          ' Update the data grid
          BindCategories()
        End Try
      End Sub
```

16. Now it's time to handle the `Click` event of the `addCategoryButton`. Double-click
    the button in Design View to have the signature generated and add the
    following lines:

```
      Private Sub addCategoryButton_Click(ByVal sender As System.Object, _
          ByVal e As System.EventArgs) Handles addCategoryButton.Click
        ' Get the department ID from the query string
        Dim departmentId As String = Request.QueryString("DepartmentID")
        ' Add the new category to the database. Apart from specifying its name
        ' and description, we also mention the department it belongs to
        CatalogAdmin.AddCategory(departmentId, _
                            nameTextBox.Text, descriptionTextBox.Text)
        ' Update the data grid
        BindCategories()
      End Sub
```

17. Finally, it's time to handle the `Click` event of the `departmentsNameLink LinkButton` control. Double-click it on the Design View, and complete its code like this:

```
Private Sub departmentNameLink_Click(ByVal sender As System.Object, _
ByVal e As System.EventArgs) Handles departmentNameLink.Click
    ' Reload admin.aspx
    Response.Redirect("admin.aspx")
End Sub
```

18. The last step in this exercise is to add the `CategoriesAdmin` user control to the second cell in the table in `admin.aspx` (see Figure 8-35). After doing this change, `admin.aspx` should look like Figure 8-35, while in Design View (note that the text has been removed from the bottom table cells).

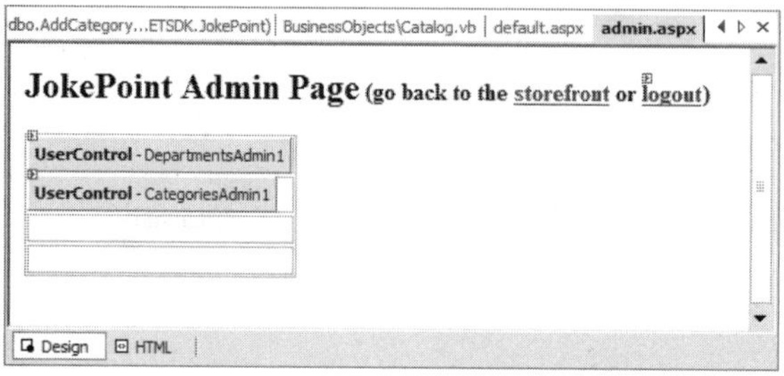

Figure 8-35. Adding the `CategoriesAdmin` *user control to the second cell in the table*

How It Works: `CategoriesAdmin.ascx`

Even though the project is not compilable yet, you can see how this user control will look when executed in Figure 8-36, to help you understand what happens there.

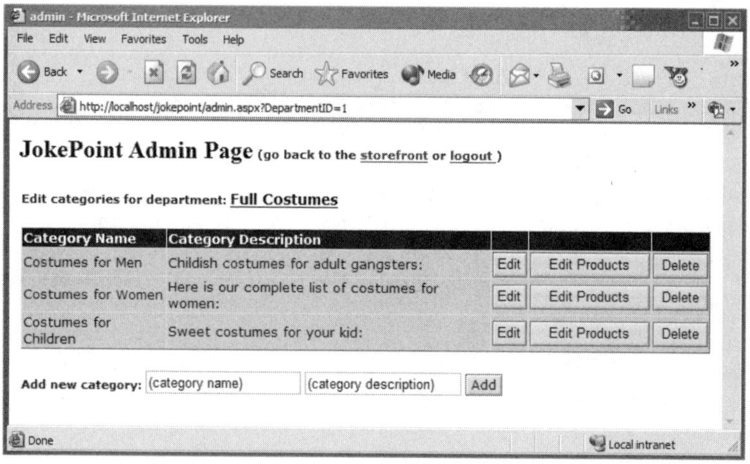

Figure 8-36. `CategoriesAdmin.ascx` *in action*

On the top of the control, you can see the name of the department, and then the list of categories that belong to it. At the bottom, you see the controls that allow you to add a new category to the selected department.

Most of the code is similar to what you did for the DepartmentsAdmin Web User Control. Still, let's recap the main points to keep in mind about the code.

Page_Load is fired when the control is loaded (or reloaded). First, the code checks whether the DepartmentID and CategoryID parameters were passed in the query string, and decides whether to display CategoriesAdmin based on their existence:

```
' Save DepartmentID from the query string to a variable
Dim departmentId As String = Request.QueryString("DepartmentID")
' Save CategoryID from the query string to a variable
Dim categoryId As String = Request.QueryString("CategoryID")
' If no department is selected, or if a category is selected
' this control should be invisible
If Not IsNumeric(departmentId) Or IsNumeric(categoryId) Then
  Me.Visible = False
```

In fact, as you can see, the code doesn't only check whether the DepartmentID and CategoryID parameters have been supplied, but also whether they have numerical values. This is a simple but effective validation method that guards against invalid (nonnumerical) DepartmentID and CategoryID values.

Then, if the conditions for showing CategoriesAdmin.ascx are passed, the code verifies that the page isn't loaded as the result of a client postback. If it is, you rely on ASP.NET to keep the user control's state, so you don't reload any data from the database:

```
ElseIf Not Page.IsPostBack Then
  ' Update the data grid
  BindCategories()
  ' Retrieve the name of the department
  Dim departmentDetails As DepartmentDetails
  departmentDetails = Catalog.GetDepartmentDetails(departmentId)
  ' Set the text of departmentNameLabel
  departmentNameLink.Text = departmentDetails.Name
End If
```

 TIP *You learned about the postback mechanism in Chapter 6.*

So the data grid is loaded from the database when the page loads for the first time. If the page is reloaded as a result of a client postback (a button is clicked for example), you don't want to access the database again, because the data is still there. This is the reason why the code first checks the value of Page.PostBack in Page_Load before updating any information in the user control.

The BindCategories method populates the grid. It calls the GetCategoriesWith-Descriptions stored procedure to get the list of categories for the currently selected department:

```
Private Sub BindCategories()
  ' Save DepartmentID from the query string to a variable
  Dim departmentId As String = Request.QueryString("DepartmentID")
  ' Supply the data grid with the list of categories
  categoriesGrid.DataSource = _
    CatalogAdmin.GetCategoriesWithDescriptions(departmentId)
```
Then, also in BindCategories, the DataKey field is set for the grid:
```
  ' The DataKey of each row is the category ID.
  categoriesGrid.DataKeyField = "CategoryID"
  ' Bind the data grid to the data source
  categoriesGrid.DataBind()
End Sub
```

The DataKey field is used when needing the ID of a category that was selected in the grid for updating, deleting, or viewing its products. The UpdateCommand and DeleteCommand event handlers receive a DataGridCommandEventArgs object named e, which is used to find out on what row of the data grid the Update or Delete button was clicked. By asking the DataKey of that row, you find out the CategoryID of the category that is being updated or deleted:

```
' CategoryID is the DataKey field for categoriesGrid
categoryId = categoriesGrid.DataKeys(e.Item.ItemIndex)
```

You also need to find out the CategoryID in the SelectedIndexChanged event (which is triggered when clicking the Edit Products button, since this is the Select button of the grid). Still, in this event handler, you don't receive a DataGridCommandEventArgs object, so you can't find out the index of the selected row using the traditional e.Item.ItemIndex. However, there is an even simpler method: when the Select button of a grid is clicked, you can get its index using the DataGrid's SelectedIndex property. Once you know the index, again it's very simple to find out the category ID:

```
' CategoryID is the DataKey field for categoriesGrid
categoryId = categoriesGrid.DataKeys(categoriesGrid.SelectedIndex)
```

The SelectedIndexChanged event handler associated with the Edit Products buttons, reloads admin.aspx by adding DepartmentID and CategoryID in the query string. When this happens, the DepartmentsAdmin.ascx and CategoriesAdmin.ascx controls will be invisible, but ProductsAdmin.ascx will show up listing the products for the selected category. You'll implement this control next.

We enter the data grid in edit mode in the EditCommand event handler; this event is raised when the visitor clicks on the Edit button in the data grid. When this happens, we set the EditItemIndex property of the DataGrid to the row we want to edit. Once this is done, the DataGrid takes care of the details, and displays editable textboxes in the fields being edited. Note that the fields can be marked as read-only from the Property Builder of the DataGrid; these fields won't be transformed to editable TextBox controls, when entering edit mode.

We cancel edit mode in the UpdateCommand and CancelCommand event handlers. Remember that the Delete and Cancel buttons appear only when the grid is in edit mode (they replace the Edit button), and after they are clicked we need to exit edit mode:

```
' Cancel edit mode
categoriesGrid.EditItemIndex = -1
```

In the `DeleteCommand` event handler, you once again use a `Try...Catch...Finally` block:

```
Try
   CatalogAdmin.DeleteCategory(categoryId)
   BindCategories()
Catch ex As Exception
   ' Here we can show an error message specifying that the category
   ' can't be deleted. At the moment we simply redisplay the grid
   ' Update the data grid
   BindCategories()
End Try
```

This error-trapping mechanism is implemented because the database might raise an error if the category you attempt to delete has related products (this would break the database integrity because it would result in orphaned `ProductCategory` records). If an exception is caught in the `Try` block code, the execution is passed to the `Catch` block. The `Catch` block simply ignores the error and updates the information in the data grid, although this update isn't really necessary because the data grid doesn't get modified if no records are deleted.

Middle-Tier Methods for Categories Administration

Now you'll write the methods of the `CatalogAdmin` class that support the functionality required by the `CategoriesAdmin` user control. These methods support the basic administrative operations with categories: `GetCategoriesWithDescriptions`, `UpdateCategory`, `DeleteCategory`, and `AddCategory`.

Add these methods to `CatalogAdmin.vb`, just after the `Departments` region (which contains similar methods for departments):

```
#Region " Categories "
  Public Shared Function GetCategoriesWithDescriptions( _
                       ByVal departmentId As String) As SqlDataReader
     ' Create the connection object
     Dim connection As New SqlConnection(connectionString)
     ' Create and initialize the command object
     Dim command As New SqlCommand("GetCategoriesWithDescriptions", connection)
     command.CommandType = CommandType.StoredProcedure
     ' Add an input parameter and supply a value for it
     command.Parameters.Add("@DepartmentID", SqlDbType.Int)
     command.Parameters("@DepartmentID").Value = departmentId
     Try
        ' Open the connection
        connection.Open()
        ' Return an SqlDataReader to the calling function
        Return command.ExecuteReader(CommandBehavior.CloseConnection)
```

```
      Catch e As Exception
        ' Close the connection and throw the exception
        connection.Close()
        Throw e
    End Try
End Function


Public Shared Function UpdateCategory(ByVal categoryId As String, _
        ByVal categoryName As String, ByVal categoryDescription As String)
    ' Create the connection object
    Dim connection As New SqlConnection(connectionString)
    ' Create and initialize the command object
    Dim command As New SqlCommand("UpdateCategory", connection)
    command.CommandType = CommandType.StoredProcedure
    ' Add an input parameter and supply a value for it
    command.Parameters.Add("@CategoryID", SqlDbType.Int)
    command.Parameters("@CategoryID").Value = categoryId
    ' Add an input parameter and supply a value for it
    command.Parameters.Add("@CategoryName", SqlDbType.VarChar, 50)
    command.Parameters("@CategoryName").Value = categoryName
    ' Add an input parameter and supply a value for it
    command.Parameters.Add("@CategoryDescription", SqlDbType.VarChar, 200)
    command.Parameters("@CategoryDescription").Value = categoryDescription
    ' Open the connection, execute the command, and close the connection
    Try
        connection.Open()
        command.ExecuteNonQuery()
    Finally
        connection.Close()
    End Try
End Function


Public Shared Function DeleteCategory(ByVal categoryId As String)
    ' Create the connection object
    Dim connection As New SqlConnection(connectionString)
    ' Create and initialize the command object
    Dim command As New SqlCommand("DeleteCategory", connection)
    command.CommandType = CommandType.StoredProcedure
    ' Add an input parameter and supply a value for it
    command.Parameters.Add("@CategoryID", SqlDbType.Int)
    command.Parameters("@CategoryID").Value = categoryId
    ' Open the connection, execute the command, and close the connection
    Try
        connection.Open()
        command.ExecuteNonQuery()
    Finally
        connection.Close()
    End Try
End Function


Public Shared Function AddCategory(ByVal departmentID As String, _
    ByVal categoryName As String, ByVal categoryDescription As String)
```

```
' Create the connection object
Dim connection As New SqlConnection(connectionString)
' Create and initialize the command object
Dim command As New SqlCommand("AddCategory", connection)
command.CommandType = CommandType.StoredProcedure
' Add an input parameter and supply a value for it
command.Parameters.Add("@DepartmentID", SqlDbType.Int)
command.Parameters("@DepartmentID").Value = departmentID
' Add an input parameter and supply a value for it
command.Parameters.Add("@CategoryName", SqlDbType.VarChar, 50)
command.Parameters("@CategoryName").Value = categoryName
' Add an input parameter and supply a value for it
command.Parameters.Add("@CategoryDescription", SqlDbType.VarChar, 200)
command.Parameters("@CategoryDescription").Value = categoryDescription
' Open the connection, execute the command, and close the connection
Try
  connection.Open()
  command.ExecuteNonQuery()
Finally
  connection.Close()
End Try
    End Function
#End Region
```

After having written these four methods, it's time to implement the stored procedures that support their functionality.

Stored Procedures for Categories Administration

The four stored procedures are each called by one of the four methods you wrote for the business tier. Add each of the stored procedures covered in the following sections to the JokePoint database.

GetCategoriesWithDescriptions

The GetCategoriesWithDescriptions stored procedure takes the ID of a department as a parameter and returns the categories that belong to that department. Unlike the GetCategories stored procedure, this one also returns their descriptions.

```
CREATE PROCEDURE GetCategoriesWithDescriptions
(@DepartmentID int)
AS

SELECT CategoryID, Name, Description
FROM Category
WHERE DepartmentID = @DepartmentID

RETURN
```

UpdateCategory

The UpdateCategory stored procedure updates the name and description of a category.

```
CREATE PROCEDURE UpdateCategory
(@CategoryID int,
@CategoryName varchar(50),
@CategoryDescription varchar(1000))
AS

UPDATE Category
SET [Name] = @CategoryName, [Description] = @CategoryDescription
WHERE CategoryID = @CategoryID

RETURN
```

DeleteCategory

DeleteCategory deletes a certain category from the database. If the category has products that belong to it, the database will raise an error because the deletion would affect the database integrity—remember that you have implemented the One-to-Many relationship between Category and Product tables using a foreign-key relationship back in Chapter 4. In this case, the error is trapped in the presentation tier (the CategoriesAdmin user control), which simply ignores the error and refreshes the information in the data grid.

```
CREATE PROCEDURE DeleteCategory
(@CategoryID int)
AS

DELETE FROM Category
WHERE CategoryID = @CategoryID

RETURN
```

AddCategory

AddCategory adds a new category to the database. Apart from the name and description of the new category, you also need a DepartmentID, which specifies the department the category belongs to. Note that you don't need to (in fact, you can't) specify a CategoryID because CategoryID is an IDENTITY column in the Category table, and its value is automatically generated by the database when inserting a new record.

```
CREATE PROCEDURE AddCategory
(@DepartmentID int,
@CategoryName varchar(50),
@CategoryDescription varchar(50))
AS
```

```
INSERT INTO Category (DepartmentID, [Name], [Description])
VALUES (@DepartmentID, @CategoryName, @CategoryDescription)

RETURN
```

Testing the CategoriesAdmin Web User Control

The code is ready; press F5 to run the project. If you want to load the project directly in Internet Explorer (without executing the project with F5), make sure to compile it first by pressing Ctrl+Shift+B.

Figure 8-37 shows the control in edit mode.

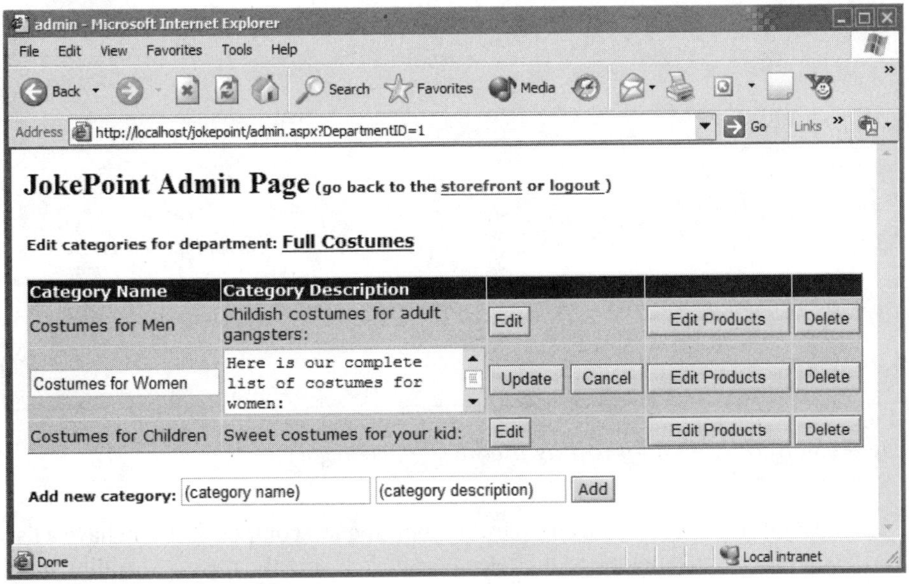

Figure 8-37. CategoriesAdmin in edit mode

Feel free to play with the options to make sure they work as advertised.

Administering Products

You are now ready for the last major part of the catalog administration page: the place where you edit the products that belong to the selected category. This one has a few more controls than the others, as shown in Figure 8-38.

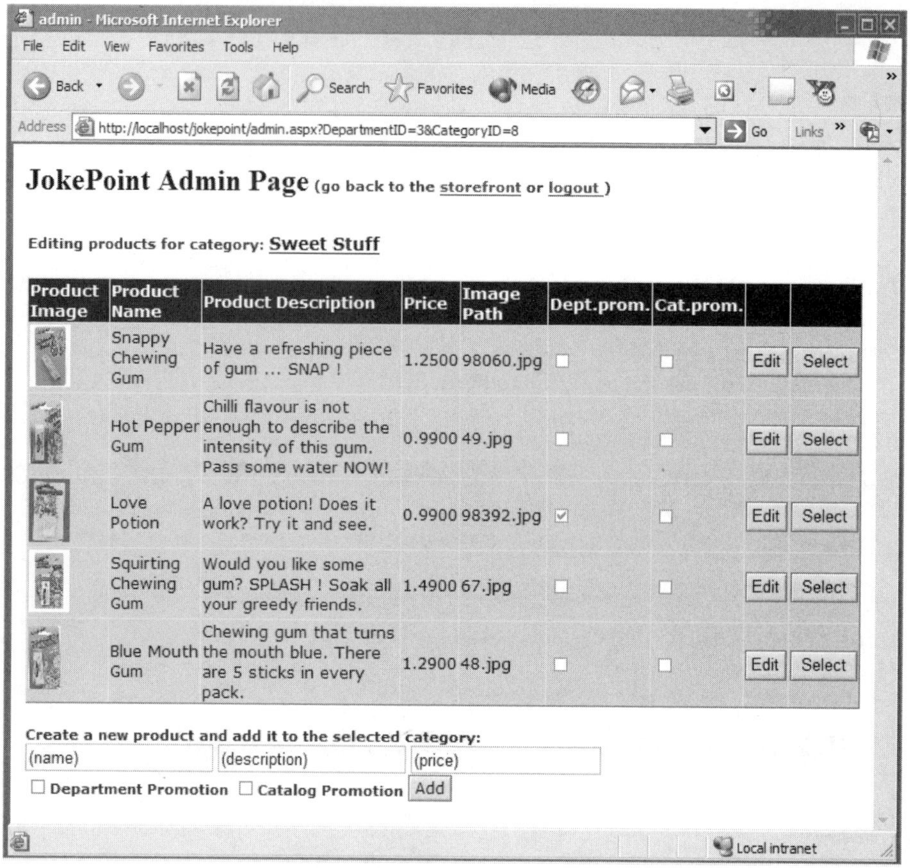

Figure 8-38. The screen for editing products in a category

The interface is a bit more complex, but nothing too complicated. You have a list with the products that belong to the selected category, and the means of adding new products to that category.

The ProductsAdmin Web User Control

You saw in Figure 8.36 what this user control will look like. Most of its functionality is similar to the previous user controls, but ProductsAdmin.ascx provides a closer look at some new error-handling techniques.

Exercise: Implementing ProductsAdmin.ascx

1. Create a new Web User Control named ProductsAdmin.ascx in the AdminUserControls folder.

2. Add labels, text boxes, buttons, check boxes, and a DataGrid as shown in Figure 8-39.

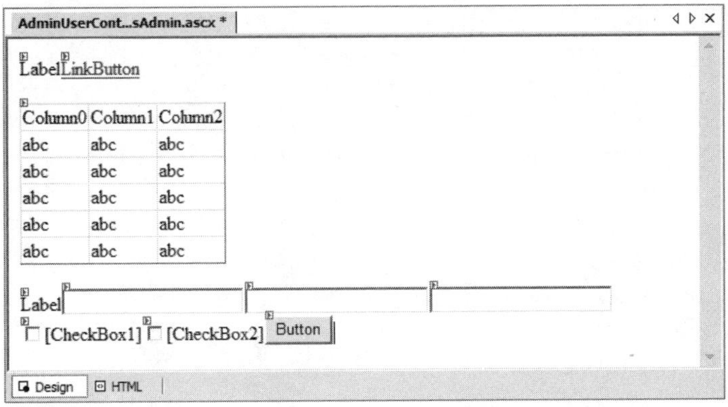

Figure 8-39. `ProductsAdmin.ascx` *in Design View*

3. Change the properties of each control to the values in the Table 8-6.

Table 8-6. Setting Controls' Properties in `ProductsAdmin.ascx`

Control Type	ID Property	Text Property	CssClass Property
Label	firstLabel	Editing products for category:	AdminPageText
LinkButton	categoryNameLink	*(should be empty)*	ListDescription
DataGrid	productsGrid		
Label	newProductLabel	Create a new product and add it to the selected category:	AdminPageText
TextBox	nameTextBox	(name)	
TextBox	descriptionTextBox	(description)	
TextBox	priceTextBox	(price)	
CheckBox	departmentPromotionCheck	Department Promotion	AdminPageText
CheckBox	catalogPromotionCheck	Catalog Promotion	AdminPageText
Button	createProductButton	Add	AdminButtonText

4. Right now, the control should look like Figure 8-40, when viewed in Design View. Remember that the CSS styles don't apply when designing the form, only when it is executed.

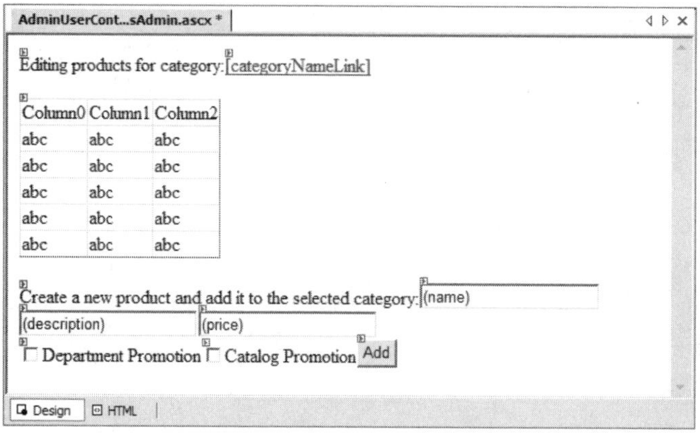

```
AdminUserCont...sAdmin.ascx *                                         ◁ ▷ ✕
```
Editing products for category: [categoryNameLink]

Column0	Column1	Column2
abc	abc	abc
abc	abc	abc
abc	abc	abc
abc	abc	abc
abc	abc	abc

Create a new product and add it to the selected category: (name)
(description)   (price)
☐ Department Promotion ☐ Catalog Promotion Add

```
⊡ Design   ⊟ HTML
```

Figure 8-40. `ProductsAdmin.ascx` *in Design View*

5. Now modify the `DataGrid`'s properties. Open the Property Builder and select the Columns page. Deselect the Create Columns Automatically at Runtime check box, and add nine columns, according to Table 8-7.

Table 8-7. Setting `DataGrid` *Field Properties*

Column Type	Header Text	Data Field	Other Properties
Bound Column	Product Image	`ImagePath`	Check the "Read Only" CheckBox
Bound Column	Product Name	`Name`	
Bound Column	Product Description	`Description`	
Bound Column	Price	`Price`	
Bound Column	Image Path	`ImagePath`	
Bound Column	Dept.prom.	`OnDepartmentPromotion`	
Bound Column	Cat.prom.	`OnCatalogPromotion`	
Edit, Update, Cancel			Button type: PushButton
Select			Button type: PushButton

TIP *There's no Delete button in the* `DataGrid` *because you'll implement the delete-product functionality later.*

6. Go back to the first bound column (Product Image), and click Convert this Column into a Template Column. Do the same for the "Product Description", "Dept.prom.", and "Cat.prom" columns. You'll update their templates after modifying the DataGrid's colors.

 TIP *The goal is to have the Product Image column show the product image instead of the image path, and the Department Promotion and Catalog Promotion columns show check boxes instead of "True"/"False" string values. The Product Description column should show a multiline text box when edited, just like the two other* DataGrids *you created earlier.*

---

7. Change the DataGrid colors as you did for the other two grids.

8. Click OK. Now you need to modify the templates for the two template columns. Switch to HTML View, and edit the Product Image template column as follows:

```
<asp:TemplateColumn HeaderText="Product Image">
  <ItemTemplate>
    <img border="0" height="50"
       src='ProductImages/<%# DataBinder.Eval(Container,
                                  "DataItem.ImagePath") %>'>
  </ItemTemplate>
</asp:TemplateColumn>
```

9. Modify EditItemTemplate of the Product Description column by updating the properties of the editing text box. This is what you did in the previous data grids, except now we show the HTML code directly:

```
<asp:TemplateColumn HeaderText="Product Description">
  <ItemTemplate>
    <asp:Label id=Label3 runat="server"
      Text='<%# DataBinder.Eval(Container, "DataItem.Description") %>'>
    </asp:Label>
  </ItemTemplate>
  <EditItemTemplate>
    <asp:TextBox id=editDescriptionTextBox runat="server"
      Text='<%# DataBinder.Eval(Container, "DataItem.Description") %>'
      TextMode="MultiLine" Width="250" Rows="3">
    </asp:TextBox>
  </EditItemTemplate>
</asp:TemplateColumn>
```

10. Modify the Department Promotion and Catalog Promotion columns as shown. Instead of displaying the data from the database (True/False) using labels, display it using check boxes. When the grid is in edit mode, the check boxes are enabled; otherwise, they are not. When they are in edit mode, they also need to be assigned names, so you can refer to them from the code-behind file.

```
<asp:TemplateColumn HeaderText="Dept.prom.">
  <ItemTemplate>
    <asp:CheckBox Text="" Enabled="False" runat="server" ID="Checkbox1"
        Checked='<%# DataBinder.Eval(Container,
                               "DataItem.OnDepartmentPromotion") %>' >
    </asp:CheckBox>
  </ItemTemplate>
  <EditItemTemplate>
    <asp:CheckBox id="deptPromListCheck" Text="" runat="server"
        Checked='<%# DataBinder.Eval(Container,
                               "DataItem.OnDepartmentPromotion") %>'>
    </asp:CheckBox>
  </EditItemTemplate>
</asp:TemplateColumn>
<asp:TemplateColumn HeaderText="Cat.prom.">
  <ItemTemplate>
    <asp:CheckBox Text="" Enabled="False" runat="server"
        Checked='<%# DataBinder.Eval(Container,
                               "DataItem.OnCatalogPromotion") %>'>
    </asp:CheckBox>
  </ItemTemplate>
  <EditItemTemplate>
    <asp:CheckBox id="catPromListCheck" Text="" runat="server"
        Checked='<%# DataBinder.Eval(Container,
                               "DataItem.OnCatalogPromotion") %>'>
    </asp:CheckBox>
  </EditItemTemplate>
</asp:TemplateColumn>
```

11. After all the changes, the user control should look Figure 8-41 when viewed in Design View:

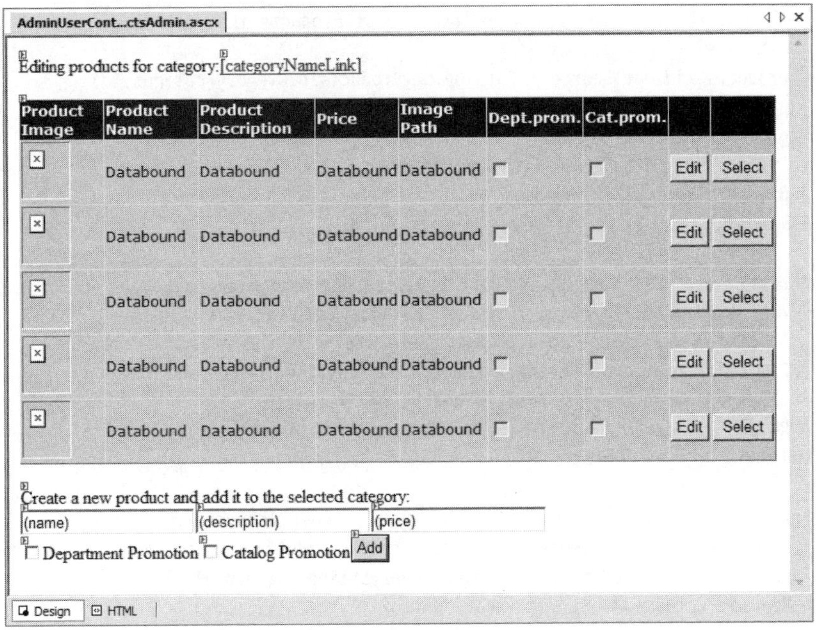

Figure 8-41. ProductsAdmin.ascx *in Design View*

12. Now it's time to write the code. Remember to use Visual Studio .NET to generate the event handler signatures for you. Here is the listing of the code-behind file ProductsAdmin.ascx.vb:

```vb
Private Sub Page_Load(ByVal sender As System.Object, _
  ByVal e As System.EventArgs) Handles MyBase.Load
  ' Obtain the Category ID from the query string
  Dim categoryId As String = Request.QueryString("CategoryID")
  ' Obtain the Product ID from the query string
  Dim productId As String = Request.QueryString("ProductID")
  ' Set the label to its initial text
  firstLabel.Text = "Editing products for category:"
  ' Hide the control if a category was not selected,
  ' or if a product was selected
  If Not IsNumeric(categoryId) Or IsNumeric(productId) Then
    Me.Visible = False
  ElseIf Not Page.IsPostBack Then
    ' Populate the data grid with products
    BindProducts()
    ' Set categoryNameLabel.Text to the name of the selected category
    categoryNameLink.Text = Catalog.GetCategoryDetails(categoryId).Name
  End If
End Sub

Private Sub BindProducts()
  ' Obtain the Category ID from the query string
  Dim categoryId As String = Request.QueryString("CategoryID")
```

```vbnet
    ' Populate the data grid with the list of products that belong to
    ' the selected category
    productsGrid.DataSource = Catalog.GetProductsInCategory(categoryId)
    ' Set the DataKey field
    productsGrid.DataKeyField = "ProductID"
    ' Bind the grid to the data source
    productsGrid.DataBind()
End Sub

Private Sub categoryNameLink_Click(ByVal sender As System.Object, _
ByVal e As System.EventArgs) Handles categoryNameLink.Click
    ' Get the department ID from the query string
    Dim departmentId As String = Request.QueryString("DepartmentID")
    ' Reload admin.aspx by specifying the DepartmentID
    Response.Redirect("admin.aspx?DepartmentID=" & departmentId)
End Sub

Private Sub createProductButton_Click(ByVal sender As System.Object, _
    ByVal e As System.EventArgs) Handles createProductButton.Click
    Dim categoryId As String = Request.QueryString("CategoryID")
    Dim productName As String = nameTextBox.Text
    Dim productDescription As String = descriptionTextBox.Text
    Dim productPrice As String = priceTextBox.Text
    Dim productImage As String = "GenericProduct.png"
    Dim onDepartmentPromotion As String = _
                                departmentPromotionCheck.Checked.ToString
    Dim onCatalogPromotion As String = _
                                catalogPromotionCheck.Checked.ToString
    Try
        ' Attempt to create the product and assign it to the category.
        ' If the operation is successful, the error message is cleared.
        CatalogAdmin.CreateProductToCategory(categoryId, productName, _
            productDescription, productPrice, productImage, _
            onDepartmentPromotion, onCatalogPromotion)
    Catch
        ' Here you can inform the user about the error.
        firstLabel.Text = "<font color=red>Could not create the product." _
                        & "Please verify the input values." _
                        & "</font><br>Editing products for category:"
    Finally
        ' Finally, no matter if an error occured or not, we update
        ' the products grid by calling BindProducts
        BindProducts()
    End Try
End Sub

Private Sub productsGrid_CancelCommand(ByVal source As Object, _
    ByVal e As System.Web.UI.WebControls.DataGridCommandEventArgs) _
    Handles productsGrid.CancelCommand
    ' Exit edit mode
    productsGrid.EditItemIndex = -1
    BindProducts()
End Sub
```

```
Private Sub productsGrid_UpdateCommand(ByVal source As Object, _
  ByVal e As System.Web.UI.WebControls.DataGridCommandEventArgs) _
  Handles productsGrid.UpdateCommand
  Dim id As String
  Dim name As String
  Dim description As String
  Dim price As String
  Dim image As String
  Dim onDepartmentPromotion As String
  Dim onCatalogPromotion As String
  ' Gather product information
  id = productsGrid.DataKeys(e.Item.ItemIndex)
  name = CType(e.Item.Cells(1).Controls(0), TextBox).Text
  description = _
      CType(e.Item.FindControl("editDescriptionTextBox"), TextBox).Text
  price = CType(e.Item.Cells(3).Controls(0), TextBox).Text
  image = CType(e.Item.Cells(4).Controls(0), TextBox).Text
  onDepartmentPromotion = _
      CType(e.Item.FindControl("deptPromListCheck"), CheckBox).Checked
  onCatalogPromotion = _
      CType(e.Item.FindControl("catPromListCheck"), CheckBox).Checked
  Try
    ' Try to update the product info. If everything is OK clear the
    ' error label.
    CatalogAdmin.UpdateProduct(id, name, description, price, image, _
      onDepartmentPromotion, onCatalogPromotion)
  Catch
    ' Tell the visitor about the error
    firstLabel.Text= "<font color=red>Could not update product info." _
                  & "Please verify the input values.</font><br>" _
                  & "Editing products for category:"
  Finally
    ' No matter if an error occurs or not we cancel edit mode and
    ' update the product's grid information
    productsGrid.EditItemIndex = -1
    BindProducts()
  End Try
End Sub

Private Sub productsGrid_EditCommand(ByVal source As Object, _
  ByVal e As System.Web.UI.WebControls.DataGridCommandEventArgs) _
  Handles productsGrid.EditCommand
  ' Enter the grid into edit mode and rebind the data grid
  productsGrid.EditItemIndex = e.Item.ItemIndex
  BindProducts()
End Sub

Private Sub productsGrid_SelectedIndexChanged( _
  ByVal sender As System.Object, ByVal e As System.EventArgs) _
  Handles productsGrid.SelectedIndexChanged
  Dim departmentId As String = Request.QueryString("DepartmentID")
  Dim categoryId As String = Request.QueryString("CategoryID")
```

```
            Dim productName As String = _
                    productsGrid.Items(productsGrid.SelectedIndex).Cells(1).Text
            Dim productId As String = _
                                productsGrid.DataKeys(productsGrid.SelectedIndex)
            Dim imagePath As String = _
                    productsGrid.Items(productsGrid.SelectedIndex).Cells(4).Text
            ' Send product info in the query string
            ' This is used in the ProductDetailsAdmin user control
            Response.Redirect("admin.aspx?DepartmentID=" & departmentId _
                & "&CategoryID=" & categoryId & "&ProductID=" & productId _
                & "&ProductName=" & productName & "&ImagePath=" & imagePath)
        End Sub
```

13. Add ProductsAdmin.ascx to the third cell of the table in admin.aspx, as shown in Figure 8-42.

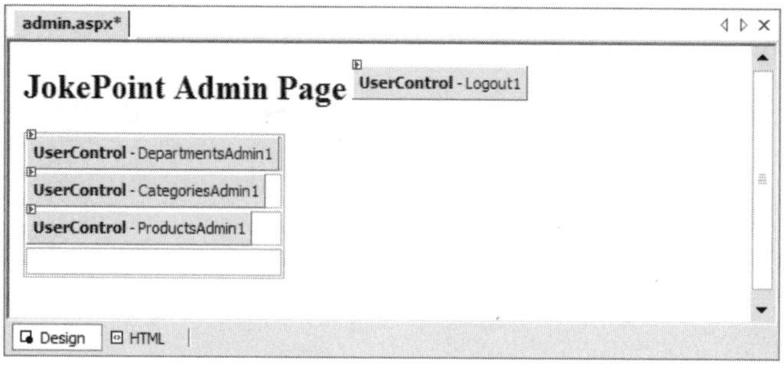

Figure 8-42. Adding ProductsAdmin.ascx *to the third cell of the table*

How It Works: ProductsAdmin.ascx

Most methods are similar to those you wrote for the previous controls. Products can be updated, deleted, or selected. When adding a new product, a generic image (GenericProduct.png) is used by default. The administrator can change the product's image using the product details admin page, which shows up when a product is selected in the list. You'll create that control later after you finish ProductsAdmin.ascx.

As usual, when selecting a product, you reload the form by adding something to the query string. In this case, you add more details (ProductID, ProductName, and ImagePath) about the product so you won't have to read them again from the database in the ProductDetailsAdmin control, which you'll write in the next section.

ProductDetailsAdmin will allow you to assign the selected product to another category, upload a picture for the product, remove the product from its category, or remove the product from the database.

Middle-Tier Methods for Products Administration

The methods you write here, CreateProductToCategory and UpdateProduct, although quite long, are similar to what you have done so far. Add the following code to CatalogAdmin.vb, just after the Categories region:

```vb
#Region "  Products  "
  Public Shared Function CreateProductToCategory(ByVal categoryId As String, _
          ByVal productName As String, ByVal productDescription As String, _
          ByVal productPrice As String, ByVal productImage As String, _
          ByVal onDepartmentPromotion As String, _
          ByVal onCatalogPromotion As String)
    ' Create the connection object
    Dim connection As New SqlConnection(connectionString)
    ' Create and initialize the command object
    Dim command As New SqlCommand("CreateProductToCategory", connection)
    command.CommandType = CommandType.StoredProcedure
    ' Add an input parameter and supply a value for it
    command.Parameters.Add("@CategoryID", SqlDbType.Int)
    command.Parameters("@CategoryID").Value = categoryId
    ' Add an input parameter and supply a value for it
    command.Parameters.Add("@ProductName", SqlDbType.VarChar, 50)
    command.Parameters("@ProductName").Value = productName
    ' Add an input parameter and supply a value for it
    command.Parameters.Add("@ProductDescription", SqlDbType.VarChar, 1000)
    command.Parameters("@ProductDescription").Value = productDescription
    ' Add an input parameter and supply a value for it
    command.Parameters.Add("@ProductPrice", SqlDbType.Money, 8)
    command.Parameters("@ProductPrice").Value = productPrice
    ' Add an input parameter and supply a value for it
    command.Parameters.Add("@ProductImage", SqlDbType.VarChar, 50)
    command.Parameters("@ProductImage").Value = productImage
    ' Add an input parameter and supply a value for it
    If onDepartmentPromotion.ToUpper = "TRUE" _
      Or onDepartmentPromotion = "1" Then
      ' If we receive "True" or "1" for onDepartmentPromotion ...
      command.Parameters.Add("@OnDepartmentPromotion", SqlDbType.Bit, 1)
      command.Parameters("@OnDepartmentPromotion").Value = 1
    Else
      ' For all the other values we assume the product is not on promotion
      command.Parameters.Add("@OnDepartmentPromotion", SqlDbType.Bit, 1)
      command.Parameters("@OnDepartmentPromotion").Value = 0
    End If
    ' Add an input parameter and supply a value for it
    If onCatalogPromotion.ToUpper = "TRUE" _
      Or onCatalogPromotion = "1" Then
      ' If we receive "True" or "1" for onCatalogPromotion ...
      command.Parameters.Add("@OnCatalogPromotion", SqlDbType.Bit, 1)
      command.Parameters("@OnCatalogPromotion").Value = 1
    Else
      ' For all the other values we assume the product is not on promotion
```

```
        command.Parameters.Add("@OnCatalogPromotion", SqlDbType.Bit, 1)
        command.Parameters("@OnCatalogPromotion").Value = 0
    End If
    ' Open the connection, execute the command, and close the connection
    Try
      connection.Open()
      command.ExecuteNonQuery()
    Finally
      connection.Close()
    End Try
  End Function


  ' This is identical to CreateProductToCategory, except that we call
  ' the UpdateProduct stored procedure instead of CreateProductToCategory
  Public Shared Function UpdateProduct(ByVal productId As String, _
          ByVal productName As String, ByVal productDescription As String, _
          ByVal productPrice As String, ByVal productImage As String, _
          ByVal onDepartmentPromotion As String, _
          ByVal onCatalogPromotion As String)
    ' Create the connection object
    Dim connection As New SqlConnection(connectionString)
    ' Create and initialize the command object
    Dim command As New SqlCommand("UpdateProduct", connection)
    command.CommandType = CommandType.StoredProcedure
    ' Add an input parameter and supply a value for it
    command.Parameters.Add("@ProductID", SqlDbType.Int)
    command.Parameters("@ProductID").Value = productId
    ' Add an input parameter and supply a value for it
    command.Parameters.Add("@ProductName", SqlDbType.VarChar, 50)
    command.Parameters("@ProductName").Value = productName
    ' Add an input parameter and supply a value for it
    command.Parameters.Add("@ProductDescription", SqlDbType.VarChar, 1000)
    command.Parameters("@ProductDescription").Value = productDescription
    ' Add an input parameter and supply a value for it
    command.Parameters.Add("@ProductPrice", SqlDbType.Money, 8)
    command.Parameters("@ProductPrice").Value = productPrice
    ' Add an input parameter and supply a value for it
    command.Parameters.Add("@ProductImage", SqlDbType.VarChar, 50)
    command.Parameters("@ProductImage").Value = productImage
    If onDepartmentPromotion.ToUpper = "TRUE" Or onDepartmentPromotion = "1" Then
        ' If we receive "True" or "1" for onDepartmentPromotion ...
        command.Parameters.Add("@OnDepartmentPromotion", SqlDbType.Bit, 1)
        command.Parameters("@OnDepartmentPromotion").Value = 1
    Else
        ' For all the other values we assume the product is not on promotion
        command.Parameters.Add("@OnDepartmentPromotion", SqlDbType.Bit, 1)
        command.Parameters("@OnDepartmentPromotion").Value = 0
    End If
    If onCatalogPromotion.ToUpper = "TRUE" Or onCatalogPromotion = "1" Then
        ' If we receive "True" or "1" for onCatalogPromotion ...
        command.Parameters.Add("@OnCatalogPromotion", SqlDbType.Bit, 1)
        command.Parameters("@OnCatalogPromotion").Value = 1
    Else
        ' For all the other values we assume the product is not on promotion
```

```
    command.Parameters.Add("@OnCatalogPromotion", SqlDbType.Bit, 1)
    command.Parameters("@OnCatalogPromotion").Value = 0
  End If
  ' Open the connection, execute the command, and close the connection
  Try
    connection.Open()
    command.ExecuteNonQuery()
  Finally
    connection.Close()
  End Try
End Function
#End Region
```

Stored Procedures for Products Administration

Two stored procedures support the UI functionality: CreateProductToCategory and UpdateProduct. The procedures are described in the following sections.

CreateProductToCategory

The CreateProductToCategory stored procedure is called when you create a new product. After creating the product, the stored procedure also assigns the product to the category mentioned as a parameter. Because the ProductID column is an identity column, you are assured that the generated value is unique. A side effect is that you can be certain the (ProductID, CategoryID) pair doesn't exist in the ProductCategory table, because the newly created ProductID didn't exist in the database before.

```
CREATE PROCEDURE CreateProductToCategory
(@CategoryID int,
 @ProductName varchar(50),
 @ProductDescription varchar(1000),
 @ProductPrice Money,
 @ProductImage varchar(50),
 @OnDepartmentPromotion bit,
 @OnCatalogPromotion bit)
AS

DECLARE @ProductID int

INSERT INTO Product
    (Name,
     Description,
     Price,
     ImagePath,
     OnDepartmentPromotion,
     OnCatalogPromotion )
VALUES
    (@ProductName,
     @ProductDescription,
```

```
        CONVERT(money,@ProductPrice),
        @ProductImage,
        @OnDepartmentPromotion,
        @OnCatalogPromotion)

SELECT @ProductID = @@Identity

INSERT INTO ProductCategory (ProductID, CategoryID)
VALUES (@ProductID, @CategoryID)

RETURN
```

This line of code is of particular importance:

```
SELECT @ProductID = @@Identity
```

Identity columns are automatically generated by the database. If you ever wondered how to determine which value has been generated, here's the answer: the @@Identity system value. This needs to be saved into a variable immediately because its value is rewritten after other SQL statements execute. After you determine which ID was generated for the new product, assign it to the category that you receive as a parameter:

```
INSERT INTO ProductCategory (ProductID, CategoryID)
VALUES (@ProductID, @CategoryID)
```

UpdateProduct

The UpdateProduct stored procedure updates the information of a product:

```
CREATE PROCEDURE UpdateProduct
(@ProductID int,
 @ProductName varchar(50),
 @ProductDescription varchar(1000),
 @ProductPrice money,
 @ProductImage varchar(50),
 @OnDepartmentPromotion bit,
 @OnCatalogPromotion bit)
AS

UPDATE Product
SET Name = @ProductName,
    Description = @ProductDescription,
    Price = CONVERT(money,@ProductPrice),
    ImagePath = @ProductImage,
    OnDepartmentPromotion = @OnDepartmentPromotion,
    OnCatalogPromotion = @OnCatalogPromotion
WHERE ProductID = @ProductID

RETURN
```

Administering Product Details

The products list you built earlier is wonderful, but it lacks a few important features.
The final control you're implementing will take care of these missing features.
ProductDetailsAdmin.ascx will allow you to

- View the product's picture.

- Remove the product from its category.

- Remove the product from the database completely.

- Assign the current product to an additional category.

- Move the current product to another category.

When it comes to product removal, things aren't straightforward: you can either
unassign the product from a category by removing the record from the ProductCategory
table, or you can effectively remove the product from the Product table. Because products are accessed in the catalog by selecting a category, you must make sure there are no
orphaned products (products that don't belong to any category), because they couldn't
be accessed using the current administration interface.

So, if you added a Delete button to the data grid, what kind of deletion would that
button have to do? Delete the product from the database? This would work, but it's
a bit awkward if you have a product assigned to multiple categories and you only want
to remove it from a single category. On the other hand, if the Delete button removes
the product from the current category, you can create orphaned products because they
exist in the Product table, but they don't belong to any category so they can't be accessed.
You could fix that by allowing the site administrator to see the complete list of products
without locating them by department and category.

The simple solution implemented in this chapter is like that: if the product belongs
to more than one category, the Delete button unassigns the product from the current
category. If the product belongs to only one category, the product is first unassigned from
the current category, and then also removed from the Product table.

For this strategy to work, you need to let the administrator know which categories
the product belongs to (so the administrator will know what the Delete button does
to that product).

With ProductsDetailsAdmin, apart from permitting the administrator to remove
products, you'll also see how to assign the currently selected product to an additional
category, or move the product to another category.

The ProductDetailsAdmin *Web User Control*

Figure 8-43 shows how the control will look for a product that belongs to a single
category.

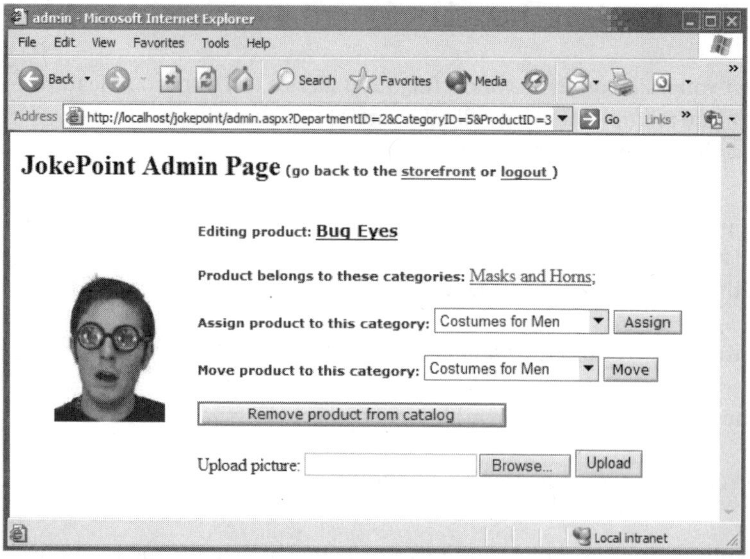

Figure 8-43. The product details admin page

You'll implement the control in the next two exercises. In the first exercise, you'll implement most of its functionality, and in the second exercise, you'll implement the file upload feature.

Exercise: Implementing `ProductDetailsAdmin.ascx`

1. Create a new user control named `ProductDetailsAdmin` in the `AdminUserControls` folder.

2. Create a table with one row and two columns, either in HTML View or by using the Table, Insert ➤ Table menu. Add an `Image` control in the left cell, and then add five `Label` controls, a `LinkButton`, two `DropDownList` controls, and three `Button` controls to the second cell, as shown in Figure 8-44.

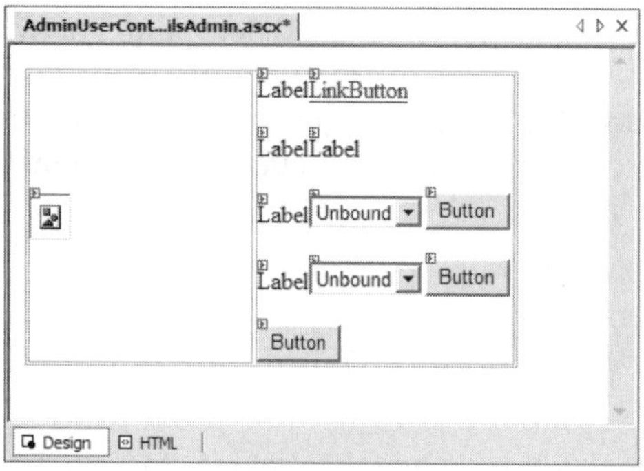

Figure 8-44. Creating a Product Details form

3. Set their properties as shown in Table 8-8.

Table 8-8. Setting Controls' Properties in ProductDetailsAdmin.ascx

Control Type	ID Property	Text Property	CssClass Property
Image	productImage	n/a	
Label	Label1	Editing product:	AdminPageText
LinkButton	productNameLink	*(clear this property)*	ListDescription
Label	Label2	Product belongs to these categories:	AdminPageText
Label	categoriesListLabel	*(clear this property)*	
Label	Label4	Assign product to this category:	AdminPageText
DropDownList	categoriesList	n/a	
Button	assignButton	Assign	AdminButtonText
Label	Label5	Move product to this category:	AdminPageText
DropDownList	categoriesList2	n/a	
Button	moveButton	Move	AdminButtonText
Button	removeButton	(We will set this in code)	AdminButtonText

4. After the changes, the control looks like Figure 8-45 in Design View.

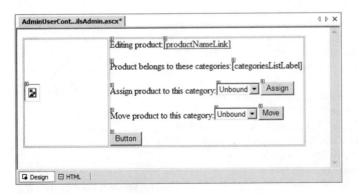

Figure 8-45. ProductDetailsAdmin.ascx *in Design View*

5. Double-click somewhere in the control, but not on one of its constituent controls, to open the Page_Load event handler. Modify it like this:

```
' Will store the number of categories associated with the selected product
Private categoriesCount As Integer = 0

Private Sub Page_Load(ByVal sender As System.Object, _
ByVal e As System.EventArgs) Handles MyBase.Load
  ' Get the ProductID from the query string
  Dim productId As String = Request.QueryString("ProductID")
  ' The control gets displayed only when a product is selected
  If Not IsNumeric(productId) Then
    Me.Visible = False
    ' Only reload data when the page is loaded for the first time
  ElseIf Not IsPostBack Then
    FillControls()
  End If
End Sub


Private Sub FillControls()
  ' Set the product name
  productNameLink.Text = Request.QueryString("ProductName")
  ' Display the product's image.
  productImage.ImageUrl = "../ProductImages/" & _
                Request.QueryString("ImagePath")
  ' Get the ProductID from the query string
  Dim productId As String = Request.QueryString("ProductID")
  ' Get the list of categories into an SqlDataReader object
  Dim reader As SqlClient.SqlDataReader
  reader = CatalogAdmin.GetCategoriesForProduct(productId)
  ' Temporary variables we'll use in this method
  Dim categoryName As String
  Dim categoryId As String
  ' Read each category and add its name to the label
  categoriesListLabel.Text = ""
  While (reader.Read)
    ' extract the category ID from the SqlDataReader
    categoryId = reader.GetValue(0).ToString()
    ' extract the category name from the SqlDataReader
    categoryName = reader.GetValue(1).ToString()
    ' append category links to the Label
    categoriesListLabel.Text += _
       "<a href=""" + Request.Url.AbsolutePath + _
       "?DepartmentID=" + Request.QueryString("DepartmentID") + _
       "&CategoryID=" + categoryId + """>" + _
       categoryName + "</a>" + "; "
    ' increase the number of categories the selected product belongs to
    categoriesCount = categoriesCount + 1
  End While
  ' Set the text of the Delete button depending on
  ' the number of categories
```

```
      If categoriesCount = 1 Then
        ' Set the text on the Remove button
        removeButton.Text = "Remove product from catalog"
      Else
        ' Obtain the Category ID from the query string
        categoryId = Request.QueryString("CategoryID")
          ' Get the name of the current category from the database
          categoryName = Catalog.GetCategoryDetails(categoryId).Name
          ' Set the text on the Remove button
          removeButton.Text="Remove product from category: " + categoryName
        End If
      ' Close the SqlDataReader. This will also close the data connection
      reader.Close()
      ' Get all the categories, to populate the DropDownList with them
      reader = CatalogAdmin.GetCategoriesForNotProduct(productId)
      ' Add the list of categories to the DropDownList objects
      categoriesList.Items.Clear()
      categoriesList2.Items.Clear()
      While (reader.Read)
        ' extract the category ID from the SqlDataReader
        categoryId = reader.GetValue(0).ToString()
        ' extract the category name from the SqlDataReader
        categoryName = reader.GetValue(1).ToString()
        ' add the category to the CategoriesList dropdown
        categoriesList.Items.Add(New ListItem(categoryName, categoryId))
        ' add the category to the CategoriesList2 dropdown
        categoriesList2.Items.Add(New ListItem(categoryName, categoryId))
      End While
      ' Close the SqlDataReader. This will also close the data connection
      reader.Close()
    End Sub
```

6. While in Design View, double-click the LinkButton, and then complete its Click event handler like this:

```
Private Sub productNameLink_Click(ByVal sender As System.Object, _
ByVal e As System.EventArgs) Handles productNameLink.Click
  BackToCategory()
End Sub

Private Sub BackToCategory()
  ' The category currently selected by the user
  Dim categoryId As String = Request.QueryString("CategoryID")
  ' The department currently selected by the user
  Dim departmentId As String = Request.QueryString("DepartmentID")
  ' Redirect to the category admin page
  Response.Redirect("admin.aspx?DepartmentID=" & _
                    departmentId & "&CategoryID=" & categoryId)
End Sub
```

7. While in Design View, double-click the first button (Assign), and then complete its Click event handler method like this:

```
Private Sub assignButton_Click(ByVal sender As System.Object, _
ByVal e As System.EventArgs) Handles assignButton.Click
  ' The product currently selected by the user
  Dim productId As String = Request.QueryString("ProductID")
  ' Extract ID of the category that was selected in the DropDownList
  Dim categoryId As String = categoriesList.SelectedItem.Value
  ' Associate the product with the category
  CatalogAdmin.AssignProductToCategory(productId, categoryId)
  ' Update the page with the new info
  FillControls()
End Sub
```

8. While in Design View, double-click the second button (Move), and then complete its Click event handler method like this:

```
Private Sub moveButton_Click(ByVal sender As System.Object, _
ByVal e As System.EventArgs) Handles moveButton.Click
  ' The product currently selected by the user
  Dim productId As String = Request.QueryString("ProductID")
  ' The category currently selected by the user
  Dim oldCategoryId As String = Request.QueryString("CategoryID")
  ' The ID of the category that was selected in the DropDownList
  Dim newCategoryId As String = categoriesList2.SelectedItem.Value
  ' Associate the product with the category
  CatalogAdmin.MoveProductToCategory(productId, oldCategoryId, newCategoryId)
  ' Update the page with the new info
  BackToCategory()
End Sub
```

9. While in Design View, double-click the third button (Remove), and then complete its event handler method like this:

```
Private Sub removeButton_Click(ByVal sender As System.Object, _
ByVal e As System.EventArgs) Handles removeButton.Click
  ' The product currently selected by the user
  Dim productId As String = Request.QueryString("ProductID")
  ' The category currently selected by the user
  Dim categoryId As String = Request.QueryString("CategoryID")
  ' The department currently selected by the user
  Dim departmentId As String = Request.QueryString("DepartmentID")
  ' Remove the product
  CatalogAdmin.RemoveFromCategoryOrDeleteProduct(productId, categoryId)
  ' Redirect to the category admin page
  Response.Redirect("admin.aspx?DepartmentID=" & _
    departmentId & "&CategoryID=" & categoryId)
End Sub
```

10. Add `ProductDetailsAdmin.ascx` to the last cell in the table from `admin.aspx`, as shown in Figure 8-46.

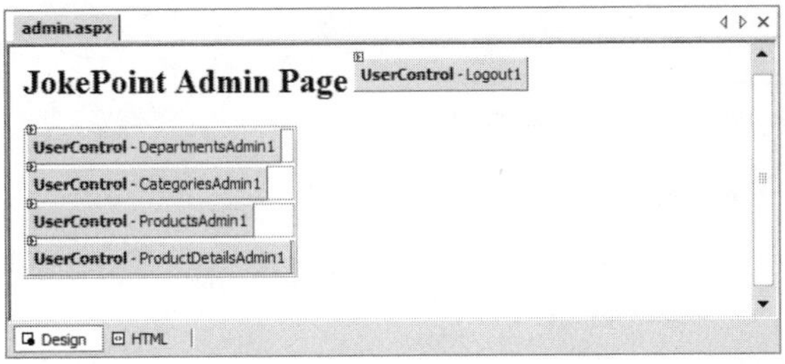

Figure 8-46. Adding `ProductDetailsAdmin.ascx` *to the last cell in the table*

How It Works: `ProductDetailsAdmin.ascx`

The `FillControls` method is responsible for populating all the form's controls with data. In this method, you manually parse `SqlDataReader` objects to populate the `categoriesListLabel` control (which lists the categories the currently selected product belongs to), and the `categoriesList` and `categoriesList2` `DropDownList` objects (which allow the administrator to assign or move the product to another category).

When filling the `DropDownLists`, you also save the categories' IDs, not only their names—you'll need these IDs in `assignButton_Click` and `moveButton_Click`, when you'll need the ID of the category selected in the `DropDownList`.

The actual functionality is performed by the middle-tier methods, which you'll implement next.

Middle-Tier Methods for Product Details Admin

Add the following methods to the `CatalogAdmin` class:

- `RemoveFromCategoryOrDeleteProduct` is called when the Delete button is clicked.

- `GetCategoriesForProduct` is used to get the list of categories that are related to the specified product.

- `GetCategoriesForNotProduct` returns the categories that are not associated with the specified product.

- `AssignProductToCategory` and `MoveProductToCategory` do what their names imply.

Because their functionality is better expressed by the stored procedures they call, we'll discuss more about them when implementing the data tier. Add the following code to the CatalogAdmin class:

```
#Region "  Product Details  "
  Public Shared Function RemoveFromCategoryOrDeleteProduct( _
  ByVal productId As String, ByVal categoryId As String)
    ' Create the connection object
    Dim connection As New SqlConnection(connectionString)
    ' Create and initialize the command object
    Dim command As New SqlCommand("RemoveFromCategoryOrDeleteProduct",connection)
    command.CommandType = CommandType.StoredProcedure
    ' Add an input parameter and supply a value for it
    command.Parameters.Add("@ProductID", SqlDbType.Int)
    command.Parameters("@ProductID").Value = productId
    ' Add an input parameter and supply a value for it
    command.Parameters.Add("@CategoryID", SqlDbType.Int)
    command.Parameters("@CategoryID").Value = categoryId
    ' Open the connection, execute the command, and close the connection
    Try
      connection.Open()
      command.ExecuteNonQuery()
    Finally
      connection.Close()
    End Try
  End Function

  Public Shared Function GetCategoriesForProduct( _
  ByVal productId As String) As SqlDataReader
    ' Create the connection object
    Dim connection As New SqlConnection(connectionString)
    ' Create and initialize the command object
    Dim command As New SqlCommand("GetCategoriesForProduct", connection)
    command.CommandType = CommandType.StoredProcedure
    ' Add an input parameter and supply a value for it
    command.Parameters.Add("@ProductID", SqlDbType.Int)
    command.Parameters("@ProductID").Value = productId
    Try
      ' Open the connection
      connection.Open()
      ' Return an SqlDataReader to the calling function
      Return command.ExecuteReader(CommandBehavior.CloseConnection)
    Catch e As Exception
      ' Close the connection and throw the exception
      connection.Close()
      Throw e
    End Try
  End Function
```

```
Public Shared Function GetCategoriesForNotProduct( _
ByVal productId As String) As SqlDataReader
  ' Create the connection object
  Dim connection As New SqlConnection(connectionString)
  ' Create and initialize the command object
  Dim command As New SqlCommand("GetCategoriesForNotProduct", connection)
  command.CommandType = CommandType.StoredProcedure
  ' Add an input parameter and supply a value for it
  command.Parameters.Add("@ProductID", SqlDbType.Int)
  command.Parameters("@ProductID").Value = productId
  Try
    ' Open the connection
    connection.Open()
    ' Return an SqlDataReader to the calling function
    Return command.ExecuteReader(CommandBehavior.CloseConnection)
  Catch e As Exception
    ' Close the connection and throw the exception
    connection.Close()
    Throw e
  End Try
End Function

Public Shared Function AssignProductToCategory(ByVal productId As String, _
ByVal categoryId As String)
  ' Create the connection object
  Dim connection As New SqlConnection(connectionString)
  ' Create and initialize the command object
  Dim command As New SqlCommand("AssignProductToCategory", connection)
  command.CommandType = CommandType.StoredProcedure
  ' Add an input parameter and supply a value for it
  command.Parameters.Add("@ProductID", SqlDbType.Int, 4)
  command.Parameters("@ProductID").Value = productId
  ' Add an input parameter and supply a value for it
  command.Parameters.Add("@CategoryID", SqlDbType.Int, 4)
  command.Parameters("@CategoryID").Value = categoryId
  ' Open the connection, execute the command, and close the connection
  Try
    connection.Open()
    command.ExecuteNonQuery()
  Finally
    connection.Close()
  End Try
End Function

Public Shared Function MoveProductToCategory(ByVal productId As String, _
ByVal oldCategoryId As String, ByVal newCategoryID As String)
  ' Create the connection object
  Dim connection As New SqlConnection(connectionString)
  ' Create and initialize the command object
  Dim command As New SqlCommand("MoveProductToCategory", connection)
  command.CommandType = CommandType.StoredProcedure
  ' Add an input parameter and supply a value for it
```

```
          command.Parameters.Add("@ProductID", SqlDbType.Int, 4)
          command.Parameters("@ProductID").Value = productId
          ' Add an input parameter and supply a value for it
          command.Parameters.Add("@OldCategoryID", SqlDbType.Int, 4)
          command.Parameters("@OldCategoryID").Value = oldCategoryId
          ' Add an input parameter and supply a value for it
          command.Parameters.Add("@NewCategoryID", SqlDbType.Int, 4)
          command.Parameters("@NewCategoryID").Value = newCategoryID
          ' Open the connection, execute the command, and close the connection
          Try
            connection.Open()
            command.ExecuteNonQuery()
          Finally
            connection.Close()
          End Try
        End Function
  #End Region
```

Stored Procedures for Product Details Admin

Here you add the following stored procedures to the JokePoint database:

- RemoveFromCategoryOrDeleteProduct

- GetCategoriesForProduct

- GetCategoriesForNotProduct

- AssignProductToCategory

- MoveProductToCategory

RemoveFromCategoryOrDeleteProduct

The RemoveFromCategoryOrDeleteProduct stored procedure verifies how many categories the product exists in. If the product exists in more than one category, the
stored procedure just removes the product from the current category (ID received as
a parameter). If the product is associated with a single category, it is first removed
from the category and then effectively deleted from the database.

```
CREATE PROCEDURE RemoveFromCategoryOrDeleteProduct
(@ProductID int, @CategoryID int)
AS

IF (SELECT COUNT(*) FROM ProductCategory WHERE ProductID=@ProductID)>1
  DELETE FROM ProductCategory
  WHERE CategoryID=@CategoryID AND ProductID=@ProductID
```

```
ELSE
 BEGIN
   DELETE FROM ProductCategory WHERE ProductID=@ProductID
   DELETE FROM Product where ProductID=@ProductID
 END

RETURN
```

GetCategoriesForProduct

The GetCategoriesForProduct stored procedure returns a list of the categories that belong to the specified product. Only their IDs and names are returned because this is the only information we're interested in.

```
CREATE PROCEDURE GetCategoriesForProduct
(@ProductID int)
AS

SELECT Category.CategoryID, Name
FROM Category INNER JOIN ProductCategory
ON Category.CategoryID = ProductCategory.CategoryID
WHERE ProductCategory.ProductID = @ProductID

RETURN
```

GetCategoriesForNotProduct

The strangely named GetCategoriesForNotProduct stored procedure returns the IDs and names of the categories that *do not* belong to the specified product. This will be called from ProductDetailsAdmin.ascx, when you need the list of categories that a product can be associated with (or moved to).

```
CREATE PROCEDURE GetCategoriesForNotProduct
(@ProductID int)
AS

SELECT Category.CategoryID, Name
FROM Category
WHERE CategoryID NOT IN
    (SELECT Category.CategoryID
     FROM Category INNER JOIN ProductCategory
     ON Category.CategoryID = ProductCategory.CategoryID
     WHERE ProductCategory.ProductID = @ProductID)

RETURN
```

AssignProductToCategory

The AssignProductToCategory stored procedure associates a product with a category by adding a (ProductID, CategoryID) value pair into the ProductCategory table.

```
CREATE PROCEDURE AssignProductToCategory
(@ProductID int, @CategoryID int)
AS

INSERT INTO ProductCategory (ProductID, CategoryID)
VALUES (@ProductID, @CategoryID)

RETURN
```

Note that you don't do any verification here. If an error occurs (because the entered ProductID is not associated with any product or the ProductID, CategoryID pair already exists in the ProductCategory table), the error is trapped at the presentation-tier level and the administrator is notified.

Still, since we talked about the error-handling techniques, it's worth noting that you can make the stored procedure smart enough to do some validation before attempting to add the (ProductID, CategorID) pair to ProductCategory table.

Following is a bulletproof version of the stored procedure, which inserts the new record into ProductCategory only if the received ProductID and CategoryID values are valid, and if the pair doesn't already exist in the database:

```
CREATE PROCEDURE AssignProductToCategory
(@ProductID int, @CategoryID int)
AS

IF EXISTS
  (SELECT [Name]
   FROM Product
   WHERE ProductID=@ProductID)
  AND EXISTS
  (SELECT [Name]
   FROM Category
   WHERE CategoryID=@CategoryID)
  AND NOT EXISTS
  (SELECT *
   FROM ProductCategory
   WHERE CategoryID=@CategoryID AND ProductID=@ProductID)
INSERT INTO ProductCategory (ProductID, CategoryID)
VALUES (@ProductID, @CategoryID)

RETURN
```

MoveProductToCategory

MoveProductToCategory is the stored procedure that moves a product from one category to another:

```
CREATE PROCEDURE MoveProductToCategory
(@ProductID int, @OldCategoryID int, @NewCategoryID int)
AS

UPDATE ProductCategory
SET CategoryID=@NewCategoryID
WHERE CategoryID=@OldCategoryID
  AND ProductID=@ProductID

RETURN
```

Testing the ProductDetailsAdmin Web User Control

To see if this works, open the details page of a product by clicking the Select button for one product in the ProductsAdmin control. You should see something like Figure 8-47.

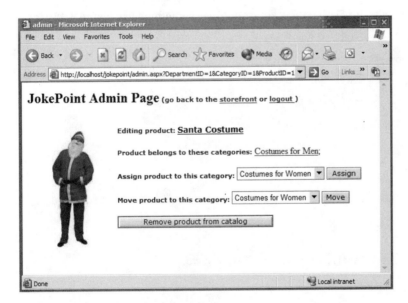

Figure 8-47. The details page of a product

Uploading Product Pictures

In this last section of the chapter, you'll add a few bits to ProductDetailsAdmin that will allow you to upload a picture for the currently selected product. You'll implement all the new functionality in the next exercise.

Exercise: *Updating* ProductDetailsAdmin.ascx *to upload product pictures*

1. Open admin.aspx, go to HTML View, and modify its <form> element by adding the enctype value:

    ```
    <form id="Form1" method="post" runat="server"
    enctype="multipart/form-data">
    ```

2. Open ProductDetailsAdmin.ascx in HTML View, and add the following HTML code below the Remove Product button.

    ```
    Upload picture:
    <input id="fileName" type="file" name="fileName" runat="server">
    <asp:button id="uploadFile" text="Upload" runat="server"></asp:Button>
    <asp:label id="uploadMessageLabel" runat="server"></asp:label>
    ```

    Now switch to Design View. You should see something like Figure 8-48.

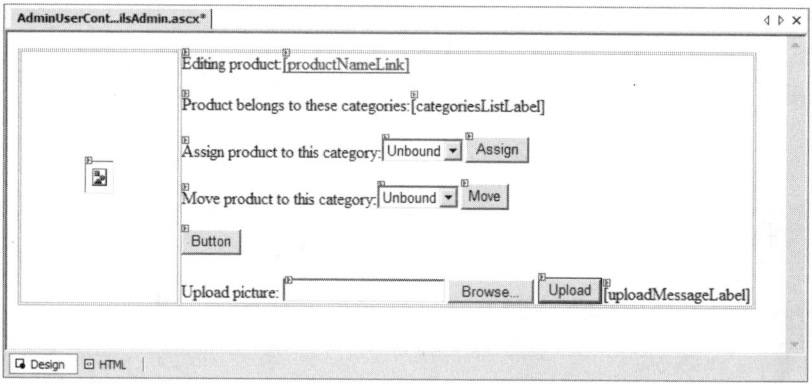

Figure 8-48. ProductDetailsAdmin.ascx *in Design View*

3. While in Design View, double-click the Upload button to generate its Click event. Modify it like this:

```
Private Sub uploadFile_Click(ByVal sender As System.Object, ByVal e As
System.EventArgs) Handles uploadFile.Click
  ' Get the full path of the downloaded file
  Dim imageFilePath As String = fileName.PostedFile.FileName
  ' Extract the file name from the path
  ' (we're not interested in the original client-side path]
  Dim imageFileName = System.IO.Path.GetFileName(imageFilePath)
  Try
    ' Save the file
    fileName.PostedFile.SaveAs(Server.MapPath("./ProductImages/") + _
                                                          imageFileName)
    ' Update the database to reflect the new image file
    Dim productId = Request.QueryString("ProductID")
    CatalogAdmin.UpdateProductPicture(productId, imageFileName)
    ' If the upload is successful, redirect to the category page
    BackToCategory()
  Catch
    ' Show update failure message
    uploadMessageLabel.Text = "<BR><font color=red>Upload failed!"
  End Try
End Sub
```

4. Add the following method to the CatalogAdmin class:

```
Public Shared Function UpdateProductPicture(ByVal productId As String,
ByVal imageFileName As String)
  ' Create the connection object
  Dim connection As New SqlConnection(connectionString)
  ' Create and initialize the command object
  Dim command As New SqlCommand("UpdateProductPicture", connection)
  command.CommandType = CommandType.StoredProcedure
  ' Add an input parameter and supply a value for it
  command.Parameters.Add("@ProductID", SqlDbType.Int)
  command.Parameters("@ProductID").Value = productId
  ' Add an input parameter and supply a value for it
  command.Parameters.Add("@ImageFileName", SqlDbType.VarChar, 50)
  command.Parameters("@ImageFileName").Value = imageFileName
  ' Open the connection, execute the command, and close the connection
  Try
    connection.Open()
    command.ExecuteNonQuery()
  Finally
    connection.Close()
  End Try
End Function
```

5.   Add the following stored procedure to the JokePoint database

```
CREATE PROCEDURE UpdateProductPicture
     (@ProductID int,
       @ImageFileName varchar(50))
AS

UPDATE Product
SET ImagePath = @ImageFileName
WHERE ProductID = @ProductID

RETURN
```

How it Works: Uploading Files with ASP.NET

The technique to upload files with ASP.NET is quite simple. The download is handled in part with HTML code by using an <input type="file"> element (which creates a text box and a Browse button), in a form marked with enctype="multipart/form-data".

The <input> element, named fileName, is marked to run at server side. You use it to save the selected file to the hard disk, when the Upload button is clicked. At the end, you update the database with the new product picture information.

Summary

You've done quite a lot of coding in this chapter. You implemented four user controls, along with their middle-tier methods and stored procedures for the data tier. You learned how to implement a simple authentication scheme so only administrators are allowed to access the catalog administration page.

You made contact with the DataGrid, which is probably the most powerful web control that comes packaged with the .NET Framework. You learned how to use its built-in features for editing, selecting, updating, and deleting records, and how to use template columns to improve its functionality.

At the end of the chapter, you learned how to upload files from the client to the server using ASP.NET.

CHAPTER 9

The Shopping Basket

WELCOME TO THE SECOND STAGE of development! At this stage, you start improving and adding new features to the already existing, fully functional e-commerce site.

So, what can you improve about it? Well, the answer to this question isn't that hard to find if you take a quick look at the popular e-commerce sites on the web. They have user personalization and product recommendations, they remember customers' preferences, and boast many other features that make the site easy to remember and hard to leave without first buying something.

Because in the first stage of development we extensively relied on a third party-payment processor (PayPal), which supplied an integrated shopping basket, we didn't record any shopping cart or order info into the database. Right now, your site isn't capable of displaying a list of "most wanted" products, or any other information about the products that have been sold through the web site, because, at this stage, you aren't tracking the products sold. This makes it impossible to implement any of the improvements listed earlier.

Obviously, saving order information into the database is your first priority and most of the features you'll want to implement next rely on having a record of the products sold. To achieve this functionality, you'll implement a custom shopping basket and a custom checkout.

In this chapter, you will implement the custom shopping basket, which will store its data in the local JokePoint database. This will provide you with more flexibility, compared to the PayPal shopping basket over which you have no control and which cannot be saved into your database for further processing and analysis. With the custom shopping basket, when the visitor clicks the Add to Cart button for a product, a new entry is created in the database and the visitor will be shown a page like Figure 9-1.

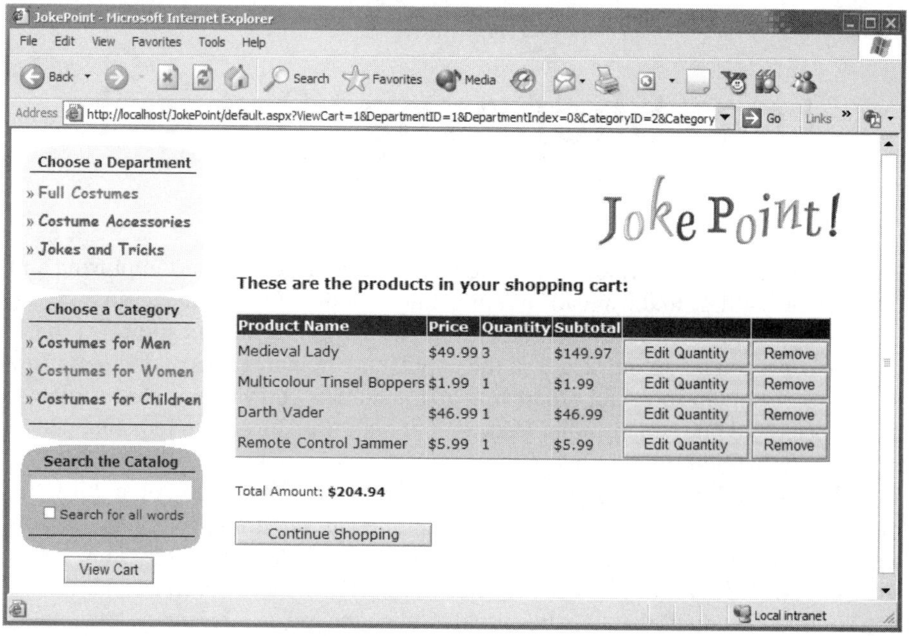

Figure 9-1. The JokePoint Shopping Cart

At the end of this chapter, you'll have a functional shopping basket, but the visitor will not yet have the ability to order the products contained in it. This will be taken care of in the next chapter, where you'll implement a custom checkout. Simply put, in the next chapter, you'll add the Proceed to Checkout button. When the visitor clicks this button, the products in the shopping basket are saved as a separate order in the database, and the visitor is redirected to a page where they can pay for them. If you integrated the PayPal shopping cart for the first development stage, starting with the next chapter, PayPal will only be used to handle payments, and you won't rely on its shopping cart any more.

Before moving to the details, let's review what you'll do in this chapter:

- Talk about how to design your shopping cart.

- Add a new database table to store shopping cart records.

- Create the stored procedures that work with the new table.

- Implement the business layer procedures.

- Implement the Add to Cart and View Cart buttons; if you implemented them to work with PayPal as explained in the PayPal chapter, here you'll make them work with the new shopping cart instead of the PayPal shopping cart.

- Implement the presentation layer part of the custom shopping cart.

Designing the Shopping Cart

Before starting to write the code for the shopping cart, take a look at an overview of what you're going to do.

First, note that you won't have any user personalization features at this stage of the site. We don't care who buys our products, we just want to know what products were sold, and when. When you add user customization features in the later chapters, your task will be fairly simple: when the visitor authenticates, the visitor's temporary (anonymous) shopping cart will be associated with the visitor's account. Because you work with temporary shopping carts, even after implementing the customer account system, the visitor isn't required to supply additional information (log in) earlier than necessary.

Having that said, probably the best way to store shopping cart information is to generate a unique cart ID for each shopping cart and save it on the visitor's computer as a cookie. When the visitor clicks the Add to Cart button, the server first verifies whether the cookie exists on the client computer. If it does, the specified product is added to the existing cart. Otherwise, the server generates another cart ID, saves it to the client's cookie, and then adds the product to the newly generated shopping cart.

In the previous chapter, you created the user controls by starting with the presentation layer components. However, this strategy doesn't work here because now you need to do a bit more design work beforehand, so we'll take the more common approach, and start with the database tier.

Storing Shopping Cart Information

We'll store all shopping cart items in a single table, named ShoppingCart. Add this table to your JokePoint database as shown in Figure 9-2, and then we'll comment on it.

Column Name	Data Type	Length	Allow Nulls
CartID	char	36	
ProductID	int	4	
Quantity	int	4	
DateProductAdded	datetime	8	

Figure 9-2. Designing the ShoppingCart *table*

CartID is the unique ID you'll generate for each shopping cart. Unlike the other unique identifiers you've seen so far, this is not an integer field. It is a char(36) field, which will be filled with a GUID string. A GUID (Globally Unique Identifier) is a value guaranteed to be unique across time and space. Two generated GUIDs will never be the same. The string representation of a GUID has 36 characters: the GUID itself is 32 bytes long, and its string representation also contains four separating dashes. An example of a GUID is ff8029a7-91e2-4ca2-b4e7-99a7588be751.

TIP   *When you know the exact length of the strings you're storing in a table field, it's better to use the* char *data type instead of* varchar.

The second field is ProductID, which, as expected, holds the ID of an existing product. To ensure that the cart doesn't hold any nonexistent products, you'll enforce the One-to-Many relationship between the ShoppingCart and Product tables through a FOREIGN KEY constraint.

It's important to note that the primary key is formed from both the CartID and ProductID fields (we have a *composite primary key*). This makes sense because a particular product can exist only once in a particular shopping cart, so a (CartID, ProductID) pair shouldn't appear more than once in the table. If the visitor adds a product more than once, the Quantity value increases. The relationship is tied between the ProductID columns in the ShoppingCart and Product tables.

Each record in ShoppingCart also has a DateProductAdded field, which is automatically populated with the current date when a new product is added to the cart, and will be useful when deleting old records.

TIP   *The current implementation of the* AddProductToCart *procedure manually fills the* DateProductAdded *field using the* GETDATE *function. Alternatively, you can specify* GETDATE *as the default value for the* DateProductAdded *field.*

Before moving on, create the ShoppingCart table as shown earlier, save it to the database, and then implement the One-to-Many relationship between the Product and ShoppingCart tables by adding a FOREIGN KEY constraint on their ProductID columns. The steps were explained in Chapter 4, so you might want to re-read some paragraphs in that chapter if you don't exactly remember the steps. Remember that you can also create this table and the relationship by using database diagrams or by running the SQL script provided in the code download for this chapter in the Downloads section of the Apress web site (http://www.apress.com).

NOTE   *Feel free to use* smalldatetime *instead of* datetime *for the* DataProductAdded *column. This stores the date with less precision, down to minutes, but occupies 4 bytes instead of 8.*

Implementing the Data Tier

Because you have already created stored procedures in the previous chapters, we'll move a bit quicker this time. You need to add the following stored procedures to the JokePoint database:

- AddProductToCart adds a product to a shopping cart.

- UpdateCartItem modifies a shopping cart record.

- RemoveProductFromCart deletes a record from the ShoppingCart table.

- GetShoppingCartProducts gets the list of products in the specified shopping cart.

- GetTotalAmount returns the total cost of the products in the specified product cart.

AddProductToCart

AddProductToCart is called when the visitor clicks the Add to Cart button for one of the products. If the selected product already exists in the shopping cart, its quantity should be increased by one; if the product doesn't exist, one unit is added to the shopping cart (a new ShoppingCart record is created).

Not surprisingly, the parameters AddProductToCart receives are CartID and ProductID.

The stored procedure first searches to determine whether the product mentioned (ProductID, CartID) pair exists in the ShoppingCart table. If it does, the stored procedure updates the current product quantity in the shopping cart by adding one unit. Otherwise, the procedure creates a new record for the product in ShoppingCart with a default quantity of 1, but not before checking whether the mentioned @ProductID is valid.

```
CREATE Procedure AddProductToCart
(@CartID char(36),
 @ProductID int)
AS

IF EXISTS
        (SELECT CartID
         FROM ShoppingCart
         WHERE ProductID = @ProductID AND CartID = @CartID)
    UPDATE ShoppingCart
    SET Quantity = Quantity + 1
    WHERE ProductID = @ProductID AND CartID = @CartID
ELSE
    IF EXISTS (SELECT Name FROM Product WHERE ProductID=@ProductID)
        INSERT INTO ShoppingCart (CartID, ProductID, Quantity, DateProductAdded)
        VALUES (@CartID, @ProductID, 1, GETDATE())

RETURN
```

You use the GETDATE system function to retrieve the current date and manually populate the DateProductAdded field, but you can set the GETDATE function as the default value of that field instead.

RemoveProductFromCart

Following is the stored procedure that removes a product from the shopping cart. This will happen when the Remove button is clicked for one of the products in the shopping cart.

```
CREATE PROCEDURE RemoveProductFromCart
(@CartID char(36),
 @ProductID int)
AS

DELETE FROM ShoppingCart
WHERE CartID = @CartID and ProductID = @ProductID

RETURN
```

UpdateCartItem

UpdateCartItem is used when you want to update the quantity of an existing shopping cart item. This will be called when editing the product quantity in the shopping cart (see Figure 9-3).

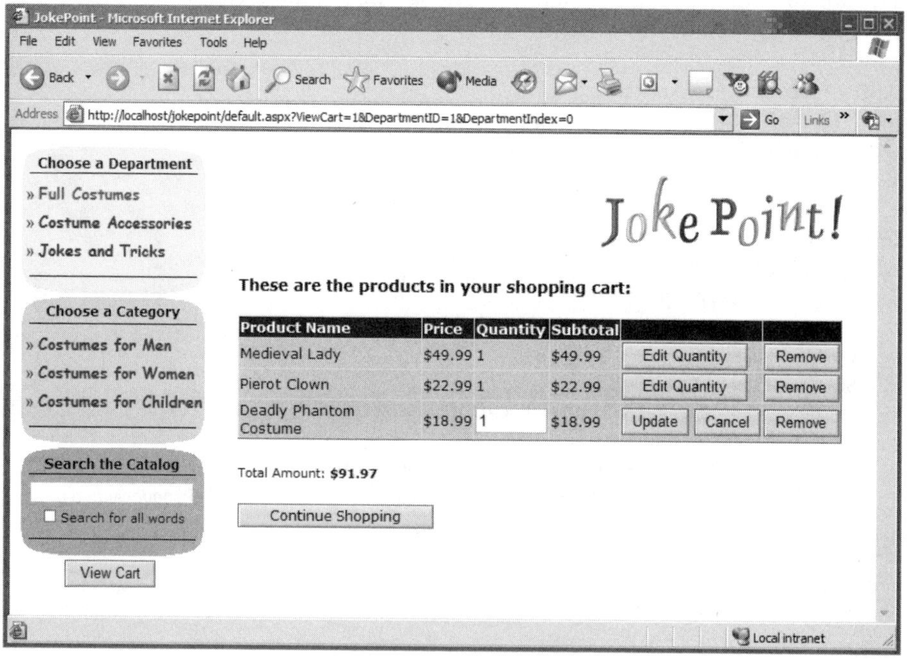

Figure 9-3. Updating a quantity in the shopping cart

UpdateCartItem receives as parameters three values: @CartID, @ProductID, and @Quantity.

If @Quantity is 0 or less, UpdateCartItem calls RemoveItemFromCart to remove the mentioned product from the shopping cart. Otherwise, it updates the quantity of the product in the shopping cart, and also updates DateProductAdded to accurately reflect the time the record was last modified.

 TIP *Updating the* DateProductAdded *field is important because the administrator will be able to remove old shopping carts from the database.*

```
CREATE Procedure UpdateCartItem
(@CartID char(36),
 @ProductID int,
 @Quantity int)
As

IF @Quantity<=0
   EXEC RemoveProductFromCart @CartID, @ProductID
ELSE
   UPDATE ShoppingCart
   SET Quantity = @Quantity, DateProductAdded=GETDATE()
   WHERE ProductID = @ProductID AND CartID = @CartID

RETURN
```

GetShoppingCartProducts

This stored procedure returns the ID, Name, Price, Quantity, and Subtotal for each product in the shopping cart. Because the ShoppingCart table only stores the ProductID for each product it stores, you need to join the ShoppingCart and Product tables to get the information you need.

```
CREATE PROCEDURE GetShoppingCartProducts
(@CartID char(36))
AS

SELECT Product.ProductID, Product.Name, Product.Price, ShoppingCart.Quantity,
       Product.Price*ShoppingCart.Quantity AS Subtotal
FROM ShoppingCart INNER JOIN Product
ON ShoppingCart.ProductID = Product.ProductID
WHERE ShoppingCart.CartID = @CartID

RETURN
```

NOTE Subtotal *is a calculated column. It doesn't exist in any of the tables you joined, but it's generated using a formula, which in this case is the price of the product multiplied by its quantity. When sending back the results,* Subtotal *will be regarded as a separate column.*

GetTotalAmount

GetTotalAmount returns the total value of the products in the shopping cart. This is called when displaying the total amount for the shopping cart.

We declare a variable named @Amount that calculates the sum of each product's price times its quantity in the shopping cart. The syntax used to calculate @Amount is interesting, and it's worth taking a closer look.

At the end, the value stored in @Amount is returned

```
CREATE PROCEDURE GetTotalAmount
(@CartID char(36))
AS

DECLARE @Amount money

SELECT ISNULL(SUM(Product.Price*ShoppingCart.Quantity),0)
FROM ShoppingCart INNER JOIN Product
ON ShoppingCart.ProductID = Product.ProductID
WHERE ShoppingCart.CartID = @CartID

RETURN
```

NOTE *The* ISNULL *method is used to return* 0 *instead of a* NULL *total amount (this happen if the shopping cart is empty). You must do this because the business tier expects to receive a numerical value as the amount.*

This stored procedure is different than the others in that it returns a single value instead of a result set. In the business tier, you'll retrieve this value using the ExecuteScalar method of the SqlCommand object.

Implementing the Business Tier

You'll write the business layer methods for the shopping cart in a separate class named ShoppingCart.

The ShoppingCart class will support the functionality required for the presentation layer of the shopping cart, and will call the stored procedures you wrote earlier. For example, when the visitor clicks the Add to Cart button, a method of the ShoppingCart class named AddProduct is called. All the methods of the ShoppingCart class receive either no parameters (such as GetTotalAmount or GetProducts), or one parameter, namely productId (AddProduct, UpdateProductQuantity, RemoveProduct). UpdateProductQuantity also has a quantity parameter.

None of the methods receives a CartID parameter, which might appear strange because all the stored procedures you've written so far do require a CartID parameter. So, how does the AddProduct method know which CartID to send to the AddProductToCart stored procedure?

Generating Shopping Cart IDs

The ShoppingCart has two properties. One of these is connectionString, which you already know from the previous chapters. The second property is shoppingCartId, which returns the cart ID of the current visitor. It's important to understand how this latter property works.

shoppingCartId is a read-only property that returns the CartID of the visitor for whom the call has been made. But how do you find out the unique CartID of the visitor? Well, the answer lies in the use of cookies. **Cookies** are client-side pieces of information that are managed by the visitor's browser; they are stored as name-value pairs. Cookies have the advantages of not consuming server resources (because they are managed at the client), and having configurable expiration. This is useful because you can set the shopping cart cookie to expire when the browser session ends (so a new shopping cart is created every time the visitor comes back to the site), or they can be set to exist indefinitely on the client computer.

 NOTE *A potential problem with using cookies is that they can be disabled at the client side. As a second choice, instead of using cookies, you could use the ASP.NET session state through the* Session *object, although by default the ASP.NET session uses cookies as part of its inner mechanism, too.*

In the shoppingCartId property, you check whether a cookie named JokePoint_CartID exists on the visitor's browser. If it does, this means that the visitor already has a shopping cart, and its ID is read from the cookie. If the cookie doesn't exist, a new GUID value is generated, and then stored in the JokePoint_CartID cookie. This way, the same GUID will be used on all subsequent calls.

You'll implement this functionality in the following exercise, and then we'll analyze its details afterwards, in the "How It Works" section.

Exercise: Implementing the ShoppingCart *Class*

1. Right-click the BusinessObjects folder in the Solution Explorer and select
   Add ➤ Add New Item.

2. Select Class from the Templates window, and name it ShoppingCart.vb.

3. After the file is in place, write its shoppingCartId and connectionString properties, as shown here:

```vb
Imports System.Data.SqlClient

Public Class ShoppingCart
  Private Shared ReadOnly Property shoppingCartId()
    Get
      Dim context As HttpContext = HttpContext.Current

      ' If the JokePoint_CartID cookie doesn't exit
      ' on client machine we create it with a new GUID
      If context.Request.Cookies("JokePoint_CartID") Is Nothing Then
        ' Generate a new GUID
        Dim cartId As Guid = Guid.NewGuid()
        ' Create the cookie and set its value
        Dim cookie As New HttpCookie("JokePoint_CartID", cartId.ToString)
        ' Current Date
        Dim currentDate As DateTime = DateTime.Now()
        ' Set the time span to 10 days
        Dim ts As New TimeSpan(10, 0, 0, 0)
        ' Expiration Date
        Dim expirationDate As DateTime = currentDate.Add(ts)
        ' Set the Expiration Date to the cookie
        cookie.Expires = expirationDate
        ' Set the cookie on client's browser
        context.Response.Cookies.Add(cookie)
        ' return the Cart ID
        Return cartId.ToString()
      Else
        ' return the value stored in JokePoint_CartID
        Return context.Request.Cookies("JokePoint_CartID").Value
      End If
    End Get
  End Property

  Private Shared ReadOnly Property connectionString() As String
    Get
      Return ConfigurationSettings.AppSettings("ConnectionString")
    End Get
  End Property

  '
  ' add the other methods here
  '

End Class
```

How It Works: Cookies

When you set an expiration time for the cookie, it becomes a persistent cookie and is saved as a file by the computer's browser. We set our cookie to expire in ten days, so the visitor's shopping cart exists for ten days from the time it is created. If an expiration date is not specified, the cookie is stored only for the current browser session.

What If the Visitor Doesn't Like Cookies?

If you want your site to work even with browsers that have cookies disabled, you can store the cart ID in the query string or in the Session object. The problem is that the ASP.NET Session, by default, works with cookies. To make the ASP.NET work without cookies, you first need to open Web.config and make this change:

```
<sessionState
      mode="InProc"
      stateConnectionString="tcpip=127.0.0.1:42424"
      sqlConnectionString="data source=127.0.0.1;Trusted_Connection=yes"
      cookieless="true"
      timeout="20" />
```

> **NOTE** *By default, the* cookieless *mode is "*false*", so ASP.NET does use cookies for storing session state.*

In cookieless mode, an ID for the session state is automatically saved by ASP.NET in the query string:

```
http://localhost/jokepoint/(vcmq0tz22y2okxzdq1bo2w45)/default.aspx
```

This looks a bit ugly, but works without using cookies. After you enable cookieless session state support, you need to update the shoppingCartId property to use the Session object instead of cookies:

```
Private ReadOnly Property shoppingCartId()
  Get
    Dim context As HttpContext = HttpContext.Current
    ' Get the value of JokePoint_CartID session variable
    ' (note that it might be void)
    Dim id As String
    id = context.Session("JokePoint_CartID")
    ' Check to see if JokePoint_CartID exists
    If id = "" Then
      ' Generate a new GUID
      Dim cartId As Guid = Guid.NewGuid()
      ' Store the generated GUID in the session state
      context.Session("JokePoint_CartID") = cartId.ToString
```

```
        id = context.Session("JokePoint_CartID")
    End If
    Return id
  End Get
End Property
```

Implementing the Methods

You have five methods in the business tier, corresponding to the five stored procedures you wrote earlier. Add the methods presented in the following sections to the ShoppingCart class.

AddProduct

AddProduct calls the AddProductToCart stored procedure. If the product already exists in the shopping cart, its quantity is increased by one. Otherwise, it's added with a default quantity of one:

```
Public Shared Function AddProduct(ByVal productId As String)
  ' Create the connection object
  Dim connection As New SqlConnection(connectionString)
  ' Create and initialize the command object
  Dim command As New SqlCommand("AddProductToCart", connection)
  command.CommandType = CommandType.StoredProcedure
  ' Add an input parameter and supply a value for it
  command.Parameters.Add("@CartID", SqlDbType.Char, 36)
  command.Parameters("@CartID").Value = shoppingCartId
  ' Add an input parameter and supply a value for it
  command.Parameters.Add("@ProductID", SqlDbType.Int)
  command.Parameters("@ProductID").Value = productId
  ' Open the connection, execute the command, and close the connection
  Try
    connection.Open()
    command.ExecuteNonQuery()
  Finally
    connection.Close()
  End Try
End Function
```

UpdateProductQuantity

UpdateProductQuantity calls the UpdateCartItem stored procedure to change the quantity of a product that already exists in the shopping cart:

```
Public Shared Function UpdateProductQuantity(ByVal productId As String, _
                                             ByVal quantity As Integer)
   ' Create the connection object
   Dim connection As New SqlConnection(connectionString)
   ' Create and initialize the command object
   Dim command As New SqlCommand("UpdateCartItem", connection)
   command.CommandType = CommandType.StoredProcedure
   ' Add an input parameter and supply a value for it
   command.Parameters.Add("@CartID", SqlDbType.Char, 36)
   command.Parameters("@CartID").Value = shoppingCartId
   ' Add an input parameter and supply a value for it
   command.Parameters.Add("@ProductID", SqlDbType.Int)
   command.Parameters("@ProductID").Value = productId
   ' Add an input parameter and supply a value for it
   command.Parameters.Add("@Quantity", SqlDbType.Int)
   command.Parameters("@Quantity").Value = quantity
   ' Open the connection, execute the command, and close the connection
   Try
      connection.Open()
      command.ExecuteNonQuery()
   Finally
      connection.Close()
   End Try
End Function
```

RemoveProduct

Now add the RemoveProduct method, which causes the removal of one product from
the customer's shopping cart:

```
Public Shared Function RemoveProduct(ByVal productId As String)
   ' Create the connection object
   Dim connection As New SqlConnection(connectionString)
   ' Create and initialize the command object
   Dim command As New SqlCommand("RemoveProductFromCart", connection)
   command.CommandType = CommandType.StoredProcedure
   ' Add an input parameter and supply a value for it
   command.Parameters.Add("@CartID", SqlDbType.Char, 36)
   command.Parameters("@CartID").Value = shoppingCartId
   ' Add an input parameter and supply a value for it
   command.Parameters.Add("@ProductID", SqlDbType.Int)
   command.Parameters("@ProductID").Value = productId
   ' Open the connection, execute the command, and close the connection
   Try
      connection.Open()
      command.ExecuteNonQuery()
   Finally
      connection.Close()
   End Try
End Function
```

GetProducts

GetProducts retrieves all the products in the customer's shopping cart. This is called from the presentation tier when the visitor wants to view its cart.

```
Public Shared Function GetProducts() As SqlDataReader
  ' Create the connection object
  Dim connection As New SqlConnection(connectionString)
  ' Create and initialize the command object
  Dim command As New SqlCommand("GetShoppingCartProducts", connection)
  command.CommandType = CommandType.StoredProcedure
  ' Add an input parameter and supply a value for it
  command.Parameters.Add("@CartID", SqlDbType.Char, 36)
  command.Parameters("@CartID").Value = shoppingCartId
  Try
    ' Open the connection and return the results
    connection.Open()
    Return command.ExecuteReader(CommandBehavior.CloseConnection)
  Catch e As Exception
    ' Close the connection and throw the exception
    connection.Close()
    Throw e
  End Try
End Function
```

GetTotalAmount

GetTotalAmount does exactly what it suggests, and it's a bit more interesting than the others because it uses SqlCommand's ExecuteScalar method, which we haven't used so far. Add it to the ShoppingCart class, and we'll discuss the details:

```
Public Shared Function GetTotalAmount() As Decimal
  ' Create the connection object
  Dim connection As New SqlConnection(connectionString)
  ' Create and initialize the command object
  Dim command As SqlCommand = New SqlCommand("GetTotalAmount", connection)
  command.CommandType = CommandType.StoredProcedure
  ' Add an input parameter and supply a value for it
  command.Parameters.Add("@CartID", SqlDbType.Char, 36)
  command.Parameters("@CartID").Value = shoppingCartId
  ' The amount has a default value of 0
  Dim amount As Decimal = 0
  Try
    ' Try to get the amount from the database
    connection.Open()
    amount = command.ExecuteScalar()
  Finally
    ' Close the connection
    connection.Close()
  End Try
  ' Return the amount
  Return amount
End Function
```

ExecuteScalar is used to execute the GetTotalAmount stored procedure. When using ExecuteScalar, you need to use an additional variable (amount, in this case) to store the retrieved value if you want to return the value back to the presentation tier function.

A common mistake is to use the ExecuteScalar method in the same way you use ExecuteNonQuery, like this:

```
' Don't try this at home
connection.Open()
Return command.ExecuteScalar()
connection.Close()
```

The problem with this code is that it returns before having the chance to close the database connection. When using ExecuteScalar, always use an intermediary variable if the value needs to be returned to the client.

Implementing the Presentation Tier

The rest of this chapter deals with building the user interface part of the shopping cart. After updating the storefront, we'll have Add to Cart buttons for each product, and a View Cart button in the left part of the page (see Figure 9-4).

Figure 9-4. The page with Add to Cart buttons and a View Cart button

If you added PayPal integration as presented in Chapter 6, you'll already have these buttons on your site, and you can update their functionality here.

When the Add to Cart button is clicked for a product, the product is added to the shopping cart. If it already exists in the shopping cart, its quantity in the cart will be increased by one. When View Cart is clicked, default.aspx is reloaded with an additional parameter (ViewCart) in the query string. This will instruct default.aspx to dynamically load ShoppingCart.ascx (which you'll build a bit later) in its pageContentsCell cell. You'll implement this logic in default.aspx.vb, in the same way you did for loading SearchResults.ascx, Catalog.ascx, or FirstPage.ascx (take a look at default.aspx.vb if you don't recall the technique).

When the visitor clicks Continue Shopping on the Shopping Cart page, default.aspx is reloaded without the ViewCart parameter in the query string. This will result in going back to the page the visitor was on before clicking the View Cart button.

Before moving on, review the main steps you'll take to implement the whole user interface of the shopping cart:

- Add the Add to Cart buttons for products and implement their functionality.

- Add the View Cart button to default.aspx.

- Modify the code-behind file of default.aspx to recognize the ViewCart query string parameters.

- Implement the ShoppingCart user control.

Creating the Add to Cart and View Cart Buttons

To have Add to Cart buttons for each product, as shown in the previous figure, you need to update ProductsList.ascx. You'll create these buttons in the following exercise.

Exercise: Creating the Add to Cart Buttons

1. If you implemented the PayPal shopping cart as shown in Chapter 7, you'll need to remove the PayPal Add to Cart buttons from ProductsList.ascx. Open the file in HTML View and remove the following code:

    ```
    <a href="JavaScript: OpenPayPalWindow('...')">
      <IMG src="Images/AddToCart.gif" border="0">
    </a>
    ```

2. Add a button in the ItemTemplate of ProductsList.ascx, just below the product price. You can see the HTML code in the following snippet, but keep in mind that you can use the Edit Template feature in Design View to generate at least part of the code. In any case, make sure you have this button in the ItemTemplate:

```
<asp:Button runat="server" Text="Add to Cart"
    CommandArgument='<%# DataBinder.Eval(Container.DataItem, "ProductID") %>'>
</asp:Button>
```

 NOTE *Clicking a button in a* DataList *fires the* DataList's ItemCommand *event. In the event handler, we read the* CommandArgument *of the button, which contains the* ID *of the product that needs to be added to the shopping cart.*

---

3. Open the code-behind file, and let Visual Studio generate the signature of the ItemCommand event of the list DataList. Then complete the function with the following code:

```
Private Sub list_ItemCommand(ByVal source As Object, ByVal e As
System.Web.UI.WebControls.DataListCommandEventArgs) Handles list.ItemCommand
    ' The CommandArgument of the Button that was clicked
    ' in the DataList contains the ProductID
    Dim productId As String = e.CommandArgument
    ' Add the product to the shopping cart
    ShoppingCart.AddProduct(productId)
End Sub
```

How It Works: The Add to Cart Buttons

After updating ProductsList.ascx, build the project (Ctrl+Shift+B), and then load the site to make sure the buttons appear okay. Now click the Add to Cart button on one of the products on the site. If you don't get any errors, the product was probably successfully added to the shopping cart; right now, you can't see this in the web site, because you still need to implement the View Cart button.

The ItemCommand event is raised by the DataList when one of its buttons is clicked. The CommandArgument parameter of the Add to Cart buttons is populated with the product ID from the database. This ID is read from the ItemCommand event handler, which passes it to ShoppingCart.AddProduct to have it added to the database.

When the View Cart button is clicked, you need to reload default.aspx with an additional parameter (named ViewCart) in the query string. You'll do this in the following exercise.

Exercise: Creating the View Cart button

1. If you had a PayPal shopping cart, open default.aspx in HTML View and remove the code that generates the PayPal View Cart button:

```
<a href="JavaScript: OpenPayPalWindow('...')">
  <IMG src="Images/ViewCart.gif" border="0">
</a>
```

2. Instead of this code, add the following Button control:

    ```
    <asp:Button id="viewCartButton" runat="server" Text="View Cart">
    </asp:Button>
    ```

    Now your page should look something like Figure 9-5, in Design View.

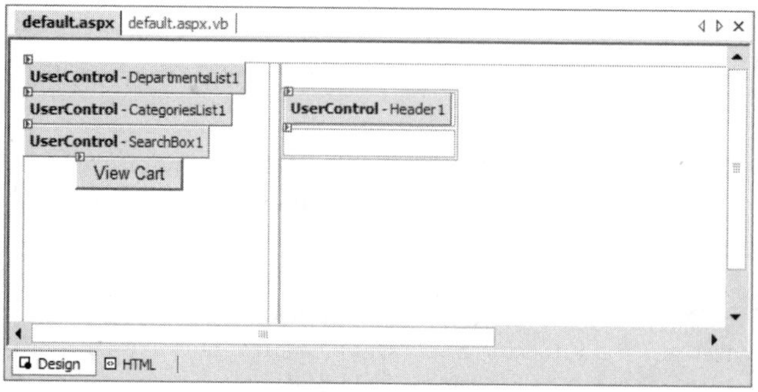

Figure 9-5. The page in Design view

3. While in Design View, double-click the button to generate its Click event handler. Add the following code to it:

    ```
    Private Sub viewCartButton_Click(ByVal sender As System.Object, ByVal e As
    System.EventArgs) Handles viewCartButton.Click
        ' Get the query string as a NameValueCollection object
        If Request.QueryString("ViewCart") Is Nothing Then
          Response.Redirect("default.aspx?ViewCart=1&" & _
            Request.QueryString.ToString())
        End If
    End Sub
    ```

How It Works: The View Cart Button

Clicking the View Cart button adds the ViewCart parameter to the existing query string with a predefined value. It doesn't matter what that value is; the simple presence of the ViewCart parameter instructs default.aspx to load the shopping cart. The code also ensures that ViewCart doesn't already exist in the shopping cart, so clicking the View Cart button multiple times won't generate additional ViewCart parameters.

Loading the Shopping Cart in `default.aspx`

Although you didn't create the `ShoppingCart.ascx` user control, you know where it will be placed and the mechanism to load it. You'll create the control a bit later, but for now you should finish your work with `default.aspx`.

Exercise: Modifying `default.aspx` ***to Load*** `ShoppingCart.ascx`

1. Open the `Page_Load` method in `default.aspx.vb` now. You want `Page_Load` to load `ShoppingCart.ascx` in `pageContentsCell` when the `ViewCart` parameter is found in the query string.

2. Update the method as shown in the following listing:

```
Private Sub Page_Load(ByVal sender As System.Object, ByVal e As System.EventArgs)
Handles MyBase.Load
    ' Save DepartmentID from the query string to a variable
    Dim departmentId As String = Request.QueryString("departmentID")
    ' Save the search string from the query string to a variable
    Dim searchString As String = Request.QueryString("Search")
    ' We need to find out if the ViewCart parameter has been supplied
    Dim viewCart As String = Request.QueryString("ViewCart")
    ' Load page contents
    If Not viewCart Is Nothing Then
      ' we display the shopping cart
      Dim control As Control
      control = Page.LoadControl("UserControls/ShoppingCart.ascx")
      pageContentsCell.Controls.Add(control)
    ElseIf Not searchString Is Nothing Then
      ' we're searching the catalog
      Dim control As Control
      control = Page.LoadControl("UserControls/SearchResults.ascx")
      pageContentsCell.Controls.Add(control)
    ElseIf Not departmentId Is Nothing Then
      Dim control As Control
      control = Page.LoadControl("UserControls/Catalog.ascx")
      pageContentsCell.Controls.Add(control)
    Else
      Dim control As Control
      control = Page.LoadControl("UserControls/FirstPage.ascx")
      pageContentsCell.Controls.Add(control)
    End If
End Sub
```

How It Works: Loading the *Shopping Cart* in default.aspx

After adding this code, default.aspx will know to load the ShoppingCart.ascx user control in its contents cell when ViewCart appears in the query string. First, it reads the value of the ViewCart query string parameter in a String variable:

```
' We need to find out if the ViewCart parameter has been supplied
Dim viewCart As String = Request.QueryString("ViewCart")
```

If that variable contains anything at all, it means ViewCart exists in the query string, and ShoppingCart.ascx loads. Because this control doesn't exist yet, now you get an error when clicking the View Cart button.

```
' Load page contents
If Not viewCart Is Nothing Then
  ' we display the shopping cart
  Dim control As Control
  control = Page.LoadControl("UserControls/ShoppingCart.ascx")
  pageContentsCell.Controls.Add(control)
```

Creating the ShoppingCart Web User Control

Right now, clicking the View Cart button generates an exception because ShoppingCart.ascx is the user control that displays the visitor's shopping cart. You'll create this control step by step, in the following exercise.

Exercise: Creating ShoppingCart.ascx

1. Create a new Web User Control named ShoppingCart.ascx in the UserControls folder.

2. Add three labels, one DataGrid, and one button to the control, as shown in Figure 9-6.

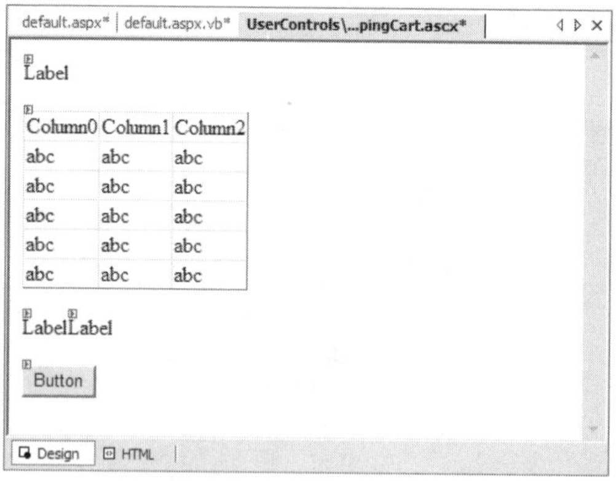

Figure 9-6. Adding controls to ShoppingCart.ascx

3. Now modify the properties for each control as shown in Table 9-1.

Table 9-1. Control Properties in ShoppingCart.ascx

Control Type	ID **Property**	Text **Property**	CssClass **Property**
Label	introLabel	These are the products in your shopping cart:	ListDescription
DataGrid	grid		
Label	Label2	Total Amount:	ProductDescription
Label	totalAmountLabel	*(should be void)*	ProductPrice
Button	continueShoppingButton	Continue Shopping	AdminButtonText

NOTE *We reused some styles that we created in the previous chapters for other parts of the web site. This is not really professional because the styles' names aren't suited for these controls and changing the style for one page results in the look of this control being changed as well. For a production-quality solution, you should create another set of styles. However, for the purpose of this chapter, we prefer to focus on the more important aspects of the control.*

Your control should now look like Figure 9-7.

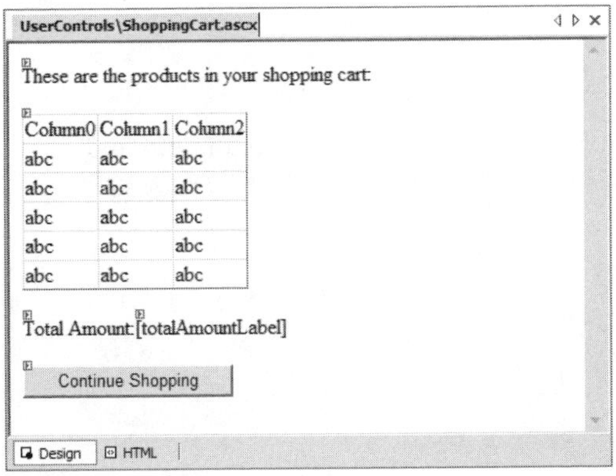

UserControls\ShoppingCart.ascx

These are the products in your shopping cart:

Column0	Column1	Column2
abc	abc	abc
abc	abc	abc
abc	abc	abc
abc	abc	abc
abc	abc	abc

Total Amount: [totalAmountLabel]

Continue Shopping

Design   HTML

Figure 9-7. ShoppingCart.ascx *in Design View*

4. Select the DataGrid and click the Property Builder link, situated in the lower part of the Properties window.

5. Select Columns from the menu on the left, and then deselect the Create Columns Automatically at Runtime check box. Add six fields and set their properties as shown in Table 9-2.

Table 9-2. Setting the Properties of the DataGrid *Control*

Column Type	Header Text	Data Field	Other Properties
Bound Column	Product Name	Name	Read Only
Bound Column	Price	Price	Read Only; Set Data Formatting Expression to {0:c}
Bound Column	Quantity	Quantity	
Bound Column	Subtotal	Subtotal	Read Only; Set Data Formatting Expression to {0:c}
Edit, Update, Cancel			Change Button type to PushButton and Edit Text to Edit Quantity.
Delete			Change Button type to PushButton and Text to Remove

NOTE *The Product Name, Price, and Subtotal columns are marked as read-only. The effect is that they won't be editable when the* DataList *enters edit mode. Also, we set the Data Formatting Expression for Price and Subtotal to* {0:c}, *which instructs the* DataList *to display the values using the currency format.*

6. Let's play a bit with the colors now. Click Format on the left menu and Header in the Objects list. Set the header's appearance properties as in Figure 9-8.

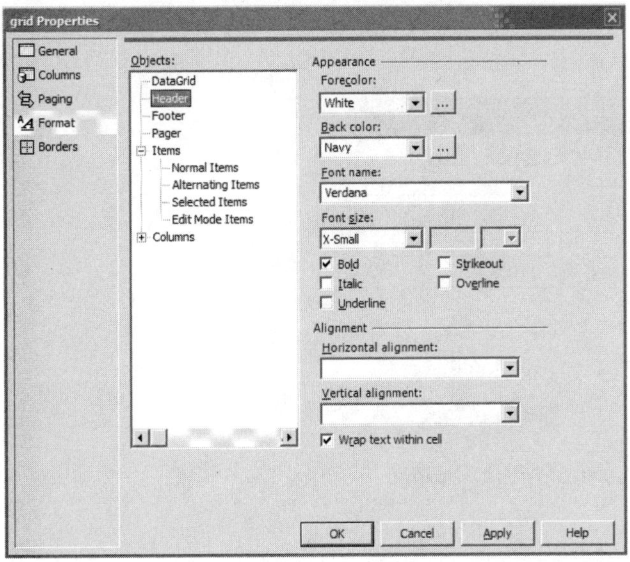

Figure 9-8. Setting appearance properties for the header

7. Now change the look for the Normal Items template (see Figure 9-9).

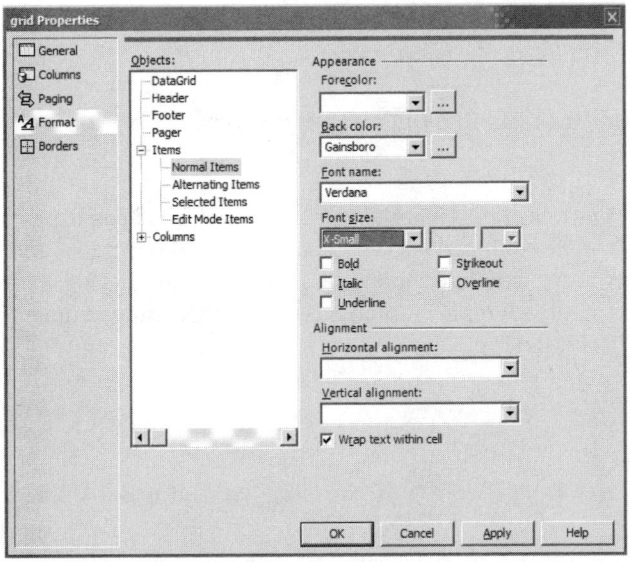

Figure 9-9. Setting properties for the Normal Items template

8. Now click OK to exit the Property Builder window. Select the DataGrid and set its Width property to 100%. This will make the grid fit very nicely onto the page, even when it is resized. Right now the ShoppingCart control looks like Figure 9-10 when viewed in Design View.

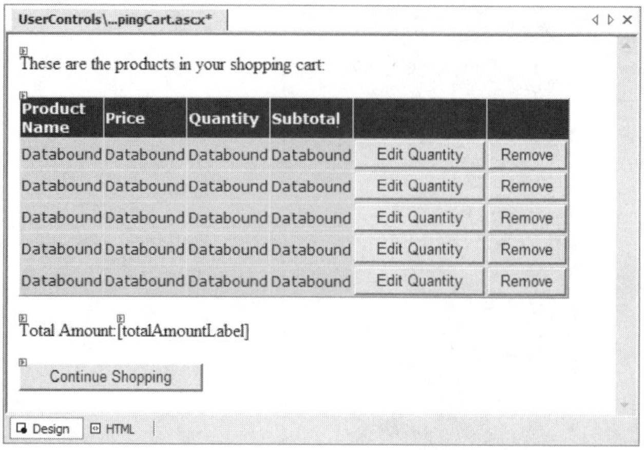

Figure 9-10. ShoppingCart *control in Design View*

9. Before implementing the code, you need to take care of a final detail. With the current settings, when entering into edit mode, the grid would look like Figure 9-11.

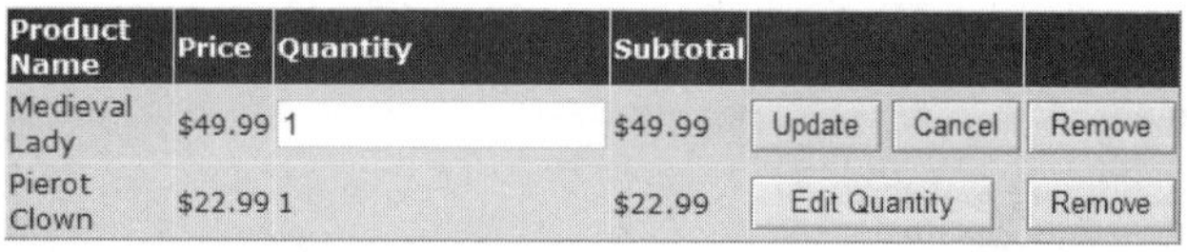

Figure 9-11. Editing the product's quantity in the shopping cart

To change the dimensions of the Quantity TextBox control, you need to change it into a template column. Visit the DataGrid properties window, and transform Quantity into a template column by selecting it and clicking Convert this column into a Template Column. Modify its Quantity template column like this, in HTML View:

```
<asp:TemplateColumn HeaderText="Quantity">
  <ItemTemplate>
    <asp:Label id=Label1 runat="server"
               Text='<%# DataBinder.Eval(Container, "DataItem.Quantity") %>'>
    </asp:Label>
  </ItemTemplate>
  <EditItemTemplate>
    <asp:TextBox id=quantityTextBox Width="65px" MaxLength="3" runat="server"
               Text='<%# DataBinder.Eval(Container, "DataItem.Quantity") %>' >
    </asp:TextBox>
  </EditItemTemplate>
</asp:TemplateColumn>
```

With this change, the Quantity TextBox control will have its size changed, and will not permit receiving more than three characters (see Figure 9-12).

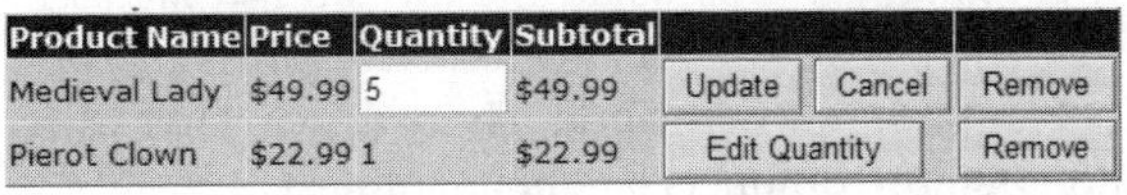

Figure 9-12. Editing the product's quantity in the shopping cart

10. The visual part is now ready. Now you can start writing the code-behind file with the Page_Load method and its helper method:

```
Private Sub Page_Load _
(ByVal sender As System.Object, ByVal e As System.EventArgs) _
Handles MyBase.Load
   If Not Page.IsPostBack Then
     ' Update the data grid
     BindShoppingCart()
   End If
End Sub


Private Sub BindShoppingCart()
   Dim amount As Decimal = ShoppingCart.GetTotalAmount()
   ' Set the total amount label using the Currency format
   totalAmountLabel.Text = String.Format("{0:c}", amount)
   If amount = 0 Then
     introLabel.Text = "Your shopping cart is empty!"
     grid.Visible = False
   Else
     ' Populate the data grid and set its DataKey field
     grid.DataSource = ShoppingCart.GetProducts
     grid.DataKeyField = "ProductID"
     grid.DataBind()
   End If
End Sub
```

How It Works: The ShoppingCart User Control

You can now build the project, load JokePoint in your favorite web browser, and test the Add to Cart and View Cart buttons. The shopping cart is not yet fully functional, in that its Continue Shopping button doesn't work, and also the grid's Remove and Edit Quantity buttons don't work.

Still, you have laid down the basis of the ShoppingCart user control. The user interface is in its final form. For the labels, you've reused some styles created earlier in this book, and you've played a little bit with the DataGrid's colors.

BindShoppingCart takes care of populating the DataGrid and the totalAmountLabel control. In BindShoppingCart, you also set the DataKeyField to ProductID, which instructs the grid to remember the ProductID for each row in the grid. This will help later when you need to update grid information (remove products or edit quantities).

The text for totalAmountLabel is returned from the ShoppingCart.GetTotalAmount function, and is presented using the currency format:

```
Dim amount As Decimal = ShoppingCart.GetTotalAmount()
' Set the total amount label using the Currency format
totalAmountLabel.Text = String.Format("{0:c}", amount)
```

You applied the same formatting to the Price and Subtotal columns of the DataGrid by setting their Data Formatting Expressions to {0:c}.

Remember, you used the same {0:c} string formatter in the ProductsList.ascx control to correctly show the product prices. The letter c is used to specify the currency display mode, and the 0 part specifies that you're applying the selected format for the first parameter (the amount variable).

In Chapter 4, when creating ProductsList.ascx, you set the culture information to en-US in Web.config to make sure the product prices are always written with the US format, no matter what is the default configuration of the computer.

Adding "Continue Shopping" Functionality

Although you have the Continue Shopping button, at this point, it doesn't do much. The two steps to make it work are presented in the next exercise.

Exercise: Implementing the Continue Shopping Button

1. Start editing ShoppingCart.ascx in Design View, and double-click the Continue Shopping button. This automatically creates the continueShoppingButton_Click event handler. Modify it like this:

```
Private Sub continueShoppingButton_Click(ByVal sender As System.Object, _
ByVal e As System.EventArgs) Handles continueShoppingButton.Click
    ' This will contain the original location
    Dim redirectPage As String
    ' For a start we initialize it with the location of default.aspx
    redirectPage = Request.Url.AbsolutePath + "?" + _
                   ShoppingCart.RemoveCartFromQueryString()
    ' Redirect to the new page
    Response.Redirect(redirectPage)
End Sub
```

2. Add a method named RemoveCartFromQueryString to the ShoppingCart class in the business tier (located in the ShoppingCart.vb file):

```vb
' Removes ViewCart parameters from the query string
Public Shared Function RemoveCartFromQueryString() As String
  ' Will contain the query string without the ViewCart parameters
  Dim newQueryString As String = String.Empty
  Try
    ' query stores the current query string
    Dim query As System.Collections.Specialized.NameValueCollection
    query = HttpContext.Current.Request.QueryString
    ' Will hold the name of each query string parameter
    Dim paramName As String
    ' Will host the value of each query string parameter
    Dim paramValue As String
   ' Used to parse the query string
    Dim i As Integer
    ' Parse every element of the query string
    For i = 0 To query.Count - 1
      ' We guard against null (Nothing) parameters
      If Not query.AllKeys(i) Is Nothing Then
        ' Get the parameter name
        paramName = query.AllKeys(i).ToString()
        ' Test to see if the parameter is not ViewCart
        If paramName.ToUpper <> "VIEWCART" Then
          ' Get the value of the parameter
          paramValue = query.Item(i)
          ' Append the parameter to the page
          newQueryString = newQueryString + paramName + "=" + paramValue + "&"
        End If
      End If
    Next
  Catch ex As Exception
    ' If something goes wrong we redirect to the main page
    Return String.Empty
  End Try
  Return newQueryString
End Function
```

How It Works: The Continue Shopping Button

This method calls ShoppingCart.RemoveCartFromQueryString that removes the ViewCart parameter from the query string, and redirects to the original page using the new query string.

RemoveCartFromQueryString might seem a bit scary at first, but actually it's very simple, provided you know a couple of details about how the query string is stored inside the Request object.

RemoveCartFromQueryString removes the ViewCart parameter from the query string. The straightforward solution would be to take the query string and do textual searches for the elements you want to remove. Still, a more powerful and flexible solution is to check the elements of the query string one by one from the parameters collection, and include only the ones different from ViewCart. Let's analyze the code and see how this is done.

The current query string is stored into a variable named query. Because you didn't import the System.Collections.Specialized namespace at the beginning of the file, you needed to specify the fully qualified name for the class when declaring the query object:

```
Dim query As System.Collections.Specialized.NameValueCollection
query = HttpContext.Current.Request.QueryString
```

NOTE   NameValueCollection *objects store a collection of (key, value) pairs. Each element in the query string collection represents a query string parameter.*

Even though the NameValueCollection class has a method named Remove, which allows removing elements from the collection, you can't use it with the query string collection, which is read-only. The consequence is that you can't simply remove the ViewCart element from the QueryString collection. Instead, you read each parameter and test whether its value is "ViewCart".

You obtain the key name (parameter name) of a specific element in the query object using query.AllKeys(i), and the value of that key using query.Item(i).

You put all the logic into a Try block. If an error happens (although it shouldn't because we did proper checking), redirectPage is automatically reset to default.aspx.

Allowing the Visitor to Change the Quantity

You learned how to work with editable DataGrids in Chapter 8. Remember that Visual Studio can help you automatically generate the event handler signatures. For this, while editing the code-behind file for ShoppingCart.ascx, you need to select the DataGrid control in the first combo box situated at the top of the code editor, and then choose the event that you want to handle from the second combo box.

Generate event handlers for the EditCommand, CancelCommand, UpdateCommand, and DeleteCommand events of the DataGrid. Now, fill each of them with code.

EditCommand

EditCommand puts the grid into edit mode. The only DataGrid editable field is Quantity, because you marked the other ones as read-only.

```
Private Sub grid_EditCommand(ByVal source As Object, ByVal e As
System.Web.UI.WebControls.DataGridCommandEventArgs) Handles grid.EditCommand
    grid.EditItemIndex = e.Item.ItemIndex
    BindShoppingCart()
End Sub
```

CancelCommand

When the grid is in edit mode and the Cancel button is clicked, the `CancelCommand` event is generated. Set `EditItemIndex` to `-1`, which cancels the edit mode:

```
Private Sub grid_CancelCommand(ByVal source As Object, ByVal e As
System.Web.UI.WebControls.DataGridCommandEventArgs) Handles grid.CancelCommand
    grid.EditItemIndex = -1
    BindShoppingCart()
End Sub
```

UpdateCommand

`UpdateCommand` comes into action when the grid is in edit mode and the Update button is clicked. The shopping cart is updated by sending the new product quantity to the `UpdateProductQuantity` method of the `ShoppingCart` class. You read the `DataKeys` property to find out the `ProductID` of the product being edited.

```
Private Sub grid_UpdateCommand(ByVal source As Object, ByVal e As
System.Web.UI.WebControls.DataGridCommandEventArgs) Handles grid.UpdateCommand
    Dim productId As String = grid.DataKeys(e.Item.ItemIndex)
    Dim quantity As String = _
                    CType(e.Item.FindControl("quantityTextBox"), TextBox).Text
    Try
        ShoppingCart.UpdateProductQuantity(productId, quantity)
    Catch ex as Exception
        ' If the update generates an error, here is the place
        ' we should warn the user about it
    Finally
        grid.EditItemIndex = -1
        BindShoppingCart()
    End Try
End Sub
```

Because the `UpdateCommand` is susceptible to generating errors (it's easy to type a string instead of a number in the Quantity box, for example), you need to implement a simple error-trapping mechanism. Here, you simply ignore the error, but it would be easy to display an error message using a `Label` control, for example.

No matter whether the update is successful or not, you exit edit mode and update the data in the `DataGrid` in the `Finally` block.

DeleteCommand

`DeleteCommand` is triggered when the Remove button is clicked. You use the `ShoppingCart-.RemoveProduct` method to remove a product from the shopping cart:

```
Private Sub grid_DeleteCommand(ByVal source As Object, ByVal e As
System.Web.UI.WebControls.DataGridCommandEventArgs) Handles grid.DeleteCommand
    Dim productId As String
    productId = grid.DataKeys(e.Item.ItemIndex)
```

```
        ShoppingCart.RemoveProduct(productId)
        BindShoppingCart()
    End Sub
```

Testing the Shopping Cart

Now that you've finished the code for this chapter, it's time to play with it and make sure everything works as expected. You might especially want to test the new data grid functionality that you just implemented. When the grid enters into edit mode, only the quantity is editable, because you set the other fields as read-only when creating the grid (see Figure 9-13).

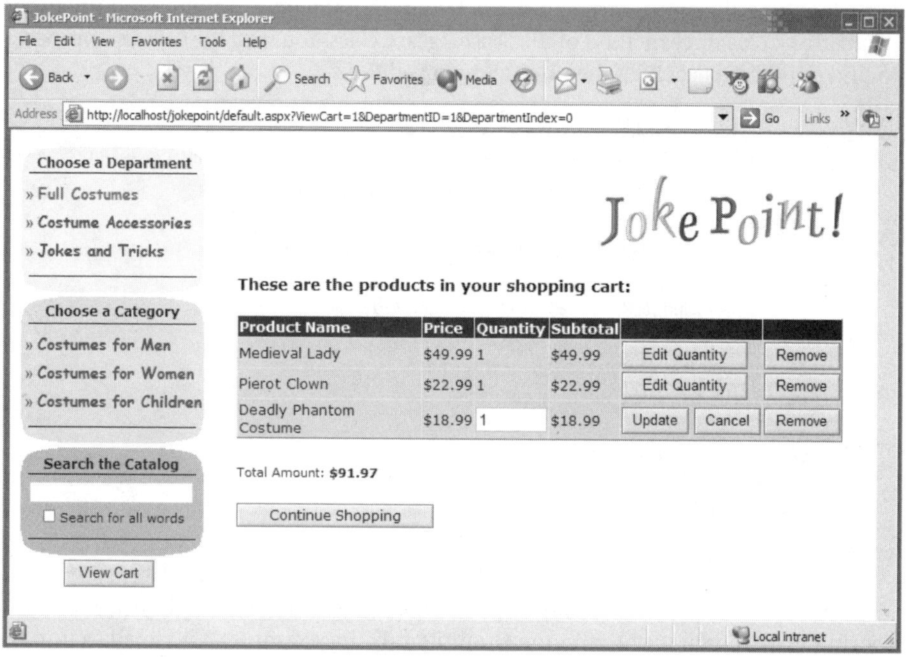

Figure 9-13. Testing the new data grid

You can now play around with testing here by adding products to the shopping cart, changing the quantity, and removing items.

Administering the Shopping Cart

Now that you have finished writing the shopping cart, there are two more things you need to take into account, both related to administration issues:

- How to delete from the product catalog a product that exists in shopping carts.

- How to remove old shopping cart elements by building a simple shopping cart administration page. This is important, because without this feature, the ShoppingCart table keeps growing.

Deleting Products that Exist in Shopping Carts

The catalog administration pages offer the possibility to completely delete products from the catalog. Before removing a product, you need to remove related records from its related tables first. If a product still has related records, the foreign-key relationships between Product and the other tables won't allow the deletion.

For example, right now the RemoveFromCategoryOrDeleteProduct stored procedure first deletes all related records from ProductCategory before deleting the record:

```
DELETE FROM ProductCategory WHERE ProductID=@ProductID
DELETE FROM Product where ProductID=@ProductID
```

Now the problem reappears with the ShoppingCart table: the Product and ShoppingCart tables are tied through a FOREIGN KEY constraint on their ProductID fields. The database doesn't allow deleting products from Product that have related ShoppingCart records. You'll fix this problem in the following exercise.

Exercise: *Updating* RemoveFromCategoryOrDeleteProduct

The solution is to update the RemoveFromCategoryOrDeleteProduct stored procedure to also remove all the references to the product from the ShoppingCart table before attempting to delete it from the database. Update the stored procedure like this, in the database:

```
ALTER PROCEDURE RemoveFromCategoryOrDeleteProduct
(@ProductID int, @CategoryID int)
AS

IF (SELECT COUNT(*) FROM ProductCategory WHERE ProductID=@ProductID)>1
  DELETE FROM ProductCategory
  WHERE CategoryID=@CategoryID AND ProductID=@ProductID
ELSE
  BEGIN
    DELETE FROM ShoppingCart WHERE ProductID=@ProductID
    DELETE FROM ProductCategory WHERE ProductID=@ProductID
    DELETE FROM Product where ProductID=@ProductID
  END

RETURN
```

How It Works: Removing ShoppingCart *Entries*

In this simple exercise, you updated the RemoveFromCategoryOrDeleteProduct stored procedure to delete a product from any shopping carts before removing it from the Product table. This avoids any errors that could happen because of the relationship between the ShoppingCart and Product tables.

Removing Old ShoppingCart *Entries*

The second problem with the shopping cart is that at this moment no mechanism exists to delete the old records from the ShoppingCart table. On a high activity web site, the ShoppingCart table can grow to very large dimensions.

With the current version of the code, shopping cart IDs are stored at the client browser for ten days. As a result, you can assume that any shopping carts that haven't been updated in the last ten days are invalid, and can be safely removed.

In the following exercise, you'll quickly implement a simple shopping cart administration page, where the administrator can see how many old shopping cart entries exist, and can delete them if necessary.

The most interesting aspect you need to understand is the logic behind the database stored procedure that calculates the records that need to be deleted. The goal is to delete all shopping carts that haven't been updated in a certain amount of time.

This isn't as simple as it sounds—at first sight, you might think all you have to do is delete all the records in ShoppingCart whose DateProductAdded is older than a specified date. However, this strategy doesn't work with shopping carts that are modified over time (say, the visitor has been adding items to the cart each week in the past three months). If the last change to the shopping cart is recent, none of its elements should be deleted, even if some are very old. In other words, you should either remove all elements in a shopping cart, or none of them. The age of a shopping cart is given by the age of its most recently modified or added product.

 TIP *If you look at the* UpdateCartItem *stored procedure, you'll notice it also updates the* DateProductAdded *field of a product each time the quantity changes.*

For the shopping cart admin page, you'll build two stored procedures (CleanShoppingCart and CountOldShoppingCartElements), but they both work using the same logic to calculate the shopping cart elements that are old and should be removed. First, you should learn a little bit about the SQL logic that retrieves the old shopping cart elements.

Take a look at the following query, which returns for each cart ID, how many days have passed since the day the last cart item was added or modified:

```
SELECT CartID,
       MIN(DATEDIFF(dd,DateProductAdded,GETDATE())) as DaysFromMostRecentRecord
FROM ShoppingCart
GROUP BY CartID
```

The DATEDIFF function returns the difference, in days (because of the dd parameter), between the date specified by DateProductAdded and the current date (specified by GETDATE). GROUP BY groups the results by CartID, and for each CartID, the MIN aggregate function calculates the most recent record.

To select all the elements from the carts that haven't been modified in the last ten days, you need a query like this:

```
SELECT CartID
FROM ShoppingCart
GROUP BY CartID
HAVING MIN(DATEDIFF(dd,DateProductAdded,GETDATE()))>10
```

You'll implement the shopping cart administration page in the next exercise. You'll implement everything, starting from the stored procedures and finishing with the presentation tier, in a single exercise.

Exercise: Implementing the Cart Admin Page

1. Add the CleanShoppingCart stored procedure to the database. It receives as a parameter the maximum number of days for a shopping cart age. All shopping carts older than that are deleted.

   ```
   CREATE PROCEDURE CleanShoppingCart
       (@Days smallint)
   AS
   DELETE FROM ShoppingCart
   WHERE CartID IN
       (SELECT CartID
        FROM ShoppingCart
        GROUP BY CartID
        HAVING MIN(DATEDIFF(dd,DateProductAdded,GETDATE()))>@Days)
   ```

2. Add CountOldShoppingCartElements, which returns the number of shopping cart elements that would be deleted by a CleanShoppingCart call.

   ```
   CREATE PROCEDURE CountOldShoppingCartElements
       (@Days smallint)
   AS
   SELECT COUNT(CartID)
   FROM ShoppingCart
   WHERE CartID IN
       (SELECT CartID
        FROM ShoppingCart
        GROUP BY CartID
        HAVING MIN(DATEDIFF(dd,DateProductAdded,GETDATE()))>@Days)
   ```

3. Add these methods in the business tier, in the ShoppingCart class (located in ShoppingCart.vb). They are used to interact with the two stored procedures you wrote earlier.

```
Public Shared Function CleanShoppingCart(ByVal days As Integer)
  ' Create the connection object
  Dim connection As New SqlConnection(connectionString)
  ' Create and initialize the command object
  Dim command As New SqlCommand("CleanShoppingCart", connection)
  command.CommandType = CommandType.StoredProcedure
  ' Add an input parameter and supply a value for it
  command.Parameters.Add("@Days", SqlDbType.SmallInt)
  command.Parameters("@Days").Value = days
  ' Open the connection, execute the command, close the connection
  Try
    connection.Open()
    command.ExecuteNonQuery()
  Finally
    connection.Close()
  End Try
End Function

Public Shared Function _
CountOldShoppingCartElements(ByVal days As Integer) As Integer
  ' Create the connection object
  Dim connection As New SqlConnection(connectionString)
  ' Create and initialize the command object
  Dim command As New _
              SqlCommand("CountOldShoppingCartElements", connection)
  command.CommandType = CommandType.StoredProcedure
  ' Add an input parameter and supply a value for it
  command.Parameters.Add("@Days", SqlDbType.SmallInt)
  command.Parameters("@Days").Value = days
  ' Execute the command and return the result
  Dim count As Integer = 0
  Try
    ' Execute the command and get the result
    connection.Open()
    count = command.ExecuteScalar()
  Finally
    ' Close the connection
    connection.Close()
  End Try
  ' Return the count value
  Return count
End Function
```

4. Create a new Web Form at the root of the JokePoint project, named shoppingCartAdmin. Switch it to Flow Layout, and add a link to JokePoint.css in the <HEAD> section:

```
<link href="JokePoint.css" type="text/css" rel="stylesheet">
```

5. Complete the `<FORM>` element with this content:

```
<form id="Form1" method="post" runat="server">
  <strong><font size="5">JokePoint Admin Page</font></strong>
  <P>
    <asp:label id="countLabel" runat="server" CssClass="AdminPageText">
      Hello!
    </asp:label></P>
  <P>
    <asp:Label id="Label1" runat="server">How many days?</asp:Label>
    <asp:DropDownList id="daysList" runat="server">
      <asp:ListItem Value="1">One</asp:ListItem>
      <asp:ListItem Value="10" Selected="True">Ten</asp:ListItem>
      <asp:ListItem Value="20">Twenty</asp:ListItem>
      <asp:ListItem Value="30">Thirty</asp:ListItem>
    </asp:DropDownList></P>
  <P>
    <asp:button id="countButton" runat="server"
              Text="Count Old Elements" CssClass="AdminButtonText">
    </asp:button>
  </P>
  <P>
    <asp:button id="deleteButton" runat="server"
              Text="Delete Old Elements" CssClass="AdminButtonText">
    </asp:button>
  </P>
</form>
```

This should generate the form shown in Figure 9-14.

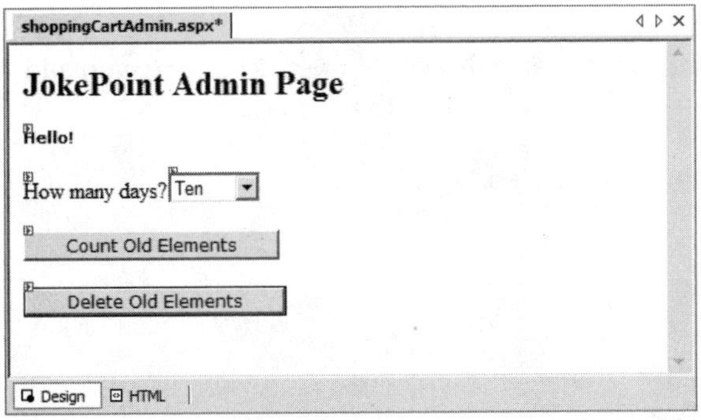

Figure 9-14. The shoppingCartAdmin *Web Form in Design View*

6. Add the `Logout.ascx` control from the Solution Explorer to `shoppingCartAdmin.ascx` as shown in Figure 9-15.

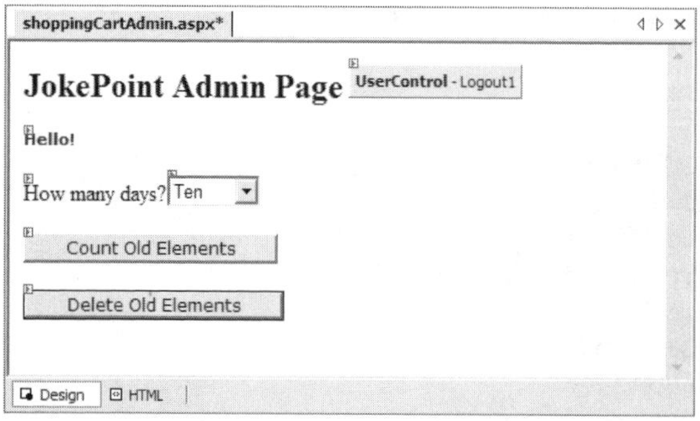

Figure 9-15. Adding the `Logout.ascx` *control to* `shoppingCartAdmin`

7. Double-click the Delete Old Elements button, and complete its `Click` event handler with the following code:

```
Private Sub deleteButton_Click _
(ByVal sender As System.Object, ByVal e As System.EventArgs) _
HandlesdeleteButton.Click
    Dim days As Integer = Integer.Parse(daysList.SelectedItem.Value)
    ShoppingCart.CleanShoppingCart(days)
    countLabel.Text = "Old elements were removed from shopping cart"
End Sub
```

8. To restrict this page to administrator-only access, open `Web.config` and add the following block, after the one that deals with `admin.aspx`:

```
<location path="shoppingCartAdmin.aspx">
  <system.web>
    <authorization>
      <allow users="admin" />
      <deny users="*" />
    </authorization>
  </system.web>
</location>
```

9. Finally, add a link to this new admin page in the FirstPage.ascx control:

```
Press here for the <a href="admin.aspx">catalog admin page</a> or
<a href="shoppingCartAdmin.aspx"> cart admin page.</a></font>
```

How It Works: The Shopping Cart Admin Page

Yep, you're done! Your new shopping cart admin page should work as expected (see Figure 9-16).

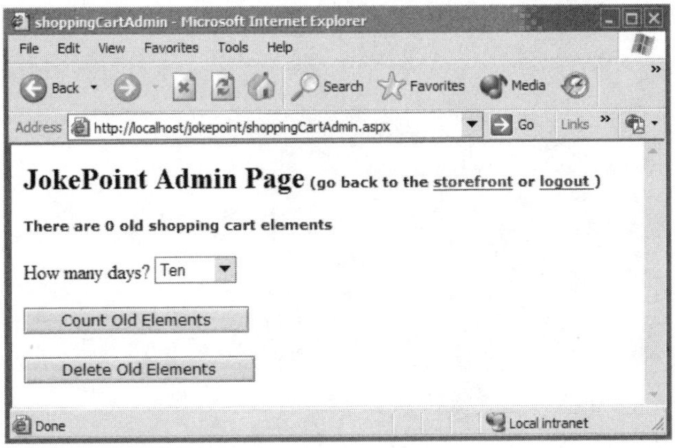

Figure 9-16. Your shopping cart admin page in action

Summary

In this chapter, you learned how to store the shopping cart information in the database, and you learned a few things in the process as well. Probably the most interesting was the way you can store the shopping cart ID as a cookie on the client, since you haven't done anything similar so far in this book.

After working through the process of creating the shopping cart, starting with the database and ending with the presentation tier, we also touched on the new administrative challenges.

You'll complete the functionality offered by the custom shopping cart in the next chapter with a custom checkout system. You'll add a "Place Order" button to the shopping cart, which will allow you to save the shopping cart information as a separate order in the database.

See you in the next chapter!

CHAPTER 10

Dealing with Customer Orders

THE GOOD NEWS IS that your brand-new shopping cart looks good and is fully functional. The bad news is that it doesn't allow the visitor to actually place an order, making it totally useless in the context of a production system.

We'll deal with that problem in this chapter, in two separate stages. In the first part of the chapter, you'll implement the client-side part of the order-placing mechanism. More precisely, you'll add a Place Order button onto the shopping cart control, which will allow the visitor to order the products in the shopping cart.

In the second part of the chapter, you'll implement a simple orders administration page where the site administrator can view and handle pending orders.

The code for each part of the site will be presented in the usual way, starting with the database tier, continuing with the business tier, and finishing with the User Interface (UI).

Implementing an Order-Placing System

The entire order placing system is related to the Place Order button mentioned earlier. Figure 10-1 shows how this button will look after you update the ShoppingCart control in this chapter.

These are the products in your shopping cart:

Product Name	Price	Quantity	Subtotal		
Medieval Lady	$49.99	1	$49.99	Edit Quantity	Remove
Police Plastic Helmet	$1.35	1	$1.35	Edit Quantity	Remove
Darth Vader	$46.99	1	$46.99	Edit Quantity	Remove
Remote Control Jammer	$5.99	1	$5.99	Edit Quantity	Remove
Skull Moving	$7.50	1	$7.50	Edit Quantity	Remove

Total amount: **$111.82**   Place Order

Continue Shopping

Figure 10-1. The Shopping Cart with a Place Order button

Looking at the picture, the button looks quite boring for something that is the center of this chapter's universe. Still, a lot of logic is hidden behind it, so consider what you want to happen when the customer clicks that button. Remember that at this stage, it doesn't matter who places the order, but it's important to store information in the database about the products that were ordered.

Basically, two things need to happen when the customer clicks the Place Order button:

- First, the order must be stored somewhere in the database. You'll save the shopping cart's products to an order named JokePoint Order *nnn,* and then clear the shopping cart.

- Secondly, the customer must be redirected to a PayPal payment page where the customer pays the necessary amount for the order.

NOTE *For the second development stage, you still don't process the payments, but use a third-party payment processor instead. You no longer need the PayPal shopping cart because you implemented your own in the previous chapter. Instead, as you'll see, you'll use the Single Item Purchases option of PayPal, which redirects the visitor directly to a payment page.*

A problem that arises when using a third-party payment processor is that the customer can change her mind and cancel the order while at the checkout page. This can result in orders that are saved to the database (the order is saved *before* the page is redirected to the payment page), but for which payment wasn't completed. This makes it obvious that a payment-confirmation system is necessary, along with a database structure able to store status information about each order.

The confirmation system that you'll implement is simple. Every payment processor, including PayPal, can be instructed to send a confirmation message after a payment has been processed. The site administrator will be able to manually check, in the administration page, which orders have been paid for. These orders will be known as **verified orders.** You'll see later in this chapter how to manage them in the orders management part of the site.

NOTE *PayPal and its competitors offer automated systems that instruct your web site when a payment has been completed or canceled. However, in this book we don't aim at visiting the intimate details of any of these payment systems—you'll need to do your homework and study the documentation of the company you choose. The PayPal Instant Payment Notification manual can be downloaded at* https://www.paypal.com/en_US/pdf/ipn.pdf.

Now that you have an idea of what the Place Order button will do, the next major concerns are *what* order information to store in the database and *how* to store it. As you saw in the previous chapters, deciding how to store information helps you have a better idea of how the whole system works.

Storing Orders in the Database

Two kinds of order information need to be stored:

- The general details about the order: the date the order was created; whether and when the products have been shipped; whether the order is verified, completed, or canceled; and a few other details.

- The products that belong to that order and their quantities.

In the order administration page that you'll create later in this chapter, you'll be able to see and modify the order information.

Two data tables in the database will store the order information. The first table is Orders, which stores general order information, and the second table is OrderDetail, which stores the order's products. Let's have a look at these tables.

Creating the New Data Tables

Due to the nature of the information you need to store, two data tables are necessary: Orders and OrderDetail. The Orders table will store information regarding the order as a whole, while OrderDetail contains the products that belong to each order.

TIP *So far, we have been consistent about naming our tables in singular form (*ShoppingCart*, *Department*, and so on). However, here we make an exception for the* Orders *table. Because* ORDER *is an SQL keyword, we can't use it as a name unless written with square brackets, like this:* [Order]*. For the purposes of this book, we prefer to break the naming convention to avoid any confusion while writing the SQL code, and generally speaking, it's not good practice to use keywords as names.*

These tables have a One-to-Many relationship, enforced through a FOREIGN KEY constraint on their OrderID fields. One-to-Many is the usual relationship implemented between an Orders table and an OrderDetail table. The OrderDetail table contains *many* records that belong to *one* order. You might want to revisit Chapter 4 where the table relationships are explained in more detail.

You'll implement the tables in the following exercise.

Exercise: Adding the Orders and the OrderDetail Tables to the Database

1. First add the Orders table nature to the database, as shown in Figure 10-2.

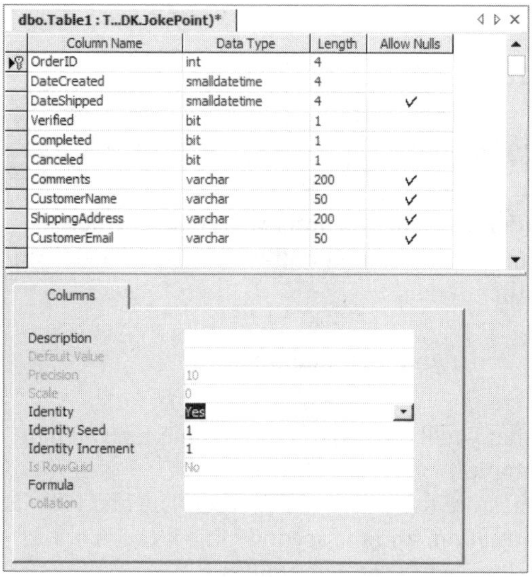

Column Name	Data Type	Length	Allow Nulls
OrderID	int	4	
DateCreated	smalldatetime	4	
DateShipped	smalldatetime	4	✓
Verified	bit	1	
Completed	bit	1	
Canceled	bit	1	
Comments	varchar	200	✓
CustomerName	varchar	50	✓
ShippingAddress	varchar	200	✓
CustomerEmail	varchar	50	✓

Columns

Description	
Default Value	
Precision	10
Scale	0
Identity	Yes
Identity Seed	1
Identity Increment	1
Is RowGuid	No
Formula	
Collation	

Figure 10-2. Adding the Orders table to the database

CAUTION *Don't forget to set OrderID as a primary key and an identity column! Leave Identity Seed and Identity Increment at their default values of 1.*

TIP *Remember that making a column an identity column tells the database to automatically generate values for it when new records are added to the table. You can't supply your own values for that field when adding new records. The generated ID value can be found by reading the @@Identity system variable. You'll use this when creating the CreateOrder stored procedure a bit later.*

2. Set the default value for the three bit fields (Verified, Completed, and Canceled) in the Orders table to 0.

3. Add the OrderDetail table (see Figure 10-3).

dbo.Table1 : T...DK.JokePoint)*					◁ ▷ ×
Column Name	Data Type	Length	Allow Nulls	▲	
▶🗝 OrderID	int	4			
🗝 ProductID	int	4			
ProductName	varchar	50			
Quantity	int	4			
UnitCost	money	8			
				▼	

Columns	
Description	
Default Value	
Precision	10
Scale	0
Identity	No
Identity Seed	
Identity Increment	
Is RowGuid	No
Formula	
Collation	

Figure 10-3. Adding the OrderDetail *table*

 CAUTION   *Don't forget to set the composite primary key formed of* OrderID *and* ProductID.

---

4. Enforce the One-to-Many relationship between the tables by adding a FOREIGN KEY constraint on the OrderID column (see Figure 10-4). If you created the tables directly in the diagram, you can create the relationship by dragging the OrderID column from one of the tables to the OrderID columns in the other table. The table where OrderID is the whole primary key (Orders in this case) will be the table in the *one* part of the relationship.

DatabaseDiagr...DK.JokePoint)*	◁ ▷ ×

OrderDetail
🗝 OrderID
🗝 ProductID
  ProductName
  Quantity
  UnitCost

Orders
🗝 OrderID
  DateCreated
  DateShipped
  Verified
  Completed
  Canceled
  Comments
  CustomerName
  ShippingAddress
  CustomerEmail

Figure 10-4. Diagram showing the relationship between Orders *and* OrderDetail.

If you're not using a diagram, you can create the FOREIGN KEY constraint by choosing View ➤ Relationships, while one of the tables is selected, as shown in Figure 10-5.

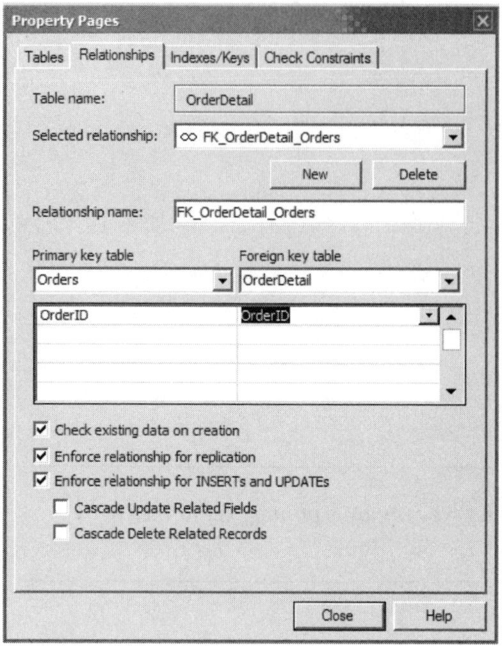

Figure 10-5. Creating the FOREIGN KEY *constraint*

> **NOTE** *Although* ProductID *is part of the primary key in* OrderDetail, *you don't place a* FOREIGN KEY *constraint on it (referencing the* Product *table), because products can change in time, or can even be removed, while the existing orders should remain unchanged.* ProductID *is used to form the primary key of* OrderDetail *because at any given time, each product has a unique* ProductID. *However, the* ProductID *in* OrderDetail *is not required to point to an existing product.*

How It Works: The Data Tables

Now that you have created the tables, take a closer look at the way they are designed.

The Orders Table

The Orders table basically contains two categories of information: data about the order itself (the first seven fields), and data about the customer that made the order (last three fields).

An alternative would be to store the customer information in a separate table named Customer and store only the customer ID in the Orders table. However, storing customer data is not one of the goals of this development stage. At this stage, we prefer to keep things simple because it doesn't matter who made the order, only what products have been sold. This allows you to focus on the task at hand. You'll deal with creating a separate Customer table in Chapter 12.

Third-party payment processors like PayPal store and manage the complete customer information, so it doesn't need to be stored in your database as well. The CustomerName, ShippingAddress, and CustomerEmail fields have been added as optional fields that can be filled by the administrator if it's easier to have this information at hand for certain (or all) orders.

Now take a look at the other fields. You have the necessary OrderID column, which is also the primary key of the table. The other required field (that doesn't allow NULL values) is DateCreated. You need to know the date when each order was created. Note that in this implementation, you'll have to manually supply a value for the DateCreated field when adding records to the table, but keep in mind that you can supply a function as the default value for it (that function would be GETDATE, which returns the current date and time).

Apart from OrderID and DateCreated, three bit fields show the status of the order: Verified, Completed, and Canceled. These fields store 0 for No and 1 for Yes. Note that instead of having more bit fields, you could have a single Status field, which would contain the order status coded as an integer value, for example 1 for Processing, 2 for Completed, 3 for Canceled, and so on.

The Verified field will be set to 1 after the payment has been confirmed by PayPal. The site administrator will do this upon receipt of the payment confirmation mail. After the payment is confirmed (and the order is verified), the products are shipped, so the DateShipped field is populated and the Completed bit is set to 1.

The administrator might want to mark an order as canceled (by setting the Canceled bit to 1) if it hasn't been verified in a certain amount of time, or for other various reasons. The Comments field will be used to record whatever special information might show up about the order.

The OrderDetail *Table*

Let's see now what information the OrderDetail table contains. Figure 10-6 shows what some typical OrderDetail records look like.

OrderID	ProductID	ProductName	Quantity	UnitCost
1	1	Santa Costume	1	14.99
1	2	Medieval Lady	2	49.99
1	28	Police Plastic Helmet	4	1.35
1	30	Bug Eyes	4	2.75
2	2	Medieval Lady	1	49.99
2	28	Police Plastic Helmet	1	1.35
2	31	Darth Vader	1	46.99
2	42	Remote Control Jammer	1	5.99
2	50	Skull Moving	1	7.5

Figure 10-6. Sample data in OrderDetail

Each record in OrderDetail represents an ordered product that belongs to the order specified by OrderID. The primary key is formed by both OrderID and ProductID because a particular product can be ordered only once in one order. A Quantity field contains the number of ordered items, so it wouldn't make any sense to have one ProductID recorded more than once for one order.

You might be wondering why apart from the product ID, you also store the price and product name in the OrderDetail table. The question is valid because if you have the product ID, you can get all of the product's details from the Product table without having any duplicated information.

We chose to duplicate the product data (the product's name and price) in the OrderDetail table to guard against product information changes; products can be removed from the database, and their name and price can change, but this shouldn't affect the orders' data.

The ProductID is stored because, apart from being the only programmatic way to link back to the original product info (if the product still exists), it is used to create the primary key of OrderDetail. ProductID comes in very handy, because having it in the composite primary key in OrderDetail saves you from needing to add another primary key field, and also ensures that you won't have the same product more than once in a single order.

Implementing the Stored Procedures

At this stage, you only need two stored procedures. The most important is CreateOrder, which takes the products from a shopping cart and creates an order with them. The other procedure is EmptyShoppingCart, which empties the visitor's cart after the order has been placed.

You'll start with EmptyShoppingCart, because this is called from CreateOrder.

EmptyShoppingCart

EmptyShoppingCart isn't the most interesting stored procedure you've ever written, but nevertheless it's important for JokePoint. The customer expects the shopping cart to be empty after buying the products. Here's the stored procedure:

```
CREATE PROCEDURE EmptyShoppingCart
(@CartID char(36))
AS

DELETE FROM ShoppingCart
WHERE CartID = @CartID

RETURN
```

CreateOrder

The heart of the order placing mechanism consists of the CreateOrder stored procedure. This procedure gets called when the customer decides that he wants to buy the products in the shopping cart and clicks the Place Order button.

The role of CreateOrder is to create a new order based on the products in the customer's shopping cart. This implies adding a new record to the Orders table and a number of records (one record for each product) in the OrderDetail table.

Create the CreateOrder stored procedure in the JokePoint database, and then we'll talk a bit more about it:

```
CREATE PROCEDURE CreateOrder
(@CartID char(36))
AS
/* Insert a new record into Orders*/
DECLARE @OrderID int
INSERT INTO Orders (DateCreated, Verified, Completed, Canceled)
           VALUES (GETDATE(), 0, 0, 0)
/* Obtain the new Order ID */
SET @OrderID = @@IDENTITY
/* Add the order details to OrderDetail */
INSERT INTO OrderDetail
     (OrderID, ProductID, ProductName, Quantity, UnitCost)
SELECT
     @OrderID, Product.ProductID, Product.Name,
     ShoppingCart.Quantity, Product.Price
FROM Product JOIN ShoppingCart
ON Product.ProductID = ShoppingCart.ProductID
WHERE ShoppingCart.CartID = @CartID
/* Clear the shopping cart */
EXEC EmptyShoppingCart @CartID
/* Return the Order ID */
SELECT @OrderID
```

The first step in this procedure is to create the new record in the Orders table. This must be done at the beginning because you need to find out what OrderID was generated for the new order. Remember that the OrderID field is an identity column and is automatically generated by the database.

```
/* Insert a new record into Orders*/
DECLARE @OrderID int
INSERT INTO Orders (DateCreated, Verified, Completed, Canceled)
           VALUES (GETDATE(), 0, 0, 0)
/* Obtain the new Order ID */
SET @OrderID = @@IDENTITY
```

This is the basic mechanism of extracting the newly generated ID. After the INSERT statement, you save the value of @@IDENTITY to a variable. You must do this immediately after inserting the new row, because the value @@IDENTITY is reset afterwards.

Using the @OrderID variable, you add the OrderDetail records by gathering information from the Product and ShoppingCart tables. From ShoppingCart, you need the list of the products and their quantities, and from Product, you get their names and prices.

> **TIP** *When joining* Product *and* ShoppingCart, *you get the* ProductID *from* Product *but you could also get it from* ShoppingCart; *the result would be the same, because the table join is made on the* ProductID *column.*

After creating the order, the visitor's shopping cart is emptied with a call to EmptyShoppingCart, which you've already seen. A stored procedure is called from within another stored procedure using the EXEC command:

```
/* Clear the shopping cart */
EXEC EmptyShoppingCart @CartID
```

The last step for the CreateOrder stored procedure is to return the OrderID to the calling function. This will be required when providing the order number to the customer.

```
/* Return the Order ID */
SELECT @OrderID
```

Updating the Business Layer

Luckily, at this stage you only need a single method named CreateOrder, which you'll add to the ShoppingCart class.

CreateOrder

Add this method to the ShoppingCart class:

```
Public Shared Function CreateOrder() As String
  ' Create the connection object
  Dim connection As New SqlConnection(connectionString)
  ' Create and initialize the command object
  Dim command As New SqlCommand("CreateOrder", connection)
  command.CommandType = CommandType.StoredProcedure
  ' Add an input parameter and supply a value for it
  command.Parameters.Add("@CartID", SqlDbType.Char, 36)
  command.Parameters("@CartID").Value = shoppingCartId
  ' Save the value that needs to be returned to a variable
  Dim orderId As String
  ' Execute the command and return the result
  Try
    ' Try to execute the command
    connection.Open()
    orderId = command.ExecuteScalar()
  Catch e As Exception
    ' Close the connection and rethrow the exception
```

```
    connection.Close()
    Throw e
  Finally
    ' Close the connection
    connection.Close()
  End Try
  ' Return the saved value
  Return orderId
End Function
```

The method calls the CreateOrder stored procedure in the usual way. It returns the OrderID of the newly created order.

ExecuteScalar is the SqlCommand method used to execute stored procedures that return a single value.

Implementing the UI

Now, you'll finally get to see the code you've written so far working for you. The UI consists of your star, the Place Order button, which allows the visitor to become a customer.

This button is the only addition on the visitor side for the custom checkout. You'll place the button in the ShoppingCart Web User Control, and then implement the functionality by handling its Click event.

You get the desired functionality by following a few simple steps. The first one involves adding the Place Order button to the shopping cart.

Adding the Place Order Button to the Form

Modify ShoppingCart.ascx in HTML View mode. Add a table between the DataGrid and the Continue Shopping button, and place the existing labels that display the total amount in the first cell of the table. Here's the code for the table:

```
<table width="100%">
  <tr>
    <td width="100%">
      <asp:label id="Label1" runat="server" CssClass="ProductDescription">
        Total amount:</asp:label> 
      <asp:label id="totalAmountLabel" runat="server"
        CssClass="ProductPrice"></asp:label>
    </td>
    <td>
      <asp:Button id="placeOrderButton" runat="server" Text="Place Order">
        </asp:Button>
    </td>
  </tr>
</table>
```

After implementing this change, `ShoppingCart.ascx` should look like Figure 10-7 when viewed in Design View.

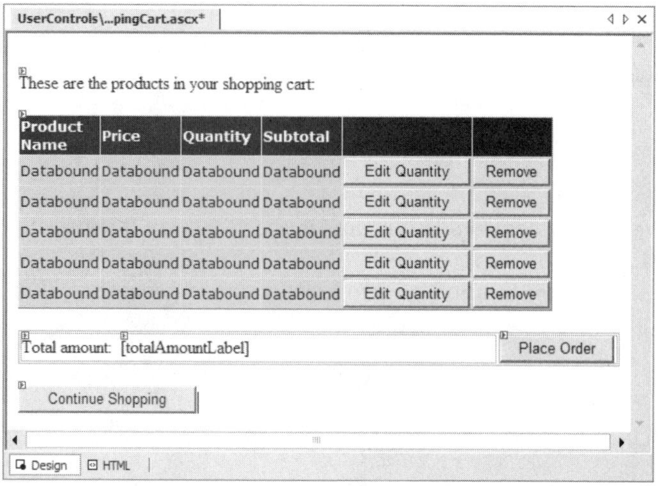

Figure 10-7. `ShoppingCart.ascx` *in Design View*

Disabling the Button If the Cart Is Empty

Cool, now you have a Place Order button in the shopping cart. This button should be enabled only when the shopping cart is not empty. Take care of this issue by modifying `BindShoppingCart` in `ShoppingCart.ascx.vb`:

```
Private Sub BindShoppingCart()
    Dim amount As Decimal = ShoppingCart.GetTotalAmount()
    ' Set the total amount label using the Currency format
    totalAmountLabel.Text = String.Format("{0:c}", amount)
    If amount = 0 Then
        introLabel.Text = "Your shopping cart is empty!"
        grid.Visible = False
        placeOrderButton.Enabled = False
    Else
        placeOrderButton.Enabled = True
        ' Populate the data grid and set its DataKey field
        grid.DataSource = ShoppingCart.GetProducts
        grid.DataKeyField = "ProductID"
        grid.DataBind()
    End If
End Sub
```

You can run the project and test the new shopping cart. You'll see that the Place Order button is enabled only when the shopping cart amount is greater than zero, which happens when there is at least one product in it.

Implementing the Place Order Functionality

Now it's time to implement the Place Order button's functionality. Because this functionality depends on the company that processes your payments, you might need to suit it for the payment-processing company you're working with.

If you use PayPal, the code that redirects the visitor to a page where he can pay was presented in the "The PayPal Single Item Purchases Feature" section of Chapter 7. Here it is again:

```
Private Sub placeOrderButton_Click(ByVal sender As System.Object, ByVal e As
System.EventArgs) Handles placeOrderButton.Click
   ' We need to store the total amount because the shopping cart
   ' is emptied when creating the order
   Dim amount As Decimal = ShoppingCart.GetTotalAmount()
   ' Create the order and store the order ID
   Dim orderId As String = ShoppingCart.CreateOrder()
   ' This will contain the PayPal request string
   Dim redirect As String
   ' Create the redirect string
   redirect += "https://www.paypal.com/xclick/business=youremail@server.com"
   redirect += "&item_name=JokePoint Order " & orderId
   redirect += "&item_number=" & orderId
   redirect += "&amount=" & String.Format("{0:c}", amount)
   redirect += "&return=http://www.YourWebSite.com"
   redirect += "&cancel_return=http://www.YourWebSite.com"
   ' Load the PayPal payment page
   Response.Redirect(redirect)
End Sub
```

If you use another company to process your payments, you'll need to modify the code accordingly.

When the Place Order button is clicked, two important actions happen. First, the order is created in the database by calling ShoppingCart.CreateOrder. This function creates a new order with the products in the shopping cart, and returns the ID of the new order:

```
Dim orderId As String = ShoppingCart.CreateOrder()
```

The second important action is the redirection to the payment page:

```
Response.Redirect(redirect)
```

Administering Orders

So your visitor just made an order. Now what?

After giving visitors the option to pay for your products, you need to make sure they actually get what they paid for.

Without a carefully designed administration page, where the administrator can quickly see the status of pending orders, JokePoint wouldn't function very well when customers start buying products.

NOTE *This chapter doesn't intend to help you create a perfect order administration system, but rather something that is simple and functional enough to get you on the right track.*

The orders administration part of the site will consist of a Web Form named `ordersAdmin.aspx` and two Web User Controls, `OrdersAdmin.ascx` and `OrderDetailsAdmin.ascx`.

`OrdersAdmin` offers the capability to see the list of orders. When first loaded, it will offer you various ways to select orders, as shown in Figure 10-8.

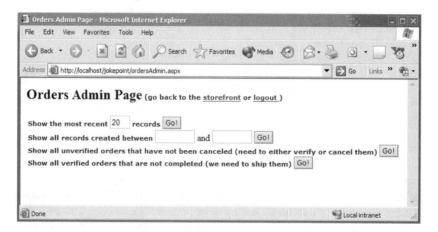

Figure 10-8. The Orders Admin page

After clicking one of the Go! buttons, the matching orders show up in a data grid, as shown in Figure 10-9.

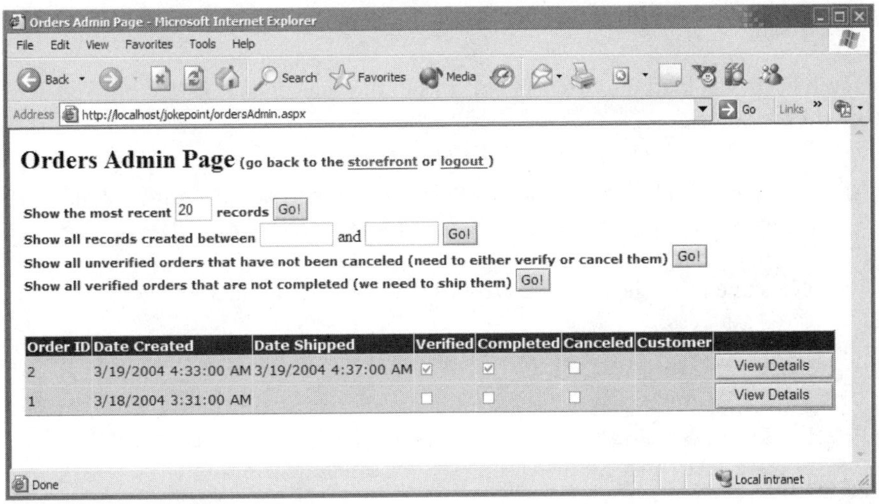

Figure 10-9. The Orders Admin page showing a list of orders

When you click the View Details button for an order, you are sent to a page where you can view and update order information (see Figure 10-10).

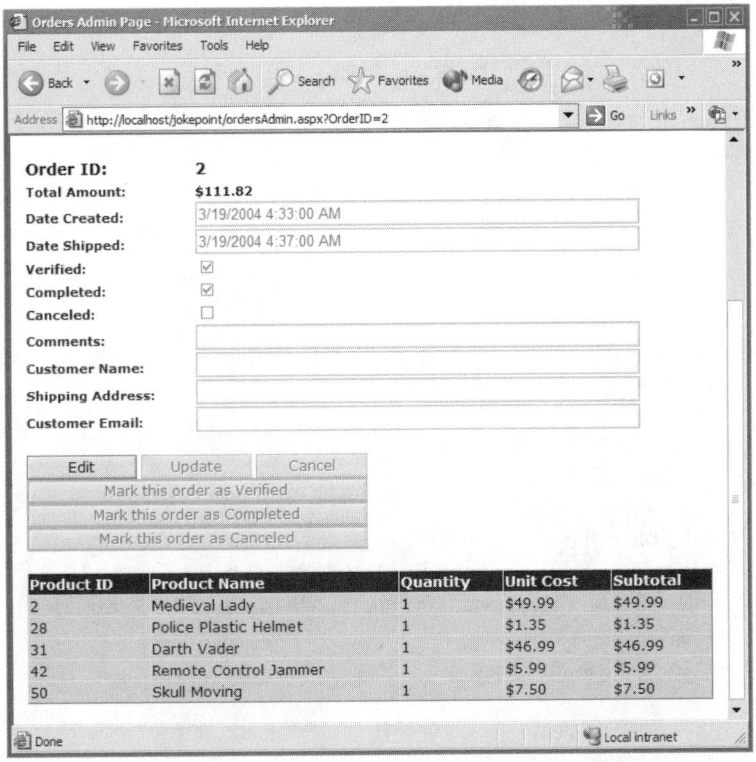

Figure 10-10. The form that allows administering order details

Creating the ordersAdmin Web Form

This Web Form will load the two user controls in the cells of an HTML table. You'll create the form here:

1. Add a new Web Form to the JokePoint project and name it ordersAdmin.aspx. After creating it, change its pageLayout property to FlowLayout.

2. Now open the file in HTML View. Add a reference to the CSS file, JokePoint.css:

    ```
    <HEAD>
        <title>Orders Admin Page</title>
        <meta name="GENERATOR" content="Microsoft Visual Studio.NET 7.0">
        <meta name="CODE_LANGUAGE" content="Visual Basic 7.0">
        <meta name="vs_defaultClientScript" content="JavaScript">
        <meta name="vs_targetSchema"

    content="http://schemas.microsoft.com/intellisense/ie5">
        <link href="JokePoint.css" type="text/css" rel="stylesheet">
    </HEAD>
    ```

3. Modify the <body> area as shown in the following code listing. This adds the table, with its two table cells, to the form.

    ```
    <body>
        <form id="Form1" method="post" runat="server">
            <strong><font size="5">Orders Admin Page</font></strong>
            <br><br>
            <table border="0">
                <tr>
                    <td>
                    </td>
                </tr>
                <tr>
                    <td runat="server" id="orderDetailsCell"></td>
                </tr>
            </table>
        </form>
    </body>
    ```

Only the second table cell is set to run at server side, because it's the only one you'll dynamically populate at runtime, with the OrderDetailsAdmin.ascx Web User Control. You'll populate the first table cell at design time, with the OrdersAdmin.ascx control.

In Design View, the page should look like Figure 10-11.

Figure 10-11. The orders admin page in Design View

While you're here, take a look at the code-behind file to make sure Visual Studio has defined variables for the table cell object, and the Button object (declared to run at server side). If it hasn't, make sure to add them at:

```
Protected WithEvents logoutButton As _
                            System.Web.UI.WebControls.LinkButton
Protected WithEvents orderDetailsCell As _
                            System.Web.UI.HtmlControls.HtmlTableCell
```

4. Add the Logout.ascx control to the form (see Figure 10-12).

Figure 10-12. Adding the Logout.ascx *control to the form*

Implementing Security

Now it's time to extend the simple security mechanism for the page you created. Modify Web.config by adding the following lines just after the ones for admin.aspx and shoppingCartAdmin.aspx:

```
<location path="ordersAdmin.aspx">
  <system.web>
    <authorization>
      <allow users="admin" />
      <deny users="*" />
    </authorization>
  </system.web>
</location>
```

Placing a Link to the Orders Admin page on the First Page

Finally, before moving on, add a link to the orders admin page by updating the FirstPage.ascx user control, which should look like Figure 10-13 when opened in Internet Explorer.

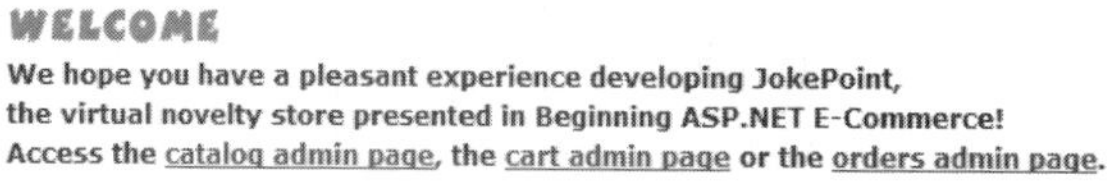

WELCOME

We hope you have a pleasant experience developing JokePoint,
the virtual novelty store presented in Beginning ASP.NET E-Commerce!
Access the <u>catalog admin page</u>, the <u>cart admin page</u> or the <u>orders admin page</u>.

Figure 10-13. The FirstPage.ascx *user control in Internet Explorer*

Open FirstPage.ascx in HTML View and add a link to ordersAdmin.aspx near the link to the catalog admin page, as in the following code snippet:

```
Access the <a href="admin.aspx">catalog admin page</a>, the
<a href="shoppingCartAdmin.aspx"> cart admin page</a> or the
<A href="ordersAdmin.aspx">orders admin page</A>.
```

The OrdersAdmin *Web User Control*

The OrdersAdmin web control fills the first table cell in the order administration page, and has the role of allowing the administrator to view the orders that have been placed on the web site. Because the orders list will become very long, it's important to have a few well-chosen filtering options.

The administrator will be allowed to select the orders by the following criteria:

- Show the most recent orders.

- Show orders that took place in a certain period of time.

- Show pending orders that have not been canceled. This will show the recent orders that have been placed and for which payment confirmation from PayPal is still pending. The administrator will need to mark these orders as Verified, when the financial transaction is confirmed. Otherwise, if the payment is not confirmed in a reasonable amount of time, the administrator will probably want to cancel the order (marking it as Canceled), so that it will not be listed when the button is clicked again at a later time.

- Show orders that need to be shipped (they are Verified, but not yet Completed). These are the orders that have been paid for, but for which the products haven't yet shipped. After the products are shipped, the administrator will mark the order as Completed.

Okay, now that you know what you need, you can start writing some code in the data tier.

The Database Stored Procedures

Add the stored procedures described in the following sections to the JokePoint database.

GetMostRecentOrders

In the GetMostRecentOrders stored procedure, the SET ROWCOUNT statement is used to limit the number of rows returned by the SELECT statement. The parameter, @Count, specifies the number of records. The SELECT command simply returns the necessary rows, in descending order of the date they were created.

```
CREATE PROCEDURE GetMostRecentOrders
(@Count smallint)
AS

SET ROWCOUNT @Count

SELECT OrderID, DateCreated, DateShipped,
       Verified, Completed, Canceled, CustomerName
FROM Orders
ORDER BY DateCreated DESC

SET ROWCOUNT 0
```

At the end, you set ROWCOUNT to 0, which tells SQL Server to stop limiting the number of returned rows.

ORDER BY is used to sort the returned results from the SELECT statement. The default sorting mode is ascending, but adding DESC sets the descending sorting mode (so the most recent orders will be listed first).

GetOrdersBetweenDates

GetOrdersBetweenDates simply returns all the records in which the current date is between the start and end dates that are supplied as parameters. The results are sorted descending by date.

```
CREATE PROCEDURE GetOrdersBetweenDates
(@StartDate smalldatetime,
 @EndDate smalldatetime)
AS

SELECT OrderID, DateCreated, DateShipped,
       Verified, Completed, Canceled, CustomerName
```

```
FROM Orders
WHERE DateCreated BETWEEN @StartDate AND @EndDate
ORDER BY DateCreated DESC
```

GetUnverifiedUncanceledOrders

GetUnverifiedUncanceledOrders returns the orders that have not been verified yet, but
have not been canceled either. In other words, you'll see the orders that need to be
either verified (and then completed when the shipment is done), or canceled (if the
payment isn't confirmed in a reasonable amount of time). The code is fairly straightforward:

```
CREATE PROCEDURE GetUnverifiedUncanceledOrders
AS

SELECT OrderID, DateCreated, DateShipped,
       Verified, Completed, Canceled, CustomerName
FROM Orders
WHERE Verified=0 AND Canceled=0
ORDER BY DateCreated DESC
```

GetVerifiedUncompletedOrders

GetVerifiedUncompletedOrders returns all the orders that have been verified, but not
yet completed. The administrator will want to see these orders when a shipment has
been done and the order needs to be marked as Completed. (When an order will be
marked as completed, the DateShipped field will also be populated.)

```
CREATE PROCEDURE GetVerifiedUncompletedOrders
AS

SELECT OrderID, DateCreated, DateShipped,
       Verified, Completed, Canceled, CustomerName
FROM Orders
WHERE Verified=1 AND Completed=0
ORDER BY DateCreated DESC
```

The Business Tier Methods

As usual, this is where you create the Visual Basic methods for the OrdersAdmin control. These methods will call the stored procedures you wrote earlier. Before writing
the new methods, you'll create a new class in the BusinessObjects folder:

Creating the OrderManager *Class*

Create a new Visual Basic class file in the BusinessObjects folder named OrderManager.vb by following these steps:

1. Right-click BusinessObjects, and then click Add ➤ Add New Item.

2. Select Class from the Templates window, and type **OrderManager.vb** (or simply **OrderManager**) for the file name.

3. Click Open.

4. Open the newly created file, add the usual connectionString property, and import the SqlClient namespace:

```
Imports System.Data.SqlClient

Public Class OrderManager
    Private Shared ReadOnly Property connectionString() As String
        Get
            Return ConfigurationSettings.AppSettings("ConnectionString")
        End Get
    End Property


    '
    ' Add methods here
    '

End Class
```

GetMostRecentOrders

Now add the GetMostRecentOrders method to the OrderManager class. This one calls the GetMostRecentOrders stored procedure and returns a list of most recent orders to the calling function, in the form of an SqlDataReader object.

```
Public Shared Function GetMostRecentOrders(ByVal count As Integer) As _
SqlDataReader
    ' Create the connection object
    Dim connection As New SqlConnection(connectionString)
    ' Create and initialize the command object
    Dim command As New SqlCommand("GetMostRecentOrders", connection)
    command.CommandType = CommandType.StoredProcedure
    ' Add an input parameter and supply a value for it
    command.Parameters.Add("@Count", SqlDbType.SmallInt)
    command.Parameters("@Count").Value = count
    ' Return the results
    Try
        ' Open the connection
        connection.Open()
        ' Return an SqlDataReader to the calling function
```

```
      Return command.ExecuteReader(CommandBehavior.CloseConnection)
    Catch e As Exception
      ' Close the connection and rethrow the exception
      connection.Close()
      Throw e
    End Try
  End Function
```

GetOrdersBetweenDates

The GetOrdersBetweenDates method returns all the orders that have been placed in a certain period of time, specified by a start date and an end date.

```
  Public Shared Function GetOrdersBetweenDates(ByVal startDate As String, ByVal _
endDate As String) As SqlDataReader
    ' Create the connection object
    Dim connection As New SqlConnection(connectionString)
    ' Create and initialize the command object
    Dim command As New SqlCommand("GetOrdersBetweenDates", connection)
    command.CommandType = CommandType.StoredProcedure
    ' Add an input parameter and supply a value for it
    command.Parameters.Add("@StartDate", SqlDbType.SmallDateTime)
    command.Parameters("@StartDate").Value = startDate
    ' Add an input parameter and supply a value for it
    command.Parameters.Add("@EndDate", SqlDbType.SmallDateTime)
    command.Parameters("@EndDate").Value = endDate
    ' Return the results
    Try
      ' Open the connection
      connection.Open()
      ' Return an SqlDataReader to the calling function
      Return command.ExecuteReader(CommandBehavior.CloseConnection)
    Catch e As Exception
      ' Close the connection and rethrow the exception
      connection.Close()
      Throw e
    End Try
  End Function
```

GetUnverifiedUncanceledOrders

The GetUnverifiedUncanceledOrders method returns a list of orders that have not been verified yet, but were not canceled either. These are the records that need to be either verified (and then set to completed when the shipment is done), or canceled (if the payment isn't confirmed in a reasonable amount of time).

```
  Public Shared Function GetUnverifiedUncanceledOrders() As SqlDataReader
    ' Create the connection object
    Dim connection As New SqlConnection(connectionString)
```

```
  ' Create and initialize the command object
  Dim command As New SqlCommand("GetUnverifiedUncanceledOrders", connection)
  command.CommandType = CommandType.StoredProcedure
  ' Return the results
  Try
    ' Open the connection
    connection.Open()
    ' Return an SqlDataReader to the calling function
    Return command.ExecuteReader(CommandBehavior.CloseConnection)
  Catch e As Exception
    ' Close the connection and rethrow the exception
    connection.Close()
    Throw e
  End Try
End Function
```

GetVerifiedUncompletedOrders

The GetVerifiedUncompletedOrders method returns all the orders that have been verified, but not yet completed. The administrator will want to see these orders when a shipment has been done to mark the order as Completed.

```
Public Shared Function GetVerifiedUncompletedOrders() As SqlDataReader
  ' Create the connection object
  Dim connection As New SqlConnection(connectionString)
  ' Create and initialize the command object
  Dim command As New SqlCommand("GetVerifiedUncompletedOrders", connection)
  command.CommandType = CommandType.StoredProcedure
  ' Return the results
  Try
    ' Open the connection
    connection.Open()
    ' Return an SqlDataReader to the calling function
    Return command.ExecuteReader(CommandBehavior.CloseConnection)
  Catch e As Exception
    ' Close the connection and rethrow the exception
    connection.Close()
    Throw e
  End Try
End Function
```

The Presentation Tier: OrdersAdmin.ascx

Now it's time to implement the OrdersAdmin control. First, you'll create the control and add the constituent controls on the form using Visual Studio's Design View mode, and then you'll write the code-behind file.

While building the UI in the following exercise, you'll also learn about the validator controls provided by the .NET Framework. This is the first (and only) place in this book they are used, so pay special attention to them.

Exercise: Creating OrdersAdmin.ascx

1.   Create a new Web User Control in the AdminUserControls folder named OrdersAdmin.ascx.

2.   Add Label controls, Button controls, and a DataGrid, as shown in Figure 10-14.

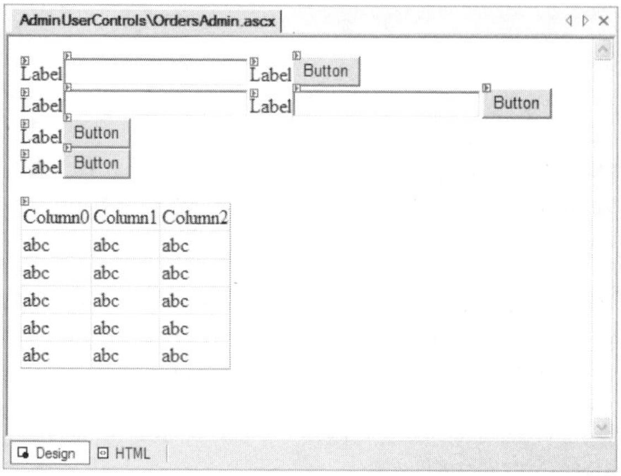

Figure 10-14. Adding controls to OrdersAdmin.ascx

TIP   *Use Shift+Enter instead of Enter to generate*
 tags between lines, instead of generating separate paragraphs.

---

3.   Set the properties for each control as described in Tables 10-1 through 10-5.

The controls for the first line should have their properties set as shown here:

TIP   *Notice that many controls, especially those of the same type, have the same* CssClass *property. You can make life easier by selecting more controls, and then setting the property for all of them in one step, instead of setting the property separately for each control.*

Table 10-1. Properties for the First Line of Controls in OrdersAdmin.ascx

Control Type	ID	Text	CssClass	Width
Label	(doesn't matter)	Show the most recent	AdminPageText	
TextBox	recordCountTextBox	20		35px
Label	(doesn't matter)	records	AdminPageText	
Button	mostRecentButton	Go!	AdminButtonText	

The property settings for the second line are shown in Table 10-2.

Table 10-2. Properties for the Second Line of Controls in OrdersAdmin.ascx

Control Type	ID	Text	CssClass	Width
Label	(doesn't matter)	Show all records created between	AdminPageText	
TextBox	startDateTextBox	(empty)		70px
Label	(doesn't matter)	and	AdminPageText	
TextBox	endDateTextBox	(empty)		70px
Button	betweenDatesButton	Go!	AdminButtonText	

The controls for the third line should be set as shown in Table 10-3.

Table 10-3. Properties for the Third Line of Controls in OrdersAdmin.ascx

Control Type	ID	Text	CssClass
Label	(doesn't matter)	Show all unverified orders that have not been canceled (need to either verify or cancel them)	AdminPageText
Button	unverifiedOrdersButton	Go!	AdminButtonText

The controls for the fourth and final lines should be set as shown in Table 10-4.

Table 10-4. Properties for the Forth and Fifth Lines of Controls in OrdersAdmin.ascx

Control Type	ID	Text	CssClass	Width
Label	(doesn't matter)	Show all verified orders that are not completed (we need to ship them)	AdminPageText	
Button	verifiedOrdersButton	Go!	AdminButtonText	
DataGrid	grid			100%

4. Open the DataGrid's Property Builder page and select the Columns tab. Deselect the Create Columns Automatically at Runtime check box. Set the data grid's columns as shown in Table 10-5.

Table 10-5. Configuring DataGrid's *Fields*

Column Type	Header Text	Data Field	Other Properties
Bound Column	Order ID	OrderID	Click the Read Only check box.
Bound Column	Date Created	DateCreated	Click the Read Only check box.
Bound Column	Date Shipped	DateShipped	Click the Read Only check box.
Bound Column	Verified	Verified	Click the Read Only check box, and then click Convert this Column into a Template Column.
Bound Column	Completed	Completed	Click the Read Only check box, and then click Convert this Column into a Template Column.
Bound Column	Canceled	Canceled	Click the Read Only check box, and then click Convert this Column into a Template Column.
Bound Column	Customer	CustomerName	
Select			Set the Text property to View Details and Button type to PushButton.

TIP   *You actually don't need to set the Header text and Data field for the Verified, Completed, and Canceled columns, because you transform them to template columns anyway. However, if you set these properties before converting them to template columns, Visual Studio will help you a little bit by generating some of the template code for you. Also, if the columns are read-only, Visual Studio will not generate their* EditItemTemplate. *All columns are read-only because you won't implement edit functionality for this data grid.*

5.   In HTML View, set the following code for the three template columns:

```
<asp:TemplateColumn HeaderText="Verified">
  <ItemTemplate>
    <asp:CheckBox id="Checkbox1" Text="" runat="server" Enabled="False"
      Checked='<%# DataBinder.Eval(Container, "DataItem.Verified") %>'>
    </asp:CheckBox>
  </ItemTemplate>
</asp:TemplateColumn>
<asp:TemplateColumn HeaderText="Completed">
  <ItemTemplate>
    <asp:CheckBox id="Checkbox2" Text="" runat="server" Enabled="False"
      Checked='<%# DataBinder.Eval(Container, "DataItem.Completed") %>'>
    </asp:CheckBox>
  </ItemTemplate>
</asp:TemplateColumn>
<asp:TemplateColumn HeaderText="Canceled">
  <ItemTemplate>
    <asp:CheckBox id="Checkbox3" Text="" runat="server" Enabled="False"
      Checked='<%# DataBinder.Eval(Container, "DataItem.Canceled") %>'>
    </asp:CheckBox>
  </ItemTemplate>
</asp:TemplateColumn>
```

6.   In the Property Builder window, click the Format link on the left and select the Header tab. Set its properties as shown in Figure 10-15.

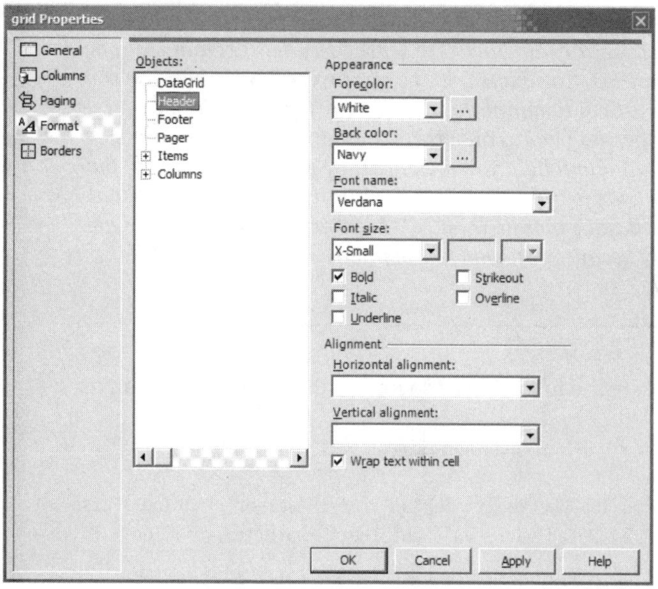

Figure 10-15. Setting DataGrid *properties*

7. Open the Normal Items template and set its properties as shown in Figure 10-16.

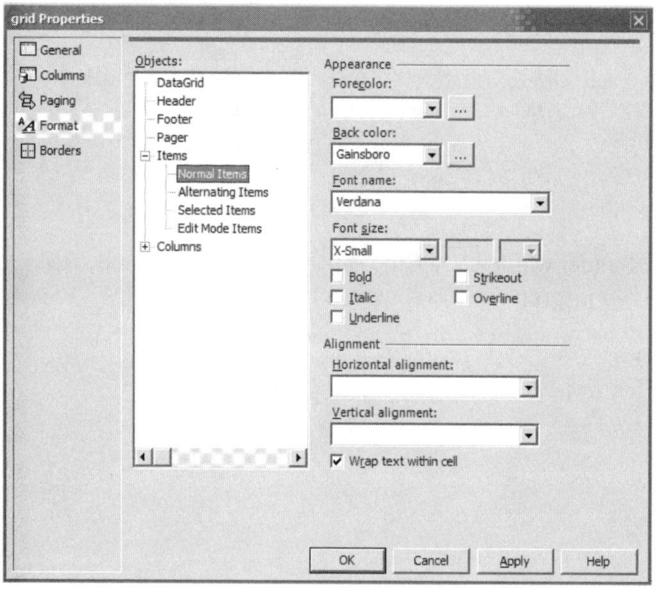

Figure 10-16. Setting DataGrid *properties*

Right now, the form should look like Figure 10-17, while in Design View.

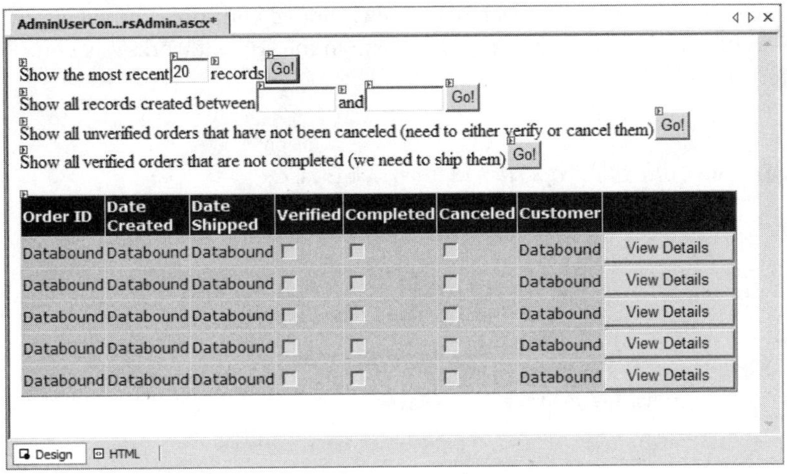

Figure 10-17. OrdersAdmin.ascx *in Design View*

8. So far, you have only added objects that you're already familiar with from the previous chapters. In this exercise, however, we introduce the **validator controls** provided by the .NET Framework. These controls provide a quick and easy way to validate the input values at the presentation-tier level. In this form, you'll test whether the values entered into the text boxes are valid before querying the business tier with them. Just above the data grid, add a Label control, two RangeValidator controls, a CompareValidator control, and a ValidationSummary control, as shown in Figure 10-18.

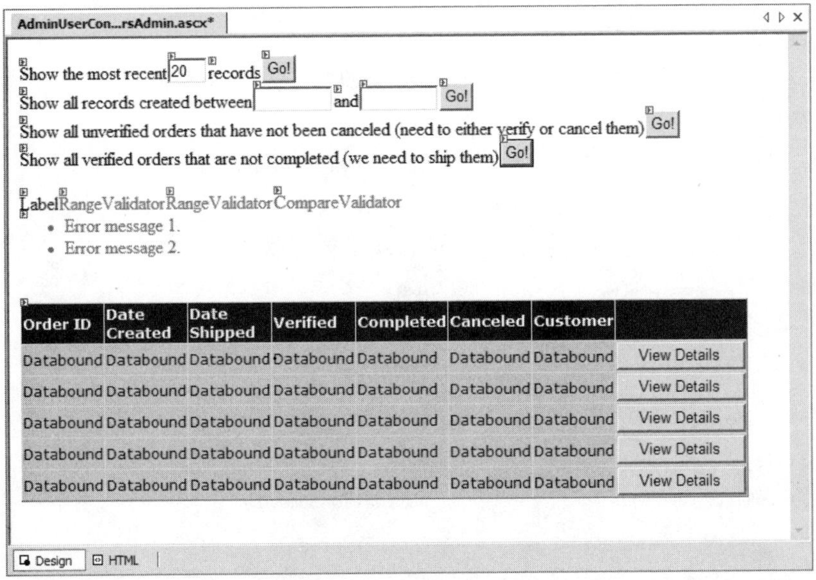

Figure 10-18. OrdersAdmin.ascx *in Design View*

9. Now set the properties for each of the newly added controls as noted in Table 10-6. (We'll take a closer look at them in the "How It Works" section, afterwards.)

Table 10-6. Setting Control's Properties in `OrdersAdmin.ascx`

Control	Property Name	Property Value
Label	(ID)	errorLabel
	Text	(should be empty)
	CssClass	AdminErrorText
	EnableViewState	False
RangeValidator	(ID)	startDateValidator
	ControlToValidate	startDateTextBox
	Display	None
	ErrorMessage	Invalid start date.
	MaximumValue	1/1/2005
	MinimumValue	1/1/1999
	Type	Date
RangeValidator	(ID)	endDateValidator
	ControlToValidate	endDateTextBox
	Display	None
	ErrorMessage	Invalid end date.
	MaximumValue	1/1/2005
	MinimumValue	1/1/1999
	Type	Date
CompareValidator	(ID)	compareDatesValidator
	ControlToCompare	endDateTextBox
	ControlToValidate	startDateTextBox
	Display	None
	ErrorMessage	Start date should be more recent than end date.
	Operator	LessThan
	Type	Date
ValidationSummary	(ID)	validationSummary
	CssClass	AdminErrorText
	HeaderText	Validation errors:

10. Add the following style to `JokePoint.css`:

```css
.AdminErrorText
{
   font-weight: bold;
   font-size: 12px;
   color: red;
   font-style: italic;
   font-family: Verdana, Helvetica, sans-serif;
}
```

11. Before ending this exercise, drag the control from the Solution Explorer and drop it into the first cell in the table in `ordersAdmin.aspx` (see Figure 10-19).

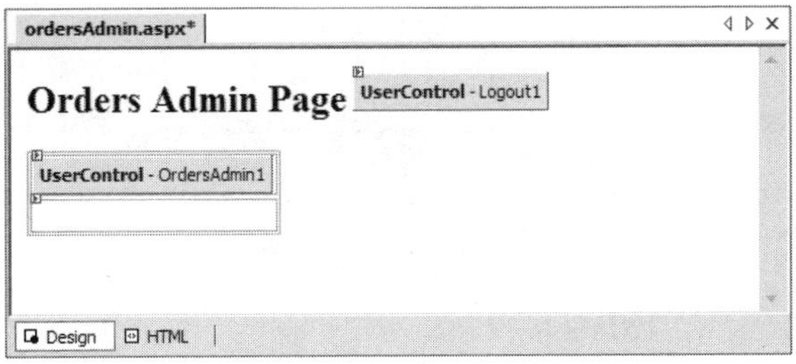

Figure 10-19. `ordersAdmin.aspx` *in DesignView*

12. Press **F5** to execute the project. Browse to the orders administration page (you'll eventually be required to supply the login info), add some invalid values in the text boxes, and click one of the Go! buttons. You should receive an error message similar to the ones in Figure 10-20.

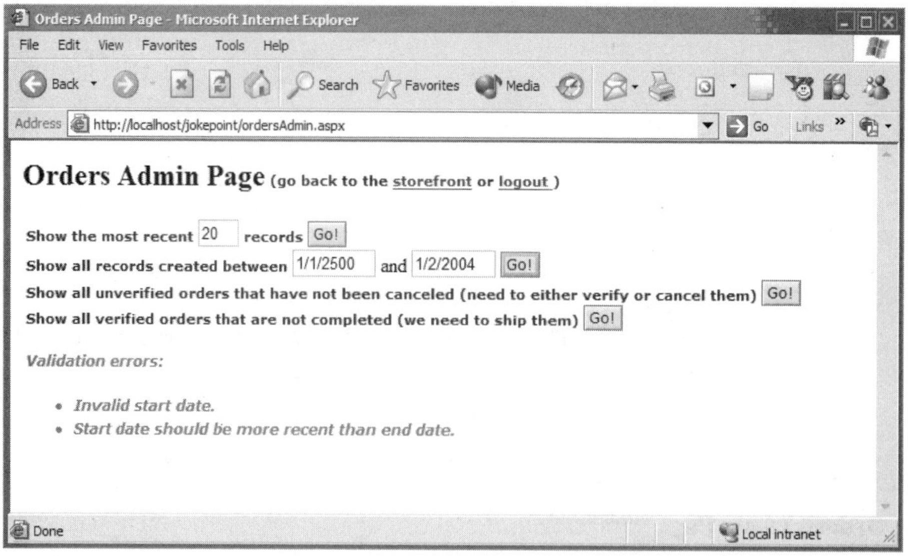

Orders Admin Page (go back to the <u>storefront</u> or <u>logout</u>)

Show the most recent 20 records Go!

Show all records created between 1/1/2500 and 1/2/2004 Go!

Show all unverified orders that have not been canceled (need to either verify or cancel them) Go!

Show all verified orders that are not completed (we need to ship them) Go!

Validation errors:

- *Invalid start date.*
- *Start date should be more recent than end date.*

Figure 10-20. An error message on the Orders Admin page

How It Works: `OrdersAdmin.ascx` *and the Validator Controls*

This is the first example in this book where you played with the validator controls. A validator control validates the value of other controls. It can be associated only with input controls—like the text boxes in our example.

For our page, you had the following requirements regarding the input text boxes:

- The values in `startDateTextBox` and `endDateTextBox` must be correctly formatted dates between 1/1/1999 and 1/1/2005.

- The start date needs to be more recent than the end date.

CAUTION *The validation controls have the power to prevent the page from being submitted to the server—if any of the validator controls signal an error, none of the Go! Buttons will work, ensuring that the business tier is only called with valid values.*

The first requirement is implemented using `RangeValidator` controls, and the second using a `CompareValidator`. The `ValidationSummary` control gets the errors from the validator controls and displays them in a single, easy-to-read list.

The .NET Framework provides more validator controls, each specialized in a certain type of validation: `RequiredFieldValidator`, `CompareValidator`, `RangeValidator`, `RegularExpressionValidator`, and `CustomValidator`.

We will only briefly analyze the way CompareValidator and RangeValidator work, because they are used for JokePoint. Still, the way all the validation controls work is similar, with the exception of CustomValidator, which is more powerful, and its validation logic can be programmed manually. You'll also work with the ValidationSummary control, which gathers all the error messages from the validation controls in the page and presents them in a separate list, as you saw in previously in Figure 10-20.

NOTE *In the previous exercise, you also added a* Label *control named* errorLabel. *This control has nothing to do with the validator controls; you'll use it for displaying other error messages a bit later in this chapter.*

So let's see how you made the three validator controls work. The two RangeValidator controls test whether the data type of each text box is correct and whether its value is in a specified range of values. When adding a new RangeValidator control, you usually will set these properties:

- *ControlToValidate*: Set this property to the control that you want to validate.

- *Display*: If you don't use a ValidationSummary control, leave this as Dynamic or Static, which results in the error message being displayed right in the place where the validator is placed. But because in this example you are using the ValidationSummary control, set the Display to None, so that the error messages aren't displayed twice.

- *ErrorMessage*: This property contains the message to be displayed if the control is not validated.

- *Type*: This property specifies the data type that should exist in the control being validated. Set this property to Date for the two text boxes.

- *MinimumValue*, MaximumValue: These specify the maximum and minimum value that should exist in the control being validated.

CompareValidator compares the values of two input controls, and has a few properties that are specific to it:

- *ControlToCompare, ControlToValidate*: The two controls that need to be compared. The one specified by ControlToValidate is the reference control.

- *Operator*: Specifies what kind of comparison should be done between the two controls. Possible values are Equal, NotEqual, GreaterThan, GreaterThanEqual, LessThan, LessThanEqual, and DataTypeCheck. When DataTypeCheck is selected, only the data type of ControlToValidate is verified, and the control specified by ControlToCompare is ignored.

For the `ValidationSummary` control, you set the `CssClass` property to a style named `AdminErrorText`. You also set the `HeaderText` property, which represents the header to be displayed before the list of errors.

Note that you can change the layout of this control by setting the `DisplayMode` property. You also can set it up to raise a dialog box by setting the `ShowMessageBox` property to `True`.

When creating the control, you also added a `Label` control named `errorLabel`, which will be used to display errors that come from the database or the business tier after the code of the Go! button executes. You set its `EnableViewState` property to false, so its value will be cleared after a successful Go! command executes. You'll populate this label in the code-behind file, which you'll implement in the next exercise.

Exercise: Implementing the Logic in `OrdersAdmin.ascx`

You need to complete five steps here: implement the `Click` event handler for each of the four Go! buttons, and then for the `SelectedIndexChanged` event of the data grid.

1. While in Design View, double-click the first Go! button, and then modify its `Click` event handler like this:

    ```
    Private Sub mostRecentButton_Click(ByVal sender As System.Object,
    ByVal e As System.EventArgs) Handles mostRecentButton.Click
        Dim recordCount As Integer
        Try
            recordCount = Int16.Parse(recordCountTextBox.Text)
            grid.DataSource = OrderManager.GetMostRecentOrders(recordCount)
            grid.DataKeyField = "OrderID"
            grid.DataBind()
        Catch ex as Exception
            errorLabel.Text = "Could not get the requested data!"
        End Try
    End Sub
    ```

    This method populates the data grid with the familiar routine. It calls the `GetMostRecentOrders` method from the middle tier, which in turn calls the `GetMostRecentOrders` stored procedure.

    You transform the text from `recordCountTextBox` into a string using the `Int16.Parse` method. This method raises an exception if the input data isn't numerical (or if it's out of range), in which case `errorLabel` gets populated with an error message.

 TIP *Of course, you can use a validator control to test the value in the* `recordCountTextBox`.

---

2. Switch to Design View, double-click the second Go! button, and then modify its Click event handler like this:

```
Private Sub betweenDatesButton_Click(ByVal sender As System.Object,
ByVal e As System.EventArgs) Handles betweenDatesButton.Click
    Dim startDate As String
    Dim endDate As String
    Try
       startDate = startDateTextBox.Text
       endDate = endDateTextBox.Text
       grid.DataSource = OrderManager.GetOrdersBetweenDates(startDate, endDate)
       grid.DataKeyField = "OrderID"
       grid.DataBind()
    Catch ex as Exception
       errorLabel.Text = "Could not get the requested data!"
    End Try
End Sub
```

This method is very similar to the preceding one. One difference is that here you send the input data from the text boxes (the two dates) as strings to the middle tier. The data type casting is done in the middle tier in this case, when the two dates are sent as SqlDbType.SmallDateTime parameters to the GetOrdersBetweenDates stored procedure.

3. Switch to Design View, double-click the third Go! button, and then modify its Click event handler like this:

```
Private Sub unverifiedOrdersButton_Click(ByVal sender As System.Object,
ByVal e As System.EventArgs) Handles unverifiedOrdersButton.Click
    Try
       grid.DataSource = OrderManager.GetUnverifiedUncanceledOrders()
       grid.DataKeyField = "OrderID"
       grid.DataBind()
    Catch ex as Exception
       errorLabel.Text = "Could not get the requested data!"
    End Try
End Sub
```

4. Switch to Design View, double-click the fourth Go! button, and then modify its Click event handler like this:

```
Private Sub verifiedOrdersButton_Click(ByVal sender As System.Object,
ByVal e As System.EventArgs) Handles verifiedOrdersButton.Click
    Try
       grid.DataSource = OrderManager.GetVerifiedUncompletedOrders()
       grid.DataKeyField = "OrderID"
       grid.DataBind()
    Catch ex as Exception
       errorLabel.Text = "Could not get the requested data!"
    End Try
End Sub
```

5. Finally, switch again to Design View and double-click the data grid to generate the signature for the SelectedIndexChanged event handler. Add these lines to it:

```
Private Sub grid_SelectedIndexChanged(ByVal sender As System.Object,
ByVal e As System.EventArgs) Handles grid.SelectedIndexChanged
    Dim orderId As String
    orderId = grid.DataKeys(grid.SelectedIndex)
    Response.Redirect("ordersAdmin.aspx?OrderID=" & orderId)
End Sub
```

Here you simply obtain the ID of the order you clicked the View Details button for—remember that View Details is the Select button of the grid, so clicking it triggers the SelectedIndexChanged event. When this happens, ordersAdmin.aspx is reloaded by adding the OrderID parameter to it. This will make ordersAdmin.aspx load the OrderDetailsAdmin user control (which you'll create later) in the second cell of the administration page.

How It Works: Showing Orders in OrderDetails.ascx

Each of the buttons' Click event handlers calls one of the methods of the OrderManager class and populates the data grid with the returned SqlDataReader.

If anything bad happens in these calls, you let the user know by setting a simple error message in the errorLabel control. This could happen, for example, if the SQL Server instance is paused or stopped. Remember that it's possible to even further fine-tune the error messages by implementing multiple Catch blocks to deal differently with each kind of error.

The SelectedIndexChanged event of the data grid is generated when you click its Select buttons, which have the View Details text. When one of these buttons is clicked, the page is reloaded with the OrderID parameter appended in the query string. Remember that OrdersAdminPage loads the OrderDetailsAdmin user control in the second table cell when an order ID is supplied.

The OrderDetailsAdmin Web User Control

The OrderDetailsAdmin user control allows the administrator to edit the details of a particular order. The most common tasks will be to mark an unverified order as either Verified or Canceled (it can't be directly marked as Completed if it isn't verified yet), and to mark a verified order as Completed when the shipment is dispatched.

Figure 10-21 shows OrderDetailsAdmin in action.

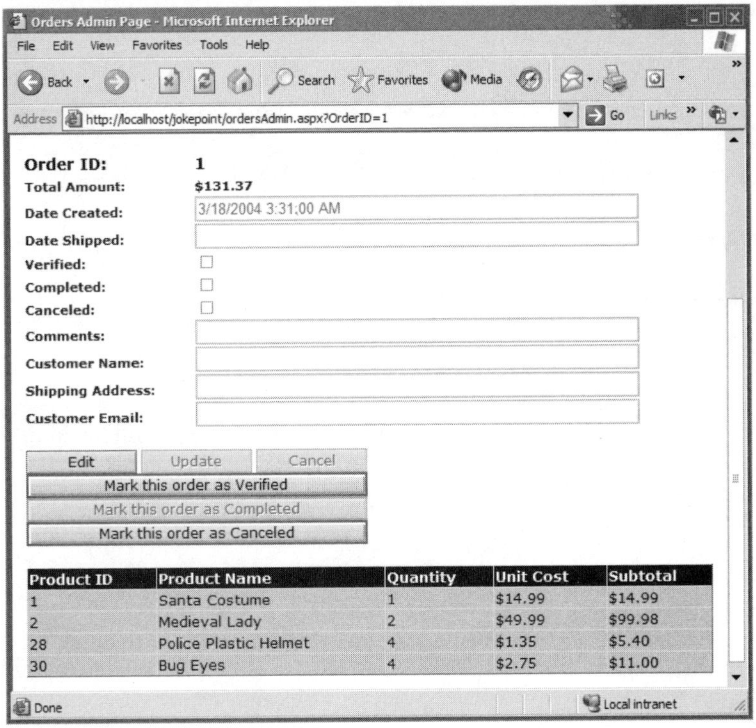

Figure 10-21. OrderDetailsAdmin in action

Here you've provided the administrator with three very useful buttons: Mark this Order as Verified, Mark this Order as Completed, and Mark this Order as Canceled. These buttons will be enabled or disabled, depending on the status of the order. The Edit, Update, and Cancel buttons allow the administrator to manually edit any of the details of an order. When the Edit button is clicked, all of the check boxes and text boxes (except for the one holding the order ID) become editable.

Now you have an idea about what you'll be doing with this control. You'll implement it in the usual style starting with the data tier.

The Database Stored Procedures

Now you'll implement the data tier logic that will support the functionality required by the UI. You'll enable the administrator to do six operations, which you'll implement with the following stored procedures:

- GetOrderInfo returns the data needed to populate the text boxes of the form with general order information, such as the total amount, date created, date shipped, and so on. You can see the complete list in the previous screenshot.

- GetOrderDetails returns all the products that belong to the selected order, and its return data fills the grid at the bottom of the form.

- UpdateOrder is called when the form is in edit mode, and you submit new data to update the selected order.

- MarkOrderAsVerified is called to set the Verified bit of the selected order to 1.

- MarkOrderAsCompleted sets the Completed bit of the order to 1.

- MarkOrderAsCanceled sets the Canceled bit of the order to 1.

You'll now implement each of these stored procedures.

GetOrderInfo

The GetOrderInfo stored procedure returns the information necessary to fill the long list of text boxes in the OrderDetailsAdmin control.

```
CREATE PROCEDURE GetOrderInfo
(@OrderID int)
AS
SELECT OrderID,
        (SELECT SUM(UnitCost*Quantity) FROM OrderDetail WHERE OrderID = @OrderID)
        AS TotalAmount,
        DateCreated,
        DateShipped,
        Verified,
        Completed,
        Canceled,
        Comments,
        CustomerName,
        ShippingAddress,
        CustomerEmail
FROM Orders
WHERE OrderID = @OrderID
```

Note that a subquery is used to generate the TotalAmount field. All the other data you need is read from the Orders table, but to get the total amount of an order, you need to look at the OrderDetail table as well.

The subquery that returns the total amount of a particular order uses the SUM function to add up the subtotal of each product in the order, as follows:

```
SELECT SUM(UnitCost*Quantity) FROM OrderDetail WHERE OrderID = @OrderID
```

This subquery gets executed for each row of the outer query, and its result is saved as a calculated column named TotalAmount.

GetOrderDetails

GetOrderDetails returns the list of products that belong to a specific order. This will be used to populate the data grid containing the order details, situated at the bottom of the control.

```
CREATE PROCEDURE GetOrderDetails
(@OrderID int)
AS

SELECT Orders.OrderID,
       ProductID,
       ProductName,
       Quantity,
       UnitCost,
       Quantity*UnitCost AS Subtotal
FROM OrderDetail JOIN Orders
ON Orders.OrderID = OrderDetail.OrderID
WHERE Orders.OrderID = @OrderID
```

UpdateOrder

The UpdateOrder procedure is called when the user is updating the order in the DataGrid.

```
CREATE PROCEDURE UpdateOrder
(@OrderID int,
 @DateCreated smalldatetime,
 @DateShipped smalldatetime = NULL,
 @Verified bit,
 @Completed bit,
 @Canceled bit,
 @Comments varchar(200),
 @CustomerName varchar(50),
 @ShippingAddress varchar(200),
 @CustomerEmail varchar(50))
AS

UPDATE Orders
SET DateCreated=@DateCreated,
    DateShipped=@DateShipped,
    Verified=@Verified,
    Completed=@Completed,
    Canceled=@Canceled,
    Comments=@Comments,
    CustomerName=@CustomerName,
    ShippingAddress=@ShippingAddress,
    CustomerEmail=@CustomerEmail
WHERE OrderID = @OrderID
```

MarkOrderAsVerified

MarkOrderAsVerified is called when the Mark this Order as Verified button is clicked.

```
CREATE PROCEDURE MarkOrderAsVerified
(@OrderID int)
AS

UPDATE Orders
SET Verified = 1
WHERE OrderID = @OrderID
```

MarkOrderAsCompleted

MarkOrderAsCompleted is called when the administrator clicks the Mark this Order as Completed button. It not only sets the Completed bit to 1, but also updates the DateShipped field because an order is completed just after the shipment has been done.

```
CREATE PROCEDURE MarkOrderAsCompleted
(@OrderID int)
AS

UPDATE Orders
SET Completed = 1,
    DateShipped = getdate()
WHERE OrderID = @OrderID
```

MarkOrderAsCanceled

MarkOrderAsCanceled is called when the Mark this Order as Canceled button is clicked.

```
CREATE PROCEDURE MarkOrderAsCanceled
(@OrderID int)
AS

UPDATE Orders
SET Canceled = 1
WHERE OrderID = @OrderID
```

The Business Tier

Apart from the usual methods that pass data back and forth between the UI and the database stored procedures, you'll create an additional class named OrderInfo. Objects of this class will store order information and will be used to pass order information from the business-tier methods to the presentation tier.

It is simpler to use such a class instead of passing SqlDataReader objects, because the constituent controls are not data-bound and you need to manually fill them with data.

The OrderInfo *Class*

Add the OrderInfo class to the OrderManager.vb file, but not inside the OrderManager class.

 NOTE *If you prefer having each class in its separate file, feel free to add a new class file to your* BusinessObjects *folder.*

```
Imports System.Data.SqlClient

Public Class OrderInfo
    Public OrderID As String
    Public TotalAmount As Decimal
    Public DateCreated As String
    Public DateShipped As String
    Public Verified As Boolean
    Public Completed As Boolean
    Public Canceled As Boolean
    Public Comments As String
    Public CustomerName As String
    Public ShippingAddress As String
    Public CustomerEmail As String
End Class

Public Class OrderManager
    ' ...
```

After this class is in place, add the following methods to the OrderManager class:

GetOrderInfo

This method gets information related to a particular order from the database, in the form of an SqlDataReader object. It then reads the SqlDataReader and saves the data into an OrderInfo object, which is then returned to the calling function.

```
Public Shared Function GetOrderInfo(ByVal orderId As String) As orderInfo
    ' Create the Connection object
    Dim connection As New SqlConnection(connectionString)
    ' Create and initialize the Command object
    Dim command As New SqlCommand("GetOrderInfo", connection)
    command.CommandType = CommandType.StoredProcedure
    ' Add an input parameter and set a value for it
    command.Parameters.Add("@OrderID", SqlDbType.Int)
    command.Parameters("@OrderID").Value = orderId
    ' The SqlDataReader object used to get the results
    Dim reader As SqlDataReader
    ' Get the results
```

```
    Try
        ' Open the connection
        connection.Open()
        ' Return an SqlDataReader to the calling function
        reader = command.ExecuteReader(CommandBehavior.CloseConnection)
    Catch e As Exception
        ' Close the connection and throw the exception
        connection.Close()
        Throw e
    End Try
    ' We move to the first (and only) record in the reader object
    ' and store the information in an OrderInfo object.
    Dim orderInfo As New OrderInfo()
    If reader.Read() Then ' returns true if there are records
        orderInfo.OrderID = reader("OrderID").ToString()
        orderInfo.TotalAmount = reader("TotalAmount").ToString()
        orderInfo.DateCreated = reader("DateCreated").ToString()
        orderInfo.DateShipped = reader("DateShipped").ToString()
        orderInfo.Verified = Boolean.Parse(reader("Verified").ToString())
        orderInfo.Completed = Boolean.Parse(reader("Completed").ToString())
        orderInfo.Canceled = Boolean.Parse(reader("Canceled").ToString())
        orderInfo.Comments = reader("Comments").ToString()
        orderInfo.CustomerName = reader("CustomerName").ToString()
        orderInfo.ShippingAddress = reader("ShippingAddress").ToString()
        orderInfo.CustomerEmail = reader("CustomerEmail").ToString()
        ' Close the reader and its connection
        reader.Close()
        connection.Close()
    End If
    ' Return the information in the form of an OrderInfo object
    Return orderInfo
End Function
```

ToString is used when reading each read field from the SqlDataReader because some fields might have NULL, which cannot be stored in a string variable. NULL fields are transformed into empty strings when ToString is called on them.

GetOrderDetails

GetOrderDetails returns the order details of the specified order.

```
Public Shared Function GetOrderDetails(ByVal orderId As String) As SqlDataReader
    ' Create the Connection object
    Dim connection As New SqlConnection(connectionString)
    ' Create and initialize the Command object
    Dim command As New SqlCommand("GetOrderDetails", connection)
    command.CommandType = CommandType.StoredProcedure
    ' Add an input parameter and set a value for it
    command.Parameters.Add("@OrderID", SqlDbType.Int)
    command.Parameters("@OrderID").Value = orderId
    ' Get the results
```

```
Try
  ' Open the connection
  connection.Open()
  ' Return an SqlDataReader to the calling function
  Return command.ExecuteReader(CommandBehavior.CloseConnection)
Catch e As Exception
  ' Close the connection and throw the exception
  connection.Close()
  Throw e
End Try
End Function
```

UpdateOrder

This stored procedure updates an order, and is called when the Update button in
OrderDetailsAdmin is clicked. It receives the order details as an OrderInfo parameter.

```
Public Shared Sub UpdateOrder(ByVal orderInfo As OrderInfo)
  ' Create the Connection object
  Dim connection As New SqlConnection(connectionString)
  ' Create and initialize the Command object
  Dim command As New SqlCommand("UpdateOrder", connection)
  command.CommandType = CommandType.StoredProcedure
  ' Add the @Verified parameter
  command.Parameters.Add("@Verified", SqlDbType.Bit)
  If orderInfo.Verified Then
    command.Parameters("@Verified").Value = 1
  Else
    command.Parameters("@Verified").Value = 0
  End If
  ' Add the @Completed parameter
  command.Parameters.Add("@Completed", SqlDbType.Bit)
  If orderInfo.Completed Then
    command.Parameters("@Completed").Value = 1
  Else
    command.Parameters("@Completed").Value = 0
  End If
  ' Add the @Canceled parameter
  command.Parameters.Add("@Canceled", SqlDbType.Bit)
  If orderInfo.Canceled Then
    command.Parameters("@Canceled").Value = 1
  Else
    command.Parameters("@Canceled").Value = 0
  End If
  ' Add the @OrderID parameter and set its value
  command.Parameters.Add("@OrderID", SqlDbType.Int)
  command.Parameters("@OrderID").Value = orderInfo.OrderID
  ' Add the @DateCreated parameter and set its value
  command.Parameters.Add("@DateCreated", SqlDbType.SmallDateTime)
  command.Parameters("@DateCreated").Value = orderInfo.DateCreated
  ' @DateShipped will be sent only if the user typed a date in that
  ' text box; otherwise we don't send this parameter, as its default
```

```
' value in the stored procedure is NULL
If orderInfo.DateShipped.Trim <> "" Then
  command.Parameters.Add("@DateShipped", SqlDbType.SmallDateTime)
  command.Parameters("@DateShipped").Value = orderInfo.DateShipped
End If
' Add the @Comments parameter and set its value
command.Parameters.Add("@Comments", SqlDbType.VarChar, 200)
command.Parameters("@Comments").Value = orderInfo.Comments
' Add the @CustomerName parameter and set its value
command.Parameters.Add("@CustomerName", SqlDbType.VarChar, 50)
command.Parameters("@CustomerName").Value = orderInfo.CustomerName
' Add the @ShippingAddress parameter and set its value
command.Parameters.Add("@ShippingAddress", SqlDbType.VarChar, 200)
command.Parameters("@ShippingAddress").Value = orderInfo.ShippingAddress
' Add the @CustomerEmail parameter and set its value
command.Parameters.Add("@CustomerEmail", SqlDbType.VarChar, 50)
command.Parameters("@CustomerEmail").Value = orderInfo.CustomerEmail
' Execute the command, making sure the connection gets closed
Try
  connection.Open()
  command.ExecuteNonQuery()
Finally
  connection.Close()
End Try
End Sub
```

MarkOrderAsVerified

The MarkOrderAsVerified method is called when the Mark this Order as Verified button is clicked, and sets the Verified bit of the specified order to 1.

```
Public Shared Sub MarkOrderAsVerified(ByVal orderId As String)
  ' Create the Connection object
  Dim connection As New SqlConnection(connectionString)
  ' Create and initialize the Command object
  Dim command As New SqlCommand("MarkOrderAsVerified", connection)
  command.CommandType = CommandType.StoredProcedure
  ' Add an input parameter and set a value for it
  command.Parameters.Add("@OrderID", SqlDbType.Int)
  command.Parameters("@OrderID").Value = orderId
  ' Execute the command, making sure the connection gets closed
  Try
    connection.Open()
    command.ExecuteNonQuery()
  Finally
    connection.Close()
  End Try
End Sub
```

MarkOrderAsCompleted

The MarkOrderAsCompleted method is called when the Mark this Order as Completed button is clicked, and sets the Completed bit of the specified order to 1.

```
Public Shared Sub MarkOrderAsCompleted(ByVal orderId As String)
  ' Create the Connection object
  Dim connection As New SqlConnection(connectionString)
  ' Create and initialize the Command object
  Dim command As New SqlCommand("MarkOrderAsCompleted", connection)
  command.CommandType = CommandType.StoredProcedure
  ' Add an input parameter and set a value for it
  command.Parameters.Add("@OrderID", SqlDbType.Int)
  command.Parameters("@OrderID").Value = orderId
  ' Execute the command, making sure the connection gets closed
  Try
    connection.Open()
    command.ExecuteNonQuery()
  Finally
    connection.Close()
  End Try
End Sub
```

MarkOrderAsCanceled

The MarkOrderAsCanceled method is called when the Mark this Order as Canceled button is clicked, and sets the Canceled bit of the specified order to 1.

```
Public Shared Sub MarkOrderAsCanceled(ByVal orderId As String)
  ' Create the Connection object
  Dim connection As New SqlConnection(connectionString)
  ' Create and initialize the Command object
  Dim command As New SqlCommand("MarkOrderAsCanceled", connection)
  command.CommandType = CommandType.StoredProcedure
  ' Add an input parameter and set a value for it
  command.Parameters.Add("@OrderID", SqlDbType.Int)
  command.Parameters("@OrderID").Value = orderId
  ' Execute the command, making sure the connection gets closed
  Try
    connection.Open()
    command.ExecuteNonQuery()
  Finally
    connection.Close()
  End Try
End Sub
```

The Presentation Tier: OrderDetailsAdmin.ascx

Once again, you've reached the place where you wrap up all the data-tier and
business-tier functionality and package it into a nice-looking UI. You'll create this
user control in the following exercise.

Exercise: Creating the OrderDetailsAdmin *Web User Control*

1. Right-click the AdminUserControls folder in Solution Explorer and select Add
   ➤ Add Web User Control. Choose OrderDetailsAdmin.ascx for the name of the
   new user control.

2. Open the control in Design View and add labels, buttons, check boxes, and
   a data grid, as shown in Figure 10-22.

 TIP   *While in Design View, Visual Studio .NET permits you to copy
and paste groups of controls. As such, you can select a label and the
text box next to it, press Ctrl+C to copy the controls, and then multiply them using Ctrl+V (Paste). Also, remember to use Shift+Enter
instead of Enter, to generate <BR> tags between the lines instead of
<P> paragraph tags.*

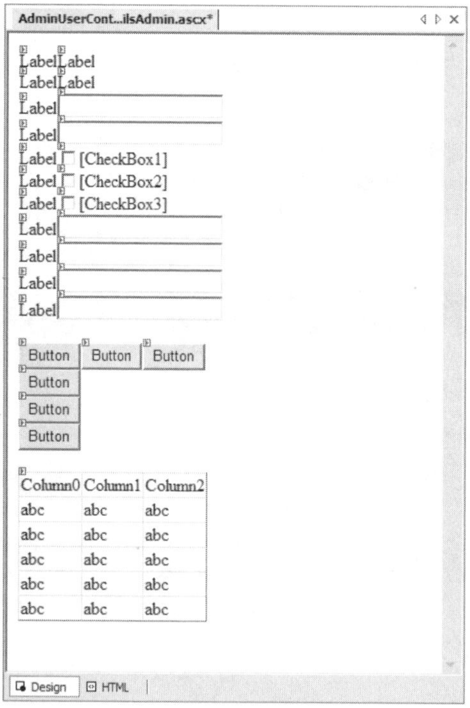

Figure 10-22. OrderDetailsAdmin.ascx *in Design View*

3. Set the properties for each constituent control as shown in Table 10-7.

 TIP *Visual Studio .NET allows you to set properties on more than one control at a time—you can select, for example, all the label controls in the left and set their* CssClass *to* AdminPageText *and* Width *to 150px, then select the* TextBox *controls on the right and set their* Width *to 400px, and so on.*

Table 10-7. Setting Controls' Properties in OrderDetailsAdmin.ascx

Control Type	ID	Text	CssClass	Width
Label	(doesn't matter)	Order ID:	ListDescription	150px
Label	orderIdLabel		ListDescription	400px
Label	(doesn't matter)	Total Amount:	AdminPageText	150px
Label	totalAmountLabel	(empty)	ProductPrice	
Label	(doesn't matter)	Date Created:	AdminPageText	150px
TextBox	dateCreatedTextBox			400px
Label	(doesn't matter)	Date Shipped:	AdminPageText	150px
TextBox	dateShippedTextBox			400px
Label	(doesn't matter)	Verified:	AdminPageText	150px
CheckBox	verifiedCheck			400px
Label	(doesn't matter)	Completed:	AdminPageText	150px
CheckBox	completedCheck			400px
Label	(doesn't matter)	Canceled:	AdminPageText	150px
CheckBox	canceledCheck			400px
Label	(doesn't matter)	Comments:	AdminPageText	150px
TextBox	commentsTextBox			400px
Label	(doesn't matter)	Customer Name:	AdminPageText	150px
TextBox	customerNameTextBox			400px
Label	(doesn't matter)	Shipping Address:	AdminPageText	150px
TextBox	shippingAddressTextBox			400px
Label	(doesn't matter)	Customer Email:	AdminPageText	150px
TextBox	customerEmailTextBox			400px
Button	editButton	Edit	AdminButtonText	100px
Button	updateButton	Update	AdminButtonText	100px
Button	cancelButton	Cancel	AdminButtonText	100px

Table 10-7. Setting Controls' Properties in OrderDetailsAdmin.ascx *(continued)*

Control Type	ID	Text	CssClass	Width
Button	markAsVerifiedButton as Verified	Mark this order	AdminButtonText	300px
Button	markAsCompletedButton as Completed	Mark this order	AdminButtonText	300px
Button	markAsCanceledButton as Canceled	Mark this order	AdminButtonText	300px
DataGrid	grid			100%

4. After setting the properties, the user control should look like Figure 10-23 when in Design View.

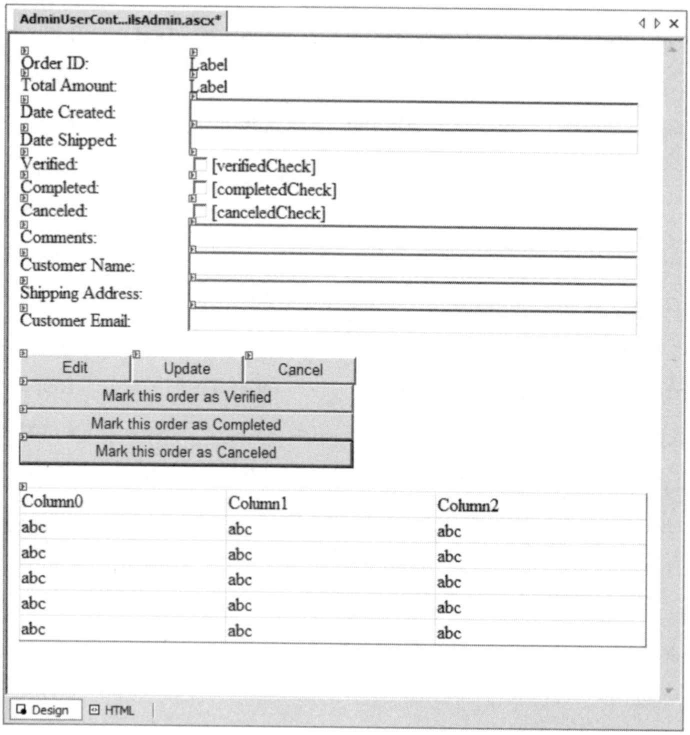

Figure 10-23. OrderDetailsAdmin.ascx in Design View

5. Open the Property Builder for the data grid, click the Columns link and dese-lect the Create Columns Automatically at Runtime check box. Now add the fields in Table 10-8 to the data grid.

Table 10-8. Setting DataGrid *Fields' Properties*

Column Type	Header Text	Data Field	Other Properties
Bound Column	Product ID	ProductID	
Bound Column	Product Name	ProductName	
Bound Column	Quantity	Quantity	
Bound Column	Unit Cost	UnitCost	Set Data formatting expression to {0:c}
Bound Column	Subtotal	Subtotal	Set Data formatting expression to {0:c}

6. Now set the colors and fonts by applying the same format properties as with the data grids you implemented until now.

    After setting all of the properties, the grid should look like Figure 10-24 when viewed in Design View.

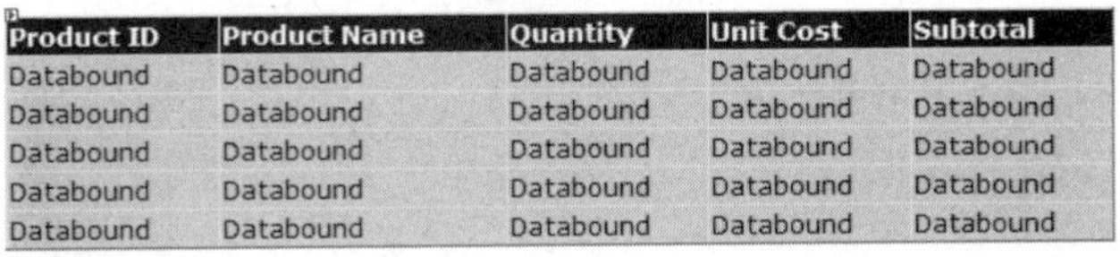

Figure 10-24. The DataGrid control in Design View

7. The visual part of the control is ready now. Before implementing the code-behind file, instruct ordersAdmin.aspx to load the control in the sec-ond table cell, when the OrderID parameter appears in the query string. Modify the Page_Load method in ordersAdmin.aspx.vb as shown:

```
Private Sub Page_Load(ByVal sender As System.Object, _
ByVal e As System.EventArgs) Handles MyBase.Load
  ' Save OrderID from the query string to a variable
  Dim orderId As String = Request.QueryString("OrderID")
  ' Load OrderDetailsAdmin only if Order ID exists in the query string
  If Not orderId Is Nothing Then
    Dim control As Control
    control = _
          Page.LoadControl("AdminUserControls/OrderDetailsAdmin.ascx")
    orderDetailsCell.Controls.Add(control)
  End If
End Sub
```

8. Start writing the code-behind logic of `OrderDetailsAdmin.ascx` by modifying the `Page_Load` method:

```
Private Sub Page_Load(ByVal sender As System.Object, _
ByVal e As System.EventArgs) Handles MyBase.Load
  If Not Page.IsPostBack Then
    ' Update information in all controls
    PopulateControls()
    ' Initially Edit mode should be disabled
    ' (administrator can't change order information)
    SetEditMode(False)
  End If
End Sub
```

In the `Page_Load` function, you use two additional methods: `PopulateControls`, which populates all the controls on the form with data, and `SetEditMode`, which disables the text boxes and check boxes for editing. These should allow editing only after the Edit button is clicked, as you'll see. First, implement the `PopulateControls` method:

9. Add `PopulateControls` just below `Page_Load`:

```
Private Sub PopulateControls()
  ' The OrderInfo object will be populated by calling
  ' OrderManager.GetOrderDetails
  Dim orderInfo As OrderInfo
  ' We receive the order ID in the query string
  Dim orderId As String = Request.Params("OrderID")
  ' Get order info by calling OrderManager.GetOrderDetails
  orderInfo = OrderManager.GetOrderInfo(orderId)
  ' Populate the text boxes with order information
  orderIdLabel.Text = orderInfo.OrderID
  totalAmountLabel.Text = String.Format("{0:c}", orderInfo.TotalAmount)
  dateCreatedTextBox.Text = orderInfo.DateCreated
  dateShippedTextBox.Text = orderInfo.DateShipped
  verifiedCheck.Checked = orderInfo.Verified
  completedCheck.Checked = orderInfo.Completed
  canceledCheck.Checked = orderInfo.Canceled
  commentsTextBox.Text = orderInfo.Comments
  customerNameTextBox.Text = orderInfo.CustomerName
  shippingAddressTextBox.Text = orderInfo.ShippingAddress
  customerEmailTextBox.Text = orderInfo.CustomerEmail
  ' By default the Edit button is enabled
  ' and the Update and Cancel buttons are disabled
  editButton.Enabled = True
  updateButton.Enabled = False
  cancelButton.Enabled = False
  ' Decide which one of the other three buttons
  ' should be enabled and which should be disabled
  If canceledCheck.Checked Or completedCheck.Checked Then
    ' if the order was canceled or completed ...
```

```
    markAsVerifiedButton.Enabled = False
    markAsCompletedButton.Enabled = False
    markAsCanceledButton.Enabled = False
ElseIf verifiedCheck.Checked Then
    ' if the order was not canceled but is verified ...
    markAsVerifiedButton.Enabled = False
    markAsCompletedButton.Enabled = True
    markAsCanceledButton.Enabled = True
Else
    ' if the order was not canceled and is not verified ...
    markAsVerifiedButton.Enabled = True
    markAsCompletedButton.Enabled = False
    markAsCanceledButton.Enabled = True
End If
' Fill the data grid with orderdetails
grid.DataSource = OrderManager.GetOrderDetails(orderId)
grid.DataKeyField = "OrderID"
grid.DataBind()
End Sub
```

This method gets the order information in an `OrderInfo` object, which was especially created for this purpose, by calling the `GetOrderInfo` method of the `OrderManager` class. Using the information from that object, the method fills the text boxes and the total amount label with data.

At the end, `OrderManager.GetOrderDetails`, which returns an `SqlDataReader` object containing the products in the specified order, is called to populate the data grid with the order details for the selected order.

10. Write the `SetEditMode` method now, which enables or disables edit mode for the information text boxes.

```
Private Sub SetEditMode(ByVal value As Boolean)
    dateCreatedTextBox.Enabled = value
    dateShippedTextBox.Enabled = value
    verifiedCheck.Enabled = value
    completedCheck.Enabled = value
    canceledCheck.Enabled = value
    commentsTextBox.Enabled = value
    customerNameTextBox.Enabled = value
    shippingAddressTextBox.Enabled = value
    customerEmailTextBox.Enabled = value
    editButton.Enabled = Not value
    updateButton.Enabled = value
    cancelButton.Enabled = value
End Sub
```

This method receives a `Boolean` parameter that specifies whether you enter or exit edit mode. When entering edit mode, all text boxes and the Update and Cancel buttons become enabled, while the Edit button is disabled.

The reverse happens when exiting edit mode, which happens when either the Cancel or Update button is clicked.

At this moment, the project is compilable so you can execute it and see how the form looks when it's populated with some order information (see Figure 10-25).

Orders Admin Page (go back to the storefront or logout)

Show the most recent 20 records Go!

Show all records created between and Go!

Show all unverified orders that have not been canceled (need to either verify or cancel them) Go!

Show all verified orders that are not completed (we need to ship them) Go!

Order ID:	1
Total Amount:	$131.37
Date Created:	3/18/2004 3:31:00 AM
Date Shipped:	
Verified:	☐
Completed:	☐
Canceled:	☐
Comments:	
Customer Name:	
Shipping Address:	
Customer Email:	

Edit	Update	Cancel

Mark this order as Verified

Mark this order as Completed

Mark this order as Canceled

Product ID	Product Name	Quantity	Unit Cost	Subtotal
1	Santa Costume	1	$14.99	$14.99
2	Medieval Lady	2	$49.99	$99.98
28	Police Plastic Helmet	4	$1.35	$5.40
30	Bug Eyes	4	$2.75	$11.00

Figure 10-25. Administering order information

11. Now, start implementing the code that allows the administrator to edit order information. To make your life easier, first double-click each of the buttons in Design View to let Visual Studio generate the signatures of the event handlers. Start with the Click event of the Edit button, which simply enters the user control into edit mode:

```
Private Sub editButton_Click(ByVal sender As System.Object, _
ByVal e As System.EventArgs) Handles editButton.Click
    SetEditMode(True)
End Sub
```

12. In the Click event handler for the Cancel button, first exit edit mode and then call PopulateControls, which restores the correct data in the form:

```
Private Sub cancelButton_Click(ByVal sender As System.Object, _
ByVal e As System.EventArgs) Handles cancelButton.Click
  SetEditMode(False)
  PopulateControls()
End Sub
```

13. Now deal with the updateButton_Click event handler, which first creates and populates an OrderInfo object with the data gathered from the text boxes and then sends it as a parameter to the OrderManager.UpdateOrder business-tier method. This takes care of updating the order info. In the end, exit edit mode and call PopulateControls once again; this way, in case the update failed, the original information appears again in the form.

```
Private Sub updateButton_Click(ByVal sender As System.Object, _
ByVal e As System.EventArgs) Handles updateButton.Click
  ' Store the new order details in an OrderInfo object
  Dim orderInfo As New OrderInfo()
  orderInfo.OrderID = orderIdLabel.Text
  orderInfo.DateCreated = dateCreatedTextBox.Text
  orderInfo.DateShipped = dateShippedTextBox.Text
  orderInfo.Verified = verifiedCheck.Checked
  orderInfo.Completed = completedCheck.Checked
  orderInfo.Canceled = canceledCheck.Checked
  orderInfo.Comments = commentsTextBox.Text
  orderInfo.CustomerName = customerNameTextBox.Text
  orderInfo.ShippingAddress = shippingAddressTextBox.Text
  orderInfo.CustomerEmail = customerEmailTextBox.Text
  Try
    ' Update the order
    OrderManager.UpdateOrder(orderInfo)
  Catch ex as Exception
    ' Do nothing in case the update fails
  End Try
  ' Exit edit mode and update controls' information
  SetEditMode(False)
  PopulateControls()
End Sub
```

NOTE *Here we didn't implement a mechanism to let the administrator know why the update failed—if something happens, we just ignore the error. You've learned various error-handling techniques in this and previous chapters, and you can choose to implement whichever technique you think is best for your application.*

14. Finally, take care of the `Click` event handlers for the final three buttons:

```
Private Sub markAsVerifiedButton_Click(ByVal sender As System.Object, _
ByVal e As System.EventArgs) Handles markAsVerifiedButton.Click
  Dim orderId As String = orderIdLabel.Text
  OrderManager.MarkOrderAsVerified(orderId)
  PopulateControls()
End Sub

Private Sub markAsCompletedButton_Click(ByVal sender As System.Object, _
ByVal e As System.EventArgs) Handles markAsCompletedButton.Click
  Dim orderId As String = orderIdLabel.Text
  OrderManager.MarkOrderAsCompleted(orderId)
  PopulateControls()
End Sub

Private Sub markAsCanceledButton_Click(ByVal sender As System.Object, _
ByVal e As System.EventArgs) Handles markAsCanceledButton.Click
  Dim orderId As String = orderIdLabel.Text
  OrderManager.MarkOrderAsCanceled(orderId)
  PopulateControls()
End Sub
```

How It Works: `OrderDetailsAdmin.ascx`

Whew, you've written a lot of code for this control. The code itself isn't complicated, but you had to deal with a lot of UI elements.

Because we talked about each method while writing the code, it should be pretty clear how the page works. Run it now and play with the buttons to make sure everything works as it should.

Summary

We covered a lot of ground in this chapter. You implemented a system by which you can both take orders and manually administer them.

You accomplished this in two separate stages. You added a Place Order button onto the shopping cart control, to allow the visitor to order the products in the shopping cart. You implemented a simple orders administration page, where the site administrator could view and handle pending orders.

In addition, we looked at the use of validation controls and also, importantly, set the scene for entirely automating the entire order system.

Because order data is now stored in the database, you can create various statistics and run calculations based on the items sold. In the next chapter, you'll learn how to implement a "Visitors who bought this also bought..." feature, which wouldn't have been possible without the order data stored in the database.

Making Recommendations

IN AN E-COMMERCE STORE, being friendly and helpful equals being efficient. If your web site knows how to suggest more products based on the visitor's preferences, there's a chance he or she will end up buying more from you than initially planned.

You can implement a product recommendations system in several ways, depending on your kind of store. Here are a few popular ones:

- *Up-selling*: Recommending the visitor alternate products for a specific product. So if the visitor is trying to buy a mask, you can recommend different types of masks.

- *Cross-selling*: Recommending the visitor complementary products for a specific product. So for a mask, you can recommend buying a similar costume.

- *Featured products on the home page*: JokePoint already permits the site administrator to choose the products featured on the main page.

- *Dynamic recommendations*: Dynamically finding products similar to a specified product, based on various criteria.

Dynamic recommendations have the advantage that they don't need manual maintenance. Because at this point, JokePoint retains what products were sold, in this chapter you will implement a "customers who bought this product also bought ..." feature.

Increasing Sales with Dynamic Recommendations

In JokePoint, you'll implement the dynamic recommendations system in the visitor's shopping cart. The shopping cart page will display what other products were bought by the customers that bought the products in the shopping cart.

After implementing this functionality, the shopping cart will look like Figure 11-1.

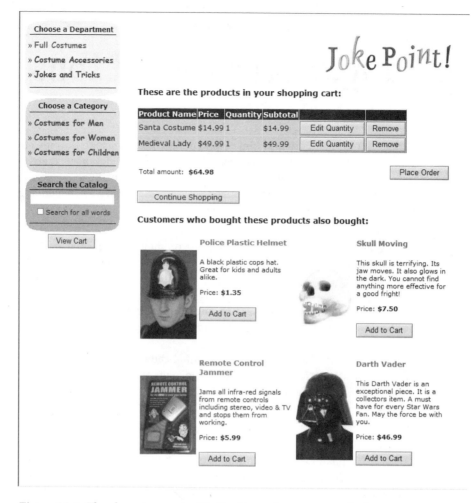

Figure 11-1. The shopping cart with the dynamic recommendations system implemented

You'll start, as usual, with the data tier component.

Implementing the Data Tier

The only stored procedure you'll write, which is the heart of the dynamic recommendations system, is GetSimilarProducts. This stored procedure receives the CartID of the customer as input parameter, and returns the products that are "similar" to the products in the mentioned cart. Add it to the database, and we'll discuss it afterwards.

Exercise: Adding the GetSimilarProducts *Stored Procedure*

Add this stored procedure to the JokePoint database:

```
CREATE PROCEDURE GetSimilarProducts
(@CartID CHAR(36))
AS
--- Returns the products that were bought by customers that
--- bought the products in the mentioned shopping cart
SELECT Product.ProductID, Product.Name, Product.Description,
       Product.Price, Product.ImagePath, Product.OnDepartmentPromotion,
       Product.OnCatalogPromotion
FROM Product
WHERE ProductID IN
   (
   -- Returns the products that exist in a list of orders
   SELECT TOP 4 ProductID
   FROM OrderDetail
   WHERE OrderID IN
      (
      -- Returns the orders that contain certain products
      SELECT DISTINCT OrderID
      FROM OrderDetail
      WHERE ProductID IN
         (
         -- Returns the products in the specified shopping cart
         SELECT ProductID
         FROM ShoppingCart
         WHERE CartID = @CartID
         )
      )
   -- Must not include products that already exist in the visitor's cart
   AND ProductID NOT IN
      (
      -- Returns the products in the specified shopping cart
      SELECT ProductID
      FROM ShoppingCart
      WHERE CartID = @CartID
      )
   -- Group the ProductID so we can calculate the rank
   GROUP BY ProductID
   -- Order descending by rank
   ORDER BY COUNT(ProductID) DESC
   )
```

How It Works: `GetSimilarProducts`

Okay, so let's see what this baby does.

The only information you receive as input parameter is a `CartID`. Having the `CartID` equals knowing the products in the shopping cart with that `CartID`. To find out the products that are "similar" to the products in the shopping cart, you first need to get the list of orders that contain the products in the shopping cart, and then find what other products are in those orders (these are the products you're looking for).

Following is the subquery that returns all the orders that contain the products in the shopping cart:

```
-- Returns the orders that contain certain products
SELECT DISTINCT OrderID
FROM OrderDetail
WHERE ProductID IN
    (
    -- Returns the products in the specified shopping cart
    SELECT ProductID
    FROM ShoppingCart
    WHERE CartID = @CartID
    )
```

Having this list of orders, you get all their products by querying the `OrderDetail` table. From the returned products list, the products that already exist in the shopping cart are removed, because you don't want to recommend a product that already exists in the shopping cart:

```
-- Returns the products that exist in a list of orders
SELECT TOP 4 ProductID
FROM OrderDetail
WHERE OrderID IN
    ( ... list of orders ... )
-- Must not include products that already exist in the visitor's cart
AND ProductID NOT IN
    (
    -- Returns the products in the specified shopping cart
    SELECT ProductID
    FROM ShoppingCart
    WHERE CartID = @CartID
    )
```

`TOP 4` makes sure you recommend no more than four products to the visitor. However, you still need to make sure to return the four products that were most popular among the other orders, rather than random products. Here's where `GROUP BY` comes in.

The fun of the whole query consists in the ranking method. The query so far returns a list of products, where each product can and usually does appear more than once, depending on how many times it has been ordered before. By grouping the results by `ProductID` and sorting the list descending on the number of appearances, you'll always get the most popular products:

```
-- Group the ProductID so we can calculate the rank
GROUP BY ProductID
-- Order descending by rank
ORDER BY COUNT(ProductID) DESC
)
```

GetSimilarProducts: *An Alternative to Using Subqueries*

Because SQL is so versatile, GetSimilarProducts can be written in a variety of ways. In this case, one popular alternative to using subqueries is using table joins. In my tests, the version with subqueries performed better, but here's the code:

```
CREATE PROCEDURE GetSimilarProducts
(@CartID CHAR(36))
AS
--- Returns the products that were bought by customers that
--- bought the products in the mentioned shopping cart
SELECT Product.ProductID,Product.[Name], Product.[Description],
       Product.Price, Product.ImagePath, Product.OnDepartmentPromotion,
       Product.OnCatalogPromotion
FROM Product
WHERE ProductID IN
    (
    -- Returns the products that exist in a list of orders
    SELECT TOP 4 od1.ProductID AS Rank
    FROM OrderDetail od1
      JOIN OrderDetail od2
        ON od1.OrderID=od2.OrderID
      JOIN ShoppingCart sp
        ON od2.ProductID = sp.ProductID
    WHERE sp.CartID = @CartID
        -- Must not include products that already exist in the visitor's cart
      AND od1.ProductID NOT IN
      (
      -- Returns the products in the specified shopping cart
      SELECT ProductID
      FROM ShoppingCart
      WHERE CartID = @CartID
      )
    -- Group the ProductID so we can calculate the rank
    GROUP BY od1.ProductID
    -- Order descending by rank
    ORDER BY COUNT(od1.ProductID) DESC
    )
```

Implementing the Business Tier

The business tier consists of the GetSimilarProducts method, which calls the GetShoppingCart stored procedure. Add the following method in the ShoppingCart class (located in ShoppingCart.vb):

```
Public Shared Function GetSimilarProducts() As SqlDataReader
  ' Create the connection object
  Dim connection As New SqlConnection(connectionString)
  ' Create and initialize the command object
  Dim command As New SqlCommand("GetSimilarProducts", connection)
  command.CommandType = CommandType.StoredProcedure
  ' Add an input parameter and supply a value for it
  command.Parameters.Add("@CartID", SqlDbType.Char, 36)
  command.Parameters("@CartID").Value = shoppingCartId
  Try
    ' Open the connection and return the results
    connection.Open()
    Return command.ExecuteReader(CommandBehavior.CloseConnection)
  Catch e As Exception
    ' Close the connection and throw the exception
    connection.Close()
    Throw e
  End Try
End Function
```

Implementing the Presentation Tier

For the User Interface (UI), you'll reuse your old friend, the ProductsList.ascx control. This control displays the list of popular products in the visitor's shopping cart. Follow the simple steps shown in the following exercise.

Exercise: Creating the UI

1. Open ShoppingCart.ascx in Design View.

2. At the bottom of the control, add a Label control named similarProductsLabel. Set its CssClass property to ListDescription, and its Text property to "Customers who bought these products also bought:".

3. Add the ProductsList.ascx control at the bottom of ShoppingCart. Now ShoppingCart should look like Figure 11-2 in Design View.

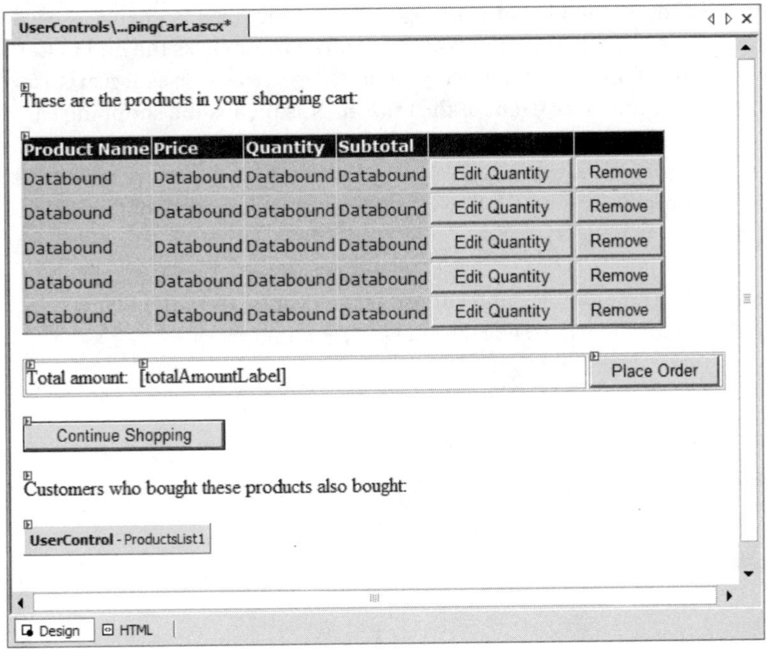

Figure 11-2. The shopping cart with the ProductsList.ascx *control added*

4. Open the code-behind file of ShoppingCart.ascx (ShoppingCart.ascx.vb),
    and make sure similarProductsLabel shows up only if the shopping cart is
    not empty:

```
Private Sub BindShoppingCart()
  Dim amount As Decimal = ShoppingCart.GetTotalAmount()
  ' Set the total amount label using the Currency format
  totalAmountLabel.Text = String.Format("{0:c}", amount)
  If amount = 0 Then
    introLabel.Text = "Your shopping cart is empty!"
    grid.Visible = False
    placeOrderButton.Enabled = False
    similarProductsLabel.Visible = False
  Else
    placeOrderButton.Enabled = True
    ' Populate the data grid and set its DataKey field
    grid.DataSource = ShoppingCart.GetProducts
    grid.DataKeyField = "ProductID"
    grid.DataBind()
  End If
End Sub
```

Also in the code-behind file of ShoppingCart.ascx, you need to change the way the shopping cart DataGrid is populated. When a visitor clicks the Add to Cart button on any of the recommended products, Page_Load in ShoppingCart.ascx executes *before* the Click event of the button. This means the shopping cart DataGrid is refreshed before the new product being added to the database. To correct this problem, you call BindShoppingCart in the PreRender event-handler method of ShoppingCart, which fires *after* the ItemCommand event of the Add to Cart buttons.

5. Open ShoppingCart.ascx.vb, and choose (Page Events) from the first combo box at the top of the page (see Figure 11-3).

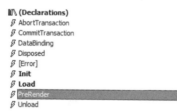

Figure 11-3. Choosing (Page Events) from ShoppingCart.ascx.vb

6. From the second combo box, select the PreRender event (see Figure 11-4).

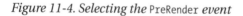

Figure 11-4. Selecting the PreRender *event*

7. This generates the Page_PreRender event-handler method, where you need to add a call to BindShoppingCart:

```
Private Sub Page_PreRender(ByVal sender As Object, _
ByVal e As System.EventArgs) Handles MyBase.PreRender
  BindShoppingCart()
End Sub
```

8. Finally, remove the call to BindShoppingCart from Page_Load to avoid loading the shopping cart twice on every page load.

9. The last step is to instruct `ProductsList` to load the product recommendations in case it's loaded from the shopping cart. Open code-behind file
   `ProductsList.ascx.vb`, and instruct the control to load the list of product
   recommendations in case `ViewCart` is present on the query string:

```vb
Private Sub Page_Load(ByVal sender As System.Object, _
ByVal e As System.EventArgs) Handles MyBase.Load
    ' Retrieve ViewCart from the query string
    Dim viewCart As String = Request.QueryString("ViewCart")
    ' Retrieve DepartmentID from the query string
    Dim departmentId As String = Request.QueryString("DepartmentID")
    ' Retrieve CategoryID from the query string
    Dim categoryId As String = Request.QueryString("CategoryID")
    ' Retrieve the SearchString from the query string
    Dim searchString As String = Request.QueryString("Search")
    ' Populate the DataList
    If Not viewCart Is Nothing Then
      ' recommendations
      list.DataSource = ShoppingCart.GetSimilarProducts()
      list.DataBind()
    ElseIf Not searchString Is Nothing Then
      ' search results
      list.DataSource = Session("SearchTable")
      list.DataBind()
      Session.Remove("SearchTable")
    ElseIf Not categoryId Is Nothing Then
      ' category
      list.DataSource = Catalog.GetProductsInCategory(categoryId)
      list.DataBind()
    ElseIf Not departmentId Is Nothing Then
      ' department
      list.DataSource = _
                Catalog.GetProductsOnDepartmentPromotion(departmentId)
      list.DataBind()
    Else
      ' main page
      list.DataSource = Catalog.GetProductsOnCatalogPromotion()
      list.DataBind()
    End If
End Sub
```

10. Execute the project and enjoy the results.

How It Works: Showing Product Recommendations

The challenge when implementing the presentation tier was to ensure that the shopping
cart `DataGrid` gets updated properly when the visitor adds products from the product
recommendations list.

You solved the problem by binding the shopping cart `DataGrid` in the `PreRender` event handler of the `ShoppingCart` control. Unlike the `Load` event in `ShoppingCart`, `PreRender` fires after the ItemCommand event in `ProductsList`, where the product is added to the database. To learn more about the life cycle of an ASP.NET Server Control, see the article at `http://msdn.microsoft.com/library/default.asp?url=/library/en-us/cpguide/html/cpconcontrolexecutionlifecycle.asp`.

Summary

In this short chapter, you added a new and interesting functionality to the JokePoint web site. With product recommendations, you have more chances to convince visitors to buy products from the JokePoint web site.

In the next chapter, you'll enter the third stage of development, by adding customer accounts functionality.

Customer Details

SO FAR IN THIS BOOK, you've built a basic (but functional) site, and have hooked it into PayPal for taking payments and confirming orders. In this section of the book, you'll take things a little further. By cutting out PayPal from the ordering process, you can gain better control as well as reduce overheads. This isn't as complicated as you might think, but you must be careful to do things right.

This chapter lays the groundwork for this, by implementing a customer account system.

To make e-commerce sites more user friendly, details such as credit card numbers are stored in a database so that users don't have to retype this information each time they place an order. The customer account system you'll implement will do this, and will include all of the web pages required for the entering such details.

As well as implementing these web pages, you'll need to take several other factors into account. First, simply placing credit card numbers, expiry dates, and so on into a database in plain text isn't ideal. This method might unwittingly expose this data to unscrupulous people with access to the database. This could occur remotely or be perpetrated by individuals within your client's organization. Rather than enforcing a prohibitively restrictive access policy to such data, it's much easier to encrypt sensitive information, and retrieve it programmatically when required. You'll create a security library to ease this functionality.

Secondly, secure communications are important because you'll be capturing sensitive information such as credit card details via the Web. You can't just put a form up for people to access via HTTP and allow them to send it to you because the data could be intercepted. You'll learn about the solution to this: using SSL over HTTPS connections.

You'll be taking the JokePoint application to the point where you can move on and implement your own backend order pipeline in the next chapter.

Handling Customer Accounts

There are many ways to handle customer account functionality in web sites. In general, though, they share the following features:

- Customers log in via a login page or dialog box to get access to secured areas of the web site.

- Once logged in, the Web Application remembers the customer until the customer logs out (either manually via a Log Out button, or automatically if the session times out or a server error occurs).

- All secure pages in a Web Application need to check whether a customer is logged in before allowing access.

First, let's look at the general implementation details for the JokePoint
e-commerce site.

Creating a JokePoint Customer Account Scheme

One simple way of enabling a check for a logged in customer is to store the customer
ID in the session state. You can then check to see whether a value is present here at the
start of your secured pages, and redirect to a login form if not. The login form can then
authenticate a user and store a value in the session state if successful, ready for later
retrieval. To log out a user, you simply remove the ID from the session state.

To log in, a customer needs to supply a username (email address is used here,
because it's guaranteed to be unique) and a password. Sending this information over
the Internet is a sensitive issue, because it's possible for third parties to eavesdrop
and capture it. Later in this chapter, we'll look at and implement secure communications over the Internet for this information. For now, however, we'll concentrate on
the authentication side of things, which is unaffected by the type of connection used
to transmit the email address and password of the customer.

Another issue related to security is the storage of user passwords. It isn't a good
idea to store user passwords in your database in plain text, because this information
is a potential target for attack. Instead, you should store what is known as the **hash** of
the password. A hash is a unique string that represents the password, but cannot be
converted back into the password itself. To validate the password entered by the user,
you simply need to generate a hash for the password entered and compare it with the
hash stored in your database. If the hashes match, the passwords entered match as
well, so you can be sure that the customer is not an imposter.

This leads us to another important task—you need to supply a method by which
new users can register. The result of registration is to add a new customer to your
database, including username and password hash information.

The specifics of the implementation of this scheme in your application are as
follows:

- A new database table to hold customer details called Customer, with associated
  stored procedures to add, modify, and retrieve information from customer
  records

- Modifications to ShoppingCart.ascx, which will now redirect the user to
  a checkout page called Checkout.aspx

- A customer login page called CustomerLogin.aspx

- A customer registration page called CustomerNew.aspx

Along the way, you'll also implement the following:

- A page for customers to edit their basic details called `CustomerEdit.aspx`

- A page for customers to enter their credit card details called `CustomerCreditCard.aspx`

- A page for customers to enter their shipping address called `CustomerAddress.aspx`

The Customer Table

So, let's build the first table. Once again, an SQL script in the code download for this chapter will build this table for you, or you can build it yourself in MSDE or SQL Enterprise Manager manually. The `Customer` table in the `JokePoint` database is shown in Table 12-1.

Table 12-1. The Customer *Table*

Column Name	Column Type	Description
CustomerID	int(4)	Primary key, also set as table identity—this column should not allow NULLs
Name	varchar(50)	Customer name—should not allow NULLs
Email	varchar(50)	Customer email address—should not allow NULLs
Password	varchar(50)	Customer password, stored as a hash—should not allow NULLs
CreditCard	varchar(512)	Customer credit card details
Address1	varchar(100)	First line of customer address
Address2	varchar(100)	Second line of customer address
City	varchar(100)	Customer address town/city information
Region	varchar(100)	Customer address region/state information
PostalCode	varchar(100)	Customer address postal code/ZIP information
Country	varchar(100)	Customer address country information
Phone	varchar(100)	Customer phone number

The credit card information for the customer is stored in an encrypted format. This is necessary because it's undesirable to store plain credit card details in the database, for the same reason that you don't want plain text passwords in there. Unlike passwords, however, you need to be able to retrieve this credit card information when required by the order pipeline, so you can't simply use a hash. The facilities for achieving this are contained in a new class library called `SecurityLib`, which we should look at now.

The SecurityLib Class Library

The two areas you've seen so far where security functionality is required are

- Password hashing

- Credit card encryption

Both tasks are carried out by classes in the SecurityLib class library. The reason for separating this functionality is that you are likely to want access to it from outside of the JokePoint application. In addition, it makes good logical sense not to bundle all this together in one place.

The SecurityLib class library project consists of the following files:

- *PasswordHasher.vb*: Contains the PasswordHasher class, which contains the shared method Hash that returns a hash for the password supplied.

- *SecureCard.vb*: Contains the SecureCard class, which represents a credit card. This class can be initialized with credit card information, which is then accessible in encrypted format. Alternatively, it can be initialized with encrypted credit card data, and supply access to the decrypted information contained therein.

- *SecureCardException.vb*: Should there be any problems during encryption or decryption, the exception contained in this file, SecureCardException, is thrown by SecureCard.

- *StringEncryptor.vb*: The class contained in this file, StringEncryptor, is used by SecureCard to encrypt and decrypt data. This means that if you want to change the encryption method, you only need to modify the code here, leaving the SecureCard class untouched.

- *StringEncryptorException.vb*: Contains the StringEncryptorException exception, thrown by StringEncryptor if an error occurs.

We'll look at the code for hashing first, followed by encryption.

Hashing

Hashing, as has already been noted, is a means by which a unique value can be obtained that represents an object. In practice, this means doing the following:

1. Serialize the object being hashed into a byte array.

2. Hash the byte array, obtaining a new, hashed byte array.

3. Convert the hashed byte array into the format required for storage.

For passwords this is simple because converting a string (which is an array of characters) into a byte array is no problem. Converting the resultant hashed byte array into a string for database storage and quick comparison is also simple.

The actual method used to convert the source byte array into a hashed byte array can vary. The `System.Security.Cryptography` namespace in .NET contains several algorithms for hashing, and allows you to provide your own if necessary, although we won't go into details of this here. The two main hashing algorithms found in the .NET Framework are SHA1 (Secure Hash Algorithm) and MD5 (Message Digest, another name for the hash code generated). SHA1 generates a 160-bit hash (regardless of the size of the input data), while MD5 generates a 128-bit hash, so SHA1 is generally considered more secure (although slower) than MD5. The Framework also contains other versions of the SHA1 hash algorithm that generate longer hashes, up to 512 bits, as well as hash algorithms that work using a key (shared secret) as well as the data to be hashed.

In the JokePoint implementation, you'll use SHA1, although it's easy to change this if you require stronger security. You'll see the code that achieves this in the `PasswordHasher` class shortly.

Exercise: Implementing the `PasswordHasher` *Class*

1. Create a new Class Library project called `SecurityLib` in the directory `C:\BegECom\Chapter12`.

2. Delete `Class1.vb` and add a new class file called `PasswordHasher.vb` with code as follows:

```
Imports System.Security.Cryptography

Public Class PasswordHasher
  Private Shared hasher As SHA1Managed = New SHA1Managed()

  Private Sub New()
    ' do nothing, make class uncreatable
  End Sub

  Public Shared Function Hash(ByVal password As String) As String
    ' convert password to byte array
    Dim passwordBytes() As Byte = _
        System.Text.ASCIIEncoding.ASCII.GetBytes(password)

    ' generate hash from byte array of password
    Dim passwordHash() As Byte = hasher.ComputeHash(passwordBytes)

    ' convert hash to string
    Return Convert.ToBase64String(passwordHash, 0, passwordHash.Length)
  End Function
End Class
```

3. Add a new console application project to the solution, called `SecurityLibTester`, and make this project the startup project (right-click it and select Set as StartUp Project).

4. Add a project reference to `SecurityLibTester`, referencing the `SecurityLib` project by right-clicking the references folder of the `SecurityLibTester` project, selecting Add Reference..., selecting the Projects tab of the dialog that appears, and selecting the only item that appears in the list—SecurityLib.

5. Modify `Module1.vb` as follows:

```vb
Imports SecurityLib

Module Module1

    Sub Main()
        Console.WriteLine("Enter your password:")
        Dim password1 As String = Console.ReadLine()
        Dim hash1 As String = PasswordHasher.Hash(password1)
        Console.WriteLine("The hash of this password is: {0}", hash1)
        Console.WriteLine("Enter your password again:")
        Dim password2 As String = Console.ReadLine()
        Dim hash2 As String = PasswordHasher.Hash(password2)
        Console.WriteLine("The hash of this password is: {0}", hash2)
        If hash1 = hash2 Then
            Console.WriteLine("The passwords match! Welcome!")
        Else
          Console.WriteLine("Password invalid." _
            & "Armed guards are on their way.")
        End If
    End Sub

End Module
```

6. Execute the application (note that to avoid the window being closed as some as the code executes, you can start without debugging by pressing Ctrl+F5, building the project, and running `SecurityTestLib.exe` from the command line, or by adding a `Console.ReadLine` statement at the end of the code). The result is shown in Figure 12-1.

Figure 12-1. Password hasher example result

How It Works: Implementing the PasswordHasher *Class*

The code in the PasswordHasher class follows the steps that were discussed earlier. First you use the utility function System.Text.ASCIIEncoding.ASCII.GetBytes to convert the password string into a byte array:

```
' convert password to byte array
Dim passwordBytes() As Byte = _
    System.Text.ASCIIEncoding.ASCII.GetBytes(password)
```

Next you use the private shared member hasher, an instance of SHA1Managed, to generate a hash byte array:

```
' generate hash from byte array of password
Dim passwordHash() As Byte = hasher.ComputeHash(passwordBytes)
```

Finally you convert the hash back into a string, using the utility function Convert.ToBase64String and return the result:

```
' convert hash to string
Return Convert.ToBase64String (passwordHash, 0, passwordHash.Length)
```

All the hash algorithm classes in the .NET Framework use this ComputeHash method to get a hash from an input array of bytes. To increase the size of the hash, you could simply replace the hasher with another one of these, for example:

```
Public Class PasswordHasher
    Private Shared hasher As SHA512Managed = New SHA512Managed()

    ...

End Class
```

This change would result in a 512-bit hash, which is probably a bit excessive in this application!

The client application, SecurityLibTest, simply hashes two passwords and compares the result. The code is basic enough to ignore for now. What is worth mentioning, however, is that the generated hashes vary a great deal for even simple changes to the input data—one of the defining features of good hash generation.

Encryption

Encryption comes in many shapes and sizes, and continues to be a hot topic. There is no definitive solution to encrypting data, although plenty of advice can be given. In general, there are two forms of encryption:

- *Symmetric encryption*: A single key is used both to encrypt and decrypt data.

- *Asymmetric encryption*: Separate keys are used to encrypt and decrypt data. The encryption key is commonly known as the public key, and anyone can use it to encrypt information. The decryption key is known as the private key, because it can only be used to decrypt data that has been encrypted using the public key.

NOTE *In some situations, such as digital signing, the private key is used for encryption and the public key for decryption. However, this doesn't apply to the techniques in this chapter.*

Symmetric encryption is faster, but can be less secure because both the encryptor and decryptor know a single key. With Internet communications, there is often no way of ensuring that this key remains a secret from third parties when it is sent to the encryptor.

Asymmetric encryption gets around this by its key-pair method of operation, because the private key need never be divulged, making it much more difficult for a third party to break the encryption. Because the key-pair method requires a lot more processing power, the normal method of operation is to use asymmetric encryption to exchange a symmetric key over the Internet this key is then used for symmetric encryption, safe in the knowledge that it hasn't been exposed to third parties.

In the `JokePoint` application, things are much simpler than with Internet communications—you just need to encrypt data for storage in the database and decrypt it again when required—so you can use a symmetric algorithm.

NOTE *Behind the scenes, asymmetric encryption is going on, however, because that is the method used to encrypt the credit card details that are sent over the Internet. You don't need to do much to enable this, as you'll see in the "Secure Connections" section later in this chapter.*

As with hashing, several algorithms can be used for both symmetric and asymmetric encryption. The .NET Framework contains implementations of several of these in the `System.Security.Cryptography` namespace.

The two available asymmetric algorithms are DSA (Digital Signature Algorithm) and RSA (Rivest-Shamir-Adleman, from the names of its inventors: Ronald Rivest, Adi Shamir, and Leonard Adleman). Of these, DSA can only be used to "sign" data so that its authenticity can be verified, while RSA is more versatile (although slower than DSA when used to generate digital signatures). DSA is the current standard for digital authentication used by the US government.

The symmetric algorithms found in the .NET Framework are DES (Data Encryption Standard), Triple DES (3DES), RC2 ("Ron's Code," or "Rivest's Cipher" depending on who you ask, also from Ronald Rivest), and Rijndael (from the names of its inventors, John Daemen and Vincent Rijman). DES has been the standard for some time now, although this is gradually changing. It uses a 64-bit key, although, in practice, only 56 of these bits are used because 8 are "parity" bits, and as such is often seen to be not strong enough to avoid being broken using today's computers (there are reports that a setup costing $400,000 managed to break DES encryption in three days). Both Triple DES and RC2 are variations of DES. Triple DES effectively encrypts data using three separate DES encryptions with three keys totaling 168 bits when parity bits are subtracted. RC2 is a variant where key lengths up to 128 bits are possible (longer keys are also possible using RC3, RC4, and so on), so it can be made weaker or stronger than DES depending on the key size. Rijndael is a completely separate encryption method, and has now been accepted as the new AES (Advanced Encryption Standard). This standard is intended to replace DES, and several competing algorithms were considered before Rijndael was chosen. This is the standard that is gradually replacing DES as the most used symmetric encryption algorithm.

The tasks that must be carried out when encrypting and decrypting data are a little more involved than hashing. The classes in the .NET Framework are optimized to work with data streams so you have a bit more work to do with data conversion. You also have to define both a key and an initialization vector (IV) to perform encryption and decryption. The IV is required due to the nature of encryption: calculating the encrypted values for one sequence of bits involves using the encrypted values of the immediately preceding sequence of bits. Because there are no such values at the start of encryption, an IV is used instead. In practice, both the IV and the key can be represented as a byte array, which in the case of DES encryption is 64 bits (8 bytes) long.

The steps required for encrypting a string into an encrypted string are as follows:

1. Convert the source string into a byte array.

2. Initialize an encryption algorithm class.

3. Use the encryption algorithm class to generate an encryptor object, supporting the ICryptoTransform interface. This requires key and IV values.

4. Use the encryptor object to initialize a cryptographic stream (CryptoStream object). This stream also needs to know that you are encrypting data, and needs a target stream to write encrypted data to.

5. Use the cryptographic stream to write encrypted data to a target memory stream, using the source byte array created previously.

6. Extract the byte data stored in the stream.

7. Convert the byte data into a string.

Decryption follows a similar scheme:

1. Convert the source string into a byte array.

2. Fill a memory stream with the contents of the byte array.

3. Initialize an encryption algorithm class.

4. Use the encryption algorithm class to generate a decryptor object, support-
    ing the ICryptoTransform interface. This requires key and IV values.

5. Use the decryptor object to initialize a cryptographic stream (CryptoStream
    object). This stream also needs to know that you are decrypting data, and
    needs a source stream to read encrypted data from.

6. Use the cryptographic stream to read decrypted data (can use the
    StreamReader.ReadToEnd method to get the result as a string).

In the JokePoint code, you'll use DES, but the code in the StringEncryptor class
could be replaced with code to use any of the algorithms specified previously.

Exercise: Implementing the StringEncryptor *Class*

1. Add a new class to the SecurityLib class library called
    StringEncryptorException with code as follows:

    ```
    Public Class StringEncryptorException
        Inherits Exception

        Public Sub New(ByVal message As String)
            MyBase.New(message)
        End Sub
    End Class
    ```

2. Add another new class to the SecurityLib class library called StringEncryptor
    with code as follows:

    ```
    Imports System.Security.Cryptography
    Imports System.IO

    Public Class StringEncryptor
        Private Sub New()
            ' do nothing, make class uncreatable
        End Sub

        Public Shared Function Encrypt(ByVal sourceData As String) As String
            ' set key and initialization vector values
            Dim key() As Byte = New Byte() {1, 2, 3, 4, 5, 6, 7, 8}
            Dim iv() As Byte = New Byte() {1, 2, 3, 4, 5, 6, 7, 8}
            Try
                ' convert data to byte array
                Dim sourceDataBytes() As Byte = _
                    System.Text.ASCIIEncoding.ASCII.GetBytes(sourceData)

                ' get target memory stream
                Dim tempStream As MemoryStream = New MemoryStream()

                ' get encryptor and encryption stream
                Dim encryptor As DESCryptoServiceProvider = _
                    New DESCryptoServiceProvider()
    ```

```vbnet
        Dim encryptionStream As CryptoStream = _
          New CryptoStream(tempStream, _
                          encryptor.CreateEncryptor(key, iv), _
                          CryptoStreamMode.Write)

        ' encrypt data
        encryptionStream.Write(sourceDataBytes, 0, _
                                        sourceDataBytes.Length)
        encryptionStream.FlushFinalBlock()

        ' put data into byte array
        Dim encryptedDataBytes() As Byte = tempStream.GetBuffer()

        ' convert encrypted data into string
        Return Convert.ToBase64String(encryptedDataBytes, 0, _
                                        tempStream.Length)
      Catch
        Throw New StringEncryptorException("Unable to encrypt data.")
      End Try
  End Function

  Public Shared Function Decrypt(ByVal sourceData As String) As String
      ' set key and initialization vector values
      Dim key() As Byte = New Byte() {1, 2, 3, 4, 5, 6, 7, 8}
      Dim iv() As Byte = New Byte() {1, 2, 3, 4, 5, 6, 7, 8}
      Try
          ' convert data to byte array
          Dim encryptedDataBytes() As Byte = _
            Convert.FromBase64String(sourceData)

          ' get source memory stream and fill it
          Dim tempStream As MemoryStream = _
            New MemoryStream(encryptedDataBytes, 0, _
                                        encryptedDataBytes.Length)

          ' get decryptor and decryption stream
          Dim decryptor As DESCryptoServiceProvider = _
            New DESCryptoServiceProvider()
          Dim decryptionStream As CryptoStream = _
            New CryptoStream(tempStream, _
                decryptor.CreateDecryptor(key, iv), _
                CryptoStreamMode.Read)

          ' decrypt data
          Dim allDataReader As StreamReader = New StreamReader(decryptionStream)
          Return allDataReader.ReadToEnd()
      Catch
          Throw New StringEncryptorException("Unable to decrypt data.")
      End Try
    End Function
End Class
```

3. Modify the code in Module1.vb in SecurityLibTester as follows:

```vb
Sub Main()
    Console.WriteLine("Enter data to encrypt:")
    Dim stringToEncrypt As String = Console.ReadLine()
    Dim encryptedString = StringEncryptor.Encrypt(stringToEncrypt)
    Console.WriteLine("Encrypted data: {0}", encryptedString)
    Console.WriteLine( _
        "Enter data to decrypt (hit enter to decrypt above data):")
    Dim stringToDecrypt As String = Console.ReadLine()
    If stringToDecrypt = "" Then
        stringToDecrypt = encryptedString
    End If
    Dim decryptedString As String = _
        StringEncryptor.Decrypt(stringToDecrypt)
    Console.WriteLine("Decrypted data: {0}", decryptedString)
End Sub
```

4. Execute the code. The result is shown in Figure 12-2.

Figure 12-2. String encryption example result

How It Works: Implementing the StringEncryptor *Class*

The StringEncryptor class has two shared methods, Encrypt and Decrypt, which encrypt and decrypt data. We'll look at each of these in turn.

Encrypt starts by defining two hard-coded byte arrays for the key and IV used in encryption:

```vb
Public Shared Function Encrypt(ByVal sourceData As String) As String
    ' set key and initialization vector values
    Dim key() As Byte = New Byte() {1, 2, 3, 4, 5, 6, 7, 8}
    Dim iv() As Byte = New Byte() {1, 2, 3, 4, 5, 6, 7, 8}
```

Both these arrays are set to temporary values here. They could just as easily take any other values, depending on the key you want to use. Alternatively, they could be loaded from disk, although having the values compiled into your code in this way could stop people from discovering the values used quite effectively. This method isn't foolproof—the data could be extracted if anyone gets access to your DLLs (Dynamic Link Libraries), but it's secure enough for our purposes. Note that you initialize these values each time the method is called rather than using constant values. One reason for this is that the iv array is modified as part of the encryption process, so the values would be different if you didn't re-initialize it. In effect, this would mean that the first few bytes of the decrypted data would be garbled. The important point to note here is that you should use your own values, not the temporary ones used in the previous code snippet. There are classes and methods in the System.Security.Cryptography namespace that you can use to generate such values automatically, or you can just insert random numbers.

TIP *You could restrict access to this assembly to code that has been compiled using a particular key. This is possible if you strongly name your assemblies and configure code access security yourself, and would prevent people from using the SecurityLib assembly to decrypt credit card details from outside the JokePoint application, unless they had access to the signature key. However, this is an advanced topic and won't be covered here.*

The encryption code is contained in a Try...Catch block in case an error occurs. The code follows the steps laid out earlier, starting with the conversion of the source string into a byte array:

```
Try
    ' convert data to byte array
    Dim sourceDataBytes() As Byte = _
        System.Text.ASCIIEncoding.ASCII.GetBytes(sourceData)
```

Next, a MemoryStream object is initialized, which will be used to store encrypted data:

```
    ' get target memory stream
    Dim tempStream As MemoryStream = New MemoryStream ()
```

Now you get the encryptor object, in this case, an instance of the DESCryptoServiceProvider class, and use it with the key and IV created earlier to generate a CryptoStream object (specifying an encryption operation via the CreateEncryptor method and CryptoStreamMode.Write mode):

```
    ' get encryptor and encryption stream
    Dim encryptor As DESCryptoServiceProvider = New DESCryptoServiceProvider()
    Dim encryptionStream As CryptoStream = _
        New CryptoStream(tempStream, encryptor.CreateEncryptor(key, iv), _
        CryptoStreamMode.Write)
```

This is the place where to change code if you wanted to substitute a different encryption algorithm (although you might also have to change the amount of data contained in the key and IV arrays if you did so).

NOTE *Note that the suffix of this class is* CryptoServiceProvider. *This indicates an unmanaged implementation of the DES encryption algorithm. There is no managed implementation of this algorithm in the .NET Framework, although there is a managed implementation of the Rijndael algorithm. In practice, however, this makes little (if any) difference to application performance.*

The next section of code performs the actual encryption, writing the resultant byte array to the MemoryStream created earlier:

```
' encrypt data
encryptionStream.Write(sourceDataBytes, 0, sourceDataBytes.Length)
encryptionStream.FlushFinalBlock()
```

The FlushFinalBlock call here is essential. Without this call, unwritten data might be left in the buffer of the CryptoStream. This call forces the stream writing to complete so that all the data you require is contained in the MemoryStream object.

Next you grab the data from the MemoryStream and place it into a byte array:

```
' put data into byte array
Dim encryptedDataBytes() As Byte = tempStream.GetBuffer()
```

Finally, you convert the resultant byte array into a string and return it:

```
' convert encrypted data into string
Return Convert.ToBase64String(encryptedDataBytes, 0, tempStream.Length)
```

Should anything go wrong during this process, a StringEncryptorException exception is thrown:

```
Catch
    Throw New StringEncryptorException("Unable to encrypt data.")
  End Try
End Function
```

Note that this exception class doesn't do very much, and you might think that just throwing a standard Exception would be good enough. However, by creating your own type, it's possible for SEH code that uses this class to test for the specific type of this new exception, filtering out StringEncryptorException exceptions from other exceptions that might occur.

The Decrypt method is very similar to Encrypt. You start in the same way by initializing the key and IV before moving into a Try...Catch block and converting the source string into a byte array:

```vb
Public Shared Function Decrypt(ByVal sourceData As String) As String
    ' set key and initialization vector values
    Dim key() As Byte = New Byte() {1, 2, 3, 4, 5, 6, 7, 8}
    Dim iv() As Byte = New Byte() {1, 2, 3, 4, 5, 6, 7, 8}
    Try
        ' convert data to byte array
        Dim encryptedDataBytes() As Byte = Convert.FromBase64String(sourceData)
```

This time, however, you need a stream that is filled with this source byte array because the CryptoStream will be reading from a stream rather than writing to one:

```vb
        ' get source memory stream and fill it
        Dim tempStream As MemoryStream = _
        New MemoryStream(encryptedDataBytes, 0, encryptedDataBytes.Length)
```

The next code is similar, although you use the CreateDecryptor method and CryptoStreamMode.Read mode to specify decryption:

```vb
        ' get decryptor and decryption stream
        Dim decryptor As DESCryptoServiceProvider = New DESCryptoServiceProvider()
        Dim decryptionStream As CryptoStream = _
            New CryptoStream(tempStream, decryptor.CreateDecryptor(key, iv), _
            CryptoStreamMode.Read)
```

Finally, you get the decrypted data out of the CryptoStream using a StreamReader object, which handily allows you to grab the data straight into a string for returning. As with Encrypt, the last step is to add the code that throws a StringEncryptorException exception if anything goes wrong:

```vb
        ' decrypt data
        Dim allDataReader As StreamReader = New StreamReader(decryptionStream)
        Return allDataReader.ReadToEnd()
    Catch
        Throw New StringEncryptorException("Unable to decrypt data.")
    End Try
    End Function
End Class
```

The client code for this class simply encrypts and decrypts data, demonstrating that things are working properly. The code for this is very simple, so it's not detailed here.

Now that you have the StringEncryptor class code, the last step in creating the SecureLib library is to add the SecureCard class.

Exercise: *Implementing the* SecureCard *Class*

1. Add a new class to the SecurityLib class library called
    SecureCardException.vb with code as follows:

```
Public Class SecureCardException
   Inherits Exception

   Public Sub New(ByVal message As String)
     MyBase.New(message)
   End Sub
End Class
```

2. Add another new file to the SecurityLib class library called SecureCard.vb
    with code as follows:

```
Imports System.Xml

Public Class SecureCard
   Private isDecrypted As Boolean = False
   Private isEncrypted As Boolean = False
   Private _cardHolder As String
   Private _cardNumber As String
   Private _issueDate As String
   Private _expiryDate As String
   Private _issueNumber As String
   Private _cardType As String
   Private _encryptedData As String
   Private _xmlCardData As XmlDocument
   Private Sub New()
     ' private default constructor
   End Sub

   Public Sub New(ByVal newEncryptedData As String)
     ' constructor for use with encrypted data
     _encryptedData = newEncryptedData
     DecryptData()
   End Sub

   Public Sub New(ByVal newCardHolder As String, _
       ByVal newCardNumber As String, _
       ByVal newIssueDate As String, ByVal newExpiryDate As String, _
       ByVal newIssueNumber As String, ByVal newCardType As String)
     ' constructor for use with decrypted data
     _cardHolder = newCardHolder
     _cardNumber = newCardNumber
     _issueDate = newIssueDate
     _expiryDate = newExpiryDate
     _issueNumber = newIssueNumber
     _cardType = newCardType
     EncryptData()
   End Sub
```

```vbnet
Private Sub CreateXml()
    ' encode card details as XML document
    _xmlCardData = New XmlDocument()
    Dim documentRoot As XmlElement = _
        _xmlCardData.CreateElement("CardDetails")
    Dim child As XmlElement

    child = _xmlCardData.CreateElement("CardHolder")
    child.InnerXml = _cardHolder
    documentRoot.AppendChild(child)

    child = _xmlCardData.CreateElement("CardNumber")
    child.InnerXml = _cardNumber
    documentRoot.AppendChild(child)

    child = _xmlCardData.CreateElement("IssueDate")
    child.InnerXml = _issueDate
    documentRoot.AppendChild(child)

    child = _xmlCardData.CreateElement("ExpiryDate")
    child.InnerXml = _expiryDate
    documentRoot.AppendChild(child)

    child = _xmlCardData.CreateElement("IssueNumber")
    child.InnerXml = _issueNumber
    documentRoot.AppendChild(child)

    child = _xmlCardData.CreateElement("CardType")
    child.InnerXml = _cardType
    documentRoot.AppendChild(child)
    _xmlCardData.AppendChild(documentRoot)
End Sub

Private Sub ExtractXml()
    ' get card details out of XML document
    _cardHolder = _
        _xmlCardData.GetElementsByTagName("CardHolder").Item(0).InnerXml
    _cardNumber = _
        _xmlCardData.GetElementsByTagName("CardNumber").Item(0).InnerXml
    _issueDate = _
        _xmlCardData.GetElementsByTagName("IssueDate").Item(0).InnerXml
    _expiryDate = _
        _xmlCardData.GetElementsByTagName("ExpiryDate").Item(0).InnerXml
    _issueNumber = _
        _xmlCardData.GetElementsByTagName("IssueNumber").Item(0).InnerXml
    _cardType = _
        _xmlCardData.GetElementsByTagName("CardType").Item(0).InnerXml
End Sub
```

```vb
Private Sub EncryptData()
  Try
    ' stuff data into XML doc
    CreateXml()

    ' encrypt data
    _encryptedData = StringEncryptor.Encrypt(_xmlCardData.OuterXml)

    ' set encrypted flag
    isEncrypted = True
  Catch
    Throw New SecureCardException("Unable to encrypt data.")
  End Try
End Sub

Private Sub DecryptData()
  Try
    ' decrypt data
    _xmlCardData = New XmlDocument()
    _xmlCardData.InnerXml = StringEncryptor.Decrypt(_encryptedData)

    ' extract data from XML
    ExtractXml()

    ' set decrypted flag
    isDecrypted = True
    Catch
      Throw New SecureCardException("Unable to decrypt data.")
  End Try
End Sub

Public ReadOnly Property CardHolder() As String
  Get
    If isDecrypted Then
      Return _cardHolder
    Else
      Throw New SecureCardException("Data not decrypted.")
    End If
  End Get
End Property

Public ReadOnly Property CardNumber() As String
  Get
    If isDecrypted Then
      Return _cardNumber
    Else
      Throw New SecureCardException("Data not decrypted.")
    End If
  End Get
End Property
```

```vbnet
Public ReadOnly Property CardNumberX() As String
  Get
    If isDecrypted Then
     Return "XXXX-XXXX-XXXX-" _
        & _cardNumber.Substring(_cardNumber.Length - 4, 4)
    Else
      Throw New SecureCardException("Data not decrypted.")
    End If
  End Get
End Property

Public ReadOnly Property IssueDate() As String
  Get
    If isDecrypted Then
      Return _issueDate
    Else
      Throw New SecureCardException("Data not decrypted.")
    End If
  End Get
End Property

Public ReadOnly Property ExpiryDate() As String
  Get
    If isDecrypted Then
      Return _expiryDate
    Else
      Throw New SecureCardException("Data not decrypted.")
    End If
  End Get
End Property

Public ReadOnly Property IssueNumber() As String
  Get
    If isDecrypted Then
      Return _issueNumber
    Else
      Throw New SecureCardException("Data not decrypted.")
    End If
  End Get
End Property

Public ReadOnly Property CardType() As String
  Get
    If isDecrypted Then
      Return _cardType
    Else
      Throw New SecureCardException("Data not decrypted.")
    End If
  End Get
End Property
```

```
            Public ReadOnly Property EncryptedData() As String
              Get
                If isEncrypted Then
                  Return _encryptedData
                Else
                  Throw New SecureCardException("Data not encrypted.")
                End If
              End Get
            End Property
          End Class
```

3. Modify the code in Module1.vb as follows:

```
    Sub Main()
      Console.WriteLine("Enter data to encrypt:")
      Console.WriteLine("Card Holder:")
      Dim cardHolder As String = Console.ReadLine()
      Console.WriteLine("Card Number:")
      Dim expiryDate As String = Console.ReadLine()
      Console.WriteLine("Issue Date:")
      Dim cardNumber As String = Console.ReadLine()
      Console.WriteLine("Expiry Date:")
      Dim issueDate As String = Console.ReadLine()
      Console.WriteLine("Issue Number:")
      Dim issueNumber As String = Console.ReadLine()
      Console.WriteLine("Card Type:")
      Dim cardType As String = Console.ReadLine()

      Dim encryptedCard As SecureCard = _
          New SecureCard(cardHolder, cardNumber, issueDate, expiryDate, _
          issueNumber, cardType)
      Console.WriteLine("Encrypted data: {0}", _
                                     encryptedCard.EncryptedData)

      Console.WriteLine( _
          "Enter data to decrypt (hit enter to decrypt above data):")
      Dim stringToDecrypt As String = Console.ReadLine()
      If stringToDecrypt = "" Then
          stringToDecrypt = encryptedCard.EncryptedData
      End If
      Dim decryptedCard As SecureCard = _
          New SecureCard(stringToDecrypt)
      Console.WriteLine("Decrypted data: {0}, {1}, {2}, {3}, {4}, {5}", _
          decryptedCard.CardHolder, decryptedCard.CardNumber, _
          decryptedCard.IssueDate, decryptedCard.ExpiryDate, _
          decryptedCard.IssueNumber, decryptedCard.CardType)
    End Sub
```

4. Execute the application. The result is shown in Figure 12-3.

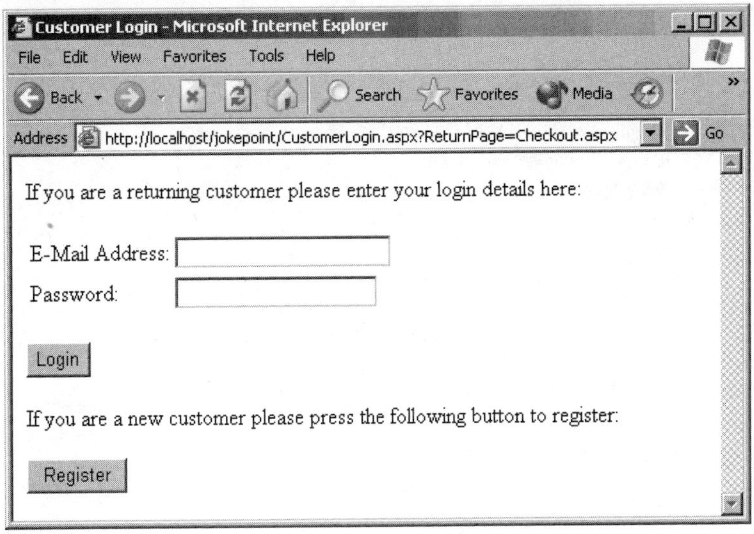

Figure 12-3. Credit card encryption example result

How It Works: Implementing the SecureCard *Class*

There is a bit more code here than in previous examples, but it's all quite simple. First you have the private member variables to hold the card details as individual strings, as an encrypted string, and in an intermediate XML document. You also have Boolean flags indicating whether the data has been successfully encrypted or decrypted:

```
Imports System.Xml

Public Class SecureCard
  Private isDecrypted As Boolean = False
  Private isEncrypted As Boolean = False
  Private _cardHolder As String
  Private _cardNumber As String
  Private _issueDate As String
  Private _expiryDate As String
  Private _issueNumber As String
  Private _cardType As String
  Private _encryptedData As String
  Private _xmlCardData As XmlDocument
```

Next there are three constructors, a private default one (because you don't want the class to be instantiated with no data), and two for encrypting or decrypting credit card data:

```
Private Sub New()
  ' private default constructor
End Sub

Public Sub New(ByVal newEncryptedData As String)
  ' constructor for use with encrypted data
  _encryptedData = newEncryptedData
  DecryptData()
End Sub

Public Sub New(ByVal newCardHolder As String, ByVal newCardNumber As String, _
    ByVal newIssueDate As String, ByVal newExpiryDate As String, _
    ByVal newIssueNumber As String, ByVal newCardType As String)
  ' constructor for use with decrypted data
  _cardHolder = newCardHolder
  _cardNumber = newCardNumber
  _issueDate = newIssueDate
  _expiryDate = newExpiryDate
  _issueNumber = newIssueNumber
  _cardType = newCardType
  EncryptData()
End Sub
```

The main work is carried out in the private `EncryptData` and `DecryptData` methods, which we'll come to shortly. First you have two utility methods for packaging and unpackaging data in XML format (which makes it easier to get at the bits you want when exchanging data with the encrypted format):

```
Private Sub CreateXml()
  ' encode card details as XML document
  _xmlCardData = New XmlDocument()
  Dim documentRoot As XmlElement = _xmlCardData.CreateElement("CardDetails")
  Dim child As XmlElement

  child = _xmlCardData.CreateElement("CardHolder")
  child.InnerXml = _cardHolder
  documentRoot.AppendChild(child)

  child = _xmlCardData.CreateElement("CardNumber")
  child.InnerXml = _cardNumber
  documentRoot.AppendChild(child)

  child = _xmlCardData.CreateElement("IssueDate")
  child.InnerXml = _issueDate
  documentRoot.AppendChild(child)

  child = _xmlCardData.CreateElement("ExpiryDate")
  child.InnerXml = _expiryDate
  documentRoot.AppendChild(child)

  child = _xmlCardData.CreateElement("IssueNumber")
  child.InnerXml = _issueNumber
  documentRoot.AppendChild(child)
```

```
        child = _xmlCardData.CreateElement("CardType")
        child.InnerXml = _cardType
        documentRoot.AppendChild(child)
        _xmlCardData.AppendChild(documentRoot)
    End Sub

    Private Sub ExtractXml()
        ' get card details out of XML document
        _cardHolder = _xmlCardData.GetElementsByTagName("CardHolder").Item(0).InnerXml
        _cardNumber = _
            _xmlCardData.GetElementsByTagName("CardNumber").Item(0).InnerXml
        _issueDate = _
            _xmlCardData.GetElementsByTagName("IssueDate").Item(0).InnerXml
        _expiryDate = _
            _xmlCardData.GetElementsByTagName("ExpiryDate").Item(0).InnerXml
        _issueNumber = _
            _xmlCardData.GetElementsByTagName("IssueNumber").Item(0).InnerXml
        _cardType = _xmlCardData.GetElementsByTagName("CardType").Item(0).InnerXml
    End Sub
```

These methods use simple XML syntax to address data elements.

The `EncryptData` method starts by using the previous `CreateXml` method to package the details supplied in the `SecureCard` constructor into XML format:

```
Private Sub EncryptData()
    Try
        ' stuff data into XML doc
        CreateXml()
```

Next, the XML string contained in the resultant XML document is encrypted into a single string and stored in the `_encryptedData` member:

```
        ' encrypt data
        _encryptedData = StringEncryptor.Encrypt(_xmlCardData.OuterXml)
```

Finally, the `isEncrypted` flag is set to `True` to indicate success—or throw a `SecureCardException` exception if anything goes wrong:

```
        ' set encrypted flag
        isEncrypted = True
    Catch
        Throw New SecureCardException("Unable to encrypt data.")
    End Try
End Sub
```

The `DecryptData` method gets the XML from its encrypted form and uses it to populate a new XML document:

```
Private Sub DecryptData()
  Try
    ' decrypt data
    _xmlCardData = New XmlDocument()
    _xmlCardData.InnerXml = StringEncryptor.Decrypt(_encryptedData)
```

Then, the method gets the data in the XML document into the private member variables for card details using ExtractXml, and either sets the isDecrypted flag to True or throws an exception depending on whether the code succeeds:

```
    ' extract data from XML
    ExtractXml()

    ' set decrypted flag
    isDecrypted = True
  Catch
    Throw New SecureCardException("Unable to decrypt data.")
  End Try
End Sub
```

Next you come to the publicly accessible properties of the class. There are quite a few of these so we won't show them all. Several are for reading card detail data, such as CardHolder:

```
Public ReadOnly Property CardHolder() As String
  Get
    If isDecrypted Then
      Return _cardHolder
    Else
      Throw New SecureCardException("Data not decrypted.")
    End If
  End Get
End Property
```

Note that the data is only accessible when isDecrypted is True, so if an exception has been thrown during decryption, then no data is available here (an exception is thrown instead). Also, note that the data isn't accessible after encryption—the data used to initialize a SecureCard object is only accessible in encrypted form. This is more a use-case decision than anything else, because this class is only really intended for encryption and decryption, not for persistently representing credit card details. After a SecureCard instance has been used to encrypt card details, you shouldn't subsequently need access to the unencrypted data, only the encrypted string.

One interesting property here is CardNumberX, which displays only a portion of the number on a credit card. This is handy when showing a user existing details, and is becoming standard practice because it lets the customer know what card they have stored without exposing the details to prying eyes:

```
Public ReadOnly Property CardNumberX() As String
  Get
    If isDecrypted Then
      Return "XXXX-XXXX-XXXX-" & _cardNumber.Substring(_cardNumber.Length - 4, 4)
```

```
      Else
         Throw New SecureCardException("Data not decrypted.")
      End If
   End Get
End Property
```

The last property worth looking at is `EncryptedData`, used when extracting the encrypted credit card details for database storage:

```
Public ReadOnly Property EncryptedData() As String
   Get
      If isEncrypted Then
         Return _encryptedData
      Else
         Throw New SecureCardException("Data not encrypted.")
      End If
   End Get
End Property
End Class
```

The structure here is much like the other properties, although this time the `isEncrypted` flag restricts access rather than the `isDecrypted` flag.

Before moving on to the client code, it's important to explain and justify one design consideration that you have probably already noticed. At no point are any of the card details validated. In fact, this class will work perfectly well with empty strings for any properties. This is so the class can remain as versatile as possible. It's more likely that credit card details will be validated as part of the UI used to enter them, or even not at all. This isn't at all dangerous—if invalid details are used, then the credit card transaction will simply fail, and you handle that using very similar logic to that required to deal with lack of funds (that is, you notify the customer of failure and request another card). Of course, there are also simple data formatting issues (dates are usually MM/YY for example), but as noted, these can be dealt with externally to the `SecureCard` class.

The client code for this class simply allows you to see how an encrypted card looks. As you can see, a lot of data is generated, hence the rather large column size in the `Customer` database. You can also see that both encryption and decryption are working perfectly, and can now move on to the customer account section of this chapter.

The Customer Login Page

Currently, `ShoppingCart.ascx` has the following code when the Place Order button is clicked:

```
Private Sub placeOrderButton_Click(ByVal sender As System.Object, _
      ByVal e As System.EventArgs) Handles placeOrderButton.Click
   ' We need to store the total amount because the shopping cart
   ' is emptied when creating the order
   Dim amount As Decimal = ShoppingCart.GetTotalAmount()
```

```
' Create the order and store the order ID
Dim orderId As String = ShoppingCart.CreateOrder()

' This will contain the PayPal request string
Dim redirect As String

' Create the redirect string
redirect += "https://www.paypal.com/xclick/business=email@server.com"
redirect += "&item_name=JokePoint Order " & orderId
redirect += "&item_number=" & orderId
redirect += "&amount=" & String.Format("{0:c}", amount)
redirect += "&return=http://www.JokePoint.com"
redirect += "&cancel_return=http://www.JokePoint.com"

' Load the PayPal payment page
Response.Redirect(redirect)
End Sub
```

This creates an entry in the Orders table using the contents of the current shopping cart and then uses this in a call to PayPal. After this processing, you have a new order and an empty shopping cart.

In your new system, you'll be removing this code from this class (although much of it will reappear later). Instead, you redirect the user to your new page, Checkout.aspx. This page will check for a logged on user by examining the session state for a variable called JokePoint_CustomerID, and will redirect the user to another new web page, CustomerLogin.aspx, if this variable isn't found (meaning that the user isn't logged in). The checkout page itself will allow users to edit their details, including credit card details, and place the order. Alternatively, they can cancel the order in progress at any time, return to the shop front, add more items to the shopping cart (which will be preserved until the order is placed), and place the order later.

In this section, you'll make the required modification to ShoppingCart.ascx, add the basic login check portion of Checkout.aspx, and implement CustomerLogin.aspx.

Exercise: Adding the Customer Login Page

1. Add a reference to the JokePoint project to the SecurityLib assembly created earlier.

2. Modify ShoppingCart.ascx as follows:

    ```
    Private Sub placeOrderButton_Click(ByVal sender As System.Object, _
        ByVal e As System.EventArgs) Handles placeOrderButton.Click
        ' Redirect to checkout page
        Response.Redirect("Checkout.aspx")
    End Sub
    ```

3. Modify the text on the Place Order button so it reads Checkout.

4. Add a new Web Form to the JokePoint application called Checkout.aspx.

5. Modify the code in Checkout.aspx.vb as follows:

```
Public Class Checkout
  Inherits System.Web.UI.Page
  Private customerID As Integer

  ...Web Form Designer Generated Code...

  Private Sub Page_Load(ByVal sender As System.Object, _
      ByVal e As System.EventArgs) Handles MyBase.Load
    If Not Page.IsPostBack Then
      If Context.Session("JokePoint_CustomerID") Is Nothing Then
        Response.Redirect("CustomerLogin.aspx?ReturnPage=Checkout.aspx")
      Else
        customerID = _
            Convert.ToInt32(Context.Session("JokePoint_CustomerID"))
      End If
    Else
      customerID = _
          Convert.ToInt32(Context.Session("JokePoint_CustomerID"))
    End If
  End Sub
End Sub
```

6. Add a new Web Form to the JokePoint application called CustomerLogin.aspx.

7. Modify the ASP.NET code as follows:

```
<!DOCTYPE HTML PUBLIC "-//W3C//DTD HTML 4.0 Transitional//EN">
<HTML>
  <HEAD>
    <title>Customer Login</title>
    <meta content="Microsoft Visual Studio.NET 7.0" name="GENERATOR">
    <meta content="Visual Basic 7.0" name="CODE_LANGUAGE">
    <meta content="JavaScript" name="vs_defaultClientScript">
    <meta content="http://schemas.microsoft.com/intellisense/ie5"
        name="vs_targetSchema">
  </HEAD>
  <body>
    <form id="Form1" method="post" runat="server">
      <p>If you are a returning customer please enter your login details
          here:</p>
      <P>
        <table>
          <tr>
            <td><asp:label id="Label1" runat="server"
                text="E-Mail Address:"/></td>
            <td><asp:textbox id="txtEmail" runat="server"/></td>
          </tr>
          <tr>
            <td><asp:label id="Label2" runat="server" text="Password:"/></td>
```

```
              <td><asp:textbox id="txtPassword" runat="server"
                    TextMode="Password"/></td>
            </tr>
          </table>
        </P>
        <P><asp:button id="btnLogin" runat="server" Text="Login" /></P>
        <P><asp:label id="lblLoginMsg" runat="server"></asp:label></P>
        <P>If you are a new customer please press the following button to
            register:</P>
        <P><asp:button id="btnRegister" runat="server"
            Text="Register"></asp:button></P>
      </form>
    </body>
  </HTML>
```

8. Add the following `Imports` statements to `CustomerLogin.aspx.vb`:

```
Imports System.Data.SqlClient
Imports SecurityLib
```

9. Add event handlers for the two buttons on the form as follows:

```
Private Sub btnLogin_Click(ByVal sender As System.Object, _
    ByVal e As System.EventArgs) Handles btnLogin.Click
    ' create instance of Connection and Command objects
    Dim connection As SqlConnection = _
        New SqlConnection( _
        ConfigurationSettings.AppSettings("ConnectionString"))
    Dim command As SqlCommand = _
        New SqlCommand("GetCustomerIDPassword", connection)
    command.CommandType = CommandType.StoredProcedure
    command.Parameters.Add("@Email", txtEmail.Text)

    ' execute command, checking for a user with the email entered
    connection.Open()
    Dim customerReader As SqlDataReader = command.ExecuteReader()
    If customerReader.Read = False Then
      ' display error, close connection, and exit method
      lblLoginMsg.Text = "Unrecognized Email."
      connection.Close()
      Return
    End If

    ' extract user information and close connection
    Dim customerID As Integer = customerReader("CustomerID")
    Dim hashedPassword As String = customerReader("Password")
    connection.Close()
```

```
' check password
If PasswordHasher.Hash(txtPassword.Text) <> hashedPassword Then
  ' display error
  lblLoginMsg.Text = "Unrecognized password."
Else
  ' set session variable, storing customer ID for later retrieval
  Context.Session("JokePoint_CustomerID") = customerID

  ' redirect user
  If Not Context.Request.QueryString("ReturnPage") Is Nothing Then
    Response.Redirect(Context.Request.QueryString("ReturnPage"))
  Else
    Response.Redirect("default.aspx")
  End If
End If
End Sub

Private Sub btnRegister_Click(ByVal sender As System.Object, _
    ByVal e As System.EventArgs) Handles btnRegister.Click
  ' redirect user
  If Not Context.Request.QueryString("ReturnPage") Is Nothing Then
    Response.Redirect("CustomerNew.aspx?ReturnPage=" _
        & Context.Request.QueryString("ReturnPage"))
  Else
    Response.Redirect("CustomerNew.aspx")
  End If
End Sub
```

10. Add the following stored procedure to the database:

```
CREATE PROCEDURE GetCustomerIDPassword
(@Email varchar(50))
AS

SELECT CustomerID, [Password]
FROM Customer
WHERE Email = @Email
GO
```

11. Compile and point your browser at the Checkout.aspx page, or go via the store front, add some items to a cart, and then click the Checkout button to take you to Checkout.aspx automatically.

    You will be redirected to the new login page (shown in Figure 12-4), although you can't log in because you haven't registered any customers.

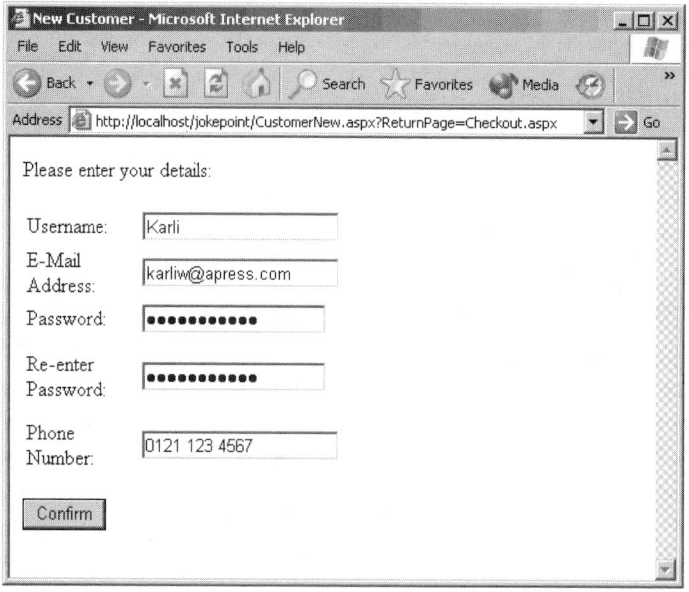

Figure 12-4. Customer login page

How It Works: Adding the Customer Login Page

As noted previously, the code entered isn't a great deal of help at this stage because there are no customers to log in and you won't be adding the customer registration page until the next section. However, you can still look through the code for the page to see how it works.

First, look at what happens in your basic Checkout.aspx page. When this page is loaded, a check is made for a logged on user by examining the Session variable JokePoint_CustomerID. If this value is present, then a user is logged in; otherwise, the browser is redirected to the login page:

```
Private Sub Page_Load(ByVal sender As System.Object, _
    ByVal e As System.EventArgs) Handles MyBase.Load
  If Not Page.IsPostBack Then
    If Context.Session("JokePoint_CustomerID") Is Nothing Then
      Response.Redirect("CustomerLogin.aspx?ReturnPage=Checkout.aspx")
    Else
      customerID = _
          Convert.ToInt32(Context.Session("JokePoint_CustomerID"))
    End If
  Else
    customerID = Convert.ToInt32(Context.Session("JokePoint_CustomerID"))
  End If
End Sub
```

If a customer is logged in, this code also stores the ID retrieved from the Session variable in the private member CustomerID. Now, let's look at CustomerLogin.aspx.

After the user has entered an email address and password, the code starts by checking to determine whether there is a user with the email address entered. It does this using the `GetCustomerIDPassword` stored procedure, which returns the ID and (hashed) password for a given customer email address:

```
Private Sub btnLogin_Click(ByVal sender As System.Object, _
                           ByVal e As System.EventArgs) Handles btnLogin.Click
    ' create instance of Connection and Command objects
    Dim connection As SqlConnection = _
        New SqlConnection(ConfigurationSettings.AppSettings("ConnectionString"))
    Dim command As SqlCommand = _
        New SqlCommand("GetCustomerIDPassword", connection)
    command.CommandType = CommandType.StoredProcedure
    command.Parameters.Add("@Email", txtEmail.Text)
```

After the command is executed using the email address entered, you check to determine whether a customer has been found by testing for a `True` result when calling the `Read` method on the data reader obtained. If you don't get the `True` result, you know that no such user exists, so you can display an appropriate message and exit the event handler:

```
    ' execute command, checking for a user with the email address entered
    connection.Open()
    Dim customerReader As SqlDataReader = command.ExecuteReader()
    If customerReader.Read = False Then
        ' display error, close connection, and exit method
        lblLoginMsg.Text = "Unrecognized Email."
        connection.Close()
        Return
    End If
```

If a user does exist, you get the `ID` and password information out of the data reader for further processing:

```
    ' extract user information and close connection
    Dim customerID As Integer = customerReader("CustomerID")
    Dim hashedPassword As String = customerReader("Password")
    connection.Close()
```

The next step is to check the password entered against the password stored. This requires you to hash the entered password because the stored password is also hashed. Again, if no match is found, you display a message and exit:

```
    ' check password
    If PasswordHasher.Hash(txtPassword.Text) <> hashedPassword Then
        ' display error
        lblLoginMsg.Text = "Unrecognized password."
```

Alternatively, if the passwords match, you can set the session variable `JokePoint_CustomerID` to the value extracted from the database and redirect the user to the page that originally sent you to the login page (or the `default.aspx` page if the `ReturnPage` query string parameter was omitted):

```
Else
    ' set session variable, storing customer ID for later retrieval
    Context.Session("JokePoint_CustomerID") = customerID

    ' redirect user
    If Not Context.Request.QueryString("ReturnPage") Is Nothing Then
        Response.Redirect(Context.Request.QueryString("ReturnPage"))
    Else
        Response.Redirect("default.aspx")
    End If
    End If
End Sub
```

NOTE   *This method suffers from a security flaw. It is possible for users to determine whether an email address exists in the database because the error messages differ—even if they are subsequently unable to guess the password. They might use this information to contact the user with this email address, and possibly even obtain the correct password illegally. For illustrative purposes, having two error messages is fine, but in production, you should return just one, for example "Illegal username/password combination."*

The other event handler, for the `Register` button, simply redirects to the customer registration page, `CustomerNew.aspx`, forwarding the `ReturnPage` query string parameter. The URL `CustomerLogin.aspx?returnPage=Checkout.aspx` is used so that the login page knows where to redirect to.

The Customer Registration Page

The customer registration page is already hooked up to the customer login page; you just need to add the code.

Exercise: Adding the Customer Registration Page

1.   Add a new Web Form to the `JokePoint` application called `CustomerNew.aspx`.

2.   Modify the ASP.NET code as follows:

```
<HTML>
    <HEAD>
        <title>New Customer</title>
            <meta content="Microsoft Visual Studio.NET 7.0" name="GENERATOR">
```

```
        <meta content="Visual Basic 7.0" name="CODE_LANGUAGE">
        <meta content="JavaScript" name="vs_defaultClientScript">
        <meta content="http://schemas.microsoft.com/intellisense/ie5"
            name="vs_targetSchema">
</HEAD>
<body>
    <form id="Form1" method="post" runat="server">
        <p>Please enter your details:</p>
        <P>
          <table>
            <tr>
                <td><asp:label id="Label3"
                    runat="server">Username:</asp:label></td>
                <td><asp:textbox id="txtUserName"
                    runat="server"></asp:textbox></td>
                <td><asp:requiredfieldvalidator id="validateUserName"
                    ErrorMessage="You must enter a user name."
                    ControlToValidate="txtUserName"
                    Runat="server"></asp:requiredfieldvalidator></td>
            </tr>
            <tr>
                <td><asp:label id="Label1"
                    runat="server">E-Mail Address:</asp:label></td>
                <td><asp:textbox id="txtEmail"
                    runat="server"></asp:textbox></td>
                <td><asp:requiredfieldvalidator id="validateEmail"
                    ErrorMessage="You must enter an e-mail address."
                    ControlToValidate="txtEmail"
                    Runat="server"></asp:requiredfieldvalidator></td>
            </tr>
            <tr>
                <td><asp:label id="Label2"
                    runat="server">Password:</asp:label></td>
                <td><asp:textbox id="txtPassword" runat="server"
                    TextMode="Password"></asp:textbox></td>
                <td><asp:requiredfieldvalidator id="validatePassword"
                    ErrorMessage="You must enter a password."
                    ControlToValidate="txtPassword"
                    Runat="server"></asp:requiredfieldvalidator></td>
            </tr>
            <tr>
                <td><asp:label id="Label4"
                    runat="server">Re-enter Password:</asp:label></td>
                <td><asp:textbox id="txtPasswordConfirm"
                    runat="server" TextMode="Password"></asp:textbox></td>
                <td><asp:requiredfieldvalidator id="validatePasswordReEntry"
                    ErrorMessage="You must re-enter your password."
                    ControlToValidate="txtPasswordConfirm"
                    Runat="server"></asp:requiredfieldvalidator>
                  <asp:comparevalidator id="validatePasswordMatch"
                    ErrorMessage="You must re-enter the same password."
```

```
                          ControlToValidate="txtPassword" Runat="server"
                          Operator="Equal"
                          ControlToCompare="txtPasswordConfirm"/></td>
               </tr>
               <tr>
                 <td><asp:label id="Label5"
                        runat="server">Phone Number:</asp:label></td>
                 <td><asp:textbox id="txtPhone"
                        runat="server"></asp:textbox></td>
                 <td><asp:requiredfieldvalidator id="validatePhone"
                        ErrorMessage="You must enter a phone number."
                        ControlToValidate="txtPhone"
                        Runat="server"></asp:requiredfieldvalidator></td>
               </tr>
             </table>
           </P>
           <P><asp:button id="btnConfirm" runat="server"
               Text="Confirm"></asp:button></P>
           <P><asp:label id="lblMsg" runat="server"></asp:label></P>
         </form>
       </body>
     </HTML>
```

3. Add the following `Imports` statements to `CustomerNew.aspx.vb`:

```
Imports System.Data.SqlClient
Imports SecurityLib
```

4. Add the following event handler for the `Confirm` button:

```
Private Sub btnConfirm_Click(ByVal sender As System.Object, _
    ByVal e As System.EventArgs) Handles btnConfirm.Click
   ' Create Instance of Connection and Command Object,
   ' check for existing user
   Dim connection As SqlConnection = _
       New SqlConnection( _
       ConfigurationSettings.AppSettings("ConnectionString"))
   Dim command As SqlCommand = _
       New SqlCommand("GetCustomerIDPassword", connection)
   command.CommandType = CommandType.StoredProcedure
   command.Parameters.Add("@Email", txtEmail.Text)

   connection.Open()
   Dim customerReader As SqlDataReader = command.ExecuteReader()
   If customerReader.Read = True Then
     lblMsg.Text = "A user with that Email address already exists."
     connection.Close()
     Return
   End If
```

```
    connection.Close()
    ' Add user
    command = New SqlCommand("AddCustomer", connection)
    command.CommandType = CommandType.StoredProcedure
    command.Parameters.Add("@Name", txtUserName.Text)
    command.Parameters.Add("@Email", txtEmail.Text)
    command.Parameters.Add("@Password", _
        PasswordHasher.Hash(txtPassword.Text))
    command.Parameters.Add("@Phone", txtPhone.Text)
    Dim customerID As Integer
    connection.Open()
    customerID = command.ExecuteScalar()
    connection.Close()
    Context.Session("JokePoint_CustomerID") = customerID
    If Not Context.Request.QueryString("ReturnPage") Is Nothing Then
        Response.Redirect(Context.Request.QueryString("ReturnPage"))
    Else
        Response.Redirect("default.aspx")
    End If
End Sub
```

5. Add the following stored procedure to the database:

```
CREATE PROCEDURE AddCustomer
(@Name varchar(50),
 @Email varchar(50),
 @Password varchar(50),
 @Phone varchar(100))
AS

DECLARE @CustomerID AS int

INSERT INTO Customer ([Name], Email, [Password], Phone)
VALUES (@Name, @Email, @Password, @Phone)
SET @CustomerID = @@IDENTITY

SELECT @CustomerID
GO
```

6. Add a customer using the new page, via Checkout.aspx and the Register button
    of CustomerLogin.aspx, as shown in Figure 12-5.

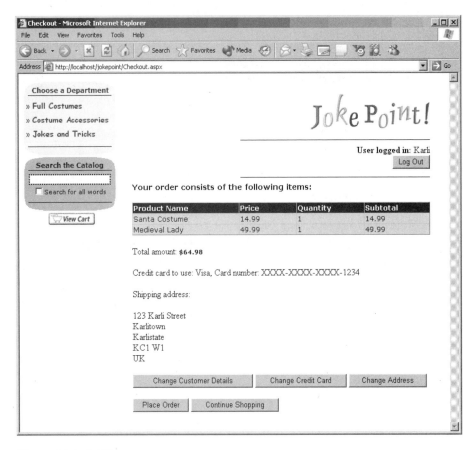

Figure 12-5. Adding a user

How It Works: Adding the Customer Registration Page

At this point, the basis of your customer account system is in place. You can now add customers and log in as a specific customer. As yet, you haven't provided a means to add more customer details (address and credit card information), but that's not a big problem.

Before moving on, let's look at the code for adding a customer. This code starts in a very similar way to the code for logging in a customer, because the first step is to ensure that no existing customer has the email address entered. This code uses the GetCustomerIDPassword stored procedure from the last section, and we needn't look at this in any more depth.

Assuming that a new email address has been entered, the next step is to add the details:

```
' Add user
command = New SqlCommand("AddCustomer", connection)
command.CommandType = CommandType.StoredProcedure
command.Parameters.Add("@Name", txtUserName.Text)
command.Parameters.Add("@Email", txtEmail.Text)
```

```
command.Parameters.Add("@Password", PasswordHasher.Hash(txtPassword.Text))
command.Parameters.Add("@Phone", txtPhone.Text)
Dim customerID As Integer
connection.Open()
customerID = command.ExecuteScalar()
connection.Close()
```

This uses the stored procedure `AddCustomer`, which returns the `ID` of the new customer as a result. You can then use this `ID` to set as the session variable for customer ID, thus removing the need for customers to log in after entering their details:

```
Context.Session("JokePoint_CustomerID") = customerID
```

Finally, you redirect the user using the `ReturnPage` query string parameter as before:

```
If Not Context.Request.QueryString("ReturnPage") Is Nothing Then
    Response.Redirect(Context.Request.QueryString("ReturnPage"))
Else
    Response.Redirect("default.aspx")
End If
End Sub
```

Customer Detail Modification Pages

There are three pages for modifying customer details:

- *CustomerEdit.aspx*: Modifies basic customer information, including email address, password, and phone number.

- *CustomerAddress.aspx*: Modifies customer address.

- *CustomerCreditCard.aspx*: Modifies customer credit card information.

These pages function in a very similar way. Each displays a simple form using ASP.NET code much like you've seen previously, allowing the customer to edit various pieces of information. Each page uses the following stored procedure, `GetCustomer`, to get the details it needs to populate text boxes with existing details:

```
CREATE PROCEDURE GetCustomer
(@CustomerID varchar(50))
AS

SELECT CustomerID, [Name], [Password], Email, CreditCard, Address1, Address2, City,
  Region, PostalCode, Country, Phone
FROM Customer
WHERE CustomerID = @CustomerID
GO
```

The following three stored procedures, UpdateCustomerDetails, UpdateAddress, and UpdateCreditCard, are used to make changes to the information in the database. UpdateCustomerDetails changes the entries for the Name, Email, Password, and Phone columns:

```
CREATE PROCEDURE UpdateCustomerDetails
(@CustomerID int,
 @Name varchar(50),
 @Email varchar(50),
 @Password varchar(50),
 @Phone varchar(100))

AS
UPDATE Customer
SET [Name] = @Name, Email = @Email, [Password] = @Password, Phone = [Phone]
WHERE CustomerID = @CustomerID
GO
```

UpdateAddress changes the entries for the Address1, Address2, City, Region, PostalCode, and Country columns:

```
CREATE PROCEDURE UpdateAddress
(@CustomerID int,
 @Address1 varchar(100),
 @Address2 varchar(100),
 @City varchar(100),
 @Region varchar(100),
 @PostalCode varchar(100),
 @Country varchar(100)
)

AS
UPDATE Customer
SET Address1 = @Address1, Address2 = @Address2, City = @City, Region = @Region,
 PostalCode = @PostalCode, Country = @Country
WHERE CustomerID = @CustomerID
GO
```

UpdateCreditCard changes the entry for the CreditCard column:

```
CREATE PROCEDURE UpdateCreditCard
(@CustomerID int,
 @CreditCard varchar(512))

AS
UPDATE Customer
SET CreditCard = @CreditCard
WHERE CustomerID = @CustomerID
GO
```

Other than that, there is very little to say about this section of the code. Refer to the code in the Downloads section of the Apress web site (http://www.apress.com) for a look at these pages, which contain comments to guide you through.

The Checkout Page

You can now add to the checkout page (so far all it does is redirect users to CustomerLogin.aspx if they aren't logged in). This page will look similar to the ShoppingCart.ascx control because you are displaying the items ordered, but will also display additional information. Because you have access to a logged in user, you can display user information and can include buttons for modifying address and credit card information. For new customers, neither address nor credit card information will have been added, so you can also disable the order button until this information has been added.

Some of the ASP.NET code will be taken from default.aspx, such that the same color scheme, header, and so on is included, although you won't include the list of links on the left-hand side.

Exercise: Updating the Checkout Page

1. Modify the ASP.NET code for Checkout.aspx as follows:

```
<%@ Register TagPrefix="uc1" TagName="Header"
          Src="UserControls/Header.ascx" %>
<%@ Register TagPrefix="uc1" TagName="DepartmentsList"
Src="UserControls/DepartmentsList.ascx" %>
<%@ Register TagPrefix="uc1" TagName="CategoriesList"
Src="UserControls/CategoriesList.ascx" %>
<%@ Register TagPrefix="uc1" TagName="SearchBox"
Src="UserControls/SearchBox.ascx" %>
<%@ Page Language="vb" AutoEventWireup="false"
          Codebehind="Checkout.aspx.vb"
      Inherits="JokePoint.Checkout"%>
<!DOCTYPE HTML PUBLIC "-//W3C//DTD HTML 4.0 Transitional//EN">
<HTML>
  <HEAD>
    <title>Checkout</title>
    <meta name="GENERATOR" content="Microsoft Visual Studio.NET 7.0">
    <meta name="CODE_LANGUAGE" content="Visual Basic 7.0">
    <meta name="vs_defaultClientScript" content="JavaScript">
    <meta name="vs_targetSchema"
        content="http://schemas.microsoft.com/intellisense/ie5">
      <link href="JokePoint.css" type="text/css" rel="stylesheet">
  </HEAD>
  <body>
    <form id="Form1" runat="server">
      <table height="100%" cellSpacing="0" cellPadding="0" width="770"
          border="0">
```

```
<tr>
    <td vAlign="top" width="190" height="100%">
        <table height="100%" cellSpacing="0" cellPadding="0"
            width="190" border="0">
          <tr>
            <td vAlign="top" height="100%">
              <uc1:departmentslist id="DepartmentsList1" runat="server">
              </uc1:departmentslist>
              <uc1:categorieslist id="CategoriesList1" runat="server">
              </uc1:categorieslist>
              <uc1:searchbox id="SearchBox1" runat="server" />
              <br>
nbsp;         
                <asp:imagebutton id="viewCartButton" runat="server"
                    ImageUrl="Images/ViewCart.gif"></asp:imagebutton>
            </td>
          </tr>
        </table>
    </td>
    <td vAlign="top" width="550"><br>
      <table>
        <tr>
          <td>
            <uc1:Header id="Header1" runat="server"></uc1:Header>
      </td>
    <tr>
      <td>
        <p align="right">
        <b>User logged in:</b>
        <asp:label id="txtUserName" runat="server"></asp:label><br>
        <asp:button id="logOutButton" runat="server"
            Text="Log Out"></asp:button><br>
        <img src="Images/1n.gif" border="0" width="350" height="1">
        </p>
      </td>
    </tr>
    <tr>
      <td id="pageContentsCell" runat="server">
        <P><asp:label id="Label1" runat="server"
                                        CssClass="ListDescription">
            Your order consists of the following items:
          </asp:label></P>
        <P><asp:datagrid id="grid" runat="server"
              AutoGenerateColumns="False" Width="100%">
            <ItemStyle Font-Size="X-Small" Font-Names="Verdana"
                BackColor="Gainsboro"></ItemStyle>
            <HeaderStyle Font-Size="X-Small"
                Font-Names="Verdana" Font-Bold="True"
                ForeColor="White" BackColor="Navy"></HeaderStyle>
              <Columns>
                <asp:BoundColumn DataField="Name"
                    ReadOnly="True" HeaderText="Product Name">
```

```
            </asp:BoundColumn>
            <asp:BoundColumn DataField="Price"
                ReadOnly="True" HeaderText="Price" />
            <asp:BoundColumn DataField="Quantity"
                ReadOnly="True" HeaderText="Quantity" />
            <asp:BoundColumn DataField="Subtotal"
                ReadOnly="True" HeaderText="Subtotal" />
          </Columns>
        </asp:datagrid></P>
        <P>
        Total amount:
        <asp:label id="totalAmountLabel" runat="server"
            CssClass="ProductPrice"></asp:label>
        <br><br>
        <asp:label id="lblCreditCardNote"
            Runat="server"></asp:label>
        <br><br>
        <asp:label id="lblAddress" Runat="server" />
        <br><br>
        <asp:button id="changeDetailsButton" runat="server"
            Text="Change Customer Details"></asp:button>
        <asp:button id="addCreditCardButton" runat="server"
            Text="Add Credit Card"></asp:button>
        <asp:button id="addAddressButton" runat="server"
            Text="Add Address"></asp:button>
        <br><br>
        <asp:button id="placeOrderButton" runat="server"
            Text="Place Order"></asp:button>
        <asp:button id="cancelOrderButton" runat="server"
            Text="Continue Shopping"></asp:button>
        </P>
      </td>
    </tr>
  </table>
    </td>
  </tr>
</table>
</form>
</body>
</HTML>
```

2. Add the following `Imports` statements to `Checkout.aspx.vb`:

```
Imports System.Data.SqlClient
Imports SecurityLib
Imports System.Text
```

3. Add the following private methods for displaying user and shopping cart details (BindShoppingCart is very similar to the method of the same name in ShoppingCart.ascx):

```
Private Sub BindShoppingCart()
    ' Populate the data grid and set its DataKey field
    Dim cart As New ShoppingCart()
    grid.DataSource = cart.GetProducts
    grid.DataKeyField = "ProductID"
    grid.DataBind()

    ' Set the total amount label using the Currency format
    totalAmountLabel.Text = String.Format("{0:c}", _
                                            cart.GetTotalAmount())
End Sub

Private Sub BindUserDetails()
    ' Create Instance of Connection and Command Object
    Dim connection As SqlConnection = _
        New SqlConnection( _
        ConfigurationSettings.AppSettings("ConnectionString"))
    Dim command As SqlCommand = _
        New SqlCommand("GetCustomer", connection)
    command.CommandType = CommandType.StoredProcedure
    command.Parameters.Add("@CustomerID", customerID)

    ' get customer details
    connection.Open()
    Dim customerReader As SqlDataReader = command.ExecuteReader()
    If customerReader.Read = False Then
        Response.Redirect("CustomerLogin.aspx?returnPage=Checkout.aspx")
    End If

    ' set customer data display
    txtUserName.Text = customerReader("Name")
    If customerReader("CreditCard").GetType() Is GetType(DBNull) Then
        lblCreditCardNote.Text = "No credit card details stored."
        placeOrderButton.Visible = False
    Else
        Dim cardDetails As SecureCard = _
            New SecureCard(customerReader("CreditCard"))
        lblCreditCardNote.Text = "Credit card to use: " _
            & cardDetails.CardType _
            & ", Card number: " & cardDetails.CardNumberX()
        addCreditCardButton.Text = "Change Credit Card"
    End If
    If customerReader("Address1").GetType() Is GetType(DBNull) Then
        lblAddress.Text = "Shipping address required to place order."
        placeOrderButton.Visible = False
    Else
        Dim addressBuilder As StringBuilder = New StringBuilder()
        addressBuilder.Append("Shipping address:<br><br>")
        addressBuilder.Append(customerReader("Address1"))
```

```
         addressBuilder.Append("<br>")
         If Not customerReader("Address2").GetType() _
               Is GetType(DBNull) Then
            If customerReader("Address2") <> "" Then
               addressBuilder.Append(customerReader("Address2"))
               addressBuilder.Append("<br>")
            End If
         End If
         addressBuilder.Append(customerReader("City"))
         addressBuilder.Append("<br>")
         addressBuilder.Append(customerReader("Region"))
         addressBuilder.Append("<br>")
         addressBuilder.Append(customerReader("PostalCode"))
         addressBuilder.Append("<br>")
         addressBuilder.Append(customerReader("Country"))
         lblAddress.Text = addressBuilder.ToString()
         addAddressButton.Text = "Change Address"
      End If
      connection.Close()
   End Sub
```

4. Modify the code in `Page_Load` to call the previous methods:

```
   Private Sub Page_Load(ByVal sender As System.Object, _
      ByVal e As System.EventArgs) Handles MyBase.Load
     If Not Page.IsPostBack Then
       If Context.Session("JokePoint_CustomerID") Is Nothing Then
         Response.Redirect("CustomerLogin.aspx?returnPage=Checkout.aspx")
       Else
         customerID = _
         Convert.ToInt32(Context.Session("JokePoint_CustomerID"))
       End If
       BindShoppingCart()
       BindUserDetails()
     Else
       customerID = _
           Convert.ToInt32(Context.Session("JokePoint_CustomerID"))
     End If
   End Sub
```

5. Add the following button event handlers for customer detail modification:

```
   Private Sub addCreditCardButton_Click(ByVal sender As System.Object, _
      ByVal e As System.EventArgs) Handles addCreditCardButton.Click
     Response.Redirect( _
        "CustomerCreditCard.aspx?ReturnPage=Checkout.aspx")
   End Sub

   Private Sub addAddressButton_Click(ByVal sender As System.Object, _
      ByVal e As System.EventArgs) Handles addAddressButton.Click
     Response.Redirect("CustomerAddress.aspx?ReturnPage=Checkout.aspx")
   End Sub
```

```
Private Sub changeDetailsButton_Click(ByVal sender As System.Object, _
    ByVal e As System.EventArgs) Handles changeDetailsButton.Click
  Response.Redirect("CustomerEdit.aspx?ReturnPage=Checkout.aspx")
End Sub


Private Sub logOutButton_Click(ByVal sender As System.Object, _
    ByVal e As System.EventArgs) Handles logOutButton.Click
  Context.Session("JokePoint_CustomerID") = Nothing
  Response.Redirect("default.aspx")
End Sub


Private Sub cancelOrderButton_Click(ByVal sender As System.Object, _
    ByVal e As System.EventArgs) Handles cancelOrderButton.Click
  Response.Redirect("default.aspx")
End Sub
```

6.   Add the following event handler for the Place Order button:

```
Private Sub placeOrderButton_Click(ByVal sender As System.Object, _
    ByVal e As System.EventArgs) Handles placeOrderButton.Click
  ' The Shopping Cart object
  Dim cart As New ShoppingCart()

  ' We need to store the total amount because the shopping cart
  ' is emptied when creating the order
  Dim amount As Decimal = cart.GetTotalAmount()

  ' Create the order and store the order ID
  Dim orderId As String = cart.CreateOrder()

  ' After saving the order into our database, we need to
  ' redirect to a page where the customer can pay for the
  ' order. Please take a look at the "Single Item Purchases"
  ' section of the PayPal appendix to see how you can
  ' integrate PayPal here

  ' Right now we redirect to default.aspx
  Response.Redirect("default.aspx")
End Sub
```

This is the logic for the main checkout page. The other three ASP pages necessary to run this application are:

- CustomerAddress.aspx

- CustomerCreditCard.aspx

- CustomerEdit.aspx

NOTE *These pages should be added to the project from the code download file for the chapter (in the Downloads section of the Apress web site). None of them contain anything that you haven't seen before, so merely add them to your project by right-clicking the project name and selecting Add ➤ Add Existing Item and copying them into your working project.*

7. Compile, login as the customer registered in the last section, add all customer details, and check out the results (shown in Figure 12-6).

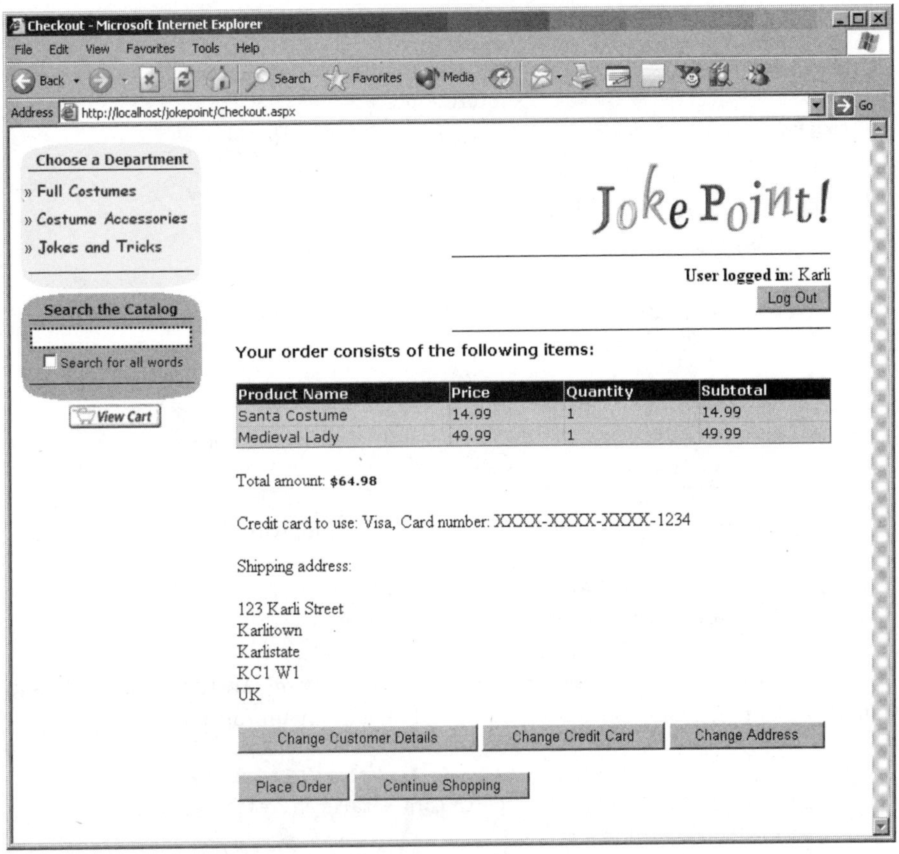

Figure 12-6. Checkout view with logged in user

How It Works: Updating the Checkout Page

Again, we haven't introduced any earth-shattering new code here. All we've done is use the GetCustomer stored procedure to get customer details and format the checkout display accordingly. If either the address or credit card information is not present, the Order Now button is hidden because placing an order requires this information. Because BindShoppingCart is practically identical to the version in ShoppingCart.ascx (the only difference being that you don't bother to check for items because users will only get to this stage via ShoppingCart.ascx), you only need to look through BindUserDetails. This method starts by getting information about the current customer from the Customer table:

```
Private Sub BindUserDetails()
  ' Create Instance of Connection and Command Object
  Dim connection As SqlConnection = _
      New SqlConnection(ConfigurationSettings.AppSettings("ConnectionString"))
  Dim command As SqlCommand = New SqlCommand("GetCustomer", connection)
  command.CommandType = CommandType.StoredProcedure
  command.Parameters.Add("@CustomerID", customerID)

  ' get customer details
  connection.Open()
  Dim customerReader As SqlDataReader = command.ExecuteReader()
```

If no customer is found, there is a problem with the login, so you redirect the user to the CustomerLogin.aspx page:

```
If customerReader.Read = False Then
  Response.Redirect("CustomerLogin.aspx?returnPage=Checkout.aspx")
End If
```

Otherwise, you begin extracting information, starting with the name of the user:

```
' set customer data display
txtUserName.Text = customerReader("Name")
```

Next you try to get the credit card details, which may or may not be present. If no data is present, you hide the Order button and display an appropriate message:

```
If customerReader("CreditCard").GetType() Is GetType(DBNull) Then
    lblCreditCardNote.Text = "No credit card details stored."
    orderButton.Visible = False
```

Alternatively, you display the required details and modify the text on the Add Credit Card button to Change Credit Card:

```
Else
  Dim cardDetails As SecureCard = _
      New SecureCard(customerReader("CreditCard"))
  lblCreditCardNote.Text = "Credit card to use: " & cardDetails.CardType _
      & ", Card number: " & cardDetails.CardNumberX()
  addCreditCardButton.Text = "Change Credit Card"
End If
```

Next you check for an address by looking at the `Address1` column and seeing if it contains any data. If it doesn't, you display a message and disable the Place Order button, as you did for credit card details:

```
If customerReader("Address1").GetType() Is GetType(DBNull) Then
    lblAddress.Text = "Shipping address required to place order."
    orderButton.Visible = False
```

If an address is present, you use a `StringBuilder` instance to assemble the address data into an HTML string for displaying on the web page:

```
Else
    Dim addressBuilder As StringBuilder = New StringBuilder()
    addressBuilder.Append("Shipping address:<br><br>")
    addressBuilder.Append(customerReader("Address1"))
    addressBuilder.Append("<br>")
    If Not customerReader("Address2").GetType() Is GetType(DBNull) Then
        If customerReader("Address2") <> "" Then
            addressBuilder.Append(customerReader("Address2"))
            addressBuilder.Append("<br>")
        End If
    End If
    addressBuilder.Append(customerReader("City"))
    addressBuilder.Append("<br>")
    addressBuilder.Append(customerReader("Region"))
    addressBuilder.Append("<br>")
    addressBuilder.Append(customerReader("PostalCode"))
    addressBuilder.Append("<br>")
    addressBuilder.Append(customerReader("Country"))
    lblAddress.Text = addressBuilder.ToString()
    addAddressButton.Text = "Change Address"
End If
```

When you have all the necessary information, close the connection:

```
    connection.Close()
End Sub
```

Currently, the code that is called when the Place Order button is clicked is identical to the old code in `ShoppingCart.ascx`. You'll get onto this and change things in the next chapter when you implement the order pipeline.

Setting Up Secure Connections

Customers can now register on your site, log in, and change details. However, the current system involves sending potentially sensitive information over HTTP. This protocol isn't secure, and the information could be intercepted and stolen. To avoid this, you need to set up the application to work with SSL (Secure Socket Layer) connections using HTTPS (HyperText Transport Protocol [Secure]).

To do this, we have a bit of groundwork to get through first. Unless you have already been using SSL connection on your web server, you are unlikely to have the correct configuration to do so. This configuration involves obtaining a security certificate for your server and installing it via IIS management.

Security certificates are basically public-private key pairs of similar form to those discussed earlier in the chapter relating to asymmetric encryption. You can generate these yourself if your domain controller is configured as a certification authority, but this has its problems. Digital signing of SSL certificates is such that browsers using such a certificate will not be able to verify the identity of your certification authority, and may therefore doubt your security. This isn't disastrous, but may affect consumer confidence, because users will be presented with a warning message when they attempt to establish a secure connection.

The alternative is to obtain SSL certificates from a known and respected organization that specializes in web security, such as VeriSign. Web browsers such as Internet Explorer have built-in root certificates from organizations such as this, and are able to authenticate the digital signature of SSL certificates supplied by them. This means that no warning message will appear, and an SSL secured connection will be available with a minimum of fuss.

This section assumes that you take this latter option, although if you want to create your own certificates, that won't affect the end result.

Obtaining an SSL Certificate from VeriSign

Obtaining a certificate from VeriSign is a relatively painless experience, and full instructions are available on the VeriSign web site, http://www.verisign.com/. You also can get test certificates from VeriSign, which are free to use for a trial period. The basic steps are as follows:

1. Sign up for a trial certificate on the VeriSign web site.

2. Generate a Certificate Signing Request (CSR) via IIS management on your web server. This involves filling out various personal information, including the name of your web site, and so on.

3. Copy the contents of the generated CSR into the VeriSign request system.

4. Shortly afterwards, you will receive a certificate from VeriSign that you copy into IIS Management to install the certificate.

There is a little more to it than that, but as noted, detailed instructions are available on the VeriSign web site, and you shouldn't run into any difficulties.

Enforcing SSL Connections

Once installed, you can access any web pages on your web server using an SSL connection, simply by replacing the http:// part of the URL used to access the page with
https:// (assuming that your firewall is set up to allow an SSL connection, which by
default uses port 443, if you use a firewall—this doesn't apply to local connections).
Obviously, you don't need SSL connections for all areas of the site, and shouldn't
enforce it in all places because it can reduce performance. However, you *do* want to
make sure that the checkout, customer login, customer registration, and customer
detail modification pages are accessible only via SSL.

To achieve this, you need to configure the individual pages via IIS management.
Looking at the properties for Checkout.aspx in IIS management, for example, shows the
File Security tab, as shown in Figure 12-7.

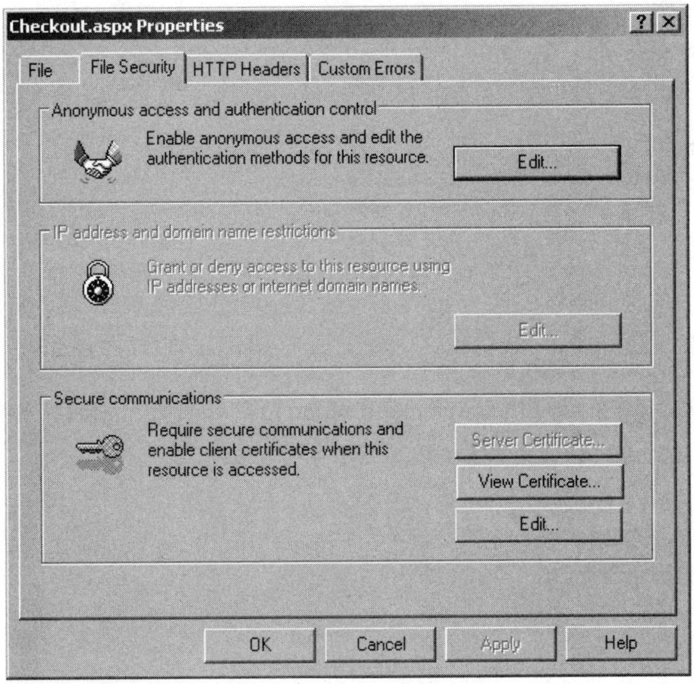

Figure 12-7. File Security property page

NOTE   *To access this dialog box, open IIS manager from the
Administrative Tools section of Control Panel, navigate through the tree
view through IIS/Local Computer/Web Sites/Default Web Site/JokePoint,
and get the properties for* Checkout.aspx.

From here, you can click the Edit button in the Secure Communications section and tick the Require Secure Channel (SSL) box in the dialog box that appears (don't need to worry about the other options), as shown in Figure 12-8.

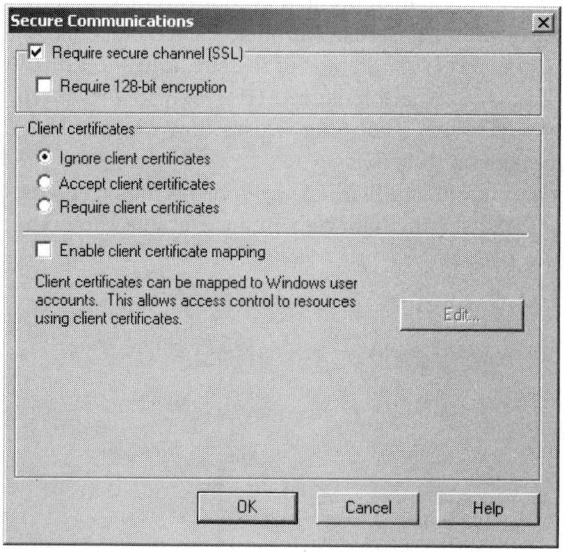

Figure 12-8. Setting the HTTPS requirement

After clicking OK, attempts to access the Checkout.aspx page using HTTP will be rejected.

You should go ahead and make the same modification to all the pages where security is essential:

- Checkout.aspx

- CustomerAddress.aspx

- CustomerCreditCard.aspx

- CustomerEdit.aspx

- CustomerLogin.aspx

- CustomerNew.aspx

Modifying Redirections to Use SSL Connections

Currently, you redirect pages using the following syntax (taking the code in ShoppingCart.ascx.vb as an example):

```
Private Sub placeOrderButton_Click(ByVal sender As System.Object, _
    ByVal e As System.EventArgs) Handles placeOrderButton.Click
  ' Redirect to checkout page
  Response.Redirect("Checkout.aspx")
End Sub
```

Unfortunately, there is no easy way to change the connection to an SSL connection and keep this simple virtual path syntax. Instead, you need to provide a full URL to the page, including the https:// string at the start of the URL. This is all very well for published web sites where you have a mapped domain name, but slightly trickier for testing. The following might seem okay:

```
Private Sub placeOrderButton _Click(ByVal sender As System.Object, _
    ByVal e As System.EventArgs) Handles placeOrderButton.Click
  ' Redirect to checkout page
  Response.Redirect("https://localhost Request.ApplicationPath & "/Checkout.aspx")
End Sub
```

However, this restricts the users that can use the site to those accessing it locally on the web server. This is fine for testing, but won't work when you deploy the application.

The solution to this is to extract the host used in the current request (which might be localhost, www.JokePoint.com, or whatever) to build the URL using code as follows:

```
Private Sub placeOrderButton _Click(ByVal sender As System.Object, _
    ByVal e As System.EventArgs) Handles placeOrderButton.Click
  ' Redirect to checkout page
  Response.Redirect("https://" & Request.Url.Host _
      & Request.ApplicationPath & "/Checkout.aspx")
End Sub
```

You also have something else to consider—in Chapter 9, we gave the option of changing things a bit by storing session information without using cookies and instead including the session ID in the URL. Unfortunately, the code shown previously won't cope with this. Instead, you need to determine whether this scheme is being used and include the session ID, if necessary, using the following code:

```
Private Sub placeOrderButton_Click(ByVal sender As System.Object, _
    ByVal e As System.EventArgs) Handles placeOrderButton.Click
  ' Redirect to checkout page
  If Session.IsCookieless Then
    Response.Redirect("https://" & Request.Url.Host _
        & Request.ApplicationPath & "/(" & Session.SessionID & ")/Checkout.aspx")
  Else
    Response.Redirect("https://" & Request.Url.Host _
        & Request.ApplicationPath & "/Checkout.aspx")
  End If
End Sub
```

`Session.IsCookieless` is a Boolean property that reflects the configured behavior in `Web.config`. This change keeps the same URL format that you've seen in earlier examples, and makes sure you don't lose the shopping cart between pages.

Further redirects will keep using HTTPS even if they are just redirects to virtual paths, so this is the only place you need to make this change. However, you don't want to continue using HTTPS when you return to `default.aspx`, because there is an appreciable overhead when using a secure connection. Instead, modify the code in `default.aspx.vb` to detect and redirect secure connections using similar code to that shown previously:

```
Private Sub Page_Load(ByVal sender As System.Object, _
    ByVal e As System.EventArgs) Handles MyBase.Load
  ' Check for HTTPS (SSL) connection
  If Context.Request.IsSecureConnection Then
    ' Redirect to standard HTTP
    If Session.IsCookieless Then
      Response.Redirect("http://" & Request.Url.Host _
          & Request.ApplicationPath & "/(" & Session.SessionID & ")/default.aspx")
    Else
      Response.Redirect("http://" & Request.Url.Host _
          & Request.ApplicationPath & "/default.aspx")
    End If
  End If
```

This ensures the persistence of shopping cart data and ends secure connections.

Summary

In this chapter, you've implemented a customer account system that customers can use to store their details ready for use during order processing. You've looked at many aspects of the customer account system, including encrypting sensitive data, and securing web connections for obtaining it.

You started by looking at a new table in your database, `Customer`, with fields for storing customer information.

Next you created a `SecurityLib` class library containing classes for hashing and encrypting strings, and a secure credit card representation that makes it easy to exchange credit card details between the encrypted and decrypted format.

After this, you used this library to help create login, registration, and customer detail editing web pages. This required a few more stored procedures to be added, but the actual code turned out to be quite simple.

Finally, we looked at how to secure data passing over the Internet using secure SSL connections. This involved obtaining a certificate from a known certification authority (VeriSign, for example), installing it, restricting access to SSL where appropriate, and modifying the redirection code slightly to use SSL connections.

In the next chapter, we'll be looking at how to create the framework for the order-processing pipeline, enabling you to automate even more of the supply process.

CHAPTER 13

Order Pipeline

THE JOKEPOINT E-COMMERCE application is shaping up nicely. You've added customer account functionality, and you're keeping track of customer addresses and credit card information, which is stored in a secure way. However, you're not currently using this information—you're delegating responsibility for this to PayPal.

In this and the next chapter, you'll build your own order-processing pipeline that deals with credit card authorization, stock checking, shipping, email notification, and so on. In fact, we'll leave the credit card processing specifics until Chapter 15, but we'll show you where this process fits in before then.

Order pipeline functionality is an extremely useful capability for an e-commerce site because it allows you to track orders at every stage in the process, and provides auditing information that you can refer to at a later date or if something goes wrong during the order processing. You can do all this without having to rely on a third party's accounting system, which also can reduce costs. The first section of this chapter discusses what we actually mean by an order pipeline, and the specifics that apply to the JokePoint application.

There are many ways of implementing such a system, and many people recommend that you use a transactional system such as MTS (Microsoft Transaction Server), or COM+ (Component Object Model+) in more recent operating systems. However, this method adds its own complications, and doesn't give you that much that you can't achieve using standard .NET assemblies. Although it's possible to create COM+ components using .NET, the code implementation is more complicated, and debugging code can be tricky. For this reason, we'll stick with the .NET platform here, which has the added advantage that it makes code easier to understand and debug. The bulk of this chapter deals with the construction of such a system, which also involves a small modification of the way things currently work, and some additions to the database you've been using. However, the code in this chapter isn't much more complicated than the code you've already been using. The real challenges are in the design of the system.

By the end of Chapter 14, customers will be able to place orders into your pipeline, and you'll be able to follow the progress of these orders as they pass through various stages. Although no real credit card processing will take place, you'll end up with a fairly complete system, including a new administration web page that can be used by suppliers to confirm that they have items in stock and to confirm that orders have been shipped. To start with, however, you need a bit more background about what we are actually trying to achieve.

Defining an Order Pipeline

Any commercial transaction, whether in a shop on the street, over the Internet, or any-where else, has several related tasks that must be carried out before it can be considered complete. For example, you can't simply remove an item of clothing from a fashion boutique without paying for it and say that you have bought it—remuneration is (unfor-tunately!) an integral part of any purchase. In addition, a transaction can only complete successfully if each of the tasks carried out completes successfully. If a customer's credit card is rejected, for example, then no funds can be taken from it, so a purchase can't be made.

The sequence of tasks carried out as part of a transaction is often thought of in terms of a pipeline. In this analogy, orders start at one end of the pipe and come out of the other end when they are completed. Along the way, they must pass through several pipeline sections, each of which is responsible for a particular task, or a related group of tasks. If any pipeline section fails to complete, then the order "gets stuck," and might require outside interaction before it can move further along the pipeline, or it might be canceled completely.

For example, the simple pipeline shown in Figure 13-1 applies to transactions in a street shop.

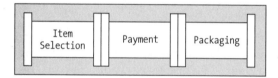

Figure 13-1. Transactions for a street shop on the street

Here the last section might be optional, and might involve additional tasks such as gift-wrapping. The payment stage might also take one of several methods of operation, because the customer could pay using cash, credit card, gift certificates, and so on.

As you'll see in the next section, the e-commerce purchasing pipeline becomes longer, but isn't really any more complicated.

Understanding the JokePoint Order Pipeline

In JokePoint, the pipeline will look like the one in Figure 13-2.

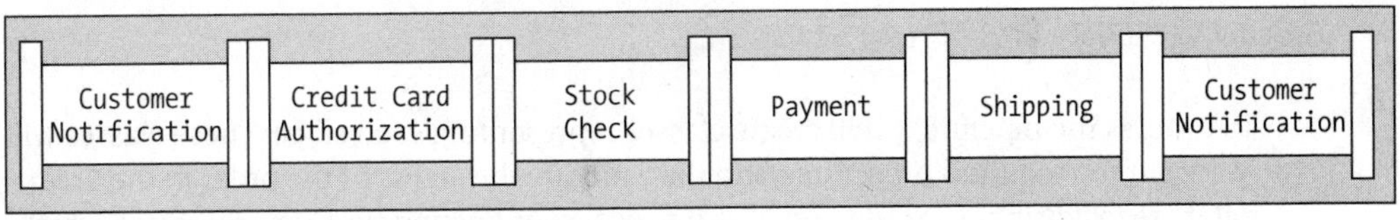

| Customer Notification | Credit Card Authorization | Stock Check | Payment | Shipping | Customer Notification |

Figure 13-2. The JokePoint order pipeline

The tasks carried out in these pipeline sections are as follows:

- *Customer Notification*: An email is sent notifying the customer that order processing has started, and confirming the items to be sent and the address that goods will be sent to.

- *Credit Card Authorization*: The credit card used for purchasing is checked, and the total order amount is set aside (although no payment is taken at this stage).

- *Stock Check*: An email is sent to the supplier with a list of the items that have been ordered. Processing continues when the supplier confirms that the goods are available.

- *Payment*: The credit card transaction is completed using the funds set aside earlier.

- *Shipping*: An email is sent to the supplier confirming that payment for the items ordered has been taken. Processing continues when the supplier confirms that the goods have been shipped.

- *Customer Notification*: An email is sent notifying the customer that the order has been shipped, and thanking them for using the JokePoint web site.

 NOTE *In terms of implementation, as you'll see shortly, there are actually more stages than this, because the stock check and shipping stages consist of two pipeline sections: one for sending the email and one that waits for confirmation.*

As orders flow through this pipeline, entries are added to a new database table called Audit. These entries can be examined to see what has happened to an order, and are an excellent way of identifying problems if they occur. Each entry in the Orders database also will be flagged with a status, identifying which point in the pipeline it has reached.

Building the Pipeline

To process the pipeline, you'll create classes representing each stage. These classes will carry out the required processing and then modify the status of the order in the Orders database to advance the order. You'll also need a coordinating class (or processor), which can be called for any order and will execute the appropriate pipeline stage class. This processor will be called once when the order is placed, and in normal operation, will be called twice more: once for stock confirmation and once for shipping confirmation.

To make life easier, you'll also define a common interface supported by each pipeline stage class to enable the order processor class to access each stage in a standard way. You'll also define several utility functions and expose several common properties in the order processor class, which will be used as and when necessary by the pipeline stages. For example, the ID of the order should be accessible to all pipeline stages, and to save code duplication, you'll put that information in the order processor class.

Now, let's get on to the specifics. You'll build an assembly called CommerceLib containing all the classes, which you'll reference from JokePoint. CommerceLib will contain the following:

- *OrderProcessor*: The main class for processing orders.

- *OrderProcessorConfiguration*: The structure containing various configuration details for the OrderProcessor class, including the administrator email address, SQL connection string, and so on.

- *OrderProcessorException*: The custom exception class for use in the order processor and pipeline sections.

- *IPipelineSection*: The interface definition for pipeline sections.

- *Customer, OrderDetails, OrderDetail*: The classes used to store data extracted from the database, for ease of access.

- *PSInitialNotification, PSCheckFunds, PSCheckStock, PSStockOK, PSTakePayment, PSShipGoods, PSShipOK, PSFinalNotification*: The pipeline section classes.

The progress of an order through the pipeline as mediated by the order processor relates to the pipeline shown earlier (see Figure 13-3).

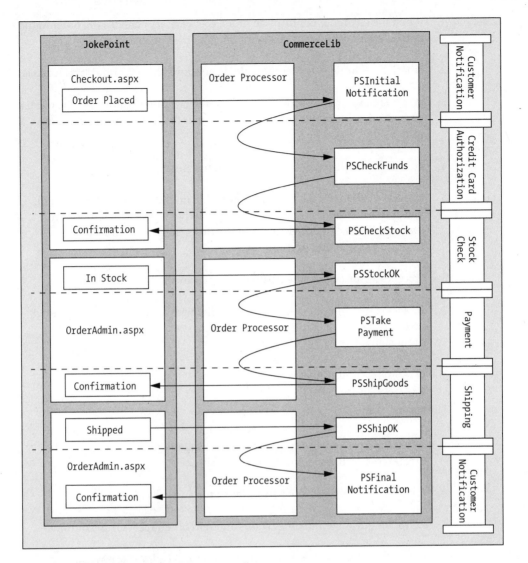

Figure 13-3. CommerceLib *pipeline processing*

The process shown in Figure 13-3 is divided into three sections as follows:

- Customer places order.

- Supplier confirms stock.

- Supplier confirms shipping.

The first stage is as follows:

1. When the customer confirms an order, Checkout.aspx creates the order in the database and calls OrderProcessor to begin order processing.

2. OrderProcessor detects that the order is new and calls PSInitialNotification.

3. PSInitialNotification sends an email to the customer confirming the order, and advances the order stage. It also instructs OrderProcessor to continue processing.

4. OrderProcessor detects the new order status and calls PSCheckFunds.

5. PSCheckFunds checks that funds are available on the customer's credit card, and stores the details required to complete the transaction if funds are available. If this is successful, then the order stage is advanced and OrderProcessor is told to continue.

6. OrderProcessor detects the new order status and calls PSCheckStock.

7. PSCheckStock sends an email to the supplier with a list of the items ordered, instructs the supplier to confirm via OrderAdmin.aspx, and advances the order status.

8. OrderProcessor terminates.

The second stage:

1. When the supplier confirms that stock is available OrderAdmin.aspx calls OrderProcessor to continue order processing.

2. OrderProcessor detects the new order status and calls PSStockOK.

3. PSStockOK advances the order status and tells OrderProcessor to continue.

4. OrderProcessor detects the new order status and calls PSTakePayment.

5. PSTakePayment uses the transaction details stored earlier by PSCheckFunds to complete the transaction, then advances the order status, and tells OrderProcessor to continue.

6. OrderProcessor detects the new order status and calls PSShipGoods.

7. PSShipGoods sends an email to the supplier with a confirmation of the items ordered, instructs the supplier to ship these goods to the customer, and advances the order status.

8. OrderProcessor terminates.

The third stage:

1. When the supplier confirms that the goods have been shipped, `OrderAdmin.aspx` calls `OrderProcessor` to continue order processing.

2. `OrderProcessor` detects the new order status and calls `PSShipOK`.

3. `PSShipOK` enters the shipment date in the database, advances the order status, and tells `OrderProcessor` to continue.

4. `OrderProcessor` detects the new order status and calls `PSFinalNotification`.

5. `PSFinalNotification` sends an email to the customer confirming that the order has been shipped and advances the order stage.

6. `OrderProcessor` terminates.

If anything goes wrong at any point in the pipeline processing, such as a credit card being declined, an email is sent to an administrator. This administrator then has all the information necessary to check what has happened, get in contact with the customer involved, and cancel or replace the order if necessary.

No point in this process is particularly complicated; it's just that quite a lot of code is required to put this into action!

Laying the Groundwork

Before you start building the components described previously, you must make a few modifications to the `JokePoint` database and Web Application.

The Audit Table

During order processing, one of the most important functions of the pipeline is to maintain an up-to-date audit trail. The implementation of this will involve adding records to a new database table called `Audit`. You need to create this table with fields as shown in Table 13-1.

Table 13-1. The Audit *Table*

Column Name	Column Type	Description
AuditID	int(4)	Primary key, also set as table identity
OrderID	int(4)	The ID of the order that the audit entry applies to
DateStamp	datetime(8)	The date and time that the audit entry was created
Message	varchar(512)	The text of the audit entry
MessageNumber	int(4)	An identifying number for the audit entry type

Entries will be added by OrderProcessor and by individual pipeline stages to indicate successes and failures. These can then be examined to see what has happened to an order, an important function when it comes to error checking.

The MessageNumber column is interesting because it allows you to associate specific messages with an identifying number. It would be possible to have another database table allowing you to match these message numbers with descriptions, although this isn't really necessary, because the scheme used for numbering (as you'll see later in the chapter) is, in itself, descriptive. In addition, the Message column already provides human-readable information.

The Orders Table

Currently the Orders table doesn't allow for as much information as you'll need to implement the order-processing pipeline. You need to add the new columns shown in Table 13-2 to the Orders table.

Table 13-2. The Orders Table

Column Name	Column Type	Description
Status	int(4)	The current status of the order, which is equivalent to what pipeline section the order has reached
CustomerID	int(4)	The ID of the customer that placed the order
AuthCode	varchar(50)	The authentication code used to complete the customer credit card transaction
Reference	varchar(50)	The unique reference code of the customer credit card transaction

The first two of these columns are self-explanatory, but the next two are related to credit card transactions, which we'll look at in Chapter 15.

Note that you won't be using some of the columns that already exist in the Orders table, such as Verified and Completed. This is because this information is now encapsulated in the Status column. The CustomerID column is used to link to the Customer table, rather than including customer information in CustomerName and the other customer-related fields.

NOTE   *To enable this database to be used with both the code in this section of the book and the code in the earlier part of this book, it's necessary to make these columns nullable, because earlier data won't supply values for them.*

The CreateCustomerOrder *Stored Procedure*

Currently, the CreateOrder stored procedure is used to add orders to the database:

```
CREATE PROCEDURE CreateOrder
(@CartID varchar(50))
AS

DECLARE @OrderID int
INSERT INTO Orders (DateCreated, Verified, Completed, Canceled)
VALUES (GETDATE(), 0, 0, 0)
SET @OrderID = @@IDENTITY

INSERT INTO OrderDetail
      (OrderID, ProductID, ProductName, Quantity, UnitCost)
SELECT
      @OrderID, Product.ProductID, Product.[Name],
      ShoppingCart.Quantity, Product.Price
FROM Product JOIN ShoppingCart
ON Product.ProductID = ShoppingCart.ProductID
WHERE ShoppingCart.CartID = @CartID

EXEC EmptyShoppingCart @CartID

SELECT @OrderID
GO
```

When an order is created, more data will be added to the database, so you need to use a different (although very similar) stored procedure, CreateCustomerOrder (the differences are shown in bold):

```
CREATE PROCEDURE CreateCustomerOrder
(@CartID varchar(50),
 @CustomerID int)
AS

DECLARE @OrderID int
INSERT INTO Orders (DateCreated, Verified, Completed, Canceled, CustomerID, Status)
VALUES (GETDATE(), 0, 0, 0, @CustomerID, 0)
SET @OrderID = @@IDENTITY

INSERT INTO OrderDetail
      (OrderID, ProductID, ProductName, Quantity, UnitCost)
SELECT
      @OrderID, Product.ProductID, Product.[Name],
      ShoppingCart.Quantity, Product.Price
FROM Product JOIN ShoppingCart
ON Product.ProductID = ShoppingCart.ProductID
WHERE ShoppingCart.CartID = @CartID
```

```
EXEC EmptyShoppingCart @CartID

SELECT @OrderID
GO
```

The two new bits here are as follows:

- Including a `CustomerID` value with the order

- Setting the `Status` column to 0, signifying that the order needs processing from the start of the order pipeline

Modifying JokePoint

To use the new stored procedure, you need to overload a method on the `ShoppingCart` class in the JokePoint application. Insert the following method into this class:

```
Public Function CreateOrder(ByVal customerID As Integer) As Integer
    ' Create the connection object
    Dim connection As New SqlConnection(connectionString)

    ' Create and initialize the command object
    Dim command As New SqlCommand("CreateCustomerOrder", connection)
    command.CommandType = CommandType.StoredProcedure

    ' Add input parameters and supply values for them
    command.Parameters.Add("@CartID", SqlDbType.VarChar, 50)
    command.Parameters("@CartID").Value = shoppingCartId
    command.Parameters.Add("@CustomerID", SqlDbType.Int, 4)
    command.Parameters("@CustomerID").Value = customerID

    ' Save the value that needs to be returned to a variable
    Dim orderId As Integer
    connection.Open()
    orderId = Convert.ToInt32(command.ExecuteScalar())

    ' Close the connection
    connection.Close()

    ' Return the saved value
    Return orderId
End Function
```

This is simply a new overload for the `CreateOrder` method used earlier in the book. You'll use this version later, when you modify the `Checkout.aspx` page to use the order-processing pipeline.

Defining Utility Classes

The first classes to consider are the OrderProcessorException exception class and the utility classes for database objects: Customer, OrderDetail, and OrderDetails. We're looking at these first because the other classes use them, so having the types defined will make entering the code for later classes easier.

Exercise: CommerceLib ***Utility Classes***

1. Create a new Class Library project called CommerceLib in the directory C:\BegECommerce\Chapter13, and remove the Class1.vb class.

2. Add a reference to the SecurityLib assembly created in the last chapter.

3. Add a new class called OrderProcessorException with code as follows:

```
Public Class OrderProcessorException
    Inherits ApplicationException

    Public Sub New(ByVal message As String, ByVal sourceStage As Integer)
        MyBase.New(message)
        _sourceStage = sourceStage
    End Sub

    Private _sourceStage As Integer

    Public ReadOnly Property SourceStage() As Integer
        Get
            Return _sourceStage
        End Get
    End Property
End Class
```

4. Add a new class called Customer with code as follows:

```
Imports SecurityLib
Imports System.Text
Imports System.Data.SqlClient

Public Class Customer
    Public CustomerID As Integer
    Public Name As String
    Public Email As String
    Public CreditCard As SecureCard
    Public Address1 As String
    Public Address2 As String
    Public City As String
    Public Region As String
    Public PostalCode As String
```

```
            Public Country As String
            Public Phone As String
            Public AddressAsString As String

            Public Sub New(ByVal reader As SqlDataReader)
                ' check for customer
                If reader.Read = False Then
                    Throw New OrderProcessorException( _
                        "Unable to obtain customer information.", 100)
                End If

                ' initialize data
                CustomerID = reader("CustomerID")
                Name = reader("Name")
                Email = reader("Email")
                Address1 = reader("Address1")
                Address2 = reader("Address2")
                City = reader("City")
                Region = reader("Region")
                PostalCode = reader("PostalCode")
                Country = reader("Country")
                Phone = reader("Phone")

                ' get credit card details
                Try
                    CreditCard = New SecureCard(reader("CreditCard"))
                Catch
                    Throw New OrderProcessorException( _
                        "Unable to retrieve credit card details.", 100)
                End Try

                ' construct address string
                Dim builder As StringBuilder = New StringBuilder()
                builder.Append(Name)
                builder.Append(Chr(10))
                builder.Append(Address1)
                builder.Append(Chr(10))
                If Address2 <> "" Then
                    builder.Append(Address2)
                    builder.Append(Chr(10))
                End If
                builder.Append(City)
                builder.Append(Chr(10))
                builder.Append(Region)
                builder.Append(Chr(10))
                builder.Append(PostalCode)
                builder.Append(Chr(10))
                builder.Append(Country)
                AddressAsString = builder.ToString()
            End Sub
        End Class
```

5. Add a new class called `OrderDetail` with code as follows:

```vbnet
Imports System.Text

Public Class OrderDetail
    Public ProductID As String
    Public ProductName As String
    Public Quantity As Double
    Public UnitCost As Double
    Public ItemAsString As String
    Public Cost As Double

    Public Sub New(ByVal newProductID As String, _
                   ByVal newProductName As String, _
                   ByVal newQuantity As Double, _
                   ByVal newUnitCost As Double)
        ' initialize data
        ProductID = newProductID
        ProductName = newProductName
        Quantity = newQuantity
        UnitCost = newUnitCost
        Cost = UnitCost * Quantity

        ' construct item string for use in emails etc.
        Dim builder As StringBuilder = New StringBuilder()
        builder.Append(Quantity.ToString())
        builder.Append(" ")
        builder.Append(ProductName)
        builder.Append(", $")
        builder.Append(UnitCost.ToString())
        builder.Append(" each, total cost $")
        builder.Append(Cost.ToString())
        ItemAsString = builder.ToString()
    End Sub
End Class
```

6. Add a new class called `OrderDetails` with code as follows:

```vbnet
Imports System.Collections
Imports System.Text
Imports System.Data.SqlClient

Public Class OrderDetails
    Inherits CollectionBase

    Public TotalCost As Double = 0
    Public ListAsString As String

    Public Sub New(ByVal reader As SqlDataReader)
        ' check for details
```

```
      If reader.Read = False Then
          Throw New OrderProcessorException( _
              "Unable to obtain order details.", 100)
      End If
      ' construct string for item list and calculate total cost
      Dim builder As StringBuilder = New StringBuilder()
      Dim newOrderDetail As OrderDetail
      Dim productsRemaining As Boolean = True
      While productsRemaining
          newOrderDetail = _
              New OrderDetail(reader("ProductID"), reader("ProductName"), _
                              Convert.ToDouble(reader("Quantity")), _
                              Convert.ToDouble(reader("UnitCost")))
          List.Add(newOrderDetail)
          builder.Append(newOrderDetail.ItemAsString)
          TotalCost += newOrderDetail.Cost
          builder.Append(Chr(10))
          productsRemaining = reader.Read()
      End While
      builder.Append(Chr(10))
      builder.Append("Total order cost: $")
      builder.Append(TotalCost.ToString())
      ListAsString = builder.ToString()
    End Sub

    Default Public Property Item(ByVal index As Integer) As OrderDetail
        Get
            Return CType(List(index), OrderDetail)
        End Get
        Set(ByVal Value As OrderDetail)
            List(index) = Value
        End Set
    End Property
End Class
```

7. Compile the preceding code, and add a new console application project to the solution to test the code, called CommerceLibTest.

8. Add references to CommerceLib and SecurityLib to CommerceLibTest, and make it the startup project.

9. Add the following code to Module1.vb, replacing the values for customerID and orderID with IDs of existing items in the JokePoint database, and changing the connection string to the one you've been using in previous chapters (if you've forgotten what it is, check out web.config for the JokePoint application):

```
Imports System.Data.SqlClient
Imports CommerceLib

Module Module1

    Sub Main()
        Dim customerID As Integer = 5
        Dim orderID As Integer = 25
        Dim Connection As SqlConnection = _
            New SqlConnection( _
                "server=(local);Integrated Security=SSPI;database=JokePoint")

        Dim customerCommand As SqlCommand = _
            New SqlCommand("GetCustomer", Connection)
        customerCommand.CommandType = CommandType.StoredProcedure
        customerCommand.Parameters.Add("@CustomerID", customerID)
        Connection.Open()
        Dim customerObj As Customer = _
            New Customer(customerCommand.ExecuteReader)
        Connection.Close()
        Console.WriteLine("Customer found. Address:")
        Console.WriteLine(customerObj.AddressAsString)
        Console.WriteLine("Customer credit card number: {0}", _
                            customerObj.CreditCard.CardNumberX)
        Console.WriteLine()

        Dim orderCommand As SqlCommand = _
            New SqlCommand("GetOrderDetails", Connection)
        orderCommand.CommandType = CommandType.StoredProcedure
        orderCommand.Parameters.Add("@OrderID", orderID)
        Connection.Open()
        Dim orderObj As OrderDetails = _
            New OrderDetails(orderCommand.ExecuteReader)
        Connection.Close()
        Console.WriteLine("Order found. Details:")
        Console.WriteLine(orderObj.ListAsString)
        Console.WriteLine()
        Console.WriteLine("List of item names:")
        Dim item As OrderDetail
        For Each item In orderObj
            Console.WriteLine(item.ProductName)
        Next
    End Sub

End Module
```

10. Execute the application. The result is shown in Figure 13-4.

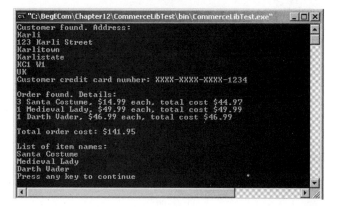

Figure 13-4: CommerceLibTest *result*

How It Works: CommerceLib *Utility Classes*

You've added quite a lot of code here, but much of it is similar to code you've already seen. First, the OrderProcessorException class is simply derived from System.Exception and adds the Integer property SourceStage. This will be used by pipeline stages to identify the source of the exception. A value of 100 (used in the Customer and OrderDetails classes) is arbitrarily chosen as meaning "no stage," because the numbering of pipeline sections starts with 0. No code in the definition of this exception requires further analysis.

The Customer class is a wrapper around a row of data from the Customer table. To initialize a Customer object, you pass an SqlDataReader to the class constructor, where this SqlReader contains all the fields in the Customer table. The test console application code uses the GetCustomer stored procedure from the last chapter to achieve this.

The constructor starts by checking for customer data in the SqlReader, and throws an exception if no data row is encountered:

```
If reader.Read = False Then
    Throw New OrderProcessorException( _
        "Unable to obtain customer information.", 100)
End If
```

Next it reads most of the data from the Customer table row into public fields, for example:

```
CustomerID = reader("CustomerID")
```

When it comes to credit card data, however, you need to decrypt the data—hence the reference to the SecurityLib assembly. If an error occurs during decryption, an exception is thrown:

```
Try
    CreditCard = New SecureCard(reader("CreditCard"))
Catch
    Throw New OrderProcessorException( _
        "Unable to retrieve credit card details.", 100)
End Try
```

The `Customer` class has one extra public field: `AddressAsString`. This provides direct access to a formatted string representing the address of the customer—which will be very useful later on when you need to notify your supplier of the address to send an order to! This string is built up from the data already stored using a `StringBuilder` object to maximize performance, which is why you have the reference to the `System.Text` namespace. The console application used to test this class displays the value of this field to show typical output.

The `OrderDetails` class is slightly more complicated because it's actually a strongly typed collection of individual `OrderDetail` objects. For this reason, we'll look at `OrderDetail` first.

`OrderDetail` is fairly standard looking class that simply groups the data for an order item in one place. The constructor for this class is simpler than that of `Customer`, because it simply takes the values to use for this data. As with `Customer`, however, this class also exposes data that is built from order item properties rather than being part of them. There are two such public fields this time, `Cost` (the product of the `Quantity` and `UnitCost` for the item), and `ItemAsString` (which is a formatted string suitable for displaying item properties in a readable way). The code for all this won't teach you anything new, so we won't examine it in any more depth here.

`OrderDetails` inherits from the `CollectionBase` class in the `System.Collections` namespace, which is a great starting point for strongly typed collection classes. If you haven't come across this class before, it should be noted that it has a protected member called `List` that stores a list of objects. This member has methods including `Add`, to add an object to a list, that we'll make use of here. It also has an indexer, handy for iterating through items where appropriate.

The constructor for the `OrderDetails` class starts in a similar way to that of `Customer`, because it checks for existing data before progressing:

```
If reader.Read = False Then
    Throw New OrderProcessorException("Unable to obtain order details.", 100)
End If
```

The remainder of the constructor reads each item from the `SqlReader`, which contains a list of records from the `OrderDetails` table. The constructor adds the items found in the `SqlReader` to the `List` member as `OrderDetail` objects, and builds another handy public field: `ListAsString`. This time, the public field is a combination of the `ItemAsString` fields of each `OrderDetail` stored and a "Total cost" string. This will come in handy when confirming orders with customers, and passing lists of items to suppliers. The code to achieve this is as follows:

```
Dim builder As StringBuilder = New StringBuilder()
Dim newOrderDetail As OrderDetail
Dim productsRemaining As Boolean = True
While productsRemaining
    newOrderDetail = _
        New OrderDetail(reader("ProductID"), reader("ProductName"), _
                        Convert.ToDouble(reader("Quantity")), _
                        Convert.ToDouble(reader("UnitCost")))
    List.Add(newOrderDetail)
    builder.Append(newOrderDetail.ItemAsString)
    TotalCost += newOrderDetail.Cost
    builder.Append(Chr(10))
    productsRemaining = reader.Read()
End While
builder.Append(Chr(10))
builder.Append("Total order cost: $")
builder.Append(TotalCost.ToString())
ListAsString = builder.ToString()
```

This code uses a StringBuilder like the other string-creating code in the classes you've seen, which is why this class also has a reference to the System.Text namespace. The code consists mainly of a single While loop, which executes until no more items are found in the SqlReader; that is, until the reader.Read method returns False.

The OrderDetails class also includes an indexer. This is implemented as the default public property Item, in standard VB .NET fashion, which will allow you to use the handy For Each syntax to access the OrderDetail objects contained in the collection (you do this in CommerceLibTest):

```
Default Public Property Item(ByVal index As Integer) As OrderDetail
    Get
        Return CType(List(index), OrderDetail)
    End Get
    Set(ByVal Value As OrderDetail)
        List(index) = Value
    End Set
End Property
```

Note that you must change the type of the objects returned to OrderDetail—List contains Object items.

The console application uses the GetOrderDetails stored procedure used in earlier chapters to initialize an instance of OrderDetails. This stored procedure simply gets all the rows in the OrderDetails table that have a specific OrderID value, supplied as a parameter. This gets all the information required for the OrderDetails constructor to carry out its data extraction.

The code in the console application tests all of the data classes added by reading data in and displaying a few properties. It also uses the indexer of OrderDetails to iterate through the OrderDetail objects it contains. If you want to make sure the OrderProcessorException class is working, simply choose a value for customerID or orderID that doesn't have associated data in the database—an OrderProcessorException exception will be thrown!

The OrderProcessor Class

As is probably apparent now, the OrderProcessor class (which is the class responsible for moving an order through the pipeline) will contain quite a bit of code. However, you can start simply, and build up additional functionality as needed. To start with, you'll create a version of the OrderProcessor class with the following functionality:

- Includes full configuration, whereby information such as the connection string to use, the mail server to send mail via, the required email addresses, and so on is loaded into the order processor when it is instantiated

- Dynamically selects a pipeline section supporting IPipelineSection

- Adds basic auditing data

- Gives access to the current order details

- Gives access to the customer for the current order

- Gives access to administrator mailing

- Mails the administrator in case of error

The configuration is carried out via a structure called OrderProcessorConfiguration. A structure is used rather than a class because the data required consists of simple values. This is a somewhat subtle distinction, but is the correct choice here.

You'll also create a single pipeline section, PSDummy, which uses some of this functionality.

To implement the functionality described in the previous list, you'll also need to add three new stored procedures:

- *GetOrderStatus*: Returns the status of an order with the given order ID

- *AddAudit*: Adds an entry to the Audit table

- *GetCustomerByOrderID*: Returns customer data associated with an order with a given order ID

The code for these stored procedures appears in the next section.

Exercise: The Basic OrderProcessor *Class*

1. Add a new structure to the CommerceLib project called
   OrderProcessorConfiguration (to create a structure, merely select Add New
   Item ➤ Add Class, renaming the class and deleting the contents before
   replacing them with the following):

```
' Configuration details for order processor
Public Structure OrderProcessorConfiguration
   Public ConnectionString As String
   Public MailServer As String
   Public AdminEmail As String
   Public CustomerServiceEmail As String
   Public OrderProcessorEmail As String
   Public SupplierEmail As String

   Public Sub New(ByVal newConnectionString As String, _
                  ByVal newMailServer As String, _
                  ByVal newAdminEmail As String, _
                  ByVal newCustomerServiceEmail As String, _
                  ByVal newOrderProcessorEmail As String, _
                  ByVal newSupplierEmail As String)
      ConnectionString = newConnectionString
      MailServer = newMailServer
      AdminEmail = newAdminEmail
      CustomerServiceEmail = newCustomerServiceEmail
      OrderProcessorEmail = newOrderProcessorEmail
      SupplierEmail = newSupplierEmail
   End Sub
End Structure
```

2. Add three new stored procedures to the JokePoint database.

   First procedure:

```
CREATE PROCEDURE GetOrderStatus
(@OrderID int)
AS

SELECT Status
FROM Orders
WHERE OrderID = @OrderID
GO
```

   Second procedure:

```
CREATE PROCEDURE AddAudit
(@OrderID int,
 @Message nvarchar(512),
 @MessageNumber int)
AS
```

```
INSERT INTO Audit (OrderID, DateStamp, Message, MessageNumber)
VALUES (@OrderID, GetDate(), @Message, @MessageNumber)
GO
```

Third procedure:

```
CREATE PROCEDURE GetCustomerByOrderID
(@OrderID int)
AS

SELECT Customer.CustomerID, Customer.[Name], Customer.Email,
 Customer.[Password], Customer.CreditCard, Customer.Address1,
 Customer.Address2, Customer.City, Customer.Region,
 Customer.PostalCode, Customer.Country, Customer.Phone
FROM Customer INNER JOIN Orders
ON Customer.CustomerID = Orders.CustomerID
WHERE Orders.OrderID = @OrderID
GO
```

3. Add a new class to the `CommerceLib` project called `OrderProcessor` with code as follows:

 TIP *Many people have had trouble using the* `System.Web.Mail`
namespace, specifically because the error `Could not create`
`CDO.Message` *object occurs, particularly on W2K systems.*

*The VS7 installation tries to replace the cdosys.dll file that the
namespace depends upon with a file called cdoex.dll, which always
fails. In the process, however, cdosys.dll is unregistered, and the infa-
mous error message will then haunt you forever after. If this happens,
simply typing in regsvr32 cdosys.dll at a command prompt will solve
the problem.*

*Also, unless the SMTP service on the developer's machine is set to
accept relays from itself (in the Access tab of the SMTP server's IIS properties window, click the Relay button and grant access to 127.0.0.1, or
localhost), the same error will occur (and it isn't set to accept relays
from itself by default).*

*In addition to these, you might have to add System.Web.dll as
a reference to the project, depending upon your installation.*

```
Imports System.Data.SqlClient
Imports System.Web.Mail

' Main class, used to obtain order information,
' run pipeline sections, audit orders, etc.
Public Class OrderProcessor
    Friend OrderID As Integer
    Friend OrderStatus As Integer
    Friend Connection As SqlConnection
    Friend Configuration As OrderProcessorConfiguration
```

```vb
Friend CurrentPipelineSection As IPipelineSection
Friend ContinueNow As Boolean
Private _currentCustomer As Customer
Private _currentOrderDetails As OrderDetails

Public Sub Process(ByVal newOrderID As Integer, _
      ByVal newConfiguration As OrderProcessorConfiguration)
    ' set order ID
    OrderID = newOrderID

    ' configure processor
    Configuration = newConfiguration
    ContinueNow = True

    ' open connection, to be shared by all data access code
    Connection = New SqlConnection(Configuration.ConnectionString)
    Connection.Open()

    ' log start of execution
    AddAudit("Order Processor started.", 10000)

    ' obtain status of order
    Dim command As SqlCommand = _
       New SqlCommand("GetOrderStatus", Connection)
    command.CommandType = CommandType.StoredProcedure
    command.Parameters.Add("@OrderID", OrderID)
    OrderStatus = CType(command.ExecuteScalar(), Integer)

    ' process pipeline section
    Try
       While ContinueNow
          ContinueNow = False
          GetCurrentPipelineSection()
          CurrentPipelineSection.Process(Me)
       End While
    Catch e As OrderProcessorException
      MailAdmin("Order Processing error occured.", _
         e.Message, e.SourceStage)
      AddAudit("Order Processing error occured.", 10002)
      Throw New OrderProcessorException( _
         "Error occured, order aborted. " _
       & "Details mailed to administrator.", 100)
    Catch e As Exception
      MailAdmin("Order Processing error occured.", e.Message, 100)
      AddAudit("Order Processing error occured.", 10002)
      Throw New OrderProcessorException( _
      "Unknown error, order aborted. " _
       & "Details mailed to administrator.", 100)
    Finally
       AddAudit("Order Processor finished.", 10001)
       Connection.Close()
    End Try
End Sub
```

```vbnet
Private Function GetCurrentPipelineSection() As IPipelineSection
    ' select pipeline section to execute based on order status
    ' for now just provide a dummy
    CurrentPipelineSection = New PSDummy()
End Function


Friend Sub MailAdmin(ByVal subject As String, _
        ByVal message As String, _
        ByVal sourceStage As Integer)
    ' Send mail to administrator
    SmtpMail.SmtpServer = Configuration.MailServer
    Dim notificationMail As MailMessage = New MailMessage()
    notificationMail.To = Configuration.AdminEmail
    notificationMail.From = Configuration.OrderProcessorEmail
    notificationMail.Subject = subject
    notificationMail.Body = "Message: " & message & Chr(10) _
        & "Source: " _
        & sourceStage.ToString() & Chr(10) & "Order ID: " _
        & OrderID.ToString()
    SmtpMail.Send(notificationMail)
End Sub


Friend Sub AddAudit(ByVal message As String, _
        ByVal messageNumber As Integer)
    ' add audit to database
    Dim command As SqlCommand = New SqlCommand("AddAudit", Connection)
    command.CommandType = CommandType.StoredProcedure
    command.Parameters.Add("@OrderID", OrderID)
    command.Parameters.Add("@Message", message)
    command.Parameters.Add("@MessageNumber", messageNumber)
    command.ExecuteNonQuery()
End Sub


Friend ReadOnly Property CurrentCustomer() As Customer
    Get
        If _currentCustomer Is Nothing Then
            ' Use ID of order to obtain customer information
            Dim command As SqlCommand = _
                New SqlCommand("GetCustomerByOrderID", Connection)
            command.CommandType = CommandType.StoredProcedure
            command.Parameters.Add("@OrderID", OrderID)
            Dim reader As SqlDataReader = command.ExecuteReader()
            Try
                _currentCustomer = New Customer(reader)
            Catch
                Throw
            Finally
                reader.Close()
            End Try
        End If
        Return _currentCustomer
    End Get
End Property
```

```
Friend ReadOnly Property CurrentOrderDetails() As OrderDetails
    Get
        If _currentOrderDetails Is Nothing Then
            ' Get list of items in order
            Dim command As SqlCommand = _
                New SqlCommand("GetOrderDetails", Connection)
            command.CommandType = CommandType.StoredProcedure
            command.Parameters.Add("@OrderID", OrderID)
            Dim reader As SqlDataReader = command.ExecuteReader()
            Try
                _currentOrderDetails = New OrderDetails(reader)
            Catch
                Throw
            Finally
                reader.Close()
            End Try
        End If
        Return _currentOrderDetails
    End Get
End Property
End Class
```

4. Add a new interface to the `CommerceLib` project called `IPipelineSection` with code as follows:

```
Public Interface IPipelineSection
    Sub Process(ByVal processor As OrderProcessor)
End Interface
```

5. Add a new class to the `CommerceLib` project called `PSDummy` with code as follows:

```
Public Class PSDummy
    Implements IPipelineSection

    Public Sub Process(ByVal processor As OrderProcessor) _
        Implements IPipelineSection.Process

        processor.AddAudit("PSDoNothing started.", 99999)
        processor.AddAudit("Customer: " _
            & processor.CurrentCustomer.Name, 99999)
        processor.AddAudit("First item in order: " _
            & processor.CurrentOrderDetails(0).ItemAsString, 99999)
        processor.MailAdmin("Test.", "Test mail from PSDummy.", 99999)
        processor.AddAudit("PSDoNothing finished.", 99999)
    End Sub
End Class
```

6. Modify the code in `Module1` in the `CommerceLibTest` project as follows, customizing the data with your own SMTP server for `MailServer`, your own email addresses for `AdminEMail` and `SupplierEMail`, and an `OrderID` that exists in the database:

```
Sub Main()
    Dim configuration As OrderProcessorConfiguration = _
        New OrderProcessorConfiguration( _
            "server=(local);Integrated Security=SSPI; " _
            & "database=JokePoint", _
            "MailServer", _
            "AdminEMail", _
            "customerservice@JokePoint.com", _
            "orderprocessor@JokePoint.com", _
            "SupplierEMail")
    Dim processor As New OrderProcessor()
' processor.Process(ByVal orderID As Integer, ByVal configuration As
' OrderProcessorConfiguration)
    processor.Process(1, configuration)
End Sub
```

7. If necessary, modify the Status field in the JokePoint database for Orders for the order selected previously, giving it a value of 0 to move it back to the start of the pipeline.

8. Modify the CustomerID filed in the JokePoint database for the order selected previously, giving it a value for a customer in the Customers table (necessary because you haven't yet modified Checkout.aspx to place orders that include this information).

9. Execute the application.

10. Check your inbox for new mail. An example of this is shown in Figure 13-5.

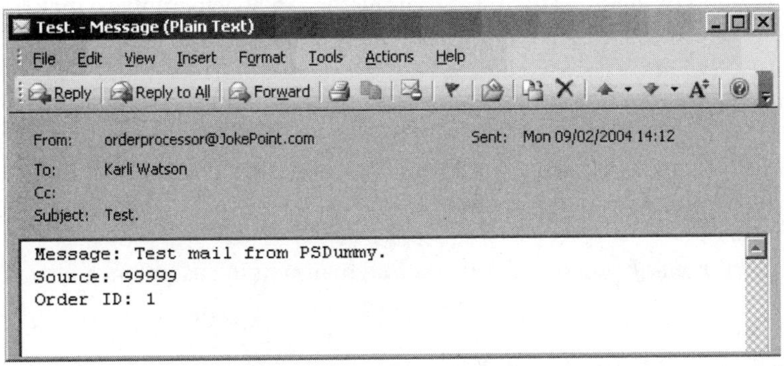

Figure 13-5: Email from PSDummy

11. Examine the `Audit` table in the database to see the new entries:

AuditID	OrderID	DateStamp	Message	MessageNumber
1	1	09/02/2004 14:11:47	Order Processor started.	10000
2	1	09/02/2004 14:11:47	PSDoNothing started.	99999
3	1	09/02/2004 14:11:47	Customer: Karli	99999
4	1	09/02/2004 14:11:47	First item in order: 1 Santa Costume, $14.99 each, total cost $14.99	99999
5	1	09/02/2004 14:11:48	PSDoNothing finished.	99999
6	1	09/02/2004 14:11:48	Order Processor finished.	10001

Figure 13-6: Audit table entries from PSDummy

How It Works: The Basic OrderProcessor *Class*

The first code added in the previous exercise was for the `OrderProcessorConfiguration` structure. This is a simple structure for grouping together the various pieces of information required to allow the `OrderProcessor` class to function. There are alternatives to this, such as storing this data in the Registry, but this method works fine and makes your code simple. It also allows the same component library to be used in multiple e-commerce applications, because it's configured dynamically. Later you'll see how to store this data in the `web.config` file of the JokePoint application before retrieving it when an order is placed.

The information stored in the `OrderProcessorConfiguration` structure, and its use, is as follows:

- *Connection string*: Used in all database communications.

- *Mail server*: The name of the SMTP server used to send email messages. This is required by the classes in the `System.Web.Mail` namespace, which is used as a simple method of sending email. This parameter can be left empty so that the local server is used, which is enough in many situations.

- *Administrator email*: The email address to send mail to if something goes wrong during order processing. This will include messages in the case of lack of funds available, allowing the administrator to take corrective action, and maybe contact the customer directly.

- *Customer server email*: The return address for email sent to customers and suppliers.

- *Order processor email*: The return address for email sent to the administrator.

- *Supplier email*: The address for email sent to the supplier.

For demonstration purposes, we set the administrator and supplier email addresses to our own email address, which should also be the address of the customer used to generate test orders. That way we can check that everything is working properly before sending mail to the outside world.

Next, we come to the stored procedures mentioned before the code. These all involve simple code and we don't need to go into any more detail.

It is, however, worth stepping through all of the code for the OrderProcessor class. To start with, you have the Imports statements for the namespaces required for database access and email functionality:

```
Imports System.Data.SqlClient
Imports System.Web.Mail
```

Following on from this, you have the class definition itself, starting with field definitions:

```
' Main class, used to obtain order information, run pipeline sections, audit
' orders, etc.
Public Class OrderProcessor
    Friend OrderID As Integer
    Friend OrderStatus As Integer
    Friend Connection As SqlConnection
    Friend Configuration As OrderProcessorConfiguration
    Friend CurrentPipelineSection As IPipelineSection
    Friend ContinueNow As Boolean = True
    Private _currentCustomer As Customer
    Private _currentOrderDetails As OrderDetails
```

Note that many of these have the Friend access modifier. This is a quick way of enabling access only to the other classes in the project, which includes all the pipeline section classes. These are all simple variables, so there is no real need to define full property access, but you do want to prevent outside code from accessing this data. You can rely on the pipeline sections not to do anything they shouldn't do with this data, because we're writing them ourselves!

The two Private members are instances of the Customer and OrderDetails utility classes examined earlier. These are exposed as properties, and you'll see why this is necessary a little later.

The main body of the OrderProcessor class is the Process method, which will be called by the Checkout.aspx and OrderAdmin.aspx pages to process an order. The order to be processed is indicated by its ID, and the configuration to use is set via an OrderProcessorConfiguration parameter:

```
    Public Sub Process(ByVal newOrderID As Integer, _
                    ByVal newConfiguration As OrderProcessorConfiguration)
        ' set order ID
        OrderID = newOrderID

        ' configure processor
        Configuration = newConfiguration
        ContinueNow = True
```

You'll see how ContinueNow fits in shortly.

To simplify the code a little, you provide a single connection to the database, used by the OrderProcessor component and all pipeline sections. Because the order processor doesn't take long to function and isn't likely to be called as often as, say, a web page listing items in a department, this makes good sense. Remember that the .NET Framework carries out connection pooling automatically. Doing things this way means that you don't have to take a connection from the pool every time the database is accessed—you just do it once, and then use it until you're finished. This will prevent other processes emptying the connection pool when you're halfway through processing, which might cause the OrderProcessor to pause for longer than you'd like. In practice, perhaps this isn't as crucial as all that, but it also has the advantage of shortening the code somewhat, because you won't be creating new connections and calling Open and Close all the time.

```
' open connection, to be shared by all data access code
Connection = New SqlConnection(Configuration.ConnectionString)
Connection.Open()
```

Here you simply open the connection using the connection string supplied in the configuration for the order processor.

Next, you use the AddAudit method (which we'll come to shortly) to add an audit entry indicating that the OrderProcessor has started:

```
' log start of execution
AddAudit("Order Processor started.", 10000)
```

 NOTE 10000 *is the message number to store for the audit entry—we'll look at these codes in more detail shortly.*

As detailed earlier, the processing of an order depends on its status, so the first thing to do is to get the status of the order using the new GetOrderStatus stored procedure:

```
' obtain status of order
Dim command As SqlCommand = New SqlCommand("GetOrderStatus", Connection)
command.CommandType = CommandType.StoredProcedure
command.Parameters.Add("@OrderID", OrderID)
OrderStatus = CType(command.ExecuteScalar(), Integer)
```

The status is stored in the OrderStatus field you saw earlier.

Next we come to the order processing itself. The model used here checks the Boolean ContinueNow field before processing a pipeline section. This allows sections to specify either that processing should continue when they're finished with the current task (by setting ContinueNow to True) or that processing should pause (by setting ContinueNow to False). This is necessary because you need to wait for external input at certain points along the pipeline, such as checking whether stock is available.

The pipeline section to process is selected by the private `GetCurrentPipelineSection` method, which will eventually select a section based on the status of the order, but currently just has the job of setting the `CurrentPipelineSection` field to an instance of `PSDummy`:

```
Private Function GetCurrentPipelineSection() As IPipelineSection
    ' select pipeline section to execute based on order status
    ' for now just provide a dummy
    CurrentPipelineSection = New PSDummy()
End Function
```

Back to `Process`, you see this method being called in a `Try` block:

```
' process pipeline section
Try
    While ContinueNow
        ContinueNow = False
        GetCurrentPipelineSection()
```

Note that `ContinueNow` is set to `False` in the `While` loop—the default behavior is to stop after each pipeline section.

After you have a pipeline section, you need to process it. All sections support the simple `IPipelineSection` interface, defined as follows:

```
Public Interface IPipelineSection
    Sub Process(ByVal processor As OrderProcessor)
End Interface
```

All pipeline sections will use a `Process` method to perform their work, and this method requires an `OrderProcessor` reference. This is because the pipeline sections need access to the `Friend` fields, methods, and properties exposed by the order processor.

The last part of the `While` loop in `OrderProcessor` calls this method:

```
        CurrentPipelineSection.Process(Me)
    End While
```

We'll come back to the `Process` method in `PSDummy` shortly.

The last part of the `Process` method in `OrderProcessor` involves catching exceptions, which might be `OrderProcessorException` instances or other exception types. In either case, you send an email to the administrator using the `MailAdmin` method (we'll cover this in a little while), add an audit entry, and throw a new `OrderProcessorException` that can be caught by users of the `OrderProcessor` class:

```
Catch e As OrderProcessorException
    MailAdmin("Order Processing error occured.", e.Message, e.SourceStage)
    AddAudit("Order Processing error occured.", 10002)
    Throw New OrderProcessorException( _
  "Error occured, order aborted. Details mailed to administrator.", 100)
Catch e As Exception
    MailAdmin("Order Processing error occured.", e.Message, 100)
```

```
    AddAudit("Order Processing error occured.", 10002)
    Throw New OrderProcessorException( _
    "Unknown error, order aborted. Details mailed to administrator.", 100)
```

Regardless of whether processing is successful, you add a final audit entry saying that the processing has completed, and close the shared connection:

```
  Finally
    AddAudit("Order Processor finished.", 10001)
    Connection.Close()
  End Try
End Sub
```

Next, the MailAdmin method simply takes a subject and message for the basic email properties, and appends an identifier for the pipeline stage that sent the mail and the ID of the order being processed. Note that the calls to this method from the Process method shown previously used a pipeline stage ID of 100, arbitrarily chosen as meaning "no pipeline stage" as mentioned earlier in the chapter. Even if you add new pipeline sections to the order pipeline, you're unlikely to have a hundred of them, so this is a safe choice!

```
Friend Sub MailAdmin(ByVal subject As String, ByVal message As String, _
                     ByVal sourceStage As Integer)
  ' Send mail to administrator
  SmtpMail.SmtpServer = Configuration.MailServer
  Dim notificationMail As MailMessage = New MailMessage()
  notificationMail.To = Configuration.AdminEmail
  notificationMail.From = Configuration.OrderProcessorEmail
  notificationMail.Subject = subject
  notificationMail.Body = "Message: " & message & Chr(10) & "Source: " _
                          & sourceStage.ToString() & Chr(10) & "Order ID: " _
                          & OrderID.ToString()
  SmtpMail.Send(notificationMail)
End Sub
```

This emailing code is the standard .NET way of sending email; we won't go into more details here, other than to point out that the mail server used is identified via the appropriate entry in the configuration of the order processor.

The AddAudit method simply calls the AddAudit stored procedure shown earlier:

```
Friend Sub AddAudit(ByVal message As String, ByVal messageNumber As Integer)
  ' add audit to database
  Dim command As SqlCommand = New SqlCommand("AddAudit", Connection)
  command.CommandType = CommandType.StoredProcedure
  command.Parameters.Add("@OrderID", OrderID)
  command.Parameters.Add("@Message", message)
  command.Parameters.Add("@MessageNumber", messageNumber)
  command.ExecuteNonQuery()
End Sub
```

At this point, it's worth examining the message number scheme chosen for order-processing audits. In all cases, the audit message number will be a five-digit number. The first digit of this number will either be 1 in the case of an audit being added by OrderProcessor, or 2 if the audit is added by a pipeline section. The next two digits are used for the pipeline stage that added the audit (which maps directly to the status of the order when the audit was added). The final two digits uniquely identify the message within this scope. For example, so far you've seen the following message numbers:

- *10000*: Order processor started.

- *10001*: Order processor finished.

- *10002*: Order processor error occurred.

Later you'll see a lot of these that start with 2, as you get on to pipeline sections, and include the necessary information for identifying the pipeline section as noted previously. Hopefully you'll agree that this scheme allows for plenty of flexibility, although you can, of course, use whatever numbers you see fit. As a final note, numbers ending in 00 and 01 are used for starting and finishing messages for both the order processor and pipeline stages, while 02 and above are for other messages. There is no real reason for this apart from con-sistency between the components.

The last part of the OrderProcessor class is the code for the CurrentCustomer and CurrentOrderDetails properties. Earlier, we promised to explain why the fields for this information were Private and required property accessors, rather than simply being Friend like the other fields. The reason is to cut back on database access. Not every pipeline stage will require this information, and it makes little sense to access it if it isn't required. Instead, both these properties obtain their data only when needed. After they have been called, their data is stored in the private fields, and there is no need to repeat database access.

 NOTE *This method of only getting information when needed is often known as **lazy initialization**, which is one of those bits of computer programming terminology that always makes me grin.*

The code for both properties is simple, using the new GetCustomerByOrderID for CurrentCustomer, and the GetOrderDetails stored procedure from earlier in the chapter in CurrentOrderDetails:

```
Friend ReadOnly Property CurrentCustomer() As Customer
    Get
        If _currentCustomer Is Nothing Then
            ' Use ID of order to obtain customer information
            Dim command As SqlCommand = _
                New SqlCommand("GetCustomerByOrderID", Connection)
            command.CommandType = CommandType.StoredProcedure
```

```
                command.Parameters.Add("@OrderID", OrderID)
                Dim reader As SqlDataReader = command.ExecuteReader()
                Try
                    _currentCustomer = New Customer(reader)
                Catch
                    Throw
                Finally
                    reader.Close()
                End Try
            End If
            Return _currentCustomer
        End Get
    End Property

    Friend ReadOnly Property CurrentOrderDetails() As OrderDetails
        Get
            If _currentOrderDetails Is Nothing Then
                ' Get list of items in order
                Dim command As SqlCommand = _
                    New SqlCommand("GetOrderDetails", Connection)
                command.CommandType = CommandType.StoredProcedure
                command.Parameters.Add("@OrderID", OrderID)
                Dim reader As SqlDataReader = command.ExecuteReader()
                Try
                    _currentOrderDetails = New OrderDetails(reader)
                Catch
                    Throw
                Finally
                    reader.Close()
                End Try
            End If
            Return _currentOrderDetails
        End Get
    End Property
End Class
```

One point to note here is the unusual way that these properties use exception handling. The reason for this is that having an open SqlReader object completely blocks your database connection. Until you close the SqlReader for either of these properties, you can't do anything using this connection—including adding audit entries! To get around this, you use an exception handling Finally block to ensure that the SqlReaders are closed before the property finishes processing, regardless of whether the data reading is successful. If an exception is thrown, you simply rethrow it—the code using the property is given the responsibility of dealing with it.

The PSDummy class that is used in this skeleton processor performs some basic functions to check that things are working correctly:

```
Public Class PSDummy
    Implements IPipelineSection

    Public Sub Process(ByVal processor As OrderProcessor) _
        Implements IPipelineSection.Process
```

```
            processor.AddAudit("PSDoNothing started.", 99999)
            processor.AddAudit("Customer: " & processor.CurrentCustomer.Name, 99999)
            processor.AddAudit("First item in order: " _
                            & processor.CurrentOrderDetails(0).ItemAsString, 99999)
            processor.MailAdmin("Test.", "Test mail from PSDummy.", 99999)
            processor.AddAudit("PSDoNothing finished.", 99999)
        End Sub
    End Class
```

The code here uses the `AddAudit` and `.MailAdmin` methods of `OrderProcessor` to generate something to show that the code has executed correctly. Note that the numbering schemes outlined previously aren't used there, as this isn't a real pipeline section.

That was a lot of code to get through, but it did have the effect of making the client code very simple:

```
        Dim configuration As OrderProcessorConfiguration = _
            New OrderProcessorConfiguration( _
                "server=(local);Integrated Security=SSPI;database=JokePoint", _
                "MailServer", _
                "AdminEMail", _
                "customerservice@JokePoint.com", _
                "orderprocessor@JokePoint.com", _
                "SupplierEMail")
        Dim processor As New OrderProcessor()
        processor.Process(1, configuration)
```

Short of setting all the configuration details, there is very little to do, because `OrderProcessor` does a *lot* of work for you. It's worth noting that the code you have at this point is for the most part a consequence of the design choices made earlier. This is an excellent example of how a strong design can lead straight to powerful and robust code.

Adding More Functionality to `OrderProcessor`

You need to add a few more bits and pieces to the `OrderProcessor` class, but it hardly seems worth going through another "Exercise" section to do so. Instead, we'll simply go through the code briefly here.

You need to look at

- Updating the status of an order

- Setting and getting credit card authentication details

- Setting the order shipment date

Updating the Status of an Order

Each pipeline section needs the capability to change the status of an order, advancing it to the next pipeline section. Rather than simply incrementing the status, this functionality is kept flexible, just in case you end up with a more complicated branched pipeline. This requires a new stored procedure, UpdateOrderStatus:

```
CREATE PROCEDURE UpdateOrderStatus
(@OrderID int,
 @Status int)
AS

UPDATE Orders
SET Status = @Status
WHERE OrderID = @OrderID
GO
```

The method that calls this stored procedure is another one with Friend access, such that it can be used from pipeline sections, and acts in much the same way as some of the other methods you've seen already:

```
Friend Sub UpdateOrderStatus(ByVal newStatus As Integer)
    ' change status of order, called by pipeline sections
Dim command As SqlCommand = New SqlCommand("UpdateOrderStatus", Connection)
    command.CommandType = CommandType.StoredProcedure
    command.Parameters.Add("@OrderID", OrderID)
    command.Parameters.Add("@Status", newStatus)
    command.ExecuteNonQuery()
    OrderStatus = newStatus
End Sub
```

Setting and Getting Credit Card Authentication Details

In the next chapter, when we deal with credit card usage, you'll need to set and retrieve data in the AuthCode and Reference fields in the Orders table.

Setting requires a new stored procedure, SetOrderAuthCode:

```
CREATE PROCEDURE SetOrderAuthCode
(@OrderID int,
 @AuthCode nvarchar(50),
 @Reference nvarchar(50))
AS

UPDATE Orders
SET AuthCode = @AuthCode, Reference = @Reference
WHERE OrderID = @OrderID
GO
```

The authorization and reference codes will be stored in private fields, because you'll use a similar method of access to that for the Customer and OrderDetails information covered earlier:

```
Private _authCode As String
Private _reference As String
```

The code to set these values in the database is as follows:

```
Friend Sub SetOrderAuthCodeAndReference(ByVal newAuthCode As String, _
                                        ByVal newReference As String)
    ' update order authorization code and reference
  Dim command As SqlCommand = New SqlCommand("SetOrderAuthCode", Connection)
    command.CommandType = CommandType.StoredProcedure
    command.Parameters.Add("@OrderID", OrderID)
    command.Parameters.Add("@AuthCode", newAuthCode)
    command.Parameters.Add("@Reference", newReference)
    command.ExecuteNonQuery()
    _authCode = newAuthCode
    _reference = newReference
  End Sub
```

This code also sets the private fields, just in case they are required before the OrderProcessor terminates. In this situation, it wouldn't make much sense to get these values from the database when you already know what the result will be.

Getting the data out also requires a new stored procedure, GetOrderAuthCode:

```
CREATE PROCEDURE GetOrderAuthCode
(@OrderID int)
AS

SELECT AuthCode,  Reference
FROM Orders
WHERE OrderID = @OrderID
GO
```

Both AuthCode and Reference will be available as properties, but will only perform a database read if no data is currently available. Because the values of these items are linked, you supply the data-access code in one place:

```
Private Sub GetOrderAuthCodeAndReference()
    ' get order authorization code and reference
  Dim command As SqlCommand = New SqlCommand("GetOrderAuthCode", Connection)
    command.CommandType = CommandType.StoredProcedure
    command.Parameters.Add("@OrderID", OrderID)
    Dim reader As SqlDataReader = command.ExecuteReader()
    Try
        reader.Read()
        _authCode = reader("AuthCode")
        _reference = reader("Reference")
```

```
        Catch
            Throw
        Finally
            reader.Close()
        End Try
    End Sub
```

This code handles the `SqlReader` returned in an exception handling block for the same reason as mentioned earlier—you don't want to block your connection by leaving an `SqlReader` open.

The properties themselves are as follows:

```
Friend ReadOnly Property AuthCode()
    Get
        If _authCode Is Nothing Then
            GetOrderAuthCodeAndReference()
        End If
        Return _authCode
    End Get
End Property

Friend ReadOnly Property Reference()
    Get
        If _reference Is Nothing Then
            GetOrderAuthCodeAndReference()
        End If
        Return _reference
    End Get
End Property
```

It would also be possible to configure read-write properties for this data, but having one method to set the values cuts down on database accesses.

Setting the Order Shipment Date

When an order is shipped, you should update the shipment date in the database, which can simply be the current date. The new stored procedure to do this, SetDateShipped, is as follows:

```
CREATE PROCEDURE SetDateShipped
(@OrderID int)
AS

UPDATE Orders
SET DateShipped = GetDate()
WHERE OrderID = @OrderID
GO
```

The code to call this stored procedure is very simple:

```
Friend Sub SetDateShipped()
    ' set the shipment date of the order
    Dim command As SqlCommand = New SqlCommand("SetDateShipped", Connection)
    command.CommandType = CommandType.StoredProcedure
    command.Parameters.Add("@OrderID", OrderID)
    command.ExecuteNonQuery()
End Sub
```

Summary

You've begun to build the backbone of the application, and prepared it for the lion's share of the order pipeline processing functionality, which you'll implement in Chapter 14.

Specifically, we've covered:

- Modifications to the JokePoint application to enable your own pipeline processing

- The basic framework for your order pipeline

- The database additions for auditing data and storing additional required data in the Orders table

In the next chapter, you'll go on to implement the order pipeline.

CHAPTER 14

Implementing
the Pipeline

IN THE LAST CHAPTER, you completed the basic functionality of the OrderProcessor
component, which is responsible for moving orders through pipeline stages. You've
seen a quick demonstration of this using a dummy pipeline section, but you haven't
yet implemented the pipeline discussed at the beginning of the last chapter.

In this chapter, you'll add the required pipeline sections so that you can process
orders from start to finish, although you won't be adding full credit card transaction
functionality until the next chapter.

We'll also look at the web administration of orders by modifying the order admin
pages added earlier in the book to take into account the new order-processing system.

Considering the Code for the Pipeline Sections

The OrderProcessor code is complete, except for one important section—the pipeline
stage selection. Rather than forcing the processor to use PSDummy, you actually want to
select one of the pipeline stages outlined in Chapter 13, depending on the status of
the order. Before you do this, let's run through the code for each of the pipeline sections
in turn, which will take you to the point where the order pipeline will be complete
apart from actual credit card authorization.

As you go through the following sections, create a new class in the CommerceLib
project, using the name of the section as the class name. It follows that the code
beneath the heading should be entered into the class (remember that this code is
available in the Downloads section of the Apress web site [http://www.apress.com]).
By the time you get to the next "Exercise" section, you should have eight new classes
with the following names:

- PSInitialNotification

- PSCheckFunds

- PSCheckStock

- PSStockOK

- PSTakePayment

- PSShipGoods

- PSShipOK

- PSFinalNotification

We'll discuss the classes you are creating as you go.

PSInitialNotification

PSInitialNotification is the first pipeline stage, and is responsible for sending an email to the customer confirming that the order has been placed. The code for this class starts off in what will soon become a very familiar fashion:

```
Imports System.Text
Imports System.Web.Mail

' 1st pipeline stage - used to send a notification email to
' the customer, confirming that the order has been received
Public Class PSInitialNotification
    Implements IPipelineSection

    Private _processor As OrderProcessor
    Private _currentCustomer As Customer
    Private _currentOrderDetails As OrderDetails

    Public Sub Process(ByVal processor As OrderProcessor) _
        Implements IPipelineSection.Process

        _processor = processor
        _processor.AddAudit("PSInitialNotification started.", 20000)
```

The code contains the required Imports statements; the class itself, which implements the IPipelineSection interface; some private fields for storing important references; and then the IPipelineSection.Process method implementation. This method starts by storing the reference to OrderProcessor, which all of the pipeline sections will do because using the methods it exposes (either in the Process method or in other methods) is essential. An audit entry is also added using the numbering scheme introduced earlier (the initial 2 signifies that it's coming from a pipeline section, the next 00 means that it's the first pipeline section, and the final 00 shows that it's the start message for the pipeline section).

Next you get the customer and order details required by the pipeline section, using the appropriate properties of OrderProcessor:

```
' get customer details
_currentCustomer = _processor.CurrentCustomer

' get order details
_currentOrderDetails = _processor.CurrentOrderDetails
```

The remainder of the `Process` method sends the email. This requires information from the customer and configuration data, which you have easy access to. A private method is used to build a message body, which we'll look at shortly:

```
Try
    ' Send mail to customer
    SmtpMail.SmtpServer = _processor.Configuration.MailServer
    Dim notificationMail As MailMessage = New MailMessage()
    notificationMail.To = _currentCustomer.Email
    notificationMail.From = _processor.Configuration.CustomerServiceEmail
    notificationMail.Subject = "Order received."
    notificationMail.Body = GetMailBody()
    SmtpMail.Send(notificationMail)
```

After the mail is sent, you add an audit message to change the status of the order, and tell the order processor that it's okay to move straight on to the next pipeline section:

```
    _processor.AddAudit("Notification e-mail sent to customer.", 20002)

    _processor.UpdateOrderStatus(1)
    _processor.ContinueNow = True
```

If an error occurs, an `OrderProcessor` exception is thrown:

```
Catch
    ' mail sending failure
    Throw _
        New OrderProcessorException("Unable to send e-mail to customer.", 0)
End Try
```

If all goes according to plan, the `Process` method finishes by adding a final audit entry:

```
    _processor.AddAudit("PSInitialNotification finished.", 20001)
End Sub
```

The `GetMailBody` method is used to build up an email body to send to the customer using a `StringBuilder` object for efficiency. The text uses customer and order data, but follows a generally accepted e-commerce email format:

```
Private Function GetMailBody() As String
    ' construct message body
    Dim bodyBuilder As StringBuilder = New StringBuilder()
    bodyBuilder.Append("Thank you for your order! The products you have " _
                      & "ordered are as follows:")
    bodyBuilder.Append(Chr(10))
    bodyBuilder.Append(Chr(10))
    bodyBuilder.Append(_currentOrderDetails.ListAsString)
```

```
              bodyBuilder.Append(Chr(10))
              bodyBuilder.Append(Chr(10))
              bodyBuilder.Append("Your order will be shipped to: ")
              bodyBuilder.Append(Chr(10))
              bodyBuilder.Append(Chr(10))
              bodyBuilder.Append(_currentCustomer.AddressAsString)
              bodyBuilder.Append(Chr(10))
              bodyBuilder.Append(Chr(10))
              bodyBuilder.Append("Order reference number: ")
              bodyBuilder.Append(_processor.OrderID.ToString())
              bodyBuilder.Append(Chr(10))
              bodyBuilder.Append(Chr(10))
              bodyBuilder.Append("You will receive a confirmation e-mail when this " _
                          & "order has been dispatched. Thank you for shopping " _
                          & "at JokePoint.com!")
          Return bodyBuilder.ToString()
      End Function
  End Class
```

When this pipeline stage finishes, processing moves straight on to PSCheckFunds.

PSCheckFunds

The PSCheckFunds pipeline stage is responsible for making sure that the customer has the required funds available on a credit card. For now, you'll provide a dummy implementation of this, and just assume that these funds are available.

The code starts in the same way as PSInitialNotification:

```
Imports SecurityLib

' 2nd pipeline stage - used to check that the customer
' has the required funds available for purchase
Public Class PSCheckFunds
    Implements IPipelineSection

    Private _processor As OrderProcessor

    Public Sub Process(ByVal processor As OrderProcessor) _
        Implements IPipelineSection.Process

        _processor = processor
        _processor.AddAudit("PSCheckFunds started.", 20100)
```

Even though you aren't actually performing a check, you set the authorization and reference codes for the transaction to make sure that the code in OrderProcessor works properly:

```
Try
    ' check customer funds
    ' assume they exist for now

    ' set order authorization code and reference
    _processor.SetOrderAuthCodeAndReference("AuthCode", "Reference")
```

You finish up with some auditing, the code required for continuation, and error checking:

```
    ' audit and continue
    _processor.AddAudit("Funds available for purchase.", 20102)
    _processor.UpdateOrderStatus(2)
    _processor.ContinueNow = True
Catch
    ' fund checking failure
    Throw _
        New OrderProcessorException("Error occured while checking funds.", 1)
End Try
_processor.AddAudit("PSCheckFunds finished.", 20101)
    End Sub
End Class
```

When this pipeline stage finishes, processing moves straight on to PSCheckStock.

PSCheckStock

The PSCheckStock pipeline stage sends an email instructing the supplier to check stock availability:

```
Imports System.Text
Imports System.Web.Mail

' 3rd pipeline stage - used to send a notification email to
' the supplier, asking whether goods are available
Public Class PSCheckStock
    Implements IPipelineSection

    Private _processor As OrderProcessor
    Private _currentOrderDetails As OrderDetails

    Public Sub Process(ByVal processor As OrderProcessor) _
        Implements IPipelineSection.Process

        _processor = processor
        _processor.AddAudit("PSCheckStock started.", 20200)
```

This time, you need access to order details, although there's no real need to get the customer details because the supplier isn't interested in who has placed the order at this stage:

```
' get order details
_currentOrderDetails = _processor.CurrentOrderDetails
```

Mail is sent in a similar way to PSInitialNotification, using a private method to build up the body:

```
Try
    ' Send mail to supplier
    SmtpMail.SmtpServer = _processor.Configuration.MailServer
    Dim notificationMail As MailMessage = New MailMessage()
    notificationMail.To = _processor.Configuration.SupplierEmail
    notificationMail.From = _processor.Configuration.AdminEmail
    notificationMail.Subject = "Stock check."
    notificationMail.Body = GetMailBody()
    SmtpMail.Send(notificationMail)
```

As before, you finish by auditing and updating the status, although this time, you don't tell the order processor to continue straight away:

```
    _processor.AddAudit("Notification e-mail sent to supplier.", 20202)

    _processor.UpdateOrderStatus(3)
Catch
    ' mail sending failure
    Throw _
        New OrderProcessorException("Unable to send e-mail to supplier.", 2)
End Try
_processor.AddAudit("PSCheckStock finished.", 20201)
End Sub
```

The code for building the message body is simple; it just lists the items in the order and tells the supplier to confirm via the JokePoint web site (using the order administration page OrdersAdminPage.aspx, which you'll modify later):

```
Private Function GetMailBody() As String

    ' construct message body
    Dim bodyBuilder As StringBuilder = New StringBuilder()
    bodyBuilder.Append("The following goods have been ordered:")
    bodyBuilder.Append(Chr(10))
    bodyBuilder.Append(Chr(10))
    bodyBuilder.Append(_currentOrderDetails.ListAsString)
```

```
        bodyBuilder.Append(Chr(10))
        bodyBuilder.Append(Chr(10))
        bodyBuilder.Append("Please check availability and confirm via " _
                            & "http://www.JokePoint.com/OrdersAdminPage.aspx")
        bodyBuilder.Append(Chr(10))
        bodyBuilder.Append(Chr(10))
        bodyBuilder.Append("Order reference number: ")
        bodyBuilder.Append(_processor.OrderID.ToString())
        Return bodyBuilder.ToString()
    End Function
End Class
```

When this pipeline stage finishes, processing pauses. Later, when the supplier confirms that stock is available, processing moves on to PSStockOK.

PSStockOK

The PSStockOK pipeline section doesn't do much at all. It just confirms that the supplier has the product in stock and moves on. Its real purpose is to look for orders that have a status corresponding to this pipeline section and know that they are currently awaiting stock confirmation.

```
' 4th pipeline stage - after confirmation that supplier has goods available
Public Class PSStockOK
    Implements IPipelineSection
    Private _processor As OrderProcessor

    Public Sub Process(ByVal processor As OrderProcessor) _
        Implements IPipelineSection.Process

        _processor = processor
        _processor.AddAudit("PSStockOK started.", 20300)

        ' the method is called when the supplier confirms that stock is available,
        ' so we don't have to do anything else here.
        _processor.AddAudit("Stock confirmed by supplier.", 20302)
        _processor.UpdateOrderStatus(4)
        _processor.ContinueNow = True
        _processor.AddAudit("PSStockOK finished.", 20301)
    End Sub
End Class
```

When this pipeline stage finishes, processing moves straight on to PSTakePayment.

PSTakePayment

The PSTakePayment pipeline section completes the transaction started by PSCheckFunds. As with that section, you only provide a dummy implementation here, although you do retrieve the authorization and reference codes to check that part of OrderProcessor.

```
' 5th pipeline stage - takes funds from customer
Public Class PSTakePayment
    Implements IPipelineSection

    Private _processor As OrderProcessor
    Private _authCode As String
    Private _reference As String

    Public Sub Process(ByVal processor As OrderProcessor) _
        Implements IPipelineSection.Process

        _processor = processor
        _processor.AddAudit("PSTakePayment started.", 20400)

        ' get authorization code and reference
        _authCode = _processor.AuthCode
        _reference = _processor.Reference

        Try
            ' take customer funds
            ' assume success for now

            ' audit and continue
            _processor.AddAudit("Funds deducted from customer credit card " _
                            & "account.", 20402)
            _processor.UpdateOrderStatus(5)
            _processor.ContinueNow = True
        Catch
            ' fund checking failure
            Throw _
                New OrderProcessorException("Error occured while taking payment.", 4)
        End Try
        _processor.AddAudit("PSTakePayment finished.", 20401)
    End Sub
End Class
```

When this pipeline stage finishes, processing moves straight on to PSShipGoods.

PSShipGoods

The PSShipGoods pipeline section is remarkably similar to PSCheckStock, because it sends a mail to the supplier and stops the pipeline until the supplier has confirmed that stock has shipped. This time you need customer information, because the supplier needs to know where to ship the order! This section should not be combined with PSCheckStock because after you've checked the goods are in stock, you need to take payment before shipping the goods.

```
Imports System.Text
Imports System.Web.Mail

' 6th pipeline stage - used to send a notification email to
' the supplier, stating that goods can be shipped
Public Class PSShipGoods
    Implements IPipelineSection

    Private _processor As OrderProcessor
    Private _currentCustomer As Customer
    Private _currentOrderDetails As OrderDetails

    Public Sub Process(ByVal processor As OrderProcessor) _
        Implements IPipelineSection.Process

        _processor = processor
        _processor.AddAudit("PSShipGoods started.", 20500)

        ' get customer details
        _currentCustomer = _processor.CurrentCustomer

        ' get order details
        _currentOrderDetails = _processor.CurrentOrderDetails
        Try
            ' Send mail to supplier
            SmtpMail.SmtpServer = _processor.Configuration.MailServer
            Dim notificationMail As MailMessage = New MailMessage()
            notificationMail.To = _processor.Configuration.SupplierEmail
            notificationMail.From = _processor.Configuration.AdminEmail
            notificationMail.Subject = "Ship Goods."
            notificationMail.Body = GetMailBody()
            SmtpMail.Send(notificationMail)
            _processor.AddAudit("Ship goods e-mail sent to supplier.", 20502)
            _processor.UpdateOrderStatus(6)
        Catch
            ' mail sending failure
            Throw _
                New OrderProcessorException("Unable to send e-mail to supplier.", 5)
        End Try
        _processor.AddAudit("PSShipGoods finished.", 20501)
    End Sub
```

As before, a private method called GetMailBody is used to build the message body for the email sent to the supplier:

```
Private Function GetMailBody() As String
    ' construct message body
    Dim bodyBuilder As StringBuilder = New StringBuilder()
    bodyBuilder.Append("Payment has been received for the following goods:")
    bodyBuilder.Append(Chr(10))
    bodyBuilder.Append(Chr(10))
    bodyBuilder.Append(_currentOrderDetails.ListAsString)
    bodyBuilder.Append(Chr(10))
    bodyBuilder.Append(Chr(10))
    bodyBuilder.Append("Please ship to:")
    bodyBuilder.Append(Chr(10))
    bodyBuilder.Append(Chr(10))
    bodyBuilder.Append(_currentCustomer.AddressAsString)
    bodyBuilder.Append(Chr(10))
    bodyBuilder.Append(Chr(10))
    bodyBuilder.Append("When goods have been shipped, please confirm via " _
                    & "http://www.JokePoint.com/OrdersAdminPage.aspx")
    bodyBuilder.Append(Chr(10))
    bodyBuilder.Append(Chr(10))
    bodyBuilder.Append("Order reference number: ")
    bodyBuilder.Append(_processor.OrderID.ToString())
    Return bodyBuilder.ToString()
End Function
End Class
```

When this pipeline stage finishes, processing pauses. Later, when the supplier confirms that the order has been shipped, processing moves on to PSShipOK.

PSShipOK

The PSShipOK pipeline section is very similar to PSStockOK, although it has slightly more to do. Because you know that items have shipped, a shipment date value can be added to the Orders table. Technically, this isn't really necessary, because all audit entries are dated. However, this method ensures that all the information is easily accessible in one database table.

```
' 7th pipeline stage - after confirmation that supplier has shipped goods
Public Class PSShipOK
    Implements IPipelineSection
    Private _processor As OrderProcessor

    Public Sub Process(ByVal processor As OrderProcessor) _
        Implements IPipelineSection.Process

        _processor = processor
        _processor.AddAudit("PSShipOK started.", 20600)
```

```
        ' set order shipment date
        _processor.SetDateShipped()
        _processor.AddAudit("Order dispatched by supplier.", 20602)
        _processor.UpdateOrderStatus(7)
        _processor.ContinueNow = True
        _processor.AddAudit("PSShipOK finished.", 20601)
    End Sub
End Class
```

When this pipeline stage finishes, processing moves straight on to PSFinalNotification.

PSFinalNotification

The last pipeline section—PSFinalNotification—is very similar to the first, in that it sends email to the customer. This section confirms that the order has shipped:

```
Imports System.Text
Imports System.Web.Mail

' 8th pipeline stage - used to send a notification email to
' the customer, confirming that the order has been shipped
Public Class PSFinalNotification
    Implements IPipelineSection

    Private _processor As OrderProcessor
    Private _currentCustomer As Customer
    Private _currentOrderDetails As OrderDetails

    Public Sub Process(ByVal processor As OrderProcessor) _
        Implements IPipelineSection.Process

        _processor = processor
        _processor.AddAudit("PSFinalNotification started.", 20700)

        ' get customer details
        _currentCustomer = _processor.CurrentCustomer

        ' get order details
        _currentOrderDetails = _processor.CurrentOrderDetails

        Try
            ' Send mail to customer
            SmtpMail.SmtpServer = _processor.Configuration.MailServer
            Dim notificationMail As MailMessage = New MailMessage()
            notificationMail.To = _currentCustomer.Email
            notificationMail.From = _processor.Configuration.CustomerServiceEmail
            notificationMail.Subject = "Order dispatched."
            notificationMail.Body = GetMailBody()
            SmtpMail.Send(notificationMail)
```

```
        _processor.AddAudit("Dispatch e-mail sent to customer.", 20702)

        _processor.UpdateOrderStatus(8)
    Catch
        ' mail sending failure
        Throw _
            New OrderProcessorException("Unable to send e-mail to customer.", 7)
    End Try
    _processor.AddAudit("PSFinalNotification finished.", 20701)
End Sub
```

It uses a familiar-looking GetMailBody method to build the body of the email:

```
Private Function GetMailBody() As String
    ' construct message body
    Dim bodyBuilder As StringBuilder = New StringBuilder()
    bodyBuilder.Append("Your order has now been dispatched! The following " _
                        & "products have been shipped:")
    bodyBuilder.Append(Chr(10))
    bodyBuilder.Append(Chr(10))
    bodyBuilder.Append(_currentOrderDetails.ListAsString)
    bodyBuilder.Append(Chr(10))
    bodyBuilder.Append(Chr(10))
    bodyBuilder.Append("Your order has beenshipped to: ")
    bodyBuilder.Append(Chr(10))
    bodyBuilder.Append(Chr(10))
    bodyBuilder.Append(_currentCustomer.AddressAsString)
    bodyBuilder.Append(Chr(10))
    bodyBuilder.Append(Chr(10))
    bodyBuilder.Append("Order reference number: ")
    bodyBuilder.Append(_processor.OrderID.ToString())
    bodyBuilder.Append(Chr(10))
    bodyBuilder.Append(Chr(10))
    bodyBuilder.Append("Thank you for shopping at JokePoint.com!")
    Return bodyBuilder.ToString()
End Function
End Class
```

When this pipeline section finishes, the order status is changed to 8, which represents a completed order. Further attempts to process the order using OrderProcessor will result in an exception being thrown.

Exercise: The Pipeline in Action

1   If you haven't already done so, ensure that the utility methods and pipeline stage classes detailed in the previous sections have been added to the CommerceLib project.

2   Modify the code of the GetCurrentPipelineSection method in OrderProcessor as follows:

```
Private Function GetCurrentPipelineSection() As IPipelineSection
    ' select pipeline section to execute based on order status
    Select Case OrderStatus
        Case 0
            CurrentPipelineSection = New PSInitialNotification()
        Case 1
            CurrentPipelineSection = New PSCheckFunds()
        Case 2
            CurrentPipelineSection = New PSCheckStock()
        Case 3
            CurrentPipelineSection = New PSStockOK()
        Case 4
            CurrentPipelineSection = New PSTakePayment()
        Case 5
            CurrentPipelineSection = New PSShipGoods()
        Case 6
            CurrentPipelineSection = New PSShipOK()
        Case 7
            CurrentPipelineSection = New PSFinalNotification()
        Case 8
            Throw New OrderProcessorException( _
                "Order has already been completed.", 100)
        Case Else
            Throw New OrderProcessorException( _
                "Unknown pipeline section requested.", 100)
    End Select
End Function
```

3. Modify the code in Module1.vb as follows, using the same values you used in
    the last example for the configuration:

```
Sub Main()
    Dim configuration As OrderProcessorConfiguration = _
        New OrderProcessorConfiguration( _
            "server=(local);Integrated Security=SSPI;" _
            & "database=JokePoint", _
            "MAILSERVER", _
            "AdminEMail", _
            "customerservice@JokePoint.com", _
            "orderprocessor@JokePoint.com", _
            "SupplierEMail")
    Dim processor As New OrderProcessor()
    ' 1st call to OrderProcessor, normally from Checkout.aspx
    processor.Process(1, configuration)
    Console.ReadLine()
    ' 2nd call to OrderProcessor, normally from OrdersAdminPage.aspx
    processor.Process(1, configuration)
    Console.ReadLine()
    ' 3rd call to OrderProcessor, normally from OrdersAdminPage.aspx
    processor.Process(1, configuration)
End Sub
```

4. Execute the code, calling `OrderProcessor.Process` for the first time.

5. Check your (customer account) mail for the customer notification email. An example is shown in Figure 14-1.

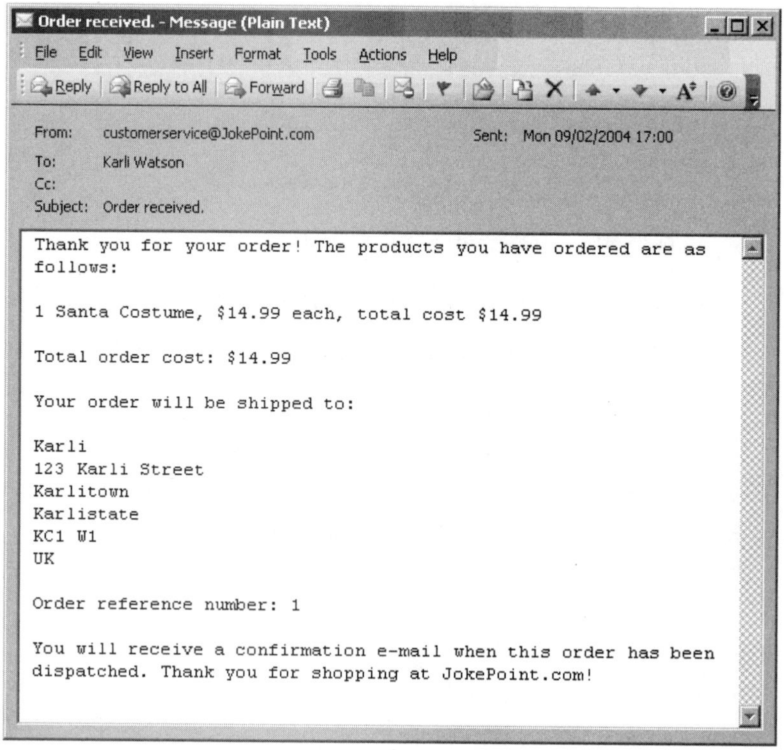

Figure 14-1. Customer order notification email

6. Check your (administrator) mail for the stock check email (see Figure 14-2).

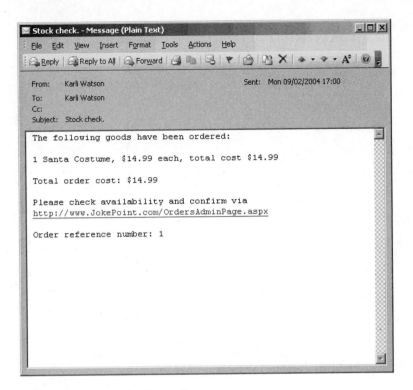

Figure 14-2. Stock check email

7. Continue processing in the `CommerceLibTest` application by pressing Enter, calling `OrderProcessor.Process` for the second time.

8. Check your mail for the ship goods email (see Figure 14-3).

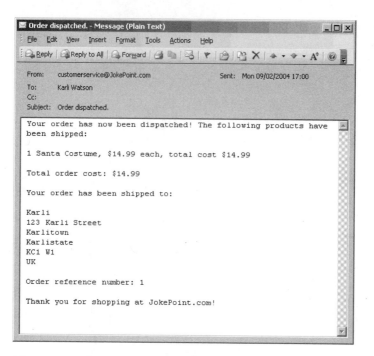

Figure 14-3. Ship goods email

9. Continue processing in the CommerceLibTest application by pressing Enter, calling OrderProcessor.Process for the third time and finishing the application.

10. Check your mail for the shipping confirmation email (see Figure 14-4).

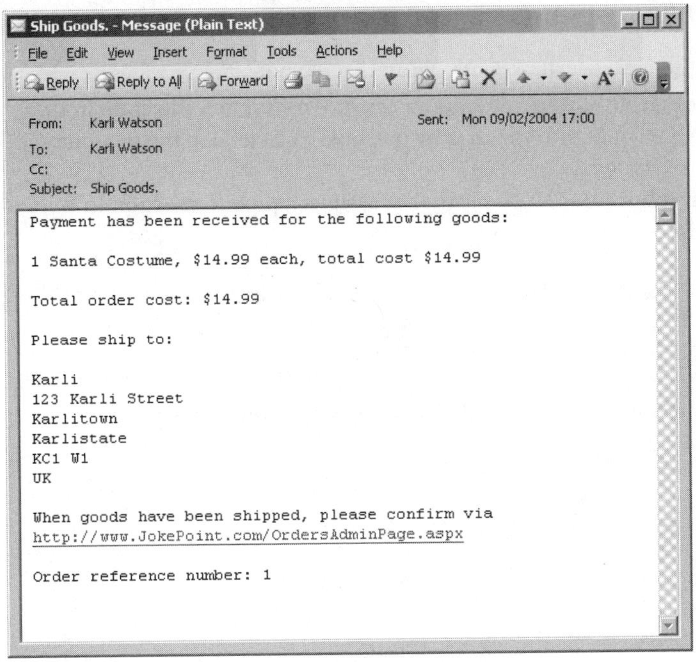

Figure 14-4. Customer shipping notification email

11. Examine the new audit entries for the order (see Figure 14-5).

AuditID	OrderID	DateStamp	Message	MessageNumber
46	1	09/02/2004 16:59:49	Order Processor started.	10000
47	1	09/02/2004 16:59:50	PSInitialNotification started.	20000
48	1	09/02/2004 16:59:50	Notification e-mail sent to customer.	20002
49	1	09/02/2004 16:59:50	PSInitialNotification finished.	20001
50	1	09/02/2004 16:59:50	PSCheckFunds started.	20100
51	1	09/02/2004 16:59:50	Funds available for purchase.	20102
52	1	09/02/2004 16:59:50	PSCheckFunds finished.	20101
53	1	09/02/2004 16:59:50	PSCheckStock started.	20200
54	1	09/02/2004 16:59:50	Notification e-mail sent to supplier.	20202
55	1	09/02/2004 16:59:50	PSCheckStock finished.	20201
56	1	09/02/2004 16:59:50	Order Processor finished.	10001
57	1	09/02/2004 16:59:55	Order Processor started.	10000
58	1	09/02/2004 16:59:55	PSStockOK started.	20300
59	1	09/02/2004 16:59:55	Stock confirmed by supplier.	20302
60	1	09/02/2004 16:59:55	PSStockOK finished.	20301
61	1	09/02/2004 16:59:55	PSTakePayment started.	20400
62	1	09/02/2004 16:59:55	Funds deducted from customer credit card account.	20402
63	1	09/02/2004 16:59:55	PSTakePayment finished.	20401
64	1	09/02/2004 16:59:55	PSShipGoods started.	20500
65	1	09/02/2004 16:59:55	Ship goods e-mail sent to supplier.	20502
66	1	09/02/2004 16:59:55	PSShipGoods finished.	20501
67	1	09/02/2004 16:59:56	Order Processor finished.	10001
68	1	09/02/2004 16:59:58	Order Processor started.	10000
69	1	09/02/2004 16:59:58	PSShipOK started.	20600
70	1	09/02/2004 16:59:58	Order dispatched by supplier.	20602
71	1	09/02/2004 16:59:58	PSShipOK finished.	20601
72	1	09/02/2004 16:59:58	PSFinalNotification started.	20700
73	1	09/02/2004 16:59:58	Dispatch e-mail sent to customer.	20702
74	1	09/02/2004 16:59:58	PSFinalNotification finished.	20701
75	1	09/02/2004 16:59:58	Order Processor finished.	10001

Figure 14-5. Audit entries for completed order

How It Works: The Pipeline in Action

We've covered how the order pipeline works, so all you need to consider here is what's going on with the new code added to OrderProcessor. We changed the code in the GetCurrentPipelineSection method, which is responsible for selecting the pipeline section that needs to be executed.

The change is simply a Select Case block that assigns a pipeline section to CurrentPipelineSection:

```
Private Function GetCurrentPipelineSection() As IPipelineSection
    ' select pipeline section to execute based on order status
    Select Case OrderStatus
        Case 0
            CurrentPipelineSection = New PSInitialNotification()
        Case 1
            CurrentPipelineSection = New PSCheckFunds()
        Case 2
            CurrentPipelineSection = New PSCheckStock()
        Case 3
            CurrentPipelineSection = New PSStockOK()
        Case 4
            CurrentPipelineSection = New PSTakePayment()
        Case 5
            CurrentPipelineSection = New PSShipGoods()
        Case 6
            CurrentPipelineSection = New PSShipOK()
        Case 7
            CurrentPipelineSection = New PSFinalNotification()
        Case 8
            Throw New OrderProcessorException( _
                "Order has already been completed.", 100)
        Case Else
            Throw New OrderProcessorException( _
                "Unknown pipeline section requested.", 100)
    End Select
End Function
```

If the order has been completed or an unknown section is requested, an exception is generated.

The test code gives you the additional opportunity of testing this exception generation, because if you run it again, you'll be processing an already completed order. Execute the application again and you should get an exception as shown in Figure 14-6.

Figure 14-6. Order completed exception

If you check your mail, you'll see the details (see Figure 14-7).

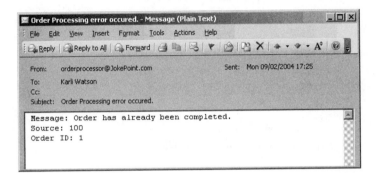

Figure 14-7. Order completion error email

The error message mailed to the administrator should be enough to get started in detective work, finding out what has happened.

Making Modifications to JokePoint

The last example forced the OrderProcessor.Process method to be called three times in a row from the test code. In practice, this won't happen—the method will be called once by Checkout.aspx when a customer places an order, and twice more by the supplier in OrdersAdminPage.aspx. You'll need to modify these web pages to enable the web interface.

Both these pages will need to configure the order processor as well, so a good starting point is to add the configuration details to web.config as follows:

```
<appSettings>
    <add key="ConnectionString"
     value="server=(local);Integrated Security=SSPI;database=JokePoint" />
    <add key="MailServer" value="MailServer" />
    <add key="AdminEmail" value="AdminEMail" />
```

```
<add key="CustomerServiceEmail"
  value="customerservice@JokePoint.com" />
<add key="OrderProcessorEmail" value="orderprocessor@JokePoint.com" />
<add key="SupplierEmail" value="SupplierEmail" />
</appSettings>
```

Again, you'll need to modify these settings to match your configuration. You also need to add a reference to the new CommerceLib assembly.

The Checkout.aspx Web Page

The modifications to the Checkout.aspx page are as follows:

```
Imports CommercLib
...
Private Sub placeOrderButton_Click(ByVal sender As System.Object, _
    ByVal e As System.EventArgs) Handles placeOrderButton.Click
  ' The Shopping Cart object
  Dim cart As New ShoppingCart()

  ' Create the order and store the order ID
  Dim orderId As Integer = cart.CreateOrder(customerID)

  ' Get configuration for order processor
  Dim processorConfiguration As OrderProcessorConfiguration = _
    New OrderProcessorConfiguration( _
      ConfigurationSettings.AppSettings("ConnectionString"), _
      ConfigurationSettings.AppSettings("MailServer"), _
      ConfigurationSettings.AppSettings("AdminEmail"), _
      ConfigurationSettings.AppSettings("CustomerServiceEmail"), _
      ConfigurationSettings.AppSettings("OrderProcessorEmail"), _
      ConfigurationSettings.AppSettings("SupplierEmail"))

  ' Process order
  Try
    Dim processor As OrderProcessor = New OrderProcessor()
    processor.Process(orderId, processorConfiguration)
  Catch ex As OrderProcessorException
    ' If an error occurs head to an error page
    Response.Redirect("OrderError.aspx?message=" & ex.Message)
  End Try

  ' On success head to an order successful page
  Response.Redirect("OrderDone.aspx")
End Sub
```

The values from web.config are used to initialize an OrderProcessor instance, and the order is processed in the same way you've seen earlier in this chapter. To round things off, the customer is redirected to OrderDone.aspx—you can create this simple page by adding the following code to its body:

```
<form id="Form1" method="post" runat="server">
    <p>Thank you for your order!</p>
    <p>A confirmation e-mail should arrive shortly.</p>
    <p><a href="default.aspx">Back to shop</a></p>
</form>
```

Alternatively, if an error occurs, the customer is redirected to another page—`OrderError.aspx`—created with the following code:

```
<form id="Form1" method="post" runat="server">
    <p>An error has occured during the processing of your order.</p>
    <p>Details:
        <asp:Label Runat="server" ID="errorLabel"></asp:Label></p>
    <p>If you have an enquiry regarding this message please e-mail
        <a href="mailto:customerservice@JokePoint.com">
        customerservice@JokePoint.com</a></p>
    <p><a href="default.aspx">Back to shop</a></p>
</form>
This page also has code in its Page_Load() event handler:
    Private Sub Page_Load(ByVal sender As System.Object, _
        ByVal e As System.EventArgs) Handles MyBase.Load
        errorLabel.Text = Request.Params("message")
    End Sub
```

You can now use the `JokePoint` Web Application to place orders, but the order process will pause when it gets to stock confirmation. To continue, you need to implement the interface suppliers and administrators will use to force orders to continue processing.

The `OrdersAdminPage.aspx` *Page*

This page could be implemented in all manner of ways. In some setups, it might be better to implement this page as a Windows Forms application, for example, if your suppliers are in-house and on the same network. Or, it might be better to combine this approach with web services.

Whichever method you choose, the basic functionality is the same: suppliers and administrators should be able to view a list of orders that need attention, and advance them in the pipeline manually. This is simply a case of calling the `OrderProcess.Process` method as described earlier.

To simplify things in this section, you'll supply a single page for both administrators and suppliers. This might not be ideal in all situations, because you might not want to expose all order details and audit information to external suppliers. However, for demonstration purposes, this reduces the amount of code you have to get through. We'll also tie in the security for this page with the administrator forms-based security used earlier in the book, assuming that people with permission to edit the site data also have permission to administer orders. In a more advanced setup, you could modify this slightly, providing roles for different types of users, and restricting the functionality available to users in different roles.

As a starting point, you'll take the existing `OrdersAdminPage.aspx` and associated user controls and classes, and rewrite them to provide the functionality required. In fact, you can simplify the code slightly to achieve this, because you won't need to update order data as completely as you did before. However, there are quite a lot of code modifications to get through, so we won't look at this example in the context of an "Exercise" section.

The first thing to do is to add a new database table.

Adding the Status Table

This table contains human-readable strings that describe the status of orders. When filtering orders, it's a lot better to filter by an order stage description than via a status number because it's easier to remember a description such as "Order Completed" than the number 8, for example. Placing this data in the database allows for future extensibility.

The new table, Status, has columns as shown in Table 14-1.

Table 14-1. Status *Table Columns*

Column Name	Column Type	Description
StatusID	int(4)	Primary key. Corresponds to a status number
Description	varchar(50)	The human-readable description of the status

Add data to this table as shown in Table 14-2.

Table 14-2. Status *Table Contents*

StatusId	Value
0	Order placed, notifying customer
1	Awaiting confirmation of funds
2	Notifying supplier—stock check
3	Awaiting stock confirmation
4	Awaiting credit card payment
5	Notifying supplier—shipping
6	Awaiting shipment confirmation
7	Sending final notification
8	Order completed

Adding Stored Procedures

You'll need to add several new stored procedures, which will be used by the OrderManager data object to get the data required for displaying order information.

Note that many of these stored procedures will be used in place of some of the stored procedures previously used by the older version of this page (or, more specifically, by the OrderManager class). Because the order data storage system has changed a little, you are now interested in different columns.

```
CREATE PROCEDURE GetStatuses
AS

SELECT StatusID, [Description]
FROM Status
GO
```

- *GetOrders*: Gets all orders.

```
CREATE PROCEDURE GetOrders
AS

SELECT Orders.OrderID, Orders.DateCreated, Orders.DateShipped,
  Orders.Status, Orders.CustomerID, Orders.AuthCode,
  Orders.Reference, Status.[Description], Customer.[Name]
FROM Orders INNER JOIN Customer
ON Customer.CustomerID = Orders.CustomerID
INNER JOIN Status
ON Status.StatusID = Orders.Status
GO
```

- *GetOrder*: Gets a specific order.

```
Create PROCEDURE GetOrder
(@OrderID as int)
AS

SELECT Orders.OrderID, Orders.DateCreated, Orders.DateShipped,
  Orders.Status, Orders.CustomerID, Status.[Description],
  Customer.[Name], Orders.AuthCode, Orders.Reference
FROM Orders INNER JOIN Customer
ON Customer.CustomerID = Orders.CustomerID
INNER JOIN Status
ON Status.StatusID = Orders.Status
WHERE Orders.OrderID = @OrderID
GO
```

- *GetOrdersByRecent*: Gets a specified number of most recent orders.

```
CREATE PROCEDURE GetOrdersByRecent
(@Count int)
AS

SET ROWCOUNT @Count

SELECT Orders.OrderID, Orders.DateCreated, Orders.DateShipped,
 Orders.Status, Orders.CustomerID, Status.[Description],
 Customer.[Name]
FROM Orders INNER JOIN Customer
ON Customer.CustomerID = Orders.CustomerID
INNER JOIN Status
ON Status.StatusID = Orders.Status
ORDER BY DateCreated DESC
SET ROWCOUNT 0
GO
```

- *GetOrdersByCustomer*: Gets all orders placed by a specified customer.

```
CREATE PROCEDURE GetOrdersByCustomer
(@CustomerID int)
AS

SELECT Orders.OrderID, Orders.DateCreated, Orders.DateShipped,
 Orders.Status, Orders.CustomerID, Status.[Description],
 Customer.[Name]
FROM Orders INNER JOIN Customer
ON Customer.CustomerID = Orders.CustomerID
INNER JOIN Status
ON Status.StatusID = Orders.Status
WHERE Orders.CustomerID = @CustomerID
GO
```

- *GetOrdersByDate*: Gets orders between two specified dates.

```
CREATE PROCEDURE GetOrdersByDate
(@StartDate datetime,
 @EndDate datetime)
AS

SELECT Orders.OrderID, Orders.DateCreated, Orders.DateShipped,
 Orders.Status, Orders.CustomerID, Status.[Description],
 Customer.[Name]
FROM Orders INNER JOIN Customer
ON Customer.CustomerID = Orders.CustomerID
INNER JOIN Status
ON Status.StatusID = Orders.Status
WHERE Orders.DateCreated > @StartDate AND Orders.DateCreated < @EndDate
GO
```

- *GetOrdersByStatus*: Gets all orders with a specific status.

```
CREATE PROCEDURE GetOrdersByStatus
(@Status int)
AS

SELECT Orders.OrderID, Orders.DateCreated, Orders.DateShipped,
  Orders.Status, Orders.CustomerID, Status.[Description],
  Customer.[Name]
FROM Orders INNER JOIN Customer
ON Customer.CustomerID = Orders.CustomerID
INNER JOIN Status
ON Status.StatusID = Orders.Status
WHERE Orders.Status = @Status
GO
```

- *GetAuditTrail*: Gets the Audit table entries associated with a specific order.

```
CREATE PROCEDURE GetAuditTrail
(@OrderID int)
AS

SELECT DateStamp, MessageNumber, Message
FROM Audit
WHERE OrderID = @OrderID
GO
```

Modifying OrderManager

You'll also have to add several new methods to the OrderManager class for the stored procedures listed previously (and, optionally, remove the methods you no longer need).

The first stored procedure, GetStatuses, is accessed using a new method also called GetStatuses:

```
Public Function GetStatuses() As SqlDataReader
    ' Create the connection object
    Dim connection As New SqlConnection(connectionString)

    ' Create and initialize the command object
    Dim command As New SqlCommand("GetStatuses", connection)
    command.CommandType = CommandType.StoredProcedure

    ' Return the results
    connection.Open()
    Return command.ExecuteReader(CommandBehavior.CloseConnection)
End Function
```

The code here looks almost identical to the code for some of the methods already included in OrderManager, and is made even simpler because this stored procedure requires no parameters.

Next the `GetOrder` stored procedure is also accessed by a method with the same name:

```
Public Function GetOrder(ByVal orderID As Integer) As SqlDataReader
    ' Create the connection object
    Dim connection As New SqlConnection(connectionString)

    ' Create and initialize the command object
    Dim command As New SqlCommand("GetOrder", connection)
    command.CommandType = CommandType.StoredProcedure

    ' Add an input parameter and supply a value for it
    command.Parameters.Add("@OrderID", SqlDbType.Int, 4)
    command.Parameters("@OrderID").Value = orderID

    ' Return the results
    connection.Open()
    Return command.ExecuteReader(CommandBehavior.CloseConnection)
End Function
```

Again, there isn't anything new here, you simply pass the ID of the order you want to retrieve to the stored procedure and return the result in `SqlDataReader` form.

The code for the methods that use the rest of the stored procedures listed previously follows the same format.

- You have `GetOrders`:

```
Public Function GetOrders() As SqlDataReader
    ' Create the connection object
    Dim connection As New SqlConnection(connectionString)

    ' Create and initialize the command object
    Dim command As New SqlCommand("GetOrders", connection)
    command.CommandType = CommandType.StoredProcedure

    ' Return the results
    connection.Open()
    Return command.ExecuteReader(CommandBehavior.CloseConnection)
End Function
```

- `GetOrdersByRecent`:

```
Public Function GetOrdersByRecent(ByVal count As Integer) As SqlDataReader
    ' Create the connection object
    Dim connection As New SqlConnection(connectionString)

    ' Create and initialize the command object
    Dim command As New SqlCommand("GetOrdersByRecent", connection)
    command.CommandType = CommandType.StoredProcedure

    ' Add an input parameter and supply a value for it
    command.Parameters.Add("@Count", SqlDbType.Int, 4)
```

```
    command.Parameters("@Count").Value = count

    ' Return the results
    connection.Open()
    Return command.ExecuteReader(CommandBehavior.CloseConnection)
End Function
```

- GetOrdersByCustomer:

```
Public Function GetOrdersByCustomer(ByVal customerID As Integer) _
    As SqlDataReader
    ' Create the connection object
    Dim connection As New SqlConnection(connectionString)

    ' Create and initialize the command object
    Dim command As New SqlCommand("GetOrdersByCustomer", connection)
    command.CommandType = CommandType.StoredProcedure

    ' Add an input parameter and supply a value for it
    command.Parameters.Add("@CustomerID", SqlDbType.Int, 4)
    command.Parameters("@CustomerID").Value = customerID

    ' Return the results
    connection.Open()
    Return command.ExecuteReader(CommandBehavior.CloseConnection)
End Function
```

- GetOrdersByDate:

```
Public Function GetOrdersByDate(ByVal startDate As String, _
    ByVal endDate As String) As SqlDataReader
    ' Create the connection object
    Dim connection As New SqlConnection(connectionString)

    ' Create and initialize the command object
    Dim command As New SqlCommand("GetOrdersByDate", connection)
    command.CommandType = CommandType.StoredProcedure

    ' Add an input parameter and supply a value for it
    command.Parameters.Add("@StartDate", SqlDbType.SmallDateTime)
    command.Parameters("@StartDate").Value = startDate

    ' Add an input parameter and supply a value for it
    command.Parameters.Add("@EndDate", SqlDbType.SmallDateTime)
    command.Parameters("@EndDate").Value = endDate

    ' Return the results
    connection.Open()
    Return command.ExecuteReader(CommandBehavior.CloseConnection)
End Function
```

- GetOrdersByStatus:

```
Public Function GetOrdersByStatus(ByVal status As Integer) As SqlDataReader
    ' Create the connection object
    Dim connection As New SqlConnection(connectionString)

    ' Create and initialize the command object
    Dim command As New SqlCommand("GetOrdersByStatus", connection)
    command.CommandType = CommandType.StoredProcedure

    ' Add an input parameter and supply a value for it
    command.Parameters.Add("@Status", SqlDbType.Int, 4)
    command.Parameters("@Status").Value = status

    ' Return the results
    connection.Open()
    Return command.ExecuteReader(CommandBehavior.CloseConnection)
End Function
```

- GetAuditTrail:

```
Public Function GetAuditTrail(ByVal orderID As Integer) As SqlDataReader
    ' Create the connection object
    Dim connection As New SqlConnection(connectionString)

    ' Create and initialize the command object
    Dim command As New SqlCommand("GetAuditTrail", connection)
    command.CommandType = CommandType.StoredProcedure

    ' Add an input parameter and supply a value for it
    command.Parameters.Add("@OrderID", SqlDbType.Int, 4)
    command.Parameters("@OrderID").Value = orderID

    ' Return the results
    connection.Open()
    Return command.ExecuteReader(CommandBehavior.CloseConnection)
End Function
```

You also have one more new method that uses a stored procedure introduced in the last chapter, GetCustomerByOrderID:

```
Public Function GetCustomerByOrderID(ByVal orderId As String) As SqlDataReader
    ' Create the Connection object
    Dim connection As New SqlConnection(connectionString)

    ' Create and initialize the Command object
    Dim command As New SqlCommand("GetCustomerByOrderID", connection)
    command.CommandType = CommandType.StoredProcedure

    ' Add an input parameter and set a value for it
    command.Parameters.Add("@OrderID", SqlDbType.Int)
    command.Parameters("@OrderID").Value = orderId
```

```
    ' Get the command results as an SqlDataReader
    connection.Open()
    Return command.ExecuteReader(CommandBehavior.CloseConnection)
  End Function
End Class
```

The only method in `OrderManager` that you need to leave in is `GetOrderDetails`:

```
Public Function GetOrderDetails(ByVal orderId As String) As SqlDataReader
    ' Create the Connection object
    Dim connection As New SqlConnection(connectionString)

    ' Create and initialize the Command object
    Dim command As New SqlCommand("GetOrderDetails", connection)
    command.CommandType = CommandType.StoredProcedure

    ' Add an input parameter and set a value for it
    command.Parameters.Add("@OrderID", SqlDbType.Int)
    command.Parameters("@OrderID").Value = orderId
    ' Get the command results as an SqlDataReader
    connection.Open()
    Return command.ExecuteReader(CommandBehavior.CloseConnection)
  End Function
```

All the rest can be removed—including the `OrderInfo` class definition at the start of the file.

TIP *Rather than deleting the unused code, it can be helpful to mark classes and methods that have been replaced with the* `Obsolete` *attribute. This attribute doesn't affect functionality, but it will cause warnings during compilation if the marked items are used. The benefit here is that older code won't break immediately, but you will be reminded to update it. However, in this situation, because you have removed all the code that uses the removed items, there is no real need to do this.*

Modifying OrdersAdmin.ascx

`OrdersAdmin.ascx` is the user control that displays a list of orders meeting certain criteria, such as orders placed between specific dates. Now that you have changed the way orders are processed, there are some filters here that are no longer required, such as searching for unverified, uncanceled orders. Instead, you add filters that take into account the new structure of your data, such as filtering orders by status or by customer ID. You also need to change what data is displayed in the data grid. This requires several modifications to the ASP.NET code for the page.

NOTE *Some of the changes shown here are changes to the IDs of items. This is to keep things in line with the names of your new stored procedures, so that it's easier to see which component relates to what.*

First, you need to make changes to the list of filters at the top of the control:

```
<%@ Control Language="vb" AutoEventWireup="false"
Codebehind="OrdersAdmin.ascx.vb"
    Inherits="JokePoint.OrdersAdmin"
    TargetSchema="http://schemas.microsoft.com/intellisense/ie5" %>
<P><asp:label id="Label1" CssClass="AdminPageText" runat="server">
    Show the most recent</asp:label>
  <asp:textbox id="recordCountTextBox" runat="server"Width="35px">
    20</asp:textbox>
  <asp:label id="Label2" CssClass="AdminPageText"runat="server">
    orders</asp:label>
  <asp:button id="ordersByRecentButton" CssClass="AdminButtonText" runat="server"
    Text="Go!"></asp:button><BR>
<P><asp:label id="Label3" CssClass="AdminPageText" runat="server">
    Show all orders created between</asp:label>
  <asp:textbox id="startDateTextBox" runat="server" Width="70px"></asp:textbox>
  <asp:label id="Label4" CssClass="AdminPageText" runat="server">
    and</asp:label>
  <asp:textbox id="endDateTextBox" runat="server" Width="70px"></asp:textbox>
  <asp:button id="ordersByDateButton" CssClass="AdminButtonText" runat="server"
    Text="Go!"></asp:button><BR>
  <asp:label id="Label5" CssClass="AdminPageText" runat="server">
    Show orders by status</asp:label>
  <asp:dropdownlist id="statusList" Runat="server"></asp:dropdownlist>
  <asp:button id="ordersByStatusButton" CssClass="AdminButtonText" runat="server"
    Text="Go!"></asp:button><BR>
  <asp:label id="Label6" CssClass="AdminPageText" runat="server">
    Show orders for customer with CustomerID</asp:label>
  <asp:textbox id="customerIDTextBox" runat="server" Width="35px">
    1</asp:textbox>
  <asp:button id="ordersByCustomerButton" CssClass="AdminButtonText"
    runat="server" Text="Go!"></asp:button><BR>
  <asp:label id="Label7" CssClass="AdminPageText" runat="server">
    Show order with OrderID</asp:label>
  <asp:textbox id="orderIDTextBox" runat="server" Width="35px">
    1</asp:textbox>
  <asp:button id="orderByIDButton" CssClass="AdminButtonText" runat="server"
    Text="Go!"></asp:button></P>
```

You also need to add the required validators for these new filters:

```
<P><asp:label id="errorLabel" CssClass="AdminErrorText" runat="server">
   </asp:label>
   <asp:requiredfieldvalidator id="recordCountValidator" runat="server"
       Display="None" ControlToValidate="recordCountTextBox"
       ErrorMessage="Invalid record count.">
   </asp:requiredfieldvalidator>
   <asp:rangevalidator id="startDateValidator" runat="server" Display="None"
       ControlToValidate="startDateTextBox" ErrorMessage="Invalid start date."
       Type="Date" MinimumValue="1/1/1999" MaximumValue="1/1/2005">
   </asp:rangevalidator>
   <asp:rangevalidator id="endDateValidator" runat="server" Display="None"
       ControlToValidate="endDateTextBox" ErrorMessage="Invalid end date."
       Type="Date" MinimumValue="1/1/1999" MaximumValue="1/1/2005">
   </asp:rangevalidator>
   <asp:requiredfieldvalidator id="customerIDValidator" Display="None"
       ControlToValidate="customerIDTextBox"
       ErrorMessage="You must enter a customer ID." Runat="server">
   </asp:requiredfieldvalidator>
   <asp:requiredfieldvalidator id="orderIDValidator" Display="None"
       ControlToValidate="orderIDTextBox"
       ErrorMessage="You must enter an order ID." Runat="server">
   </asp:requiredfieldvalidator>
   <asp:comparevalidator id="compareDatesValidator" runat="server" Display="None"
       ControlToValidate="startDateTextBox"
       ErrorMessage="End date should be more recent than start date." Type="Date"
       Operator="LessThan" ControlToCompare="endDateTextBox">
   </asp:comparevalidator>
   <asp:validationsummary id="ValidationSummary" CssClass="AdminErrorText"
       runat="server" HeaderText="Validation errors:">
   </asp:validationsummary>
```

Next, the data grid needs to show a status description, customer ID, and customer name from a different column (from the data extracted from the Customer table by the stored procedures, rather than from the now redundant CustomerName field in the Orders table):

```
<asp:datagrid id="grid" runat="server" Width="100%"
    AutoGenerateColumns="False">
    <ItemStyle Font-Size="X-Small" Font-Names="Verdana"
        BackColor="Gainsboro"></ItemStyle>
    <HeaderStyle Font-Size="X-Small" Font-Names="Verdana" Font-Bold="True"
        ForeColor="White" BackColor="Navy"></HeaderStyle>
    <Columns>
        <asp:BoundColumn DataField="OrderID"
            HeaderText="Order ID"></asp:BoundColumn>
        <asp:BoundColumn DataField="DateCreated"
            HeaderText="Date Created"></asp:BoundColumn>
        <asp:BoundColumn DataField="DateShipped"
            HeaderText="Date Shipped"></asp:BoundColumn>
        <asp:BoundColumn DataField="Description"
            HeaderText="Status"></asp:BoundColumn>
        <asp:BoundColumn DataField="CustomerID"
```

```
                HeaderText="Customer ID"></asp:BoundColumn>
            <asp:BoundColumn DataField="Name"
                HeaderText="Customer Name"></asp:BoundColumn>
            <asp:ButtonColumn Text="View Details" ButtonType="PushButton"
                CommandName="Select"></asp:ButtonColumn>
        </Columns>
    </asp:datagrid></P>
```

Next, the code behind this form, `OrdersAdmin.ascx.vb`, requires a little extra work in the `Page_Load` handler to list an individual order if the `OrderID` query string parameter is used, and to get a list of status descriptions for drop-down list selection:

```
Private Sub Page_Load(ByVal sender As System.Object, _
        ByVal e As System.EventArgs) Handles MyBase.Load
    errorLabel.Text = ""

    If Not IsPostBack Then
        Dim om As New OrderManager()
        If Not Request.Params("OrderID") Is Nothing Then
            ' Set OrderID text box to selected order
            orderIDTextBox.Text = Request.Params("OrderID")

            ' Get selected Order
            grid.DataSource = _
                om.GetOrder(Convert.ToInt32(Request.Params("OrderID")))
            grid.DataKeyField = "OrderID"
            grid.DataBind()
        End If

        statusList.DataSource = om.GetStatuses()
        statusList.DataTextField = "Description"
        statusList.DataValueField = "StatusID"
        statusList.DataBind()
    End If
End Sub
```

The `SelectedIndexChanged` method is the only other one of the existing methods required:

```
Private Sub grid_SelectedIndexChanged(ByVal sender As System.Object, _
        ByVal e As System.EventArgs) Handles grid.SelectedIndexChanged
    Dim orderId As String
    orderId = grid.DataKeys(grid.SelectedIndex)
    Response.Redirect("orders.aspx?OrderID=" & orderId)
End Sub
```

Next, the various button click handlers for the Go! buttons on the form are all very similar, like the methods you looked at for `OrderManager`. First you have `ordersByStatusButton_Click`:

```
Private Sub ordersByStatusButton_Click(ByVal sender As System.Object, _
        ByVal e As System.EventArgs) Handles ordersByStatusButton.Click
    Dim om As New OrderManager()
    Dim status As Integer

    Try
        status = statusList.SelectedItem.Value

        grid.DataSource = om.GetOrdersByStatus(status)
        grid.DataKeyField = "OrderID"
        grid.DataBind()
    Catch
        errorLabel.Text = "Could not get the requested data!"
    End Try
End Sub
```

You get the status value from the drop-down list statusList and use that in the
OrderManager.GetOrdersByStatus method to get an SqlDataReader containing a list of
orders with the specified status. This is then bound to the data grid to display them.

Next, you have ordersByCustomerButton_Click, which works in the same way but
gets orders according to customer:

```
Private Sub ordersByCustomerButton_Click(ByVal sender As System.Object, _
        ByVal e As System.EventArgs) Handles ordersByCustomerButton.Click
    Dim om As New OrderManager()
    Dim customerID As Integer

    Try
        customerID = Int32.Parse(customerIDTextBox.Text)

        grid.DataSource = om.GetOrdersByCustomer(customerID)
        grid.DataKeyField = "OrderID"
        grid.DataBind()
    Catch
        errorLabel.Text = "Could not get the requested data!"
    End Try
End Sub
```

Next you have orderByIDButton_Click, which gets orders according to ID:

```
Private Sub orderByIDButton_Click(ByVal sender As System.Object, _
        ByVal e As System.EventArgs) Handles orderByIDButton.Click
    Dim om As New OrderManager()
    Dim orderID As Integer

    Try
        orderID = Int32.Parse(orderIDTextBox.Text)
        grid.DataSource = om.GetOrder(orderID)
        grid.DataKeyField = "OrderID"
        grid.DataBind()
```

```
    Catch
        errorLabel.Text = "Could not get the requested data!"
    End Try
End Sub
```

Next, ordersByRecentButton_Click, **which gets the most recent orders:**

```
Private Sub ordersByRecentButton_Click(ByVal sender As System.Object, _
        ByVal e As System.EventArgs) Handles ordersByRecentButton.Click
    Dim om As New OrderManager()
    Dim recordCount As Integer

    Try
        recordCount = Int32.Parse(recordCountTextBox.Text)

        grid.DataSource = om.GetOrdersByRecent(recordCount)
        grid.DataKeyField = "OrderID"
        grid.DataBind()
    Catch
        errorLabel.Text = "Could not get the requested data!"
    End Try
End Sub
```

Finally, ordersByDateButton_Click, **which gets orders by date:**

```
Private Sub ordersByDateButton_Click(ByVal sender As System.Object, _
        ByVal e As System.EventArgs) Handles ordersByDateButton.Click
    Dim om As New OrderManager()
    Dim startDate As String
    Dim endDate As String

    Try
        startDate = startDateTextBox.Text
        endDate = endDateTextBox.Text

        grid.DataSource = om.GetOrdersByDate(startDate, endDate)
        grid.DataKeyField = "OrderID"
        grid.DataBind()
    Catch
        errorLabel.Text = "Could not get the requested data!"
    End Try
End Sub
```

Changing OrderDetailsAdmin.ascx

The last control to modify is OrderDetailsAdmin.ascx, which shows the details of an
order. Earlier in the book, this control also included the capability to modify order
data, but we're removing this here. Instead, we provide the capability for orders to be

pushed along the pipeline when they are stuck at the Awaiting Confirmation of Stock and Awaiting Confirmation of Shipment stages.

A few other modifications are also necessary. Now that you have more detailed customer information, you can display all available data (apart from credit card and password information) for the customer who placed the order in a new data grid. You can also display all the audit information for the order in another new data grid. Because you have these new sources of information, you can also cut back a little on the other information displayed for the order, which is displayed in read-only text boxes above the data grids:

```
<%@ Control Language="vb" AutoEventWireup="false"
    Codebehind="OrderDetailsAdmin.ascx.vb"
    Inherits="JokePoint.OrderDetailsAdmin"
    TargetSchema="http://schemas.microsoft.com/intellisense/ie5" %>
<P><asp:label id="Label1" CssClass="AdminPageText" Width="150px" runat="server">
      Order ID:</asp:label>
    <asp:textbox id="orderIdTextBox" Width="400px" runat="server"
      ReadOnly="True"></asp:textbox><BR>
    <asp:label id="Label4" CssClass="AdminPageText" Width="150px" runat="server">
      Date Created:</asp:label>
    <asp:textbox id="dateCreatedTextBox" Width="400px" runat="server"
      ReadOnly="True"></asp:textbox><BR>
    <asp:label id="Label5" CssClass="AdminPageText" Width="150px" runat="server">
      Date Shipped:</asp:label>
    <asp:textbox id="dateShippedTextBox" Width="400px" runat="server"
      ReadOnly="True"></asp:textbox><BR>
```

However, fields are added to display the order status, AuthCode, and Reference:

```
<asp:label id="Label6" CssClass="AdminPageText" Width="150px" runat="server">
    Status:</asp:label>
<asp:textbox id="statusTextBox" Width="400px" runat="server"
    ReadOnly="True"></asp:textbox><BR>
<asp:label id="Label7" CssClass="AdminPageText" Width="150px" runat="server">
    AuthCode:</asp:label>
<asp:textbox id="authCodeTextBox" Width="400px" runat="server"
    ReadOnly="True"></asp:textbox><BR>
<asp:label id="Label8" CssClass="AdminPageText" Width="150px" runat="server">
    Reference:</asp:label>
<asp:textbox id="referenceTextBox" Width="400px" runat="server"
    ReadOnly="True"></asp:textbox></P>
```

Next the button for processing orders in the pipeline is only displayed for orders with the statuses noted previously:

```
<asp:button id="processButton" CssClass="AdminButtonText" Width="302px"
    runat="server" Text="Process Button"></asp:button></P>
```

After this, the list of items in the order is one section of code you don't need to modify. However, you can add a descriptive label because you'll now have three data grids and you don't want to get them mixed up:

```
<P><asp:label id="Label2" CssClass="AdminPageText" Width="150px" runat="server">
    Order Details:</asp:label>
  <asp:datagrid id="orderDetailsGrid" Width="100%" runat="server"
    AutoGenerateColumns="False">
    <ItemStyle Font-Size="X-Small" Font-Names="Verdana"
      BackColor="Gainsboro"></ItemStyle>
    <HeaderStyle Font-Size="X-Small" Font-Names="Verdana" Font-Bold="True"
      ForeColor="White" BackColor="Navy"></HeaderStyle>
    <Columns>
      <asp:BoundColumn DataField="ProductID"
        HeaderText="Product ID"></asp:BoundColumn>
      <asp:BoundColumn DataField="ProductName"
        HeaderText="Product Name"></asp:BoundColumn>
      <asp:BoundColumn DataField="Quantity"
        HeaderText="Quantity"></asp:BoundColumn>
      <asp:BoundColumn DataField="UnitCost"
        HeaderText="Unit Cost"></asp:BoundColumn>
      <asp:BoundColumn DataField="Subtotal"
        HeaderText="Subtotal"></asp:BoundColumn>
    </Columns>
  </asp:datagrid></P>
```

Now you come to your two new data grids, starting with the one for displaying customer information:

```
<P><asp:label id="Label11" CssClass="AdminPageText" Width="150px" runat="server">
    Customer Details:</asp:label>
  <asp:datagrid id="customerGrid" Width="100%" runat="server"
    AutoGenerateColumns="False">
    <ItemStyle Font-Size="X-Small" Font-Names="Verdana"
      BackColor="Gainsboro"></ItemStyle>
    <HeaderStyle Font-Size="X-Small" Font-Names="Verdana" Font-Bold="True"
      ForeColor="White" BackColor="Navy"></HeaderStyle>
    <Columns>
      <asp:BoundColumn DataField="CustomerID"
        HeaderText="ID"></asp:BoundColumn>
      <asp:BoundColumn DataField="Name"
        HeaderText="Name"></asp:BoundColumn>
      <asp:BoundColumn DataField="Email"
        HeaderText="EMail"></asp:BoundColumn>
      <asp:BoundColumn DataField="Address1"
        HeaderText="Address1"></asp:BoundColumn>
      <asp:BoundColumn DataField="Address2"
        HeaderText="Address2"></asp:BoundColumn>
      <asp:BoundColumn DataField="City"
        HeaderText="Town/City"></asp:BoundColumn>
      <asp:BoundColumn DataField="Region"
        HeaderText="Region/State"></asp:BoundColumn>
```

```
        <asp:BoundColumn DataField="PostalCode"
            HeaderText="Postal Code/ZIP"></asp:BoundColumn>
        <asp:BoundColumn DataField="Country"
            HeaderText="Country"></asp:BoundColumn>
        <asp:BoundColumn DataField="Phone"
            HeaderText="Phone"></asp:BoundColumn>
    </Columns>
  </asp:datagrid></P>
```

Finally, the data grid for showing the audit trail for the order:

```
<P><asp:label id="Label3" CssClass="AdminPageText" Width="150px" runat="server">
    Audit Trail:</asp:label>
  <asp:datagrid id="auditGrid" Width="100%" runat="server"
    AutoGenerateColumns="False">
    <ItemStyle Font-Size="X-Small" Font-Names="Verdana"
        BackColor="Gainsboro"></ItemStyle>
    <HeaderStyle Font-Size="X-Small" Font-Names="Verdana" Font-Bold="True"
        ForeColor="White" BackColor="Navy"></HeaderStyle>
    <Columns>
        <asp:BoundColumn DataField="DateStamp"
            HeaderText="Date Recorded"></asp:BoundColumn>
        <asp:BoundColumn DataField="Message"
            HeaderText="Message"></asp:BoundColumn>
        <asp:BoundColumn DataField="MessageNumber"
            HeaderText="Message Number"></asp:BoundColumn>
    </Columns>
  </asp:datagrid></P>
```

Next you come to the code behind OrderDetailsAdmins.ascx. The first modification here is to add the following:

```
Imports System.Data
Imports System.Data.SqlClient
Imports CommerceLib
```

This is necessary because you'll need to use OrderProcessor to push orders along the pipeline.

For the rest of the code, you take out almost as much as you add. The Page_Load event handler no longer needs to worry about whether the control is in edit mode, so the code is shortened there:

```
    Private Sub Page_Load(ByVal sender As System.Object, _
        ByVal e As System.EventArgs) Handles MyBase.Load
        'Put user code to initialize the page here
        If Not Page.IsPostBack Then
            ' Update information in all controls
            PopulateControls()
        End If
    End Sub
```

The PopulateControls method called here also changes. This time there are several reasons: the OrderInfo class is no longer used, more data grids are available to populate, edit mode is not a concern, and the Process button must be considered.

Taking it from the top, you start by getting the data for the order selected in the form of an SqlDataReader:

```
Private Sub PopulateControls()
    ' Create the OrderManager object which has the GetOrderDetails method
    Dim om As New OrderManager()

    ' Get orderID from request parameters
    Dim orderID As Integer = Convert.ToInt32(Request.Params("OrderID"))

    ' The Order information is extracted using om.GetOrder
    Dim orderReader As SqlDataReader = om.GetOrder(orderID)
```

First you check for data and abort if none is found:

```
If Not orderReader.Read() Then
    ' no data to display
    Return
End If
```

Next, you extract order information for placing in the text boxes, first checking to determine whether certain fields are NULL (you only need to check this for the fields where NULL values are allowed):

```
    ' Populate the text boxes with order information
    orderIdTextBox.Text = orderReader("OrderID")
    dateCreatedTextBox.Text = orderReader("DateCreated")
    If Not orderReader("DateShipped").GetType() Is GetType(DBNull) Then
        dateShippedTextBox.Text = orderReader("DateShipped")
    End If
    statusTextBox.Text = orderReader("Description")
    If Not orderReader("AuthCode").GetType() Is GetType(DBNull) Then
        authCodeTextBox.Text = orderReader("AuthCode")
        referenceTextBox.Text = orderReader("Reference")
    End If
```

Note that the AuthCode and Reference data fields are linked, so if one of them is NULL then the other one will be as well, hence the single check for a NULL value in the preceding code rather than checking both fields.

The Process button will only be available for orders with a status of 3 or 6, and should be formatted accordingly:

```
    ' Name or hide Process button
    If orderReader("Status") = 3 Then
        processButton.Text = "Confirm Stock"
```

```
    ElseIf orderReader("Status") = 6 Then
        processButton.Text = "Confirm Shipment"
    Else
        processButton.Visible = False
    End If
```

Finally, you close the data reader:

```
    ' close reader
    orderReader.Close()
```

The last part of this method populates the three data grids using the following simple code:

```
    ' Fill the data grid with orderdetails
    orderDetailsGrid.DataSource = om.GetOrderDetails(orderID)
    orderDetailsGrid.DataKeyField = "OrderID"
    orderDetailsGrid.DataBind()

    ' Get full customer details
    customerGrid.DataSource = om.GetCustomerByOrderID(orderID)
    customerGrid.DataBind()

    ' Fill the audit trail with data
    auditGrid.DataSource = om.GetAuditTrail(orderID)
    auditGrid.DataKeyField = "DateStamp"
    auditGrid.DataBind()
End Sub
```

The only user interaction that is now possible for an order is clicking the Process button. When you do this, code is called that is very similar to that in Checkout.aspx.vb, because you're using OrderProcessor to push an order along the pipeline:

```
Private Sub processButton_Click(ByVal sender As System.Object, _
        ByVal e As System.EventArgs) Handles processButton.Click
    ' Get orderID from request parameters
    Dim orderID As Integer = Convert.ToInt32(Request.Params("OrderID"))

    ' Get configuration for order processor
    Dim processorConfiguration As OrderProcessorConfiguration = _
        New OrderProcessorConfiguration( _
            ConfigurationSettings.AppSettings("ConnectionString"), _
            ConfigurationSettings.AppSettings("MailServer"), _
            ConfigurationSettings.AppSettings("AdminEmail"), _
            ConfigurationSettings.AppSettings("CustomerServiceEmail"), _
            ConfigurationSettings.AppSettings("OrderProcessorEmail"), _
            ConfigurationSettings.AppSettings("SupplierEmail"))
```

```
' Process order, ignore errors as they will be apparent when
' nothing changes!
Try
    Dim processor As OrderProcessor = New OrderProcessor()
    processor.Process(orderID, processorConfiguration)
Catch ex As OrderProcessorException
    ' If an error occurs head to an error page
End Try

    Response.Redirect("orders.aspx?OrderID=" & orderID.ToString())
End Sub
```

Testing the Order Administration Page

All that remains now is to check that everything is working properly. To do this, use the web interface to place an order, and then check it out via the orders admin link on default.aspx. You should see that the order is awaiting confirmation of stock, as shown in Figure 14-8.

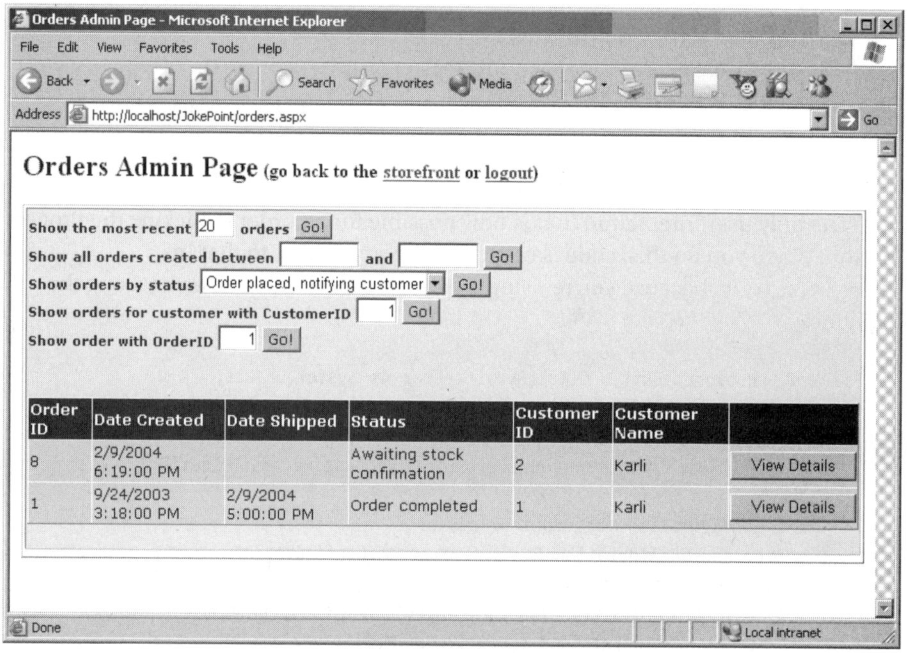

Figure 14-8. Order awaiting stock confirmation

Click View Details, and scroll down until the button for confirming stock appears, as shown in Figure 14-9.

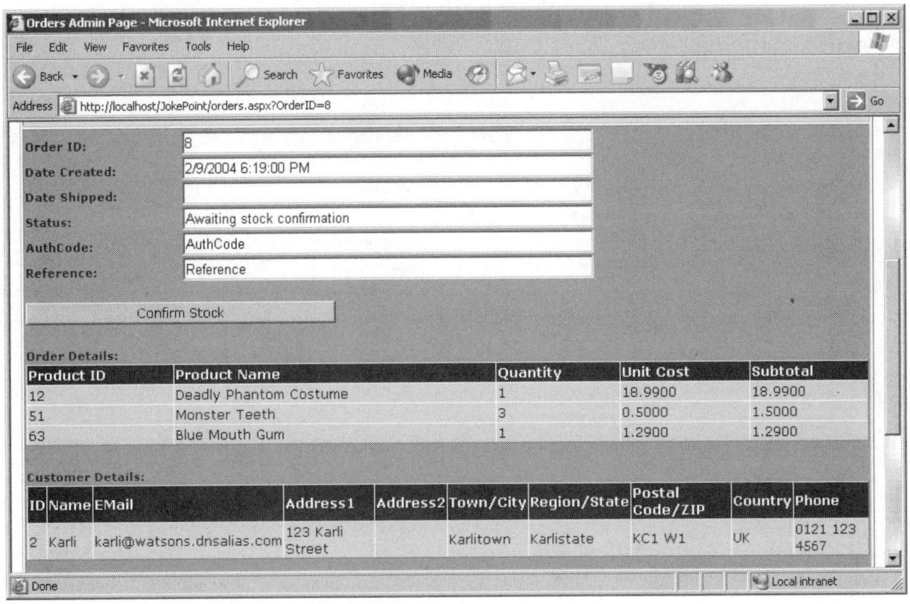

Figure 14-9. Confirm Stock button

Click the Confirm Stock button and the order is processed. Because this happens very quickly, you are soon presented with the next stage, a prompt to confirm shipment, as shown in Figure 14.10.

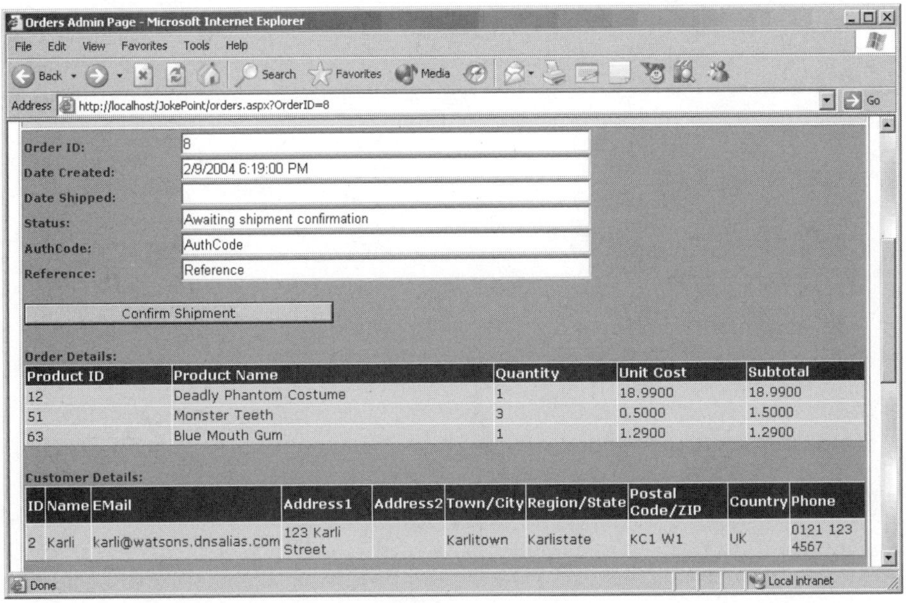

Figure 14-10. Prompt to confirm shipment

Clicking Confirm Shipment shows you that the order has been completed, as shown in Figure 14-11.

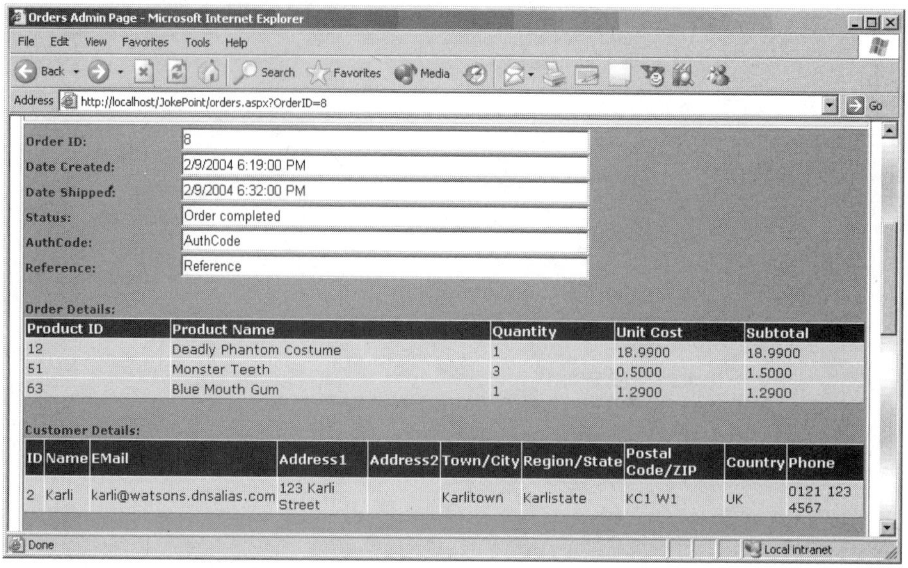

Figure 14-11. Order completed status

If you scroll down further, you can see all audit trail messages that have been stored in the database concerning this order, as shown in Figure 14-12.

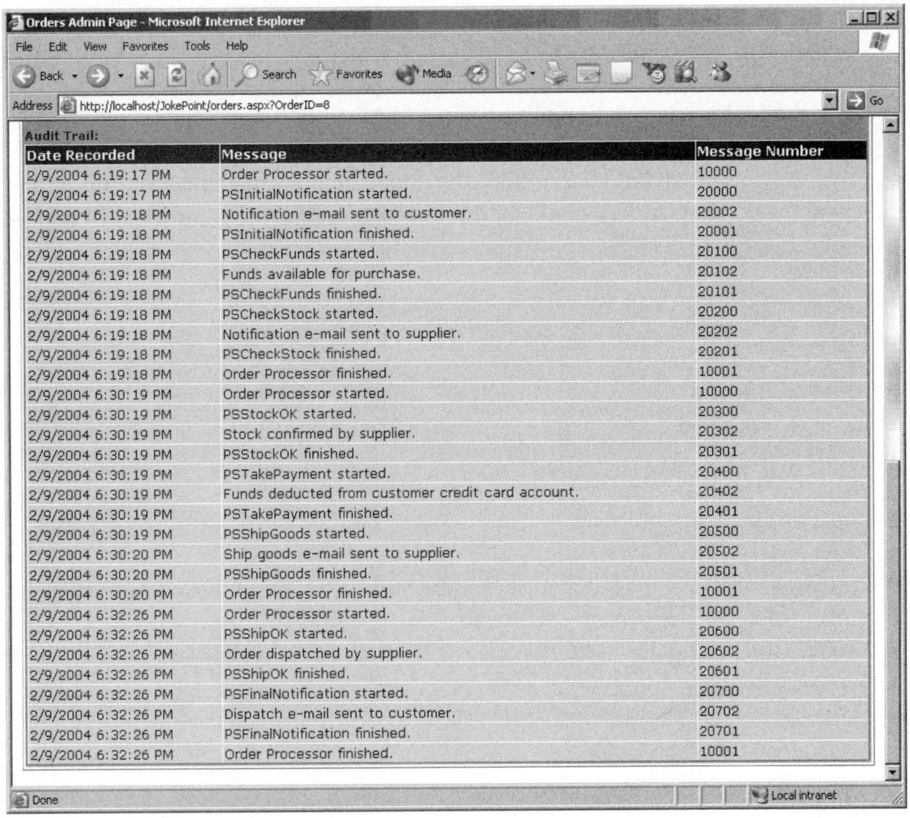

Date Recorded	Message	Message Number
2/9/2004 6:19:17 PM	Order Processor started.	10000
2/9/2004 6:19:17 PM	PSInitialNotification started.	20000
2/9/2004 6:19:18 PM	Notification e-mail sent to customer.	20002
2/9/2004 6:19:18 PM	PSInitialNotification finished.	20001
2/9/2004 6:19:18 PM	PSCheckFunds started.	20100
2/9/2004 6:19:18 PM	Funds available for purchase.	20102
2/9/2004 6:19:18 PM	PSCheckFunds finished.	20101
2/9/2004 6:19:18 PM	PSCheckStock started.	20200
2/9/2004 6:19:18 PM	Notification e-mail sent to supplier.	20202
2/9/2004 6:19:18 PM	PSCheckStock finished.	20201
2/9/2004 6:19:18 PM	Order Processor finished.	10001
2/9/2004 6:30:19 PM	Order Processor started.	10000
2/9/2004 6:30:19 PM	PSStockOK started.	20300
2/9/2004 6:30:19 PM	Stock confirmed by supplier.	20302
2/9/2004 6:30:19 PM	PSStockOK finished.	20301
2/9/2004 6:30:19 PM	PSTakePayment started.	20400
2/9/2004 6:30:19 PM	Funds deducted from customer credit card account.	20402
2/9/2004 6:30:19 PM	PSTakePayment finished.	20401
2/9/2004 6:30:19 PM	PSShipGoods started.	20500
2/9/2004 6:30:20 PM	Ship goods e-mail sent to supplier.	20502
2/9/2004 6:30:20 PM	PSShipGoods finished.	20501
2/9/2004 6:30:20 PM	Order Processor finished.	10001
2/9/2004 6:32:26 PM	Order Processor started.	10000
2/9/2004 6:32:26 PM	PSShipOK started.	20600
2/9/2004 6:32:26 PM	Order dispatched by supplier.	20602
2/9/2004 6:32:26 PM	PSShipOK finished.	20601
2/9/2004 6:32:26 PM	PSFinalNotification started.	20700
2/9/2004 6:32:26 PM	Dispatch e-mail sent to customer.	20702
2/9/2004 6:32:26 PM	PSFinalNotification finished.	20701
2/9/2004 6:32:26 PM	Order Processor finished.	10001

Figure 14-12. Audit trail messages for this order

Summary

You've taken giant strides toward completing your e-commerce application in this chapter. Now you have a fully audited, secure backbone for the application.

Specifically, we've covered:

- Modifications to the JokePoint application to enable your own pipeline processing
- The basic framework for the order pipeline
- The database additions for auditing data and storing additional required data in the `Orders` table

- The implementation of most of the order pipeline, apart from those sections that deal with credit cards

- A simple implementation of an order administration web page

The only thing missing that needs to be added before you can deliver this application to the outside world is credit card processing functionality, which we'll look at in the next chapter.

CHAPTER 15

Credit Card Transactions

THE LAST THING YOU need to do before launching the e-commerce site is enable credit card processing. In this chapter, we will look at how you can build this into the pipeline you created in the last chapter.

We'll start by looking at the theory behind credit card transactions, the sort of organizations that help you achieve credit card processing, and the sort of transactions that are possible. Moving on, we'll take two example organizations and discuss the specifics of their transaction APIs (Application Program Interfaces, the means by which you access credit card transaction functionality). After this, you'll build a new class library that helps you use one of these transaction APIs via some simple test code.

Finally, you'll integrate the API with the JokePoint e-commerce application and order-processing pipeline.

Learning the Credit Card Transaction Fundamentals

Banks and other financial institutions use secure networks for their transactions, based on the X.25 protocol rather than TCP/IP (Transmission Control Protocol/Internet Protocol, the primary means by which data is transmitted across the Internet). X.25 isn't something you need to know anything about, apart from the fact that it's a different protocol for networking and isn't compatible with TCP/IP. As such, X.25 networks are completely separate from the Internet, and although it's possible to get direct access to them, this is unlikely to be a reasonable option. To do so, you might have to enter into some serious negotiation with the owner of the network you want to use. The owner will want to be 100% sure that you are a reliable customer who is capable of enforcing the necessary safeguards to prevent an attack on their system. The owner of the network won't be handing out these licenses to just anyone, because most people won't be able to afford the security measures required (which include locking your servers in a cage, sending daily backup tapes down a secure chute, having three individuals with separate keys to access these tapes, and so on).

The alternative is to go via a gateway provider. This enables you to perform your side of the credit card transaction protocol over the Internet (using a secure protocol), while relying on your chosen gateway to communicate with X.25 networks. Although there is likely to be a cost involved with this, the provider will have reached some deal with financial institutions that enables them to keep costs low, and the savings will be passed on to you (after the gateway takes its share), so it's likely to be much cheaper than having your own X.25 connection. This method is also likely to be cheaper than using a third party such as PayPal, because you only need the minimum functionality when you are handling your own order pipeline. There is no need, for example, to use all the order-auditing functionality offered by a company such as PayPal, because in the last chapter, you already built all this functionality.

Working with Credit Card Payment Gateways

To work with a gateway organization, you first need to open a merchant bank account. This can be done at most banks, and will get you a merchant ID that you can use when signing up with the gateway. The next step is to find a suitable gateway. Unfortunately, this can be a lot of hard work!

It isn't hard to find a gateway; but it is hard to find the right one. Literally hundreds of companies are ready to take a cut of your sales. A quick search on the Internet for "credit card gateway" will get you a long list. The web sites of these companies are for the most part pure brochureware—you'll find yourself reading through pages of text about how they are the best and most secure at what they do, only to end up with a form to fill in so that a customer service representative can call you to "discuss your needs." In the long run, you can rest assured that at least you will probably only have to go through the procedure once.

You'll probably find that most of the organizations offering this service offer similar packages, so there may be very little that influences your choice. However, key points to look for include which banks they will do business with (your merchant bank account will have to be at one of these), which currencies they deal in, and, of course, what the costs are.

In this chapter, we'll look at two of the few organizations that are easy to deal with—DataCash and VeriSign PayFlow Pro.

Table 15-1 shows some of the gateway services available.

Table 15-1. Gateway Services

United States	Web Address	United Kingdom	Web Address
CyberCash	http://www.cybercash.com/	Arcot	http://www.arcot.com/onlinepayments.html
First Data	http://www.firstdata.com/	WorldPay	http://www.worldpay.com/
Cardservice International	http://www.cardservice.com/	DataCash	http://www.datacash.com/
VeriSign Pay Flow Pro	http://www.verisign.com/products/payflow/pro/	VeriSign Pay Flow Pro	http://www.verisign.com/products/payflow/pro/
ICVerify	http://www.icverify.com/		

DataCash

DataCash is a UK-based credit card gateway organization. Unfortunately, this means that you'll need a UK merchant bank account if you want to use it in your final application, but you don't have to worry about this for now. The reason for using DataCash in this chapter is that you don't have to do very much to get access to a rather useful test account—you don't even need a merchant bank account. As you'll see later in this chapter, you'll be able to perform test transactions using so-called "magic" credit card numbers supplied by DataCash, which will accept or decline transactions without performing any actual financial transactions. This is fantastic for development purposes, because you don't want to use your own credit cards for testing!

The important point to bear in mind is that the techniques covered in this chapter apply to every credit card gateway there is. The specifics may change slightly if you switch to a different organization, but you'll have done most of the hard work already.

Before you ask, no, we're not sales representatives for DataCash. It's just that we've spent many hours (days?) looking into credit card transactions, and so far we've yet to find a more developer-friendly way of getting started.

PayFlow Pro

PayFlow Pro is a service supplied by the globally recognized Internet company VeriSign. This company has established itself as an excellent resource for Internet security and e-commerce applications, so it comes as no surprise that VeriSign has an entry in the competitive credit card gateway arena.

In fact, the first edition of this book did not cover the PayFlow Pro service. However, because readers have had great success with it, we feel obliged to cover it here.

NOTE *The authors of this book are in no way affiliated with VeriSign.*

Understanding Credit Card Transactions

Whichever gateway you use; the basic principles of credit card transactions are the same. First, the sort of transactions you'll be dealing with in an e-commerce web site are known as Card Not Present (CNP) transactions, which means you don't have the credit card in front of you, and you can't check the customer signature. This isn't a problem; after all you've probably been performing CNP transactions for some time now: online, over the phone, by mail, and so on. It's just something to be aware of should you see the CNP acronym.

Several advanced services are offered by various gateways, including cardholder address verification, security code checking, fraud screening, and so on. Each of these adds an additional layer of complexity to your credit card processing, and we're not going to go into details here. Rather, this chapter provides a starting point from which you can add these services if required. With all of these optional extras, the choice will involve how much money is passing through your system, and a trade off between the costs of implementation and the potential costs if something goes wrong that could be prevented if you use these extra services. If you are interested in these services, the "customer service representative" mentioned previously will be happy to explain things.

You can perform several types of transaction, including

- *Authorization*: Basic type, checks card for funds and deducts them.

- *Pre-authorization*: Checks cards for funds and allocates them if available, but doesn't deduct them immediately.

- *Fulfillment*: Completes a pre-authorization transaction, deducting the funds already allocated.

- *Refund*: Refunds a completed transaction, or simply puts money on a credit card.

Again, the specifics vary, but these are the basic types.

In this chapter, you'll use the pre/`fulfill` model, in which you don't take payment until just before you instruct your supplier to ship goods. This has been hinted at previously by the structure of the pipeline you created in the last chapter.

Implementing Credit Card Processing

Now that we've covered the basics, we need to look at how to get things working in the JokePoint application using the DataCash system. First, you need to obtain a test account with DataCash:

1. Point your browser at `http://www.datacash.com/`.

2. Head to the Support ➤ Integration Info section of the web site.

3. Enter your details and submit.

4. From the email you receive, make a note of your account username and password, as well as the additional information required for accessing the DataCash reporting system.

The next step would normally be to download one of DataCash's toolkits for easy integration. However, because DataCash doesn't provide a .NET-compatible implementation, you must use the XML API for performing transactions. Basically, this involves sending XML requests to a certain URL using an SSL connection, and deciphering the XML result. This is easy to do in .NET.

NOTE   *After we have looked at DataCash in detail, we'll examine the PayFlow Pro system, although we won't show the code implementation. The code is, however, available in the Downloads section on the Apress web site (http://www.apress.com) for this book.*

Considering the DataCash XML API

You'll be doing a lot of XML manipulation when communicating with DataCash, because you'll need to create XML documents to send to DataCash, and extract data from XML responses. In this section, we will take a quick look at the XML required for the operations you'll be performing, and the responses you can expect.

Pre-authentication Request

When you send a pre-authentication request to DataCash, you need to include the following information:

- DataCash username (known as the DataCash Client)

- DataCash password

- A unique transaction reference number (explained later in this section)

- The amount of money to be debited

- The currency used for the transaction (USD, GBP, and so on)

- The type of the transaction (for pre-authentication, the code pre is used)

- The credit card number

- The credit card expiry date

- The credit card issue date (if applicable to the type of credit card being used)

- The credit card issue number (if applicable to the type of credit card being used)

The reference number must be a number between 6 and 12 digits long, which you choose to uniquely identify the transaction with an order. Because you can't use a short number, you can't just use the order ID values you've been using until now for orders. However, you can use this order ID as the starting point for creating a reference number, simply by adding a high number, such as 1,000,000. You can't duplicate the reference number in any future transactions, so you can be sure that after a transaction is completed, it won't execute again, which might otherwise result in charging the customer twice. This does mean, however, that if a credit card is rejected, you might need to create a whole new order for the customer, but that shouldn't be a problem if required.

The XML request is formatted in the following way, with the values detailed previously shown in bold:

```
<?xml version="1.0" encoding="UTF-8"?>
<Request>
  <Authentication>
    <password>DataCash password</password>
    <client>DataCash client</client>
  </Authentication>
  <Transaction>
    <TxnDetails>
      <merchantreference>Unique reference number</merchantreference>
      <amount currency='Currency Type'>Cash amount</amount>
    </TxnDetails>
    <CardTxn>
      <method>pre</method>
      <Card>
        <pan>Credit card number</pan>
        <expirydate>Credit card expiry date</expirydate>
      </Card>
    </CardTxn>
  </Transaction>
</Request>
```

Response to Pre-authentication Request

The response to a pre-authentication request includes the following information:

- A status code number indicating what happened; 1 if the transaction was successful, or one of several other codes if something else happens. For a complete list of return codes for a DataCash server, see `https://testserver.datacash.com/software/returncodes.html`.

- A reason for the status, which is basically a string explaining the status in English. For a status of 1, this string is ACCEPTED.

- An authentication code used to fulfill the transaction.

- A reference code for use by DataCash.

- The time that the transaction was processed.

- The mode of the transaction, which is TEST when using the test account.

- Confirmation of the type of credit card used.

- Confirmation of the country that the credit card was issued in.

- The authorization code used by the bank (for reference only).

The XML for this is formatted as follows:

```
<?xml version="1.0" encoding="utf-8"?>
<Response>
  <status>Status code</status>
  <reason>Reason</reason>
  <merchantreference>Authentication code</merchantreference>
  <datacash_reference>Reference number</datacash_reference>
  <time>Time</time>
  <mode>TEST</mode>
  <CardTxn>
    <card_scheme>Card Type</card_scheme>
    <country>Country</country>
    <authcode>Bank authorization code</authcode>
  </CardTxn>
</Response>
```

Fulfillment Request

For a fulfillment request, you need to send the following information:

- DataCash username (known as the DataCash Client)

- DataCash password

- The type of the transaction (for fulfillment, you use the code fulfil)

- The authentication code received earlier

- The reference number received earlier

Optionally, you can include additional information, such as a confirmation of the amount to be debited from the credit card, although this isn't really necessary.
This is formatted as follows:

```
<?xml version="1.0" encoding="UTF-8"?>
<Request>
  <Authentication>
    <password>DataCash password</password>
    <client>DataCash client</client>
  </Authentication>
  <Transaction>
    <HistoricTxn>
      <reference>Reference Number</reference>
      <authcode>Authentication code</authcode>
```

```
      <method>fulfil</method>
    </HistoricTxn>
  </Transaction>
</Request>
```

Fulfillment Response

The response to a fulfillment request includes the following information:

- A status code number indicating what happened; 1 if the transaction was successful, or one of several other codes if something else happens. Again for a complete list of the codes, see `https://testserver.datacash.com/software/returncodes.html`.

- A reason for the status, which is basically a string explaining the status in English. For a status of 1, this string is FULFILLED OK.

- Two copies of the reference code for use by DataCash.

- The time that the transaction was processed.

- The mode of the transaction, which is TEST when using the test account.

The XML for this is formatted as follows:

```
<?xml version="1.0" encoding="utf-8"?>
<Response>
   <status>Status code</status>
   <reason>Reason</reason>
   <merchantreference>Reference Code</merchantreference>
   <datacash_reference>Reference Code</datacash_reference>
   <time>Time</time>
   <mode>TEST</mode>
</Response>
```

Exchanging XML Data

You could build up the XML documents shown previously piece by piece, but the .NET Framework allows you to do things in a much better way. The solution presented here involves XML serialization. It's possible to configure any .NET class in such a way that it can be serialized as an XML document, and also that XML documents can be used to instantiate classes. This involves converting all public fields and properties into XML data, and is the basis for the web services functionality in .NET.

The default behavior for this is to create XML documents with elements named the same as the public fields and properties that you are serializing. For example, you might have the following class and member:

```
Public Class TestClass
   Public TestMember as String
End Class
```

This would be serialized as follows:

```
<?xml version="1.0" encoding="utf-8"?>
<TestClass>
   <TestMember>Value</TestMember>
</TestClass>
```

You can override this behavior using XML serialization attributes. You can force pieces of data to be formatted in elements with custom names, as attributes, as plain text, and so on.

For example, you could force the previous class to serialize as an attribute as follows:

```
Public Class TestClass
   <XmlAttributeAttribute("TestAttribute")>
   Public TestMember as String
End Class
```

The `<XmlAttributeAttribute()>` part means that the member that follows should be serialized as an attribute, and the string parameter names the attribute. This class would now serialize as follows:

```
<?xml version="1.0" encoding="utf-8"?>
<TestClass TestAttribute="Value">
</TestClass>
```

You can use several of these attributes, and you'll see some of them in the example that follows. This example demonstrates how you can create classes that represent DataCash requests and responses, which will be capable of serializing to and deserializing from an XML representation. This has two benefits:

- It makes sending data to DataCash easy.

- You can use the full power of .NET classes to provide an intelligent way of accessing data.

In the example that follows, you'll create the classes necessary to exchange data with DataCash, and try out these classes using some simple client code. Note that several classes are used to build up the XML because the structure involves several nested elements rather than a flat structure.

Exercise: Communicating with DataCash

1. Create a new Class Library project in `C:\BegECom\Chapter15` called `DataCashLib`.

2. Remove the default `Class1` class.

3. Add the following classes starting with `AmountClass`:

```
Imports System.Xml.Serialization

Public Class AmountClass
  <XmlAttributeAttribute("currency")> _
  Public Currency As String

  <XmlText()> _
  Public Amount As String
End Class
```

4. Add the following class, `AuthenticationClass`:

```
Imports System.Xml.Serialization

Public Class AuthenticationClass
  <XmlElement("password")> _
  Public Password As String

  <XmlElement("client")> _
  Public Client As String
End Class
```

5. Add the following class, CardClass:

```
Imports System.Xml.Serialization

Public Class CardClass
  <XmlElement("pan")> _
  Public CardNumber As String

  <XmlElement("expirydate")> _
  Public ExpiryDate As String

  <XmlElement("startdate")> _
  Public StartDate As String

  <XmlElement("issuenumber")> _
  Public IssueNumber As String
End Class
```

6. Add the following class, CardTxnRequestClass:

```vb
Imports System.Xml.Serialization

Public Class CardTxnRequestClass
    <XmlElement("method")> _
    Public Method As String

    <XmlElement("Card")> _
    Public Card As CardClass = New CardClass()
End Class
```

7. Add the following class, CardTxnResponseClass:

```vb
Imports System.Xml.Serialization

Public Class CardTxnResponseClass
    <XmlElement("card_scheme")> _
    Public CardScheme As String
    <XmlElement("country")> _
    Public Country As String

    <XmlElement("issuer")> _
    Public Issuer As String

    <XmlElement("authcode")> _
    Public AuthCode As String
End Class
```

8. Add the following class, HistoricTxnClass:

```vb
Imports System.Xml.Serialization

Public Class HistoricTxnClass
    <XmlElement("reference")> _
    Public Reference As String

    <XmlElement("authcode")> _
    Public AuthCode As String

    <XmlElement("method")> _
    Public Method As String

    <XmlElement("tran_code")> _
    Public TranCode As String

    <XmlElement("duedate")> _
    Public DueDate As String
End Class
```

9. Add the following class, `TxnDetailsClass`:

```
Imports System.Xml.Serialization

Public Class TxnDetailsClass
  <XmlElement("merchantreference")> _
  Public MerchantReference As String

  <XmlElement("amount")> _
  Public Amount As AmountClass = New AmountClass()
End Class
```

10. Add the following class, `TransactionClass`:

```
Imports System.Xml.Serialization

Public Class TransactionClass
  <XmlElement("TxnDetails")> _
  Public TxnDetails As TxnDetailsClass = New TxnDetailsClass()
  Private _cardTxn As CardTxnRequestClass

  Private _historicTxn As HistoricTxnClass

  <XmlElement("CardTxn")> _
  Public Property CardTxn() As CardTxnRequestClass
    Get
      If _historicTxn Is Nothing Then
        If _cardTxn Is Nothing Then
          _cardTxn = New CardTxnRequestClass()
        End If
        Return _cardTxn
      Else
        Return Nothing
      End If
    End Get
    Set(ByVal Value As CardTxnRequestClass)
      _cardTxn = Value
    End Set
  End Property

  <XmlElement("HistoricTxn")> _
  Public Property HistoricTxn() As HistoricTxnClass
    Get
      If _cardTxn Is Nothing Then
        If _historicTxn Is Nothing Then
          _historicTxn = New HistoricTxnClass()
        End If
        Return _historicTxn
      Else
        Return Nothing
      End If
    End Get
```

```
      Set(ByVal Value As HistoricTxnClass)
        _historicTxn = Value
      End Set
    End Property
  End Class
```

11. Add the following class, DataCashRequest:

```
Imports System.Net
Imports System.IO
Imports System.Text
Imports System.Xml.Serialization

<XmlRoot("Request")> _
Public Class DataCashRequest
  <XmlElement("Authentication")> _
  Public Authentication As AuthenticationClass = _
    New AuthenticationClass()

  <XmlElement("Transaction")> _
  Public Transaction As TransactionClass = New TransactionClass()
  Public Function GetResponse(ByVal url As String) As DataCashResponse
    ' Configure HTTP Request
    Dim httpRequest As HttpWebRequest
    httpRequest = WebRequest.Create(url)
    httpRequest.Method = "POST"

    ' Prepare correct encoding for XML serialization
    Dim encoding As UTF8Encoding = New UTF8Encoding()

    ' Use Xml property to obtain serialized XML data
    ' Convert into bytes using encoding specified above and get length
    Dim bodyBytes() As Byte = encoding.GetBytes(Xml)
    httpRequest.ContentLength = bodyBytes.Length

    ' Get HTTP Request stream for putting XML data into
    Dim httpRequestBodyStream As Stream = _
      httpRequest.GetRequestStream()

    ' Fill stream with serialized XML data
    httpRequestBodyStream.Write(bodyBytes, 0, bodyBytes.Length)
    httpRequestBodyStream.Close()

    ' Get HTTP Response
    Dim httpResponseStream As StreamReader
    Dim httpResponse As HttpWebResponse = httpRequest.GetResponse()
    httpResponseStream = _
      New StreamReader(httpResponse.GetResponseStream(), _
                       System.Text.Encoding.ASCII)

    Dim httpResponseBody As String
```

```
        ' Extract XML from response
        httpResponseBody = httpResponseStream.ReadToEnd()
        httpResponseStream.Close()

        ' Ignore everything that isn't XML by removing headers
        httpResponseBody = _
          httpResponseBody.Substring(httpResponseBody.IndexOf("<?xml"))

        ' Deserialize XML into DataCashResponse
        Dim serializer As XmlSerializer = _
          New XmlSerializer(GetType(DataCashResponse))
        Dim responseReader As StringReader = _
          New StringReader(httpResponseBody)

        ' Return DataCashResponse result
        Return CType(serializer.Deserialize(responseReader), _
          DataCashResponse)
    End Function

    <XmlIgnore()> _
    Public ReadOnly Property Xml()
        Get
            ' Prepare XML serializer
            Dim serializer As XmlSerializer = _
              New XmlSerializer(GetType(DataCashRequest))

            ' Serialize into StringBuilder
            Dim bodyBuilder As StringBuilder = New StringBuilder()
            Dim bodyWriter As StringWriter = New StringWriter(bodyBuilder)
            serializer.Serialize(bodyWriter, Me)

            ' Replace UTF-16 encoding with UTF-8 encoding
            Dim body As String = bodyBuilder.ToString()
            body = body.Replace("utf-16", "utf-8")
            Return body
        End Get
    End Property
End Class
```

12. Add the following class, DataCashResponse:

```
Imports System.IO
Imports System.Text
Imports System.Xml.Serialization

<XmlRoot("Response")> _
Public Class DataCashResponse
    <XmlElement("status")> _
    Public Status As String
```

```
<XmlElement("reason")> _
Public Reason As String

<XmlElement("information")> _
Public Information As String

<XmlElement("merchantreference")> _
Public MerchantReference As String

<XmlElement("datacash_reference")> _
Public DatacashReference As String

<XmlElement("time")> _
Public Time As String

<XmlElement("mode")> _
Public Mode As String

<XmlElement("CardTxn")> _
Public CardTxn As CardTxnResponseClass

<XmlIgnore()> _
Public ReadOnly Property Xml()
  Get
    ' Prepare XML serializer
    Dim serializer As XmlSerializer = _
      New XmlSerializer(GetType(DataCashResponse))
    ' Serialize into StringBuilder
    Dim bodyBuilder As StringBuilder = New StringBuilder()
    Dim bodyWriter As StringWriter = New StringWriter(bodyBuilder)
    serializer.Serialize(bodyWriter, Me)

    ' Replace UTF-16 encoding with UTF-8 encoding
    Dim body As String = bodyBuilder.ToString()
    body = body.Replace("utf-16", "utf-8")
    Return body
  End Get
End Property
End Class
```

13. Now you've finished adding the classes, and can now add a new console application project to the solution called DataCashLibTest.

14. Add a reference to DataCashLib to the DataCashLibTest project, and set the project as the startup application.

15. Modify the code in Module1.vb as follows, replacing the values for dataCashClient and dataCashPassword with your own values (obtained when you signed up with DataCash). You will also have to change the Merchant Reference number to be a different value or else you will get a duplicate reference response returned to you:

```vb
Imports DataCashLib
Imports System.Xml.Serialization
Imports System.Text
Imports System.IO

Module Module1
  Sub Main()
    ' Initialize variables
    Dim request As DataCashRequest
    Dim requestSerializer As XmlSerializer = _
      New XmlSerializer(GetType(DataCashRequest))
    Dim response As DataCashResponse
    Dim responseSerializer As XmlSerializer = _
      New XmlSerializer(GetType(DataCashResponse))
    Dim xmlBuilder As StringBuilder
    Dim xmlWriter As StringWriter
    Dim dataCashUrl As String = _
      "https://testserver.datacash.com/Transaction"
    Dim dataCashClient As String = "99110400"
    Dim dataCashPassword As String = "rUD27uD"

    ' Construct pre request
    request = New DataCashRequest()
    request.Authentication.Client = dataCashClient
    request.Authentication.Password = dataCashPassword
    request.Transaction.TxnDetails.MerchantReference = "9999999"
    request.Transaction.TxnDetails.Amount.Amount = "49.99"
    request.Transaction.TxnDetails.Amount.Currency = "GBP"
    request.Transaction.CardTxn.Method = "pre"
    request.Transaction.CardTxn.Card.CardNumber = "4444333322221111"
    request.Transaction.CardTxn.Card.ExpiryDate = "10/04"

    ' Display pre request
    Console.WriteLine("Pre Request:")
    xmlBuilder = New StringBuilder()
    xmlWriter = New StringWriter(xmlBuilder)
    requestSerializer.Serialize(xmlWriter, request)
    Console.WriteLine(xmlBuilder.ToString())
    Console.WriteLine()

    ' Get pre response
    response = request.GetResponse(dataCashUrl)

    ' Display pre response
    Console.WriteLine("Pre Response:")
    xmlBuilder = New StringBuilder()
    xmlWriter = New StringWriter(xmlBuilder)
    responseSerializer.Serialize(xmlWriter, response)
    Console.WriteLine(xmlBuilder.ToString())
    Console.WriteLine()
```

```
' Construct fulfil request
request = New DataCashRequest()
request.Authentication.Client = dataCashClient
request.Authentication.Password = dataCashPassword
request.Transaction.HistoricTxn.Method = "fulfill"
request.Transaction.HistoricTxn.AuthCode = _
  response.MerchantReference
request.Transaction.HistoricTxn.Reference = _
  response.DatacashReference

' Display fulfil request
Console.WriteLine("Fulfil Request:")
xmlBuilder = New StringBuilder()
xmlWriter = New StringWriter(xmlBuilder)
requestSerializer.Serialize(xmlWriter, request)
Console.WriteLine(xmlBuilder.ToString())
Console.WriteLine()

' Get fulfil response
response = request.GetResponse(dataCashUrl)

' Display fulfil response
Console.WriteLine("Fulfil Response:")
xmlBuilder = New StringBuilder()
xmlWriter = New StringWriter(xmlBuilder)
responseSerializer.Serialize(xmlWriter, response)
Console.WriteLine(xmlBuilder.ToString())
  End Sub
End Module
```

16. Now build the solution and run the program from the command line. Go to
    C:\BegECom\Chapter15\DataCashLibTest\bin and enter DataCashLibTest.
    The first part of the result is shown in Figure 15-1.

Figure 15-1. `DataCashLib` *transaction result*

17. Log on to https://testserver.datacash.com/reporting2 to see the transaction log for your DataCash account (note that this view takes a while to update, so you might not see the transaction right away). This report is shown in Figure 15-2, with a more detailed view in Figure 15-3.

Figure 15-2. DataCash transaction report

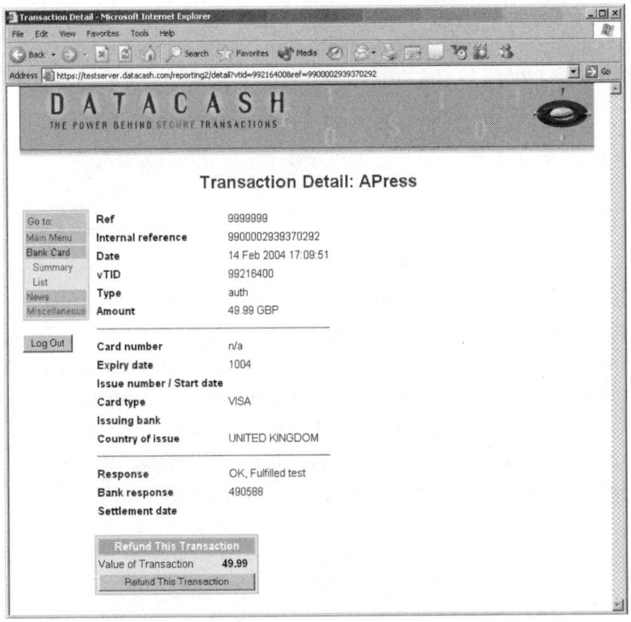

Figure 15-3. DataCash transaction report details

How It Works: Communicating with DataCash

You've created code to represent the XML documents that you're exchanging. Two root classes—DataCashRequest and DataCashResponse—encapsulate XML requests and responses. These classes contain instances of the other classes defined, which contain instances of other classes, and so on, relating to the structure of the XML documents described earlier.

Each of the members of these classes has an associated XML serialization attribute, matching the data with the way it will be formatted when the request or response classes are serialized. For example, many of the String members appear as follows:

```
<XmlElement("status")> _
Public Status As String
```

The Status field will be formatted as follows:

```
<status>Status data</status>
```

The correct capitalization is included while at the same time allowing you to set the status data using standard Pascal Casing format.

 NOTE *Pascal Casing is where variable names start with a capital letter and each subsequent word in the name also has a capital letter, such as* ThisIsAVariable. *One alternative scheme is camel Casing, where the first word isn't capitalized, for example* thisIsAVariable. *The capitalization in the names of these casing schemes serves as a reminder of their usage.*

One of the classes used, TransactionClass, is slightly more complicated than the others, because the <Transaction> element contains one of either <CardTxn> or <HistoricTxn>, depending on whether the request is a pre request or a fulfil request. Instead of using fields, this class uses properties that ensure that only one of these two elements is used.

The DataCashRequest class also has a method called GetResponse that sends the request, and packages the returned response as a DataCashResponse class. In the code to do this, you start by creating an HttpWebRequest instance for the URL supplied as a parameter:

```
Public Function GetResponse(ByVal url As String) As DataCashResponse
    Dim httpRequest As HttpWebRequest
    httpRequest = WebRequest.Create(url)
```

This request is then defined as a POST request with the appropriate encoding:

```
httpRequest.Method = "POST"
Dim encoding As UTF8Encoding = New UTF8Encoding()
```

NOTE *HTTP requests can be sent in a number of formats, the most common being* GET *and* POST. *The difference here is that* GET *requests have just a URL and header information;* POST *requests have all this plus a message body. Think of an HTTP* POST *request as if it was an email, with the HTTP response being the email reply. In both cases, header information is like the address and subject of the email, and body information is like the message body of an email.*

Next you need to supply the body of the POST request, which is the XML document you want to send. To do this, you get the serialized version of the data contained in the object via the Xml property (which simply serializes the DataCashRequest instance into XML, making use of the XML serialization attributes):

```
Dim bodyBytes() As Byte = encoding.GetBytes(Xml)
```

You also need to specify the length of the data contained in the HTTP header for the request:

```
httpRequest.ContentLength = bodyBytes.Length
```

Next you take the XML data and place it into the request via standard stream manipulation code:

```
Dim httpRequestBodyStream As Stream = httpRequest.GetRequestStream()
httpRequestBodyStream.Write(bodyBytes, 0, bodyBytes.Length)
httpRequestBodyStream.Close()
```

Once you have the request class, you can obtain the response, also via stream manipulation:

```
Dim httpResponseStream As StreamReader
Dim httpResponse As HttpWebResponse = httpRequest.GetResponse()
httpResponseStream = _
   New StreamReader(httpResponse.GetResponseStream(), _
                    System.Text.Encoding.ASCII)
Dim httpResponseBody As String
httpResponseBody = httpResponseStream.ReadToEnd()
httpResponseStream.Close()
```

You only need the XML data contained in this stream, so clip off the headers at the beginning of the data returned before deserializing it. We do this using the String.Substring method to obtain the section of the string that starts with "<?xml", the location of which is found using the String.IndexOf method.

```
httpResponseBody = _
   httpResponseBody.Substring(httpResponseBody.IndexOf("<?xml"))
Dim serializer As XmlSerializer = _
```

```
New XmlSerializer(GetType(DataCashResponse))
Dim responseReader As StringReader = New StringReader(httpResponseBody)
```

Finally, you cast the deserialized object into a DataCashResponse object for further manipulation:

```
Return CType(serializer.Deserialize(responseReader), DataCashResponse)
End Function
```

After the transaction has completed, you can check that everything has worked properly via the DataCash reporting web interface.

Integrating DataCash with JokePoint

Now you have a new class library that you can use to perform credit card transactions. However, you need to modify a few things to integrate it with your existing e-commerce application and pipeline.

Modifying the OrderProcessor *Configuration*

You now have three new pieces of information that CommerceLib requires to operate:

- DataCash client

- DataCash password

- DataCash URL

You can place all this information into the OrderProcessorConfiguration class you are using to initialize OrderProcessor as follows:

```
' Configuration details for order processor
Public Structure OrderProcessorConfiguration
    Public ConnectionString As String
    Public MailServer As String
    Public AdminEmail As String
    Public CustomerServiceEmail As String
    Public OrderProcessorEmail As String
    Public SupplierEmail As String
    Public DataCashClient As String
    Public DataCashPassword As String
    Public DataCashUrl As String

    Public Sub New(ByVal newConnectionString As String, _
                    ByVal newMailServer As String, _
                    ByVal newAdminEmail As String, _
                    ByVal newCustomerServiceEmail As String, _
                    ByVal newOrderProcessorEmail As String, _
```

```
                ByVal newSupplierEmail As String, _
                ByVal newDataCashClient As String, _
                ByVal newDataCashPassword As String, _
                ByVal newDataCashUrl As String)
      ConnectionString = newConnectionString
      MailServer = newMailServer
      AdminEmail = newAdminEmail
      CustomerServiceEmail = newCustomerServiceEmail
      OrderProcessorEmail = newOrderProcessorEmail
      SupplierEmail = newSupplierEmail
      DataCashClient = newDataCashClient
      DataCashPassword = newDataCashPassword
      DataCashUrl = newDataCashUrl
    End Sub
End Structure
```

> **NOTE** *Making this change will break any code that uses the*
> CommerceLib *library. Don't worry about this for now; by the time you*
> *use it, you'll have corrected things. However, you might want to remove*
> CommerceLibTest *from the* CommerceLib *solution because you we won't*
> *be needing it any more, and it will be annoying to see it fail to compile*
> *every time. Alternatively, you could modify* CommerceLibTest *to make it*
> *work with this new scheme and use it for testing, although this isn't*
> *really necessary at this stage.*

You can store this information in the web.config file of JokePoint just as you did
the other data:

```
<appSettings>
    <add key="ConnectionString"
     value="server=(local);Integrated Security=SSPI;database=JokePoint" />
    <add key="MailServer" value="MailServer" />
    <add key="AdminEmail" value="AdminEmail" />
    <add key="CustomerServiceEmail"
     value="customerservice@JokePoint.com" />
    <add key="OrderProcessorEmail" value="orderprocessor@JokePoint.com" />
    <add key="SupplierEmail" value="SupplierEmail" />
    <add key="DataCashClient" value="99110400" />
    <add key="DataCashPassword" value="rUD27uD" />
    <add key="DataCashUrl"
     value="https://testserver.datacash.com/Transaction" />
</appSettings>
```

You also need to change the placeOrderButton_Click event handler in
Checkout.aspx.vb to include this information:

```
Private Sub placeOrderButton_Click(ByVal sender As System.Object, _
    ByVal e As System.EventArgs) Handles orderButton.Click
  Dim cart As New ShoppingCart()
```

```
Dim processorConfiguration As OrderProcessorConfiguration = _
  New OrderProcessorConfiguration( _
    ConfigurationSettings.AppSettings("ConnectionString"), _
    ConfigurationSettings.AppSettings("MailServer"), _
    ConfigurationSettings.AppSettings("AdminEmail"), _
    ConfigurationSettings.AppSettings("CustomerServiceEmail"), _
    ConfigurationSettings.AppSettings("OrderProcessorEmail"), _
    ConfigurationSettings.AppSettings("SupplierEmail"), _
    ConfigurationSettings.AppSettings("DataCashClient"), _
    ConfigurationSettings.AppSettings("DataCashPassword"), _
    ConfigurationSettings.AppSettings("DataCashUrl"))
Dim processor As OrderProcessor = New OrderProcessor()
processor.Process(cart.CreateOrder(customerID), processorConfiguration)
Response.Redirect("OrderDone.aspx")
End Sub
```

Exactly the same change also needs to be made to the code in
OrderDetailsAdmin.aspx.vb.

Modifying the Pipeline

The final changes involve modifying the pipeline section classes that deal with
credit card transactions. The infrastructure for storing and retrieving authentication code and reference information has already been included, via the
OrderProcessor.SetOrderAuthCodeAndReference method and the AuthCode and
Reference properties.

After you add a reference to DataCashLib to CommerceLib, the modifications to
PSCheckFunds are as follows:

```
' 2nd pipeline stage - used to check that the customer
' has the required funds available for purchase
Imports DataCashLib
Imports SecurityLib

Public Class PSCheckFunds
  Implements IPipelineSection

  Private _processor As OrderProcessor
  Private _currentCustomer As Customer
  Private _currentOrderDetails As OrderDetails

  Public Sub Process(ByVal processor As OrderProcessor) _
    Implements IPipelineSection.Process

    _processor = processor
    _processor.AddAudit("PSCheckFunds started.", 20100)
    ' get customer details
    _currentCustomer = _processor.CurrentCustomer
```

```vbnet
' get order details
_currentOrderDetails = _processor.CurrentOrderDetails

Try
  ' check customer funds via DataCash gateway
  ' configure DataCash XML request
  Dim request As DataCashRequest = New DataCashRequest()
  request.Authentication.Client = _processor.Configuration.DataCashClient
  request.Authentication.Password = _
    _processor.Configuration.DataCashPassword
  request.Transaction.TxnDetails.MerchantReference = _
    _processor.OrderID.ToString().PadLeft(6, "0"c).PadLeft(7, "5"c)
  request.Transaction.TxnDetails.Amount.Amount = _
    _currentOrderDetails.TotalCost.ToString()
  request.Transaction.TxnDetails.Amount.Currency = "GBP"
  request.Transaction.CardTxn.Method = "pre"
  request.Transaction.CardTxn.Card.CardNumber = _
    _currentCustomer.CreditCard.CardNumber
  request.Transaction.CardTxn.Card.ExpiryDate = _
    _currentCustomer.CreditCard.ExpiryDate
  If _currentCustomer.CreditCard.IssueDate <> "" Then
    request.Transaction.CardTxn.Card.StartDate = _
      _currentCustomer.CreditCard.IssueDate
  End If
  If _currentCustomer.CreditCard.IssueNumber <> "" Then
    request.Transaction.CardTxn.Card.IssueNumber = _
      _currentCustomer.CreditCard.IssueNumber
  End If

  ' Get DataCash response
  Dim response As DataCashResponse = _
    request.GetResponse(_processor.Configuration.DataCashUrl)
  If response.Status = "1" Then
    ' update order authorization code and reference
    _processor.SetOrderAuthCodeAndReference(response.MerchantReference, _
                                      response.DatacashReference)

    ' audit and continue
    _processor.AddAudit("Funds available for purchase.", 20102)
    _processor.UpdateOrderStatus(2)
    _processor.ContinueNow = True
  Else
    _processor.AddAudit("Funds not available for purchase.", 20103)
    _processor.MailAdmin("Credit card declined.", "XML data exchanged:" _
      & Chr(10) & request.Xml & Chr(10) & Chr(10) & response.Xml, 1)
  End If
Catch
  ' fund checking failure
  Throw _
    New OrderProcessorException("Error occured while checking funds.", 1)
End Try
_processor.AddAudit("PSCheckFunds finished.", 20101)
```

```
      End Sub
End Class
```

The modifications to PSTakePayment are as follows:

```
' 5th pipeline stage - takes funds from customer
Imports DataCashLib

Public Class PSTakePayment
  Implements IPipelineSection

  Private _processor As OrderProcessor
  Private _authCode As String
  Private _reference As String

  Public Sub Process(ByVal processor As OrderProcessor) _
    Implements IPipelineSection.Process

    _processor = processor
    _processor.AddAudit("PSTakePayment started.", 20400)

    ' get authorization code and reference
    _authCode = _processor.AuthCode
    _reference = _processor.Reference

    Try
      ' take customer funds via DataCash gateway
      ' configure DataCash XML request
      Dim request As DataCashRequest = New DataCashRequest()
      request.Authentication.Client = _processor.Configuration.DataCashClient
      request.Authentication.Password = _
        _processor.Configuration.DataCashPassword
      request.Transaction.HistoricTxn.Method = "fulfill"
      request.Transaction.HistoricTxn.AuthCode = _authCode
      request.Transaction.HistoricTxn.Reference = _reference

      Dim response As DataCashResponse = _
        request.GetResponse(_processor.Configuration.DataCashUrl)
      If response.Status = "1" Then
        ' audit and continue
        _processor.AddAudit( _
          "Funds deducted from customer credit card account.", 20402)
        _processor.UpdateOrderStatus(5)
        _processor.ContinueNow = True
      Else
        _processor.AddAudit( _
          "Error taking funds from customer credit card account.", 20403)
        _processor.MailAdmin("Credit card fulfillment declined.", _
          "XML data exchanged:" & Chr(10) & request.Xml & Chr(10) & Chr(10) _
          & response.Xml, 1)
      End If
    Catch
```

```
        ' fund checking failure
        Throw _
            New OrderProcessorException("Error occured while taking payment.", 4)
        End Try
        _processor.AddAudit("PSTakePayment finished.", 20401)
    End Sub
End Class
```

Testing

Now that you have all this in place, it's important to test with a few orders. This is easily done by making sure you create a customer with "magic" credit card details. As mentioned earlier in the chapter, these are numbers that DataCash supplies for testing purposes, and can be used to obtain specific responses from DataCash. A sample of these numbers is shown in Table 15-2; a full list is available on the DataCash web site.

Table 15-2. DataCash Credit Card Test Numbers

Card Type	Card Number	Return Code	Description	Sample Message
Switch	4936000000000000001	1	Authorized with random auth code.	AUTH CODE ??????
	4936000000000000019	7	Decline the transaction.	DECLINED
	6333000000000005	1	Authorized with random auth code.	AUTH CODE ??????
	6333000000000013	7	Decline the transaction.	DECLINED
	6333000000123450	1	Authorized with random auth code.	AUTH CODE ??????
Visa	4242424242424242	7	Decline the transaction.	DECLINED
	4444333322221111	1	Authorized with random auth code.	AUTH CODE ??????
	4546389010000131	1	Authorized with random auth code.	AUTH CODE ??????

Going Live

Moving from the test account to the live one is now simply a matter of replacing the DataCash information in web.config. After you have set up a merchant bank account, you can use these details to set up a new DataCash account, obtaining new client and password data along the way. You also need to change the URL that you send data to—it needs to be the live server. The URL for this is https://transaction.datacash.com/Transaction. Other than removing the test user accounts from the database, this is all you need to do before exposing your newly completed e-commerce application to customers.

Using the PayFlow Pro API

To use PayFlow Pro, you need to sign up via the web site, which you can access at http://www.verisign.com/products/payflow/pro/. After you register, you can log on to the VerisSign Manager web site and download the API and documentation necessary to use PayFlow Pro.

One advantage that PayFlow Pro has over DataCash is the provision of a .NET API, simplifying communications with the credit card gateway. However, one disadvantage is that the syntax required to use it is a little more convoluted. Instead of sending and receiving XML files, you send and receive strings consisting of name-value pairs, separated by ampersands. Effectively, you use a similar syntax to query strings appended to URLs.

The .NET API comes with instructions for installing the various DLLs necessary to communicate with the PayFlow Pro gateway, and includes sample code to test things out. The VB test application starts with the following declarations:

```
Sub Main()
    Dim pfpro As New PFPro
    Dim Response As String
    Dim pCtlx As Integer

    Dim User As String
    Dim Vendor As String
    Dim Partner As String
    Dim Password As String

    Dim HostAddress As String
    Dim HostPort As Integer
    Dim ParmList As String
    Dim Timeout As Integer
    Dim ProxyAddress As String
    Dim ProxyPort As Integer
    Dim ProxyLogon As String
    Dim ProxyPassword As String

    Dim UserAuth As String
```

These variables are used to send and receive a string that authorizes a credit card transaction. Four of these, shown here, must be set to values used when signing up with PayFlow Pro:

```
User = "user"
Vendor = "vendor"
Partner = "partner"
Password = "password"
```

You probably won't have to change the following variable definitions in this example unless you use a proxy server. Note that port 443 is used for communications, which is the same as saying, "use https"; that is, it causes an SSL connection to be used.

```
HostAddress = "test-payflow.verisign.com"
HostPort = 443
ParmList =
"&TRXTYPE=S&TENDER=C&ACCT=5105105105105100&EXPDATE=1209&AMT=14.42&
COMMENT1[3]=123&COMMENT2=Good
Customer&INVNUM=1234567890&STREET=5199 JOHNSON&ZIP=94588"
Timeout = 30
ProxyAddress = ""
ProxyPort = 0
ProxyLogon = ""
ProxyPassword = ""
```

The most important variable here is ParmList, which includes most of the parameters required for the transaction, including the credit card details, transaction amount, and transaction type. A transaction type of S (shorthand for Sale) is used, which is an Authorization type transaction in PayFlow Pro. Alternatively, you can use transaction types of A (for Authorization) and D (for Delayed Capture) to perform a pre/fulfil type transaction.

The rest of the parameters required are created from the values set earlier in the code, and the two parameter strings are concatenated:

```
UserAuth = "USER=" + User + "&VENDOR=" + Vendor + "&PARTNER=" + Partner +
"&PWD=" + Password

ParmList = UserAuth + ParmList
```

Next, after some basic information output, the transaction is carried out. This involves creating a context in which to carry out the transaction, which just means configuring the API with host information, and so on, getting a response to the transaction query, and destroying the context:

```
Console.WriteLine("Running PFProdotNETExample using VB...")
Console.WriteLine("")

pCtlx = pfpro.CreateContext(HostAddress, HostPort, Timeout, _
    ProxyAddress, ProxyPort, ProxyLogon, ProxyPassword)

Response = pfpro.SubmitTransaction(pCtlx, ParmList)

pfpro.DestroyContext(pCtlx)
```

577

```
    Console.WriteLine(Response)
End Sub
```

The result is along the lines of:

```
RESULT=0&PNREF=VXYZ00912465&ERRCODE=00&AUTHCODE=09TEST&AVSADDR=Y&AVSZIP=N&
```

 NOTE *To carry out a successful transaction, you must first configure your account in the VeriSign Manager. Specifically, most test transactions will fail due to no transaction amount ceiling being set and failure of address verification (AVS). If you set a suitably high amount ceiling and disable AVS, you will be able to carry out successful transactions.*

You can use the information in the PayFlow Pro documentation to decipher this as follows:

- *RESULT=0*: A value of 0, as shown here, means a successful transaction. Any other number indicates an error.

- *PNREF= VXYZ00912465*: A unique reference number assigned by VeriSign.

- *ERRCODE=00*: Error code.

- *AUTHCODE=09TEST*: Approval code.

- *AVSADDR=Y&AVSZIP=N*: Address verification information.

When using pre/fulfil transactions, you need to use the PNREF value as the ORIGID parameter in the fulfillment stage.

Integrating PayFlow Pro with JokePoint

As with DataCash, you need to modify things in a few places to use this API. Rather than showing all the code for this, we can just review the steps required:

- Add configuration settings to web.config. For PayFlow Pro, you need to set user, vendor, partner, and password settings for verification, and the host to send data to (test-payflow.verisign.com for testing). Optionally, you could configure other context information here, matching the values shown in the test code in the last section (port, timeout, and proxy information).

- Modify OrderProcessorConfiguration to accept these configured values.

- Modify `Checkout.aspx.vb` and `OrderDetailsAdmin.aspx.vb` to use this new version of the configuration.

- Modify `PSCheckFunds` and `PSTakePayment` to use this new information to communicate with PayFlow Pro. This involves building a request string and interpreting response strings, and storing authorization codes in the database as with DataCash.

In addition, to use the PayFlow Pro library, you need to add a reference to `CommerceLib` to use `PFProdotNET.dll` (the .NET API for PayFlow Pro), and copy the `certs` directory to the `C:\WINDOWS\system32` directory (as described in the sample application documentation).

The downloadable code for this chapter includes a version of `CommerceLib` modified to use PayFlow Pro, and the modifications to JokePoint required to use this new library.

Summary

In this chapter, you've completed the e-commerce application by integrating JokePoint with credit card authorization. Short of putting your own products in, hooking it up with your suppliers, getting a merchant bank account, and putting it on the web, you're ready to go. Okay, so that's still quite a lot of work, but none of it is particularly difficult. We've done the hard work for you.

Specifically, in this chapter, we have looked at the theory behind credit card transactions on the web and looked at one full implementation—DataCash. You created a library that can be used to access DataCash and integrated it with your application. We also looked at PayFlow Pro. The code required to use this credit card gateway is included in the Downloads section for this book on the Apress web site (http://www.apress.com).

Creating Class Libraries and Installing IIS, MSDE, and OSQL

IN THIS APPENDIX, we'll cover a few bits and pieces that you'll need to know to run the code in this book. You may or may not already be familiar with this material, so feel free to dip in and out for just what you need.

In this appendix, we'll cover:

- Installing and working with the IIS 5.x Web Server

- Installing MSDE

- Using OSQL

- Creating class libraries

Let's begin by looking at how to install your IIS Web Server.

Installing the IIS 5.x Web Server

We'll look at the installation process for IIS on Windows 2000 Professional and Windows XP Professional together because they don't differ significantly. The main difference is that Windows 2000 installs IIS 5.0, while Windows XP installs IIS 5.1. The options for installing are exactly the same; the only thing that might differ is the look of the dialog boxes.

It's worth noting that you can't install IIS on Windows XP Home Edition, and therefore you can't run ASP.NET on it. It will only work on Windows XP Professional.

Because your computer might be already running IIS 5.x, we'll describe a process for checking whether this is the case as part of the installation process. You should also note that to install anything (not just ASP.NET, but literally anything) on Windows 2000/XP, you need to be logged in as a user with administrative rights.

Installing IIS 5.x on a Web Server Machine

Go to the Control Panel and select the Add or Remove Programs icon. The dialog box shown in Figure A-1 appears, displaying a list of your currently installed programs:

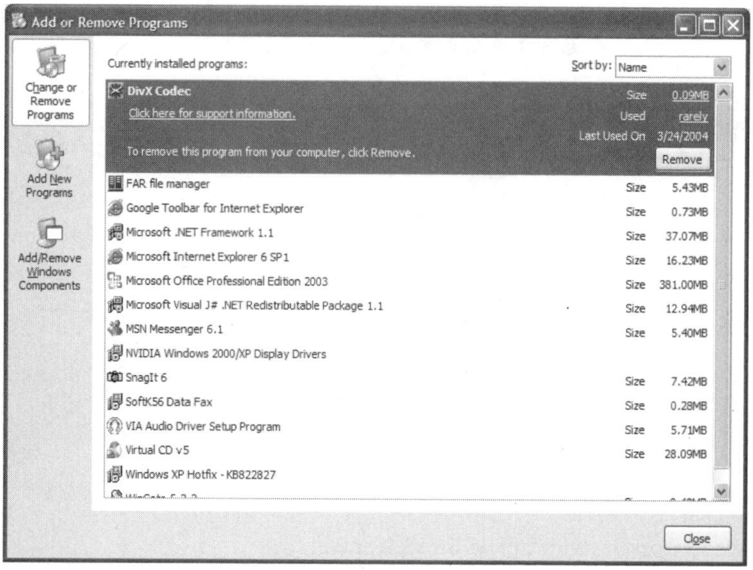

Figure A-1. The Add or Remove Programs window

Select the Add/Remove Windows Components icon on the left side of the dialog box to get to the screen that allows you to install new Windows components (see Figure A-2). Make sure the Internet Information Services (IIS) check box is checked.

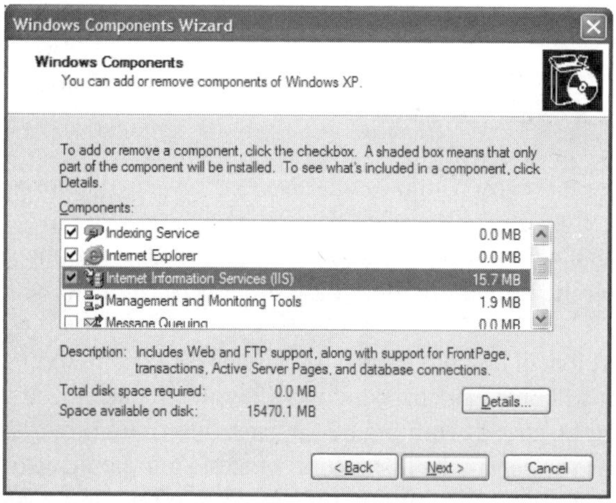

Figure A-2. Installing new Windows components

While Internet Information Services (IIS) is checked, click the Details button. This will take you to the dialog box shown in Figure A-3. There are a few options here for the installation of various optional bits of functionality. Make sure the FrontPage 2000 Server Extensions entry is checked. The Internet Information Services Snap-In is also very desirable, as you'll see in the book, so make sure this is checked, too. You need to check SMTP Service if you'll want to send administrative emails through your own server, as shown in Chapter 4. The last component, World Wide Web Server, is the most important, because it's the server that allows your computer to serve web pages to its clients.

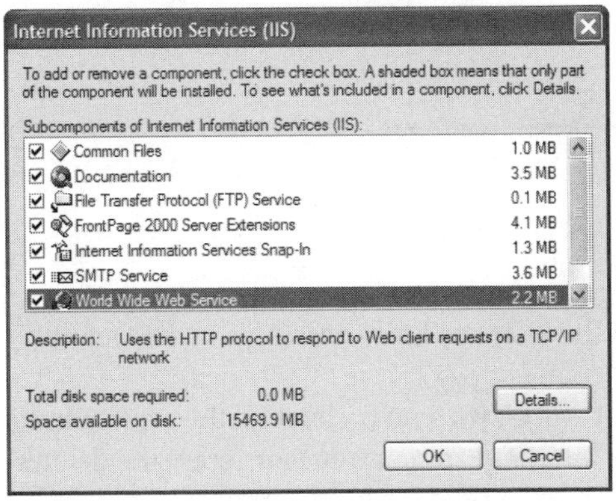

Figure A-3. IIS dialog box

For the purpose of this installation, make sure all the check boxes in this dialog box are checked. Then click OK to return to the previous dialog box.

IIS starts up automatically as soon as your installation is complete, and thereafter whenever you boot up Windows.

IIS installs most of its bits and pieces under the (`Windows root`)\system32\inetsrv directory. However, more interesting to you at the moment is the \Inetpub\wwwroot directory, which is also created at this time. This directory is the default root web directory, and contains subdirectories that will provide the home for the web page files that you create. When loading http://localhost/ in Internet Explorer, the application in \Inetpub\wwwroot is loaded by default. In Chapter 2, you learn how to create the JokePoint virtual directory under the root virtual directory (so it's accessible through http://localhost/JokePoint), and make it point to a custom physical folder (not a sub-folder of \Inetpub\wwwroot).

Working with IIS

Having installed IIS web server software onto your machine, you'll need some means of administering its contents and settings. In this section, you'll meet the User Interface (UI) provided for IIS 5.*x*.

Whenever you need to administer IIS, you can simply call up the Internet Information Services administration applet by choosing Control Panel ➤ Administrative Tools (see Figure A-4).

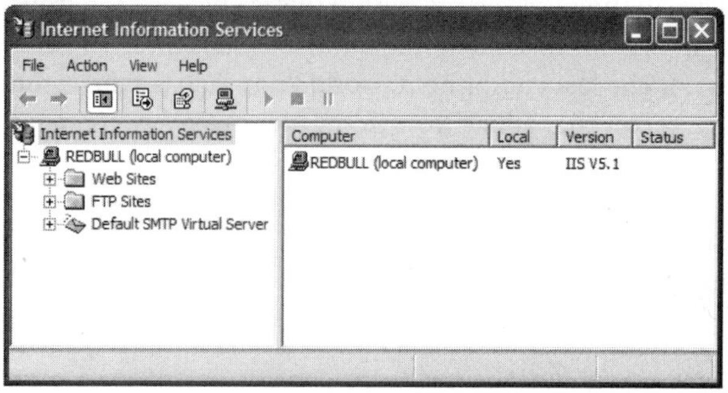

Figure A-4. The IIS Administration tool

Having opened the IIS applet, you can perform all of your web-management tasks from this window. The properties of the web site are accessible via the Default Web Site node.

To test that your IIS installation actually works, you can try loading the web address of your computer in a web browser such as Internet Explorer. You can access the default address through http://127.0.0.1/ (127.0.0.1 is the IP of the local computer), or alternatively through http://localhost/ (localhost is an alias for the 127.0.0.1 address), or http://*computer_name*/. You can view or change your computer's name through the Control Panel ➤ System applet (there you'll find a tab named Computer Name or Network Identification).

In the book, in any examples that require you to specify a web server name, the server name will be shown as localhost, implicitly assuming that your web server and browser are being run on the same machine. If they reside on different machines, you simply need to substitute the computer name of the appropriate web server machine.

Let's now move on to look at installing MSDE.

Installing MSDE

The first thing to say about MSDE is that it's entirely compatible with SQL Server, which is truly an enterprise-class database server. This means that the things you learn while using MSDE will stand you in good stead when you come to use SQL Server itself—it behaves in exactly the same way. From our perspective, however, the immediate benefits of MSDE are that it is

- Freely distributable.

- Currently available on your Visual Studio .NET 2002 discs. If you have Visual Studio .NET 2003, you'll need to download the installation kit from the Internet.

This means that as well as providing the perfect system for you to learn and experiment with, a complete Web Application can initially be produced and distributed without incurring any costs for the database server. If the system expands at a later date, it can be ported to the commercial distribution of SQL Server with next to no effort.

SQL Server also supports all of the features that MSDE supports. The converse is not true; some of the richer functionality of SQL Server is not present in MSDE. However, none of this functionality is required for any of the code in this book to operate correctly. Unlike SQL Server, MSDE is optimized for (but not limited to) up to five simultaneous connections, the maximum database size is limited to 2GB, and some enterprise features are absent.

In this book, the code samples and text will assume that MSDE is being used as the data provider. To ensure that the code in the book all functions correctly, the next section details the installation of MSDE.

Obtaining and Installing MSDE

MSDE doesn't ship with Visual Studio .NET 2003, but it can be freely downloaded from the Internet. Go to the Start ➤ All Programs menu, select Microsoft .NET Framework v1.1 and then Samples and Quickstart Tutorials (see Figure A-5).

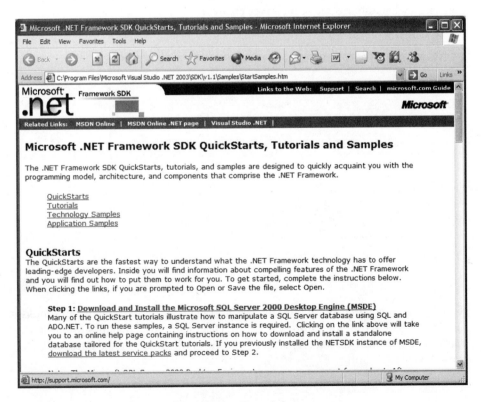

Figure A-5. The Samples and Quickstart Tutorials page

This page is self-explanatory: clicking the first link takes you to a page where you can download MSDE. When executing the downloaded file (sqk2kdesksp3.exe for MSDE with Service Pack 3), it asks you where to unpack itself. The folder you select is the folder where the MSDE setup kit will be unpacked.

Navigate to that folder and execute the setup program (setup.exe) with the following parameters:

```
setup INSTANCENAME="NetSDK" SAPWD="password" SECURITYMODE=SQL
```

The INSTANCENAME parameter specifies the name of the SQL Server instance to install (there can be more SQL Server instances installed on the same Windows installation). If the instance name is NetSDK, then SQL Server can be accessed through computer_name\NetSDK.

SAPWD specifies the password of the System Administrator (sa) account.

Setting SECURITYMODE to SQL allows SQL Server to accept authenticating connections through SQL Server Authentication mode. See the "Configuring SQL Server Security" section in Chapter 3 for more details about why you might need to enable this authentication option.

After it has been successfully installed on the local machine, you need to make sure that the MSDE service has started (you might need to reboot your machine first). One way is to verify the SQL Server service, using the Services applet you can find in Control Panel ➤ Administrative Tools (see Figure A-6).

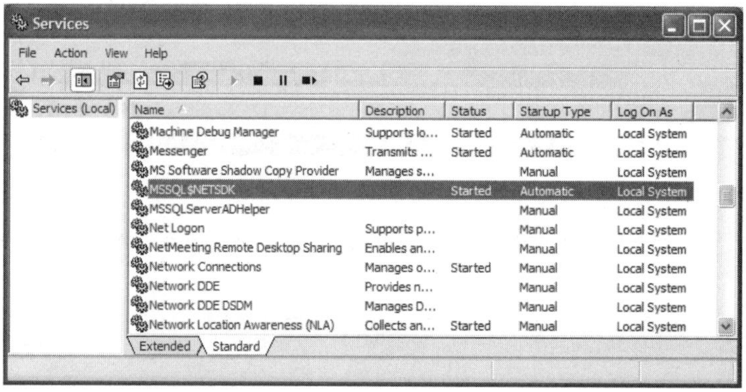

Figure A-6. The SQL Server service

Alternatively, you can use the SQL Server Manager program, which you should find in the system tray, after installing MSDE (see Figure A-7). It allows you to start, pause, and stop an SQL Server instance, and control whether it should automatically start at Windows startup.

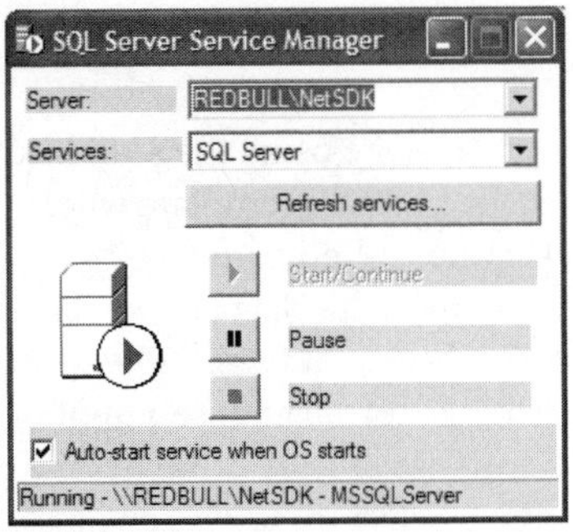

Figure A-7. The SQL Server Manager program

Running Scripts with osql

Unlike SQL Server, MSDE doesn't ship with graphical utility programs, such as Enterprise Manager or Query Analyzer. The utility that ships with MSDE and lets you execute various commands on the database is osql.

osql can also be used to run the SQL scripts from the code download, which create various database structures or populate the JokePoint database. The syntax of the command that executes an SQL script is shown here (make sure the case of the switches is exactly as shown):

```
osql -S localhost\NetSDK -d JokePoint -E -i ShoppingCart.sql
```

Table A-1 describes the switches in this script.

Table A-1 Parameters You Can Use with osql

Switch	Description
S	The name of the server on which your instance of SQL Server is running (can also be *server name\instance name*).
U	Username (if not using Windows Authentication for the database access).
P	Password (f not using integrated security for the database access).
d	The name of the database you want to use. If you intend to create other databases, you can connect to the master database first.
E	Tells the program that you are using a trusted connection (using Windows Authentication).
i	Full path of the SQL script file you want to run.

Creating Class Libraries

In Chapter 12, you'll need to create a class library project. If you're using the Standard Edition of Visual Basic .NET, you're not provided with a Class Library template when building a new project, so you'll need to do a little trick, as described here.

Start Visual Studio .NET, go to File ➤ New ➤ Project to open the New Project dialog box, and create a new console application project named `MyClassLibrary`. The new project has a default module called `Module1.vb`. Right-click `Module1.vb` in the Solution Explorer and choose Delete. Confirm the choice by clicking OK.

Now close the solution by selecting File ➤ Close Solution. Select Yes to save changes.

Browse to the folder where you saved the project, and open `MyClassLibrary.vbproj` with a text editor, such as Notepad. `MyClassLibrary.vbproj` is an XML file that keeps track of all the files in the project, as well as settings that apply to the whole project. You are going to edit this file to transform the console application project into a class library project. The line we are interested in is this one—about 19 lines down the file:

```
DelaySign = "false"
OutputType = "Exe"
OptionCompare = "Binary"
```

Change the bold line to:

```
OutputType = "Library"
```

Take care not to change anything else. Now save the file, close Notepad, and open the solution again in Visual Studio .NET. That's it, you have a class library project now.

This process is more complicated than using a full version of Visual Studio .NET. Behind the scenes, however, things are very similar. You want to create a class library, but no template is available. The closest one is a console application (because it doesn't bring up a designer, for example), so you create one. This creates a default module—Module1. You don't want this, so you delete it. A console application is a program—it can run on its own. You need to change it so that instead of it building to something runnable, it builds to a library. Visual Basic .NET Standard Edition offers no way for you to do this, but the information that makes the decision is in the VBPROJ file that Visual Basic .NET Standard creates. So, to get around the problem, you change the file.

APPENDIX B

Project Management Considerations

by Lucian Gheorghe

IT FEELS GREAT TO FINISH building a complete e-commerce store, doesn't it? For the purposes of this book, we dealt with many design issues on a chapter-by-chapter basis, while also learning the theory concepts. However, in real-world projects, many times you'll need to do the whole design work from the start. This appendix discusses how to manage building complete solutions in a professional manner.

Maybe it seems easier to just start coding without any up-front design, and with some luck, you might even create something that works the second day; however, when it comes to large projects, you'll face a lot of problems in the long term by doing that.

A project's life cycle includes more than simply coding away and building something ready to run—it should not be done hastily. For example, for almost any real-world software project, a critical part of its success is the database design, even if it only counts for a small part of the project's cycle. This makes perfect sense if you think that e-commerce sites, web portals, search engines, customer interfaces for service providers (banking, IT, insurance, and so on) are all basically interfaces to a backend database.

Of course, the way you display the data and the reports you present to the visitor also play an important role in the success of the software. However, you can think of the database as the foundation of a house; if you did something wrong there, no matter how nice or trendy the house looks, it will still be torn down by the first wind.

Developing Software Solutions

In fact, the technical design of a software solution is only a part of the software project's life cycle. To give you an idea of the steps involved in managing a complete software solution, imagine a real-world example, such as building an ERP (Enterprise Resource Planning) application for a clothing factory.

First of all, you need to know exactly what the client needs from the software, so you talk to the client about the goals of implementing such software in its network. This is the stage of gathering system requirements and software requirements for the application you need to build.

After the project manager fully understands the customer's requirements and discusses a budget allocation and a timeline for the project, a team of analysts works with the customer's commercial office to get information about the tasks performed in the factory, the work schedule, and the manufacturing equipment they have. Your analysts must be in touch with the region's economic regime, the employer's legal obligations, the import-export conditions, and so on—facts that are clarified with the commercial, economic, and personnel departments of the company. The analysts build the database, and describe the reports and the operations that the software must do.

After adjustments (if necessary) by the customer, the analytical part ends by adding a written annex to the contract with all these features agreed on by the customer and a timeline. After this, any modification in the database structure, the reports, or software functionality will be charged extra.

Next, the design team creates a user-friendly, attractive interface that can be presented to the customer and changed to fit the customer's artistic taste. After this phase is completed, the coding part begins. This shouldn't take a long time because the programmers know exactly what they need to do. When they finish coding, the software is installed on a test platform at the customer site and the customer team simulates using the software for a definite period of time. During the testing period, the eventual programming and design bugs are revealed and fixed by the programmers. At the end of this phase, the customer should have a software application that runs by the agreed specifications, and deploys on the production machines. That's the end of the project; the final payments are made, and every modification the customer asks in the future is billed.

That was a short version of a story about commercial software. Of course, the theory doesn't apply the same for all software projects. In the case of smaller projects, such as many e-commerce sites, several, if not all, the tasks can be performed by a single person.

Considering the Theory Behind Project Management

Many theories exist about how to manage the software development life cycle (SDLC). There is no model you can say is the best one, as choosing a SDLC model depends on the particularities of your project. We'll take a look at the most popular project-management theories in the following pages.

The Waterfall (or Traditional) Method

The Waterfall method, also known as the traditional method, is the father of all methodologies. It consists of breaking the software project in six or seven phases that must be processed in sequential order to deliver the final product. The input of each phase consists of the output of the preceding one (see Figure B-1).

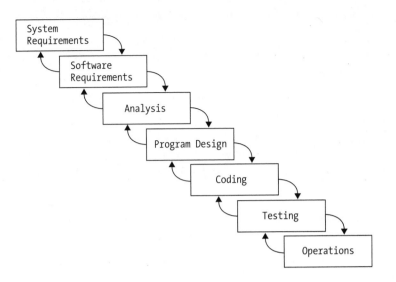

Figure B-1. The Waterfall model

Establishing the requirements is the first phase and can be divided in two as shown in Figure B-1. First, you must establish the system requirements of the project; at the end of this phase, you have a paper describing all the hardware needed for implementation, testing, and deployment of the application. You also need the software platforms your application will be developed and tested on. The first two phases must include an opportunity study at the beginning and a feasibility study at the end. Basically, the first question says "Do we really need this from the business point of view?" after you establish the requirements, the feasibility study provides a high-level cost and benefit analysis so that a ROI (return of investment) can be estimated.

In the Analysis phase, the analysts work with the customer to fully understand the customer needs. They have to spend time with the customer's staff to define the software functionalities, transcribing them in a professional analysis for the software engineers.

In the Program Design phase, the design team reads the specifications of the analysis and develops some prototypes that the customer must agree on. Usually, that is throwaway code.

In the Coding phase, programmers effectively code the application. This happens after the customer agrees on the software design delivered by the Program Design phase.

If a testing platform is provided, the programmers will install the application there and test all the functionalities of the software. All the bugs discovered are corrected, and at the end of the testing phase, the software must be ready to go in production. If a testing platform is not provided, the programmers have to simulate or conduct the testing on the actual platform the software will run on; however, at the end of the testing phase, the programmers have to install a fresh copy of the bug-free software they created.

Everything is completed after deployment at the beginning of the Operation phase.

NOTE   *Every phase has a feedback to the precedent phase where new ideas can be added and errors are corrected.*

Advantages of the Waterfall Theory

The main advantages of the Waterfall method are its simplicity and the fact that everything is documented and agreed upon with the customer. This leads to some important benefits:

- Because everything is planned from the start, it's easy for the project manager to correctly estimate project costs and timelines.

- The rigorous initial planning makes the project goals clear.

- All requirements are analyzed and validated by the customer, so the customer can estimate the benefits incurred by the software application before it's actually implemented.

Disadvantages of the Waterfall Theory

The disadvantages of the Waterfall model are

- The customer is not able to see the product until it's completely finished. At that stage, it can be very expensive to make any changes to the project.

- It has little flexibility for scope changes during the project's development.

- The architecture limitations are often not discovered until late in the development cycle.

- Because testing happens at the end of the coding phase, unexpected problems with the code might force developers to find quick fixes at the expense of the planned architecture.

- The Waterfall method doesn't work on projects whose requirements can't be rigorously planned from the start.

The Spiral Method

As a development of the Waterfall method, the Spiral method is more suitable for large, expensive, and complicated projects. Barry Boehm first described it in 1988 as an iterative waterfall in which every iteration provides increased software capability (see Figure B-2, which represents the diagram created by Barry Boehm).

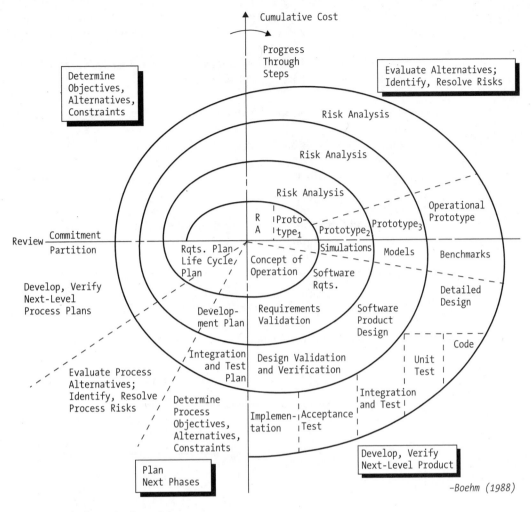

Figure B-2. The Spiral model

It consists of a spiral divided into four quadrants. Each quadrant represents a management process: Identify, Design, Construct, and Evaluate. The system goes through four cycles of these four processes:

1. *Proof-of-concept cycle*: Define the business goals, capture the requirements, develop a conceptual design, construct a "proof-of-concept," establish test plans, and conduct a risk analysis. Share results with user.

2. *First-build cycle*: Derive system requirements, develop logic design, construct first build, and evaluate results. Share results with user.

3. *Second-build cycle*: Derive subsystem requirements, produce physical design, construct second build, and evaluate results. Share results with user.

4. *Final-build cycle*: Derive unit requirements, produce final design, construct final build, and test all levels. Seek user acceptance.

The main advantages of the Spiral method proposed by Boehm are

- The entire application is built working with the client.

- Any gaps in the Requirement phase of the Waterfall method are identified as work progresses.

- The spiral representation conveys very clearly the cyclic nature of the project and the progression through its lifespan.

However, the Spiral method has some disadvantages of its own:

- Requires serious discipline on the part of the client.

- Executive control can be difficult because in most projects the client is not responsible for the schedule and budget.

NOTE   *The Spiral method is more suitable for software where the entire problem is well defined from the start, such as modeling and simulating software.*

The Rapid Application Development (RAD) Method

RAD is another common project-management method that is, in essence, "try before you buy." Whereas in the Waterfall and even Spiral methods, the client was working with a lot of documentation, in the RAD approach the client works with the software as it is being developed. The belief is that the client can produce a better feedback when working with a live system as opposed to working strictly with documentation. When using RAD as a project-management method, there are significantly less cases of customer rejection when going in production.

The RAD method consists of the following phases:

- Business modeling

- Data modeling

- Process modeling

- Application generation

- Testing and turnover

The RAD approach allows rapid generation and change of UI features. The client works with the software just like in the production environment.

The main disadvantage of RAD is that the client will always want more enhancements to the software—not always important ones—and the developer must try to satisfy the client's needs. This can result in an unending cycle of requirements, going away from the main purpose of the project.

Extreme Programming (XP) Methodology

Extreme Programming (XP) is a very controversial method not only because it's the newest, but also because it eliminates a lot of phases from the traditional Waterfall methodology. XP is simple and based on communication, feedback, and courage.

The professional analysts are replaced with the client, who is very active in the process. The client writes a document named "User Stories," which is a simple description of the desired functionality of the software. The programmers read the document and give an estimated time frame of every functionality implementation. After receiving the time estimates, the customer chooses a group of functionalities to be developed first. This is called an **iteration**.

The developers use a **test driven** design in the implementation phase, meaning that a testing method for the desired functionality is conceived before the code is actually written. Usually, every piece of code is written by a programmer under the supervision of another programmer who tests the functionality of the code.

After the code for the entire iteration is complete, it's then given an acceptance test with the customer, who approves (or disapproves) the iteration. The programmer keeps developing or improving code for that iteration until it passes the acceptance test.

The software is deployed in a number of `releases`, composed of one or more iterations; the software gets to the final release when all iterations that contain all the functionalities described in the User Stories document pass the acceptance test.

Picking a Method

There are more project management methods than the ones described so far. Because there is no single best method, a good project manager must know in theory a little about all of them so he can choose the best one for the current project. Choosing the wrong tactic for a project might lead to failure, so the project manager needs to carefully consider all options before choosing how to deal with a particular project. A strategy like this will never work: "Okay, we have to build an e-commerce site. Let's do XP with this one, and maybe we'll spiral the next one!"

In many cases, it's best to use a mix of methods to suit your project. For example, if the client doesn't know for sure what she wants, you can use bits of XP and collaborate closely with the client during the development, based on a User Stories document, add a few steps from the Waterfall method, and do some RAD on the way.

Anyway, it's very important to keep some of these procedures in mind for your next projects, because the way you manage your projects can save you time, money, and stress.

Understanding the E-Commerce Project Cycle

For most e-commerce projects, your best bet will be something with a Waterfall flavor, but with a bit of changes here or there.

If you have some knowledge about management and a good artistic spirit for web design, after you read this book, the e-commerce project can be a "one man show." First of all, you need to organize the tasks so that they take place in a logical, sequential order.

Understanding the customer needs should not be difficult. The customer wants an e-store where a range of products can be advertised and bought. You need to know the type of products the customer wants on the site and a little about future strategy (today the customer is only selling hardware components, but in the future the customer might want to sell laptops). This is very important because the database and the whole architecture must be designed from the start to support future changes. You might also want to find out about how the shipping department is organized to optimize the handling and shipping process.

Most of the customers require artistic and functional design, so, in most cases, the next phase is **creating a web prototype**. Whether you do it yourself or hire a web designer, the prototype should be only a web site template—only HTML code with something like "Product name Here" instead of an actual product, without the need of any databases. Depending on the artistic taste of the customer, you might have to build several prototypes until you agree on a design.

Designing the database is, as we said, a critical phase of the project. The logical database design is developed from the Requirements gathering phase, and is agreed on with the customer. The logical design of a database describes what data you need to store and the relationships between different entities of data (such as the relationship between products and departments), but doesn't include strict implementation details such as the associate table used to physically implement Many-to-Many relationships. If you're an advanced database designer, you'll create an optimal physical database structure yourself.

A number of tools—such as Microsoft Visio—enable you to design the database visually. These tools have very powerful features for designing relational database structures, and even generate the SQL code to turn them into real databases. Regardless of the database engine you're using, design your tables in a visual way (even with a pen and paper) rather than start writing SQL queries.

If you don't have resources to buy such an expensive program (yeah, the really professional ones can be very expensive), you can use Microsoft Access, which is another visual tool that can be successfully used to design databases and also has the capability to generate SQL code. Also, Access can export any database to external data sources, assuming you have the appropriate drivers to connect to them.

Next, you **implement the data tier objects**. This is the place you start playing with your database, because you need to implement the data access logic that will support the other tiers in your application. In the process, you'll probably want to populate the database with some fictive examples to have a base for testing your queries. Before writing the queries as data tier objects, test them using a visual interface to the database engine that allows executing and debugging SQL queries. This will make your life easier when debugging the SQL code, because as all SQL developers know, the code doesn't always work as you expect it to the first time.

After the data tier is in place, you can continue by **building the middle tier** of your application. In the middle tier, you implement the error handling, data-manipulation strategies and the business logic for your project. In this book, you learned some good techniques, but you might want to choose other ones for your particular project.

Building the ASP.NET Web Forms and ASP.NET Web Controls should be the next step. You already have a prototype that is usable only for design, because at the stage you created the prototypes, you didn't have a functional foundation. Usually, interface prototypes in software projects are throwaway code, but the ASP.NET forms and controls generate the actual look of your web site (with the design the customer agreed on).

A final testing phase is very important at the end of the project. The database will be populated with real records and a simulation is made to test the efficiency of the ordering process. Every process should be tested before going in production, so you must give your customer enough time to test every functionality of the site, to make some test orders, and to evaluate the shipping process. During this stage, any programming errors should be revealed for you to correct.

After the code is ready and tested on your local machine, the next step is to **find/provide a hosting solution**. Perhaps the best strategy is to host the project at a specialized provider, and if the site proves to be successful, the customer can invest in its own hosting solution.

Maintaining Relationships with Your Customers

In the ideal project, you include all the possible clauses in a contract; after you deliver the site and finish the project, you never want to hear from the customer again, except for developing new functionalities or changing the design, in which case, you charge the customer extra.

The most unwanted thing would be for the customer to ask you to make changes without paying for them, and that's possible if you are not careful with the contract and with the tools you provide the customer for administration.

For example, many e-commerce sites have poor catalog admin pages, which are nightmares for the programmers. Avoiding such a nightmare can be possible by providing proper tools and interfaces for the customer and, most importantly, describing how they work (eventually a user's manual). Many programmers don't take this detail seriously and prefer to bring the site up with an incomplete or hard to use catalog admin page, not knowing what's coming.

If the database is complicated, you must describe all the fields in a manual and how they must be completed; if an error occurs when the customer tries to submit a form to a database, you have to make the error page as eloquent as possible. Also, try to work with the persons who will use the tools you provide in the design stage and take a couple of hours to instruct them personally on how to use the tools. This will save you a lot of explanations over the phone or even going to the customer's office without being paid.

Index

H

forums.apress.com

FOR PROFESSIONALS BY PROFESSIONALS™

JOIN THE APRESS FORUMS AND BE PART OF OUR COMMUNITY. You'll find discussions that cover topics of interest to IT professionals, programmers, and enthusiasts just like you. If you post a query to one of our forums, you can expect that some of the best minds in the business—especially Apress authors, who all write with *The Expert's Voice*™—will chime in to help you. Why not aim to become one of our most valuable participants (MVPs) and win cool stuff? Here's a sampling of what you'll find:

DATABASES
Data drives everything.

Share information, exchange ideas, and discuss any database programming or administration issues.

INTERNET TECHNOLOGIES AND NETWORKING
Try living without plumbing (and eventually IPv6).

Talk about networking topics including protocols, design, administration, wireless, wired, storage, backup, certifications, trends, and new technologies.

JAVA
We've come a long way from the old Oak tree.

Hang out and discuss Java in whatever flavor you choose: J2SE, J2EE, J2ME, Jakarta, and so on.

MAC OS X
All about the Zen of OS X.

OS X is both the present and the future for Mac apps. Make suggestions, offer up ideas, or boast about your new hardware.

OPEN SOURCE
Source code is good; understanding (open) source is better.

Discuss open source technologies and related topics such as PHP, MySQL, Linux, Perl, Apache, Python, and more.

PROGRAMMING/BUSINESS
Unfortunately, it is.

Talk about the Apress line of books that cover software methodology, best practices, and how programmers interact with the "suits."

WEB DEVELOPMENT/DESIGN
Ugly doesn't cut it anymore, and CGI is absurd.

Help is in sight for your site. Find design solutions for your projects and get ideas for building an interactive Web site.

SECURITY
Lots of bad guys out there—the good guys need help.

Discuss computer and network security issues here. Just don't let anyone else know the answers!

TECHNOLOGY IN ACTION
Cool things. Fun things.

It's after hours. It's time to play. Whether you're into LEGO® MINDSTORMS™ or turning an old PC into a DVR, this is where technology turns into fun.

WINDOWS
No defenestration here.

Ask questions about all aspects of Windows programming, get help on Microsoft technologies covered in Apress books, or provide feedback on any Apress Windows book.

HOW TO PARTICIPATE:
Go to the Apress Forums site at **http://forums.apress.com/**.
Click the New User link.